The Media Student's Book

Third Edition

The Media Student's Book is a comprehensive introduction for students of media studies. It covers all the key topics you will encounter in media studies and provides a detailed and accessible guide to concepts and debates. This third edition has been thoroughly revised and updated throughout with up-to-the-minute examples and expanded coverage of important issues in media studies. It is structured in three parts, addressing key media concepts, media practices, and media debates.

Individual chapters include:

Meanings and media • Narratives • Genres and other classifications • Questions of representation • Ideologies and power • Audiences • Institutions • Industries • Research • Production organisation • Production techniques • Promotion and circulation • Advertising and branding • Postmodernisms • Globalisation • Technologies • Realisms • Regulation

Chapters are supported by individual case studies which include:

Analysing images • *Psycho* and news narratives • *Buffy the Vampire Slayer* • Stardom and celebrity • News • Selling audiences • Television as industry and institution • The music industry, technology and convergence • Producing in the British film industry

The Media Student's Book has been written by two experienced writers, researchers and teachers who are aware of the needs of media students at both pre-undergraduate and introductory undergraduate level. The book has been specially designed to be easy to use and understand with:

- marginal terms and references and a useful glossary
- follow-up activities, suggestions for further reading, useful websites and resource centres
- references and examples from a rich range of media forms, including advertising, films, radio, television, newspapers, magazines, photography and the Internet.

Gill Branston is a Senior Lecturer in Journalism, Media and Cultural Studies at Cardiff University. **Roy Stafford** is a Freelance Lecturer in Media Education and Training.

What readers said about the first edition of *The Media Student's Book*:

'Imaginative, accessible, comprehensive and shrewd – all textbooks should be like this. No student could read it without coming away thoroughly prepared for the pleasures, pitfalls and challenges of Media Studies, and no teacher in the field could fail to find it a superb and timely source of ideas.' Andy Medhurst, *Lecturer in Media Studies, University of Sussex*

'An exemplary textbook for Media Studies, especially but not exclusively at undergraduate level . . . they write in a lively, engaging style . . . they offer a strong sense of argument, debating the ideas of referenced authorities by asserting their own sense of where their positions lie . . . They deal with the widest imaginable, exhaustive and enviable range of references . . . they are not frightened to explore the most difficult theories and they do so with enviable explanatory skill, constant references and exemplification . . . An extraordinary feat of writing for an audience at this educational level. I've no doubt future publications will be judged by the standards it sets.' David Lusted, *English and Media Magazine no. 35, Autumn 1996*

What readers said about the second edition:

'Finally! A textbook especially designed for a critical introductory course in media studies . . . It is the perfect introduction to complex concepts and the authors do a wonderful job of explaining key critical theories in terms accessible to undergraduate students. I am a passionate fan of the book.' Clemencia Rodriguez, *University of Texas, San Antonio*

'A model textbook, one which never stops encouraging its readers to go further, to develop their ideas through independent thought and study. It is very attractively presented and accessibly written but never talks down – or dumbs down. A wide range of important terms, concepts and approaches are introduced to students without any skating over of complexities and difficulties . . . But most of all it is the intellectual excitement that the book conveys and transmits to readers that makes it such an invaluable learning resource.' Professor Jeremy Hawthorn, *Norwegian University of Science and Technology, Trondheim*

'An outstanding book that will be valuable as a resource for both students and teachers.' David Carr, *Weald College, Middlesex*

'A book which no college or first-year undergraduate student of media studies can afford to ignore . . . indispensable.' Andrew Beck, *Coventry University*

'An essential introduction to the subject. . . . Easy to use and lively to read, this second edition offers an up-to-the-minute guide for beginning Media Studies. The writing of all new sections is clear and concise, the selection of material very contemporary and accessible to younger students.' Jonathan Bignall, *University of Reading*

The Media Student's Book

Third Edition

GILL BRANSTON
and
ROY STAFFORD

Routledge
Taylor & Francis Group

LONDON AND NEW YORK

First published 1996
by Routledge

Reprinted 1996 (twice), 1997, 1998

Second edition first published 1999

Reprinted 2000, 2001, 2002

This third edition first published 2003
by Routledge
11 New Fetter Lane, London EC4P 4EE

Simultaneously published in the USA and Canada
by Routledge
West 35th Street, New York, NY 10001

Routledge is an imprint of the Taylor & Francis Group

The right of Gill Branston and Roy Stafford to be identified as the
Authors of this Work has been asserted by them in accordance with
the Copyright, Designs and Patents Act 1988

Typeset in Garamond 3 10½/14 and Gill Sans 9½/14
by Keystroke, Jacaranda Lodge, Wolverhampton
Printed and bound in Great Britain by St Edmundsbury Press,
Bury St Edmunds, Suffolk

British Library Cataloguing in Publication Data
A catalogue record for this book is available from the British Library

Library of Congress Cataloging in Publication Data
Branston, Gill.
    The media student's book / Gill Branston and Roy Stafford.–3rd ed.
        p. cm.
    Includes bibliographical references and index.
        1. Mass media. I. Stafford, Roy. II. Title.

P90 .B6764 2003
302.23–dc21   2002027545

ISBN 0–415–25610–0 (hbk)
ISBN 0–415–25611–9 (pbk)

Contents

CONTENTS

CONTENTS

Illustrations

Acknowledgements

Thanks to Rod Brookes, Glen Creeber, Sue Crockford, Malcolm Hoddy (Editor, the *Keighley News*), Matt Hills, Joost Hunningher, Rob John, Nick Lacey, Justin Lewis, Sharon Magill, Alison O'Rourke, Rob Seago, Peter Twaites, Justin Vaughan of the Open University Press, Wowo Wauters, Granville Williams, Tana Wollen, Alex Liddle, Laura Hutchinson, Ross Marklew, Rachel Bonde.

To the readers and contributors to *in the picture* magazine.

To Rebecca Barden, Chris Cudmore and Moira Taylor for their rare combination of enthusiasm and patience during the lengthy process of making this third edition. To John Banks for scrupulous copy editing.

To Lauren Branston, Lucy Branston, Marion Pencavel and Rob Seago for many virtues, not least tolerating the authors.

Finally, and emphatically, none of this would have been possible without the help of all the students and teachers and media practitioners with whom we have worked over many years.

Introduction

Media Studies is now an established area of work in further and higher education. This book is designed to help you through a subject which *both*

- relates very intimately to the sharpest contemporary cultural pleasures, *and*
- has to draw on a range of difficult theories to understand these experiences.

We have all grown up in environments saturated with media experiences. 'The media' are familiar and one of our first aims will be to make them 'strange' – to allow you to distance yourself from something you know, in order to look at it differently. This familiarity, and the expectations it arouses, also create problems for a Media Studies textbook. Television, from children's programmes, through educational television, to the vast range of broadcast material, has probably taught you a great deal, in ways which books cannot hope to emulate. You may also have quite sophisticated experience of computers, at home and at college, including interactive forms such as CD-ROMs and the Internet.

Such ways of learning have real implications for anyone setting out to write a textbook. We've tried to produce a guide which allows us to develop quite complicated arguments, where this needs to be done, in longish chapters. But we've also recognised that you will need to make all kinds of connections between ideas and will wish to exploit the possibilities of following links, as you might on a website. You will therefore find plenty of cross-references and key terms, shown in **bold**, which can be traced through the glossary. Information is offered in different-sized chunks and formats. We hope you'll like and use the jokes and quotations in the margins, the case studies, the activities and the feel of a book which is trying to work with a mixture of materials.

Modern technologies have dazzling capacities. It is now possible, using **digital imaging**, to make it seem as though Marilyn Monroe and Brad Pitt are playing a scene together, or that the Earth can 'morph' into an apple before our eyes; to broadcast such scenes simultaneously across continents; and to accompany them with music created entirely by computer. The Internet has been touted, like many earlier technologies, as a kind of utopian

Figure 0.1 Times Square, New York, 1977

space where information about 'the universe and everything' is readily available and all questions can be answered. There are two potential dangers attached to this view:

- The ease of use of technologies – 'just push the button' – can make theories and histories seem irrelevant.
- Technologies are not equally distributed, nor are they accessible or affordable for everyone.

Terms in Media Studies

Some students have problems in Media Studies because of its terminology. Words which have fairly straightforward meanings in everyday life (such as 'sign' or 'closed') take on rather different ones within this subject. This can be confusing and we've tried, wherever possible, to warn you of such likely misunderstandings.

There again, the development of Media Studies has been quite often 'driven' by developments in higher education. From the 1960s onwards, many academics, trying to get modern media taken seriously as objects for study, had to present arguments couched in very specialised language. Along with an excitement with theoretical developments such as structuralism and semiotics, which seemed to promise radical political possibilities, this produced a very difficult set of theoretical terms – especially for those who had not been involved in the years of struggling through, applying and familiarising themselves with these terms.

Now the dust has settled, the real gains of some of these approaches can be brought into study of the media. Other parts of what has become almost the official language of the subject in higher education are less useful, and often depend on such a huge amount of study that we have left them out.

Yes, the technologies are terrific – exciting and disturbing at the same time. But we hope you enjoy our sections on their histories, distribution and ways of working, rather than feeling them to be a tedious diversion from the delights of simply celebrating 'virtual reality'. However convincingly you have Marilyn and Brad in the same frame together, however much information is at your fingertips on the Internet, you can't rely on virtual decisions about what dialogue they will speak, or how they will be lit, framed and directed to move. Nor can you make use of the Internet without some sense of what information you need, and what information from it is likely to be reliable.

Media Studies is still a young subject area and the syllabuses – the official definitions – offered by the various examining bodies are still being developed. We hope we've covered all the basic concepts you will encounter and quite a few of the debates or issues which are addressed by Media A Levels, by Access courses and many undergraduate modules as well. Media theories have directly influenced work in other subjects including Sociology, English and Cultural Studies; media production practice increasingly spills over into Art, Design and Photography, and most degree courses try to incorporate some media material, if only via 'images of the subject area'. Our 'target audience' includes many different groups of students and so don't be surprised if you find things that aren't on your syllabus. Dip into them anyway – we hope you'll find that they increase your understanding of the key concepts (and they may well be required for the next course you take).

We haven't included any essay questions as such, because no one particular syllabus is targeted and we would rather try to support your basic understanding of concepts and debates. We've suggested a wide range of 'activities', some very simple and others more complex. Most of these you can pursue on your own. We hope they are enjoyable and worthwhile in their own right rather than dry 'exercises'.

This is a genuine new edition of the book. We've looked at everything and updated or revised it where necessary. We've altered the shape of the book and introduced new material, drawing on current debates and reflecting on the contemporary media environment. There are now short case studies 'embedded' in some chapters and longer 'stand-alone' case studies. New and completely reworked chapters and case studies include:

- *Buffy the Vampire Slayer*
- Stardom and celebrity
- *Big Brother*
- The reception of *The Silence of the Lambs*
- The British film industry
- Viacom
- '11 September' and news values
- Internet culture.

The two of us 'combined' have worked in most levels of further and higher education, and in media education generally for over twenty years. We 'entered the field' because we enjoyed popular culture in all its forms and recognised its importance in the contemporary world. We hope that this enthusiasm comes through in the writing – Media Studies should be challenging and fun. Whatever your interest, in passing an exam or simply understanding the 'media society', enjoy reading and working with the book and let us know, by writing to the publishers, about your ideas for improving it. Even better, e-mail us direct with your comments: BranstonGA@cardiff.ac.uk or Roy@itpmag.demon.co.uk.

How the book is organised

There are three parts in the book. Part I sets out the 'key concepts' of Media Studies, exploring in detail the theoretical background you will need for work in any part of your course. The case studies, both embedded in the chapter and following it, should give you an idea of how the key concepts can be applied in the study of a particular topic. The longer case studies are distinguished by page design. Chapters use a single column and a margin for extra material, but case studies are presented in two columns without margins. We expect you will need to keep 'dipping in' to the main chapters, but that you might read the case studies straight through.

In Part II we look more closely at media 'practice', following through the media production process from research to distribution. We hope that this will help you with your own production tasks and that it will also give you a much clearer idea of how media industries work. We've taken advertising to be a distinct media industry and given it a separate chapter in this section – although, because of our emphasis on 'integrating' work, you will find references to advertising in other chapters as well.

In Part III we offer five 'media debates' – examples of often long-running, but also contemporary, arguments about media theory and practice. These are likely to throw up issues you will be asked to investigate on your course and we show you how you can put your knowledge of the key concepts and media practice to good use.

Finding material

The book isn't organised like a 'set text' – there is no correct way to use it. Instead, it is designed for your support, so it is important that, whatever you need, you can find it easily. At the start of all chapters and case studies is a list of main headings. In chapters the appropriate headings are repeated in a computer-style menu at the top of each page. 'Running heads' at the top of each page always let you know where you are.

If you want to find a key term, look in the glossary for a quick definition and in the index for specific page references. The first time a key term appears in a chapter it is presented in bold type.

References

As all media researchers will tell you, good references are invaluable. They provide evidence of the origins of material and they point to further sources which could be used. We've adopted a number of strategies. Whenever we quote another writer, we have placed a name and a date in the text e.g. (Barthes 1972). This refers you to a book written by Barthes and published in 1972. The full reference (which includes title and publisher) is then given at the end of the chapter or case study. You should learn to list this full reference, for any books you use, at the end of your essays. We've explained this in more detail in Chapter 9.

The list at the end of a chapter includes the sources we have used and perhaps some other material we think relevant. Some of our sources are quite difficult, both to obtain and to read, so we don't always expect you to go to them direct. At the end of the book we have included a 'selected' list of important (and accessible) texts which we recommend you do look at. We also list useful websites.

The titles of films, television and radio programmes, newspapers and magazines are usually given in italics. Again, this is a convention that you might usefully copy, especially if you word-process your work. It makes it much easier to read essays. We have given the country of origin and the date of release of films to help you find them in reference sources. We have tried to use film examples which are well-referenced, so, even if you've never heard of them, you should be able to find out more, often via the Internet.

Part I
Key Concepts

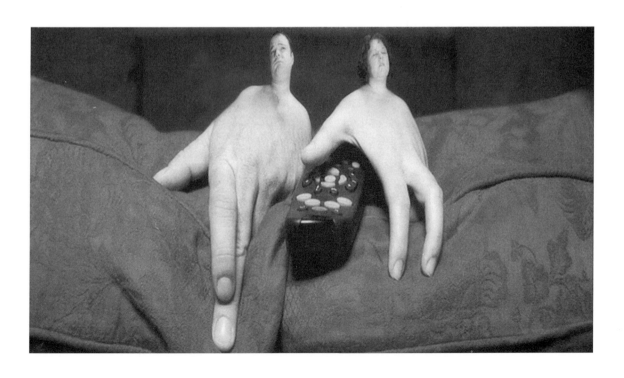

1 Meanings and media

- Semiotics
- Structuralism
- Denotation and connotation
- Debates
- References
- Further reading

The media are not so much 'things' as places which most of us inhabit. Their pleasures and messages seem to flow around and through us most of our waking lives, and there's little problem with understanding or enjoying them. Yet many feel that the processes involved in all this, the audio-visual and verbal 'languages' or sets of representations we have become used to, are worth studying seriously as a key part of the modern world.

Modern media are often thought of as a kind of conveyor belt of meaning between, or in the middle of, 'the world' and audiences, producing images 'about' or 'from' this or that debate, event or place. Sometimes this involves news, or the hidden secrets of celebrities, or the inaccessible sea depths of *Blue Planet*. This chapter, by contrast, does not assume that the media work as simple channels of communication, as 'windows on the world'. Instead, it argues, they actually *structure* the very realities which they seem to 'describe' or 'stand in for'. In particular we want to give you a grasp of **semiotics**, one of the ways to study how meaning is socially produced, whether through words, colour, gesture, music or fashion, to take a few examples.

The chapter is not an easy read; you need to spend a bit of time with it. The semiotic terms you'll be trying out are not explicitly used, all the time, in media analysis. Many of them are shared with other approaches, and they have been debated, criticised and qualified in recent years. But semiotic approaches are very much part of the subject area, and indeed of mainstream television, press and fashion, with their frequent discussions of style differences, deconstruction, signs, and of 'spinning' or making things and events *signify*. You may find you already know more about them than you at first imagine! Or that you've always wondered why Media Studies is peppered with terms such as '**construct**' and 'signify'.

The word 'media' comes from the Latin word *medium* meaning 'middle'.

A Tory MP commenting on the previous week's Labour Party conference: 'Tony Blair wearing a red tie: what greater signifier could there be than that?' (4 October 2000)

Semiotics

When the media were first seriously studied, in the late 1950s, existing methods of literary, social science and art criticism were applied to them. Value was set on 'good dialogue' or 'convincing characters' or 'beautiful compositions'. But it soon became clear that simply to discuss a film or television programme by such methods was not enough. People began to question the critical terms used and to ask: 'good' or 'convincing' or 'beautiful' according to what criteria? For whom? At the same time a whole body of ideas, now known as **structuralism** and *semiotics*, was brought into play. This asked radical questions of how meanings are constructed in language and cultures, and then applied these to the audio-visual workings of media. Finally, these approaches tried to 'hold off' older questions of the value of different stories or images in order to explore the ways that meaning is constructed.

Semiotics is also called 'semiology', and we can define it as the study of **signs**, or of the social production of meaning by sign systems, of how things come to have significance. Let's explore this a little. Drawing largely on the work of the linguists Saussure, Peirce and **Barthes**, semiotics argues that verbal language is just one of many systems of meaning. These include gesture, clothing, architecture, etc. which can be studied like verbal languages.

But how do these languages, or sets of representations, work? At the time when semiotics was first developed, there were two main models for understanding language/representations:

- language as a *reflection* of the world, where meaning itself is already fixed ('the Truth') and lies in events, people, objects waiting for language to try to 'get at' or 'express' it (in 'realistic' photographic or film styles for example)
- language as based in the *intentions* of the 'author', that is, language as predominantly the way in which we each express ideas, feelings which are unique to ourselves (this approach would value eccentric styles of writing or photography, as being 'individual').

Of course there is a lot of point to both these positions (language trying to 'capture' the real outside the speaker, *and* language use as always unique and individual). But semiotics rejected both these models and made a third emphasis:

- language is both *constructed* and *inherited*, by people using it within existing cultures, to produce meanings. Things and events in themselves do not have inherent meaning. Of course they exist. But neither they, nor the ways we describe or photograph or even perceive them, are ever experienced 'raw' or unmediated'. It is the ways that cultures, through

Roland Barthes (1913–80) French linguist who pioneered semiotic analysis of cultural and media forms. Most famous for *Mythologies* (1972, originally published 1957) a collection of essays applying his theories wittily to ads, wrestling, Greta Garbo's face and so on. (See later for *Saussure* and *Peirce*.)

their changing use of language, have 'agreed' to perceive, and then to name, things and events that determines how they get defined or valued.

And this social 'agreement' means we cannot ever produce completely private languages of our own, however characteristic our individual language use will indeed be, whether in words or fashions or the photos we take.

Semiotics used the term *signs* to describe the ways that meanings are socially produced. Signs have several characteristics:

- First, a sign has physical form, called the **signifier**. This might be a haircut, a traffic light, a finger print. It might be a word – though as signifiers words offer meaning in two main ways. The *signifiers* or physical forms are sometimes marks on paper (R-O-S-E), sometimes sounds in the air (the spoken word 'rose').

- Second, a sign refers to something other than itself. This is called the **signified** and it is important to grasp that it is a concept, not a real thing in the world. Though it's hard to separate the sounds of 'rose' when you hear them from your concept of a rose, semiotics *emphasises* this distinction. Indeed, it adds a third term, that of the **referent**, which is what both the signifier and the signified refer to: real roses, in all their different colours and shapes, which will inevitably differ from the single, rough and ready concept any one of us conjures up when we see or hear the word.

- Third, semiotics emphasise that our perception of reality is itself *constructed* and *shaped* by the words and signs we use, in various social contexts. By dividing the world into imaginative *categories*, rather than simply labelling it, language crucially determines much of our sense of things. The most famous example is snow – whereas English mostly uses only a few nouns – snow, slush, sleet – to differentiate snowy conditions, the Inuit (Eskimo) language makes subtle and detailed distinctions between different kinds of snow (which English can only describe with words such as 'light', 'soft', 'packed', 'waterlogged', 'shorefast', 'lying on surface', 'drifting on a surface' and so on). (See Hall 1997, pp. 22–3.)

These categories, into which verbal and other media languages divide the world, work by means of **differences**, such as those between kinds of snow, or between hotly contested terms which often attempt to re-signify the same thing or process. A famous example is the change from the signifier 'terrorist' to the signifier 'freedom fighter' and later 'hero of liberation' for Nelson Mandela performing identical activities during the years of anti-apartheid struggle in South Africa. This emphasis on differences as key to meaning-making was one which semiotics shared with structuralism. To understand it properly, we need to explore this field a little.

Figure 1.1 'Rose' signified in iconic (the drawing) and arbitrary (the written verbal) forms. Further connotations are embodied in the two different typefaces.

You can try to apply these terms to the process called 'signing' for hearing-impaired viewers on television; for example, where meanings are signified through gesture. What seem to be the reasons for the choice of particular signed gestures?

Structuralism

This is a set of ideas and positions which broadly emphasised two things.

First, structuralism argued all human organisation is determined by large social or psychological structures with *their own* irresistible logic, independent of human will or intention. **Freud** and **Marx** in the nineteenth century had begun to interpret the social world in this *structured* way. Freud argued that the human psyche (especially the unconscious mind) was one such structure, making us act in ways of which we're not aware, but which are glimpsed in the meanings of certain dreams, slips of the tongue and so on. Marx argued that economic life, and particularly people's relationship to the means of production (do they own them, or do they work for the owners of them?), was another, which determined political sympathies etc.

Second, and later, structuralism argued that meanings can be understood only within these systematic structures and the differences or distinctions which they generate. For example, structuralist **anthropology** might study how a culture organises its rules on food as a system:

- by rules of exclusion (the English see eating frogs and snails as a barbaric French custom)
- by signifying oppositions (savoury and sweet courses are not eaten together in most western cuisine)
- and by rules of association (steak and chips followed by ice cream: OK; steak and ice cream followed by chips: not OK).

Only within such rules would particular combinations or menus be valued, or seen as 'wrong', or as rebellious, or innovative.

Sigmund Freud (1856–1939) Austrian founder of **psychoanalysis** or the theory and practice of treating neuroses, and the theories of 'normal' unconscious mental processes obtained from its procedures.

Karl Marx (1818–83) German political intellectual and activist, analysing and seeking to overthrow by revolutionary means the emerging industrial capitalist social order of nineteenth-century Europe.

Anthropology the study of human groups, usually of other cultures than that of the researcher.

ACTIVITY 1.1

Jot down other examples of these structures in other food systems you know, for example Chinese or Indian or Jamaican food.
- Can you list any such oppositions or rules of combination in the way you and your friends dress?
- Does your school or college operate any such rules, for example around the length of haircuts, or jewellery which may and may not be worn?

Claude Lévi-Strauss (b. 1908) French anthropologist (*not* the inventor of the jeans). Most active from the 1950s, studying myths, totems and kinship systems of tribal cultures in North and South America.

Lévi-Strauss was a structuralist anthropologist whose work has had a great influence on semiotics. He emphasised the importance of **structuring oppositions** in **myth** systems and in language (also sometimes called **binary oppositions** because the qualities can be grouped into pairs of opposites). These produce key boundaries or differences within cultures, usually with unequal weight or value attached to one side of the pairing. **Saussure** applied this to the ways that language produces meanings, often through defining terms as being the opposite of other terms: black/white; hot/cold etc. We have learnt to grasp very quickly that the word 'man', for example, means different things in contexts where it is opposed to 'boy', or to 'woman', or to a 'god', or even to a 'beast'. So 'woman' is almost always defined in relation to 'man', or 'femininity' in relation to its differences from 'masculinity'.

Ferdinand de Saussure
(1857–1913) French linguist who pioneered the semiotic study of language as a system of signs, organised in codes and structures. He distinguished between *langue* as a system of speech (which children, for example, need to learn) and *parole* as acts of speaking. These may be much more various and creative than the rules of the langue might suggest. See Culler 1976.

Many familiar meaning systems work with dual oppositions as a key part of their structure: God and the Devil or Good and Evil in religions; Yin and Yang in Chinese Taoist thought; male/female in most social orders. Popular stories and entertainments often work through related formal 'pairings' or oppositions: black/white (see hats in early westerns); night/day; East/West; brunette/blonde and so on.

Figure 1.2 Branding and advertising depend largely on successfully claiming difference for some products and brands from other, often very similar, ones. The distinction claimed for this vodka, as opposed to its very similar competitors, is constructed visually by embodying (though not spelling out) contrasts of gender (male/female); history (pre-human/human); biology (human/non-human) and posture (crouching/upright) differences.

However we learn to associate words, and media products, with each other, as well as to differentiate them. **Genre** is an inseparable part of understanding how meanings are encountered in practice and its blend of *repetition and difference* is key to understanding broader areas of meaning making (see Chapter 3).

Example: Titanic

To deconstruct a television ad, film etc. in semiotic terms involves trying to see which parts of it seem to be in systematic opposition. For example the narrative of *Titanic* (US 1997) works partly by differences such as upper

Figure 1.3 How many of the structuring oppositions of this film are visible here?

deck/lower deck; upper class/lower class; American/European, which are worked through in signifiers of types of music, of dress, of colours, of sets etc.

In many semiotic analyses a further step is to explore the extent to which one side of an opposition (or binary, as it's sometimes called) is always valued less than the other. In this case, the lively, egalitarian 'lower deck/lower class' passengers, represented by Jack/DiCaprio, are valued more highly by the film than the upper classes on the upper decks. This set of oppositions is part of why Rose/Winslet's development and decisions through the plot are given more than romantic weight: the character is constructed as throwing in her lot with a more democratic future through this system of difference. (You might like to think about the connotations of the characters' names in this context.)

Another example is advertising campaigns. In planning meetings there will often be 'brain storming' sessions where the qualities which will be attributed to the product (or celebrity to be associated with it) are contrasted, in a classic list of binary oppositions, to qualities which are 'not-Levi's' or 'not-BMW' or 'not-Coca-Cola'.

See Chapter 2 on syntagmatic and paradigmatic systems for a fuller discussion.

ACTIVITY 1.2

See whether you can apply this method to an ad, or the most recent film you have seen.

• Chart those qualities, colours, music, kinds of settings etc. which seem systematically grouped together, and in contrast or opposition to others, in your chosen text.

This structuralist emphasis on oppositions helps explain semiotics' insistence that signs are fully understood only by reference to their difference from other signs in their particular representing system or code. For example, once colour becomes possible in cinema or photography, the potential meaning of black and white is changed. It then signifies differently to produce a photo or a film in black and white (as with *Schindler's List* (US 1993)) since black and white can then signify 'seriousness' or 'pastness' or even just quirkiness.

You need to grasp the extent to which visual and verbal representation are composed of such material signs, working partly through differences, partly through associations with each other, especially via genre and other ways of classifying into groups. Signs have relationships among themselves, as well as in the ways they represent the world. Words can rhyme or be punned upon; colours can be echoed (or 'rhymed'?) across a film, a pop video, an ad.

Post-structuralists take these 'constructionist' positions even further. They argue that no shared meanings are possible because *everything* is understood *only* through difference. It's important to note however that meaningful differences (e.g. black/white) differentiate things that *share* certain qualities: here as parts of the colour spectrum. See Andermahr *et al.* (1997).

> When images of the Earth were first sent back from space, it became easier to conceive of the planet as one whole system. This became an enormous resource for environmental politics of global care for the planet, and an example of the material effects of certain images.

Denotation and connotation

Signs, then, signify or name or **denote** different aspects of our experience, the world. The word 'red' *denotes* a certain part of the colour spectrum, differentiated by language from other parts (such as 'blue' or 'pink') in what is in fact a continuous spectrum.

But signs also **connote**, or link as well as define things. They may link things by association with broader cultural concepts and values, or with meanings from personal history and experience. Let's take the ways that colours are signified.

The word 'red' *denotes* or tries to mark off one part of the colour spectrum. Broadly (merging sometimes into pink and orange of course) it can be used to describe blood, fires, sunsets, blushing complexions. This perhaps indicates why, in certain cultures, the colour and the word have gathered *connotations* of fierceness, passion, danger. In *Pretty Woman* (US 1990) there is a scene where Vivien/Julia Roberts wears a red, quite formal dress (after her multicoloured hooker's gear in the first scene, and before a black, even more formal, dress in a later scene). At this point in the film it could plausibly be argued to signify a growing confidence and passion in her feelings about her relationship with Edward/Richard Gere. But 'red' does this both by means of its 'passionate'

LEARN to make this last LONGER

Figure 1.4

'To an optimist the glass of water is always half full, to a pessimist, half empty.'

associations, and also partly through its deliberate *difference* from her other costumes in that film – and from the cultural awareness of readers that red is unlikely in this film to denote 'communism' or 'STOP' or 'danger' – as it might in other fictional structures.

The word 'gold' again *denotes* or marks off both a part of the colour spectrum and a particular metal. But it has historically developed *connotations* within certain cultures (deriving partly from its prizing for jewellery, special ceremonies and as a currency) which are much wider. These surface in such phrases as 'golden opportunity', 'good as gold' and so on. In cigarette ads, under conditions of severe censorship for the sake of health, it can work as part of a structure signifying 'Benson & Hedges'.

See the following case study for an example of this flag's meanings now.

The US flag, the 'Stars and Stripes', originally signified or *denoted*, in the abstract way that flags do, the union of the different states after the Civil War (1861–5) between the North and the slave-owning South. There are now fifty stars, to represent the number of states, and the red stripes represent the original thirteen British colonies and the blood of the revolutionary war of independence against the British. Its *connotations*, as emblem of the activities of one of the most powerful nations on the planet, are now clearly very different for those who support and those who oppose particular US policies.

ACTIVITY 1.3

Look at these logos for the RAC (Royal Automobile Club, now selling services to motorists but beginning as an exclusive social and sports club).
- Why do you think the badges and logos have changed over the years?
- What kind of connotations seem to be attempted in the latest logo?
- Can you describe the connotations of the different kinds of lettering?

1909 - 1911

1912 - 1936

1937 - 1938

1939 - 1945

1946 - 1955

1955 - 1973

1973 - 1996

1997

Figure 1.5 Evolution of the RAC image.

Different kinds of signs

Let's look in more detail at how semiotics has explored visual representation systems, as well as words. A key distinction is made (initially by **Peirce**) between **iconic**, **indexical**, **arbitrary** and **symbolic signs**. Verbal language, spoken and written, is mostly composed of *arbitrary* signifiers in the sense that there is no necessary resemblance between the black marks on the page: 'daffodil' and those plants in the rest of the world that share the name 'daffodil'. Any pronounceable combination of letters could have been originally decided on to signify 'daffodils' (as is clear if you know a language other than English).

Iconic signifiers, on the other hand, always resemble what they signify. There is a physical similarity between a photo, or a good drawing of a daffodil, and most people's experience of those flowers, and for this reason the photo is called an iconic signifier. Such distinctions are especially useful in drawing attention to the ways that photographs, film, television images and so on, though often seeming to be a record or even a trace of the real, are in fact as constructed as verbal (arbitrary) accounts. They only *seem* like 'a window on the world'.

The term *indexical* is used to describe signifiers that act as a kind of evidence: smoke of a fire; sweat of effort; spots of measles and so on. Or to use the distinction of analogue and digital, thermometers or sundials are indexical signs of heat or of time passing, whereas digital technologies (translating music into number signals, which are then reassembled) act like arbitrary signs.

The term *symbolic* is used of visual signs (as opposed to words, which are usually 'arbitrary') that are arbitrarily linked to referents. Flags are nearly always symbolic, since they have to try to unite so much in one sign. The diamond hats often worn by monarchs are called crowns, and symbolise monarchy. Thirty years ago the road sign used to warn drivers to take care near a school was the image of the 'torch of learning' (see Figure 1.6(a)): it was meant to stand as symbol of the place where that learning happened. But this conventional (i.e. socially agreed) meaning became unfamiliar, and the sign was changed to the 'two children crossing' sign (see Figure 1.6(b)). In other words, it was changed to a more iconic sign.

Charles Sanders Peirce (1839–1914) American pioneer of semiotics, usually quoted for his distinctions between different kinds of sign: iconic, indexical, arbitrary and symbolic.

Icon originally referred to visual emblems or portraits of saints, rather than their written or spoken names. Confusingly though, global stars such as Madonna are sometimes called 'icons', partly to suggest that they are like saints in a very visual culture.

See Chapter 5.

(a)  (b)

Figure 1.6

Codes

So signs, far from 'naturally' just 'labelling' the real world, are never as 'natural' as they often seem. The choice of 'green' for the traffic sign meaning 'GO' could be replaced by 'pink', if that were the agreed colour for 'GO'. Similarly words in different languages ('chien' in French and 'dog' in English) can refer to the same signified.

But it's worth emphasising the broad cultural or social *agreement* (or sometimes *force*) needed for meaning to be produced – as well as its arbitrariness or slipperiness. We learn to read signs in relation to wider systems of meaning, to which the term **codes** is often given. These have by definition have to be broadly *shared*. Roland Barthes began exploration of this area, using terms such as 'rhetoric', 'myths' and 'mythologies'. Stuart Hall used the term 'codes' both for the 'professional assumptions' of production (see Chapter 11) and for wider sets of values with which they connect. So a cosmetics ad may depend on the accepted ways to light 'glamorously' the face of a woman widely considered beautiful, and could be said to express the 'dominant code' that all women should be glamorous and beautiful for men (Rose 2001: 89). Later in this book we use more politically emphatic words such as 'ideologies' and 'discourses', and the important struggles for meaning which they signal. There's also a danger, in using the word 'code': it can make communication always sound like a conspiracy on the part of the 'encoders'.

Paradoxically, it is because signs have to be employed by us, the 'readers' or 'users', to produce meanings at all that they are inherently ambiguous or unstable. In this process of being socially used and often shared by many people the meanings of signs are neither fixed nor single, but **polysemic**, or capable of having several meanings. The Union Jack has stood as symbol of the unity of the United Kingdom, and by extension the monarchy that rules it. But for Republican groups in Wales, Ireland or Scotland, or punk fashions, or opponents in war, it is used and understood in quite other ways. Fan studies have looked at the ways that fans will often produce versions of favourite media products (such as Buffy or Britney) on the Internet which are wildly different from those officially circulated.

One way in which control is attempted over the always potentially disruptive polysemy or ambiguity of visual images, especially for news purposes, is through the use of captions or commentary. Semiotics calls this **anchoring**, a process which tries to select and therefore control the meanings which could legitimately be made by a reader. (Think of it as similar to the way that an anchor tries to limit the movements of a boat or ship in the sea.)

The only exceptions are spoken words called 'onomatopoeic', where a sound resembles what it signifies: like 'rumble' or 'hiss'.

Figure 1.7 Geri Halliwell: Cool Britannia? Part of moves to re-signify 'Britishness' in the 1990s.

The word 'polysemy' – 'having many meanings' – comes from the Greek words *poly* meaning 'many' and *semeion* meaning sign.

ACTIVITY 1.4

Take three photos, either from the press or your family album.

- Devise captions for them which will *anchor* their *connotations* very differently from the way in which the original press or family album setting had done.

ACTIVITY 1.5

- Cut out a few pictures at random from a paper or magazine.
- Cut out the same number of phrases, again at random, from the same sources.
- Mix them all up and pick out, face down, one picture, and one phrase, at random.

See whether the phrase, even though randomly chosen, seems to have a kind of authority as 'caption' anchoring the meaning of the picture. However wild, most captions can seem to make a kind of sense of the picture.

Such shifting cultural 'agreements' on meanings mean that signification is never 'secure' or fixed – not even for the makers of this book! Such shifts mean also that struggles can take place over signification, over how a sign is to be 'officially' read. For example:

- In the 1960s the centuries-old connotations of the word 'black' in western cultures were challenged by the US Civil Rights movement with the slogan 'Black is Beautiful'.
- The words 'cool', 'wicked', 'hectic' and 'bad' have, in some contexts, completely lost or even reversed their previous meanings in the last few years: a 'slippage' has occurred as slang terms have entered more mainstream circulation.
- The traffic sign for 'Caution, older people crossing the road' signified by stooped, stereotypical figures of 'the old' has been objected to (a 'struggle over the sign' begun) by some groups of older people.
- Television and print newsrooms sometimes debate how they should describe certain acts: are they performed by terrorists? Freedom fighters? Guerrillas? Is an announcement about redundancies in a particular industry to be worded as 'massive job losses', 'letting go' certain workers; 'rationalisation', 'downsizing' or 'slimming down the workforce'?

Figure 1.8

ACTIVITY 1.6

Look at the front and back covers of this book, and of a book you consider very different.

- What do you think the designers were trying to signify? What particular signs and connotations are your evidence?
- Is there any slippage between what seem to have been their intentions and the meanings you take from the designs?

You may be interested to learn that we had long discussions about whether to include images from '11 September' or '9:11' as it is now called in the US.

ACTIVITY 1.7

Make notes on the next news headlines or lead stories you encounter with an eye to such verbal constructions. (They can also be visual: which of many possible photos of a celebrity or politican has been chosen?)

- Think how *else* particular events could be signified through different word or image choices. You might even build up a collection of pictures and alternative words for further news work.

Overall, semiotics has been enormously useful in rethinking the key social activity of meaning making. But semiotic and post-structuralist emphases have often been taken up as part of a crippling sense of powerlessness in the face of modern political and social developments. Language and representation have been emphasised as being *only* untrustworthy, slippery, commercially hireable through the work of 'spin doctors' and of very limited use in understanding the world, let alone helping to change it.

Debates

Several key questions have now been posed of semiotic approaches (see Corner 1998; Hall 1997):

- The preference of semiotics for detailed readings of individual images raises questions about the representativeness and **replicability** of its analyses. How representative of ads in general, for example, are those chosen by Williamson (1978), or Barthes (1972)? Would someone else have come up with the same conclusions?
- Semiotics has developed an elaborate, even over-elaborate terminology. Sometimes this is confusing or unnecessary (see Rose 2001: 97–8).

Replicability unambiguous quality of a research method, so that 'different researchers at different times using the same categories would [interpret] the images in exactly the same way' (Rose 2001: 62).

- Semiotics rightly makes a heavy emphasis on meaning as constructed. But does this sometimes *over*-emphasise the arbitrariness of signs, and *under*-emphasise the extent to which they have to be shared, to have associations, in order to produce meaning at all? (Think about this when you try to apply 'denotation' and 'connotation'.) This has important implications for the way in which some semioticians dismiss such notions as 'identification' (based on a sense of what is held in common) or 'empathy' and, following on from that, the kinds of politics based on such feelings.

- How far can such slippery matters as 'interpetation' and 'meaning' be objectively and scientifically mapped? This certainty is implied by the tone of some semioticians' writing, and by many terms in semiotics. 'Codes', for example, with its roots in signals technologies, can often seem to embody a fairly simple notion of communication. Now we might say that the 'texts' that you study offer a *meaning potential* not a fixed 'code' to be cracked once you've learnt it, like semaphore or traffic signs.

- Does semiotics' heavy emphasis on 'meaning' ignore the extent to which pleasure, irrational play with texts, and the often mischievous misreadings of audiences come into the picture (see Nowell-Smith 2000)? Despite the idea of 'polysemy', semiotics has been fairly uninterested in how audiences engage with texts.

- Is semiotics right to be quite so uninterested in **empirical**, rather than highly speculative, research into what actual audiences make of 'texts'?

One term which has the potential to help us think about the relationship between signifiers and audiences is **mode of address**. Coming out of linguistics, it refers to the ways a text seems to 'speak to' its audience, 'who it thinks we are'. A good comparison might be with how, in everyday encounters, our way of addressing a friend, a teacher, a bank manager incorporates a (different) 'position' for each of those people within what we are saying: as someone being treated respectfully, with intimacy or with caution. The further implication is that when *we* are addressed in certain ways (as 'naughty children'; as newly 'grown-up' etc.) we 'play along' and may partly even assume or perform the identity thus constructed for us, at least temporarily. Such textual work suggests that modes of address:

- are linked to assumptions about audiences, and the desire to attract or maximise them or to target specialised ones

- may also reinforce or even help to *create* these assumed identities, and to define or informally 'teach' them.

Empirical relying on observed experience as evidence for positions. A controversial term, often caricatured by opponents to imply an approach opposed to any kind of theory and relying on sense experience or simplistic facts alone.

If your course involves practical work you will be expected to think carefully about how to address your audience. In academic work you will have to learn how to address an essay to an imagined audience: how much knowledge are you supposed to assume they have? How much 'proof' (references etc.) do they need of statements in essays?

ACTIVITY 1.8

Take a current affairs programme, e.g. *Newsnight*, and make notes on its mode of address. Look at such signifiers as title sequence; studio set-up, if any; voices, accents, dress of presenters; whether the programme takes a position on its subject; use or avoidance of 'you', 'us' etc. by the presenter.

• How would you describe its mode of address overall? Respectful? Boisterous and irreverent? A mix of the two, and if so, in relation to which items?

ACTIVITY 1.9

Take a tabloid and a broadsheet newspaper and compare their modes of address. Look at such signifiers as: headline and typeface size; kind of language used, e.g. are slang or racy abbreviation present? Is it implied that this is 'plain speaking' or 'common sense'? The proportion of the page taken up by photographs; any use of 'we' or 'you' especially in the Editorial slot where the paper 'speaks its mind'; ads and how they seem to be addressing their assumed audiences.

Media Studies still goes against the trend of some media to present meanings as 'natural' and 'obvious', insisting instead that the meanings of representations are never 'given' but are always going to be slippery, fluid, and contestable. Indeed, this may be part of understanding the contemporary western preoccupation with 'spin' and struggles over how key words and images are to be understood.

Bear these questions in mind as you test out the usefulness of these approaches. The rest of this book tries to help you apply them, and takes them into much wider arenas of power and battles to secure one meaning for a word, a flag, a motto, etc. over others, in the everyday responses and creativity of audiences. Indeed one of the challenges of the subject is in trying to hold a balance between appreciating audience activities, and exploring how texts themselves do offer some meanings and pleasures, and try to cut off others.

References

Andermahr, Sonya, Lovell, Terry and Wolkowitz, Carol (1997) *A Concise Glossary of Feminist Theory*, London and New York: Arnold.

Barthes, Roland (1972) *Mythologies* (originally published 1957), London: Paladin.

Corner, John (1998) *Studying Media Problems of Theory and Method*, Edinburgh: Edinburgh University Press (esp. Introduction, and Chs 3 and 6).

Hall, Stuart (ed.) (1997) *Representation: Cultural Representations and Signifying Practices*, London, Thousand Oaks and New Delhi: Sage (to which this chapter is indebted).

Nowell-Smith, Geoffrey (2000) 'How films mean, or, from aesthetics to semiotics and half-way back again', in Christine Gledhill and Linda Williams (eds) *Reinventing Film Studies*, London and New York: Arnold.

Rose, Gillian (2001) *Visual Methodologies*, London: Sage.

Further reading

Bignell, Jonathan (1997) *Media Semiotics: An Introduction*, Manchester and New York: Manchester University Press (from which several activities in this chaper are adapted).

Eagleton, Terry (1983) *Literary Theory: An Introduction*, Oxford: Blackwell (esp. Chapter 3).

Myers, G. (1994) *Words in Ads*, London and New York: Arnold.

Strinati, Dominic (1995) *An Introduction to Theories of Popular Culture*, London: Routledge.

Tolson, Andrew (1996) *Mediations: Text and Discourse in Media Studies*, London and New York: Arnold.

Williamson, Judith (1978) *Decoding Advertisements: Ideology and Meaning in Advertising*, London: Marion Boyars.

CASE STUDY: ANALYSING IMAGES

- Advertising images
- Images from photojournalism
- Voices and sound images
- References

This case study takes still advertising and photojournalist images and tries to give you confidence in analysing them, using semiotic, along with more traditional, compositional approaches, and referring to debates from Chapter 1. We also suggest ways of analysing **sound 'images'**. We have deliberately not analysed a set of moving audio-visual images because this is so hard to do adequately on the page. But Chapter 11 contains many of the terms you will need for this, and the method of applying them is similar to that outlined here.

Advertising images

Figure 1.9a 'The new Corolla is supported by Toyota's biggest ever television and cinema campaign . . . launched . . . on New Year's Day [2002] by showing all 6 ads in the new Corolla 'a car to be proud of' series, back to back, in one epic ad break. The ads will be coming to the web soon' (Toyota website).

The Toyota Corolla (according to the *Guardian*'s car correspondent, 29 January 2002) is the world's biggest

selling car – so any relaunch is potentially very risky and needs to be carefully designed. The ad we've chosen was part of a series for the whole range: in print forms (billboard and press), on the website and on television.

In textual analysis with any image, you need to observe its formal or rhetorical strategies, especially:

Q how does it seem to address its readers?

- Examine the areas of composition, framing, colours, choice of words, if any (verbal elements are always worth focus), setting, lighting, key signifiers, references to other texts (inter-textuality), including other ads.

Focus on the question:

- What is my evidence for arguing that this mode of address seems to be at work?

Some advice:
- The analysis need not be overlong. Don't make it sound like a mechanical checklist – important to make one, but it should be done beforehand. Below we suggest one possible way of concisely analysing the Corolla ad, italicising words which show you have considered key concepts.
- Beware of writing as though the ad is having a predictable or momentous *effect* on readers ('the ad makes us . . . forces us to . . .' etc.), a common mistake. It can only make *invitations* to

meanings, to jokey connections which the reader may or may not 'get' or decide to go along with etc., and we should describe it accordingly. We can only speculate about the *intentions* of its makers.

- Analysis of ads often benefits from locating them in the broader 'meaning system' from which they derive part of their power (recall Lévi-Strauss). Even if car ads seem to ignore such debates, the design meetings will most likely have discussed them. At present such fields of meaning include:

  - a definition of the car against rivals, including the ways in which its brand is evoked. This may involve intertextual connections to how other cars are advertised (e.g. by ironic reference to, or deliberate ignoring of, semi-nude 'babes' draped across vehicles, or testosterone-fuelled fantasies of isolated speed and status)

  - a definition within other 'meaning systems', such as the debates around the globally polluting role of cars and the oil economy in general.

This ad was published in magazines (where 'browsing' time is usually assumed to be available for the reader to absorb fine detail). The car is, unusually, not centre stage or a prominent part of the *composition*: it takes up only about one-fifteenth of the whole *frame*, though it is easy to make out its design and look. It is pictured as part of a 'wanted' poster (*signified* by the plainly lettered question 'Have you seen this car?' and the telephone number to contact). These *verbal signifiers*, along with the second part of the poster, 'Nice isn't it?', associate the brand with a low-key wit, reversing 'wanted' as in hunted, and making it mean 'desired'. However the older *verbal brand identity* is also present, in the small top-right-hand corner slogan, 'The car in front is a Toyota', with its play both on 'in front' as market leader, and also the (faster) car which you've had the experience of being behind.

There is another poster visible on the next tree along (rather like appeals for help with loved missing pets) but the joke of the ad, its *play with signifiers* if you like, is that it's not a 'missing' car that's wanted, but the fact that you, the reader, have perhaps missed seeing it yet. Someone, the joke of the ad suggests, has put up the ads to advertise the car. Then, in a further move, the telephone number is that of someone at Toyota who can answer your query about the new car. The words 'Nice, isn't it?' and 'Phone Phil' (*abbreviated and colloquial*) suggests a 'no-nonsense' almost casual *address to the reader*, for this, the cheapest car in the new range. It is also, by ignoring more glamorous ways of advertising cars, effectively defining this one as 'not-Audi, not-Ford Mondeo' etc.

The setting in the 'wanted' poster is '*aspirational*', i.e. of a higher social class to which it's *assumed the reader might aspire* (*signified* by a rather 'grand'-looking house, the car parked in a driveway with sweeping trees etc). It is as though the car has been stolen from, really belongs with, a richer owner, though this *possible* meaning is *available* only if you spend time considering the ad.

The setting is 'suburban' side street or road: fairly prosperous-looking half-timbered, detached houses with clipped hedges, clean, tree-lined pavements. This avoids, as do most ads now, the actual stresses of driving on crowded streets or motorways – it's a refusal to associate with one *meaning system*, of urban pollution. It also seems from the setting that the ad is *addressing* a particular *demographic* (not teenagers, for example: there's no attempt to evoke popular youth cultural forms) who might live, or aspire to live, in such a place. The season is hard to tell – green leaves and green clipped hedges are clearly visible, though autumn leaves lie on the pavement. Such *ambiguity* is no bad thing for an ad campaign which may extend from December, the date of launch, through the year.

Figure 1.9b Here is another ad in the series, for a more expensive version of the car. Can you make a similar analysis of this image? Often such a 'launch' series of car ads work with *intertextual reference* or teasing connections to each other.

Images from photojournalism

Advertising images are, often openly and playfully, constructed in planning meetings, studios, specially chosen locations, real or digitalised. But the evidence or even thrill of photojournalism is that, though 'constructed' (at the very least, the published image has been chosen from possibly hundreds of others), it seems 'caught', a kind of trace off the real. This is perhaps why readers are disappointed when they learn that a news photo has been digitally 'doctored'.

Such photos also often work within meaning systems, the resonances of other images: e.g. the mother and child famine victims framed to resemble Madonna and child from countless western religious paintings. We will briefly consider two ways in which the resonance of one famous photo has worked recently.

When you analyse such photos, again try to consider sets of 'codes' at play which are both 'textual' and meaning-related:

- *photographic and technical codes* such as lighting; camera angle; colour or black and white stock; distance from subject; kind of focus; any evidence of whether amateur or professional photographer; developing techniques. Of course some of these will have to be approximately described or researched outside the image itself: you can rarely

know exactly what film stock, or developing process has been used, though you may be able to find out.
- *codes related to broad cultural and aesthetic frames of reference*: the choice of what to include and what to leave out via framing, for example; why this framing decision was made, rather than others which seem possible; how the whole composition has been arranged; are any verbal elements used to 'anchor' an otherwise ambiguous image?
- *codes of intertextuality*: what other images might this photo connect with, consciously or not, for its readers?

The photo below is at one and the same time

- an *iconic sign* (it is an analogue, not digital, photograph of real people: the *sign* visually resembles its *referent* and as such is vivid in ways that written accounts cannot be. Some seem to feel it is authentic in ways words cannot be.)
- an *indexical sign*. The sky, light and shadows in the scene seem to act as a kind of *evidence* of 'outdoors' – given that the photo is not one from the era of digitalisation.

Figure 1.10 On 19 February 1945, towards the end of the Second World War, 30,000 US troops invaded the Pacific island of Iwo Jima. After four days, 5,563 dead and 17,000 wounded, they took their two targets: Mount Suribachi and one of the island's two airfields. As they captured the main ridge of Suribachi, Joe Rosenthal recorded the US flag being planted in an image made famous by being awarded the Pulitzer prize, becoming the inspiration for a popular film, and for thousands of other images.

Its *composition* is striking. It has some of the qualities of classical painting and sculpture, with a triangular form at the centre providing dramatic tension between the flag's tilt to the left and the men's bodies, straining to the right. As Barker speculates, 'the flag at the apex somehow doesn't overshadow the men who plant it. Instead it seems to reach to the sky, to rise above them and crown their efforts' (Barker 1991). It is also not a victoriously, or easily, flying flag – it is only partly unfurled (see Chapter 5 on the ways a displayed flag signifies: institutions for example rarely allow their flag to trail on the ground). The amount of space given to the sky is clearly part of this sense of the men straining towards something bigger than themselves, and sky (or heavens) for some readers may have religious *signification*.

The group of soldiers has a monumental quality (indeed, the photo was later the model for a sculptured monument in Washington). Their helmets (we cannot see their faces, or age, or degree of beauty, or skin colour), and their apparent obliviousness to the camera (no *eye contact*) emphasise their anonymity. Perhaps this opens space for our wonderings about them, as well as avoiding any clear *signifiers* of ethnic or class origin, so they can be more easily read as signifying simply 'American soldiers'.

Though the photo's pose echoes classical 'certainties' it also works *difference within repetition* of this 'classical' code. For example it contains *signifiers* of the difficulty of this very masculine enterprise – the man whose hand is trying but just failing to grasp the flagpole. This difficulty seems graded through the group, so the stance of the soldier on the right is one of absolute certainty and effort. The rubble and wreckage at their feet seems to *signify* the damage of war (and for those involved, the thousands of deaths on the island) out of which this flag rises. It seems crucial that the *framing* has chosen to include this debris.

Some writers have suggested that the Second World War posed for US film-makers the problem of how

to forge collective heroism, when so much US myth is based on the individualism of the frontier. How might this image work in such context? (There was a successful John Wayne film made four years later, *Sands of Iwo Jima* (US 1949)).

Rosenthal had taken a photo a few minutes earlier of a group of some sixteen US soldiers waving their rifles triumphantly to camera around the fully flying US flag but this perhaps connected too well with the codes of the holiday snap, or family album to resonate as the famous shot did.

'On a routine night in his . . . office, John Bodkin, the AP (Associated Press) photo editor in Guam casually picked up a . . . print. He looked at it, . . . paused, shook his head in wonder, and whistled. 'Here's one for all time!' . . . Then, without wasting another second, he radiophotoed the image to AP headquarters in New York at 7 a.m. Eastern War Time. Soon afterward, wirephoto machines in newsrooms across the country were picking up the AP image. Newspaper editors, accustomed to sorting through endless battle photographs, would . . . stand fascinated. "Lead photo, page one, above the fold," they would bark'. (Bradley, James and Powers, Ron (2001) *Flags of Our Fathers*, New York: Bantam)

In periods of intense patriotism, such as the US is currently enduring, the next image (Figure 1.11) seems near to a '*closed text*', strongly encouraging only one *reading*: 'heroic American firemen struggle to raise the flag in the aftermath of a terrorist attack on New York'. Yet like any image this is *polysemic*; it cannot guarantee that it will be read in only one way. We can just about imagine that a member of al-Qaida might read it differently, an extremely deviant reading. Or that some of the firemen laid off after 'Ground Zero' might make a 'negotiated' or ambiguous reading (see Chapter 6).

Figure 1.11

- Finally, instead of the open sky of Iwo Jima, the dusty wreckage of the World Trade Center is the background to their efforts. This qualifies and undercuts the confidence of a 'gung-ho' patriotic reading.

ACTIVITY 1.10

Try to devise your own newspaper captions for the picture, across a wide range of meanings. How easy was this?

Once you have seen the celebrated Iwo Jima image it is easy to speculate that the photographer who took this photo was prompted by the way the firemen's position echoed the earlier shot. This time the flag raising produces the thrill of *repetition with difference*:

- They are civilian workers, not soldiers, though perhaps the uniforms and air of fatigue resonate with the 'front line' feel.
- They are men who do not appear to work like a unified military unit. The signifiers of uncertainty in their faces and the pose of the man on the left, as well as their denim overalls, helmets etc. are a marked contrast to, as well as an echo of, the earlier shot.
- They are all 'white', and, oddly enough in an era when much imagery is aware of the need to try to be representative by including members of other groups, this perhaps adds to the 'authentic' 'captured' quality of the shot.

Though this is a relatively 'smooth', unblurred photo, readers often understand the technical qualities of blurring as 'truthful-because-not-polished-looking'. This is partly because numerous pieces of dangerously obtained pieces of photojournalism, both still and moving, are necessarily blurred: there's an *indexical* link between the event and the photo, if you like. But this blur can be faked or constructed, as in several notorious examples of 'arranged' war footage, or, more recently, in television codes such as the deliberately awkward, documentary 'snatched'-looking filming of *ER* or the partly digitalised imagery of *Black Hawk Down* (US 2001) (see Chapter 17).

Here we enter fascinating areas of how we read 'realist' codes: what do we take as (indexical) evidence that something 'really' happened? To some extent (and especially in an era of computer-fakeable imagery) we have to rely on evidence from outside the photo, or 'text', to answer these questions, for example evidence of the trustworthiness of the institution which produced and circulated it.

The second image (Figure 1.12) which *refers intertextually* to 'Iwo Jima' is by the celebrated cartoonist Steve Bell, who often makes his political comments by referring to classical paintings and 'remaking' them in cartoon form, where of course

Figure 1.12 Steve Bell, Mazar-I-Sharif, 29 November 2001: a cartoonist's comment on controversial US treatment of prisoners during the attacks on Afghanistan after 11 September 2001.

'anything can happen', unlike photojournalism which is a kind of trace of the real. Bell signs the cartoon, captions or 'anchors' it with a verbal pun, 'Raising the standard of International Justice, Mazar-i-Sharif', and writes a copyright sign at top side left (thereby staking *authorship* claims over it, especially important for political artists in preventing misuse of their copy-righted images).

He takes the Rosenthal image as a 'classic' but changes its *key signifiers* to produce an oppositional reading of the patriotism so firmly embedded in the other two pictures. Key signifiers:

- The stars and stripes of the flag have been altered. Flags are symbolic signs, in Peirce's sense of being abstract. In the 'Stars and Stripes' the stars *signify* the number of states in the US; the red stripes are less easily agreed on: most say they signify the blood of those who made a violent revolution against the British for independence in the eighteenth century. In the days after 11 September however the 'star-spangled banner' was a symbol of national mourning, and then of more traditional defiance to enemies. Bell, two months and many US bombings later, makes the stripes seem to be made of dripping blood, and the stars of the skull and crossbones of death.

- Though the bodies echo the original pose, they are clearly not all American, judging from the signifiers of uniforms and turbans.
- Finally, instead of the debris and wreckage which the men seem to 'come out of' (both *compositionally* and *ideologically*) in Rosenthal's photo, here the ghastly damage of war – human bodies – is strewn all around *the foreground*, *the middle ground* and into the distance.

Voices and sound images

Finally, 'images' need not always be visual. Sound is coded, and signifies, in ways as complex as photographic images, though, after decades of developed analysis, the visual image is more readily recognised as 'made up'. Sound is difficult to discuss: we can't offer you a sound 'text' on the page, for one thing. We have had to ignore music, sound effects etc., though these, in the background, can be key to how voices signify within films and television (try it with your own voice). But to ignore sound, for audio-visual media, can mean that a whole dimension is missing from analysis and appreciation.

Imagine: you can't see a person, but you can hear their voice. What does this tell you about them?

- *pitch*: is the voice 'high' or 'low'?
- *volume*: 'loud' or 'quiet'?
- *texture*: 'rough' or 'smooth', 'soft' or 'hard'?
- *shape*: 'round' or 'flat'?
- *rhythm or cadence*: does the voice rise and fall or keep a continuous pace and tone? Recently an upward inflection at the end of sentences, making them sound like questions, has spread like wildfire across the English-speaking world, some say from Australian soap operas.

Key components of voices will be in play:

- *accent*, which usually refers to pronunciation (and often rhythm, cadence) and inflection. British voices are particularly characterised by accents: flattened or 'extended' vowels, missed consonants.

In *Star Wars: Phantom Menace* (US 1999) a debate raged on the film's release about the decisions taken on some of the voices (for example Jar Jar Binks, Watto and the Neimoidians). George Lucas defended himself with a thoughtlessly ethnocentric statement (which also reveals an odd sense of 'the real world' and SF): 'To me it always seems phoney when characters in science fiction movies speak English perfectly, with no accent. That's not the way the world is.' (See Brooker 2001 and Chapter 4.)

- *dialect*: everyone in the UK speaks a dialect, a sub-language which differs from a notional 'standard English'. So-called 'received pronunciation' or 'BBC English' is the dialect of the southern English middle class. Dialects also have differences of vocabulary and syntax as well as pronunciation, and dialect and accent together are read as key signifiers of class origin.
- *language register*: the vocabulary and syntax (grammar) we use to suit particular circumstances. Most of us are capable of changing this, from formal to informal modes for example.

ACTIVITY 1.11

Take a cassette recorder and a good-quality external microphone, and tape several different people talking in a variety of situations (classroom, pub, at home). Play back the recordings and try to ignore what they say, just listen to the sound of the voices.

- Can you recognise any of the codes listed above?
- Use them to describe the sound of any one voice.
- Can you relate the sound to the age or gender of the person? Surprisingly, some 'old' voices sound 'young' and vice versa. Perhaps it is other voice qualities which suggest someone is old or young?

Star presence across a range of media involves not just looks, but also voices and those who work on processing them for the sound track.

A voice is understood by most audiences as less constructed, more authentic than visible appearance, as a 'trace' off the body: size, gender, even smoking habits (see Branston 1995). From the 1930s to the 1950s the irritation of many British audiences with the upper-class voices in British films was expressed around 'the two types of people in our films – the Cockney and the Oxford accent type'.

A little later, the Scottish accent and brusque delivery of lines by Sean Connery as James Bond in 1962 were crucial signifiers of the more classless 'modern' social world of Bond-as-scripted-and-performed-in-the-Broccoli-films, compared to the upper-class John-Buchan-hero-in-the-Cold-War agent of Fleming's novels (see Branston 2000). The voice is arguably as important to this early reinvention of Bond as Connery's working-class star image and rugged, rather than suave, Pierce-Brosnan-style beauty and smoother 'trans-Atlantic' voice.

In radio and television it's been argued that the powerfully controversial written journalism of Julie Burchill has not led to television or radio success because of the light, unauthoritative quality of her voice.

Unlike that of most of the voices we encounter at college or at home, the technical quality of radio voices has been 'coded' by radio technologies. What we hear is a reproduction of the original voice, dependent on:

- the acoustics of the studio: a room with hard, shiny surfaces will produce a harsh, 'bright' edge to the voice; a studio with absorbent surfaces will soften the voice
- the choice of microphone
- the engineer's processing of the signal, for example in an echo chamber.

These *institutional and technical codes* are tremendously important. Radio 5, for example, has a different *mode of address* to its listener from Radio 4, partly through the voices of the presenters, and callers, especially those with distinctive regional accents, and also through the ways the Radio 4 and Radio 5 engineers process the voices differently. Maybe you imagine the studios of the two stations differently, just from the sound of the voices in them.

ACTIVITY 1.12

Run up and down the array of stations on your radio dial. Stop briefly at each voice you hear.

- Do you recognise the station immediately? Through a combination of codes?
- Does BBC local radio use more recognisably 'local' voices? Are commercial stations more likely to be staffed by presenters with an all-purpose 'music radio' voice?
- Why do you think this might be so?

This takes us into realism debates. Just like the blurred photographic image, the overlapping of voices on discussion programmes on radio (i.e. everyone talking at once) often signifies 'authentic lively debate' – and of course can be constructed, or faked, as can other aural signifiers.

ACTIVITY 1.13

Listen to a radio play or serial and make notes on how the signifiers (of 'childishness', of 'heated discussion' or foreign location or 'danger' etc.) are constructed.

We hope these brief introductory ideas about a 'semiotics of sound' will help you think about voices in audio-visual forms, and in your approaches to recording voices for your own productions.

References

Barker, Martin (1991) 'Iwo Jima: the photograph as symbol', *Magazine of Cultural Studies*, autumn.

Branston, Gill (1995) 'Viewer, I listened to him . . . voices, masculinity, *In the Line of Fire*' in Pat Kirkham and Janet Thumim (eds), *Me Jane: Masculinity, Movies and Women*, Lawrence and Wishart.

Branston, Gill (2000) *Cinema and Cultural Modernity*, Buckingham: Open University Press.

Brooker, Will (2001) 'Readings of racism: interpretation, stereotyping and *The Phantom Menace*', *Continuum*, vol. 15, no. 1.

Crisell, Andrew (1994, 2nd edition) *Understanding Radio*, London: Routledge.

Rose, Gillian (2001) *Visual Methodologies*, London: Sage.

Scannell, Paddy (1996) *Radio, Television and Modern Life*, Oxford: Blackwell.

Vulliamy, Ed (2001) 'Waving not drowning', *Guardian*, 23 September.

Wells, Liz (ed.) (2000, 2nd edition) *Photography: A Critical Introduction*, London and New York: Routledge.

Wilby, Peter and Conroy, Andy (1994) *The Radio Handbook*, London: Routledge.

2 Narratives

- Making **narratives**, or stories, is a key way in which meanings and pleasures get constructed and organised both in and outside the media.
- Both factual and fiction forms are subject to this kind of shaping.

Most of us spend a lot of time telling stories: gossiping about friends; telling jokes; filling family photo albums with appropriate events (rarely photos of stays in hospital) and highly constructed characters: the 'proud graduate' (never the 'hard-pressed student') at the 'happy ending' of one story, for example. All cultures seem to make stories as an involving and enjoyable way of creating sense and meanings in the world. Two points about systematic study of narrative in modern media:

- Narrative theory suggests that stories in whatever media and whatever culture share certain features.
- But particular media are able to 'tell' stories in different ways.

It is worth adding that you will hardly ever encounter a story separate from expectations about it, usually those of **genre**. Bear this in mind as you try out this chapter, and try to read it with Chapter 3.

General theories of narrative

This chapter explores the main narrative theories which have been used in Media Studies. These try to understand the devices and conventions governing how stories (fictional or factual) are organised into sequence, and the invitations these may make to audiences to become involved in various ways, and not others. Like much Media Studies, this suggests that quite ordinary activities are often connected to dominant sets of values.

Of course there are other ways of thinking about the telling and writing of stories, and names you will come across. If you are interested in producing

Like most semiotic approaches, these isolate texts from their context and uses *for the purpose of analysis*. Of course very few of us see a filmed or television story without any kind of knowledge of its genre or star or without the expectations set up by reviews.

rather than studying narrative you may be on a scriptwriting course and have come across the work of Syd Field. His books argue that all successful screenplays have a similar three-part structure (Set-Up, Confrontation, Resolution) and try to explore this in Hollywood films. Joseph Campbell (cited with respect by Field) is another name – an anthropologist interested in myths, or ancient stories which can be argued to be shared across cultures. He is said by film-makers such as George Lucas to be a key influence on films such as the *Star Wars* series.

The publication of *Hero With a Thousand Faces* (1949) established Joseph Campbell as a comparative mythologist, using a Jungian psychological framework to argue that 'eternal' myths or stories are shared by all cultures. Some have suggested that they:

- flatten important differences between the ways myths and stories are used and circulated in various cultures
- are used to give high cultural and quasi-religious status to commercially powerful products such as *Star Trek*, or the Lucas *Star Wars* films
- thereby conveniently avoid offending global audiences by not being too specific about exactly which 'god' or religion is being invoked.

Joseph Campbell (1904–87) influenced by Carl G. Jung (1875–1961), who argued that certain myths and symbols represent 'archetypal' patterns which have been central to human existence (e.g. the anima or 'feminine' side of men etc.).

Most Media Studies, however, is not involved in trying to produce stories (a wildly unpredictable process, too often thought to be reducible to formulas). It tries to understand them, especially in terms of their possible social and ideological roles. A good definition of narrative for these purposes (which of course applies to both fiction and non-fiction forms) is given by Branigan (1992: 3), who argues it is 'a way of organising spatial and temporal data into a cause-effect chain of events with a beginning, a middle and end that embodies a judgement about the nature of events'. Important theorists for this approach include **Propp**, Barthes, Todorov and Lévi-Strauss, who worked mostly with myths, novels and folk tales to try to understand how narrative shapings and values act within particular cultures. Here are the bare bones of these influential **structuralist** approaches to narrative.

Propp examined hundreds of examples of one kind of folk tale, the 'heroic wondertale', to see whether they shared any structures. He argued that whatever the surface differences (i.e. whether the stories dealt with poor woodcutters or youngest princes) it was possible to group its characters and actions into:

Vladimir Propp (1895–1970) Russian critic and folklorist whose influential book on narrative, translated as *Morphology of the Folk Tale*, was first published in 1928.

- eight character roles (or 'spheres of action' as he called them, to indicate how inseparable are character and action: think about it)
- thirty-one functions (such as 'a prohibition or ban is imposed on the hero' or 'the villain learns something about his victim') which move the story along, often in a highly predictable order. For example 'the punishment of the villain' always occurs at the end of a story, and the 'interdiction' or forbidding of some act, always comes at the beginning. What is apparently the same act can function in different ways for different narratives. For example, the 'prince' may build a castle as:
  - preparation for a wedding
  - defiance of a prohibition
  - solution of a task set.

Roles or spheres of action, Propp argued, make sense of the ways in which many very different figures (witch, woodcutter, dragon, etc.), could be reduced to eight character roles – not the same as the actual characters since one character can occupy several roles or 'spheres of action'. These are:

1 the *villain*
2 the *hero*, or character who seeks something, usually motivated by an initial lack – of money, or a mother, for example. ('Hero' is one of those terms that does not mean the same within theory as it does in life outside, where 'hero' usually refers to a male, and 'heroic' has moral connotations of 'admirable' or 'good'. Here the words are closer to describing someone who actively carries the events of a story, whether Buffy or Bart Simpson.)
3 the *donor*, who provides an object with some magic property
4 the *helper*, who aids the hero

The very terms 'prince' and 'princess' are much more than job descriptions. They come to us loaded with narrative expectations and connotations. **Q** How are these expectations played with in the series *Xena: Warrior Princess*?

5 the *princess*, reward for the hero (though see above) and object of the villain's schemes
6 her *father*, who rewards the hero
7 the *dispatcher*, who sends the hero on his way
8 the *false hero*.

Diana, Princess of Wales, could be seen as having had her life repeatedly narrativised in different media. An early narrative 'ended' at her wedding in 1981, and was a classic fairy tale, where her 'lack' (unhappy childhood, desertion by her mother, desire to 'fit in', few formal educational qualifications) was resolved by the magical transformation of 'becoming a princess' – the 'happy ending'. At the time this was signified by the kiss on the balcony of Buckingham Palace, repeated over and over in the media. (See Geraghty 1998.)

Such work on stories is inevitably bound up with the times and social orders which produced them. Propp's original study, for example, worked

Figure 2.1   Happy ending for the new princess?

Figure 2.2   Xena: 'warrior princess' and Proppian 'hero'.

with fairy tales from a period when many women would die in childbirth, and the role of ('wicked') stepmothers could therefore be a shared reference point. It's worth noting that now the hero can often be a female character, like Xena or Buffy, especially since the word 'heroine' (Propp's 'princess') designates a character who hangs around looking decorative until the hero is ready to sweep her away. (Many commentators prefer to use 'sought-for person' instead of 'princess'.)

Yet fairy tales, or versions of them, are still familiar to us. Think of *Shrek* (2001) and other animated films; the *Star Wars* series, the *Harry Potter* or *Lord of the Rings* books and films (2001), with their stories of male initiation, good versus evil and so on. Propp's approach continues to be influential, trying as it did to uncover structures beneath the surface differences of such widely circulated, popular forms. It reminds us that, though characters in stories may seem very 'real' (especially in cinema and television), they must be understood as *constructed characters*. Though played by actors who are cast for their resemblance to how we might imagine the character, they in fact have *roles to play for the sake of the story* and often get perceived very quickly, by audiences, in these roles – as 'hero', 'villain', 'helper' and so on. Even though most people are not aware of these roles, we tend to feel it very sharply when the person we thought was the hero or helper turns out to be the villain, as in *The Usual Suspects* (US 1995) or in *Psycho* (US 1960) where, to the shock of its first audiences, the female hero (and star) is killed off a third of the way through the film, and the shy young man who seemed to be a helper turns out to be something very different. Other media forms (see following case study) also construct villains – perhaps you are a fan of American wrestling with its over-the-top melodramatic oppositions of 'good' and 'evil'?

We do not have space to go into the many ways in which other cultures make narratives, from the 'magic realism' of Latin American forms to the ways in which Aboriginal culture tells its tales. If you can research them it will give you an idea of *both* how universally *shared* and how *differentiated* is this human activity.

Other narrative forms, such as the *Mahabharata* from Indian culture, or indeed western forms such as the musical or 'woman's film' take pleasure in much less action-driven narratives, using instead convoluted patterns (often circular) and several climaxes, and with scenes of spectacle, fantasy and humour given real narrative weight – for example in musical and 'Bollywood' forms.

'This was Nature at her most unforgiving' (BBC News reporter on floods in Italy, May 1998).

ACTIVITY 2.1

Check that you can identify narrative roles in your favourite *fictional* media text. Then try watching a *non-fiction* form (such as the news) for the way that media language will attribute narrative roles and thus construct 'characters'. Even in *weather forecasts* characters will often be made of natural forces: winds, isobars and so on may be called 'the villain' or 'to blame'; a warm front is 'coming to the rescue'.

- Does language used to describe illness or disease (such as cancer or AIDS) often construct it in dramatically villainous terms? (There is much medical debate about whether such 'imaging' is helpful or destructive for the sufferer.)

Tzvetan Todorov Bulgarian structuralist linguist (b. 1939) publishing influential work on narrative from the 1960s onwards.

Todorov argued that all stories begin with an '**equilibrium**' where any potentially opposing forces are 'in balance' – the 'once upon a time' moment. This is disrupted by some event, setting in train a series of other events, to close with a second, but different 'equilibrium' or status quo. His theory may sound just like the cliché that every story has a beginning, a middle and an end. But it's more interesting than that. His idea of 'equilibrium' labels a state of affairs, a status quo, and how this is 'set up' in certain ways and not others. 'Workers today decided to reject a pay offer of 1%', for instance, begins a news story with an apparent disruption to an equilibrium (of contented workers and fair management) but in fact we know about only one side of that 'balance'. We don't know for what kinds of trade-off the pay rise is being offered, after what length of negotiations, etc. How, where and when *else* the story could have begun are always good questions to ask.

'"The Royals" is the longest-running soap opera in Britain . . . the long running story of an extremely wealthy and powerful family . . . The fact that "The Royals" is loosely based on reality only adds to its fascination' (Coward (1984: 163 – written well before the success of *The Royle Family*).

Princess Diana's life, in its second period, was often 'told' by the media as a 'new story' which begins with the question: what does her presence in the British Royal Family mean? What kind of 'disruption' to that set-up was it: breath of fresh air, or neurotic selfishness, like 'Fergie's'? The *Panorama* interview can be seen as an attempt by her to 'tell her own story': this time, as one of moral virtue. (See Geraghty 1998.)

If you have seen the film *Memento* (US 2000) you will know that it experiments with narrative by having as hero a man who has lost his short-term memory and who uses notes and tattoos to remind himself of the past he painfully reconstructs as he hunt his wife's killer.

- If you haven't seen the film, try to sketch how such a narrative might proceed. What are its difficulties, and its pleasures?

Barthes suggested that narrative works with five different **codes** which activate the reader to make sense of it. This is an intricate theory, using deliberately unfamiliar terms, and Barthes is not at pains to make it accessible. But particularly interesting is his suggestion that an 'enigma code' works to keep setting up little puzzles to be solved (and not only at the beginning of the story), to delay the story's ending pleasurably: e.g. how will Tom Cruise get out of this predicament? What is in the locked room? How does *x* really feel about *y*? An action code will be read by means of accumulated details (looks, significant words) which relate to our cultural knowledge of what are often highly stereotypical models of such actions as 'falling in love' or 'being tempted into a robbery'. Barthes is important for this early attempt at building the possible involvement of 'readers' and their culturally formed expectations into a model of how narratives 'work' textually.

Such structuralist approaches have been applied not just to individual fictions but also to non-fiction forms such as major news stories, to see whether narrative drives 'set up' certain expectations and puzzles, look for (and in fact construct) tidy 'beginnings' and 'endings' etc. This can mean that complex historical and political explanations are structured out of the story-telling.

Lévi-Strauss argued that an abiding structure of all meaning-making, not just narratives, was a dependence on **binary oppositions**, or a conflict between two qualities or terms. Less interested in the order in which events were arranged in the plot (called **syntagmatic** relations), he looked 'beneath' them for deeper or **paradigmatic** arrangements of themes. Though this theory can be applied to individual stories and can act as a useful 'way in', strictly speaking it should be applied to sets of narratives, as in the western genre. Writers suggested that the different sheriffs, outlaws, schoolmarms, Native Americans etc. of hundreds of westerns could not only be usefully analysed in Proppian narrative terms (Native Americans as thrilling 'villains' whose motives were often witheld, for example), but could be seen as being organised, over time, according to systematic oppositions, among others:

A reversal of the usual narrative shape of strike stories by Jeremy Hardy, the *Guardian*, 2nd May 1998: 'Magnet [the kitchen manufacturers] have imposed all the conditions they were demanding when the strike began, including cuts in bereavement and paternity leave, and the scrapping of the pension scheme. I shouldn't say 'demanded' because, as we know, workers "demand" and employers "offer".'

For specialists: the five codes are the action or proairetic; the enigma or hermeneutic; the semic; the symbolic and the cultural or referential code.

See following case study on *Psycho*.

Paradigm a class of objects or concepts.

Syntagm an element which follows another in a particular sequence. Imagine choosing from a menu. Paradigmatic elements are those from which you choose (starters, main courses, desserts). The syntagm is the sequence into which they are arranged. Sometimes these structures are treated as 'horizontal' (across time) and 'vertical' (along values) aspects of narratives.

37

homesteaders	Native Americans
Christian	pagan
domestic	savage
weak	strong
garden	wilderness
inside society	outside society

Q It is also suggested that gender difference is entwined with these opposing lists. Which list would you say is closer to qualities called 'feminine'?

Narration, story and plot

The term **narration** describes *how* stories are told, how their material is selected and arranged in order to achieve particular effects with their audiences.

    Plot and **story** are key terms here (though a useful distinction is the one used by Russian theorists in the 1920s between *syuzhet* and *fabula*, used instead of plot and story partly because the meanings of those terms are often slippery, and get confused with each other). Bordwell and Thompson (2001: 61) usefully define story as consisting of 'all the events in a narrative, both explicitly presented and inferred'. The plot, on the other hand, is 'everything visibly and audibly present in the film before us; in other words those highly selected parts of the story which the narrative puts before us'. You can think of the story as something you are able to assemble at the end of the narrative. It would include routine events, like washing, which we assume carry on happening during a story, but would be tedious as part of the plot. It may also include material we only find out by the end of the story, having been busy trying to piece things together throughout, such as Norman's mental condition in *Psycho*.

    Other writers have explored this area in terms of the knowledge which the 'reader' has compared to the characters: is it the same, or more? When? How much more? How has this been contrived? For example, we should feel at the end of a good detective story or thriller that we have been enjoyably puzzled, so that the 'solution', our piecing together of the story in its proper order out of the evidence offered by the plot, will come as a pleasure. We should not feel that the plot has cheated; that parts of the story have suddenly been revealed which we couldn't possibly have guessed at. The butler cannot, at the last minute, suddenly be revealed to have been a poisons expert.

Soap operas often work in terms of secrets, of knowledge sometimes kept all from other characters – but not the viewer.

Q How might this affect the pleasures of narrative suspense for viewers? What pleasures might take its place?

One of the pleasures of Sherlock Holmes or *Inspector Morse* stories is that though we can never be as brilliant as Holmes/Morse, we can catch up through Dr Watson/Lewis – and also enjoy the satisfaction of feeling that we will never be that 'slow'.

ACTIVITY 2.2

Take one of your favourite stories and tell it in flashback form.

- What effect does this have on how you get to find things out, how your sympathies flow?

As an example, take the story of Red Riding Hood:

- Who would have to be speaking, and to whom, to tell this story in flashback? The wolf in 'A Wolf's Afterlife'? Red Riding Hood herself? What effects would this have on suspense?
- How would you apply such questions to a genre where suspense is not as important as it is in thrillers, for example romance or sitcom?

Figure 2.3 What if the story began here?

Another part of the construction of narratives involves the 'voice' telling the story. A first-person narration will use 'I' as the voice of the teller, and should not give the reader access to events which that 'I' could not have witnessed, or known of. A third-person or impersonal narration however refers to a story which seems to 'get itself told', as in 'Once upon a time there was a prince . . .'. Though cinema and many television or video narratives begin with a literal 'voice over' telling us the story from a personal point of view, they usually settle into the mode of impersonal narration, voiceless, and just seeming to unfold before us.

Spectacular cheats are possible: *Sunset Boulevard* (US 1950) tells the story through a first-person narrator who is in fact dead in the story's 'present'. *The Usual Suspects* (US 1995) relies for its surprise on a long, misleading flashback. If you've seen *The Others* (2001) you may like to discuss whether you feel it 'cheats' successfully.

ACTIVITY 2.3

Look at a few ads from television. Ask yourself of each:

- Is this a narrative? Does it 'begin' rather than just 'start', and 'end' rather than 'stop'?
- How do I know? Are the people in it constructed as 'characters'? How is this done?
- Or is it simply a list of claims or prices, or an image of a situation in which the product seems attractive?

It's well worth looking in detail at how ads work, since there has normally been a lot of effort put into constructing their little narratives so as to be read easily. If using narrative form, an ad will group its events in cause and effect order. Non-narrative ads won't do this. They may simply consist of a set of claims about a product, as in supermarket ads which list prices, or of setting up a glamorous mood linked to the product, as in many car ads.

Even in a few seconds, a narrative ad will create a sense of characters, action and perhaps enigma codes through economical use of signs and stereotypical traits – blonde hair, certain glances etc. These work as Propp suggests: the same traits that help us build up a sense of them as 'real people' are simultaneously crucial for the action, the furthering of the plot. For such audio-visual forms casting will work with its own 'cues' to the audience: blonde hair, a certain accent, height, star image etc. will all imply certain (different) consequences within particular narrative (or generic) contexts.

There will be a discernible 'hero' who carries the plot along (though often you may feel that in the conventional sense of the word the 'hero' is usually the product). There will be, as Todorov suggests, some sense of an initial situation, which is disrupted or altered and then happily resolved at the end – usually, of course, through the magical intervention of the product being sold.

You will also probably be able to distinguish the *story* as you can reassemble it having gone through a narrative, and the *plot* which has kept you surprised or held throughout it. Even if flashback is not used, try to imagine the same events told differently, from the point of view of another character, for example, or with different amounts of time, and therefore emphasis, given to different segments of the narrative.

Applying Lévi-Strauss's approach, television ads can often be analysed so as to show a systematic grouping of recurring signs, situations or characters in opposition to each other, with one set of terms privileged. Levi's jeans ads for example, still often group qualities as the following sets of oppositions, with Levi's associated with one side, the preferred set:

1912: two polar bears see a newspaper headline about the (real) sinking of the *Titanic*. One says to the newsvendor: 'My friend wants to know: what happened to the iceberg?'

young	old
hip	uncool
young generation	parental figures
sexy	asexual
rule-breaking/weird	rule-enforcing/'straight'
Levi's jeans	not Levi's

Narratives in different media

These broad structures, which seem to govern all story-making and story-telling, have to work differently in different media, and for different cultures. This is worth bearing in mind if you're involved in a project which asks you to *choose* a medium in which to make a story: what can *x* medium do (strip cartoon, say, or radio) that *y* cannot, and vice versa? These differences are partly due to the nature of different media and technologies.

Photography

This might seem an odd example of a narrative form, since it deals in frozen moments of time (like stained-glass windows, or cartoons). But often the impact of a powerful news or advertising photo lies in what it makes us imagine has gone before, or is about to happen. In this sense narrative is often signalled, depending on angle, information given, construction of imagined characters – and whether or not black and white film stock is involved. The difference between black and white and colour often signals 'pastness' and 'presentness' in the story.

ACTIVITY 2.4

Look for ads which use the black and white/colour contrast in the way suggested above.
* How do they set in play narrative expectations and knowledge?

Comic strips

Comic strips (and by extension animation) tell their stories by a compelling combination of
* words (including thought bubbles)
* line drawings. These can streamline characters and events more than even the highest budget movie. You never have to worry about spots on the

star's face, or problems with lighting or expensive sets in comic strip and animation.

- flashpoint illustrations of key moments involving extreme angles and exaggerations.

Q What difference does this 'speed' and clarity or capacity for exaggeration make to the kinds of narratives which can be told in animation? Do you think *South Park* or *The Simpsons* tell different kinds of stories partly because of their different styles of animation?

Cinema

Like video and audio recordings, this is a 'time-based' medium, manipulating time and space rather than image or words alone. The average feature film length of about two hours, and the way audiences pay to see it all at one sitting, can give it some of the intensity of a short story. It may lead to an experience different from that of longer fictions like soaps, serials or novels, read or viewed over days, weeks, even years, while we do many other things in between. Chapter 10 will explore further the ways we have become accustomed to stories being partly 'told' via conventions of setting, editing, sound, framing, camera positioning etc. in both cinema and television.

Radio

This is a medium using sounds and silence, which affects the way it can handle narrative. It has to construct, through voices, noises, sound effects and silence, the illusion of space between characters, and time between segments. It cannot give up much narrative time to features on which cinema might want to linger, as evidence of how the movie has spent its resources (say the display of visual special effects, or of costumes). Characters cannot stay silent for long periods of time (like the Tim Roth character, mostly silent, dying 'onstage' in *Reservoir Dogs* (US 1992)), since they would seem to have 'disappeared'. Since radio's signifiers are relatively cheap and easy to produce, it is free to construct the most bizarre and exotic stories, from time travel to a play about memories flashing through the head of a drowning woman. If you are a fan of *The Hitchhiker's Guide to the Galaxy* you might like to compare how its narrative is shaped in radio, television and book forms.

Institutions and narratives 1: broadcasting and soaps

Differences between the ways stories get told in different media are partly, then, to do with the material (sound, celluloid, computer screens, line drawings, image and sound, words alone) of that medium. But they are

also to do with *institutional* or *industrial* demands. The box below
suggests differences in how 'closed' or single and 'open' or serial narratives
tend to work in those different media institutions, 'cinema' and
'broadcasting'.

'Closed' narrative	'Open' narrative
e.g. films in cinema	e.g. television and radio soap opera
1 'Tight' reading involved; audience aware it's watching a complete story and therefore reading with the likely end in mind.	1 Casual reading, without the sense of an ending; soaps proceed as though they could go on for ever – even when one is terminated.
2 Relatively few *central* characters; 'depth' of audience knowledge often set up, with even interior voice overs giving characters' thoughts, hallucinations etc.	2 Many more characters, naturalistically represented and producing a *multi-strand plot*.
3 Characters arranged in a 'hierarchy' (central, cameo, supporting roles, extras, etc.).	3 Characters not usually in a marked hierarchy but shift in and out of prominence (partly to suit the production needs of the serial).
4 Often with audience invited to make 'verdicts' on them, identifying narrative roles, as in hero, villain, victim.	4 Characters shift also in and out of narrative function. Today's villain may be next week's helper or even hero.
5 Time usually very compressed: typical two hours of screen time constructs events as happening over months, years, sometimes centuries.	5 Time usually corresponds to 'real world time' *within* the segments of each episode, though *across* it time is compressed, as in cinema. Flashbacks rare.
6 Time and events are usually special to this particular story, and need have no resemblance to the viewer's world, though *specific* reference is possible as are flashbacks and even flashforwards.	6 The differences between time in the serial and outside are blurred. Episodes may make *broad* reference to real-life events going on at the same time, such as elections, Christmas.
7 Reader or viewer *usually* has evidence about the characters only from this single text – plus star, publicity and genre expectations (though **synergy** and the prevalence of sequels complicate this).	7 Audiences are assumed to have different kind of memory, and knowledge of a long-running soap. Magazines, television, the press often speculate about actors' contracts, and thus the fate of characters.
8 The same audience can be assumed to watch the film from beginning to end.	8 Each episode has to try to address both experienced and new viewers.
9 Often elaborate visual image, and music as integral part of the narrative.	9 Relatively rare use of music, especially in British soaps, and relatively simple visual image.

The open-ended serial form broadcast across fifty-two weeks of the year (a rough definition of a soap opera) developed first on US radio in the 1930s as a cheap way of involving housewives, whose buying choices the detergent manufacturers (and other businesses) wanted to influence. It seemed an ideal form both for commercial television in the 1960s, keen to sell the promise of audiences' regular attention to advertisers and for the BBC to revive in 1985 with *EastEnders*, wanting to boost its early evening audiences. This was partly in the hope they would stay with the channel all evening, and also to help the BBC produce evidence of large audience numbers when making its arguments for the level of the next licence fee. Now one could argue that major soaps act like big news programmes, or major serials. Such products used to be called 'flagship programmes' but now seem to help to **brand** channels in the international television market.

Though soap opera is one of the most familiar and discussed forms of media, it is not just 'one thing'. Even on British television there are Australian, American, Welsh and other British soaps, made within different kinds of broadcasting institutions (**public service broadcasting**; commercially funded etc.). These in turn divide into high- and low-budget products, and have different relationships to documentary forms, to ideas of glamour, to sitcom, romance, regional identities, and also male audiences. Nevertheless, we can generalise that one of British soap's attractions for its producers has been that costs can be kept down, partly because narrative can be centred on a few key locations (e.g. the hotel, pub, launderette or café). These are meeting places, one of the staples of the narrative, and also key to soaps' economies and production needs. Since a soap usually has to go out for two or three nights a week, many storylines are necessary, so that particular ones can swing in and out of prominence, allowing:

- time for rehearsals, and for actors' holidays, pantomime contracts, pregnancies, illnesses etc.
- a wide appeal through several stories happening at once so as to involve different sections of the audience. If you're impatient with one 'strand', you know that another, which interests you more, will probably be along in half a minute or so. The meeting places give both a chance for storylines to meet and switch, and also coherence and the feeling of 'community' so central to soap's pleasures.

Soap narratives may also change as a result of attempts to shift the composition of their audiences – and advertisers. Over the last few years several soaps have moved 'upmarket' in terms of their sets, situations and some character types, as part of the attempt to sell more expensive ad slots addressing more affluent audiences. After the success of *Brookside*, other soaps tried to attract male audiences to this traditionally female form by means of 'tough' story lines and characters, as in *The Bill*, which falls between a soap

(continuous production, never a 'closed' ending to an episode) and a series
(self-contained story lines each week, as in *X-Files* or *ER*). Serials (including
'classic' serials) and 'mini-series' (often a pilot project) are other narrative
forms designed to meet particular scheduling needs.

Soaps have also often covered controversial themes in order to aggregate
audiences. In October 2001 *EastEnders* dealt with child abuse via Kat being
discovered as the mother of Zoe (a character until then treated as her sister in
the series) as a result of in-family abuse when she was a very young adult.
Blanket publicity and coverage of this storyline, for example in the press, on
television etc., on the morning of the revelatory episode stressed the care
taken by the programme-makers with this topic, contacting the Samaritans,
NPSCC etc. What was then interesting was how skilfully the narrative itself
was written (by Tony Jordan) and performed so as to maintain the
involvement of an audience who 'knew what was going to happen' in an
obvious sense.

ACTIVITY 2.5

If you hear that any other such controversial, well 'flagged' episodes are coming up,
try to see how such narrative turns are managed, and kept interesting for audiences
who know their broad outcome. One trick is to stop the tape and ask yourself
'how would I end this scene? What lines would I write?' and then see how it has in
fact been achieved.

It also seems that soap has actual advantages over more prestigious drama
forms in its long-runningness (*Coronation Street* has been running for over forty
years!). This means that the long-term, often invisible consequences of 'social
issues' (such as rape, unemployment, child abuse, the trauma of serving in a
war) can be dealt with and re-surface for a particular character over many
years – as in real life. This gives it certain advantages over single narratives
such as 'issue films' or plays. Of course soap opera also has limitations to its
realism: when have you ever heard characters in a television soap discussing
election issues, with the names of politicians, or other television soaps, as
most of us do?

Radio, because cheaper to produce, can work differently, at least in relation
to its 'up-to-date-ness'. In *The Archers*, November 2001, for example, a young
character complained 'I'm missing *Hollyoaks* for this'. And the first case of foot
and mouth, with its disastrous consequences for farming, was mentioned by
the end of the week in which it was first reported in a way that would have
been very difficult for a television soap.

Can you research when the foot
and mouth outbreak was dealt
with on the television soap
Emmerdale?

ACTIVITY 2.6

Make notes on an episode of your favourite soap.

- How many storylines does that episode contain?
- To which sections of the audience do you think they appeal?
- Which are the main storylines? The same as a few weeks ago? Changed? Why?
- How is time managed in the episode?
- How many sets are used? Why have these places been chosen?
- Are there any rumours circulating about the fate of particular characters or actors, in the press, on television, or fanzines?
- How does your knowledge of these affect your viewing? Does it add to your pleasure? How?
- How does the soap story try to address both experienced and new viewers? How are repeated use of characters' names, repeated updatings of the storylines and so on managed so as to inform new viewers, yet not bore regular ones?
- If it's on a commercial channel, what do the ads before, during and after suggest about the expected audience?
- Is it making reference to a current news issue? If so, in what way?

Institutions and narratives 2: the influence(s) of computer culture

You might like to consider how your favourite computer game both constructs its narrative and attempts to draw you in. Is this just a matter of the game's special effects, or is the construction of character and story also key to games which you find 'satisfying'?

Contemporary Hollywood cinema is mostly produced by huge conglomerate companies with interests in the spin-off computer games, music tracks, clothes, videos, CDs which their films may help to market. It's been suggested (see Branston 2000) that we are getting used to new narrative possiblities as a result of two related developments:

- these commercial links between 'blockbuster movies' and the computer games they often sell
- many people's increasing cultural familiarity with the ways that computers allow us to re-try possibilities – in games, drafts of essays, as well as hypertext novels, where readers can select their own route by clicking on active links to new text which changes the story. These experiences may be producing new kinds of narrative.

For example: not only does a blockbuster film such as *Star Wars: The Phantom Menace* (US 1999) function, narratively, so as to resemble an extended games

**Institutions and narratives 2:
the influence(s) of computer
culture**

or toy ad, with the same kinds of action puzzles, spectacle, suspenseful situations etc. – in other words as a kind of ad for the game which the same corporation will try to sell you. But it also has a 'prequel/sequel' narrative aspect which seems to resemble the possibility we now experience, with computers, of going back over previous ground in a story and 're-playing' it. This has happened before of course. Every new version of Charles Dickens's *A Christmas Carol* uses the structure. But crucially this nineteenth-century vision of 'replaying' was for moral and religious purposes – of repentance and a 'second chance'. Much contemporary cinema seems fascinated simply by the possibility of having a games-like control over the way the 'narrative' turns out. This is part both of Hollywood blockbusters and of less mainstream cinemas.

You may yourself use phrases which express a subjective experience of computer games and other technological forms: 'I wanted to just rewind the whole incident' or 'Fast forward please'.

Groundhog Day (US 1993) and *Sliding Doors* (UK 1998) as well as *Possible Loves* (Brazil 2001) re-run their romantic and comic narratives rather like a game or a tape; *eXistenZ* (Canada/France/UK 1999) explicitly moves between the reality levels of movies and games; *Antz* (US 1999) has the mental landscape of a multi-level game; *Memento* (US 2000) uses the narrative device of damage to the hero's memory to 'play the story backwards'; and *Run, Lola, Run* (Germany 1999) plays the same 'story' several times, suggesting that small differences are crucial ones. Though not all of these share the corporate marketing connections of those who distribute blockbusters, they are interested in quite new possibilities for narrative which seem to be related to our widespread experience of computers.

ACTIVITY 2.7

Explore the process of how you 'read' a film or ad for *narrative* developments in your next viewing.

- Then note how it relates to the kinds of knowledge usually available *before* entering a cinema or renting a video or watching ads.
- Have you ever seen a film or ad with no *generic* knowledge (e.g. via poster in cinema foyer, friends' comments) of what to expect?

This takes us to Chapter 3, *Genres* and how these expectations are prepared, and played with.

References

Barthes, Roland (1977) *Introduction to the Structural Analysis of Narratives*, London: Fontana.

Bordwell, David and Thompson Kirstin (2001, 6th edition) *Film Art: An Introduction*, New York: McGraw Hill, and excellent related Online Learning Center http://www.mhhe.com/socscience/art-film/bordwell_6_filmart/

Branigan, Edward (1992) *Narrative Comprehension and Film*, London: Routledge.

Branston, Gill (2000) *Cinema and Cultural Modernity*, Buckingham: Open University Press.

Campbell, Joseph (1949) *The Hero with a Thousand Faces*, reprint Myrkos, 1972.

Coward, Ros (1984) *Female Desire: Women's Sexuality Today*, London: Paladin.

Field, Syd (1994) *Four Screenplays: Studies in the American Screenplay*, New York: Dell.

Geraghty, Christine (1991) *Women and Soap Opera*, London: Polity Press.

Geraghty, Christine (1998) 'Story' in 'Flowers and tears: the death of Diana, Princess of Wales', *Screen*, vol. 39, Spring.

Lévi-Strauss, Claude (1972) 'The structural study of myth', in R. and F. De George (eds), *The Structuralists from Marx to Lévi-Strauss*, New York: Doubleday Anchor.

Propp, Vladimir (1975) *The Morphology of the Folk Tale*, Austin: University of Texas Press.

Todorov, Tzvetan (1977) *The Poetics of Prose*, Oxford: Blackwell.

Further reading

Eagleton, Terry (1983) *Literary Theory: An Introduction*, Oxford: Blackwell, Chapter 3.

Perkins, Victor (1990) *Film as Film*, London: Penguin.

CASE STUDY: *PSYCHO* AND NEWS NARRATIVES

- Synopsis
- *Psycho* and narrative theories
- Story and plot in *Psycho*
- *Psycho* as a cinematic narrative
- Non-fiction narrative forms: news
- References
- Further reading

Psycho (US 1960) is one of the best-known films ever made, which is why we chose it for this case study. Not only are its visual images (and director Alfred Hitchcock) famous, but echoes and uses of its musical score regularly remind audiences of its celebrated powers to shock. A second version was made in 1998, in colour, with almost identical music and script, Anne Heche in the Janet Leigh role and Vince Vaughn playing Norman Bates. Though poorly received (see Rosenbaum 1998), it makes an interesting point of comparison if you have time to watch it: how do meanings, resonances and narrative itself change when a film-maker uses 'the same' shots, very similar script, but different actors, set design and colour instead of black and white film stock? However, if you have somehow missed seeing the original *Psycho*, read this synopsis of its plot.

Synopsis

Marion Crane (Janet Leigh) and her lover Sam (John Gavin) meet in her lunch break in a hotel room, as happens whenever he can come to Phoenix. He is divorced, working in a hardware store, and since he's paying maintenance to his ex-wife, and for his father's debts, he feels they cannot afford to get married. She goes back to her work as a secretary, where her boss entrusts her with $40,000 in cash, asking her to bank it.

Later, she drives out of Phoenix with the money. After being stopped by a patrolman and exchanging her car to evade detection, she stops at a motel, run by Norman Bates (Anthony Perkins) whose mother can be glimpsed and heard in the house nearby. Unbeknown to Marion, Bates watches her undressing through a concealed hole in the wall. She seems about to return to Phoenix to confess to the theft and return the money, but is brutally stabbed to death in the shower. Norman, finding her body, puts it into a car (unwittingly also putting the money with her) which he pushes into a swamp.

Lila, Marion's sister, arrives at Sam's workplace and they begin the hunt for Marion, at the same time as Arbogast, a private detective investigating the missing $40,000, arrives on the scene. Arbogast questions Norman, who at first denies Marion's visit to the motel. Returning later to investigate further, Arbogast is brutally stabbed to death.

When he fails to return, Lila persuades Sam to accompany her to the deputy sheriff who tells them that Mrs Bates has been dead for ten years, having poisoned the man she was involved with when she discovered he was married, and then killing herself. The bodies were found by Norman. We hear Norman speaking to his mother and insisting on taking her down to the cellar.

Lila and Sam check into the motel and begin to search it. Lila is shocked to discover a woman's stuffed corpse in the cellar and Norman, dressed in old-fashioned woman's clothing, enters, trying to stab her. Later, a psychiatrist explains that the now incarcerated Norman is schizophrenic, and had murdered his possessive mother two years after his father died, as he was jealous of her lover. He had then taken on her personality, especially at times when he was attracted to a woman, as he had been to Marion.

ACTIVITY 2.8

How different is this verbal account from the movie itself as you experienced it?

- Do you have any disagreements with particular emphases?
- Begin writing your own synopsis. How would you do it? Where would you begin?
- How much knowledge would you release to your reader? When?

Psycho and narrative theories

We will apply narrative theories to the film, though it is hard to separate these from the cues given by generic familiarity with the horror genre and detective thriller.

The Internet Movie Database is full of plot summaries of other films, if you want to try these exercises on one of them.

Q How would you describe the initial situation or equilibrium in the film (i.e. after Todorov)?

A It seems to consist of simply a secretary and her lover (Marion and Sam) who want to marry but cannot afford to.

Q And the disruption to this?

A Marion's decision to steal the $40,000 her boss asks her to bank.

We are partly prepared for this disruption by our generic expectations as well as, arguably, Barthes's action codes. We 'read' not just the lovers' conversation about money but also the dates superimposed on the film's opening shots with the knowledge of what they usually signal in crime genres and especially the group now known as 'film noir',

often involving a guilty couple drawn into deadly crimes.

Yet that caption:

PHOENIX, ARIZONA, FRIDAY, DECEMBER THE ELEVENTH, TWO FORTY-THREE P.M.

is a kind of visual cheat, since by the end of the film the theft has ceased to matter at all. It was a 'red herring', though important in character terms for our sense of Marion's change of mind just before she's murdered. When, to our surprise, this happens, a second equilibrium is set up. The surprise is partly one that would occur in whatever medium the narrative were told since Marion was the hero or central figure (with her boss as dispatcher, to use more of Propp's terms) and we expect her to carry that role for most of the story.

But Marion/Leigh's death is also a play with the conventions of a particular media institution: the cinema of the star system. Janet Leigh *stars* as Marion, and we expect stars to play in the film to the end. After her death, the hero role is split between Sam and Lila (with Arbogast as helper). The audience's attitude towards Norman probably changes, but is always partly formed as Propp and Barthes suggest.

Viewers or readers do seem to try to make sense of characters by exactly the kinds of 'spheres of action' which Propp suggests and which we have grown accustomed to in several genres:

- Is Norman going to turn out to be a helper or victim, as the scene clearing up the shower suggests?
- Is he the false hero we expect for a while, when we may suspect he's clearing up after his mother's killing, and we anticipate that the film may turn out to be about his defence of his mad mother?

Psycho, like any detective or mystery fiction, depends on setting up characters, codes of enigma and codes of action which mislead the audience. These will work with stereotypical features of characters' actions (and within particular genres, and budgets). Does Norman's angular appearance, accentuated by lighting and camera angles in his encounters with Marion, signify 'shy young man' or 'strange neurotic'? We busily read the signs or clues, as Barthes suggests, puzzling about what's going on, what will happen next, and expecting, as Todorov suggests, the pleasure of solution with the final equilibrium or closure. In the case of *Psycho*, this consists of:

- Norman incarcerated and diagnosed by the psychiatrist as criminally insane
- Lila and Sam safe, but knowing now Marion is dead
- an unknown number of bodies, including those of Marion and Arbogast, in the swamp, as well as the $40,000, which the audience has probably forgotten about.

Q What values are confirmed in the final equilibrium? What sense of good or evil?

Story and plot in *Psycho*

Q Think back to the initial equilibrium. What changes would occur to the narrative if this were constructed around Norman?

A Sympathy, knowledge and identification would be affected: the illusion that Mrs Bates is still alive would have to go, and Norman's madness would have to be signified. Sympathy and identification would be affected by this rearranged knowledge: for example, the plot could hardly begin with the arrival of Marion at the motel, since she would not yet be a character known to us, and her death would not therefore invite as much involvement, and horror.

'Norman Bates heard a noise and a shock went through him. It sounded as though somebody was tapping on the windowpane . . .' Thus begins the novel on which the film *Psycho* was based.

- How would you continue from here?
- How would you preserve suspense, especially around the mother's identity?

To help focus on plotting and time shifts, make notes on moments when the film goes into extended 'real time' (i.e. when the length of time taken by events on screen corresponds almost exactly to the length of time they would take in real life). When does this happen, and why do you think it happens?

One example: when Norman discovers Marion's body, and begins to clean up the bathroom. The scene begins with his cry 'Mother! Oh God! Mother, Mother! Blood, blood!' over shots of the house and his running from it towards the motel. This comparatively long scene seems partly constructed to allow audiences to recover from the shock of the killing. The audience reaction was much more extreme when the film was first released: indeed, according to Anthony Perkins, the entire scene in the hardware store following the shower murder was usually inaudible thanks to leftover howls after the shower scene. Hitchcock is even said to have asked Paramount to allow him to remix the sound to allow for the audience's reaction (see Rebello 1991).

The scene also swings suspicion away from this 'nervous young man'. If audiences suspected too early on that he was the killer, it might spoil some of the 'finding out' pleasures of this mystery/thriller/horror movie.

Clearly the careful arrangement of events in the plotting is crucial to most films, even ones that don't proceed by flashback, or seek to create tight suspense. Here, if the plot's ordering of events corresponded exactly to that of the story, we'd have a quite different kind of film, something like a psychological study of Norman. Our point of view would be affected: we'd be 'with' Norman at the beginning, and he could less easily function as the 'monster' in a suspenseful horror movie, outside understanding and sympathy (a narrative role which the word 'psycho' evokes in newspaper headlines).

Instead we'd be offered the pleasures of a developing understanding of this 'case history'. Knowledge, sympathy and of course possible styles of filming would be affected. In other stories using flashback, the moments when the plot goes into the past are often trying to elicit sympathy for a character. In Emily Brontë's novel *Wuthering Heights*, for example, much is revealed about Heathcliff's childhood towards the end of the narrative, by which time he seems almost monstrous, and the insight into his treatment in childhood suddenly swings our sympathies right round, back to him for a while (see Figure 2.4).

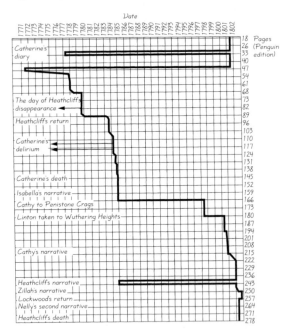

Figure 2.4 The narrative structure of the novel *Wuthering Heights* shown as a graph. It illustrates the ways that 'flashbacks' (via characters talking about earlier parts of their lives, diaries discovered, etc.) adjust the delivery of the story so as to manipulate audience interest and sympathy.

ACTIVITY 2.9

- Try to draw a graph or chart which will show how *Psycho* has been plotted in terms of time shifts. Draw a line that runs across the top of the graph to represent the actual time covered by the story (i.e. from Norman's childhood to his monologue in the police station. We're told he killed his parents ten years previously).

- Then draw, at the side of the graph, a line roughly representing plot or *syuzhet* time. This, of course, will be much less than the ten to fifteen years of the story. Try to proportion it according to the sections of the film, e.g. Lila and Sam set out about half-way through.
- When does the film go into flashbacks? Remember that events can be represented verbally in a film narrative, through conversations.
- What effects might these have on audience knowledge of events, or sympathy towards certain characters?

Applying Lévi-Strauss

Lévi-Strauss is less interested in the chronological plotting of a story (though that is part of his 'syntagmatic' group) than in repeated elements and their systematic relationship, usually across many stories, which he called the 'paradigmatic' aspect of myths.

ACTIVITY 2.10

Jot down any repeated oppositions which strike you in this film, such as: dead/alive; mother/son; the past/the present; dark/light.

- Do they seem to fall into groups that might help to account for the movie's power?

Lévi-Strauss's approach has been fruitfully applied to film and television. Underlying patterns are normally traced over a series, or a whole genre (the western; the gangster movie) or even an author's output (Hitchcock being the prime example of someone who is credited with this 'single author' influence over the films he directed). It is more problematic when applied to a single film such as this. Still, you may feel it helps you to understand how the plot has been structured. Does it support the feeling that Mother is set up as the 'real' villain? She is the only main character (remember they can be constructed offscreen, by verbal accounts) whose story, or presence, or point of view we are not given. We know her only through the psychiatrist's account (very sympathetic to Norman), with phrases such as 'His mother was a clinging, demanding woman' and 'Matricide is probably the most unbearable crime of all – most unbearable to the son who commits it.' Pretty uncomfortable for the mother too, but the film's plot gives us little room to feel this. Applying Lévi-Strauss might help us see whether mothers, or the malign powers of dead or older women, are constructed in this way in other films by Hitchcock.

Psycho as a cinematic narrative

Like most movies, this one is told in an 'impersonal' way. The camerawork and plotting, let alone any voice over, do not position us with any one character's point of view. (Try to imagine it told from the point of view of Marion, or Norman, or Lila.) And, working in the classic continuity system, events mostly just seem to unfold.

There are a few exceptions to the rule, when the camera seems to be openly 'telling the story'. In the scene just after Marion has been entrusted with $40,000, we see her dressing, the money lying on the bed. The camera, with suspenseful music on sound track, moves from the money to her handbag and back again, as though to offer her temptation. It's like the moment after the murder, when Norman takes a last look round the bedroom and the camera 'tells the story', reminding us of the money lying wrapped in a newspaper.

Though different media tell stories in different ways (**Q** what would be the literary equivalent of these shots?) some narrative effects can be shared by different media.

- The repetition of certain compositions, or musical themes, or phrases in film and television. In *Psycho* Bernard Herrmann's score works with two main repeated themes, one suggesting flight and pursuit, the other resembling a series of screams (most

famously in the shower scene). These are an important part of how we experience the 'clues' of the narrative. They also provide formal pleasures over and above that, as we register 'a story well told', as a joke can be well or badly told.

- The repeated use of certain compositions (such as a full-screen menacing face in *Psycho*) is both a narrative and a broader formal device, rather like the use of rhyme in poetry to point up connections and contrasts, or like refrains in songs.

It may be that when we see the full-screen face of Mother near the end, it's disturbing partly because it is reminiscent of the face of the traffic policeman, his eye sockets replaced by huge sunglasses, who gives Marion (and the audience) a nasty shock early on in the movie. It's also reminiscent of Norman's face, when lit so as to hollow out his eye sockets. The two sets of associations or connotations are brought together in the final shots of the film where, if you look carefully, you will see Norman's face merge with Mother's mummified one, then both dissolve into the image of a car being lifted from the swamp.

Critics have suggested the final shots are particularly satisfying because at the end of such a puzzling narrative we suddenly have explanation, and also an image of something coming into the light of day after so much repression and darkness. At any rate, it is a very visual and intensely narrative moment.

ACTIVITY 2.11

Look at other ways in which film and television construct narratives (such as lighting, costume, music, cutting, voices: see Chapter 11). Explore how they work in this movie, in a particular scene. How would you represent the chosen scene, and such elements within it:

- on radio?
- in written form?
- in comic strip form?

Figure 2.5 **Q** Looking at this poster for the re-release of the original film, what expectations do you think audiences might have had as they began to watch the film?

Non-fiction narrative forms: news

Though news is a 'factual' form, it is striking how often, especially in radio and television, such 'reality-based' programmes themselves take on a narrative shape – those teases around the ad breaks for example, or the 'happy ending', perhaps of a medical breakthrough, with which news bulletins often end. And of course all news reporters are trained in how to construct a 'good story'. This, especially for tabloid forms, involves shaping along the lines of suspense, marking clearly the story's beginning and ending, and allocating roles such as heroes, villains and victims to people who may in fact themselves overlap the actions evoked by those

terms – someone who is both a consumer of rail services and a worker on the railway, for example.

'Reality television' and narrative

One of the appeals of the first series of the British *Big Brother* was produced by the construction of narrative expectations and characters across what everyone knew was a live, '24/7' and therefore unpredictable series. This was especially vivid if you visited the website where the 'rushes' could be viewed each day and, if you had time, you could see clearly the construction of the 'story' by the programme's editing decisions.

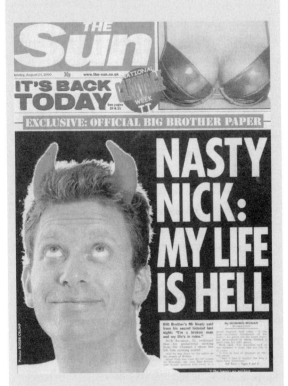

Figure 2.6 Nick from *Big Brother*: a villain function is born!

Although the 'ending' was that of a quiz show (the elimination from the house of all but the prizewinning contestant) we can understand it also as constructed via traditional visual narrative processes. Look at:

- casting – there were 45,000 application forms returned, and final selections made from 300 videoed interviews. All the 'characters' were under forty. This alone makes some narratives likely and others much less so.
- editing – which was very much 'on the lookout for' the beginning of certain 'scripts' involving romance, competition, distrust (see Chapter 3)
- set design – half trendy prison, half designer open plan
- lighting – how differently would low key or more 'realistic' lighting have worked to set up narrative expectations in the series?

All this, plus the constant surveillance, was worked to produce the most dramatic 'character' eruption in the series, that of 'the villainous Nick', constructed by both the programme and the tabloids linked with it.

Several live competitive entertainment forms seem now to construct particular figures as 'villainlike' or 'the nasty you love to hate': think of the judge Simon Cowell in *Pop Idol* (2002) or Anne Robinson's persona on *The Weakest Link*.

Long-running news stories are especially interesting. When an event is constructed as news, it can be 'run' in a number of ways, without clear hero or villain roles. But if it goes on for long enough, it is often then structured, by news staff, into a narrative shape. At the other end of news, once a 'story', or a newsworthy individual life, ends (as with Princess Diana's death, or Michael Hutchence's drug overdose), events before it will be told in the light of that ending and often seen as 'leading up to it' – tragically unexpected or 'just what s/he deserved' – in other words as part of a coherent and satisfying story.

'Unlike the Gulf War, the coming conflict [following the events of 11 September 2001] features no clear enemy in a single location. There's also the question of whether viewers will lose interest in a story without a clear beginning, middle and end' ('Newsies weigh cost of war', *Variety* (US trade magazine) 25 September 2001)

Many have claimed an authoritative version of Diana, Princess of Wales's story through their interpretations of its ending. Immediately afterwards, Internet messages tried to 'fix' the meaning of the car accident into conspiracies. 'Sick' jokes and critical questions played up her privilege and her often frivolous lifestyle, ending in a drink-driving accident. Others claimed saintliness for this young death, in the flowers and messages on the site of the Paris car crash, outside Harrods, Buckingham Palace etc. Since then there have been attempts to shift the role of other

Figure 2.7 Diana shrine outside Harrods, 1997.

'characters' in the story, such as Prince Charles, moving from 'villain' to 'hero', in his role as father to 'Will' and 'Harry', or in the attempts to legitimise his long-running affair with Camilla Parker-Bowles, and in the process to construct him in turn as the victim of a cold and ruthless Royal family. What do not fit so easily into all this are questions about what has happened to news of the anti-landmines campaigns, so important to Diana before her death (see case study Stardom and celebrity following Chapter 4).

Complex historical events and motives are often left out of long-running items, in exchange for the pleasures of a good story, as in the events following 11 September 2001, which were soon called, or shaped into, a 'war on terrorism' even though war had not officially been declared, and 'terrorism' is a notoriously slippery term.

Applying Todorov: beginnings and endings

What was so stunning about the suicide bombings of New York and Washington on 11 September 2001 was that, unprecedentedly, they seemed to come from nowhere predictable, that a 'new story' had, really, for once, 'begun'. Later it was possible to see out of what conflicts they arguably emerged. But the lack of much US foreign coverage of the 'Middle East', as well as existing perceptions of that region as 'backward' and the sheer 'modern' spectacle of the New York attacks, seeming to echo disaster movies such as *Independence Day* (US 1996), meant that much news coverage was at a loss for the sort of comment or information which news is supposed to exist to provide.

Wars eventually finish, often only for the time being. But narratives don't just finish, or come to a halt, or stop – they *end*, in a way which 'rounds things off', assigns blame and praise etc. (the 'new equilibrium'). The media have often structured the end of long-running events such as wars so as to leave out stubborn elements that in fact don't end but go on

happening (soldiers' post-traumatic stress syndrome; long recovery from physical injuries; the continuing arms trade etc.). But so deep are the satisfactions of 'the happy ending' that newsrooms will try hard to find signifiers of some happy foreign or domestic event, suggesting a return to normality – very like the 'and so they all lived happily ever after' of the fairy tale. Sometimes it will take the shape of a correspondent making his way (it's usually a male reporter) into the now-said-to-be-liberated war zone: the BBC's John Simpson entering Kabul in November 2001, Max Hastings of the *Evening Standard* into Port Stanley, the Falkland Islands in 1982.

One of the problems of handling the narrative of the post-11 September events as it has been constructed is that the US declared 'war on terrorism', particularly the al-Qaida network. However victory was achieved, almost incidentally, over the brutal Taliban regime in Afghanistan. This was greeted as though it was the 'end of the story' by some parts of the media, and the long-continued bombing was ignored. This, even though women, in particular, had been lobbying for energetic action against the Taliban for several years with no response from the US.

In the past the sign of such stories happily concluding have been: ships sailing back; soldiers talking of their pleasure at a job well done, and eventually the welcome home by the women and children. Such a sense of a narrative ending is much more difficult to achieve for such a nebulous process as the announced 'war against terrorism'.

Applying Propp: heroes and villains

To understand the construction of Osama bin Laden in 2001 we need, as so often with narrative theory, to apply knowledge of **genre**. He was constructed, not without reason, as a particular kind of villain:

- He resonated with generations of action adventure stories, books and films drawing on orientalist imagery of inscrutably evil men pitted against the West.

Figure 2.8 The Magic Carpet (US 1951): 'evil orientals' – figures which have been fascinating for the West and are regularly played with in action forms. But such images also get called on, or remembered, in more dangerous political discourses.

- More specifically his media construction sometimes resonated with James Bond villains, or the ultra-millionaire Lex Luthor villain, avowed enemy of *Superman* and often holed up in underground lairs (see Holland 2001).
- He was also perceived as villain from a western in the posters 'Wanted dead or alive' which appeared, drawing on the words of President George W. Bush.

Contrastingly, the SAS and other special forces became the 'heroes' of many accounts, drawing on the small group daring of masked men in so many stories, not least James Bond again.

Such narrative constructions do not exist in isolation from other processes of meaning construction. These range from long-standing stereotypes of 'the Orient' to the difficulty of justifying a distant, expensive, long-running 'story' around pictures of night-time bombing raids.

'Reconnaissance planes fly invisibly overhead; special forces may be infiltrating the country in secret; and media companies have expended huge amounts of time and effort to get people and equipment into this . . . remote region – only to find that the story is, in the military phrase, "beyond visual range" . . . the

bombing of Kabul looked like a tropical thunderstorm flickering behind the mountains which hide the city from the front line.' (Tim Lambon, 'Letter from Jabal Saraj', *Times Literary Supplement*, 19 October 2001)

Applying Lévi-Strauss: structured by oppositions

It is often possible to group together, in two opposing lists, the qualities which get structured into the conflict of most long-running news stories. For the fighting in Afghanistan (and the earlier Gulf War of 1991) these might include:

East	West
barbarism	civilisation
feudal	modern
despotism	democracy
fundamentalism	freedom
backward 'dirty' weapons	modern 'clean' weapons ('surgical strikes' etc.)
evil	good

Of course some of these oppositions have some justification, especially around the position of women under the Taliban regime. But these polarised (and comforting) ways of organising a story are part of the disappearance of more complex and troubling questions (hotly debated on websites at the time, such as www.opendemocracy.com):

- Who exactly manufactures, sells and profits from the arms used in such wars, whether modern or less up to date? (see *Baltimore Chronicle* web reference).
- What commercial interests, such as the importance of Afghanistan as a route for US oil exports to the developing Asian and Chinese economies, were at play in these events?
- How to come to terms with the combination of modernity and Islamic fundamentalism in the figure of Osama bin Laden, a Saudi millionaire, hiding in a cave but connected globally, via technology, and

who had been trained by the CIA as part of earlier Afghanistan wars.

ACTIVITY 2.12

Take any story, preferably a long-running one, from recent news and consider:

- How has the initial equilibrium, the 'once-upon-a-timeness', been set up?
- How has the disruption to that ('something has happened') been constructed?
- How do you think this narrative will 'end' or 'close'?
- What may be left out of that ending?
- How else could the story have begun, with what other 'equilibrium', and from whose point of view?
- Have any of the people involved been constructed as characters with narrative roles such as hero, villain, victim, donor, etc.? Do any of these overlap? (For example people driven to take strike action are often, wrongly, portrayed as quite separate from, and hostile to, the 'victims' of a strike.)

References

Anobile, Richard (ed.) (1974) *Alfred Hitchcock's* Psycho, London: Macmillan.

Holland, Gale (2001) 'Cartoon villain', *Guardian*, 19 October, reprinted from www.Salon.com.

Rebello, Stephen (1991) *Alfred Hitchcock and the Making of Psycho*, New York: Harper Perennial.

Rosenbaum, Jonathan, review of 1998 version of *Psycho* on www.chireader.com.

See Barnett's and Richard's articles for www.opendemocracy.net and the interview with Heikal, *Guardian*, 10 October 2001.

See http://baltimorechronicle.com/media3_oct01.shtml.

Further reading

Billig, Michael (1993) *Speaking of the Royal Family*, London: Sage.

Cook, Pam and Bernink, Mieke (eds) (1999 2nd edition) *The Cinema Book*, London: BFI.

Jancovich, Mark (1996) *Rational Fears: American Horror in the 1950s*, Manchester and New York: Manchester University Press, Part Three, Chapter 1: 'Re-situating *Psycho*'.

Kapsis, Robert E. (1992) *Hitchcock: The Making of a Reputation*, Chicago: University of Chicago Press.

Modleski, Tania (1988) *The Women Who Knew Too Much*, London: Methuen.

Perkins, V.F. (1993) *Film as Film*, London: Da Capo.

Williams, Linda (1994) 'Learning to scream', *Sight and Sound*, December 1994.

Williams, Linda (2002) 'Discipline and fun: *Psycho* and postmodern cinema', in Christine Gledhill and Linda Williams (eds) *Reinventing Film Studios*, London and New York: Arnold.

3 'Genres' and other classifications

All media output is classified. This classifying is made by

- its makers
- its commentators, reviewers or other official classifiers
- its 'consumers'.

These classifications (horror or SF?; 'R18' or 'PG' rated?; 'art' or 'entertainment'?; 'quality' or 'schlock'?) have material effects on the ways we enjoy and understand media, and on their status and therefore ability to withstand attack and censorship, justify adequate budgets etc. This chapter focuses on the concept of 'genre', though it also ranges into other fields, such as formats, censorship and the creation of expectations via reviewing and other practices.

'**Genre**' is simply a French word for type or kind, as in biological classifications of plants and animals. An example: a lightbulb joke depends on the same kinds of knowledge and expectations for its audience as any genre product. Unless you've never heard one before, when you hear the question you know that a joke is involved (a genre, one whose aim is to produce laughter) and are therefore likely to begin thinking in certain directions rather than others for the answer. In other words you swiftly operate a kind of classification of it – as not being a serious question, as likely to involve certain kinds of answers. But if you enjoy lightbulb jokes, part of your pleasure is that you both sort-of-know and don't-quite-know what to expect from it. In other words, a *system of expectation* is set up around it, one which involves both **repetition** and **difference**, and which depends on a **classification**.

'Taste classifies, and classifies the
classifier', Pierre Bourdieu (1984).

Q How many folksingers does it take to change a lightbulb?

A Six. One to change the bulb and five to sing about how good the old one was.

Q How many Real Men does it take to change a lightbulb?

A Real Men aren't afraid of the dark.

Q How many cockroaches does it take to change a lightbulb?

A Can't tell. The minute you switch the light on they all disappear. (from *A Bug's Life*)

The repetition is of the bare framework of elements: a lightbulb, a group of people about which certain stereotypes exist, a number which relates the two in an amusing way. The difference lies in *how* the particular connections between those elements will be made *this* time. It's the particular combination of elements, rather than something called 'difference' alone, which makes the new joke enjoyable. As the genre becomes established, play can be made with its conventions. Part of the pleasure of the riddles is their satirical reference to well-known stereotypes, and thus to your feelings about real-world groups of which you may know very little.

Television and cinema: economics and classification

Media products are classified in a variety of ways by viewers, reviewers or regulators, and makers. Genres and, increasingly for television, formats are terms used by the bodies producing and trading in media.

ACTIVITY 3.1

'Television' and 'art' status

Scan the television reviews in newspapers.

- Do they generally appear with the rest of 'arts' reviews (with other entertainment disciplines) or somewhere else? Where is this?
- What is the tone of television reviewing? Is it respectful of endings (as is film reviewing) for viewers who may have taped programmes?
- Is it a place where you look forward primarily to a display of wit by the reviewer rather than serious engagement with the programmes?
- How often is television itself covered by the television arts programmes?

Case study: *Big Brother*

Big Brother, which its makers describe as a 'format', has attracted large audiences worldwide over several series – an estimated 67 per cent of the UK population watched the first series at least once, and over ten million viewers tuned in for the final episode (Hill 2002).

'**Format**' is currently a category often used in television. It tends to overlap with 'genre', so both *The Weakest Link* and *Who Wants to Be a Millionaire?* would belong to the genre 'quiz show' though their formats or set-ups differ. When a television format is sold it can include everything from the presenting links, type of set, lighting, music, etc. even down to the senior producer, who may be included as part of the contract. Jon Dovey calls *Big Brother* 'the first truly international new television genre of the twenty first century' (2001: 137). 'Formats have emerged as scheduling weapon of choice . . . a hit parade of reality and game fare around the globe' (*Variety* trade magazine, 21–7 January 2002), allowing for the trading of a broadcasting concept across national boundaries (*Big Brother* lists nineteen countries on its part of the Endemol television website). *Pop Idol* (2002) is another example, the twenty-part format sold to US Fox television for a rumoured $1m per episode after the hugely successful UK series.

Big Brother has a loose and interesting 'repertoire of elements'. It innovatively works with:

- 'reality television' (it is a kind of documentary, using surveillance camerawork)
- a combination with game show structures and visual style
- both teams and the individuals within them competing against each other (see Ellis 2001)
- highly selected contestants of only a certain age range
- bright showbiz lighting in the house – how different would it be with low-key lighting?
- audience involvement via interactive technology, including (hugely profitable) phone votes.

It has proved to be a globally mobile structure with lots of room for local cultural adaptations, developed under licence from the originator (*Big Brother* was originally developed in the Netherlands by Endemol Entertainment). These involve the terms of the rules about expulsion; choice of setting; coverage of nudity and sex, visits to the bathroom; the use of celebrities coming into the house etc. For example the British version featured contestants who took the rules very seriously; the Australian version was located in a theme park (Dreamworld on the Gold Coast) where for many the show became 'a human zoo with the performances projected onto the world of the theme park where larger than life spectacles are expected' (Roscoe 2001). In all of this, whether you call it a genre or a format, the idea of a **'repertoire of elements'**, which can be selected from or played in many ways, is useful in thinking about classification (see below). Though such programmes may all seem the same, to be just 'reality television' or 'docu-soaps', we should try to distinguish these terms.

'Reality television' has become the term used to describe 'high impact examples of the new factual television' which increased hugely on British television between 1989 and 1999, often in prime-time pre- and post-watershed slots (see Dovey 2000: 135). The term was first applied to magazine-format programmes based on crime, accident and health stories or 'trauma television' (*Crimewatch UK*; *Lifesavers*; *America's Most Wanted* . . .). 'It often blends apparently "raw" authentic material with the gravitas of a news magazine, combining the commercial success of tabloid content with a public service mode of address' (Dovey 2000: 135).

As you will have noticed, the term has widened recently, often now simply meaning programmes which use 'ordinary people' as part of forms blending information and entertainment. This happens to classifications which try to organise (in order to think about) the cutting edge of fast-moving industries and technologies.

Docu-soap a hybrid blending elements of *soap* (its serial nature with character-driven narratives and a focus on emotional or 'gossipy' aspects of everyday life) with the codes and conventions of one kind of *documentary* (vérité camerawork, which looks hand-held or to be moving spontaneously in response to events; real people not actors; real places not locations). John Corner suggests that the combination presents 'documentary as diversion' and produces 'nosy sociability', positioning the viewer as 'an amused bystander in the mixture and mess and routine in other people's working lives' (Corner 2000).

Big Brother was attacked along familiar lines – as being about trivialisation, as being boring to watch (which lots of it was). Yet the reasons for its success are not simply reasons to despair of television audiences or civilisation as we know it, as some imply. For example, though the first series of *Survivor* may have seemed similar to *Big Brother*, it was very different. It was not broadcast live – the audience knew that this was 'dead television' and thus not in the same relation to 'the real', or, importantly, to viewers' ability to affect events by their votes.

The huge audiences for the first British *Big Brother* series suggest that scheduling and other decisions were key to the success of this 'local' version of a globally formatted product. The US version was, according to John Ellis (2001), 'badly miscast (too many bearded survivalists) and crucially, staged its evictions fortnightly rather than weekly'. In the UK the programme was first broadcast by Channel 4 as an end-of-evening event for the 'youth audience' (another classification) then, flexibly, moved to prime time and its slots increased when it caught a wider public interest. Newspapers covered events in the household and outside it, when contestants were evicted. The whole thing was continuously filmed (9,000 hours of video, 26 cameras, 55 microphones, 150 crew) and broadcast live on the Net: the term 'cross-platform delivery' is one of the ways Endemol describes its multimedia product. This was not cheap television, as many critics called it.

Figure 3.1   Big Brother 2 (UK): part of the evidence of Web liveness was 'blips': when it seemed that Craig might hit Nick, the website was switched off and the technicians forgot to switch it on again for a while. Television footage avoided such problems because it was always edited and therefore, by definition, not live.

As a way of organising the costly and volatile business of making films and television the predicable production genres and formats help to minimise risk and predict expenditure. **Economies of scale** operate and require **standardisation of production**. Even so, we need to hold that 'repetition

Standardisation has a double meaning: it can signify 'sameness'; but can also denote the maintenance of standards, in the sense of quality. Another point to bear in mind in the huge debates around 'sameness' and 'difference' in Media and Cultural Studies.

and difference' tension in mind: the standardisation is in order to reach *different* audiences, through *different* genres and formats. Television companies, for example, depend on predictable annual income from the licence fee (BBC) or selling advertising space (ITV) or selling ad space plus subscription fees (cable and satellite companies). They divide up budgets according to departments such as Entertainment, Drama, News and Current Affairs. Some genres are particularly useful in the attempt to standardise, to render predictable the schedules and the audiences the advertisers would like to be sure they have access to. Traditionally soaps, for example, have been key to building audiences in the early evening. This scheduling capacity made it worth investing in a whole close of modern houses for Brookside Productions Ltd, or for Granada to build a permanent set and employ a serial historian to avoid embarrassing mistakes in the long-running *Coronation Street*.

But recent developments in broadcasting (since the founding of Channel 4 in 1982) which have fragmented 'the audience' have led to attempts to target ever more specialised, small audience segments or **niches** of potential audience. The term **narrowcasting** distinguishes such developments from an older media ecology where fewer channels (BBC and ITV for television in the UK) had the power to 'broad-cast' to larger audiences. Media forms have consequently become more and more **cross-generic** or **hybrid**, as audiences grew accustomed to a huge amount of media output, so that different kinds of music, television and film clash and mix genres: cyberpunk, docu-soaps etc.

Niche originally meant a little nest or recess in a wall; **niche marketing** now refers to attempts to reach specialised but highly profitable groups of potential consumers with particular media products or aspects of products.

Hybridity originally used of the crossbreeding of plants, here describes media products mixing different sets of cultural values, technologies and/or formal properties: e.g. bhangra 'crossover hits' in pop music; *Buffy*'s complex mix etc.

This is sometimes called '**postmodernism**'. But genre films, for example, have always involved some kind of 'hybridity' and are never 'pure' westerns or musicals or horror films. Hollywood (and earlier nineteenth-century cultural forms) have always tried to attract as many audience segments as possible, and, for example, one way of guaranteeing some female audience for 'male' genres, such as action adventures and SF, was assumed to be a romance strand in the plot. There are of course, provisional boundaries – which however can mutate. Each film is slightly different in the way it plays the possiblities of its mixings and meldings.

This has also led to the phenomenon known as **intertextuality**, which refers to the variety of ways in which media and other texts interact with each other, rather than being unique or distinct. Though it is greatly used now because of the proliferation of media forms and audience familiarity with them, it's nevertheless the case that media products are still marketed according to familiar categories, even if mixed. Genre is one of the ways of making these categorisations, product-reputations if you like, which help determine how we encounter a whole range of media products. As Bennett

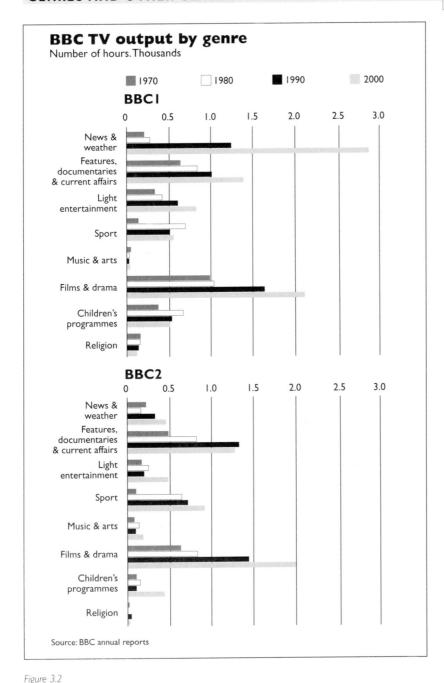

Figure 3.2

and Woollacott put it, in a study of the James Bond films: 'the same text may, in different social and ideological relations of reading, be drawn into association with different genres. The determination as to which genre rules will . . . [operate] is thus, in the last instance, cultural and variable rather than textual and fixed' (Bennett and Woollacott 1987: 81). (We explore this statement in more detail in the following *Buffy* case study.)

ACTIVITY 3.2

Zap through the channels on your television or radio. Look at title sequences.

- How quickly are you able to tell what kind of programme or music is on offer? In seconds?
- *How* were you able to tell? What kinds of differences are signalled through music, colours, kinds of dialogue, voices, pace of editing, costume, lighting etc.?

Try turning down the sound on the title sequence of a television genre and substituting another kind of music.

- What difference does this make?
- Can you tell gardening or cookery programmes from motor racing coverage just by the title music for example? Or by the kinds of voices used?

Censorship, art, reviewing

Censorship is used of decisive acts of forbidding or preventing publication or distribution of media products, or parts of those products, by those with the power, either economic or legislative, to do so.

Other ways of classifying also have the power to position media products in some ways and not others. An obvious one is the formal classification or censorship system itself, as operated in the UK for film and video by the regulatory body the **BBFC** (British Board of Film Classification) and for television by the code of the **ITC** (Independent Television Commission). The classifying bodies decide for which audiences a product is presumed to be suitable and sometimes amend or cut it to fit the nature of this presumed audience. In cinema these categories of expectation would include 'accompanied by a parent' and 'Only when over 18'. The BBFC (see its very informative website) works on five major principles, including:

- decisions based sometimes on rules (e.g. about language in junior categories) and sometimes on guidelines, for more discussion (e.g. the concept of 'harm' to children)
- 'balancing context against detail, with due weight given to the intention of the work as well as the actual images shown'.

'[more recently] the board has taken a fairly relaxed view on horror films because we recognise that going to horror movies is a roller-coaster experience. However, just as there are certain people, for instance, those below a certain height, who are not allowed on certain roller coasters, so we say that people below certain ages can't legally have this roller-coaster horror experience' (Robin Duvall, Chair of BBFC, in interview with Julian Petley, 2001)

Figure 3.3 The history of the UK category system

Year	Media	Unrestricted category	Advisory category	Restrictive category
1913	Film	U-Universal	A – more suitable for adults (no film certified that was not clean and wholesome)	None
1921	Film			London County Council – no entrance to young people at 'A' films, except with parent or guardian
1932	Film		H – indicated horror and was advisory	
1951	Film			X – incorporated old 'H' and limited audience to those over 16 years
1970	Film	U-Universal	A – advisory	AA – admission to children of 14 years or over X – raised from 16 to 18 years
1982		U-Universal	PG – Parental Guidance – general viewing but some scenes may be unsuitable for young children	15 – no person under the age of 15 to be admitted. 18 – no person under the age of 18 to be admitted R18 – for films containing more explicit sexual depictions
1985	Film	Uc-Universal, particularly suitable for unsupervised children U – as above	PG – as above	15 – suitable only for persons of 15 years and over 18 – suitable only for persons of 18 years and over R18 – restricted to distribution in licensed premises – no one under 18 to be admitted
1989	Film			12 – no person under the age of 12 to be admitted
1994	Video			12 – suitable only for persons of twelve and over

Source: BBFC

Of course censorship does not exist on its own but is part of a spectrum of *institutional* assumptions and classifications which include:

- pre-censorship or self-censorship by film-makers ('vetting' of scripts, or 'just knowing' that some subjects are 'unacceptable' for example). During the years of struggle against apartheid and its effects on sport in South Africa, it 'just wasn't done', within the discourses of cricket commentary, to bring such politics into match coverage.

- a combination of reshooting and re-editing, as practised by Miramax with many of the independent films it acquires, so that the product is adjusted to meet the demands of the assumed 'typical audience'.

- previews and test screenings, as used from the earliest days of cinema.

- formal certification and classification by age (re certain kinds of content) as well as the sense of whether or not the text is 'art' or 'not-art' and therefore likely to be experienced by a particular set of audiences in certain settings (late-night television; film society; arts theatre).

- other small discouragements that can take place in 'the nicest possible way': by critics calling certain forms (such as drama-documentary) a 'mishmash' or 'inappropriate mix' (of conventions which are never entirely separate). Certain genres are taken as the place where some but not other closely related kinds of activity are appropriately handled. In television, for example, recent events in the real world are categorised as part of the *news genre*. After a certain time, though, such events are classified as the *history genre* and come under quite different rules, notably involving less need for impartiality (see the screenings of *Sunday* (C4 2001) and *Bloody Sunday* (ITV 2002) about events in Northern Ireland in 1972 – presumably now 'history' and therefore open to partisan treatment).

Related to the power of such practices is the ability, by some makers and reviewers of films for example, to have them successfully categorised as 'art'. There is much controversy over whether the BBFC is making different classification decisions (on representing sexual activity, for example) depending on whether the text has won the battle to be considered 'art' and is therefore assumed to circulate in 'safer' environments than 'popular' cinema (see Petley 2001).

'in order for the representation of sex to be taken seriously [in English film criticism] it has to be sad, dour and ugly' (letter from Joseph De Lappe to *Sight and Sound*, August 2001)

Case study: *The Silence of the Lambs*

Such 'demarcating' work can be performed around films, and encourages reviewers to perceive them in certain ways. *The Silence of the Lambs* (US 1991) was in fact the second film use made of Thomas Harris's literary character Hannibal Lecter. The first adaptation, *Manhunter* (US 1987) was made by Michael Mann, then known mainly for his work on the television series *Miami Vice* and therefore not as high-status a film director as Jonathan Demme. In many obvious ways *Silence of the Lambs* was a horror film (though a self-reflexive one: see the opening words: 'Hurt Agony Pain – Love it Or Die'). In terms of its first distribution (it was released on Valentine's Day 1991) it fitted the slot sanctioned as an excuse for physical contact for teenage couples. As *Premiere* magazine put it: 'If it is a choice between this and chocolates for Valentine's Day, the bon bons might be a better choice, but then again, *The Silence* promises to be so terrifying, you're bound to end up in your sweetheart's arms.'

But it also sought a very different status. It tried to distinguish itself from 'run of the mill' horror, whose elements it, and the prestigious book it was based on, both draw on and refresh (see Jancovich) at both pre- and production stages; for example:

- The figures of psychiatrist and serial killer, separated in the horror genre from *Psycho* onwards, are here fused in the 'fascinating' figure of Hannibal Lecter.
- The 'final girl' (Carol Clover's phrase) of slasher movies is here the figure of Clarice Starling, FBI agent, played by Jodie Foster.

Further strategies to move the status of the film *towards that of art and away from horror* included

- encouraging press avoidance of the connection to horror genre. In place of generic classifications, adjectives abound which produce a sense of ambivalence about the film: it is 'terrifying'; 'brutally real'; 'macabre'; 'dark' – all of which avoid the obvious classification: it is a horror film.
- an emphasis on Jonathan Demme as a certain kind of serious auteur-director. This ignored the fact that he worked for Roger Corman (who has a cameo role, in *Silence*, as an FBI man) on exploitation movies such as *Caged Heat* (US 1974).
- an emphasis on the film's restrained use of violence and avoidance of voyeurism.
- emphasis on the 'serious' star image of Jodie Foster (Yale graduate, feminist sympathies) and the work of her performance (e.g. she spent a week at FBI HQ, seen as an effort towards 'realism'). She and Demme

had worked to Oscar-winning purpose together before, on the acclaimed *The Accused* (US 1988).

- an emphasis on high-status themes e.g. 'violence and American society'; 'the position of women *vis-à-vis* serial killers'. The set design (and the designer, interviewed at length in one prestige television preview programme) also expressed such themes and claims to connect to the real: the US flag in several scenes; the imagery of Francis Bacon in Lecter's imprisonment; a reference to those Nazis who were said to have listened to Mozart while overseeing the gas chambers etc.

Q See whether you can research Foster's 2002 hit *Panic Room* for evidence of the same kinds of strategies around what is basically a horror film.

Do you think the strategies remain the same e.g. emphasis on 'top flight' director; on the film's visual style; on the status of the actors involved, on the film's relation to 'serious' topical themes, even '11 September' in some reviews?

Or is the whole status of this genre changing, perhaps along with the importance of younger audiences?

For British television, classification has been operated largely by the timing of the programme ('before or after 10 p.m.?' etc.) within what is called the Family Viewing Policy, based on, and helping to reinforce, a particular conception of the usual household. Like genre classifications, these processes have material effects. A programme (such as *Buffy*) which falls between 'teen' and older presumed audiences may find itself cut when screened on BBC2 at 6.45 but uncut for a late evening showing.

See Selling audiences case study following Chapter 6.

At the other extreme, if a media text can successfully claim 'artistic' or fully 'authored' status for itself, whether film, print or television (perhaps via publicity around its main author, or the established reputations as 'artists' of leading players and workers), then it is likely to be protected from censorship, and may well occupy special media spaces. John Pilger, for example, is allowed to present controversial reports on topics such as the continuing bombing of Iraq; he is given comparatively large budgets to do so, and is usually announced in such a way as to distance the host television channel from too close association with his potentially awkwardly outspoken political positions. The later dramas of Dennis Potter were allowed much more 'artistic licence' than works by less celebrated authors.

Genres and escapism

Though most of us, as audience members, are able to operate *genre awareness* quite speedily, media theorists have been interested in genre because of:

- its importance in understanding the *low status* of mass-produced media products in relation to *higher-status* art forms
- its focus on how *entertainment* or **escapist** forms might work to organise and either to narrow or to expand the expectations and **identities** through which we understand and imagine the world and its possibilities.

Mass-produced movies, pop music, magazines, television etc. have long been classified as a lower kind of cultural production than 'true art' simply because they involved industrial production and were aimed at non-elite audiences. Hollywood's products, for example, were initially intended to entertain working-class audiences for an evening between one day's work and the next, rather than to be pondered over or sampled at elite gatherings. In addition, certain snobberies about America as inferior to Europe meant that Hollywood was assumed for years to be incapable of producing anything worthy of serious attention. A low estimate of the audience has always been inseparable from contempt for popular or genre forms. Such suspicion surfaces in the (highly classed and gendered) metaphors still used to dismiss genre products, as well as their fans, though now the dominance of US values, products and media corporations means such objections have far less power than previously.

> 'the so-called "fun" of commercial American cinema ... would feel less oppressive if it didn't already inform the experience in the US of news, politics, fast food, sports, economics, religion and leisure in general, making it less an escape than the very (enforced) essence of American life' (Rosenbaum 2002: 150–1).

Entertainment forms have also been described, contradictorily, as *both*

- the carriers of capitalist **propaganda** or ideology (i.e. related to 'the real') *and yet*
- pernicious because they encourage audiences to escape from 'real' questions via fantasy.

Clearly, though all stories and entertainments are imaginary, not 'real life' in one sense, they are a material part of most of our real lives in several others. We pay money to experience them, directly or indirectly; we spend time and imaginative energy 'playing' in their worlds; and genre forms such as soap operas, appearing several times a week, sometimes find themselves entwined with news debates. When such debates enter the news agenda, they are often

Escapist, meaning 'one who seeks escape, especially from reality' is a term used disparagingly of mass cultural forms, seen as encouraging their audiences simply to escape from, and not to face up to, the stern demands of 'the real'. Often used as synonymous with 'entertainment'. (Origin: *es-cape*: literally, taking off one's cloak and thus 'throwing off restraint'.)

Terms such as 'fodder', 'run of the mill', 'familiar recipe', 'served up', 'staple diet', 'junk food culture', 'pap', 'pulp' (referring to books made from poor-quality wood pulp), 'the Dream Factory' all emphasise repetition and inferior quality, as though films were just like the output of any other factory – or kitchen.

71

reported in terms which make their fans look stupid or gullible. Newspapers love to focus on the relatively few people who seem to believe in the soap's events as though they were real (even if, on the next page, the journalists may be contributing to the confusion by writing of an actor as though s/he was really the character they perform). Yet, arguably, being asked, night after night, to imagine, through identification with a soap character, what it is like to be a single parent, or unemployed, is a crucial part of thoughtful public debate on the key news issues.

ACTIVITY 3.3

Make a note of the different kinds of fiction you enter into this week.
- How much time do you spend in each fictional world?
- Which is your favourite genre? Why?

Utopia originally a word coined, by Sir Thomas More in his book *Utopia* (1516), from the Greek, combining *outopia* or no-place, and *eutopia*, 'good place'. It has been used, especially in science fiction, as a way of imagining ideal social orders, though we more commonly now encounter **dystopic** images of the future, such as *The Matrix* (US 1999).

Ernst Bloch (1885–1977) German Marxist cultural theorist of utopian impulses in art (*The Principle of Hope*, 1954–9) was written during exile in the US.

Mikhail Bakhtin Russian cultural theorist (1895–1975), wrote (published 1984) on sixteenth-century carnival as an expression of desires to 'turn the world upside down' in a moment of utopian celebration.

There are other positions which try to link even less 'realistic' aspects of genre forms to the real. Richard Dyer (1977) has argued that entertainment or genre forms are pleasurable and even '**utopian**' (the hostile term would be 'escapist' or even 'fantasist') precisely because they allow a kind of fantasy escape from a reality often experienced as full of scarcity, exhaustion, dreariness, fragmentation and alienation into a fictional world coded (through lighting, set design, exuberant plot lines, audiences performing exuberant happiness etc.) as abundant, energetic, intense, transparent, and with moments of full 'community'.

Following the Russian literary theorists **Bloch** and **Bakhtin**, Dyer called these **utopian** pleasures, in the sense not that they literally represent or speak about political utopias, but that key moments and qualities give sensuous expression to such feelings that 'things could be better'. His work was originally with musical forms, but has been applied to less obviously 'escapist' genres. Jackie Stacey (1993) has argued that Dyer's categories need to be thought through more specifically, in relation to gender, class, ethnicity and different historical periods, as well as to the places where entertainment happens, such as the very real escapes into luxurious cinemas for women and working-class audiences in the 1930s and 1940s. It could also be argued that many 'fan communities' now produce a kind of other space, in their Internet chatrooms, or rewritings of episodes of favourite serials, or indeed the space of their passion for the 'world' of a series such as *Xena* or *Buffy* or *Star Wars*.

Figure 3.4 The *Pop Idol* set: does this embody Dyer's 'utopian' qualities of abundance; energy; intensity (of disappointment, or of ecstasy at success); transparency (ordinary contestants shown behind the scenes etc.); community of audience and ordinary people trying to be stars?

The real and 'verisimilitude'

All media forms, from television news to heavy metal music, are constructed, working with codes and conventions: there is no neat division to be made between 'the real' and 'the imagined'. Yet some genres are perceived as having more **verisimilitude**, or connection to the 'real', and this generally gives them (and their audiences) higher cultural status than others. For example, the first step taken by many media campaigners on excessive violence on television is to *mistake* how far cartoons are connected to reality for their audiences.

This 'real-seemingness', the ways that media forms will combine systems of what seems 'real', 'likely' or 'probable' in texts, involves two areas:

- *generic verisimilitude*: sets of expectations which are internal to the genre, such as how a 'proper' or 'real' vampire film or science fiction film should proceed (respectively: with garlic as magical, not a cooking ingredient; and with scientists as probably mad, not sane). These can, in some cases, produce a highly pleasurable degree of fantasy and opportunity to play with identities and situations.
- *cultural verisimilitude*: the genre's relationship to expectations about the world outside the genre.

For example, the gangster film or the 'courtroom drama' have always had higher status than, say, the musical, because they make more explicit reference to public or political events from the world outside the film (using newspaper headlines, naming real-life politicians or criminals, and so on). In

Verisimilitude from the Latin for truth (*veritas*) and *similis* = like, similar.

It is often suggested that male paramilitaries in Northern Ireland are represented via two genres. Images of Loyalists tend to be shaped via the gangster genre, while Republicans are imagined via the visual traditions of Catholic martyrdom (for example *In the Name of the Father*, UK 1993).

Q Do you think this is changing?

their style of filming, these genres have traditionally worked in black and white or perhaps the sombre colours of the *Godfather* series or *The Sopranos* (often seen as closer to the realist codes of documentary and history), and until relatively recently made little use of the flamboyant colour, camera angles and movements enjoyed by fans of the musical (and felt to be 'unrealistic' by non-fans). Similarly the happy ending (so 'proper' for a musical) is not considered realistic in Hollywood gangster movies, even though many real-life gangsters are alive and well and living in expectation of a comfortable death. This was one of the ways that the ending of *Goodfellas* (US 1990) was seen as refreshing the conventions of the genre. On the other hand Jackie Chan, Jet Li and others have been argued to bring martial arts grace and the lightness almost of the musical to the gangster-like Hong Kong action movies. Generic elements change from culture to culture.

Relating '11 September' to action-entertainment escapism

The attacks on the US of 11 September 2001 produced fascinating discussion about the relation of 'escapist' genre forms (normally taken to be comedies, romance and so on) and the rest of the real world.

First, it was suggested 'that . . . the film industry might begin to reassess its dependence on ever-escalating images of destruction' (Greg Killday, *Hollywood Reporter*, quoted in Hari 2001) and that

> Hong Kong's reputation as a voracious market for action films may be set to change – a faltering economy and widespread distaste for violence post-September 11 means that light-hearted films are expected to outperform traditional action fare during the all-important Christmas and Chinese New Year holiday season.
> (*Screen International* (trade journal) 21 November 2001)

However, US video stores (according to Blockbuster charts) experienced an increase in demand for terrorist-themed films (Hari 2001) and there were some big-budget military-action films such as *Black Hawk Down* released quickly and successfully in 2002.

Second, action adventure can be understood as escapist, perhaps into fantasies of certain kinds of masculinity, or into the imaginative spaces of well-choreographed escape from real-seeming danger, complication, the mundane world of the everyday. However, it is usually more traditional 'feminine' genres (romance, musical) which get classified as 'escapist'. Action adventure is often valued through its supposed connection to the 'real' (see publicity around *Saving Private Ryan* and other war movies about the 'real' training undergone by the actors and stars, how hard it was, etc.). However, other connections to the real are underplayed:

> Some of Hollywood's top action filmmakers – men behind such thrillers as 'Die Hard' and 'Delta Force One' as well as the directors of 'Fight Club' and of 'Being John Malkovitch' – are helping the U.S. Army dream up possible terrorist threats [to America] and how to handle them.
>
> The counter-terrorism brainstorming sessions are the latest focus of the Institute for Creative Technologies, formed in 1999 under a $45 million U.S. Army grant at the University of Southern California to develop advanced training programs for the Army, institute officials said Tuesday. The institute originally was formed as a partnership among academics, video game makers and creative talent in Hollywood to design advanced 'virtual reality' and simulation training systems for the military.
>
> (Summarised from Reuters item, Los Angeles, on
> http://dailynews.yahoo.com/h/nm/20011009/re/attack_
> hollywood_dc_1.html)

Only a few commentators saw this as a ludicrous idea, given the implausibility of many Hollywood action adventure plots and the mistaken idea that action adventure has a close relationship to 'the real'. Sylvester Stallone was said to be working on *Rambo IV*, the latest of a series of films which have related very closely to the military rhetoric or propaganda of increasingly right-wing US regimes (see Sartelle 1996) whose presidents, from the ex-Hollywood actor Ronald Reagan onwards, have quoted movies in policy statements.

US President (and ex-film actor) Ronald Reagan quoted: 'Go ahead, make my day!' (from *Sudden Impact*); 'the Force is with us' (from *Star Wars*); named a huge US arms initiative 'Star Wars' and is said to have designed it from memories of wagon trains and encirclement in westerns.
US President George W. Bush used the tag line from countless westerns – 'Wanted Dead or Alive', about his desire for the capture of Osama bin Laden in 2001.

Rambo III (1988) is the only big Hollywood film to be set (though not actually filmed) in Afghanistan (and ends with the words 'This film is dedicated to the gallant people of Afghanistan') at a time in the 1980s when US forces were allied to the radical Islamic Mojahedin (who later became the Taliban) against Russian occupying forces and, incidentally, through the CIA, were training Osama bin Laden.

Figure 3.5 Rambo First Blood Part Three (US 1988) the only big Hollywood film which was even 'set,' let alone shot, in Afghanistan.

It will be fascinating to see how the new Rambo film will deal with or try to obliterate such ideological contortions and connections, and how the (now fading) star image of Stallone will play in the Rambo role, along with young audiences' probable lack of knowledge of the longer histories on which the film may draw.

> '[If *Black Hawk Down*] is a remake of anything, it's a remake of *Rambo: First Blood Part Two*, "Do we get to win this time, sir?" "Sure we do, son. Sure we do"' (John Patterson (2002) on the role of Hollywood in re-imagining the US defeat in Vietnam through later war movies).

What complicates things even more is that in a media-image-saturated culture, the conventions of fictional genres are often used not just in advertising but also to make news stories more vivid. The alleged serial killer Frederick West's home was called 'The House of Horror' in tabloid headlines, triggering the horror genre's resonances. News and documentary stories of the struggles against the Mafia regularly use music from and even shots that resemble gangster films, in order to add glamour to the story in a ratings-conscious television system. Such images often feed back into the 'reality effect' of the next gangster movie or television series, and so on, in that process called **intertextuality**.

Repertoires of elements

One of the most widespread ways of dismissing genre, entertainment or popular forms is the charge that 'They're all the same' or 'If you've seen one, you've seen them all'. For the owners of media industries, standardised practices are a profitable part of making genre products. But the emphasis on 'sameness', 'repetition' or 'standardisation' does not work when we come to audiences' enjoyment of genres. Not only are there different genres to appeal to different audiences, and then mixes or hybrid forms of these. But even separate genres are not the same as other industrial products. You may be happy to stick to your favourite brand of toothpaste, and indeed *hope* that each tube will be very similar, but you do not want absolute repetition in cultural products.

> Even the apparently most repetitious form – the 'cover' version in pop music, where an artist makes his/her 'repeat' of a well-known song – sells precisely on its *blend of the familiar and the new*.

The most important development in thinking about familiar entertainment genres was to put them into the context of audiences' and then, more recently, fans' understandings and activities. Genres are no longer seen as sets of fixed elements, constantly repeated, but as working with '**repertoires of elements**' or fluid systems of conventions and expectations. These are shared by makers and audiences, who are *both* active on *both* sides of meaning-making. The Internet has meant that fans can even produce alternative versions of their favourite products, and the entry of fans into higher education has partly been the reason for this greater visiblity to audience creativity.

These conventions and the expectations they can invoke, include the areas of

- *narrative* – how films' stories begin and conclude; what kinds of characters are at the centre of the fiction etc.
- *audio-visual codes of signification* (for which the terms **iconography** or **mise en scene** are still sometimes used), which would include settings (the western's classic landscape; the hi-tech arena of SF), costumes, lighting

Intertextuality the variety of ways in which media and other texts interact with each other, rather than being unique or distinct. It is different from 'allusion', which is a more conscious referencing by one text of another. In post-structuralist theory it is used to emphasise the 'always already there' nature of language, working to structure us without our being aware of it.

The point is often made that it's almost impossible to find a pure-genre Hollywood film. Most of them, for example, combine, in a **hybrid** or mixed form, a romance story with their other main genre elements. Can you think of a pure-genre film or television fiction?

Iconography The term comes from art history, where it refers to books of the fifteenth and sixteenth century guiding artists as to the correct colours, gestures, facial expressions etc. with which to encode Christian doctrine. Since cinema and television work with moving, audio-visual images, the term **signification** (see Chapter 1) is probably more useful.

- *broadly ideological themes*, such as the handling of nineteenth-century rural and military US history through the western, and nearer, urban history through the gangster film.

> The term **convention** is usually understood very conservatively, as a form which is able only to reinforce and repeat normative values. But conventions, precisely in order to survive, need to be able to adapt and shift in more dynamic ways than this.
>
> Critics of popular forms, for example, often imply that they would prefer each product to be utterly different. But if any story, or video game, or melody, were utterly different from all others, we would have no means by which to understand it.
>
> For example *Reservoir Dogs* (US 1992) was praised for its 'difference' and 'originality' when it came out. But these qualities were to some extent dependent on generic conventions. It was in many ways an arthouse movie which played with and against the expectations of the male-centred action adventure film: a crime; intense relationships exclusively between men; violence. Within this 'sameness' or familiarity, the pacing and arrangement of the elements from the repertoire could be experienced as comprehensible 'difference': the unusual plot and story shape; the importance given to a quirky kind of dialogue; the handling of violence; the use of pop music and so on.

The still low-status **romance** genre (such as the 'chick flick' or 'Mills and Boon' novel) will work with *narratives* whose starting point will predictably be the arrival into the life of the female hero of a male who, shall we say, interests her romantically. This sets in play issues such as the nature of intimate relations between men and women, and expectations about the family, work and marriage. The narrative will often proceed by means of intimate conversations and encounters, coincidences, mistakes and so on, delaying and thus intensifying the audience's desire for the couple(s) to 'get it together' (though sometimes desire is prolonged by this not happening). *Casablanca* (US 1942) plays with the elements in combination with those of a political thriller, and a male central character, while *Titanic* (US 1997) is an example of a lavish blockbuster centred on romance in combination with an unusual action-adventure narrative. *Shrek* (US 2001), the most purchased video of 2001, played with Disney-esque assumptions about beauty and romance, and, boldly, carried this through to the ending.

At the level of *audio-visual conventions*, romance has had particular traditions: lavish clothes and domestic settings; much greater use of close-ups, especially focused on the eyes, for male and female actors; less use of fetishised shots of women's bodies; certain styles of intimate acting and dialogue; use of female stars in strong roles; all amplified by a particular kind of music: sweeping chords, piano and string sections of the orchestra.

Male genres have traditionally had higher status, in terms of budgets and critical esteem, and, as outlined above, have *apparently* been less emotional (or have dealt with different kinds of emotion) and more concerned with public issues, situations, references. A famous moment from a **gangster** movie illustrates the crystallisation of generic elements with other classifying struggles from the early gangster repertoire. The pressure of censorship bodies on Hollywood to 'punish the gangster' (a very popular figure in Depression America's cinema) by public death (usually on the street) is visible here. The policeman seems to represent a public calling to account, or punishment for the gangster, while the woman, often cradling the gangster's head, perhaps embodies audience affection for him. The church steps have, for experienced gangster film fans, resonances of repentance (from the early years of the genre), as well as providing a sumptuous setting for a tableau or frozen expressive moment, which Hollywood inherited and reworked from stage melodrama.

Melodrama (from Classical Greek *melos* = Classical Greek song and Classical Greek *drama* = drama) term for a kind of theatre which emerged from censored seventeenth-century drama which was not allowed to use words. It evolved an elaborate language of gesture and spectacle, much of it inherited by early cinema. Normally a term used derogatorily. See Gledhill (1987).

Figure 3.6 Death tableau from *The Roaring Twenties* (US 1939).

The bulk of this chapter has tried to argue that cultural forms require and indeed produce a certain amount of **innovation**, not simply repetition. Yet key questions remain:

- What kinds of innovation are unacceptable in commercial genres?
- Unacceptable to whom? Why?

● How can we contest the unargued power of statements made by producing institutions such as: 'but the audience wants a happy ending' or 'you can't have a political film ending like that'?

A cultural or ideological approach to genres and formats is interested in such questions. It asks whether some of the repetitions within genres, such as the sense of what constitutes a 'happy ending', excludes some identities and imaginings, and might be reinforcing dominant and sometimes oppressive sets of values. Equally the pleasures of a particular genre or format can often reveal surprising connections to the working and leisure structures we all have to make our ways through.

A final example from a television format

The first British series of *Big Brother* was accused of simply 'dumbing down' television and making us all into voyeurs. John Ellis suggested a rather different version of its fascination, which related it to the dominant or widely experienced values and structures of our world: 'the participants face a very modern dilemma. Thrown together by circumstances, they are mutually dependent but in order to survive have to stab each other in the back by making their nominations for eviction. The experience is akin to a modern workplace with its project-based impermanence, appraisal processes and often ruthless corporate management. We watch as men and women with relatively little experience negotiate their way through it' (Ellis 2001).

References

Bennet, Tony and Wollacott, Janet (1987) *Bond and Beyond: The Political Career of a Popular Hero*, London: Macmillan.

Bourdieu, Pierre (1980) 'The aristocracy of culture', reprinted in R. Collins *et al.* (eds) *Media, Culture & Society: A Critical Reader*, London and Beverly Hills: Sage.

Corner, John (2000) 'What do we know about documentary?', *Media, Culture & Society*, vol. 22, no. 5.

Dovey, Jon (2001) 'Reality TV', in Creeber, Glen (ed.) *The Television Genre Book*, London: BFI.

Dyer, Richard (1977) 'Entertainment and Utopia', reprinted in *Only Entertainment* (1992), London: Routledge.

Ellis, John (2001) 'Mirror, mirror', *Sight and Sound*, August.

Gledhill, Christine (ed.) (1987) *Home Is Where the Heart Is*, London: BFI.

Hari, Johann (2001) 'Law of the jungle', *New Statesman*, 10 December.

Hill, Annette (2002) 'Big Brother: the real audience', *Television and Media*.

Jancovich, Mark (2000) '"A Real Shocker": authenticity, genre and the struggle for distinction', *Continuum: Journal of Media and Cultural Studies*, vol. 14, no. 1: 23–35.

O'Sullivan, Tim and Jewkes, Yvonne (eds) (1998) *The Media Studies Reader*, London and New York: Arnold.

Patterson, John (2002) 'Do we get to win this time?', the *Guardian*, 1 February.

Petley, Julian (2001) 'Raising the bar: interview with BBFC director Robin Duvall', *Sight and Sound*, December.

Roscoe, Jane and Hawkins, Guy (2001) 'New television formats' in *Media International Australia*, August.

Rosenbaum, Jonathan (2002) *Movie Wars: How Hollywood and the Media Conspire to Limit What Films We Can See*, London: Wallflower Press.

Sartelle, Joseph (1996) 'Dreams and nightmares in the Hollywood Blockbuster', in Geoffrey Nowell-Smith (ed.) *The Oxford History of World Cinema*, Oxford and New York: Oxford University Press.

Further reading

Barker, Martin (1989) *Comics: Ideology, Power and the Critics*, Manchester: Manchester University Press.

Buscombe, Ed (ed.) (1988) *The BFI Companion to the Western*, London: André Deutsch/BFI.

Gledhill, Christine (1997) 'Genre and gender: the case of soap opera', in Stuart Hall (ed.) *Representation: Cultural Representations and Signifying Practices*, London, Thousand Oaks, New Delhi: Sage (to which this chapter is indebted).

Goodwin, Andrew and Whannel, Gary (1990) *Understanding Television*, London: Routledge.

Lusted, David (1998) 'The popular culture debate and light entertainment', in Christine Geraghty and David Lusted (eds) *The Television Studies Book*, London and New York: Arnold.

Neale, Steve (1990) 'Questions of genre', *Screen*, vol. 31, no. 1.

Ryall, Tom (1998) 'Genre and Hollywood', in John Hill and Pamela Church Gibson (eds) *The Oxford Guide to Film Studies*, Oxford: Oxford University Press.

Stacey, Jackie (1993) *Star Gazing: Hollywood Cinema and Female Spectatorship*, London: Routledge.

CASE STUDY: *BUFFY THE VAMPIRE SLAYER*

- *Buffy*: 'unique' and 'authored'?
- *Buffy* as cross-generic

- Horror, romance and scheduling
- References

Buffy the Vampire Slayer (henceforward *BTVS*) makes an interesting case study through which to explore:

- the play of repetition and difference in a popular television series
- the different kinds of generic knowledge and speculation which the series and its promoters activate in various, overlapping 'readerships'
- the importance of hybridity in *both* the economics of television production and the pleasures of audiences
- how all the above complicates traditional emphases that any text has a clear, intrinsic nature in and of itself.

Buffy: 'unique' and 'authored'?

BTVS is based in a modern California awash with demons, witches and vampires, erupting into the world through the 'Hellmouth' of Sunnydale town. In the first series, the ex-cheerleader Buffy, daughter of a single parent, arrives at her new school in Sunnydale, having discovered herself to be a demon slayer. Here she meets her 'watcher', Giles the English school librarian with archaic knowledge of demons and teams up with two classmates, Willow and Xander. In each episode they expose and destroy a new demon threat, and Buffy 'wisecracks her way through fights with vampires twice her size while dressed in heels and a party dress' (Johnson 2001: 42).

We can describe the series in this way, but when it comes to its possible meanings things are less clear cut. As Tony Bennett and Susan Woollacott (1987) have argued, no reader can make whatever s/he wants of a 'text' because we always encounter 'texts' already

Figure 3.7 Buffy: a new kind of 'vampire slayer'

encrusted with meanings, associations and, in the case of British television, scheduling decisions. Genre is one (but not the only one) of the ways of making categorisations and reputations which help determine how we encounter (or have difficulty encountering) a whole range of media products.

'the same text may, in different social and ideological relations of reading, be drawn into association with different genres. The determination as to which genre rules will . . . [operate] is thus, in the last instance, cultural and variable rather than textual and fixed' (Bennett and Woollacott 1987: 81).

Within this play of different 'readings' some will be more culturally and economically powerful than others, such as the official guide to *BTVS*. This opens with a 'Mythology of Buffy', trying to produce an integrated sense of the 'Buffyverse' or the universe of characters and events in this now long-running series. As Matt Hills (to whom this case study is indebted) suggests (2002a), the 'proprietorial' connections offered by such publicity or promotional material consistently defines the significant relations of reading as being relations between episodes of *BTVS* rather than between the series and other genres or authors. These echo very traditional authorship discourses in the emphasis on Joss Whedon (the writer-director-executive producer, who had previously worked on *Roseanne* and *Toy Story*) as prime source of this organic creation with its 'intrinsic potential to evolve and grow' (Whedon), in other words the 'Buffyverse'.

This emphasis seems to work partly as a way in which *BTVS* emerges from the 'decentred' world of US commercial networks as a unique and authored piece of work. It was made by 20th Century Fox but shown, from 1997, on the Warner Brothers network as part of its move into prime-time hour-long drama, helping to solidify its signature as the 'family network' with strong appeal to the valuable teen market (see Johnson 2001: 42). Such series cannot expect an automatic huge audience share (as could the BBC which produced *Dr Who*, for example, a much earlier key series for the attention of fans) and need to create and trade on viewer loyalty if at all possible. One way of doing this is to suggest that these products are unique and distinctive within the television marketplace, as

well as to invite as wide a range of viewers as possible to enjoy the whole 'Buffyverse' of characters, generic echoes and situations.

Interestingly, *BTVS*'s publicity materials and their emphasis on this hermetic 'Buffyverse' seem to be adopted quite happily by fans in expressing their love of the show. This is different from earlier 'fan' emphases which stress the differences and struggles between fan and production perspectives (for example around the much older *Dr Who* series, produced within a much narrower British broadcasting ecology, in which the BBC often assumed rather autocratic powers as arbiters of taste).

Buffy as cross-generic

To recap: genre films have always involved some kind of 'hybridity' and are never 'pure' westerns or horror films etc. Hollywood has always tried to attract as many audience segments as possible. There are, of course, provisional boundaries – which however can mutate. Each case is slightly different in the way it plays the possiblities of its mixings and meldings.

Paradoxically, though not unusually, *BTVS*'s 'uniqueness' is formulated, by Whedon, the series 'maker', as cross-generic and even formulaic. He is quoted as saying:

> In the movie, the director took an action/horror/comedy script and went only with the comedy. In the television show we're keeping to the original formula. We take our horror genre seriously. We are not doing spoof. It's larger than life but we are very much involved with these characters. This is not *Clueless* . . . The description I liked best is *My So-Called Life* meets *The X-Files*.
>
> (Whedon cited in Tracy 1998: 22)

This, like a lot of the publicity material, tries to appeal to an audience composed of

- viewers interested in following a (female-centred) 'teen fiction' with its promise of romance and exploration of the problems of the 'in-between' period of adolescence.
- those interested in the paranormal, in science-fiction resonances drawn on by *The X-Files*.
- and those interested in both. *The X-Files* has a long-running undercurrent of potential romance between its two lead characters, and many 'teen' films and television series 'give the sense that to be a teenager is to be not quite human' (Moseley 2001: 43).
- Overlapping these are audience members who also relish the mode (rather than genre) of comedy and the series' smart, articulate dialogue and glossy, high production values (skilful shooting, imaginative and well crafted sets, well choreographed fight sequences etc).

- See Buffy's deadpan line 'While we're still young, Giles' as he gives a lengthy and learned genealogy of the hyena monsters.
- Or the 'cool' twists of word order and form: 'We so don't have time'; 'You're acting a little overly, aren't you?'; 'I'll talk to you later, when you've visited Decaf Land'.
- As Willow says in an episode where Buffy is missing: 'I've always been amazed with how Buffy fights, but in a way I feel like we took her punning for granted.' (See Williams 2001.)

In making his claims for the series Whedon uses the language of 'high concept' from cinema marketing ('*My So-Called Life* meets *The X-Files*'). It also signals both 'repetition' (the formula of many horror films) and 'difference' (the repeated tributes to *BTVS*'s originality) as well as distinguishing between the film and television versions of, and attitude to Buffy's 'world'. This world is like others (such as the 'world' of *Xena: Warrior Princess*) in which strange and fantastical things can

happen, involving all kinds of ruptures to generic expectation. It thereby potentially widens the audience base of the series (though it also risks alienating a significant number of viewers).

BTVS has even played with the musical genre, for many the opposite of horror. The www.jumptheshark.com website (which charts the votes of fans about the moment when their favourite series 'lost it' or 'jumped the shark') reported in January 2002 that the majority vote of those disaffected with *BTVS* was for the musical episode of the new series, 'Once More, With Feeling'. In this episode, the latest demon cursed the inhabitants of Sunnydale to interact with each other only in song and dance, during which time they had to sing their most closely guarded secrets.

Some suspected that the makers of a show for whom fan buzz is so key deliberately responded to the challenge of the website's finding that many other shows 'bombed' when they 'went musical'. Certainly the programme-makers are very aware of fans as audience and, for example, have playfully set up the sixth series' 'geek mafia' villains as James Bond fans.

The great thing about Buffy is that it is so baroque and strange and fantastical that you can actually get away with certain things; whether it be a musical episode or whatever, it all makes perfect sense in the Buffy universe.

(Whedon quoted in Hills 2002a: 9)

The worlds of such intensely experienced fictions can also be signalled by, and entered through, their main character or star, as in the old 'star-genre' pairing of Hollywood cinema:

Images of Sarah Michelle Gellar (usually blonde but never dumb, pouting and physically fit, yet too petit (sic) for the catwalk and far removed from the manufactured 'beauties' of *Baywatch*) have become indelibly linked with the series' rising profile.

(Wyman 2000: 72)

This fan's description, like the earlier Whedon quotation, again signals both repetition (blonde, pouting etc.) and difference (especially the image as being 'not-*Baywatch*' and 'not-catwalk') within certain kinds of generic familiarity. Interestingly, though Gellar's youthful yet grave (excuse the pun) appearance seems to fit the requirements of the 'teen' school or college series or films, the role turns out to be simultaneously one from the vampire sub-genre of horror, traditionally featuring dark (middle European?) slayers and blonde victims. (The blonde babe potential or opposite is expertly parodied in the episode where Spike has a compliant and eagerly sexual robot double made of her.) Gellar has also featured briefly, in a parallel discourse, in ads for Maybelline cosmetics, drawing on 'the codes of 'busy professionalism' which could be read as reference to Gellar and/or the character 'Buffy' (see Hills 2002a) whom Zoe Williams (2001) suggests is 'the only heroine to come out of mainstream telly in the past decade who is both sexy and awesomely competent'. So the 'star-genre promise' (Branston 2000: 209) of the series via Gellar is quite a complex one.

The series' reliance on the high school or teen-comedy or drama both in production and in marketing, draws on a categorisation which, unexpectedly perhaps, can easily overlap with that of 'vampire horror'.

Q How many examples of the 'high school' or college TV series or films can you think of for US and UK cinema today?

There are widely spread discourses which seek to understand the generic elements of 'vampire' in *BTVS* rather than the direct or 'realist' high school elements, as codings for teenage dilemmas and experiences.

- 'on Buffy, we . . . use monsters to kind o metaphorise . . . situations that teenagers . people encounter' (Noxon quoted in Gross
- 'At least one unofficial fan episode guide strongly emphasises this aspect of the show, featuring a section on each episode entitled 'The Real Horror' which examines the teenage experiences which have supposedly been textually encoded' (Hills 2002a: 13).
- 'Vampires, in *Buffy*, mutate horribly when they are about to "suck blood" (for which read, "have sex") – they are aping the bodily aspects of puberty with their furry weirdness. Buffy, in killing them, normalises and controls the transition of adolescence, and acts as the guardian of her entire generation. It's quite a feel-good show on some levels' (Williams 2001).

Though the average age of *BTVS* viewers in the US is cited by Ono (2000) as twenty-nine, this powerful 'teen' classification via channel placement, publicity materials and also fan literature means that fan magazines can engage with discussions of whether the show is too sophisticated to be understood by teen audiences (provoking fan teens to enjoyably vigorous response). Yet the power of very traditional discourses is also striking. Part of the defence of the show, whether by fans or makers, often involves the still highly culturally valued classification as 'art'. *BTVS* is 'television art'

- say the owners of the series
- say the teen fans
- say the horror and fantasy fans, contesting the widespread cultural denigration of their enthusiasms
- say the cult viewers, claiming their superior knowledge and devotion to the series.

All of them use and cluster around the claims that *BTVS* should be classified as 'art'.

Horror, romance and scheduling

BTVS draws on one of the most popular and long-lived strands of the culturally despised and often banned horror genre: vampire fictions. Horror has always been presumed to have negative effects on 'children', and has always had a special relationship to its fans, partly because of this status. It has often been defined as aimed at 'the youth market' or 'adolescents of whatever age' and has more recently been offered as linked with romance via marketing strategies, e.g. the release of key horror films on Valentine's Day (see Chapter 3).

The genre has had a mixed heritage of inputs and developments, unlike the integrated development attributed to the western or gangster genre, with their much more direct and prestigious links to US history and less rigid conventions (for example *always* connecting garlic and vampires; vampires and mirrors; stakes and vampires' deaths etc). In cinema it has been argued to be a 'body genre', given low status because it seeks to produce 'mere' bodily response (evidence of fear, bluntly). It is now often argued more positively that its pleasures are those of allowing audiences to engage vividly with a range of fears about the body and the shifting boundaries of the abnormal and the normal (hairiness, physical disintegration, appetites etc.). More recently the knowingness of the genre has been celebrated, its capacity to play with how much we can stand to see, drawing on prior audience knowledge (and because of the low status we're often discussing keen fans here) to reflect on the nature of cinema itself.

Within British television the horror strand of *BTVS* has led to many scheduling anomalies (see Hill and Calcutt 2001 for an excellent account). UK television channels do not perceive imported 'cult television', let alone series involving horror, as suitable for prime-time programming at 8 or 9 p.m., partly owing to the so called Family Viewing Policy (see Selling audiences case study following Chapter 6) before the 9 p.m. watershed. So *BTVS* has been screening partly early evening on BBC2 (where most of whose viewers are aged forty-plus) where it has been open to cuts for 'scenes of violence, sexual innuendo or bad language' (Hill and Calcutt 2001: 3). It has also been screened later in the evening on BBC2, minus such censorship, but comparison has been possible with the SkyOne screenings (of the 'next' series showing in the US) at 8 p.m. (the earlier watershed time for premium encrypted subscription channels). This has led to vigorous 'consumer activism' around the series, specifically focused on British conditons of viewing (see www.buffyuk.org).

Back to horror. Within the genre the figure of the vampire can be understood and 'played with' in many ways by both producers and audiences. (see Gledhill 1999). The figure (located in a central mythical location of the genre 'Transylvania') emerges in the nineteenth century with the publication of Bram Stoker's *Dracula* (1897) and has been categorised, among other things, as a metaphor of

- the ways that capitalists feed off the labour of the working class
- other kinds of oppression and resistance such as those around race, gender and sexuality
- the simultaneous attraction and terror of sexuality itself
- old, eastern Europe leeching off 'modern' western Europe (a metaphor which connects to negative images of asylum seekers)
- more recently, in Coppola's film version, the embodiment of fears about the blood-borne affliction AIDS.

One final note relevant to *BTVS*: Joke Hermes quotes Carol Clover's observation of how boys watching slasher films cheer the killer on as he assaults his victims 'then reverse their sympathies so as to cheer the survivor on as she assaults the killers' (1999: 23). Hermes suggests:

> Feminism has given us woman as a credible and forceful avenger . . . The popularity of horror as a genre . . . only makes sense against the broader

dynamics of social change. Without feminism there would have been no final girl or avenging woman. Nor would the young men experience the amount of gender confusion that makes horror an ideal testing laboratory [for them].

(Hermes 1999: 79)

'I got tired of [watching] girls get killed in horror movies. I thought, "Somebody should beat the holy shit out of the monsters . . ."' (Whedon quoted in *Guardian Guide*, 5–11 January 2002).

How does *BTVS* draw on these possibilities? Clearly the size of most television screens and the domestic context of viewing does not make it ideal as a vehicle for full 'body horror', and the resulting possibility of nightmares for the younger 'family audience' has to be borne in mind by makers and schedulers. The horror genre (in film and book form) has gone through many stages and been claimed for varied readings which there is no space to go into here. But it is interesting that the makers of the programme claim:

Whedon went back to an interpretation of ancient vampire mythology that few but scholars remember: some legends say that vampires are not humans at all but demons who have taken up residence inside human corpses.

(Golden and Holder 1998: 125)

In fact rather more than 'a few' know such theories, since the work of the popular novelist Anne Rice had done much to circulate them. She suggests in her novel *The Vampire Lestat* (1985) that vampires have their origin in a demonic 'infection' of human bodies. The post-Rice 'new vampire' has also been said to be 'multiple, communal and familial, living with and relating to other vampires.' (Zanger 1997: 18) as in the Hollywood movie of her novel *Interview with the Vampire* (1981).

Interestingly for the balance of 'repetition and difference' claimed for the series, *BTVS The Watcher's*

Guide omits to mention Rice's earlier take on this part of the mythology and claims, again, its 'uniqueness' or difference for Whedon alone. Hills (2002a: 16) suggests that this is because of the much lower status of the vampire 'reading formation' or genre, and the series proprietors' desire to aggregate vampire fans as audience but also distance the series from their interests. This goes along with *BTVS*'s return to an emphasis, within the repertoire of vampire fictions, on 'the slayer' of vampires and therefore the element of the 'return to normality' (see also Buffy's repeated desire for 'a normal life') rather than the relishing of the abnormal and perverse places into which the vampire will take you, which has always been a large part of the figure's appeal.

'Whereas the early series were certificated as "12" on video, the later series are "15"' (Stafford 2001).

However the series seems to have responded to its fans in this area (one of the ways in which many genres change). 'The Master' vampire in the first series was seen by some fans as a conventional lead villain, a demon king almost out of pantomime. But the figure of Angel was different. He is Buffy's main 'love interest', but a vampire, whose human soul has been restored by a gypsy curse so that one moment of perfect happiness – say with Buffy – will break the curse and turn him back into a vampire, indeed the most fiendish vampire ever known. This is clearly a complex figure, much like Louis in the film of Rice's *Interview with the Vampire*.

Dru and Spike, as a couple (fitting into a 'coupling' emphasis for romance readers, like most of the characters in *BTVS*), then introduced even more sympathetic groupings of vampires, which resembled Rice's 'new vampire' pattern. Indeed Spike in the fourth series is softened as a character, and included in the central group of 'hero' protagonists. The high incidence of couples in *BTVS* opens the series to the engagement of fans of the romance genre, though this is far from being as sharply gender-divided as the following quotation suggests:

> It's one of those genres where women and men can watch and get into it on different levels. Guys are looking at it as pure horror and most of the women look at it as a sexual and romantic metaphor. To be taken and made eternal – that's pretty hot.
>
> (Noxon quoted in Gross 2000: 87)

Nevertheless, it seems that the type of cinematic horror that women audiences most enjoy is the vampire film (see Cherry 1999), which many read in a similar way to romance fiction, identifying the relationship between the vampires, or the vampire and victim, as a major source of pleasure. Others have noted an important aspect for Gothic romances, which flow into horror: they often employ a double 'hero', dark and brooding, melancholy, enigmatic, one who embodies all that women fear and who is at the same time a safe haven from all that – rather like Angel, the reformed vampire whom Buffy fell in love with without knowing. The Buffy–Angel relationship hence allows the series to play with instabilities, especially of the transitional teen self, and the resulting difficulties and tensions of romantic relationships. Zoe Williams, like others, sees the Angel–Buffy cruel dilemma as metaphoric, to put it in a banal way, of the decision of a young girl whether to have sex with her boyfriend:

> You now have the situation rendered, not as adults remember it, but as it really was: crucial, apocalyptic, heart-shattering. The evil beasts are both metaphors for aspects of life, and portals for the adult imagination into the teenage one.
>
> (Williams 2001: 36)

The romance strand, with its expectations of difficulties in the way of the lovers which will prolong the pleasures of the viewer or reader, works in a striking way for *BTVS*. Angel's character left the programme except for occasional return visits (Whedon said that 'it became increasingly clear to us

that Buffy's and Angel's two worlds really are separate' Hills 2000a: 21). Even though television's industrial and economic determinants mean that Angel will not return full-time to the series, viewers approaching the series from the romance perspective can still see him as a potential partner for Buffy.

Meantime a BBC spinoff is planned for Giles (the actor wanted to return to England). Again, Whedon has made statements which stress his **authorship** and the further genres from which the spin off can draw, though perhaps still distancing himself from the full flavour of 'horror': 'I wanted to do a show that isn't so much about kickboxing demons as it is about English history and classical ghost stories' (Whedon quoted in *Guardian Guide*, 5–11 January 2002).

References

Bennet, Tony and Woollacott, Janet (1987) *Bond and Beyond: The Political Career of a Popular Hero*, London: Macmillan.

Branston, Gill (2001) *Cinema and Cultural Modernity*, Buckingham: Open University Press.

Cherry, Bridget (1999) 'Refusing to refuse to look: female viewers of the horror film', in Melvyn Stokes and Richard Maltby (eds) *Identifying Hollywood's Audiences:Cultural Identity and the Movies*, London: BFI.

Gledhill, Christine (1999, 2nd edition) 'Science fiction and horror', in Pam Cook and Mieke Bernink *The Cinema Book*, London: BFI.

Golden, Christopher and Holder, Nancy (1998) *Buffy the Vampire Slayer: The Watcher's Guide*, New York: Pocket Books.

Gross, Ed (2000) 'Angel Delight' *SFX* 61, February: 80–7.

Hermes, Joke (1999) 'Media figures in identity construction', in Pertti Alasuutari (ed.) *Rethinking the Media Audience*, London: Sage.

Hill, Annette and Calcutt, Ian (2001) 'Vampire hunters: the scheduling and reception of "Buffy the Vampire Slayer" and "Angel" in the UK', *Intensities* online journal.

Hills, Matt (2002a) 'Reading the (official/cult/star/teen/ vampire/romance) text of *Buffy the Vampire Slayer*: reading formation theory and the rising stakes of generic hybridity', in Elana Levine and Lisa Parks (eds) *Red Noise: Television Studies and 'Buffy the Vampire Slayer'*, London and Durham: Duke University Press.

Hills, Matt (2002b) *Fan Cultures*, London and New York: Routledge.

Johnson, Catherine (2001) 'Buffy the Vampire Slayer', in Glen Creeber (ed.) *The Television Genre Book*, London: BFI.

Kaveney, Roz (ed.) (2001) *Reading the Vampire Slayer*, Tauris Parke.

Moseley, Rachel (2001) 'The teen series', in Glen Creeber (ed.) *The Television Genre Book*, London: BFI.

Ono, Kent A. (2000) 'To be a vampire on *Buffy the Vampire Slayer*: race and ("other") socially marginalising positions on horror television', in R. H. Elyce (ed.) *Fantasy Girls: Gender in the New Universe of Science Fiction and Fantasy Televison*, Lanham: Rowman and Littlefield.

Stafford, Roy (2001) 'Keep a "watch", on Buffy' *in the picture* magazine, no. 42, September.

Tracy, Kathleen (1998) *The Girl's Got Bite: The Unofficial Guide to Buffy's World*, Los Angeles: Renaissance Books.

Williams, Zoe (2001) 'The lady and the vamp, *Guardian Weekend*, November 17.

Wyman, Mark (2000) 'Slay Belle: how Buffy hits the mark', *television Zone Special*, 36, March: 68–72.

Zanger, Jules (1997) 'Metaphor into metonymy: the vampire next door', in Joan Gordon and Veronica Hollinger (eds) *Blood Read: The Vampire as Metaphor in Contemporary Culture*, Philadelphia: University of Pennsylvania Press.

Website information

Intensities: The Journal of Cult Media www.cult-media.com
www.jumptheshark.com
www.buffyuk.org

4 Questions of representation

- Case study: Stereotyping
- Representations and gender
- Representations and the real
- Questions of positive and negative images
- Other ways of changing representations
- References
- Further reading

One of the key terms of Media Studies is 'representation', a rich term with several related meanings.

- It emphasises that, however realistic or plausible media images seem, they never simply *present* the world direct. They are always a construction, a **re**-presentation, not a transparent window on to the real.
- It also prompts the question: how have groups, or possible identities, or events that exist partly 'outside' the media, been represented in the media? This has broadly political implications, related to the world of (broadly) political representatives: people who 'stand in' for us – as union reps, or our representatives in Parliament etc.
- It also signals the way some media *re*-present certain events, stories etc. over and over again, and tend to marginalise or even exclude others, and thereby make them unfamiliar or even threatening.

The power of repeated imagery?

New York, 11 September 2001: a witness who was standing near the World Trade Center Twin Towers when they collapsed and who fled only after the first tower went said: 'I just felt safe. It was a movie set and I was an extra, so nothing could hurt me' (summarised from Hari 2001).

The media give us ways of imagining particular situations, identities and groups. These imaginings exist materially, as industries which employ people, and can also have material effects on how people experience the world, and how they in turn get understood, or legislated for, or perhaps beaten up in the street by others.

Stereotyping in this context has been a key issue. It raises such questions as:

- Do the media, in the identities and understandings they so powerfully circulate, suggest to large audiences that *x* or *y* character is typical of that group, and therefore that the whole group should be viewed in certain ways?
- Are these ways best described as negative?
- How does the relationship between media images and particular groups or identities get changed?

Stereotype comes from Greek '*stereo* = solid', a printer's term for the solid blocks of type which could be used to represent something which would otherwise need considerable work with individual pieces of type to show fine detail. Just as electronic publishing has replaced 'solid' print, so this concept of stereotyping may now need to be rethought.

Case study: stereotyping

Stereotypes are not actual people but *widely circulated ideas or assumptions* about particular groups. They are often assumed to be 'lies', and to need to be 'done away with' so we can all 'get rid of our prejudices' and meet as equals. The term is more derogatory than 'type' or even 'archetype' (which mean very similar things but have higher status as terms).

Stereotypes have the following characteristics:

1 They involve both a categorising and an evaluation of the group being stereotyped.

2 They usually emphasise some easily grasped feature(s) of the group in question and suggest that these are the cause of the group's (usually negative) position.

3 Relatedly, the evaluation carried by a stereotype is often, though not always, a negative one.

4 Stereotypes often try to insist on absolute differences where in fact the idea of a *spectrum* of difference is more appropriate, whether about the skin colours of human beings or about degrees of 'masculine' and 'feminine' attributes across the sexes.

(1) and (4)   Stereotyping is a *process of categorisation* necessary to make sense of the world, and the flood of information and impressions we receive minute by minute. We all have to be 'prejudiced', in its root sense of 'pre-judging', in order to carve our way through any situation. We make mental maps of our worlds to navigate our way through them, and maps only ever represent parts of the real world, and in particular ways.

- We all employ typifications in certain situations.
- We all belong to groups that can be typified, and stereotyped in this way. We make sense of people on the basis of gestures, dress, voice and so on, very much as we construct a sense of characters in the media.

(2) Stereotypes work by taking some easily grasped features presumed to belong to a group, putting them at the centre of the description, and implying that all members of the group always have those features.

They then suggest that these characteristics, which are often the result of a historical process, are themselves the cause of the group's position. One of the strengths of stereotypes is that they can point to features that apparently have 'a grain of truth'. But the stereotype then repeats, across a whole range of media and informal exchanges, that this characteristic is *always* the *central* truth about that group.

For example, for many years, in Hollywood cinema and other discourses, black slaves working on cotton plantations before the American Civil War of 1861–5 were often stereotyped through such signs, among others, as:

- a shuffling walk
- musical rhythm, and a tendency to burst into song and dance readily
- (in characterisations of female house slaves) bodily fatness, uneducated foolishness, and childlike qualities – see 'Mammy' and Prissy in *Gone With the Wind* (US 1939).

Figure 4.1 Hattie McDaniel as 'Mammy' arguing with Scarlett (Vivien Leigh) in *Gone with the Wind* (US 1939). See Bogle (1994: 86–92) for a detailed discussion of this character, played by this performer, who was one of very few black actors ever to gain an Oscar (for her supporting role in this film).

To say that these demeaning stereotypes embody a grain of truth may seem insulting, but consider the following facts:

- Slaves on the Southern plantations in the nineteenth century had their calf muscles cut if they tried to run away from slavery (the shuffling gait of the stereotype).

- Slaves were given hardly any educational opportunities. (Hostile use of the stereotype demeans efforts to make music and dance out of very simple resources to hand. It attributes 'rhythm' to primitive, animal qualities, thus justifying slave owners' positions such as 'they couldn't benefit from education anyway'.)

- The women were often treated simply as breeding stock by the slave owners. When this function was over, once they had given birth to numbers of new slaves and their bodies were perhaps enlarged by repeated pregnancies, they were often moved into the main house and used as nursemaids to the white children. Again, hostile use of the stereotype invites us to account for the Mammy's size in terms of physical laziness or ignorance rather than her exploitation at the hands of the slave system.

(3) Though large, historically oppressed groups such as black American slaves, or Irish people, have been heavily stereotyped, this usually happens through more than one stereotype. They can be used sympathetically, as in black Civil Rights reformist propaganda, or the broadly sympathetic if sentimental use of Irishness in *Titanic* (US 1997).

(4) Stereotypes seem to insist on absolute difference, whereas there exist spectrums of differences (think of gender, age, racial differentiation etc.). This is not the way in which stereotypes are usually argued against, which involves one of the dominant values of western culture: that we are all unique individuals. In some ways this is true (however much it ignores the social regimentations of school, family, work etc.). But it is more helpful to think of differences as involving *shared* structures of social experience. These make it possible to understand many of the experiences we have as being typical. Indeed, it's arguable that our differences are due not to 'unique essences' but to the particular ways in which very typical forces (such as class, gender and ethnicity) have intersected in your or my unique instance. Crucially this broadens the opportunities both for understanding other people's experiences, and for changing the social structures that produce them. Certainly there is plenty of evidence that stereotypes can be changed and shifted over time.

Representations and gender

The distinction between sex and gender is still very useful (even though there exist confusing differences in the ways the terms are used). Sex in this context is not the same as sexuality (which refers to people's sexual orientation, their object choice, sexual activities and imaginings). *Sex difference* refers here to the division of people into male and female, depending on physical characteristics: sex organs, hormonal make-up and so on.

Gender differences are culturally formed. They exist on the basis of the biological, 'the body', but build a huge system of differentiation over and above it. So whereas your sex will determine broadly whether or not you can bear a child, for example (though even this is not a universal truth), gender-based arguments have insisted that because women bear children, therefore they should be the ones to stay at home and bring them up. 'It's only natural' says a whole social system of laws, tax arrangements, childcare – and media images.

'Lesbian and gay studies does for *sex* and *sexuality* approximately what Women's Studies does for gender' (Henry Abelove *et al.* quoted in Medhurst and Munt 1997: 68).

Figure 4.2

ACTIVITY 4.1

- How can you tell which of the very simply drawn characters in Figure 4.2 is male and which female?
- Which lines on the drawing told you?
- Try to find other, similar examples in birthday cards, or children's comics and cartoon characters.
- What does this suggest about the ease with which assumptions of gender difference circulate in our culture?

To put it another way, sex says 'It's a boy'; gender says 'Oh, good' and gets out the blue baby clothes, the train set and guns, and a whole set of assumptions. (Adapted from Branston 1984)

Some of these assumptions are circulated through the media, and **feminist** positions keen to challenge them have developed key approaches to representation. **Content analysis** is a valuable starting point. It tries to assess the frequency with which a certain carefully chosen category appears in media texts (say 'women in the kitchen'; 'asylum seekers as criminals'; 'men as always tough'). Such studies of gender roles in magazines and advertising, for example, show that women are still represented according to long-standing cultural stereotypes. Some elements have changed since the late 1970s and early 1980s when, for example:

See Chapter 13.

- only 13 per cent of central characters in UK ads were women while they made up 41 per cent of UK employees.
- women were repeatedly shown 'as housewives, mothers, home-makers' while men were often represented 'in situations of authority and dominance over women', aided by the use of male **voice overs** (usually signifying authority on the soundtrack), or roles where only men are scientists or knowledgeable experts about the product which women 'just' consume.

Q   How true does this seem to you now, in the twenty-first century?

Would you be more careful if it was you that got pregnant?

Contraception is one of the facts of life.
Anyone, married or single, can get free advice on contraception from their doctor or family planning clinic.
You can find your local clinic under Family Planning in the telephone directory or Yellow Pages.
The Health Education Council
78 New Oxford Street, London WC1A 1AH

Figure 4.3 Family Planning Association ad, 1970: the shock of a reverse-stereotyped image.

ACTIVITY 4.2

Conduct your own random survey across one to three hours of television ads. Take a category such as age, ethnicity or gender (as in the examples above) and try to discover how that group or identity is now represented according to:

- the numbers of characters in ads who visibly belong to the group.
- how they are represented – as narrative heroes? As consumers or as experts? With or without dialogue? In what kinds of genres: comic? Serious? For cheap or expensive products?
- whether the voice-overs seem to belong to the group being represented.
- whether they are repeatedly shown in some situations but not others, e.g. at work or in the home; as people preoccupied with their appearance.

Nintendo ad for the game *Zelda*, 1999: 'Willst thou get the girl . . . or play like one?'

Such quantitative evidence is striking, though objections have been made to content analysis and simple approaches to stereotyping. In altering how gender difference is presented, a basic assumption of quantitative approaches can imply that more images of a particular group are needed; then that what are needed are more realistic portrayals (e.g. of women) since the media are said to reflect society, and such reflections should always be accurate. This raises questions such as:

- Might wider structures of economic and political power make it arguably 'realistic' to show more women than men active in the home, for example?
- How do *different* genres affect these imaginings? What of the needs of comedy or fantasy for example?
- Is it *only* irrational or ignorant prejudice that accounts for stereotyping?
- Is it true that the media have huge powers all on their own to socialise people into beliefs, roles and behaviour? There is plenty of evidence that people are not always successfully socialised in this way.

I'll
be a
post
feminist
in
post
patriarchy

Figure 4.4

The term '**post-feminism**' suggests that we are now 'beyond' the need to struggle for gender equality: 'postmodern' playfulness or irony is the proper response to oppression. Young women are now said to take for granted the respect, equal pay etc. struggled for by earlier feminists. 'It's OK to enjoy shopping and wear lipstick' points to the pleasure of 'trying on' identities, as well as to the need to reread a woman's sexualised appearance as not necessarily subordinating her to men.

Yet some women feel that the balance of representation has tilted back towards sexist images and language, merely updated by the 'alibi' of irony ('I was only joking. Don't you have a sense of humour?'), for example in the 'laddishness' of breakfast television or music radio; of magazines such as *FHM*; or the use of women in traditionally 'sex object' casting poses (Wonderbra ads, *Playboy* magazine etc.).

Q How satisfying do you find 'girl power' media images of female 'empowerment' (such as the remake of *Charlie's Angels* (US 2001) or the character Lara Croft)?

Q How far do they fit with what's sketched here as 'post feminist'?

Q How far can such imagery always be read ironically, as 'postmodern play'? After all, making and circulating it does involve real jobs, advertising budgets, space taken up – and also involves other images being thereby excluded.

Representations and the real

Calls for 'realism' or positive images of disadvantaged groups can ignore the ways that media texts do not have a straightforward relationship to the rest of the real. To say that a media text is 'distorted' or 'unrepresentative' may ignore the following points:

- It is a representation in the other sense of the word: a construction with its own formal rules and fascinations. It therefore needs to work differently with different materials: time-based film and television, with their ability to stage action forms, or radio, relying on more personal spoken words etc.

- Its images may belong to a genre (radio comedy, or horror film) which is not experienced by audiences in the same way as, say, the news. Audiences' (and especially fans') degree of familiarity with a genre's conventions is important for its 'reality effect': in action adventure genres, violence, for example, may be taken for granted as 'staged', as needed to dramatise the story. It may therefore be difficult to 'read off it' implications for masculine identities (see Connell 2001). In news or children's fictions violence may however be deeply disturbing, because there it is seen as more closely related to the real world.

  Conversely it seems that soaps, for all their reputation as 'unrealistic', can treat certain issues (such as rape, or traumatisation after military service) vividly through the way the issue persists as a problem in the long term, sometimes over years.

- The idea of reflection is far too straightforward and mirror-like, especially for fantasy forms (e.g. horror, SF or romance). It suggests there is a fairly simple thing called 'reality' to be 'reflected' in a one-to-one, undistorted way, whereas some forms, such as comedy, have been argued to *depend* on the exaggerations of stereotyping, understood playfully by audiences.

THE MEDIA STUDENT'S BOOK

After the release of *Star Wars Episode One: Phantom Menace* (US 1999), there were heated and fascinating debates over the allegations that some of the characters were negatively stereotyped, especially Jar Jar Binks (said to be an offensive caricature of Caribbean, Jamaican or African-American culture, interestingly through the construction of the voice) and the Meimoidians, said to be negatively stereotyped as 'Japanese'. See Brooker (2001) for summary and discussion.

When Les Dawson said the line: 'I knew it was the mother-in-law 'cause when they heard her coming, the mice started throwing themselves on the traps', there were several pleasures on offer:

- his delivery, gravelly Northern voice and timing, especially as contrasted with –
- the verbal surprise of the comic exaggeration – the image of those mice!
- the economic elegance of a well-crafted joke, well delivered.

However this joke's economy is not detached from its social history and context. It is able to work only because a quickly recognisable stereotype is in play (the 'mother-in-law') which could be said to offer the pleasure of community, of feeling a 'we'-ness and a 'them'-ness for a moment.

Questions that then need asking include:

- From whose point of view is it being told? Whose point of view is excluded; who is the 'them' outside this cosy community?
- How is the audience positioned, not only by the joke but by the context in which it is told: all-male club or television show or radio documentary?
- How does the group on the receiving end of the joke seem to be treated in the rest of the media? Does that change how we might experience the joke?

To make this last point clearer: in the case of mothers-in-law, we may feel OK to laugh, since this is rather an outmoded target. Changes in family structures have eroded the considerable power of the mother-in-law of many working-class couples who had to live in her home for the first few years of married life. We may even feel that the degree of exaggeration itself signals the joke's distance from reality. To put it in *semiotic* language: pleasure is more from the play of the *signifiers* than from agreement with the way the *sign* represents its *referent*.

However, you might feel differently if you were an older woman, and the object of a great number of contemptuous jokes and comedy sketches. (Or you might not, if this were only a relatively unimportant one of your several identities.)

And when jokes centre, say, on a group that is being abused on the streets or in the home, for whom there are fewer 'communities of feeling' to enter, it becomes a much less easy thing to laugh along with them.

Moreover some contemporary figures, such as Ali G, Eddie Izzard or Eminem, deliberately confuse what were previously thought to be stable distinctions of race, gender, ethnicity etc. As Paul Gilroy put it in a fascinating article:

huge amounts of energy are being wasted worrying about whether Ali G is a white Jew pretending to be black, a white Jew pretending to be a white pretending to be black, a white Jew pretending to be an Asian pretending to be black and so on.

. . . No one knows for certain what Ali is. Hatred, fear and anxiety appear in response to his ability to confound the categories that hold contemporary Britain stable.

(Paul Gilroy, 'Ali G and the Oscars', www.opendemocracy.com, 4 April 2002)

Questions of positive and negative images

History suggests that, once an oppressed group, such as women or 'black' people, perceives its political and social oppression, it begins to try to change that oppression at the level of representation. After struggling sometimes for simple visibility, it will then often try to replace 'negative' with 'positive' images. This, however, is a complex process, involving the following areas:

- debates around how to define the 'community' being represented
- questions of what is to count as 'positive' representations
- the effect of employment practices in the media on such images
- the differences that the understandings of different audiences will make to the meanings of certain kinds of images, including genre competence, religious beliefs etc.

Groups that are heavily stereotyped (as 'problems') are likely to have less **access** to influential positions in the media, or to other kinds of power. This can set up a vicious circle of unemployment. There may also be few images or stories that centre on them sympathetically (as opposed to ones where they feature as villainous or untrustworthy: see long histories of the stereotyping of gays; of ethnic 'others' such as Mexicans or Native Americans in westerns; Arabs in contemporary Hollywood or Irish people in British culture). This may be the result of violent historical processes, including wars or colonialism, which have left a long legacy of trivialising or insulting images.

'Gay characters and references to the existence of homosexuality were routinely laundered off the screen for . . . half a century' (Russo 1981: 63).

99

Racism the 'stigmatising of difference in order to justify advantage or the abuse of power, whether that advantage or abuse be economic, political, cultural or psychological' (Shohat and Stam 1994). The black activist Du Bois emphasised the obsession with 'colour, hair and bone' used to construct absolute (binary) difference between 'black' and 'white'. See Hall 1996.

In the case of asylum seekers it may even be the case that they dare not be photographed or quoted by name, for fear of reprisals in their homelands.

THERE WERE THESE THICK PADDIES........

Figure 4.5

When images of the group do begin to be produced, they have to bear what has been called the **burden of representation**. This involves questions such as:

- What is taken to be the (enormous) group which is the object of representation? What 'reality' is being represented? For groups such as women, or 'British-Asians', which members of the group are doing the defining of 'the community'? Or of defining what is positive and what is negative about an image? To imply that 'British-Asian' is a homogeneous group, all sharing the same experiences of age, class, religion, and so on, is clearly foolish. The success of the BBC television series *Goodness Gracious Me* (you may remember the 'Let's go for an English' sketch) and its spinoffs can be seen as part of a claim of younger British Asians to define their own group(s), sometimes in oppositon to the images of an older generation.

'There is a sense of urgency to say it all, or at least to signal as much as we could in one film. Sometimes we couldn't afford to hold anything back for another time, another conversation or another film. There is the reality of our experience – sometimes we only get the one chance to make ourselves heard' (Pines 1992: 101).

QUESTIONS OF REPRESENTATION

- (There is also the question of how to construct characters belonging to the group (particularly visible in the case of skin colour) if they have been relatively absent from media images previously. This can mean that they are now often read as 'representing' the whole community – a real burden to those trying to constuct the newly visible images.)

'Sunrise Radio, the biggest commercial broadcaster directed at ethnic minority communities in Britain, is proposing to drop the use of the word "Asian" following complaints from Hindu and Sikh listeners that they were being too closely associated with Muslims. Some . . . said they were being targeted following . . . September 11th' (Wells 2002).

For many years there were very few images of black British people on television, and those images which did exist were of blacks as 'problems' or (more sympathetic, if patronising) as 'victims'. When black characters *did* appear, they were often felt to need to 'stand in for' or *represent* the whole of their particular 'community'. These 'positive' images sometimes produced characterisations of strict parents, near-noble teachers and so on – clearly a narrowing of the range of representation compared to the roles available to white characters. As a result, some members of such groups felt that being represented in various and ordinary, even 'negative' ways would be a positive step. |

Meera Syal (scriptwriter, *Bhaji on the Beach* (UK 1994)) described 'how an Asian man, bloody angry, rang me up to abuse me for showing our community in such a negative light. How dare you show women doing such things? Talking about sex, and, what's worse, doing it before marriage . . . Painting our men as violent, when the real violence is against us by the white people' (Dunant 1994: 13).

'I like the sissy [stereotype of gay men]. Is it used in "negative" ways? Yeah. But my view has always been: visibility at any cost. Negative is better than nothing.' (Harvey Fierstein in Russo 1981).

ACTIVITY 4.3

Asian and Afro-Caribbean British have, after many generations' residence, begun to be imaged differently. Other ethnic groups are nevertheless often represented in very thin, or negative terms.

- Take a week's news coverage, across as many media forms as possible (radio, television, press) of eastern European refugees, or 'gypsies', or asylum seekers in Britain. How do racists (e.g. in British National Party propaganda) construct their 'otherness'?

- Are there any students in your school or college whom you could interview about their experiences of such representations?

EastEnders' variety of black characters – some involved in petty crime, some parents coping with family difficulties, some in love and so on – was argued as a kind of advance. Others, in the mid-1980s, picketed the film *My Beautiful Laundrette* (UK 1985) because of its images of gay and drug-dealing

Disabled people are the largest 'minority' group in the UK (estimated at 10–12%). Jessica Evans argues: 'Most of us will at some point in our lives be disabled – whether congenitally, or through old age, illness, or accident and so on . . . our culture is dangerously close to denying the inevitability and necessity of . . . messy or "negative" feelings, as part of normal life' (Evans in Briggs and Cobley 1998: 349).

See *Pulp Fiction* case study in Chapter 14.

See discussion of Tarantino's practices in Chapter 14.

Asian-British characters. 'Negative' images are not always best opposed by (someone's idea of) 'positive', but by the availability of a range of fuller ways of being imagined. This is arguably easier in a soap opera than in a feature film, and is certainly easier when plenty of the group in question are employed in the meaning-making industries.

> A different group and approach: there's a lovely moment at the end of the film *Sleep With Me* (US 1995) involving a character who, throughout the film, has been a keen card player. Only in the very last shot do we see him away from the card table, and suddenly realise he is in a wheelchair. Without any reference to disability, he has been constructed for most of the film as 'just the same as the other characters'.

There is another, quite different attitude towards 'positive' and 'negative'. Supposing members of a group with good grounds for surliness, and for lack of co-operation with a social system or situation (slaves in plantation conditions, as imaged in *Gone With the Wind*), are represented as always smiling and whistling contentedly at their lot? They may well wonder whether this image is 'positive' only for those who want to be reassured that all is well with an unjust set-up. So sometimes members of heavily stereotyped groups have responded by taking on the denigrated identity that an abusive nickname gives them. Examples would be black people calling themselves 'niggers', or gays calling themselves 'queens' or 'queers'. (There is heated debate about whether people outside those groups have the right to apply such labels.)

Figure 4.6 One image of cotton picking in the US in the period before the Civil War (1860–5). **Q** From whose point of view is this peaceful scene constructed? By what means? How else might an encounter between black cotton workers and plantation owners have been represented?

It seems there is no such thing as the '100 per cent right on text' or 'positive image' which will guarantee to change audiences in progressive ways all on its own. Texts have always to be understood in the context of audience formations and understandings, power structures and production practices. Fictional and other entertainment forms in particular have an extremely complex relationship to audiences' sense of the real.

Other ways of changing representations

Representations, discourses, stereotypes are an inextricable part of the material world, never just an add-on, 'airy-fairy' extra. But it is important that debates over representations should not be restricted to the level of textual analysis but should bear in mind media industries and their material processes. Such broader social activities are crucial in shifting taken-for-granted assumptions. See for example:

- political change and the ways it can widen (or narrow) imaginings and the range of images possible (such as the black Civil Rights struggles in 1950s and 1960s US or the success of the anti-corporate globalisation movement to put on the agenda different images of how to organise global resources: see www.Adbusters.com)

- employment patterns and struggles in the media industries. These often have names such as *affirmative action* or *equal opportunities* policies and mean that, wherever possible, people from particular groups (women, or those with disabilities for example) are appointed to jobs *if their suitability is more or less equivalent to that of other candidates*. These can be 'positive' in helping to produce expectations and role models other than the unspoken conviction that 'women or blacks or gays can't do that work because I've never seen one doing it'. The assumption that a woman would be too frail or scatty to get together a big-budget action film is dispelled by Mimi Leder's work, or Gale Anne Hurd's role in producing the *Terminator* films for example. In addition, affirmative action may also open up a newsroom or documentary unit or soap opera to workplace discussions and experiences which are far from those of people usually inside the group. If people with disabilities work on a newspaper, it makes it harder to resort to the stereotype that 'disabled people are always helpless victims'. Several black journalists have commented that racist headlines in **tabloid** papers would be harder to justify in the newsroom if there were more non-white British journalists employed there.

- access to dissenting mechanisms like the **right of reply**. Newspapers such as the *Sun* during Margaret Thatcher's years in power were large institutions with massive power to circulate headlines, employ cartoonists or angle photos which maintained hostile images of groups such as Irish

'Julia Roberts, J. K. Rowling and Madonna are among the most powerful women in entertainment, but ... women comprise only 17% of producers on the 250 top-grossing pictures and 24% of the producers, directors, writers, cinematographers and creators of primetime television shows [said Martha Lauzen, San Diego State University]'
(Campbell 2001)

'By the mid to late 1990s ... of a workforce of some 3,000 journalists working on national newspapers ... 20 were black. The NUJ estimated that in 1998 only 1.8% of their 27,000 strong membership were black, compared to the national minority population of 5.27%'
(*Guardian*, 2002 Race in the Media supplement).

Figure 4.7

STATEMENT ON RACE REPORTING

1. The NUJ believes that the development of racist attitudes and the growth of fascist parties pose a threat to democracy, the rights of trade union organisations, a free press and the development of social harmony and well-being.

2. The NUJ believes that its members cannot avoid a measure of responsibility in fighting the evil of racism as expressed through the mass media.

3. The NUJ reaffirms its total opposition to censorship but equally reaffirms the belief that press freedom must be conditioned by responsibility and an acknowledgement by all media workers of the need not to allow press freedom to be abused to slander a section of the community or to promote the evil of racism.

4. The NUJ believes that the methods and the lies of the racists should be publicly and vigorously exposed.

5. The NUJ believes that newspapers and magazines should not originate material which encourages discrimination on grounds of race or colour as expressed in the NUJ's Rule Book and Code of Conduct.

6. The NUJ recognises the right of members to withhold their labour on grounds of conscience where employers are providing a platform for racist propaganda.

7. The NUJ believes that editors should ensure that coverage of race stories be placed in a balanced context.

8. The NUJ will continue to monitor the development of media coverage in this area and give support to members seeking to enforce the above aims.

Guidelines on Race reporting

● Race Reporting

Only mention someone's race if it is strictly relevant. Check to make sure you have it right. Would you mention race if the person was white?

Do not sensationalise race relations issues, it harms Black people and it could harm you.

Think carefully about the words you use. Words which were once in common usage are now considered offensive, e.g. half-caste and coloured. Use mixed-race and Black instead. Black can cover people of Arab, Asian, Chinese and African origin. Ask people how they define themselves.

Immigrant is often used as a term of abuse. Do not use it unless the person really is an immigrant. Most Black people in Britain were born here and most immigrants are white.

Do not make assumptions about a person's cultural background – whether it is their name or religious detail. Ask them, or where this is not possible check with the local race equality council.

Investigate the treatment of Black people in education, health, employment and housing. Do not forget travellers and gypsies. Cover their lives and concerns. Seek the views of their representatives.

Remember that Black communities are culturally diverse. Get a full and correct view from representative organisations.

Press for equal opportunities for employment of Black staff.

Be wary of disinformation. Just because a source is traditional does not mean it is accurate.

● Reporting Racist Organisations

When interviewing representatives of racist organisations or reporting meetings or statements or claims, journalists should carefully check all reports for accuracy and seek rebutting or opposing comments. The anti-social nature of such views should be exposed.

Do not sensationalise by reports, photographs, film or presentation the activities of racist organisations.

Seek to publish or broadcast material exposing the myths and lies of racist organisations and their anti-social behaviour.

Do not allow the letters column or 'phone-in' programmes to be used to spread racial hatred in whatever guise.

GUIDELINES ON TRAVELLERS

Only mention the word gypsy or traveller if strictly relevant or accurate.

Give balanced reports seeking travellers' views as well as those of others, consulting the local travellers where possible.

Resist the temptation to sensationalise issues involving travellers, especially in their relations with settled communities over issues such as housing and settlement programmes and schooling.

Try to give wider coverage to travellers' lives and the problems they face.

Strive to promote the realisation that the travellers' community is comprised of full citizens of Great Britain and Ireland whose civil rights are seldom adequately vindicated, who often suffer much hurt and damage through misuse by the media and who have a right to have their special contributions to Irish and British life, especially in music and craftwork and other cultural activities, properly acknowledged and reported.

---

people, or the then GLC leader Ken Livingstone. Those targeted had far less power to circulate their positions and were often discredited by unfounded allegations which were later quietly retracted in an obscure part of the newspaper. The right of reply lobby (see the work of the Campaign for Press and Broadcasting Freedom) asks for the reply to such stories to be given equal prominence to the original story. Thus an untrue *front-page* headline would have to be corrected on a later *front page*. This is important for people without access to the expensive lawyers whom the wealthy can employ to maintain their reputations – a very different kind of 'right of reply'.

- activities which broaden audiences' ability to come across, and feel comfortable with a wide range of media forms and imaginings. This may involve challenging the power of certain lobbying groups. For example, abortion now seems to be a sensitive issue for soaps. Often it is not explored even as an option to be rejected (contrast the treatment of Michelle Fowler's pregnancy a few years ago on *EastEnders*). This seems to be due not so much to audience hostility as to that of religious and other pressure groups. Or it may involve campaigns around the conditions for licensing and regulating broadcast and press forms, and ways to encourage the sympathetic reviewing and exhibition of 'different' images and works.

A Chicago film critic on US isolationism and cinema: 'Precisely for this reason, even bad or mediocre foreign movies have important things to teach us. Consider them . . . precious news bulletins, breaths of air, (fresh or stale) from diverse corners of the globe; however you look at them, they're proof positive that Americans aren't the only human beings' (Rosenbaum 2001: 108).

References

Aintey, Beulah (1998) *Black Journalists, White Media*, London: Trentham Books.

Bogle, Donald (1994, 2nd edition) *Toms, Coons, Mulattoes, Mammies and Bucks: An Interpretative History of Blacks in American Films*, New York: Continuum.

Briggs, Adam and Cobley, Paul (eds) (1998) *The Media: An Introduction*, Harlow: Longman.

Brooker, Will (2001) 'Readings of racism: interpretation, stereotyping and *The Phantom Menace*', *Continuum*, vol. 15, no. 1.

Campbell, Duncan (2001) 'Hollywood still prefers men', *Guardian*, 5 December.

Connell, Robert W. (2000) *The Men and the Boys*, Cambridge: Polity.

Dunant, Sarah (ed.) (1994) *The War of the Words: The Political Correctness Debate*, London: Virago.

Durkin, Kevin (1985) *Television, Sex Roles and Children*, Milton Keynes: Open University Press.

Hari, Johann (2001) 'Law of the jungle', *New Statesman*, 10 December.

Lewis, Justin (1991) *The Ideological Octopus*, New York and London: Routledge, esp. Chapter 7.

Medhurst, Andy and Munt, Sally R. (eds) (1997) *Lesbian and Gay Studies: A Critical Introduction*, London and Herndon: Cassell.

Pines, Jim (ed.) (1992) *Black and White in Colour: Black People in British Television since 1936*, London: BFI.

Rosenbaum, Jonathan (2002) *Movie Wars: How Hollywood and the Media Conspire to Limit What Films We Can See*, London: Wallflower.

Russo, Vito (1981) *The Celluloid Closet: Homosexuality in the Movies*, New York: Harper & Row.

Shohat, Elaine and Stam, Robert (1994) *Unthinking EuroCentrism: Multiculturalism and the Media*, London and New York: Routledge.

Wells, Matt (2002) 'Ethnic minority push by BBC', *Guardian*, 25 January.

Further reading

Baehr, Helen and Dyer, Gillian (eds) (1987) *Boxed In: Women and Television*, London: Pandora..

Branston, Gill (1984) *Film and Gender*, London: Film Education.

Branston, Gill (2001) 'Toward a critical politics of representation' in *Cinema and Cultural Modernity*, Buckingham: Open University Press.

Brunsdon, Charlotte (1997) 'Post-feminism and shopping films' in *Screen Tastes: Soap Opera to Satellite Dishes*, London and New York: Routledge.

Hall, Stuart (1996) *Race, the Floating Signifier*, videotape available from the Media Education Foundation.

Macdonald, Myra (1995) *Representing Women: Myths of Femininity in the Popular Media*, London and New York: Arnold.

Malik, Sarita (2001) *Representing Black Britain: Black and Asian Images on Television*, London: Sage.

Stafford, Roy (2001) *Representation: An Introduction*, London: BFI/*in the picture*.

CASE STUDY: STARDOM AND CELEBRITY

- The construction of Hollywood stars
- 'Authenticity'
- Stardom or celebrity and news
- References
- Further reading

'Media representation' is often discussed

- through information-led and 'realist' forms, such as news, documentaries
- through content analysis, 'counting' elements recurring across many texts (such as 'woman as sex object', 'the villainous Arab') which are then said to 'represent' groups in particular ways.

Yet it can also be argued that

- entertainment and especially **celebrity** forms are now more widespread and commonly encountered than news forms. They are therefore important *in their own right* in thinking about how the values and dilemmas of a culture get represented.
- celebrity and entertainment forms also blend into news, through scandal, gossip etc., in ways which are often seen as only negative
- even though 'counting' elements of fact or fiction forms can be useful, we need to get closer to whatever it is that's going on in our fascination with stars, celebrities and scandal, especially if we want to think its role in how factual forms represent the world to us.

We will try to focus this through the histories of stardom in Hollywood; how stardom has changed in the last forty years or so, and how the fantasy and *personalisation* associated with celebrity entertainment forms enters into news and information media.

The construction of Hollywood stars

'Economically stardom is a patent on a unique set of human characteristics . . . [which] include purely physical aspects' (Wyatt 1994).

'a **star** is a performer in a particular medium whose figure enters into subsidiary forms of circulation and then feeds back into future performances.' (Ellis 1992: 91)

Film and then Media Studies have explored cinematic forms of stardom (interest in 'celebrities' came later). Seeking to move away from accounts of stars which emphasised their 'authenticity', 'giftedness' or 'magic', Richard Dyer (1998) stressed that stars are different from their 'star images' or 'personae'. He focused on

- economic factors such as the labour involved in the construction of stars' presence on screens
- the key *parallel narratives* of their lives, also partly constructed and circulated by studio workers via 'promotion' and 'publicity'. These were intended to make up a perpetual invitation to audiences to check out the star in their latest role, which usually had some reference to their offscreen life. (Film and Media Studies try to keep separate the star actor or image and the role they are playing in the convention of writing, for example 'Danny Ocean/ George Clooney'.)

- questions such as: what might be the representational, or broadly cultural-ideological effects of such constructed presences, both on and off screens?

'Everyone wanted to be Cary Grant. Even I wanted to be Cary Grant' (Cary Grant, born Archibald Leach, in Bristol).

The 'star phenomenon' began in theatrical advertising of certain actors' names in the 1820s. It was not immediately transferred to Hollywood, nor to the many other film industries developing in parallel across the globe. Hollywood studios at first (from about 1909 to 1914) ignored 'stars' – actors in whose offscreen lifestyles and personalities audiences demonstrated a particular interest. This was partly because of the costs involved in 'manufacturing stardom' on a scale which the studios could translate into measurable box-office revenue, and for fear of the power which stars might then wield.

Stars need all kinds of resources lavished on their construction: privileged access to screen and narrative space, to lighting, to the care of costumers, make-up workers, voice coaches, personal trainers etc., as well as to audience interest through previews, supply of publicity materials etc. Skilful casting is also important, though rarely discussed in work on stars, perhaps because it is seen to detract from the star's own intentions in a performance (see Lovell and Kramer 1999). Key career decisions involve a star's choice of casting agency, or the choices made by a particular film's casting director.

Though perhaps the least of the concerns of Afro-Americans in the studio years, the priorities of film technology simply ignored them. Skin colour, and the lag in technological developments in film stock for the expressive lighting and filming of black skins, helped to determine the unequal allocation of star roles, often

dependent on close-up and clearly perceptible facial gesture (see Dyer 1998).

'a good director . . . doesn't direct you, he casts you properly in a film. If he casts you right in the part, then you're going to be great in the part' (Tony Curtis (see Branston 2000: 119)).

Gillian Anderson's performance in the 'arthouse' costume drama *The House of Mirth* (US 2000) is partly the result of fine casting for role. Her physical presence reminded the director of certain nineteenth century paintings he wanted to evoke and at the level of her star image the role was a way for her to break the long association with *The X-Files* (which nevertheless was a fascination for some audiences of the film).

Once established, the star system worked lucratively for the studios. Stars were used as part of the studio's 'branding' or promise of certain kinds of narrative and production values. They were useful in 'differentiating' studios' films ('an Errol Flynn swashbuckler'; a 'Bette Davis weepie'). Stars were literally part of the studios' capital, like plant and equipment, and could be traded as such. James Stewart, making an interesting comparison with sports celebrities, said once: 'Your studio could trade you around like ball players. I was traded once to Universal for the use of their back lot for three weeks' (quoted in Bordwell, Staiger and Thompson 1985). Stars' large salaries (said to be due to nebulous qualities such as 'talent' or 'charisma') worked to negate the powers of acting unions, who might otherwise have been able to calculate acting labour and ask for more equal distribution of profits.

And stars have *always* functioned as a key part of Hollywood's relationship to broader capitalist structures. In the 1930s, for example, over-production of manufactured goods had reached crisis point in

North America, and the large banks funding Hollywood sought its help in shifting goods from warehouses to consumers.

Two adjacent changes occurred throughout the mid-1930s: Hollywood stars showcasing make-up, clothing and other items of dress-up sensibility; and direct tie-ins between screen texts and particular products . . . By the Depression, Hollywood stars were the third biggest source of news in the United States.

(Miller: 599)

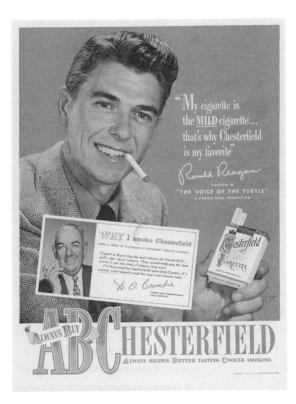

Figure 4.8 Ronald Reagan (B movie actor, later US President, then 'celebrity'), who illustrates the overlap of the discourses of advertising, stardom/celebrity, politics and commercial sponsorship.

Jackie Stacey (1994) studied, via a selection of letters, the memories of female cinema audiences in 1940s Britain. Their enjoyment of female stars (half-

pretending to be the star; emphasising some imagined physical similarity to the star in order to associate with the image and so on) was all made possible by and heavily bound up with the products which stars were used to advertise – new kinds of hairstyle, make-up, dress etc.

The break-up of the studio system (1940s to 1950s) saw the rise of 'package unit' production and promotion of films on a more one-by-one basis, organised by agencies such as ICM and CAA. Film stars, no longer under seven-year contracts, became increasingly responsible for their own images. Since the biggest stars were crucial to the studios' hugely financially risky projects, their costs rose. Contracts now also often include large proportions of box-office take – stars began to have more power in saying what they would or would not take part in. One result was that salaries escalated to their present grotesque levels. The term 'bankable' is often used now as a shorthand for stars' success, though major stars are also defined like a 'brand' (defined for other products as an image which persuades consumers of quality prior to purchase or experience). This translates literally for cinema into 'a performer who can open a film on the strength of their name alone' (see Chapter 13).

'In [US based] *Advertising Age*'s annual Top Marketing 100 list of 1997's best brands, there was a new arrival: The Spice Girls . . . [who also] ranked number 6 in *Forbes* magazine's inaugural "Celebrity Power 100" in May 1999, a new ranking based not on fame or fortune but on stars' brand "franchise"' (Klein 2000: 49).

Struggle over control of 'the star's own image' or 'brand' (i.e. the revenues from it) had always taken place, for example in tussles over the studio system's seven-year contracts which tied a star to a particular studio (before stars such as Bette Davis and Olivia de Havilland challenged those contracts).

Leonardo DiCaprio refused to allow a doll in his likeness to be made as a *Titanic* tie-in product, and later trademarked his name.

Tom Hanks's voice (only) was used for Woody's character in *Toy Story 2*. He refused to let the toy be made in his visual likeness (not used in the film) but gave interviews, for press as well as radio, letting his whole star image as well as his voice be associated the film.

See www.cmgww.com for details of one of the world's largest star and celebrity licensing agencies.

A fascinating aspect of star study (which partly transfers to celebrities) is the nature of the *symbolic* commodity ('the star') which is being traded within that industry of pleasure, cinema. What fantasies and cultural positions might stars, on and off screen, circulate?

'Authenticity'

One important aspect of the way stars and celebrities are constructed is through the idea of 'authenticity'. The whole studio system *construction* of the star image off screen was paradoxically designed to produce a sense of *authenticity* in a performance. Gay studio system actors such as Rock Hudson or bisexuals such as Barbara Stanwyck had to perform heterosexual relationships off screen as well as on.

Cinema stars can no longer be publicised by the studios as being identical with the roles they play – partly owing to the sheer amount of coverage of stars and celebrities (including tabloid press attention which leaks over into surveillance and real intrusion into personal space). Instead the *effort* involved in a performance is emphasised, sometimes via stories, inside and outside films, of bodily transformation, whether in a gym or in a fat suit. The star's versatility, necessary to survive in a 'package unit' system, is highlighted, as well as some attempt to suggest they

are worth astronomical payments – for which perhaps the myth of natural 'gifts' and 'star quality persists.

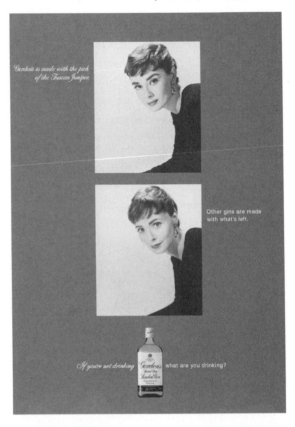

Figure 4.9 Audrey Hepburn: this ad plays with the idea of the 'authentic' and unique physical presence of a major film star, and parallels that to the aura of the branded product.

This is a hangover in many ways from nineteenth-century Romantic theories of the individual. It surfaces in the mysterious 'x factor' which the judges of *Pop Idol*, for example were forever mentioning as they told the (undoubtedly talented) final contestants 'You *are* a star'. It has huge importance in the economics of the entertainment business (see above), not least in the way it invites emphasis on the single talented individual rather than representing the always collaborative nature of production – even of a 'star'. This almost certainly impacts on training for media industries.

ACTIVITY 4.4

Check out star and celebrity Internet sites for evidence of the idea of 'authenticity' in stories of the 'real' Russell Crowe, Britney Spears, Sarah Michelle Gellar or whoever.

How is this suggested? By supposed likeness of life story to performances? By incidents taken to be the marks of authenticity – involving tears, embarrassment, joy etc.?

A key strand of star study has been to ask how stars and their images, their stories on and off screen, seem to embody or represent key tensions within a culture. An example is Julia Roberts.

Julia Roberts's star image

Julia Roberts is rare example of a woman 'A' list star (i.e. one consistently attracting more than $100 million to the North American box office) with a reputed fee of $17 million per film (Campbell 2001). Dyer (in *The Late Show*, BBC 2, 1991) suggests that her obvious cinematic strengths (conventional beauty, some acting ability etc.) are nevertheless not enough to explain her phenomenal success. 'Subsidiary forms of circulation of her image' (Internet sites, fan magazines, gossip columns, fashion magazine, newspaper articles) and her performances coalesce, as so often, around the familiar theme of *authenticity*, understood in highly gendered ways: the sudden (spontaneous?) burst of 'the smile' in many films as well as life off screen; the way her often troubled personal relationships seem to be 'told' and referred to in films; plus a relationship to 'post-feminism', especially in the identity-try-on pleasures of shopping in *Pretty Woman* (see Brunsdon 1997).

The roles she plays have had a powerful mix of strength and vulnerability, all the way from *Pretty Woman* (US 1990) to *Runaway Bride* (US 1998), *Erin Brockovitch* (US 1999) and *Notting Hill* (US 1999) and especially the 'confessional' dinner speech on stardom in that film.

Dyer suggested she embodied a key contradiction at the heart of western commercial culture's relation to feminism in the 1980s:

> Roberts embraces feminism insofar as it is no longer creditable to be a bimbo or a housewife for the female audience. At the same time, she doesn't suppress the bimbo or housewife so far that she fails to appeal to male audience . . . She's no victim, yet there are some disturbing implications of female desirability – she's vulnerable, that is to say eminently hurtable'.

in addition Roberts has formed her own film company (Shoelace Films: see http://www.hollywoodactor.com/actors_companies.html for details of this and other actors' production companies), a kind of business activity which is often played down in accounts of major stars and celebrities (such as 'Posh Spice' or Jodie Foster) – perhaps because 'authenticity' is thought to be the reverse of the calculations needed in business?

Celebrity and news

The term 'stardom' is now spread wide, to cover sport, television and popular music, for example. It overlaps with the term 'celebrities' (see Geraghty 2000 for an illuminating discussion). They are understood as having the same access to fame as stars, but are not always as closely associated with specific areas of achievement. Indeed they are sometimes seen as having no major talent apart from an appetite for celebrity and an ability to appear dressed spectacularly at hugely publicised premieres. Openly 'constructed' bands (such as Hear'Say, The Spice Girls) and music celebrities have focused on the importance of skills of self-promotion and the determination to be 'famous'. Nevertheless their bodies and lives, like those of stars, often focus or represent widespread cultural fantasies and wonderings in a *personalised* way.

Q Does radio produce 'stars'? If not, why not?

The range of other cultural forms (often owned by the same corporations) for the construction of fame now include

- popular music (especially via music videos), often produced by one of the huge entertainment corporations which own much of the film industry
- television, increasingly dependent on its own stars (and 'anchors' or presenters) to 'open a show'. British television stars sometimes migrate to Hollywood cinema (see the careers of Catherine Zeta Jones, Ewan McGregor, Robert Carlyle etc.) and many shows seem cast for 'filmic' glamour
- figures in the news, from politics, royalty and even the world of business
- sport. This makes an interesting comparison to cinema, producing hugely paid celebrities or stars (the two terms are used interchangeably) on the basis of performance and image construction by corporations who have purchased sports stars' branding power (see Klein 2000, especially p. 52). Sport is now a key site for publicly airing questions around national identity; debates around 'appropriate bodies' for men and women, or the limits of competitiveness (as figured in drug debates) and how far human bodies should be pushed within such performance.

ACTIVITY 4.5

Consider the star or celebrity image of the couple 'Becks and Posh' and their son Brooklyn.
Discuss the following suggestion:

- However gifted a footballer David Beckham is, and however important his control over his image via his contract with Manchester United, it is 'Posh Spice' who 'makes' him a major star. They have been called the pop King and Queen of England, and their wedding played with this idea and was then recycled in *Footballers' Wives*, tales of their life at 'Beckingham

Palace', etc. Because he is married to Victoria, Beckham is much more available than, say, Michael Owen for tabloid narrative speculation around such themes as family, work versus family, jealousy within a high-profile marriage etc.

Other stars with less high-profile marriages seem to fit other, perhaps more limited narrative functions: 'Saint Lineker'; the addict (Paul Merson, Tony Adams), the thug (Ian Bowyer), the wife-beater (Stan Collymore, Paul Gascoigne) etc.

The role of celebrities along with scandal or gossip in the area of news is often described in denigrating terms: as 'dumbing down', 'trivialisation', even 'mass hysteria'; or as 'tabloidisation' when applied to television factual forms. Yet it seems that all media need a certain amount of 'personalisation'. This includes news as much as popular fictions, even though the ideology of news production tends to be that it is 'serious' and 'objective', 'factual'.

Hermes (1999) suggests that the pleasures of celebrity news operates within a context where two approaches seem to be working in audience understandings:

- 'the extended family repertoire' (Hermes 1999: 80) where gossip brings the powerful down to the level of ordinary human beings, imagined as part of the family, and a place where readers or viewers can test scenarios (divorce, parenthood or the desire for it, ambition etc.) in case they occur in their own lives (Hermes 1999: 81). This may be especially true of coverage of 'the Royals' in the UK, who have since the nineteenth century been called 'the Royal family'.
- 'the repertoire of **melodrama**', a form stretching from nineteenth-century theatre and involving highly polarised struggles between Vice and Virtue: the wicked lord and the innocent maiden etc. (see Gledhill 1987). The satisfactions involved in such long-established melodramatic polarising still seem to be active in much celebrity

23/10/02 1:13 PM

                         CD'S DVD'S MD'S
                                                                TUNER'S AMP'S   WEEKLY E-MAIL FROM
                                                                SPEAKERS   hellomagazine.com
                                                                HOME CINEMA   CLICK HERE

Wednesday October 23, 2002   **About HELLO!**

UPDATES

Who's in the news?

The news in pictures

ALL THE NEWS ON...

Celebrities

Actors and actresses

Musicians

Fashion and models

Royalty and statesmen

HELLO! ALBUM

Special reports

Profiles

THE HELLO! CLUB

Postcards

Games

Competitions

Most attractive woman

Most attractive man

Most elegant woman

Contact us

Register

HELLO! MAGAZINE

This week's issue

¡HOLA!   OH LA!

THE STORY OF THE MAGAZINE

When HELLO! burst onto the newsstands in 1988, the British public - and the rest of the British media - had never seen anything like it. Part of a multinational publishing company established almost 60 years ago, HELLO! was launched with a cover story that immediately defined its character: an in-depth interview with the Princess Royal, who spoke to us at length not only about her public duties but also her personal feelings and perceptions.

 The first issue of HELLO! May 21, 1988

Over the past 13 years, that characteristic blend of international news, glamour and human interest has made HELLO! "an icon appealing to the most amazing range of of people."
HELLO! does not just cover the news - we make it. Our regular readers will have noticed we've even scooped the newspapers, and our exclusive stories are frequently picked up by the papers as soon as we hit the newsstands.

And our regular readership is growing all the time. Despite being a British publication, HELLO!, distributed in 65 countries, has a truly global outlook covering world events and international celebrities. When HELLO! won the prestigious International Magazine Of The Year in 1999 at the BSME awards - it has also won a whole raft of domestic awards - the judges commented, "Its performance overseas has been outstanding, with high sell throughout new markets."

Around 400,000 people in Britain buy HELLO! every week, and each of those copies is read by at least another four people. And, should you be flicking through the publication in a hairdressers, you will be one of no fewer than 70 individuals to have turned the pages of that HELLO!

Figure 4.10 An astonishing sales story for a magazine based almost entirely on celebrity gossip, interviews and lifestyle features.

coverage, a deep sense that the world is unjust, which points to a more collective sense of social inequality. To enjoy it when things go badly for 'rich and famous people' is a way of imagining cosmic (rather than political) justice taking its toll. Commiseration and indignation are equal ingredients of the pleasure of [such] . . . gossip.

(Hermes 1999: 81)

Figure 4.11 'Saint Diana': a figure combining glamour and virtue.
Q How much news have you read about anti-landmine campaigns since her death?
Q What might this suggest about celebrity-led news?

Two US examples of melodrama's legacy for news

A striking example of the persistence of US melodramatic imagery in news seems to have been at play in two huge 1990s US news stories which transfixed the attention of US audiences. In 1994 a black motorist, Rodney King, was beaten to the ground by Los Angeles police. The beating was captured on video, but the police were acquitted in a controversial and much-watched trial. A little later O. J. Simpson, an African-American sports celebrity, commentator, Hertz rental car spokesman and film actor, was acquitted of the stabbing to death of his white wife, Nicole Brown Simpson. A hundred million viewers watched helicopter shots and listened to cellular phone contact as LA police cars trailed O. J. Simpson's car as he tried to evade arrest and threatened suicide (see McLaughlin 1998).

Arguably *part* of the power of these two personalized news stories (only one of which involved a celebrity) was the way they 'replayed' two key nineteenth-century US fictional melodramatic moments, two whose icons and images have dominated the imagination of mainstream US media. The best-selling novel *Uncle Tom's Cabin* by Harriet Beecher Stowe (1852) generated white sympathy for black victims of slavery through an iconography of racial violence and the moving image of the black slave beaten to death (a resonance for the Rodney King story). The hit silent film *The Birth of a Nation* (US 1915) 'answered' this with images of black man as sexual threat to white woman (a resonance for many, though not all, US blacks who took the side of 'OJ': see Williams 2001).

We need to understand this power of fictional shapings within 'factual' news in order, as Linda Williams puts it, 'to get beyond the grip of a melodramatic habit of mind'. Although undoubtedly some of 'the OJ story' discussed the very problem of the ways that celebrity coverage turned the trial into a 'media circus', this took attention away from another part of the murder trial which was not available for such resonance. The harrowing playback in court of the tape of a 1993 emergency phone call (classified by police as 'potentially life-threatening') from Nicole Simpson could not, in the same way, become part of such resonant imagery. 'The differences that are associated with the routinised, everyday nature of domestic abuse "do not perform well" in court or in a public sphere where spectacles hold powerful sway' (McLaughlin 1998: 89).

ACTIVITY 4.6

Think of the most memorable news story involving celebrities which you encountered recently.

- Can you trace the two approaches Hermes outlines in the way you, or others you know, seemed to engage with it?

- Which were the 'melodramatic' elements of response, and which the 'extended family' ones?

Such work suggests that fans are far from being totally identified with, or losing their own identities in favour of, their admired celebrity or gossipy news items. Hermes suggests that the engagement with the admired figure takes place in a kind of 'playground of identity construction' (see the *Buffy* case study following Chapter 3) and quotes Ehrenreich *et al.* in a study of 'Beatlemania' in the 1960s, suggesting that 'The appeal of the male star was that you would never marry him; the romance would never end in the tedium of marriage . . . The star could be loved non-instrumentally, for his own sake, and with complete abandon' (Hermes 1999: 80).

Of course there is literally another side to celebrity, star cultures and ordinary people. You may like, as a final activity, to consider the following issues of privacy:

- 'the public's right to know': how far should this extend, especially in the case of elected politicians? What is at stake?
- the extent to which new surveillance technologies should be deployed in the search for 'news' about celebrities or stars or Royals?
- the power to protest successfully at intrusions into 'private space'. How equally distributed is it? Celebrities (and 'Royals') have behind them, usually, not only the power of corporations but also teams of advisers, lawyers etc. – and sometimes the sympathy of regulatory bodies such as the Press Complaints Commission (see website at www.pcc.org.uk and controversies, in February 2002, about the number of Royal complaints against the press which were being upheld). This success of the Royals in this lobbying is very different from the four years it took for the *Sun* to retract the slurs it made on Liverpool fans after Hillsborough; the intrusion into private grief of the photos and tapes

of Frederick West's victims released after his trial (see Scraton 1999 and 2000); or the possibility that tabloid coverage of the search for and arrest of those charged with killing Holly Wells and Jessica Chapman (2002) not only distressed the girls' families and hampered police efforts, but may also mean no fair trial can be held.

References

Bordwell, David, Staiger, Janet and Thompson, Kristin (1985) *Film History: An Introduction*. New York: McGraw Hill.

Branston, Gill (2000) 'Stars, bodies, galaxies' in *Cinema and Cultural Modernity*, Buckingham: Open University Press.

Brundson, Charlotte (1997) 'Post-feminism and shopping films' in *Screen Tastes: Soap Opera to Satellite Dishes*, London: Routledge.

Campbell, Duncan (2001) 'Trouble in Tinseltown', *Guardian*, 20 January.

Dyer, Richard (1987) *Heavenly Bodies*, London: Macmillan/BFI.

Dyer, Richard (1990) *Now You See It*, London: Routledge.

Dyer, Richard (1998, 2nd edition) *Stars*, London: BFI.

Ellis, John (1992, 2nd edition) *Visible Fictions*, London: Routledge.

Geraghty, Christine (2000) 'Re-examining stardom: questions of texts bodies and performance' in C. Gledhill and L. Williams (eds) *Reinventing Film Studies*, London and New York: Arnold.

Gledhill, Christine (ed.) (1987) *Home Is Where the Heart Is*, London: BFI.

Hermes, Joke (1999) 'Media figures in identity construction' in Alasuutari Pertti (ed.), *Re-thinking the Media Audience*, London: Sage.

Klein, Naomi (2000) *No Logo*, London: Flamingo.

Lovell, Alan and Kramer, Peter (1999) *Screen Acting*, London: Routledge.

McLaughlin, Lisa (1998) 'Gender, privacy and publicity in "media event space"' in, C. Carter, G. Branston and S. Allan (eds) *News Gender and Power*, London and New York: Routledge.

Miller, Toby (1998) 'Hollywood and the world' in John Hill and Pamela Church Gibson (eds) *The Oxford Guide to Film Studies*, Oxford: Oxford University Press.

Rojek, Chris (2001) *Celebrity*, London: Reaktion Books.

Scraton, Phil (1999) *Hillsborough: The Truth*, Edinburgh: Mainstream.

Scraton, Phil (2000) *Disaster, Trauma, Aftermath*, London: Lawrence and Wishart.

Stacey, Jackie (1994) *Star Gazing: Hollywood Cinema and Female Spectatorship*, London: Routledge.

Steinberg, Cobbett (1981) *Reel Facts*, London: Penguin.

Thompson, John B., (2000) *Political Scandal: Power and Visibility in the Media Age*, Cambridge: Polity.

Williams, Linda (2001) 'Black and white', letter to *Sight and Sound*, September.

Wyatt, Justin (1994) *High Concept: Movies and Marketing in Hollywood*, Austin: University of Texas Press.

Further reading

Rojek, Chris (2001) *Celebrity*, London: Reaktion Books.

Useful websites

www.cpbf.org.uk

www.cmgww.com

www.hollywoodactor.com/actor_companies.html

www.pcc.org.uk

www.presswise.org.uk

5 Ideologies and power

- Origins of the term: Marxist approaches
- Post-Marxism and critical pluralism
- Discourses and lived cultures
- References
- Further reading

The concept of **ideology** has been a key one for Media Studies. It is often replaced now by 'values', so that the term 'ideologies' gets reserved for 'fringe' or non-mainstream party political positions, such as environmental politics or extreme nationalisms. We believe the term still has a key role to play in suggesting very ordinary connections between media and different kinds of power. It refers to:

- sets of ideas which give some account of the social world, usually a partial and selective one
- the relationship of these ideas or values to the ways in which power is distributed socially
- the way in which such values and meanings are usually posed as 'natural' and 'obvious' rather than socially aligned with or against particular power groupings.

Check out Politics syllabuses and how they define ideologies. One UK A level Board for example lists 4 belief systems: Socialism, Conservatism, Liberalism, Environmentalism – but not, say, consumerism or sexism.

Origins of the term: Marxist approaches

The first time it was argued that ideas are not free-floating but instead systematically linked to social power was in France, in the period leading up to the 1789 Revolution. Most discussion of ideology in Media and Cultural Studies comes out of the work of **Marx**, who, writing in the nineteenth century, questioned another, supposedly 'natural' but unequal order of things. He analysed the new profit- and market-dominated system – **capitalism** – and the power of two classes within it, the rising industrial manufacturers (or capitalists) and the working class (or proletariat).

Some ideas, though they form a system and are quite rigid, are not classified as 'ideological'. Someone may have obsessive *ideas* about personal cleanliness, and relate them *systematically* to the fullness of the moon, but these would not necessarily be called ideological since they cannot be shown to relate to the distribution of social power.

A key European world view before the sixteenth century was that the earth was made by God, with the sun revolving round it, and that everything on earth had its natural place in a divinely designed order which could not be questioned. This was eventually challenged by scientists such as Galileo (1564–42).

Capitalism a competitive social system, emerging in the late feudal period in Europe, based on **commodification** and the drive of the owners of the means of production to maximise the profits of their companies.

Class Marxism defines class in terms of the antagonistic social formations created and perpetuated in the process of production (i.e. owners of and workers within various industries).

A Marxist objection to ads is that they make products appear as if by magic, obliterating the central importance of people's labour in production processes. Key ideological questions would be: Who produces these goods? Under what conditions? In what relationships to the profits and policies of the company?

Antonio Gramsci Italian Marxist activist (1891–1937) who took part in complex political struggles in Italy, involving Church and State, North and South, peasants and modern industrial workers. As a result his theories showed a keen awareness of the need for complex struggles and negotiations.

Marx emphasised the importance of **class** difference, or people's different relationships to the means of production, as key to the kinds of values and political ideas that they have. Do they *own* factories, banks, country estates, or do they have to earn their living by *working for* the owners of factories, banks and so on? He was especially interested in capitalists' relationship to their employees, the working class, who, he argued, had the power to change history by its united action.

He used (loosely) the concept of ideology to account for how the capitalist class protected and preserved its economic interests, even during years of unrest and attempted revolutions. Three of his emphases have been particularly important for Media Studies:

- The **dominant** ideas (which become the '**common sense**') of any society are those which work in the interests of the ruling class, to secure its rule or dominance. Those who own the means of production thereby, also, control the means of producing and circulating the most important ideas in any social order. This is the key to why the meaning-making bodies (which now include the modern media even in their entertainment and leisure forms) in any society represent political issues as they do. It implies that the working class needs to develop its own ideas and struggle for the means of circulating them if it is successfully to oppose the capitalist class.

- Related to this, he argued a **base–superstructure** model of the social role of institutions such as the media. The ways the basic needs of a social order are met (via industrial capitalist, or landlord–peasant, relations, for example) determine its superstructure, i.e. its 'secondary', less basic, ideological and political institutions, such as religion and cultural life. Such a model is also often called **economic determinist**, since the economic 'base' is argued crucially to determine, not just to influence, cultural and political activity.

- A final important step is the argument that, through these sets of power relationships, the dominant class is able to make workers believe that existing relations of exploitation and oppression are natural and inevitable. This power 'mystifies' the real conditions of existence, and how they might be changed, and conceals the interest it has in preventing change.

Gramsci's term '**hegemony**' was a development of this model. It became a key way of thinking how dominant value systems change through struggle, and how they are are related to everyday *lived cultures* (see below) and to 'common sense', which he suggests (see below) is very mixed, the result of all kinds of historical 'traces'. Instead of an emphasis on the imposed dominance of a ruling class, and the determining power of the economic base, Gramsci argued that particular social groups in modern democracies struggle for ascendancy or hegemony. In this they use persuasion and consent as well as occasional brute force. Because of this, power is never secured once and for all but has to be constantly negotiated in a to-and-fro tussle. The key point from this for Media Studies is that people are not forced, or duped into a false consciousness of the world, but have their consent actively fought for all the time, nowadays almost exclusively through the media.

'The personality is strangely composite: it contains Stone Age elements and principles of a more advanced science ... the historical process to date ... has deposited in you an infinity of traces, without leaving an inventory [list]. The first thing to do is to make such an inventory' (Gramsci 1971: 324).

Additionally there are often struggles around competing definitions or versions of such key ideas as 'masculinity'. 'Common sense' takes hegemony for granted, but, as Connell suggests, it is always defined in particular contexts, and therefore in relation to other important categories, such as femininity, or gay identity, and often to national identity (see Connell 2000 for interesting discussion).

Defining 'the global'

The processes of **globalisation** are handled in highly ideological ways. The *hegemonic* version emphasises globalisation as being

- such an enormous process as to be irresistible
- associated with instantaneous, global technologies which are simply baffling and therefore beyond most people's control
- related to theories which urge anyway that the world cannot be rationally and morally accounted for
- implicitly an Americanising process, for example in the ways that the words 'new world order' or 'modernity' are imaged (see Billig 1995).

Such emphases encourage the (admittedly complex) processes of globalisation to be seen as utterly beyond the control and regulation of human beings, as a force which renders us powerless. This, of course, is convenient for the corporate multinational companies benefiting from global power, since it tends to damp down enthusiasm for atttempts to direct, or regulate, them differently.

Counter-hegemonic views include those of movements now sometimes, crudely, called 'anti-globalisation' ('anti-corporate' might be a better term). These argue that

- there *is* some provable cause–effect relationship between 'local' actions (such as the US refusal to sign the 1997 and 2001 Kyoto agreements on

The popular computer game *Sim City* works like a globalised simulation. Yet it always works with a US model of what life has to be like, assuming that getting and spending, taxation, full employment, constant growth are all obvious, good and natural social forms.

pollution control) and global results (the widespread gales, floods and fogs of a polluted planet). These should therefore be regulated.

- the 'debt' of the world's poorer nations to the World Bank should be cancelled so as allow their economies to develop and trade on a more equal footing

- there is a need to publicise how unequally the multinational corporations and richest nations operate

- an emphasis on 'small' technologies for certain purposes is preferable to many bigger projects (such as the controversial Ilisu dam project in Turkey) which involve much larger profits for western corporations.

Thus counter-hegemonic positions see globalisation not as inscrutable and irresistible but as open to *some* kinds of regulation and political action.

Figure 5.1 'Green' and anti-consumerist ideas often circulate in the small-scale medium of the postcard. Meanwhile major motor ads show cars driving fast and elegantly through pristine, deserted landscapes which oil-burning cars are guaranteed to pollute.

ACTIVITY 5.1

- Collect ads which seem to be evoking a sense of the global (perhaps literally by using a globe).

- How is this 'globe' or 'world' or 'planet' represented?

- Are there traces in the ads of a struggle (for hegemony) with surrounding definitions (for example, by implication, those of environmental protest)?

The two activities of **propaganda** and overt **censorship** can be seen to reveal moments and areas where the struggle for willing consent (one form of hegemony) has come under intense pressure, and where a resort is made to more conscious manipulation of ideological positions (often accompanied by physical force). Of course this is part of a spectrum of activities which are related to censorship, beginning with the ways we all self-censor what we say or write before committing to it and ranging through routine examples of state control such as

- occasional direct government pressure on news and current affairs (as in several British governments' objections to critical *Panorama*, *Newsnight* and Radio 4 *Today* programmes and interview styles)
- the key everyday processes of news-shaping by 'official sources', the lobby system, self-censorship as a 'good professional' etc.

Propaganda direct manipulation of information for certain purposes, usually by governments or political parties. It can be understood as a kind of **discourse**, one which openly presents itself as wanting to persuade its audience. Though it usually urges political positions ('Vote for *x* or *y* party'), it may also be used for apolitical messages (e.g. not to drink and drive). Arguably advertising is also a propaganda system.

Huge conglomerates such as News Corporation, whose incomes can be the size of many nation states, also wield powers of censorship – see Rupert Murdoch's intervention in 1998 to prevent publication of former Hong Kong Governor General Chris Patten's memoirs, critical of the Chinese regime at a time when Murdoch was developing business links with them. There have also been reports that his friendship with Ariel Sharon, Israel's Prime Minister, and his extensive Israeli investments led executives terrified of irritating him on his paper *The Times* to rewrite articles extensively (see *Guardian*, 6 September 2001). And the anti-Europe stance of his British newspapers may be connected to the resistance in Europe to his attempts to take over sectors of their media (see www.cpbf.org).

See Chapter 8 for more discussion.

Nevertheless key political moments produce qualitatively different ways of circulating information and entertainment forms. Government nationalist propaganda is used at times which it has the power to define as 'national emergency' (e.g. wars; important strikes) when it will try to control and shape public perceptions in particularly coercive ways, such as:

- direct censorship of reports, especially of casualties or enemy successes, as occurred with the refusal by the US government to broadcast later tapes by Osama bin Laden in the 'anti-terror' war following 11 September 2001.
- allowing only a certain 'pool' of approved journalists into a war zone (as in the 1982 Falklands and 1991 Gulf War). This has become more difficult with the growth of satellite technologies. But there was justifiable controversy around the US bombing of an independent Saudi news agency, al-Jazeera, which had broadcast tapes from Osama bin Laden during the 2001/2 war in Afghanistan.

• encouraging an atmosphere in which government itself bans fiction and entertainment material which it perceives as related to the war, or encourages others to do so. For example, *Greg the Bunny*, set backstage at a children's show, was pulled from the US Fox channel schedules in September 2001 because of a passing reference to a suicide bomber (*The Independent*, 23 September 2001).

Marx's original emphasis on the determining role of ownership is still active in **political-economy** approaches such as those of Peter Golding or Graham Murdock in the UK and Robert McChesney or Janet Wasko in the US. These models are often seen as a corrective to media theory's arguable overemphasis on textual, audience or cultural elements, though at their best they work with those other approaches. As Janet Wasko puts it:

> Mosco has defined . . . political economy as 'the study of the social relations, particularly power relations, that mutually constitute the production, distribution and consumption of resources'. Although analyzing the political economy of media is not sufficient to fully understand the meanings and impact of cultural products, . . . it is an indispensable point of departure . . . economic factors set limitations and exert pressures on the commodities that are produced (and influence what is not produced), as well as how, where, and to whom those products are (or are not) distributed.
>
> (Wasko 2001: 29)

This, rather than simpler models of ownership or control, gives space for the ways in which oppositional or alternative ideas (such as those of the 'anti-globalisation' movement, or of socialist **feminists**) struggle for and often obtain **access** to the media, or in which a corporation such as Disney experiences contradictions within its huge marketing successes. But the increasing concentration of power in the hands of a very few enormous media corporations, and of a very few executives within those, inevitably leads to

• a decline in the range of material available (e.g. in satellite and cable television programming, or cinema) as global conglomerates exclude or swallow up all but the most commercially successful operators (hence the obsession with ratings) or those remaining few which are state-funded

• a tendency to exclude the voices of those lacking economic power, or wishing to argue against, say, high consumer capitalism and grossly unequal pay structures as ways of organising society

• the prevalence of 'easily understood, popular, formulated, undisturbing, assimilable fictional material' (see Wasko's account of Disney for a fascinating exploration of a key example of this)

'Disney's executives have received special attention because of the size of their compensation. While Michael Eisner's salary has been set at $750,000 a year, he also receives bonuses . . . In 1992 Eisner sold $32.6 million in Disney stock and held remaining options reported to be worth around $350m. In 1993 he received more than $203 million in salary and stock options' (Wasko 2001: 42).

- the dominance of corporate advertising and branding within culture
  generally (especially on many 'lightly regulated' US television
  channels, where advertising sometimes seems almost to equal programme
  time).

Post-Marxism and critical pluralism

Several recent changes in the world have affected the power of 'classic' Marxist
theories:

- the collapse of eastern bloc state socialism (often said to be the same as
  'Marxism') from 1989
- accompanying this, the renewed power of consumer capitalist 'free market'
  emphases (and their media theory equivalent: a tendency to celebrate
  audiences' powers *simply* in relation to media, rather than at the same time
  weighing corporate media ownership and the limits it sets to fans'
  activities, for example: see Hills 2002)
- the influence of some **postmodern** positions, which despite their
  'deconstructive'charge often seem to have abandoned any kind of attempt
  at constructing an accountable or improvable world
- a growing scepticism about the claims of science to either absolute truth
  or necessarily benign consequences. (This matters, since Marxism had often
  claimed scientific status for its theories.)

These changes also involved and led to

- the suggestion that to talk of one dominant ideology directly related
  to economic power implies an improbably coherent, argument-free
  ruling class, smoothly 'making' the rest of us go along with its interests.
  Such analysis often makes very patronising assumptions about anyone
  other than the person doing the analysing. If the wheels of ideology
  roll so perfectly smoothly to produce conformity, how has the person
  analysing their workings come to have his or her 'outsider'
  perceptions?
- the challenge of newer politics based on gender, ethnicity, sexuality, often
  seen as crucially 'affecting life chances' rather than being absolute
  determinants. These have tended to replace economic, class-focused
  Marxist analysis. **Identity politics**, as it is often known, has become a new
  way of analysing other kinds of inequality.

  For example, feminists have pointed out that inequality derives not
  only from unequal pay etc. in the realm of production but also from the
  realm of *reproduction* (in the sense of both the reproduction of future
  generations and the household work needed to reproduce social orders).
  Men's social position and power can often be shown to exploit women's
  work for them and their children (see Andermahr *et al*. 1997). Black

theorists have explored the ways in which inequalities between races have been constructed and maintained and have often cut across class and gender difference.

Figure 5.2 Cartoon by Posy Simmonds published in the *Guardian* in the 1970s: Taken-for-granted phrases and words form a key part of negative discourses around particular social groups.

'The richest 1% of the world have income equivalent to the poorest 57%. Four fifths of the world's population live below what countries in North America and Europe consider to be the poverty line' (Branko Milnovic of the World Bank, in *Guardian*, 18 January 2002).

We still live in deeply unequal capitalist societies, driven by the needs and practices of profit and competition, but these now operate on a global scale, with relations of exploitation spread more emphatically than ever across and between continents. It is not surprising that Marxist interest in economic power, inequalities and their relationship to social transformation has continued to be highly relevant.

At the other extreme to Marxism, however, **pluralist** models have developed, seeing the media as floating free of power, rather as the 'free market' suggests a realm of pure and equal exchange of goods for money. They emphasise the apparent diversity and choice of media forms and products. They argue that, if certain values or fiction forms are dominant, it is because they are 'genuinely popular'and have won out in this 'free market of ideas'. These voices include some of the biggest media corporations, such as Disney and AOL Time Warner, keen to downplay the economic clout of their far-flung empires, or their control over copyright enforcement and labour policies.

Of course, in the media-dominated and 'deregulated' world we inhabit, it is obvious that many different ideas and identities circulate and mix in the media. But we still need an account of power to understand how some ideas and imaginings to circulate much more freely than others. Thus, developing the original Marxist and Gramscian emphases, others (such as Thompson 1995) suggest we now live in times of a complex play between several kinds of power:

- economic power
- political power
- coercive, especially military power
- 'symbolic power', i.e. the means of information and communication, including Churches, schools and universities, and the images circulated by the media.

Such approaches are sometimes called **critical pluralism**. These acknowledge that there may be a struggle between competing discourses or accounts of the world, but insists that this is not an amicable free-for-all. Some discourses are parts of powerful institutions and have easier access to material resources, legal power, publicity and legitimacy, access which will be fought for if necessary. An important example would be what has been called 'the commercial speech of the consumer system' (i.e. marketing and advertising) and the identities and desires it has vast powers to encourage.

A suggestion: if there is a dominant ideology at the beginning of the twenty-first century, it is this: 'Everything is relative. There are no big power structures. We all have lots of freedoms. There is no such thing as a dominant ideology.'

'Once upon a time it was a small gathering of people around a fire listening to the storyteller with his tales of magic and fantasy. And now it's the whole world . . . It's not "domination" by American cinema. It's just the magic of storytelling, and it unites the world' (Steven Spielberg, *Variety*, 7 December 1993: 62).

Discourses and lived cultures

Even within the (still very influential) Gramscian emphasis on hegemony or struggles for dominance, the weighting given to 'dominant ideology' was challenged by writers such as Abercrombie, Hill and Turner (1980). They argued that, though dominant ideologies do exist, they are not the most important means for making social orders hang together. The fact that huge state bodies for surveillance and armed control exist suggests in fact that we do *not* inhabit unified social orders, running contentedly along. As well as the power of state force we need to understand the 'dull compulsion of the

economic' (and, feminists argue, of domestic labour). This leaves us little
room, time or power to challenge systems of values which most people either
disagree with or feel to be personally irrelevant. This brings us to the terms
'discourses' and 'lived cultures', which suggest a more dispersed, less binary
sense of how sets of power maintain themselves.

Media Studies tends now not to use the model of a single dominant and a
single oppositional set of ideas which can always be traced back simply to
class struggle (a model going back to Marxism). Instead it has turned to ideas
of powerful and not so powerful ideolog*ies* and identit*ies* connected to
ethnicity, religion, disability, sexuality etc. as well as to class, which operate
through *lived cultures* and powerful or marginalised *discourses*. Let's look at the
components of this more fragmented, less binary approach.

Discourses

The term '**discourse**' has a long history. For our purposes we can trace it
emerging from the work of the French theorist **Foucault** and also from
language study. Discourse analysis is interested in exploring what values and
identitites are contained, prevented or perhaps encouraged by the day-in, day-
out practices and (often unspoken) rules of a particular discourse. Though this
usually refers to verbal language, which is key for media, it can of course also
include visual 'languages' (which photos of a terrorist are to be chosen for the
news report? how will the terrorist be cast, lit, made up, scripted in the
feature film?). 'Discourses' can be usefully understood as socially constructed
knowledges. These 'knowledges' (of the law, computer science, fashion etc.)
involve regulated systems of statements or language use, that is, their
appropriate language operates rules, conventions and therefore assumptions
and exclusions. Sometimes single words can highlight the power of
dominant groups and their discourses to insist on some meanings and exclude
others.

Michel Foucault post-
structuralist philosopher,
sociologist and historian of
knowledge (1926–84). Best
known for his work on the
relationship of power and
knowledge, involving the power
of *discourses*, especially in the
areas of madness and sexuality.

Example 1: terrorism

The term 'terrorist' involves a key power to define certain acts of force in
negative ways, as non-justifiable. As such it operates within political and also
legal, sentencing discourses (with the power, in some regions, of life or death
for those successfully accused of being a terrorist) and has always been hotly
debated. Many people now understand that yesterday's 'terrorist', as defined
by the more powerful (the leaders of the American Revolution against British
rule in the eighteenth century; Nelson Mandela when fighting the apartheid

regime in South Africa; even certain acts of the suffragettes) is today's 'freedom fighter' or perhaps official statesman (as in the case of Mandela, or Gerry Adams in Northern Ireland).

But it is still the case that governments, aided by the media, usually operate this key power to label a whole range of actions 'terrorist', as happened with the 'coalition against terrorism' following '11 September', a term used to justify hugely wide-ranging attacks outside the US. It is only comparatively minority-oppositional discourses which struggle to argue that the violent actions of the more powerful (e.g. US armed and violent interventions against many regimes with which it has disagreed) might be labelled 'state-sponsored terrorism', or that certain violent acts (of resistance to Nazi Germany, for example) should not thus be labelled. So the same acts are not always and everywhere 'evil' or even violent, but key discourses and bodies of power are able to label them thus, with huge consequences. The hegemony or naturaliness of the term 'terrorist' is bound up with both forceful state powers of censorship and repression and the power to simply use it over and over again. So most people tend to take it for granted – or, if they disagree, are unable to channel that disagreement into organisations which can challenge state power.

Example 2: single parenting

'It may or may not be true that single parenting inevitably leads to delinquency and crime. But if everyone believes so, and punishes single parents accordingly, this will have real consequences for both parents and children and will become true in terms of its real effects' (Hall 1997: 49). Discourses contains evidence of struggles, for example in the common use now of the word 'single parent' (which sometimes indicates a male parent) rather than the earlier 'unmarried' or 'divorced' 'mother'.

Example 3: scientific discourse

If you have studied science you may have used 'scientific discourse' to describe experiments. 'Scientific impersonality' will be signified in writing up an experiment. The account will ideally seem to come from nowhere (no mention of the person who conducted it), and therefore to conceal its human fallibility in favour of a kind of remote authority. (British television news often operates in a similar way.)

Related to this is the way that language and metaphor work in the apparently neutral area of science called sociobiology (relating the study of

Some of Foucault's writing argues that discourses actually create 'regimes of truth' and therefore our perceptions. The term 'child' has not always been used of 'young adults' and is notoriously hard to define in years, and between different cultures. But the *power to define* someone as a 'child' has enormous legal, financial and other implications. (See Holland 1992; Scraton 1997).

genetics and the natural world to the human world). This often has embedded in it 'taken-for-granted' ideological assumptions which fit perfectly into a capitalist, profit-and-competition-centred world view. These, revealed in terms such as 'the selfish gene', involve the assertion that all human beings are 'naturally' acquisitive, competitive and selfish. A counter view would be interested in:

- examples from the natural world that justify other metaphors, of a non-competitive kind
- emphasising that people are formed by their capacity to change their culture as well as by 'natural' capacities
- tracing whether and how this way of understanding 'nature' seems to accompany the rise of positions celebrating (or stating as natural) a ruthless 'survival of the fittest' version of capitalism in the 1980s and 1990s.

'Greed . . . is good. Greed is right. Greed . . . captures the essence of the evolutionary spirit. Greed has marked the upward surge of mankind' (Michael Douglas playing Gordon Gekko, a real-life US stockbroker, in Oliver Stone's *Wall Street* (US 1987)).

Example 4: the discourse of 'famine' and its 'relief' in the 'Third World'

The word 'famine' echoes a Biblical discourse, in which mysterious scourges descend upon people from God, and are uncontrollable by human action or politics. Unlike discourses of, say, 'food supply crisis', the term 'famine' obscures financial–political relations between those who buy food, within long histories of exploitation. Involved in the discourse is the power to circulate knowledge, or perpetuate ignorance, about

- western 'food mountains' (to keep prices high) which might be used to relieve shortage
- price fixing and speculation around poorer countries' harvests in the interests of the West
- the 'futures' speculation on commodities (i.e. crops) on western stock exchanges. This often results in prices which, overnight, wipe out the profits of a whole year's work for poor farmers
- struggles around the policies of the IMF (International Monetary Fund) and the WTO (World Trade Organisation) as well as the global corporations who largely control food supply

The other side of these verbal discourses includes words and images of 'relief'. Well-meaning charity appeals or news items about the victims of food shortages have often used:

- the camera positioned above the pitiful victim, preferably a child, in its mother's arms
- a child who is given no name, or access to the sound track or translation facilities.

Figure 5.3 An attempt by the World Development Movement to counter the hegemony of one set of emphases within debates over 'globalisation'.

This unwittingly (we're all often unaware of the discourses we operate) suggests that they exist in a victim's dependency relationship to the West, and even helps perpetuate the situation by excluding a sense of such people as active in their own fates.

'The Third World' is itself a term with huge and rather patronising assumptions. It has been challenged in environmental discourses by terms such as 'the developing world', 'the South' or even 'the Majority World'.

ACTIVITY 5.2

Jot down some key phrases of financial reporting e.g. 'the pound had a bad day/was buoyant'; 'the Footsie (FTSE or Financial Times Stock Exchange list of key shareholding institutions) bounced back'.

- What do they mean?
- What kinds of knowledge, information do they exclude, for example, around the relationship of 'the West' to the 'developing world'?
- How do they image Stock Exchange activities?

Lived cultures

An interest in 'lived cultures' comes partly out of the work of Gramsci (see above). He argued that 'common sense', such an 'obvious' guide to many people's sense of the world, could be explored as being partly a complex set of traces rather than a simple class-based ideology. These traces may come from hundreds of years ago (for example in religious sayings) and may be somewhat contradictory ('God helps those who help themselves') but are also constantly changing.

He emphasised too the ways that hegemony is a lived process, never simply imposed or floating free in ideas alone. The power of common sense comes from the way it relates to dominant assumptions with material existence – in cultural practices, rituals and activities. (This is one of the points where Media Studies comes closest to Cultural Studies.)

This sounds daunting, so let's take an example. Billig usefully explores the construction of *national identity*, arguably so useful to those who wield political power when they make stirring speeches to persuade young men and women to fight and even die in wars of economic interest. He suggests that such a 'strong' version of national identity is not something that is constantly 'there'. Instead 'one needs to look for the reasons why people in the contemporary world *do not forget* their nationality' (1995: 7: emphasis added), which can then be called upon in moments of hegemonic struggle. This is achieved in the established nations by what he calls 'banal nationalism', a set of banal, or everyday, lived practices. These form a continuous 'flagging' via everyday tiny reminders of nationhood; not a flag waved with fervent passion in the sports parade or the war but the 'flag hanging unnoticed on the public building' or the national symbols on the coinage, or in the use of words such as 'we', 'us', 'them', 'home' and 'foreign' news categories, the daily salute to the Stars and Stripes in US schools etc.

'Since Sept. 11, many newsies have – like many Americans – rallied around the flag. The Stars and Stripes have been conspicuously displayed in the logos of most of the news nets, and some anchors – Fox News' Brit Hume and NBC's Tim Russert, for example – have taken to wearing flag pins on their lapels (*Variety* (US trade journal), 25 September 2001).

Other everyday lived cultural practices, involving visual as well as verbal discourses, relate to ideologies of gender and the family, whether those be 'happy endings' (i.e. love and marriage) of countless fairy tales and romance forms, or the 'familiar' family photo album and the occasions when this is added to. These photo collections usually (without anything ever being said) exclude certain kinds of imagery – thus family arguments, the unequal sharing of work in the home, child labour in the paper round (let alone child abuse) are not part of the discourse. Other poses and arrangements *are*, e.g. those which emphasise 'the family' as a harmonious, happy unit, involving certain 'dependencies' – of male on female, young on old, by height, gesture, positioning etc. All of this works to make more deviant the discourses around single parenting we outlined above – how do you assemble a comparably resonant family album for a single parent? (See Spence 1986.)

ACTIVITY 5.3

See whether you can find examples of discourses around childhood in your family photo albums. Try to devise photos which would challenge them. How do these images relate to the ways 'children' are defined, sexualised etc. in the discourses of advertising photography? (See Spence 1986, Holland 1992.)

Likewise the lived cultures of sport, especially as constructed by corporate media, could be examined for the ways they reproduce and 'refresh' our sense of such categories as gender, race and nationality, as well as the desirability of physical and financial power (the 'big hitters', 'size matters') – rather like that of the corporations. Large economic determinants clearly shape some of our sense of the relative importance of men's and women's sports. Overall media coverage of men's sports massively exceeds women's, which is given less than 10 per cent of time available, except of course when the Olympics take place.

'The sports pages in newspapers are not optional extras . . . There are always sports pages, and these are never left empty. Every day, the world over, millions upon millions of men scan these pages, sharing in defeats and victories, feeling at home in this world of waved flags' (Billig 1995: 122).

But linguistic marking and other 'natural-seeming' practices of media also construct the ideological differences of gendered sports. Thus

- Women's sports are likely to be subject to gender-marking, e.g. in women's basketball, the images of the players are typically subject to sexualisation (see Brookes 2002). In tennis Anna Kournikova is not a top-ranked tennis player yet attained celebrity status arguably because of her appearance – a lesson perhaps not lost on little girls?
- Sportswomen are sometimes still infantilised in television commentary, as 'girls' (it's rare to hear male sports people called 'boys'); by the use of the first name; by repeated reference to their marital or family status (e.g. the tennis achievements of the Williams sisters are often related to their father's coaching in a way not seen with male sports stars).

- Women's achievement is less often held up as representation of the nation (as happens for rugby teams etc.). It is more usually seen as a personal affair, partly perhaps because they are less likely to be competing in the big team sports which depend on institutional support and funding all the way from early schooling.

Q Explore the ways that commentary, descriptive terms used, interviewing styles, camera angles etc. carry broader values around such areas as power, gender, nationhood and race.

Finally, it's worth emphasising the danger of the tempting reliance on 'common sense' or the practices of news reporting at moments of crisis. Such routines can encourage some kinds of speedy assumptions and discourage others. For example, in 1995 a federal US government building in Oklahoma City was bombed, resulting in nearly two hundred dead and harrowing scenes on television news. For days there was speculation about who the bombers were, mostly focusing on Islamic extremists.

Yet only hours after the bombing a tiny agency, Inter Press, pointed the finger, accurately as it turned out, at the American far-right militia movement (see the Timothy McVeigh trial much later). It worked not on inside information but on simple deduction, involving

- the date (the anniversary of the ending of the Waco siege, highly significant for the militias)
- the fact that a government building was bombed (given the US militia's hatred of central government)
- the proximity of Oklahoma to Waco.

They were proved correct, and the 'rush to judgement', along with the rush to get 'the story' first, shown to be a very dangerous professional practice.

Q Do any events following 11 September 2001 suggest that this is still the case?

In summary, the Marxist emphasis on economics and class struggle as the basis of ideology has been replaced by an interest in other kinds of

- inequality
- power
- ways of circulating and changing dominant assumptions.

Bias originally meant 'oblique line', and by the end of the sixteenth century was applied to the game of bowls. It is now a term for ideological 'slant' in debates around factual reporting, though its origins suggest a reliance on a very 'truth/falsity' view of the plural values and pleasures which may be struggling for dominance in any news story.

Likewise Media Studies' early focus on '**bias**'-centred ideological studies of news processes, with the implication that the media 'conceal' or 'mask' the 'true' processes of class struggle, have been replaced by an exploration of fiction, entertainment and fantasy forms, and an interest in how audiences form an active rather than duped part of the processes of media. The pleasures of entertainment forms are no longer seen as simply the 'sugar on the pill' which helps the 'medicine' (ideology) go down.

References

Abercrombie, Nicholas, Hill, Stephen and Turner, Bryan S. (1980) *The Dominant Ideology Thesis*, London: Allen & Unwin.

Andermahr, Sonya, Lovell, Terry and Wolkowitz, Carol (1997) *A Concise Glossary of Feminist Theory*, London and New York: Arnold.

Billig, Michael (1995) *Banal Nationalism*, London: Sage.

Brookes, Rod (2002) *Representing Sport*, London and New York: Arnold.

Connell, Robert (1995) *Masculinities*, Cambridge: Polity.

Connell, Robert (2000) *The Men and the Boys*, Cambridge: Polity.

Golding, Peter and Murdock, Graham (1991) 'Culture, communications and political economy', in James Curran and Michael Gurevitch (eds) *Mass Media and Society*, London: Edward Arnold.

Hills, Matt (2002) *Fan Cultures*, London: Routledge.

Holland, Pat (1992) *What Is a Child? Popular Images of Childhood*, London: Virago Press.

Scraton, Phil (ed.) 1997 *'Childhood' in 'Crisis'?*, London: UCL Press.

Spence, Jo (1986) *Putting Myself in the Picture*, Camden Press.

Thompson, John B. (1990) 'Ideology and modern culture: critical theory,' in *The Age of Mass Communications*, Stanford, CA.: Stanford University Press, p. 7.

Thompson, John B. (1997) *The Media and Modernity: A Social Theory of the Media*, Cambridge: Polity.

Wasko, Janet (2001) *Understanding Disney: The Manufacture of Fantasy*, Cambridge: Polity.

Further reading

Eagleton, Terry (1994) 'Ideology' in Regan, Stephen (ed.), *The Eagleton Reader*, Oxford: Blackwell, 1998.

Foucault, Michel (1988) *Politics, Philosophy, Culture: Interviews and Other Writings 1977–1984*, London: Routledge.

Gramsci, Antonio (1994) *Selected Writings from the Prison Notebooks*, London: Lawrence and Wishart.

Hall, Stuart (ed.) (1997) *Representation: Cultural Representations and Signifying Practices*, London, Thousand Oaks, New Delhi: Sage.

Marx, Karl and Engels, Frederick (1965: first published 1888) *The German Ideology*, London: Lawrence and Wishart.

Strinati, Dominic (1995) *An Introduction to Theories of Popular Culture*, London: Routledge, esp. Chapters 2 and 4.

CASE STUDY: NEWS

- News and dominant values
- News values
- 'News professionals' and news cultures

- Impartiality and news
- References
- Further reading

News is a globally important media form. It flows at incredible speed, 24/7, across several technologies, and for both local and international contexts. Its satellite form is available, for example, in most bars, worldwide. Not only that, but its major reports can have a swift impact on politicians, on stock markets and other sites of power. Its codes have been learnt and are often attempted by those opposing vested power, anxious for their chance to be 'heard'.

It therefore still matters greatly what kind of news is made, the spaces it occupies, and the support or criticism it is given by its audiences. For example, it can either give politicians the incentive to reinforce crudely simplistic values ('a war on evil terrorists') or it can give them and their voters incentives to think about the complexity of *why* terrorists exist (see www.reportingtheworld.org).

The audience for the main British television news bulletins each night is consistently 7 to 8 million, and on days of real political significance many more (17 million watched BBC's 10 p.m. news on 11 September 2001). In 1998 although slightly more people read the *Sun* newspaper than watched television news (roughly ten million), nevertheless according to the ITC 62 per cent of people said that television is their preferred source of news; only 17 per cent said this for newspapers. The BBC Radio 4 *Today* programme, broadcast most mornings until 9 a.m., claims an audience of around 2 million (check the BBC website for the latest figures). It is influential in setting the day's news and often also the domestic political agenda, perhaps via an interview with a politician. Internet news forms are increasingly important: BBC News Online, for example, reported 2,261,428 hits during the week of 8 October 2001.

This case study explores:

- the relationship of news to dominant discourses and values
- how these are negotiated and expressed as parts of news institutions.

News and dominant values

Two points are often made about news within Media Studies:

- It is not transparent, not unbiased, not the 'window on the world' it often sets itself up to be.
- Its constructed versions of events usually serve dominant interests. This matters particularly with television news, from which most people get their sense of the world's happenings, especially at moments of perceived crisis.

A key landmark in British studies of news has been the work, from the 1970s onwards, of the Glasgow University Media Group (GUMG), who were among the first to argue an ideological influence for the ways in which the news is constructed. Yet much has changed in the news landscape since the 1970s, when the BBC and ITN news programmes (which GUMG began by analysing) claimed enormous authority for themselves. The strikes and war stories that GUMG investigated were interpreted by them as more polarised (split into only two sides, often around economics or social class) than now seems the case. In a post-Cold-War, 'deregulated' world, there is more awareness of issues such as gender, ethnicity, religion, sexuality as they shape our lives. And Media Studies now tends to make more modest claims for the influence of particular news bulletins, given:

- the proliferation of news technologies and forms, leading to '24-hour news'
- new styles of television news (e.g. Channel 5) claiming less 'on-high' authority for themselves and often resembling tabloid print forms in their reliance on celebrity gossip and scandal
- lower budgets for such news (except for 'star' presenters' salaries) allow little time for extended items, meaning less expensive foreign or expert coverage and a tendency to go with speculation or rumour (e.g. about the MMR vaccine) rather than informed debate
- the deployment of huge amounts of PR information and '**spin**' both inside and outside news
- the increasing overlap between news and 'comment' of current affairs.

Nevertheless, though news programmes may not *directly* affect belief, many would argue that they can hugely *influence* audiences and politicians, if only by their selection of items for inclusion as 'news' or by the ways they set up issues and encourage them to be understood in particular ways. They are still able to *set the agenda* of issues which we find ourselves thinking about (sometimes called **gatekeeping**), selecting some information for consideration and leaving some unexplored or unannounced. And news is still often able to set the agenda for giving the 'green light' to current affairs and investigative documentaries teams. All this makes news still hugely powerful, though sometimes in unexpected ways. It may, for example, encourage those already confident of sharing majority opinion to voice their views, while those who do not conform fall silent – as happened to peace protesters when 'the war on terrorism' became increasingly used in the US after the events of 11 September 2001 even though no declaration of war had been made. Or as, when Diana, Princess of Wales was killed in a drink-driving accident in 1997, it became difficult to describe the crash in that way, or to say that you were not

particularly moved, or were even annoyed by the scale of the news coverage. Elizabeth Noelle-Neumann (1993), writing of the related influence of opinion polls, has described this as a 'spiral of silence' (see Lewis 2001).

> An **agenda** is a list of items to be discussed at a meeting, usually drawn up by the person chairing the meeting, who has the power to arrange them in order of importance. In relation to news, terms such as 'hidden agenda' or 'agenda-setting' draw attention to the importance of this power to channel audiences' attention and discussions in some directions and not others.

ACTIVITY 5.4

Make a note of a day's major news headlines. Think whether they affect what you and your friends talk about (i.e. have they 'set the agenda' for your talk?). Then note the headlines a few weeks later.

- Do you wonder what happened to stories which, in the first set of headlines, seemed urgent and important?
- When and how did they recede into less important status?

> 'I suddenly felt things were "back to normal" a couple of days later when Ground Zero stopped being the only news item' (Anon).

ACTIVITY 5.5

Watch the title sequences of late evening BBC and ITV news bulletins. How do they announce the nature (or genre) of the programme to follow? Note:

- the kinds of imagery and music used (futuristic hi-tech studio? an emphasis on speedy news-gathering technology and lots of staff behind the scenes – the trustworthiness of the institution producing the news? or the informal low budget setting of Channel 5?)

- the dress, demeanour, accent, tones, positioning of the presenter(s)

  Q Are such arrangements trying to claim authority for the news? If not, what sort of programme is being announced?

- Examine an Internet news site. Can you apply to it any similar questions of how authoritativeness has been claimed?

News values

However dispersed 'news' is now, it is not as obvious a 'thing' as it may seem to be. Important theories of **news values** argue that news does not exist, free-floating, waiting to be discovered in the world outside the newsroom, as is suggested in many images of and dramas about news reporting. These values are argued to systematically *construct* rather than simply *accompany* the 'gathering' of news. They are not consciously held values. Indeed, many journalists would say that their main ideal is the achievement of

Figure 5.4 CNN.com 'front page'

objectivity or truth, and this remains an important aspiration, whatever the problems with stating it as an *absolute* standard.

> 'Isn't it amazing that the amount of news that happens in the world every day always just exactly fits the newspaper?' (*Guardian Unlimited* ad, 2001).

Nevertheless news is the end product of complex processes of evaluation which begin with a systematic sorting and selecting of events and topics according to professionalised news values (and lived practices), defined as 'the professional codes used in the selection, construction and presentation of news stories in corporately produced press and broadcasting' (O'Sullivan *et al.* 1994). There have been many different definitions of news values since Galtung and Ruge laid out a now famous pioneering list in 1965. Though dated now, their argument that news is structured according to unspoken values rather than 'discovered' remains a key one. We will outline and update several of their key terms, namely: frequency (and the closely allied ideas of proximity and threshold); negativity; predictability; continuity; composition; personalisation and narrativisation.

- *Frequency* or the time scale of events perceived as 'newsworthy'. Those events which become news stories will be of about the same frequency as many news bulletins, i.e. of about a daily span. An oil spillage will be perceived as a news story; the slow work over time of legislation or protest which makes it less (or more) likely to occur will not feature as news. However, such protest might be treated in current affairs or documentary programmes, especially if Greenpeace, say, staged an effective demonstration which coincided with the frequency of the news bulletins.
- *Threshold* or the 'size' of an event that's needed to be considered 'newsworthy'. Commonly occurring events happening to individuals will not usually count (except for local news) unless they involve

either a celebrity or an unusually violent or sensational happening.

- *Proximity* or the perceived closeness of an item to the audiences for that news institution. News is circulated, on the whole, by national broadcasting organisations or by regional arms ('CNN Europe') of news conglomerates. It is perhaps understandable that it often consists of items relating to that region. Though many people may be involved in a boat capsizing in Thailand, it is not likely to compete for British news space with a boat capsizing in the Channel, with fewer casualties but a chance that near relatives or friends are involved. Problems arise with the way that such 'First World' stories often constitute much of the material of the big news agencies selling news to 'Third World' broadcasting stations. And with the corresponding way in which western audiences are often given, in return, little of 'Third World news' except through 'coups crises and famines' or the same official figures getting in and out of cars, addressing news conferences etc.

ACTIVITY 5.6
Try turning down the sound on coverage of a 'big' diplomatic story whose content you know already and assess how informative the visuals are.

> 'The further away, both geographically and culturally, the more a country's affairs are likely to be portrayed in the activities of one or two senior political figures, until in remoter countries only the head of state is visible' (Golding 1981: 255).

This circle of what gets recognised as a 'big story' can be a rather vicious one. It is reinforced by the broader language processes and everyday practices: e.g. the use of 'we', 'us' and 'them' in news language; the sense of where is 'here' and where 'somewhere foreign' even in a globalised world. Why are countries still referred to as 'the Middle East' or 'the Far East'? Far away from where exactly? Why are military commanders called 'warlords' in the 'Third World' (including Bosnia) but 'Chiefs of Staff' in the West?

- *Negativity*: 'If it's news, it's bad news' sums up the feeling that long-term, constructive events are much less likely to feature as news than a catastrophe or images of violence. Despite the use of 'positive' stories, especially of medical breakthroughs as the 'happy ending' of some news bulletins, news tends to take the normal or everyday for granted, and is driven to make stories out of the deviant: crime, dissidence, disaster. In turn, news processes often augment the stereotyping and scapegoating of 'out' groups, because of the ways it feeds on the thrill of their deviancy. It may shape news coverage of 'Third World' issues in terms of 'coups, crises and famine', now joined by 'terrorism' or 'ancient hatreds' as explanation of complex processes such as the Israeli–Arab conflict.

These seem 'obvious' to many hard-pressed reporters, perhaps because they fit neatly into existing understandings in echoing fictional images and discourses (see Chapter 2). Then, in a kind of loop, the realistic 'charge' of news images feeds back into the apparent realisms of some fiction forms, shaky camera and all. In such an ecology of news, small, hopeful initiatives, such as charities which adapt bicycle technology to help villages, stand little chance of being publicised.

- *Predictability*: though news is taken to consist of random events 'out there', a lot of time is spent (often at 'editorial conferences') trying to anticipate what will be 'newsworthy', deciding where on the planet to employ expensive overseas-based staff, equipment etc. Or if the media expect a particular turn (say, 'violence') to certain events, the drive will be to report according to those expectations. Examples include large demonstrations, big football matches, world trade protests, the Notting Hill Carnival (until quite recently). Even if these turn out to be mostly peaceful, the few skirmishes which occur are often heavily focused upon (as

Children's mobile library

Figure 5.5 An example of sustainable technology: a schoolchildren's mobile library in Sri Lanka. Not, however, a story likely to make the news.

'newsworthy'), partly to justify the numbers of reporters assigned to the expected violent event.

'If it bleeds, it leads' (journalistic wisdom).

'On the day of her death Diana became, unproblematically, a news story . . . the news agenda was very quickly established and the . . . blame for the accident placed on the activities of the paparazzi and the tabloid press . . . the discussions of that day were a classic example of the way in which news stories take hypotheses as fact and preclude alternative explanation. Monday's announcement of the results of blood tests on the driver were shocking; not just for what it revealed, but for the way . . . it threatened the neatness of the news story . . . established the previous day' (Geraghty 1998).

Another meaning for 'predictable' is that events termed 'news' are often known about weeks and months ahead (in the case of PR-based material) or years in advance for conferences, anniversaries, annual reports, sporting events, book or film launches and so on. 'The news should really be called the olds' as someone once put it. Some newspapers even publish 'diaries' for the week ahead.

ACTIVITY 5.7

Find a newspaper (e.g. the *Guardian*) which publishes such a diary.

- Compare its list of events with the events which it reported in the week predicted.
- How much of an overlap was there?
- Where did reporters seem to be located, ready for stories?

Figure 5.6 An unusually vivid shot of the work of constructing 'news' of a much trailed 'fact' or event: Tony Blair's speech to the Labour Party conference after the events of 11 September 2001.

Of course, other kinds of highly predictable events, such as famines, or the long-term effects of pesticides, are not usually part of the diary, since they cannot be 'dated' nor are they 'cut and dried' in terms of their beginnings. 'By the time the pictures are horrific enough to move people, it is almost too late', as one journalist put it. Where there are big but steadily present 'domestic' issues, such as unemployment or homelessness, there's a feeling that, though they go on happening, the journalist cannot keep on writing the same story. S/he looks for a 'twist', perhaps a way of personalising or even sensationalising it, or simply leaves it as 'not news'.

- *Continuity*: if an event is defined by the powerful news companies as big enough, resources will be diverted to it for some time, and often even 'non-events' which seem part of that story will be covered. 'The driver of the car in which Diana, Princess of Wales, was killed has still not regained consciousness.' Of course this takes resources away from other areas where crucial events might be happening.
- *Composition*: the 'story' will be selected and arranged according to the editor's sense of the balance of the whole bulletin, or page. If many home stories have been used, even a fairly unimportant 'foreign' story may be included.

ACTIVITY 5.8

Look at the balance of items in a radio or television news bulletin. Again, using broadsheet papers as your source of a fuller news agenda, see whether you feel the composition has been adjusted as suggested above.

- Within the bulletin, do certain items seem ordered so as to be grouped together, either for contrast or to suggest connections?
- List the items in an order that would invite different connections.

- *Personalisation*: wherever possible, events are seen as the actions of people as individuals. This runs all the way from endless shots of politicians getting in and out of cars (respectable 'personalisation') through hospital waiting lists being put on the agenda by 'Baby *x*' or a pensioner not getting the attention s/he needs, to 'celebrity gossip and scandal' which is usually dismissed as 'trivial', part of 'dumbing down' etc.

Thompson (2000) and others have argued that political scandal (such as that involving Lord Archer in 2001) within a 'culture of visibility' means that, despite the money poured into PR attempts to 'secure consent' to certain versions of events, and the fiercely restrictive UK libel laws, politicians have to take note of the charges. Political scandal can lead to reforms (see the Nolan Committee's recommendations after the Tory 'sleaze' scandals of the 1990s) and can rightly highlight questionable activities and also hypocrisies. For someone who is legislating strict anti-gay measures to be secretly gay himself or herself, for example, is arguably a matter of real public concern. To take the argument further, so is the failure actually to experience run-down public services by those legislating (from the privilege of private education, or travel, or health arrangements) against their proper funding.

Yet even news forms driven by PR-mediated 'celebrity' and scandal, within news institutions obsessed with ratings and circulation figures, raise more complex issues than at first it seems. Stories such as coverage of the life and death of Diana, Princess of Wales allowed public voice to hitherto ignored experiences such as bulimia, or the pain of divorce (see Stardom and celebrity case study following Chapter 4).

Two other areas of the construction of news deserve mention: narrativisation (which Galton and Ruge list) and visual imperatives.

- *Narrativisation*: items are from the start called 'stories' and they are shaped into narrative form as soon as possible. (See case study following Chapter 2.) The Falklands War coverage drew on an existing repertoire from Second World War narratives (themes such as 'War is Hell but it makes Heroes', 'The Women Wait while the Men Fight'). After '11 September' the rhetoric of this 'good war' against Hitler, via references to the London Blitz, was drawn upon to justify the US–UK bombing of Afghanistan, a more controversial process.

- *Visual imperatives* are said to be especially important in television news (and of course unimportant in radio, where sound codes are key). These imperatives drive towards stories that have 'strong' pictures, whether this means pictures celebrities, or 'Biblical-looking' famines, or ones which resemble a blockbuster film, as in the shots of people fleeing from the explosions at the World Trade Center. Increasingly, if wars are heavily censored or inaccessible to picture technology, computer-aided graphics are used to give a sense of what might be happening. Debates on visual imperatives need critical consideration. For example:

Figure 5.7 'Hard news' from the 'visual imperative'? A comfortingly convincing-looking image from the early stages of the 'war on terrorism'. What does it say of such 'news', given the failure of massive and prolonged bombing of Afghanistan to find Osama bin Laden?

- Radio's agenda is very similar to television's, although it cannot operate 'visual imperatives'. Why is this, if the visual is so important to news?
- Television or press stories lacking pictures but deemed important use computer-aided graphics to assist visualisation. Thus photographs do not always 'lead'.
- 'Less newsworthy' controversial or speculative stories, or ones involved with long-term processes, are rarely helped in this way, even though they could be. Again, the visual imperatives tend to *follow*, not *lead* existing news priorities.
- 'Soundbites', or vivid short phrases used over and over again in coverage of some stories, could be argued as equally important, and as deriving from *verbal*, radio and print-related forms. It was a key part of the story that verbal shifts occurred around what to call the attacks on the World Trade Center and the Pentagon: 'Attacks on Amercia'; 'Ground Zero'; '11 September'; and '9:11', which is also the US emergency telephone dialling code (like 999). Yet verbal elements often go unexplored in media study compared to visual determinants.

ACTIVITY 5.9

Listen to the BBC World Service (and/or watch CNN, or the ITN or BBC 24-hour programmes) to see how different is the sense of a news agenda and the coverage of 'non-domestic' items to that of

- the tabloid press
- the broadsheet press
- terrestrial television news programmes.

'11 September' and 'proximity'

Proximity, threshold. Clearly by any standards this was a huge event ('threshold') if only in terms of the numbers of people killed, and it was easy to feel close ('proximity') to those affected by the 11 September bombings. For millions of people the televised events took place in real time; with uncensored and horrifying footage, unprecedented sharing of material between the main news channels and disruption to important schedules. And, after the second plane crashed into the World Trade Center, the instantaneous storytelling held the terror of it being impossible to guess what might come next.

The idea that the 'proximity' of news stories is always 'phoney' or a kind of ideological false consciousness needs some rethinking. Consider these points:

- New York is an example of the routine, globalised mix and linkages of world cities – see the list of those killed. People in many parts of the world had real contacts with these workers and tourists. Thus the feeling of proximity is not simply an illusion, though it does depend on the kinds of global power, symbolic and financial, located in New York. Interestingly, the Pentagon deaths, at the heart of the US military machine, were much less focused on, as was the role of the World Trade Organisation.
- New York is probably the most visited, filmed and photographed city in the world, and an iconic setting for films. Hence the comments that 'it felt like a movie', *though this comment itself shows an awareness that it was not a movie.*
- New York is arguably the world's media centre (television pictures were usually fed to news companies across the globe by microwave dishes on top of the WTC). There was thus no shortage of immediate pictures, journalists on the spot, first-hand comment and then involvement by millions of people.

Nevertheless, it is striking how soon it was assumed that there could only be one position to take on the atrocity, and how soon it became named '9:11'. Such namings are a key factor in soliciting support for some positions and not others.

To say that 'there was no mental preparation for a

story like this', as some commentators did, is to ignore:

- the fact that the New York images were both familiar and horribly strange. They echoed, but on a vaster scale, other images, especially from Palestine, but rarely from the US (despite the Oklahoma bombing by Timothy McVeigh in 1995).
- the extent to which US media in particular have failed to cover the 'Third World' and the ways US power has operated there. This could to an extent have prepared audiences. It forms a kind of 'proximity' – between uninformed news values and uninformed audiences?

Many commented on the way that US television showed the explosions over and over in the first days. Repetition is partly a common way of coping with trauma. But it also seemed that the capacity of news to give informed comment to its audiences at this critical moment was simply not there. Soon, comment from the rest of the world, and from radio and print forms, was available, but the initial gap and silence were striking. No wonder Americans fleeing from the horror could ask, in genuine bafflement, 'How could anyone hate America enough to do this?' But this question itself became a dangerous headline for serious news coverage, given the US government's emphasis on much simpler slogans: 'if you're not with us you're against us'; 'fighting evil' and 'wanted dead or alive'.

Figure 5.8

'News professionals' and news cultures

News values are professionalised: they have to be acquired in order

- to become a journalist, through training on the job, or achieving qualifications
- to function effectively as a journalist (which may involve less formal learning contexts, such as canteen gossip about who's a good 'source'; what is now the 'house style' of your paper or radio station).

Yet they are a good illustration of the 'taken-for-granted discourses' and 'lived cultures' we discussed in Chapter 5, all the more powerful because so taken for granted. For example, it is often argued (by Schlesinger 1987 from his observations within news rooms) that, like most television professionals, journalists make programmes for other television professionals, partly because their sense of their majority audience is very flimsy. 'They won't understand it', 'We'd love to run the story but the public just don't want to hear about it' are statements often made on the basis of very little systematic attempt to find out exactly what audiences might want (only simple overnight ratings figures are now quickly available).

Though news is often thought to be about 'reporting the facts', news teams quickly develop a sense of *news sources* – 'whom to rely on' for 'hard stories' i.e. stories full of facts, statistics and quotations from official sources which don't risk libel action. Studies (see Schlesinger 1987) show that journalists tend to rely on white, middle-class, middle-aged professional males as sources, especially when 'expert' opinion is accessed. These tend to work in either accredited bodies such as a big world news agency – Reuters, Press Association, Associated Press or United Press International, which send stories directly into the computer systems of bodies such as News International – or, increasingly, one of the big PR (Public Relations) or corporate communications companies. Controversy has raged in recent years over the degree to which government *spin doctors* or highly skilled press officers should try to construct news, though this has always happened (via the timing of press releases etc.).

All these are the preferred sources of news for its primary definers. They are sorted so that 'copy tasters' can select items to be used. Most newsrooms scan the morning newspapers and listen to the radio from early in the day. This is now more of a two-way street than it once was, as up-to-the-minute television news, and even television news pictures, as well as Internet items, often constitute newspapers' headlines the next day. But whatever the direction of the flow, such news structures tend to favour those who already have enough power to employ press officers, to distribute press releases and publicity and to hire Reuters to make up a *VNR* (Video News Release).

Frenzied circulation and ratings wars between organisations have accelerated the professionals' emphasis on being 'first with the big story' rather than 'the one that got the story right'. This trend is accentuated by new technology, such as digital cameras, portable computers and satellite phones. These mean that a reporter can input a story with photos into a newsdesk terminal almost as soon as it is written. The Internet has become a volatile (and only partly reliable) source of news stories taken up very quickly by mainstream media.

Partly as a result of such pressures, far fewer foreign correspondents are now permanently employed to develop expert, intimate knowledge of a particular country. This tendency may be intensified by the ability of news agencies to arrange speedy satellite or videophone transmission of instant judgements from someone based in a fairly comfortable hotel.

'In the 1960s a third of Fleet Street journalists were based outside London, either in the regions or on foreign postings. Now 90% of national newspaper staff work in London' (Nick Cohen, writing on the current growth of lifestyle, opinion and 'light' columns as compared to investigative or first-hand reporting, *New Statesman*, 22 May 1998). See www.reportingtheworld.org.

'CNN has occupied 30 rooms in the Islamabad Marriott at $200 per night each. That's nothing compared to the cost of $8,000 satellite telephones and . . . $70,000 for shipping and setup of satellite equipement' (*New York Times*, 8 October 2001).

Foreign news often highlights a very gendered aspect to news in general (which stories do women get to cover?). It has until recently been seen as a 'hard' form unsuited to women, despite the distinguished careers of women from Martha Gelhorn in the 1930s to Kate Adie, Maggie O'Kane and Orla Guerin more recently.

'In the 1950s, women reporters interviewing people on the streets were assumed to be soliciting. More recently Associated Press reporter and Vietnam correspondent Edie Lederer had to get an "I am not a prostitute" certificate from the authorities before she could travel in Saudi Arabia to report the Gulf War' (Sebba 1994).

On the stories which women reporters might be expected to 'pick up on': 'Kate Adie once told me that a little documented aspect of the Afghan war against the Soviet Union was the high casualty rate of rural women. The men had taken up positions in the surrounding hills. Traditional restrictive laws meant that women were forbidden to leave [their] quarters. Attacks by Russian helicopters bore down on the villages killing thousands of women. It is believed that more women than fighting men died in that war (Abdela 2001).

Correspondents may also learn a professional, distant, authoritative language with which, for example, to sanitise wars. We now often hear about atrocious modern weapons through a veil of language: 'smart bombs'; 'daisy cutters'; 'surgical strikes', implying that this is an operation for 'the patient's' own good'; 'carpet bombing' (sounds like vacuuming); 'taking people out' instead of assassinations; and so on. The early stages of the bombing of Afghanistan in 2001–2 produced the statement that this, one of the poorest countries in the world, was 'not a target rich environment'. Some have also asked how accurate the term 'defence' can be for the huge amounts spent by the US government on arms, given the absence of any credible threat from another nation state (see Lewis 2001).

'Professional' reporting of financial news also uses obscuring metaphors such as 'the pound had a bad day', 'the NASDAQ dived' or 'getting the economy back on the rails' which remystify the already mysterious workings of stock exchanges.

Impartiality and news

Broadcast media in Britain (unlike the press) are legally required to be politically impartial: i.e. broadcasters cannot express a point of view on 'major matters' but, in a linked phrase, have to make balanced reports. But a balance is always between certain forces, and these tend to be those points of view that are assumed to reflect existing public opinion. Thirty years ago, this was defended as reflecting the Labour–Conservative axis of parliamentary politics, with a stopwatch eye to how much time each party was given on television. Now, the political spectrum stretches further (though opinion that falls outside 'parliamentary democracy' is still often deemed unacceptable by BBC and ITV).

The Glasgow University Media Group has since the mid-1970s employed content analysis (see Chapter 6), often involving hundreds of hours of recorded news broadcasts, focused initially on industrial items such as strikes. They argued that the news consistently favours the interpretations of the already powerful because journalists share assumptions about the real world which are rarely seriously questioned, such as the view that strikes are harmful and disruptive. Furthermore, journalists rely on official sources to an extent that systematically outlaws different accounts of events. It is crucial that such critical positions on news continue to be tested. But, especially when dealing with arguments which put all the blame on 'spin' (or attempts to secure hegemony), as though a fully objective account existed somewhere, you should bear in mind that objectivity or impartiality is an impossible goal for any statement or story because:

- to decide to select an item for the news is to make a decision about other items that cannot be told, because of time or space restrictions. Therefore any story has already been prioritised, or had some value set on it.
- since there are always several positions from which to tell a story, and it is impossible to produce an account from completely 'outside', a position on it will inevitably have been chosen.
- to say that objectivity is possible is to imply that an unarguable interpretation of an event exists prior to the report or story.

Nevertheless, we can reasonably argue that news can and should be *as adequate and informative as possible for particular purposes*. Revelations in the UK about 'fakery' in television documentaries and the hiring of actors to pose as guests on talk shows rightly produced strong reactions in the late 1990s. An important breach of the ethical standards of those programmes, designed to offer reliable and factual information, had taken place. When audiences (or 'citizenry' in these contexts?) need to be informed about the justification for and conduct of, say, a war or major government spending decisions, or how to lessen the incidence of rape, it is right to object to unnecessary censorship or 'spin' or fakery in such stories – especially if these exclude 'limit' or critical positions from outside the conventional spectrum of opinion.

To return to the beginning of the chapter: the argument that television news is constructed, not transparent, is no longer surprising. 'News' exists now not just as BBC or ITV news. Twenty-four-hour television news services inevitably offer somewhat different accounts of events, and pose different problems for news managers. The proliferation of radio stations offers more sources of news, as do news-related forms such as phone-ins and chat shows. The Internet, said to be unpoliceable and unregulatable, is a growing source of news stories, dissent and ways of organising around them. Even the 'rule' that music is never to be used as accompaniment to television news stories is occasionally broken. Television programmes such as *It'll Be Alright on the Night* take for granted, and add to, audience knowledge of news codes and constructions. Do they, however, help audiences to understand the broader processes of news construction as they relate to dominant values?

It is clear that

- 'dominant values' now go further than stories of strikes and wars. The debate needs to include discourses around the complexities of globalised capitalism, or the ways that powerful identities such as ethnicity, age and sexuality are formed along some lines and not others.

- news images need to be understood in closer relation to the circulation of entertainment images (see Stardom and Celebrity case study following Chapter 4).

- audiences' use of news needs to be understood when its influence is discussed. There are striking examples of their rejection of certain stories. During the events which began at the World Trade Center in September 2001 it was notable that critical voices, such as those of the peace movement, or of critics of US policy in the 'Third World', were not given proportional time to those assuming that war was the best response to terrorist attack. Nevertheless in many programmes, where members of the public were invited to express views, such opinions had clearly been

seized upon, or even sought out, often via the Internet . Similarly boycotts, such as that of *The Sun* on Merseyside for libelling Liverpool soccer fans after the Hillsborough tragedy (see Scraton 1999), occasionally take place, and are a key site of consumer power in this area. This is worth mentioning since Media Studies usually reserves consideration of fan or consumer power for 'entertainment' forms, so examples of resistant understandings of news deserve celebration.

References

Abdela, Lesley (2001) 'Diary', *New Statesman*, 24 September.

Eldridge, John (ed.) (1995) *The Glasgow University Media Reader*, vol. 1, London: Routledge.

Galtung, J. and Ruge, M. (1981) 'The structure of foreign news: the presentation of the Congo, Cuba and Cyprus crises in four foreign newspapers', extract in S. Cohen and J. Young (eds) *The Manufacture of News*, London: Constable.

Golding, Peter (1981) 'The missing dimension – news media and the management of change', in T. O'Sullivan and Y. Jewkes (eds) *The Media Studies Reader*, London and New York: Arnold, 1997.

Lewis, Justin (2001) *Constructing Public Opinion: How Political Elites Do What They Like and Why We Seem to Go Along with It*, New York: Columbia University Press.

Noelle-Neumann, Elizabeth (1993) *The Spiral of Silence*, Chicago: University of Chicago Press.

O'Sullivan, Tim, Dutton, Brian and Rayner, Philip (1994, 2nd edition) *Studying the Media*, London: Arnold.

Philo, Greg (ed.) (1995) *The Glasgow Media Group Reader*, vol. 2, London and New York: Routledge.

Schlesinger, Philip (1987) *Putting 'Reality' Together*, London: Methuen.

Scraton, Phil (1999) *Hillsborough: The Truth*, Edinburgh: Mainstream.

Sebba, A. (1994) *Battling for News*, London: Sceptre.

Thompson, John T., (2000) *Political Scandal: Power and Visibility in the Media Age*, Cambridge: Polity.

Further reading

Allan, Stuart (2000) *News Culture*, Buckingham: Open University Press.

Bennett, W. and Paletz, D. (eds) (1994) *Taken By Storm: The Media Public Opinion and US Foreign Policy in the Gulf War*, Chicago: University of Chicago Press.

Carter, Cynthia, Branston, Gill and Allan, Stuart (eds) (1998) *News, Gender and Power*, London and New York: Routledge.

Chomsky, Noam (2001) *9–11*, New York: Seven Stories.

Curran, James and Seaton, Jean (1997) *Power Without Responsibility: The Press and Broadcasting in Britain*, London and New York: Routledge.

Hood, Stuart and Tabary-Peterssen, Thalia (1997, 4th edition) *On Television*, London: Pluto.

Philips, D. (1992) *Evaluating Press Coverage*, London: Kogan Page.

Philo, Greg (1990) *Seeing and Believing: The Influence of Television*, London and New York: Routledge.

Rose, Chris (1998) *The Turning of the 'Spar*, London: Greenpeace.

Schudson, Michael (1991) 'The sociology of news production revisited', in James Curran and Michael Gurevitch (eds) *Mass Media and Society*, London: Arnold.

'Alternative' Internet resources for '11 September' and events which followed

www.cjr.org
www.IndyMedia.com
www.medialens.org
www.opendemocracy.net
www.reportingtheworld.org
www.ZNet.org

6 Audiences

- Ways of thinking about 'audiences'
- The effects model
- The uses and gratifications model
- Research methods and assumptions about audiences
- Semiotics and audiences
- Contexts of reception and 'cultural competences'
- Finally: the audience 'in' the media
- References
- Further reading

Ways of thinking about 'audiences'

Note: This chapter explores some of the methods through which understanding of 'audiences' have been attempted. Strictly speaking, it's about methods of analysing texts. Some of these (e.g. content analysis) have little to say about how actual audiences might be engaging with them. They have, however, been very powerful in debates about audiences, and therefore part of the way we/they are imaged, so we have placed them here.

In Media Studies *audience* refers to the groups and individuals addressed and often partly 'constructed' by media industries. Research into audiences has been far from straightforward, and different models tend to get very different kinds of funding (see Gray 1999). However, two extremes tend to recur in a set of fascinating arguments: the **effects model** and the **uses and gratifications model**. Let's broadly outline these.

The effects model (also called the **hypodermic model**) is the name given to approaches that emphasise what the media do *to* their audiences. Power is assumed to lie with the 'message' here. The media in such work are often called 'the mass media' or 'mass communications' so as to emphasise the size and scale of their operations. The language used in this model often implies that meanings are 'injected' into the mass audience by powerful, syringe-like media. The next step is often to describe the media as working like a drug, and then to suggest that the audience is drugged, addicted, doped or duped.

> 'There are in fact no "masses" but only ways of seeing people as masses' (Raymond Williams, 'Culture is ordinary', 1958).

On the other hand, the uses and gratifications model emphasises what the audiences and readerships of media products do *with* them. Power is argued to lie with the individual **consumer** of media, who is imagined as consciously using particular programmes, films or magazines to gratify certain needs and interests. Far from being duped by the media, the audience is seen as made up of individuals free to reject, use or play with media meanings as they choose. The needs to be gratified would include those for diversion and escapism, for information, for comparing relationships and lifestyle of characters with one's own, or for sexual stimulation.

The effects model

The effects model has tended to be associated with what are called **quantitative** research methods: counting items (for example in answers to questionnaires) and drawing conclusions. Let's look in more detail at some effects approaches.

- The **Frankfurt School** theorised (rather than quantity-surveyed) the possible effects of modern media, especially in response to German fascism's use of radio and film for **propaganda** purposes. Later, in exile from Nazi Germany, the major Frankfurt theorists explored the early power of US media, including advertising and entertainments forms. Its members developed a variant of Marxism known as *critical theory* at a time when 'it seemed as though the possibility of radical social change had been smashed between the twin cudgels of concentration camps and television for the masses' (quoted in Strinati 1995). They emphasised the power of corporate capitalism, owning and controlling new media, to restrict and control cultural life in unprecedented ways, creating what they called a 'mass culture' of stupefying conformity, with no space for innovation or originality.

- A slightly different emphasis on effects was developed by researchers into what was then the new phenomenon of television in the US in the 1950s and 1960s. They were alarmed by a perceived increase in violent acts and their possible relationship to violence as represented on television, though they were uninterested in linking these to a critical analysis of late capitalist society, as the Frankfurt School had attempted. Again, though, they focused on the power of television to do things *to* people – or rather, to *other* people. Contemporary self-styled 'moral majority' movements such as the National Viewers' and Listeners' Association (NVLA) in Britain or parental movements in the US try to have television and other media more closely censored, on the assumption that they are the most important causes of a society perceived as increasingly violent.

- Other 'effects' researchers from the 1940s on were interested in issues such as whether or not television affected people's political attitudes, as measured in acts such as voting in elections.

Many researchers, especially those studying the effects of media on children, were influenced by the work of *behavioural* scientists who tried to understand

'In 1976, a group of friends from Los Angeles who often gathered together . . . to indulge in hours long sessions of television viewing, decided to call themselves "couch potatoes". With tongue in cheek publications such as *The Official Couch Potato Handbook* . . . and *The Couch Potato Guide to Life* . . . they started a mock-serious grassroots viewers' movement' (I Ang (1991) *Desperately Seeking the Audience*, London: Routledge).

The **Frankfurt School** was set up in 1923, mostly composed of left-wing German Jewish intellectuals. Key members were Theodor Adorno (1903–70), Herbert Marcuse (1898–1973) and Max Horkheimer (1895–1973). After Nazism consolidated its power in 1933 the group worked in exile in the US.

Burrhus Frederic Skinner
US behaviourist scientist
(1904–90), argued that all
behaviour is explainable solely in
terms of genetic dispositions in
individuals which interact with
'reinforcements' (punishments)
or rewards.

On the Bobo doll work Jane Root
(now Controller of BBC2) quotes
the following: 'As she entered a
laboratory, one small four-year-
old girl was heard to say "Look,
Mummy, there's the doll we have
to hit"' (*Open the Box* London:
Comedia, 1986).

human *social* behaviour by modifying the *laboratory* behaviour of animals. **B. F. Skinner** is one of the most famous **behaviourists**. You have probably also heard of Pavlov's dogs, laboratory animals whose feeding times were accompanied by a bell ringing, until eventually they would salivate whenever the bell rang, with or without the food. Clearly their laboratory behaviour had been violently modified, and scientists working on such experiments hoped that control by reinforcement could also be applied to human behaviour – though in different ways. American advertisers were interested, and some media researchers felt that there might be similarities in the 'repeated messages' or 'reinforcement' of television and their effects on audiences.

A now much-criticised piece of research was called the 'Bobo doll experiment' (Bandura and Walters 1963). It showed children some film of adults acting aggressively towards a 'Bobo doll', then recorded children acting in a similar way later when left alone with it. The implication (that children copy violent behaviour) was then extended to violent media content, which was asserted to have similar effects. Of course there are problems in trying to transfer findings from (unfortunate) laboratory animals to human beings:

- People (a group which includes children!) are often very willing to please those conducting experiments (and also have a shrewd sense of what responses are required to do this) – or to mess it up entertainingly.

- A simple, controlled laboratory experiment has very limited application to the complicated conditions under which we interact with the various media in our social lives.

- If people are seen as being like laboratory animals, they will be assumed to be empty vessels, passively absorbing simple television messages. **Cognitive psychologists** have argued instead that children actively construct, rather than passively receive, meanings from the media, and that these interpretations are affected by prior knowledge and experience.

- Entertainment and fiction forms, involving fantasy, group and 'cult' viewings and invitations to 'try out' identifications are much more complex media texts for those studying audiences.

- The 'effect' of watching television may not be shown in our measurable *outward* behaviour, such as voting, or shopping – or violent acts.

Other problems with the effects model

Within the effects model the influence of the media, especially television, is usually assumed to be negative, never positive. For example, if you look closely at the kinds of writing (e.g. tabloid editorials) that urge censorship, they often fall into one of two apparently contradictory positions, sometimes contributing to **moral panics**:

- The media produce inactivity, make us into 'couch potatoes', or into students who won't pass their exams or unemployed 'box-watchers' who make no effort to get a job.
- The media produce activity, but of a bad kind, such as violent 'copycat' behaviour, or mindless shopping in response to advertisements.

Of course media messages can have 'effects' of a quite simple, though immediate kind: a weather forecast may encourage you to put a coat on; the flashings of strobe lighting in films can be dangerous for epileptics. But usually the word 'effects' is claiming broader, more ideological influence for the media.

ACTIVITY 6.1

Take any recent panic over media effects. Make notes on the language of the pro-censorship writers, including

- the tell-tale use of 'them' rather than any admission of the 'we' of researchers' or campaigners' own involvement in viewing
- implications that 'things were all right' in some earlier age, often thirty years or so ago
- visual stereotyping or 'other-ing' of the group or person being panicked over.

'The mass audience' here is usually assumed to consist of the 'weaker' members of society such as women, and children, especially of the 'lower orders'. In the nineteenth century, novels were thought to be potentially harmful for such women; more recently there have been similar fears that romantic novels, and then **soaps**, render women passive, helpless, drugged with trivia.

Children also feature in such discourses: worried over in the 1950s because of the supposed harm done by American comics; then in the 1980s and 1990s in relation to 'video nasties', computer games, mobile phones. The problem is not that there are important concerns raised in these discourses (such as the radiation effects of intensive mobile phone use on still-developing brain cells) but the ways these get voiced in much of the media.

Such worries are usually strikingly isolated from other factors affecting children's use of media, such as

- underfunded or unstimulating childcare, school and leisure activities
- children's awareness and 'play' with fictional conventions, in particular the special effects of horror movies
- children's awareness that the computer skills acquired through playing games are highly job-marketable, as well as entertaining

'Let us go into the houses of the poor, and . . . discover what is the effect on the maiden mind of the trash the maiden buys . . . the . . . pretensions of the young girls of the period, their dislike of manual work and love of freedom, spring largely from notions imbibed in . . . perusal of their penny fiction' (Edward Salmon 1888).

• the pleasure of 'escaping' into the text messaging of mobile phones, as well as the safety and convenience with making arrangements they can offer.

Figure 6.1 Debates have raged over the effect on child audiences of characters such as the BBC's *Teletubbies* (offering the media, and us, a chance to print the Teletubbies' picture).

Thinking about the models underlying different approaches makes it easier to see when the logic of a particular model has led researchers to 'throw out the baby with the bathwater', as has happened with some effects work.

More sophisticated research into broader *influences* of the media emphasise the capacity of television to affect our *perceptions* of violence, politics, strikes etc.

• Gerbner and Gross (1976) produced work in the US which suggested that the more television you watch, the more likely you are to have a fearful attitude to the world outside the home. (These questions have been revived recently around British television programmes such as *Crimewatch*.)

- Lazarsfeld *et al.* (1944) explored, over six months, the influence exerted on voters by the media during an American presidential campaign. They concluded that voters were very resistant to media influence since individual predispositions or political preference influenced which media they consulted. The term *two-step flow* was coined to describe the important influence of local opinion leaders, whose views often mediated those offered by the media. Media effect began to be seen as one of reinforcement and *intervening variables* rather than radical change, or brainwashing.

- Greg Philo's (1990) work some years after the British coal strike of 1984–5 suggested another form of 'effect'. Over a period of time audiences tended to forget details of news reporting but they did remember key themes and phrases, such as 'picket line violence'. These, through repetition, became part of popular consciousness, and then memory about the strike, even if it could be shown at the time that they were mythical or exaggerated.

When the coal strike was over, the National Council for Civil Liberties reported that 'contrary to the impression created by the media, most of the picketing during the strike has been orderly and on a modest scale'.

The uses and gratifications model

The uses and gratifications model first found expression in the US in the 1940s and has usually been associated with television, and with socio-psychological approaches to media. More recently it has been discussed as though it was the same approach as socio-cultural approaches to audience negotiations with media (see Gray 1999 and below). Those are in fact rather different.

In the 1950s however the US research seemed like a breath of fresh air, resisting the easy pessimism and crudely behaviourist emphases of effects work. Researchers (often well funded and sometimes associated with advertisers) questioned people as to why they watched television, and concluded that 'personality types' in the audience gave rise 'to certain needs, some of which are directed to the mass media for satisfaction' (Morley 1991). These needs were grouped in such categories as cognitive (learning); affective (emotional satisfaction); tension release (relaxation); personal integrative (help with issues of personal identity); social integrative (help with issues of social identity) etc.

Unlike the Frankfurt School's position, this model was clearly not interested in critiquing capitalist mass culture. Indeed some of its extreme adherents came close to denying *any* influence for the media, and never explored critically such concepts as 'social integration' – integrated into what, exactly? Just as metaphors of drugs, addiction, passivity characterise the 'effects' tradition, so the largely US 'uses' approaches positively buzz with words like 'choice', 'consuming' and 'users'. This has one big attraction: we're

Figure 6.2 An audience illustrating the 'uses and gratifications' model?

much more likely to *want* to identify ourselves as active readers, zap-happy operators of the television remote control, than as the passive dupes of some brainwashing media corporation. (There are fascinating comparisons with free-market imagery in general here.)

Later writers (see Lewis 1992; Jenkins 2000; Barker and Brooks 1998; Hills 2002) explored the activity of **fans** and 'cult' viewers, whose pleasure in certain texts could be miles away from either the meaning intended by their makers or the meaning produced by most other viewers. Moreover, with the development of the Internet, these fans were able, in a limited way, to become 'producers' of their own episodes of favourite shows (such as *Xena* or *Buffy*) as well as consumer activists, lobbying television companies who wrote out a favourite character for example.

Research methods and assumptions about audiences

Content analysis

Quantitative analysis is often compared to *qualitative analysis*, which is usually conducted with many fewer interviewees, often within exploratory interview conditions, perhaps over some time. This can lead to 'a stand-off between theories of mass audiences, on the one hand, and increasingly detailed accounts of particular instances on the other' (Geraghty in 1998).

Content or *quantitative* analysis, as it's also called, is based on counting the frequency of certain elements in a clearly defined sample, and then analysing those frequencies (see Rose 2001: 56). The selected quantities must be 'coded', that is a set of descriptive categories or labels are attached to them, such as 'headlines involving the word "asylum seeker"'. These should be unambiguous, such that 'different researchers at different times using the same categories would code the images in exactly the same way' (Rose 2001: 62), which it is claimed makes the process **replicable**. It's a useful method because, as Lutz and Collins (1993) explain of their magazine photos research, 'It does allow . . . discovery of patterns that are too subtle to be visible on casual inspection and protection against an unconscious search through the magazine for only those which confirm one's sense of what the photos say or do' (Lutz and Collins 1993: 89).

ACTIVITY 6.2

Take a question which you're curious about (e.g. 'How are "boy" and "girl" bands represented across "teen" magazines in a chosen week?').

• Flick through, say, the magazines and jot down your impression of the proportion of your two chosen 'categories'.

• Then conduct a content analysis (perhaps of column inches, or numbers of photos, articles etc.) and see how the two results compare. Do they confirm what Lutz and Collins suggest?

Content analysis is popular also partly because numbers, unlike languages, form a universal 'currency', and can be read even when their author is not there to explain them. It is seen as more 'scientific', more full of 'hard facts' than other approaches. Partly as a result it is a powerful, often well-funded model of research into audiences. Unfortunately a jump is often made from its quantitative research findings to media speculation about the 'obvious' evidence of the supposed effects of the media. The **violence debate** for example is full of 'countings'. Rightly concerned when horrible murders etc. take place, campaigners then make the huge leap of arguing that these might be prevented by censoring 'violence on television', meaning *countable* 'acts of violence'. This ignores

'Content analysis: counting what you (think you) see' (Rose 2001: 54).

- the problem of defining the violence that is to be counted. It may seem quite a simple thing to decide what to count as 'violence' or 'violent acts' on television or in computer games. Yet the question of what, in our culture, gets *perceived* as 'violence' is a huge one. Some kinds of activity are labelled 'violent' and others aren't: the latter are sometimes called 'threatening' or 'restraining' or 'keeping the peace', for example.

- the differences between the many *kinds* of media representations that get counted. A familiar example: is the 'violence' in a *Tom and Jerry* cartoon, or a Nintendo game the same as the violence seen in a news bulletin?

So it is crucial to emphasise that what matters is the quality of the questions asked, and then the conclusions drawn. These can be much more difficult for visual or audio-visual forms than for printed ones.

'Since the late '20s an entire research tradition (on violence and media) whose total expenditure must run into hundreds of millions of dollars and pounds, and . . . guaranteed serious political reception and "front page" media coverage . . . , has dominated the media research agenda – and achieved nothing' (Martin Barker, letter to *Sight and Sound*, August 1995).

Rose (2001) focuses on the Lutz and Collins work researching into *National Geographic* magazines. They suggest four themes emerge from their content analysis: the depiction of Third World peoples as exotic, idealized, naturalized and sexualised. These did not appear in their list of coding categories but emerged by amalgamating those with the theoretical and empirical literature on which their study drew.

> Thus 'idealized' was formed from a number of codes: 'smiling in a photo', 'group size', 'aggressive activity' and 'wealth indicators' . . . Non-Westerners are not shown as ill or very poor or hungry or deformed: instead they are given the qualities that the North American *National Geographic* would like to see: happy, not too badly off; hard-working, content.
>
> (Rose 2001: 65)

As with any media text, *the counting of elements that can be counted* is a circular process, which sometimes ignores the ways codes and resonances of meaning are combined, let alone what audiences might be doing with 'texts'. If researchers talked about 'counting combinations', it might be clearer what a

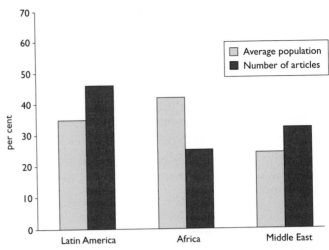

Figure 6.3 Communicating the results of content analysis by means of a graph: actual proportion of regional populations compared to *National Geographic* articles published on Latin America, Africa and the Middle East as a percentage of the total articles in the magazine, 1950–86 (Lutz and Collins 1993: 121).

complex business this would be. In the case of film or television, for instance, it would have to combine the 'act of violence' with

- its place in the narrative
- the stance that the audience is *invited*, but only 'invited', to take up in relation to it (by camera movement, positioning, editing, costume, lighting, set design etc.)
- casting (e.g. is a sympathetic star involved?)
- intertextual reference (is a joke being made about another text which somewhat changes the status of the act?)
- the historical stage of its genre (is it a western or horror film at a stage when audiences are likely to be blasé about special effects of violent death?) (see Barker and Petley (eds) 2001)
- the full social context in which it 'plays' (e.g. are guns widely available, represented as desirable possessions?)

'It is the height of hypocrisy for Senator Dole [powerful US Republican politician], who wants to repeal the assault weapons ban, to blame Hollywood for the violence in our society' (Oliver Stone, June 1995).

ACTIVITY 6.3

Take a recent film or television programme which was called 'violent'. Decide what genre it is part of. Go through the above list and decide:

- What would you say is its 'message' about violence?
- How would you argue this (see checklist above)?
- How might this strike: (1) an audience experienced in its genre? (2) an audience inexperienced in its genre?

Finally, it's worth noting that certain vivid representations of violence may have not negative but positive effects in the revulsion they invite us to feel, for example at certain kinds of assault, or military power, or bullying.

ACTIVITY 6.4

Think back to the most horrifying or frightening moment in a media text that you have ever experienced.

- How does it fit into the discussion above?
- Why was it so horrifying for you?
- Did anyone else share your feeling?
- What kind of text, what kind of genre was it part of? Fairy tale? Cartoon? News?
- Did this make a difference to how you understood it?

Semiotics and audiences

Semiotic and structuralist approaches to meaning were explored in Britain from the 1960s onwards. Questions such as

See Chapter 1.

- How does this programme or ad or movie *produce meaning?*
- With what *codes and conventions* is it operating?

promised to understand the making of meaning as a much more mediated, active and social process than the simple counting of elements in media texts.

But the theories, along with speculation from psychoanalytic approaches, were often applied in extremely text-isolated ways (notably to films in *Screen* in the 1970s, and later to television by others). One example was an emphasis on the assumed powers of the Hollywood editing system (and later television) to 'suture' (stitch) or position 'the spectator' in certain ways, making only one reading possible, however unconscious readers were of that position. Most influential was Laura Mulvey's 1975 argument, heavily couched in psychoanalytic terms (*fetishism, voyeurism, scopophilia*), that audiences were put into masculine, and therefore inevitably **voyeuristic** positions by Hollywood films through the ways in which women on screen are rendered 'to-be-looked-at' (by lighting, editing, positioning as well as narrative placement) while it is usually the male characters who are doing that looking and have control over it, and over the narrative. Key questions put to this immensely influential position, by writers who included the later Mulvey herself, included:

Voyeurism the pleasure of looking while unseen (here accounted for in Freudian terms), used in thinking about male pleasure in the ways cinema constructs women as 'objects of the gaze'. 'In the 1970s the feminist slogan "Who does this ad think you are?" pasted across street advertisements, sought to expose the hidden power of *address* to position women as subordinate' (Gledhill 1997: 370).

- How do women in the audience respond to such moments? Is there no escape from this predetermined 'position'?
- What of lesbian viewers, who might be reluctant to go along with such attacks on taking pleasure in the female image?

- What happens in genres which try to address a female audience directly (e.g. the 'woman's film' or romantic comedies)?
- Can the theory be applied to television, with its very different, less compelling screen size, its more 'open' unending soap narratives, its more fluid invitations to identify via a glancing rather than gazing 'look'?

Despite using the language of revolution (with terms such as *regime*, *subversion*, *radical*), *Screen* theory was often almost totally uninterested in what actual audiences might be doing with these 'texts'. A key, though slippery, distinction began to be made. These *'ideal spectators'* (or 'subject-positions created by the text', and by such theories) could be distinguished from the *social audience* for those texts at any given period in time (e.g. groups who were interviewed, and therefore constructed, by a more **empirical** approach).

The encoding/decoding model

See Chapter 5.

At the same time, during the 1970s, the Centre for Contemporary Cultural Studies (**CCCS**) at Birmingham University, under Stuart Hall, worked with a combination of semiotic, structuralist and more sociological approaches (see Gray 1999 for fuller account). Hall's position paper 'The television discourse – encoding and decoding' (1974) opposed or 'refreshed' several key approaches. It was written in opposition to 'content analysis' and other approaches assuming an easily measurable if not transparent relation between text and audience. It was also a move within Marxist debates, away from the 'single' idea of a dominant ideology to Gramsci's more complex model of a hegemony which has to be constantly struggled for and negotiated.

Hall's position also went beyond then current uses and gratifications approaches, insisting instead that, far from being autonomous and utterly individualised, audience members share certain frameworks of interpretation and that they worked at **decoding** media texts rather than being 'affected' in a passive way. David Morley's (again very underfunded) work, some with Charlotte Brunsdon, on the *Nationwide* early evening magazine programme tried to focus on

- power structures *outside* the text which shape audience members: class, gender, ethnicity, age and so on
- power structures *within* the text and media institutions. These mean that such programmes are often under pressure, or try to promote, a 'preferred reading' which is argued to be in line with dominant ideologies, but which struggles with other possible meanings in a text.

This broadly Gramscian model of hegemonic power in the media (power which was constantly having to work to win consent, rather than just being imposed from above) went along with Hall's three types of audience readings:

- **dominant**, or *dominant hegemonic*, where the reader recognises what a programme's 'preferred' or offered meaning is and broadly agrees with it (the flag-waving patriot who responds enthusiastically to President George W. Bush's latest speech)
- **oppositional**, where the dominant meaning is recognised but rejected for cultural, political or ideological reasons (the pacifist who understands the speech but rejects it)
- **negotiated**, where the reader accepts, rejects or refines elements of the programme in the light of previously held views (the viewer who agrees with the need to respond to the attacks of 11 September 2001 but does not agree with the military means which Bush announces).

Questions were later raised about this work, not least by David Morley. These are useful to get a sense of debates in the field:

- Does it still see media as a kind of conveyor belt for pre-made (especially ideological) meanings or messages?
- Does it blur together a number of processes? Are viewers' activities better thought of as 'comprehension/incomprehension' rather than 'agreement/disagreement' or 'decoding', for example?
- How is class defined in this context of 'dominant/oppositional'? Is it equated too easily with occupation? What of age, gender, ethnicity, sexual orientation for example?
- What about *entertainment* forms? Much other audience work had stayed with 'hard' news and documentary, though *Nationwide* was a mix of entertainment and current affairs. Where pleasure and play are even more central, can we still use the idea of a single preferred meaning?
- Questioning people about videotaped programmes in a college setting (and on a low research budget) is fine. But how likely would they be to watch those kinds of programmes outside that setting? This leads to considerations of **genres**, **discourses** and *domestic contexts for viewing* (see below).

Overall, however, Hall's work and the *Nationwide* studies are important because they

- saw both audience and text as social structures, within relations of power
- opened up interest in more empirical studies of television audiences
- drew attention to the place of entertainment and fiction forms
- drew attention to the specific domestic contexts in which viewing usually takes place.

Audience ethnographies

More recently there has been a turn to audience **ethnographies**, or fieldwork research, largely derived from **anthropology**, where the researcher attempts to enter intensively into the culture of a particular group and provide an account of its meanings and activities 'from the inside'. He or she often employs *participant observation* methods, participating in the lives of the groups to be studied for an extended period of time, asking questions and observing what goes on. When the research is written up, it often tries to show a respect for the group studied by providing life histories, case studies and verbatim quotes from them. Problems remain:

- How can the observer ever know the extent to which his or her questions, presence even, have affected the group 'under observation'?
- Have questions, and what the researcher hears in the answers to them, been selected to fit his or her pre-existing agenda or theory?
- There is usually an imbalance in power between researcher and researched. How might this affect the findings?

Nevertheless, it seems likely that more can be learnt from careful ethnographic accounts than from the assertions of theory on its own, or from simple, number-crunched questionnaires alone. The key areas which recent media ethnographic work has investigated include

- the domestic contexts of reception
- genre and cultural competence
- technologies and consumption, including 'eavesdropping' on Internet users (see Gray forthcoming).

Contexts of reception and 'cultural competences'

Morley (1986), Gray (1992) and others (see Geraghty 1998) explored ways in which the home – or rather, the 'domestic context' for most television viewing – structures viewing. Such research suggested that the home, far from being simply 'the private sphere', our 'retreat from the world', is in fact as cross-cut by social power as anywhere else. In particular, television viewing is often structured by gender and age power relations. A few examples:

- For men, often coming home after work or a day spent outside it, viewing can be an experience very different from what it is for women, who, whether or not they work outside the home, are likely to see it as a place of (house)work. It's much easier for men to watch in an uninterrupted way than it is for women, who are often expected to manage the interruptions and disputes that break out among children.
- Because women's (house)work is always there, in the home, women have spoken of their pleasure in carving out time for themselves to refuse their domestic duties for a while and enjoy a video, or a novel.
- The remote control, and who wields it, has long been a key symbol of power within families (and other groups). Even when many children have a television or computer screen in their own room, it remains significant.

All this has powerful implications for theories which imply a very concentrated relationship of viewer or text. Television viewing has never really felt like that a lot of the time. This is partly because of the **flow** which Raymond Williams (1974) and others have suggested is the characteristic experience of television, especially in commercially funded systems, keen to keep fingers off channel buttons so as to sell more audience attention to advertisers.

Television is now not the only media technology in the home. Research from the London School of Economics in 1999 suggested that computer games, CD-Roms and the Internet (not to mention mobile phones) have created a new world of 'living together separately' in the home. Two out of three children now have their own television set in their bedroom. Even more working-class children (71 per cent) than middle-class children (54 per cent) have their own sets. Yet, asked what their definition of a good time was, young people opted for 'going out with my friends'. Watching television was frequently mentioned as involved in a boring day (see *Guardian* editorial 'Bedroom culture: children want more than television', 20 March 1999).

Williams argued, on first experience of US television, that television and radio are not experienced as composed of separate items or programmes but more often as a *flow* of similar segments ('watching television'). If you have seen any US television *in the US* you will know how confusingly adverts flow into and through programmes, without any separation.

ACTIVITY 6.5

Interview your friends or other students to find out:

- How many televisions do you have in your household? Where are they? Are they all colour sets, all the same quality and size? Who uses which?
- Have you ever successfully waged, or needed to wage, a struggle for the remote control? How did you do this? With what results?
- Do you watch any programmes because you know you'll disagree with them, or enjoy ridiculing them?
- Do you have 'special occasion' viewing? If so, what arrangements do you make? Does this make television viewing more like cinema going?
- Do you use television as part of a relationship – to mend it, or help begin one, or even to avoid conversation?

Bourdieu's concept of **cultural competence** is useful in understanding the cultural contexts of media use, and the pleasures which particular audiences or readerships take in different media forms. It suggests that the media or art forms that we feel easy and familiar with are related to our social class position via the *cultural competences* we have acquired (competence here does not mean correctness or efficiency but shared knowledge and perspectives). Of course, in turn, media or art forms are socially valued in different ways, so we now need to add 'technologies' to the list of processes which involve status and competences.

Pierre Bourdieu French cultural sociologist and later anti-globalisation activist (1930–2002). Began ethnographic work after being conscripted into the French army during the Algerian War of 1958. *Distinction: A Social Critique of the Judgement of Taste* (1984) explored how the supposedly natural, universal quality of 'taste' is actually formed along class, cultural and educational lines.

Contexts of reception and 'cultural competences'

'So what was the significance of that little look then?' (much-used male query on soaps and everyday interactions within them).

'When I was 3 or 4 my mother was already teaching me to see dust and other people's feelings' (woman interviewed by Shere Hite 1988).

As an example of the role of this theory, it was assumed, for example, until the 1970s that women's soaps and magazines were an inferior media form, which anyone could understand, though in which only a rather stupid or trivial-minded audience would be interested. But feminist work such as Charlotte Brunsdon's (1981) suggested that the pleasures offered to women by soap opera required particular 'feminine' learnt skills and competencies, for example reading 'emotional turmoil, understanding the complexities of familiar relationships' (Gray 1999: 28). Women were more likely to realise the significance of certain kinds of looks between characters, small-scale gestures, silences and so on, or to feel easy with a lot of 'relationship talk' ('yakkety yak' to those hostile to soaps). Their involvement in the skills of the domestic meant that they were competent to pick up on key parts of soaps' narratives, carried by such intimate gesture and talk.

Women are argued to have access to such competences through years of informal training for their presumed future role as caring mothers; or as carers in jobs such as nursing or teaching; or through their confinement to the home, except in periods of high male unemployment. We don't want to argue that no male viewers ever come upon, or have developed, the competences to enjoy romances or soaps, nor that some women may not be irritated by those forms. But informal gender training from early on means that certain responses to some genres (like the sad-ending romance) are from very early on made unacceptable for some groups ('big boys don't cry') and natural-seeming for others.

From the male side of *gendered competences* it's been argued that boys are socialised from early on into acting tough in the face of 18-rated videos, computer games and horror films, which they sometimes find hard to stomach. Our culture still expects men, in the end, to differentiate themselves from women along the lines of 'toughness'. Young men are encouraged not to cry, not to explore feelings and to try to appear as decisive and hard as the heroes of action adventures. (The swift decisions necessitated in computer gaming often seem to embody these qualities.) Fortunately they do not all follow this encouragement.

ACTIVITY 6.6

To explore the relative status of cultural competences in your household:

- Jot down whether certain people seem to find some genres difficult to follow and need to have help in finding out 'what's going on'. Does this relate to what might be called 'cultural competences' in some genres and not others?
- Are any of your viewing choices ever ridiculed by other members of your household?
- If so, in what terms, and about what kinds of programmes?

- How insistent or lighthearted or serious is the ridiculing?
- Does it ever prevent you from watching the programme?
- It could be argued that, with recent changes in employment patterns and the rethinkings of masculinity which some argue have followed, males are now as likely as women to make such readings. What is your experience? Use your favourite soap and observations of the gendered nature of how friends 'read' these parts of it.

The Simpsons often operates a 'double mode of address', using 'adult' allusions and jokes, which may fly 'over the head' of the assumed child audience. *Xena: Warrior Princess* has likewise been said to produce the possibility of a 'parallel' lesbian reading alongside the 'children's adventure story' of its main marketing.

Bourdieu suggested that in capitalist societies there is an analogy or likeness between the ways in which access to capital (economic power) is distributed between different groups, and the ways that some groups will have access to 'cultural competences' that have higher status than others (such as knowledge of literary allusions, or, now, of computer terminology). Some theorists of **cult** forms (such as 'trash television' or movies) have suggested that fans have the privilege of 'double access' to both 'naive' enjoyment of the form 'for itself', and a knowing humour at its codes. Further, they suggest that this, rather than older familiarities with 'high' cultural forms such as Shakespeare or opera, is the form which cultural privilege or 'capital' now takes. Such knowingness seems particularly marked in some fan cultures.

See *Buffy* case study following Chapter 3.

ACTIVITY 6.7

- Do you ever describe yourself as an 'addict' of a media form (programme, magazine, novel)?
- Do you think this is a way of apologising for your interest in it?

Others interested in 'cultural competences' have researched the reasons for young women's reluctance to use computers. This work suggests not that young women are incapable of using machines or technology but that they resist, or feel ill at ease in, the world of the 'computer virtuosos', the 'techno-heads' – young men who seem to be involved in an intimate relationship with their machines, one which is often strongly competitive and macho – 'mine's bigger and faster than yours' – centred on very masculine games genres, such as the action adventure and science fiction, and valuing the playing skill of decisiveness. Attempts are being made to counter such perceptions, both in television programmes and in schools, since a very real fear is that the predicted 'information-rich' and 'information-poor' distinction will work along the lines not simply of class, and the world's North–South divide, but also of gender.

'According to the Sixth World Wide Web User Survey, almost 70% of users are male . . . Alan Durndell [a researcher] found that by the time they were 15 or 16, when important career choices were being made, girls were turned off by "violent and immature" computer games' (*Guardian*, 21 December 1996).

Figure 6.4 An ad which tries to visualise the huge 'audience' for the Net, and to shift notions of the typical user.

ACTIVITY 6.8

Do you experience such gender contrasts? Collect some recent images of scientists and computers in PC magazine advertising and television programmes such as *Tomorrow's World*.

- How far do they conform to the suggestions above? How do they represent machines? What efforts seem to be being made to change the gender balance of such images?

Finally: the audience 'in' the media?

There have been many ways in which audience members have tried to 'enter' media so as to influence media practices. **Access** for example, has traditionally meant programme-making where power, including editorial control, is handed over to a group or individual outside the broadcasting institutions. The BBC's *Open Space* slot, or Channel 4's *Right to Reply* are examples. These question old ideas of 'balance between two sides' in broadcasting, and instead try to represent a plurality of voices, especially those from outside television's often cosy world, where professionals are often said to make programmes partly for each other's approval.

The audience-in-the-media can also be thought of in the expansion of (cheap) daytime television talk shows and in interactive computer technologies (and indeed the potential merging of the two in digital television). Radio and television phone-ins, magazines, access television and chat shows routinely allow parts of the audience 'into' the media, though on rather special terms.

ACTIVITY 6.9

Take your favourite radio phone-in or television chat show and examine on what terms members of the audience manage to get a hearing. Look at the following:

- What does the title sequence promise?
- How is the studio set up, both visually and aurally?
- How does the host organise things such as interruptions, noise levels, 'expert' contributions, escalation of conflict?
- How is the show concluded or summed up?
- What kinds of ideas and positions can be most easily circulated or marginalised through such shows?
- What seem to have been the criteria for choosing the experts used in it?
- What is the most surprising or unfamiliar position you have ever heard voiced on such shows? How was it treated?

So many people organised by e-mail to put 'Knights of the Jedi' on their official census form as a 'religion' (10,000 were needed) that the ONS (Office on National Statistics) has given the creed an official numerical code, 896, making it a religion within the 'other' [religion] category. (report in *Independent*, 11 October 2001)

Again, in relation to news forms, **opinion polls** are a crucial form in which a rather weird 'snapshot' of a supposedly representative sample of the audience is given media space (see Lewis 2001). These are highly constructed: the pollsters construct the questions; key phrases designed to trigger certain responses (such as 'asylum seekers') are often used to structure the parameters of discussion; and the work of street questioning is poorly paid and hard to check. Then, the print and television media select which parts of the results to emphasise, amplify or ignore – as in such as repeated evidence in both the UK and US that people polled want good health, education and public services and would consider higher taxes to pay for them. Repeatedly in elections, for example, polling is interested not so much in discussion of such policies as in the 'horse-race' aspect of politics: who's ahead? There is some pressure to ban such polls during elections, given their potential influence on the perceived result. (Lewis (2001) argues that for US polls it is probably more important to watch how the huge money from corporate sponsors is coming in, as it did for George W. Bush in 2001.) Altogether they form a fascinating case study of myths of audience participation. Both Blair and Clinton have been represented as 'poll-driven' or 'focus-group politicians' whereas the evidence is that such moments of 'audience' visibility are ignored where they conflict with elite interests or drives.

The other huge new area for the apparent 'visibility' of audiences in media forms has been around fandom as it relates to new technologies, especially the Internet, and to entertainment forms. We've already mentioned the way that the Internet allows fans to produce alternative versions of their favourite shows or films (being followed now by digital versions of *Stars Wars*, for example: see Hills 2002). The entry of fans into higher education has also led, via writings on fandom, to greater visibility to such audience creativity and pressure on media makers. New television formats such as *Big Brother*, *Pop Stars* and *Pop Idol* have not only put sections of 'the audience' literally on stage, in auditions for example, but has also, through lucrative tie-in deals with mobile phone companies, allowed viewers to vote on which contestants should be eliminated from the shows.

'The internet has allowed the three core [Trinidad-ian] values to be realised for the first time in one individual: . . . being in the vanguard of style; maximising oneself through education in designer schools; and displaying entrepreneurial acumen by successfully by-passing standard channels of education. No wonder this has made the net "hot" and explains how it is greeted with the "heady aura" of carnival rather than as a bastion of high-tech super-geekdom' (Aniruddho Sanyal, reviewing Miller and Slater 2001, *Times Higher Education Supplement*, 7 December 2001).

> 8.7 million viewers phoned in to vote in the final of *Pop Idol*, beating all other phone polls. There were so many viewers that the National Grid called ITV to find out what time the ad breaks were taking place, so that they could prevent the nation from being plunged into a power cut. Controversy raged the next Monday as to whether there were enough phone lines to take the full capacity of the votes. The website also broke a record, with 60,000 logging on (partly summarised from the *Pop Idol* official website, 9 February 2002).

Such developments demonstrate one of the key early positions of Media Studies: that makers and audiences are each active on both sides of meaning-making. However, we also need to bear in mind the inequalities and structuring of these developments, as well as the hype with which such 'active freedoms' are often announced. Some inequalities are 'of necessity': all media, especially television and cinema, are expensive; and since their audiences are counted in billions it is hard to imagine how 'the audience' could ever have full access to the media, let alone all have appreciative audiences for their own creations.

But other kinds of structuring can be understood in terms of the continued power of the producing institutions to wield control, though never absolute control, over 'texts'. Fans love the characters and utopian 'spaces for play' made available by the producers of *Buffy* or the *Star Wars* series but equally they resent the huge powers of copyright, cost, censorship, scheduling and publicity decisions which the producing corporations maintain and patrol.

It has been argued, in some celebrations of new types of 'programmes' such as *Big Brother* (or *Pop Idol*) that 'the audience' become part of 'the text'. (There's often a slip back into ideas of 'an audience' in discussions of such television, for example, in assertions such as 'a definition of who the audience might be is revolutionised by the multi-platform access of *Big Brother*'. In fact media theory has for some years been aware of the need to think of various 'audiences' and their different relations with media, rather than 'the audience' of the block figures announced by ratings or box office receipts.)

As well as consisting of 'ordinary' people and showcasing a range of social identities in the chosen characters who got through all the auditions, *Big Brother* enabled its audiences to vote and thereby change the outcomes of the ongoing 'narrative'. They could participate in discussions and votes in other media (especially the Internet, and tabloid print forms) which could then enter into the programme itself, for example in decisions as to what the voice over and editing might emphasise in the following episode. Moreover for people who accessed *Big Brother* by the continuous webcam there was the chance to see (almost) all of the material from which the edited, broadcast version was made up.

But again the power of the producing institution and the limits to democratisation of the media both risk being underestimated in such celebrations. Let's take a few examples. 'The actual range of opportunities available to the audience . . . was . . . confined to removing or holding on to one or two of the nominated contestants' (Tincknell and Raghuram 2002: 211). The key sense of liveness was produced by large amounts of editing as well as by the use of apparently unmediated surveillance camerawork. Viewers' votes were highly conditioned by the repeated offering, by the 'down-to-earth' northern male voice-over, of a 'preferred' version of events which 'centred on the sexual behaviour of the contestants' (Tincknell and Raghuram 2002: 210). In these processes, like the daytime talk shows on which it drew, the programme tended to support a particular, hegemonic definition of 'ordinary people' as those who are not experts, not even fans with expert knowledge, nor people greatly interested in the outside world (a 'sealing off' which was built into the programme's design).

See Chapter 3 for more on the economics, 'multi-platform delivery' pleasures and whole design of *Big Brother*.

The Channel 4 website chat line for *Beneath the Veil* (2001), Saira Shah's personal television documentary about her dangerous journey into the heart of her father's country, Afghanistan, made before 11 September 2001, broke all precedents in the history of Channel 4. It turned out to be the most extensive chat service the channel had ever hosted; chatters continued until they crashed Channel 4's servers at 3 a.m. Undaunted, they started again the next day. No chat on the *Big Brother* site has ever reached this level of activity (www.channel4.co.uk/plus/afghanistan).

Nevertheless the international success of *Big Brother* made visible a lot of the excitement and hopes around a democratised media. This poses a key question for news and other non-fiction genres. Corporate media and 'deregulated' markets have profitably catered for enthusiasm and some audience participation in fiction or entertainment forms. For news perhaps we need to argue that those who are passionately involved in anti-corporate global politics and the Internet are 'fans of political discussion' who deserve equally imaginative media forms?

References

Bandura, A. and Walters, R. (1963) *Social Learning and Personality Development*, New York: Holt, Rinehart & Winston.

Barker, Martin and Brooks, Kate (1998) *Knowing Audiences 'Judge Dredd': Its Friends, Fans and Foes*, Luton: University of Luton Press.

Barker, Martin and Petley, Julian (eds) (2001, 2nd edition) *Ill Effects: The Media/Violence Debate*, London and New York: Routledge.

Bourdieu, Pierre (1984) *Distinction: A Social Critique of the Judgement of Taste*, London: Routledge.

Brunsdon, Charlotte (1981) '*Crossroads:* notes on soap opera', *Screen*, vol. 22, no. 4: 52–7.

Cohen, S. (1972) *Folk Devils and Moral Panics*, Oxford: Martin Robertson.

Geraghty, Christine (1991) *Women and Soap Opera: A Study of Prime Time Soaps*, London: Polity.

Geraghty, Christine (1998) 'Audiences and "ethnography": questions of practice', in C. Geraghty and D. Lusted (eds) *The Television Studies Book*, London and New York: Arnold.

Gerbner, G. and Gross, L. (1976) 'Living with television: the violence profile', *Journal of Communication*, no. 28.

Gledhill, Christine (1997) 'Genre and gender: the case of soap opera', in Stuart Hall (ed.) *Representation: Cultural Representations and Signifying Practices*, London, Thousand Oaks, New Delhi: Sage.

Gray, Ann (1992) *Video Playtime: The Gendering of a Leisure Technology*, London: Routledge.

Gray, Ann (1999) 'Audience and reception research in retrospective: the trouble with audiences', in Pertti Alasuutari (ed.) *Rethinking the Media Audience*, London: Sage.

Hall, Stuart (1974) 'The television discourse – encoding and decoding', *Education and Culture* no. 25 (UNESCO), reprinted in Ann Gray and Jim McGuigan (eds) (1997), *Studying Culture*, London: Arnold.

Hills, Matt (2002) *Fan Cultures*, London and New York: Routledge.

Hite, Shere (1988) *The Hite Report on Women and Love: A Cultural Revolution in Progress*, London: Viking.

Jenkins, Henry (2000) 'Reception theory and audience research: the mystery of the vampire's kiss', in Christine Gledhill and Linda Williams (eds) *Reinventing Film Studies*, London and New York: Arnold.

Lazarsfeld, P., Berelson, B. and Gaudet, H. (1944) *The People's Choice*, New York: Duell, Sloan and Pearce.

Lewis, Justin (2001) *Constructing Public Opinion: How Political Elites Do What They Like and Why We Seem to Go Along With It*, New York: Columbia University Press.

Lewis, Lisa, (ed.) (1992) *The Adoring Audience: Fan Culture and Popular Media*, London: Routledge.

Lutz, Catherine and Collins, Jane (1993) *Reading National Geographic*, Chicago: University of Chicago Press

Miller, Daniel and Slater, Don (2001) *The Internet: An Ethnographic Approach*, Oxford: Berg.

Morley, David (1980) *The Nationwide Audience*, London: BFI.

Morley, David (1986) *Family Television: Cultural Power and Domestic Leisure*, London: Comedia.

Morley, David (1991) 'Changing paradigms in audience studies', in E. Seiter, H. Borchers, G. Krentzner and E. Warth (eds) *Remote Control Television: Audiences and Cultural Power*, London and New York: Routledge.

Philo, Greg (1990) *Seeing and Believing: The Influence of Television*, London and New York: Routledge.

Rose, Gillian (2001) *Visual Methodologies*, London: Sage.

Strinati, Dominic (1995) *An Introduction to Theories of Popular Culture*, London and New York: Routledge.

Ticknell, Estella and Raghuram, Parvati (2002) '*Big Brother*: reconfiguring the "active" audience of cultural studies?', *European Journal of Cultural Studies*, vol. 5, no. 2.

Williams, Raymond (1958) 'Culture is ordinary', in *Resources of Hope: Culture, Democracy, Socialism*, London and New York: Verso, 1988.

Williams, Raymond (1974, 2nd edition 1990) *Television: Technology and Cultural Form*, London: Fontana.

Further reading

Billig, Michael (1993) *Speaking of the Royal Family*, London: Sage.

Gray, Ann (forthcoming) *Lived Cultures: Ethnographic Methods in Cultural Studies*, London: Sage.

Moores, Sean (1993) *Interpreting Audiences: The Ethnography of Media Consumption*, London: Sage.

Staiger, Janet (1992) *Interpreting Films: Studies in the Historical Reception of American Cinema*, Princeton: Princeton University Press.

CASE STUDY: SELLING AUDIENCES

- Advertising agencies
- Television and advertising
- Scheduling
- A note on the reporting of television funding
- References
- Further reading

Academic research is a tiny body of work compared to advertising research. Remember, as you study contemporary advertising and its relation to audiences:

- The effects model of readers' engagement with the media is alive and well here. Whatever the playfulness and irony within the ads, advertising agencies need to persuade companies using them that they affect customers' buying habits. In an important sense they set out to *sell audiences* (sometimes called 'eyeballs') or at least '*audiences' attention*' to their clients.

- Yet contemporary marketing talk sounds innocent of any desire to affect people. Terms such as 'level playing field', 'the market', 'the discriminating consumer' attribute power to the picking and choosing consumer (as theorised in the uses and gratifications model). This is surprising given the time spent on researching the audience to be 'targeted'.

- Whatever the arguments about the effects on our buying habits, the very act of targeting particular groups helps to create and consolidate them. The previously unknown concept of 'the teenager', for example, was, by the late 1950s, an accepted part of advertising (and political) rhetoric. It helped to create a new identity for people in a certain age range with growing spending powers.

Advertising agencies

Ad agencies exist to devise, produce and place ads and other marketing activities for their clients, the manufacturers of (often branded) products. They are usually divided into departments specialising in ad/brand design (the 'creative' team); those buying 'suitable' spaces on television etc. (media buyers) and those who oversee the operation (account managers).

Advertisers in newspapers and magazines still use the JICNARS (Joint Industry Committee for Newspaper Advertising Research) scales (culled from the NRS or National Readership Surveys: see Stoessl 1998), originally designed to investigate magazine and newspaper sales distribution. The JICNARS scale currently divides audiences into:

Group A   upper middle class, e.g. successful business or professional

Group B   middle class, e.g. senior business or professional, but not at the top of their business etc.

Group C1 white-collar lower middle class, e.g. small tradespeople and non-manual workers

Group C2 blue-collar, skilled working class

Group D   semi- or unskilled manual workers

Group E   those at the lowest levels of subsistence, 'casual workers or those who, through sickness or unemployment, are dependent on social security schemes'.

You, dear reader, are being targeted!

'A one-day marketing conference (admission £450–£500) in June 1998 on students is advertised thus: "Love 'em or hate 'em – they're a valuable consumer group spending over £5bn per annum and that's before they've left college. Catch them now and they're yours for life"' (*Campaign* magazine, 3 April 1998).

Though such indicators of social class are important, several objections have been made to the occupation-based surveys of readerships:

- The NRS questions rely on the occupation of the 'head of the household' and assume that to be a man. But in many households the main wage-earner is a woman, or the income is made up of part-time work by both partners.
- They see the family as a single consuming unit, without generational or life-stage distinctions and conflicts.
- They underestimate the ways in which a 'flexible labour market' has brought about rapid changes of occupation, and kinds of work that no longer smoothly fit the groups used.

'40% of the population no longer has a job that fits the system at all' (*Guardian* report (17 July 1995) on the government's decision to change the way class is measured by the Office of Population Censuses and Surveys).

From the 1970s onwards agencies began to use new categories, aimed at specific audience groups, by means of **demographics** which 'measured the population in terms of occupational class, age, sex and region to read off certain values and assumptions about spending' (Brierley 1998). These often divide potential buyers by geographical location (using postcodes or national census returns). Figure 6.5 shows the kind of research offered by ACORN (A Classification of Residential Neighbourhoods).

The sale of data

The following is a sales pitch to potential buyers from an organisation which sells data about audiences which have been collected by Census return. See www.datasets.com/pages/1991cens.htm.

Data is provided at postcode sector level, at 1991 Census ward (postcode sector in Scotland) level or at Census ED level for the whole of Great Britain.

Social class categories

For familiar JICNARS social class categories (AB, C1, C2, DE), choose Census data from MapInfo. The Census offices and many other data suppliers provide data in the less well-known Census social class categories (I, II, III(M), III(N), IV). MapInfo has researched the social class definitions used and carefully re-aggregated the social class data in its Census data packs from the detailed socio-economic group (SEG) categories in the raw Census data. Interpret your data and analyse your results more easily using the traditional marketing-style social class categories AB, C1, C2, DE provided here.

- Primary Demographics Pack (Ward £995; postcode sector £995; ED £8650)

The most popular set of Census counts. Includes all the counts supplied in the Extended Key Counts Pack plus age 0–4, age 5–14, age 15–24, age 25–34, age 35–44, age 45–54, age 55–64, age 65–74, age 75+, ethnic white, ethnic black, ethnic Indian, ethnic Chinese, ethnic other Asian, single person households, social class AB, social class C1, social class C2, social class DE, armed forces, households 0 cars, households 1 car, households 2 cars, households 3+ cars, tenure owner occupied, tenure rented privately, tenure rented LA etc, dwellings detached, dwellings semi-detached, dwellings terraced, dwellings flat, dwellings other permanent, dwellings non-permanent, economically active males 16–64, economically active females 16–59, unemployed males 16–64, unemployed females 16–59, employed full time, employed part time. Includes the latest Population Updates and a table of Great Britain totals.

Psychographic profiles are another, very different approach to occupational and geographical models. They use questionnaires mailed to members of a panel who are invited to respond to statements such as: 'A woman's place is in the home' or 'The use of cannabis

---

THE MOST IMPORTANT GAP IN YOUR MARKET PLACE

We can target your leaflets one of three ways, making sure that your advertising message is delivered to the heart of your market. Our professional sales team will help you to plan your campaign. You can select by demographical breakdown, geographical area or by postcode areas.

DEMOGRAPHICAL BREAKDOWN

To make sure that your message reaches exactly the right target you can plan your campaign by demographical breakdown ie: distributing to terraced housing only. You can also use this type of targeting in conjunction with either geographical area or postcodes.

Have a look at the demographical breakdown below to see which category would suit your campaign.

CATEGORY DESCRIPTION

A Affluent Suburban Housing
B Modern Housing Higher Income
C Older Housing Intermediate Status
D Terraced Housing
E Better Off Council
F Less Well Off Council
G Poorest Council

GEOGRAPHICAL AREA

Plan your campaign by geographical area, just select the towns or villages you wish to target, i.e. West Cross, Skewen and Trallwn and we can let you know how many leaflets are needed to cover those areas. This can also be used with the demographical breakdown i.e. targeting B type households only within those areas.

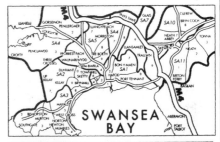

POSTCODES

You can plan your campaign by postcode areas and sectors. Just consult the map and select the sectors you wish to reach i.e. SA3 Sector 5 and we can let you know how many leaflets are required to cover your selected area. This can also be used with the demographical breakdown i.e. private housing in SA3 Sector 5.

CONTACT LORNA DAVIES

OR CONTACT NICHOLA LEWIS

Herald Direct Distribution, Cambrian House, Cambrian Place, Swansea SA1 1RH Telephone (0792) 468833 Ext 3540/3600 Fax No. (0792) 472208

Figure 6.5 Herald Direct distribution ad.

should be made legal'. On the basis of such exchanges consumers have been classified as belonging to a number of lifestyle categories – a typical model for these would be the American VALS (Values and Lifestyles) system which classifies people into: needs-driven, outer-directed, inner-directed and integrated.

Agencies may also research consumers' feelings about a product using **focus groups** of a few selected consumers presented with an issue to work on by loosely ranging talk, or asked about the image a particular product has for them, again in a freely associational way.

The availability of remote controls, video, the Internet, and more television channels and radio stations for advertising means that audiences' habits have become less easy to predict, whatever the skills of an agency's media buyers, who are assumed to know the most effective medium, and the best vehicle in that medium to carry a specific campaign.

A new medium

The Internet is being used by advertisers, and not only via the ads on many websites. 'Cookies', or small files which collect information about what users do when they visit websites, can give some picture of the user – as a potential consumer. They can be valuable not simply for market research purposes but also for targeting users with ads and offers. (See Myers 1999 and also www.cookiecentral.com.)

UK trade group rallies to save cookies

'The cookie, a . . . tag that most Internet users unknowingly carry when surfing the Web, [may be] outlawed under a proposed privacy directive from the European Commission. The legislation has triggered concern in Europe's Internet advertising community. The Interactive Advertising Bureau UK (IAB) said British companies could lose $271.8 million (£187 million) if the directive is ratified.

' "Cookies have been branded as spyware tools, or some kind of subversive software," said Danny Meadows-Klue, chairman of the IAB UK. "But it's what we use every day." ' . . . (www.cookiecentral.com, 12 November 2001).

Television and advertising

Most commercial or 'independent' television is funded through the sale of advertising space by the television companies, also described as selling audiences to advertisers. Actually it is audiences' attention which advertisers hope to purchase.

It's worth noting that, since the 1990 Broadcasting Act, sponsorship has also become a part of UK television. (It was deliberately not chosen as the main funding mechanism in the Television Act of 1954 which established commercial television.) Sponsorship is seen as a way of catching the zapping viewer with a sponsor's credit rather than (or as well as) ads during programmes, as in Vizzavi mobile phone company's sponsorship of *Pop Idol* (2002):

> Your brand is closer to the programme . . . a message before other advertising cuts in . . . It . . . allows the advertiser to build a closer relationship with a consumer . . . it's like saying 'We know what you're into and we support it too.'
>
> (*Observer*, 8 January 1995)

But the major funding system for television is one of buying and selling ad time and therefore access to certain audiences (the opposite of the notion of non-commercial public service still at work within the BBC). It began in the US during the 1930s Depression, with radio the perfect medium for advertisers wanting access to audiences confined to the home. The huge success of soap-company-funded serials (soaps) soon went along with a construction or selling of housewives' attention during the day and in the evening of men still in employment and some children. Scheduling, and the selling of advertising space in programmes likely to attract particular groups, took off, determining, and not simply following, the programmes themselves. Commercial television and radio programmes are now routinely made to attract audiences in order that advertisers can buy time or 'slots' (and more recently sponsorship deals) to catch their attention. Sometimes a guaranteed-numbers audience will be 'purchased' (measured in CPTs or Cost Per Thousand), spread across a number of slots.

'If television buyers think ITV is driving a hard bargain in its World Cup negotiations, they should ask NBC the price of a 30-second spot in *Seinfeld*. Advertisers . . . will have to pay as much as $2m [for a slot in the final episode]' (*Campaign* magazine, 3 April 1998).

ACTIVITY 6.10

Record or take notes on four or five advertising or sponsorship slots from commercial radio and television across the day, e.g. one from early morning, another from 9 a.m. or so, through to late night or early morning.

- What does this suggest about the kinds of audiences advertisers expect to be watching or listening?
- How do the surrounding programmes relate to these ads?
- Repeat the activity for broadsheet and tabloid newspapers. Look especially at the difference between 'small ads' and whole-page ones.

Huge amounts of money, time and energy are invested in audience measurement as competition between the television networks and the cable companies intensifies. This emphasis began in 1955 with the advent of ITV. 'Advertisers were terrified that people would not stay with the commercial break . . . the frequent, nervy measurement of audience totals began at this moment' (Beckett 2001). Now the main

audience assessment for BBC and ITV is conducted by **BARB** the British Audience Research Bureau, set up in 1981 to clarify the competing claims of BBC and ITV as to which had the biggest audiences. Until then the BBC had also used an 'Appreciation Index' (AI) of comments on programmes, sent in periodically by selected viewers, which were then circulated privately. (A version of this process continues today for radio, and some argue (see Bell 2001) that the system might well be revived and adapted for television via new technologies.)

BARB is a limited company, jointly owned by the BBC, ITV, Channel 4, Channel 5, BSkyB and the Institute of Practitioners in Advertising. Its data are available only to BARB subscribers, who pay a £3,000 annual registration fee and an annual subscription fee which depends on the subscriber's business (see BARB website). The company subcontracts every stage of the **ratings**-gathering process to other companies (see Beckett 2001). It compiles 'ratings' of programmes, suggesting how many, and what kinds of, viewers are watching them. These crude but 'fast' numbers are the main way in which audience appreciation of programmes is measured. They can be measured on a minute-by-minute basis, collected and digested overnight, and distributed at meetings the next morning to allow easy comparisons to be made with rivals' ratings.

These ratings are made by recording the viewing habits of a sample of viewers. (The size varies depending on how much the television company will spend.) Machines called People Meters (or 'black boxes') are attached to these viewers' television sets, and record, every five seconds, which channel the set is tuned to and which members of the household are watching. In addition the amount of VCR recording is measured, the playback of broadcast programmes which carry an electronic code, and playback of 'non-coded', bought or hired videos, in an attempt to chart audiences who are now partly freed from the schedules (see Stoessl 1998 for fuller detail).

Granada
Net Homes 2,803,000 Share 11.7

	Granada 000's	Share %
Homes	2840	100.0
Housewives and children	839	29.5
Housewives ABC 1	1167	41.1
Adults	5351	100.0
Adults 16–24	740	13.8
Adults 16–34	1787	33.4
Adults ABC 1	2323	43.4
Men	2588	48.4
Men 16–34	909	17.0
Men ABC 1	1136	21.2
Women	2763	51.6
Women 16–34	878	16.4
Women ABC 1	1187	22.2
Individuals 4+	6481	100.0
Children	1130	100.0

Source: BARB/RSMB Establishment Survey June 2000

Package A	10"	20"	30"
10 spots			
3 peak	£10,740	£14,320	£17,900

Package C	10"	20"	30"
20 spots			
7 peak	£21,480	£28,640	£35,800

Package B	10"	20"	30"
15 spots			
5 peak	£16,110	£21,480	£26,850

Package D	10"	20"	30"
25 spots			
9 peak	£26,850	£35,800	£44,750

Figure 6.6 The selling of audience attention to advertisers. ('Peaks' are ads shown between 19.15 and 23.00 hours – an interesting difference from the 'watershed' times of television's regulators. 'Spots' are ads of only 10 seconds each.)

On BARB audience arrangements: 'Officially, every time she and her boyfriend watch television now, each of them is supposed to push a button on a special remote control [as do guests who watch television]. If any one leaves the room . . . the remote control must be prodded again . . . In return she will receive regular gift vouchers, worth £10 each, to spend at shops such as Superdrug and Asda' (Beckett 2001).

However, after the recent fragmentation of British broadcasting, first by video (allowing viewers to 'reschedule' programmes), the arrival of Channel 4, and then cable, satellite and now digital and broadband forms, it has become increasingly difficult to register the small numbers of viewers for some channels. Indeed, of the three hundred television channels licensed to broadcast in the UK in 2002, several registered zero viewers on the December 2001 BARB figures.

Scheduling

Scheduling is related to ratings. John Corner defines it as a strategy within television institutions which tries to 'identify particular times of the day and particular sequences of programming in order to obtain either specific kinds of audiences or the broadest possible audience, and to obtain the best audience responses' (Corner 1991: 13).

This choice of where and when to place a programme on radio or television is usually made with a competitor's programming in mind. The classic, most notorious example was the death of Grace Archer in the then phenomenally popular radio soap *The Archers*, timed to coincide with, and draw publicity away from the launch of ITV in 1955. But broadcasters have traditionally worked with ideas such as **prime time**, the period from around 7.30 p.m. to 10.30 p.m., when large audiences are watching, though more recently the younger, hipper audiences presumed to be available after pub closing times have accounted for the later placement of some 'quality product' such as *The Mark Thomas Comedy Hour*.

It is not the case, if it ever was, that advertising simply seeks to reach the largest possible audience. At both national and global level, regional differences are carefully studied and 'pitched' to. Products are test-marketed in particular areas, for example, and some magazines produce London supplements to try to catch the attention of a concentrated and relatively affluent young audience.

However, amongst all this 'diversity' certain assumptions remain in place. Because all British broadcasting is partly public-service-regulated, both ITV and BBC have worked with the regulated Family Viewing Policy (FVP) which, drawing on effects approaches, has responded to lobbying groups such as the NVLA (National Viewers' and Listeners' Association). The FVP constructs profiles of audience availability and type, and then an image of family life from which is prescribed what should be viewable at particular times:

- 16.15 to 17.15 on weekdays is 'children's hour'.
- 17.15 to 19.30 is presumed to be family viewing time, but with all material broadcast suitable for children to view alone.
- 19.30 to 21.00 is when no material unsuitable for children viewing with the family is broadcast.
- 21.00 onwards: it is assumed that parents are responsible for any children who may still be watching. This relates to the so-called 'nine o'clock watershed', a barrier to certain kinds of language and violent or sexual imagery. Interestingly, it does not exist for radio broadcasting. (Currently the audience survey board for radio is called **RAJAR** (Radio Joint Audience Research), owned jointly by the BBC and the commercial radio stations.)

Schedulers have traditionally used the following terms:

- *pre-scheduling* Starting a programme five minutes before its rival programme on the other channel.
- *inheritance factor* Some audiences seem to 'trust' and watch one channel for most of the evening, so programmes of lesser appeal are put on after popular ones, in the hope that the audience will continue watching.
- *pre-echo* Audiences watch part of the programme before the one they want so they don't miss the beginning. This is used to try to build up an audience for the less popular programmes, and a voice over advertising upcoming programmes on the same channel now regularly accompanies the end credits of *EastEnders*, for example.
- *common junction points* Where two programmes start at the same time on BBC1 and 2, for example, the chance for cross-trailing arises: 'And now a choice of viewing on BBC.'

ACTIVITY 6.11

Watch a few hours of television on BBC or ITV at the weekend.

- What scheduling decisions seem to have been made?

- Which programmes are pitched 'against' each other within terrestrial broadcasting?
- How do the programmes connect to the ads being shown during them?
- About how much time is spent per hour advertising forthcoming programmes on the channel you are watching?

Ratings-consciousness does not apply only to commercial broadcasting. The BBC needs to justify the licence fee, and an important marker of such success is judged to be how many people are watching or listening to its programmes. Hence ratings and scheduling battles exist even where actual *sales* of audiences' attention are not involved.

There is now much emphasis on the difficulty of scheduling. Video, cable, digital, Internet and other multi-channel developments, as well as 'zapping' and the fragmentation of older 'certainties' such as family structure, all make it seem a more volatile process than previously. At the same time huge amounts of money hang on this, and the ratings process. After the somewhat chaotic launch of an enlarged (to a reported 5,300) ratings panel in January 2002, an executive with the Sci-Fi channel pointed out that the figures

determine how an estimated £3bn of advertising revenue is distributed this year. Booking of new campaigns has been affected as advertisers . . . stay away rather than trade in the dark or rely on old data. Broadcasters may be incurring substantial debts down the line as they sell time at a certain level and can't tell whether they are actually delivering the audiences the buyers expected.

(Goldsmith 2002)

It's often said that viewers are completely unpredictable, too busy 'surfing' the networks, 'grazing' across channels to be drawn in by ads, or measured by ratings. Yet

- programme-makers and advertisers still battle for 'good' slots, i.e. regular ones, and ones within prime time. Programmes (such as the controversial US sitcom *Ellen*) can be effectively stopped, not at the production level but by constantly moving them around the schedules so that viewers can't find them. This acts as a kind of censoring activity.
- effective schedulers are highly sought-after within television and radio. Witness the careers and salaries of people such as Michael Grade, renowned for his scheduling skills.
- some audiences do 'graze', at certain times of the day, but most need to have fixed viewing or listening slots in their routines which schedulers are keen to discover, and to target
- in both Britain and the US key episodes of hit dramas and comedies are not videotaped but watched as they go out. It seems that the idea of a communal viewing experience is alive and well.

Nevertheless there are many problems in relying on simple 'black box' methods for measuring television audiences and ratings, and then scheduling programmes:

- Ratings figures are not transparent in their meanings. High ratings for various programmes may be due to curiosity, the weather, the fact that there was little on other channels, etc.
- Like the use of 'testcards' for panels viewing new Hollywood releases, the emphasis on ratings often means that the unfamiliar, the new, is not given time to take root but too quickly shifted from that prime 9 p.m. or 10 p.m. slot – see Bell (2001).
- Ratings-derived advertising funding also plays havoc with one of the original arguments for the British adaptation of US commercial television: that the ITV system would be made up of regionally based companies serving and sustaining local identities. In fact the 'big three' companies (Carlton, Granada and Scottish Media Group) dominate programming; only rarely does a 'regional' programme get on to

CASE STUDY: SELLING AUDIENCES

prime-time commercial television. HTV is an interesting example, consisting of HTV West and the much bigger area, geographically, of HTV Wales simply because Wales on its own is not considered advertiser-lucrative enough to sustain major programming.

'The man [from BARB's subcontractor] had tried fitting a box to the video but couldn't manage it. He did not bother with the one in the kitchen, . . . high up on a precarious pedestal. "That's where we see the late night Channel 5 stuff that we don't want recorded" says x [BARB panel member needing to remain anonymous] with a half-joking smile . . . she also . . . likes to turn the sound off and put the radio on instead' (Beckett 2001).

'last week . . . the advertising agency Lowe Howard-Spink Lowe . . . found that at least one third of the audience "vigorously and continuously" tries to escape television commercials . . . the most zealous practitioners of this "ad avoidance" are that most desirable group, "young and early middle-aged fully employed males" (Observer, 21 May 1995).

Moreover the regional nature of commercial television allows additional advertising pressure to be applied in any region where sales are slumping. Overall, advertisers have disturbing amounts of power to shape broadcasting by niche marketing, encouraging the making of certain television genres and constructing others as unprofitable or even undesirable. Worryingly, it has been suggested that advertisers

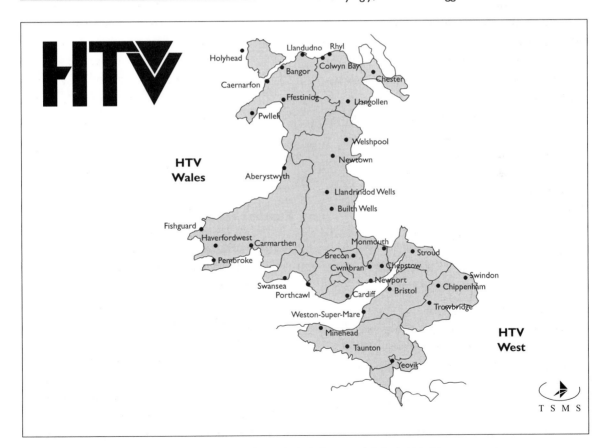

Figure 6.7 Geographical spread versus consumer power in one 'region' of commercially funded television.

179

sometimes prefer programmes that are not too involving and so do not detract from attention to the ads (Curran and Seaton 1997: 223). And Wasko (1994) argued that it is spreading to cinema, in the form of 'advertiser-preferred projects', i.e. film proposals with 'placement' potential.

A note on the reporting of television funding

It is worth remembering in debates led by the press about deregulation, the selling off of the BBC etc. that the press also lives largely by advertising revenue. The position taken by particular newspapers on television controversies exists in relation to often contradictory drives, in addition to the political sympathies of those who own and control those industries:

- *Deregulation* How far would the extension of television advertising (for example, if the BBC were to be completely commercialised) undercut newspaper advertising revenues by bringing down costs and widening the pool of media available to advertisers?
- *Ownership* Who owns the paper which is arguing against the BBC? Is it News Corporation which owns a large share of the British press and broadcasting and has a particular interest in acquiring more?
- *Representative voices* How appropriate is it that newspapers with circulation of a few hundred thousand accuse television programmes of attracting 'only' four or five million viewers (see Lawson 2001)?

'the rightwing press that prepared the way for Thatcher's deregulation of television in the '80s [argued] that one of the objections to the licence fee was its expense. Yet people are now paying around £1,000 a season (nine or more licence fees) . . . to see all the football matches they want from various non-terrestrial channels' (Lawson 2001).

References

Ang, Ien (1991) *Desperately Seeking the Audience*, London: Routledge.

Beckett, Andy (2001) 'Numbers game', *Guardian*, 20 November.

Bell, Emily (2001) 'Free us from the black box', *Guardian*, 20 November.

Brierley, Sean (1998) 'Advertising and marketing: advertising and the new media environment', in Adam Briggs and Paul Cobley (eds) *The Media: An Introduction*, Harlow: Longman.

Corner, John (1991) *Popular Television in Britain: Studies in Cultural History*, London: BFI.

Curran, James and Seaton, Jean (1997) *Power Without Responsibility: The Press and Broadcasting in Britain*, London: Routledge.

Goldsmith, Janet (2002) 'The view from where?' *Guardian*, 21 January.

Lawson, Mark (2001) 'What's on?', *Guardian*, 19 November.

Stoessl, Sue (1998) 'Audience feedback: administrative research of audiences', in Adam Briggs and Paul Cobley (eds) *The Media: An Introduction*, Harlow: Longman.

Wasko, Janet (1994) *Hollywood in the Information Age: Beyond the Silver Screen*, Cambridge: Polity.

Further reading

Ang, Ien (1996) *Living Room Wars: Rethinking Media Audiences for a Postmodern World*, London: Routledge.

Braithwaite, Brian (1998) 'Magazines', in Adam Briggs and Paul Cobley (eds) *The Media: An Introduction*, Harlow: Longman.

Brierley, Sean (1995) *The Advertising Handbook*, London and New York: Routledge.

Kent, R. (1994) *Measuring Media Audiences*, London: Routledge.

Paterson, Richard (1990) 'A suitable schedule for the family', in Andrew Goodwin and Gary Whannel (eds) *Understanding Television*, London and New York: Routledge.

Names of useful journals are given in the Useful Information section. You might also try approaching an ad agency and asking for a back copy of *BRAD* (*British Rates and Data*), which will give you the current rate in every UK publication, including broadcasting. You may find that your school or college has a staff member responsible for publicity who can lend you one.

Websites

www.barb.co.uk
www.cookiecentral.com
www.itc.co.uk
www.mpaa.org/useconomicreview/index.htm
www.pearlanddean.com
www.rajar.co.uk

7 Institutions

- Defining 'institution'
- An institutional analysis of photography
- Applying ideas about media institutions

- Media institutions and society
- References
- Further reading

'Why did they do that?' It's a question you have probably asked, coming out of a film or listening to a CD for the first time. We are puzzled because we have expectations about an artist – a director, an actor, a musician – or a particular genre. Behind the question is a suspicion that some faceless media corporation has imposed a new ending on the film or persuaded a band to use a new producer. If Media Studies had adopted the auteur or author principle as a means of understanding texts, the answer to the question would be simple – go and ask the artist. But Media Studies doesn't do that because it recognises that production is mainly an industrial and commercial process and it takes place in a social, political and cultural context. The shorthand way of describing the impact of the type of production process used, and the context of production, is to refer to it as 'institutional'.

The concept of *institution* in Media Studies sometimes gets rolled up with 'industry', but we are keeping them separate. Chapter 8 deals with the economic and financial or business activities of media producers. The concept of institution deals with ideas drawn from sociology, psychology and politics. As such, the institutional aspects of media activities are sometimes difficult to grasp because they refer to less tangible processes and relationships than, say, company balance sheets or employment contracts. This chapter attempts to define what we mean by 'institutional' in Media Studies by working through an example of a specific media institution and then applying the ideas raised to a series of key debates which can in turn be picked up in several of the other chapters and case studies, allowing you to integrate 'institutional analysis' with such key concepts for our chosen institutions as '**objectivity**' and '**quality**'. Chapter 18 deals with regulation.

Defining 'institution'

enduring regulatory and organising structures of any society, which constrain and control individuals and individuality – the underlying principles and values according to which many social and cultural practices are organised and co-ordinated – the major social sources of codes, rules and relations.

(O'Sullivan *et al.* 1994)

O'Sullivan here is referring to institutions generally, but let's think about the different kinds of institutions you may have experienced.

We all grow up within a range of different institutions. Some of these are 'formal' – education, the health service, the legal system. We are part of these institutions. We know what to expect of the services they offer; we know how to behave within them. We share (or perhaps tolerate and sometimes come actively to oppose) their values. They are formal because we are often legally 'registered' with them. But we also belong to a range of social institutions such as the family, a church perhaps or just a group of friends who meet for social activities. Within this group too, our behaviours are controlled or constrained even as we may share ideas and values. We all act, to some extent, in an institutional manner. Everyone working with or dealing with a sector of the media industries will also be subject to 'institutional constraints'.

Let's take a simple example, a visit to a local multiplex cinema. The film we are going to see has been produced in an institutional context, 'Hollywood'. It will be roughly 100–120 minutes long, in colour. It will probably have stars and feature a music soundtrack. Many of the decisions about how the film was made are economic, but others are institutional – they are concerned with how the production team work together, how they have been trained to think about 'quality', 'professionalism', 'art', 'entertainment' and the audience.

Cinema is also a 'social institution' – as audiences we share certain values with the producers and we behave in the auditorium in a particular way. In the UK we don't talk through the film and we watch it in the dark – it isn't like this everywhere. The cinema is probably a CEA (Cinema Exhibitors' Association) member and the adverts we see are subject to the **ASA** code and monitored by the CAA (Cinema Advertising Association).

See Chapter 18.

The institutional nature of cinema means that we know how to 'suspend our disbelief' and enjoy a movie. The events of 11 September 2001 exposed the institutional aspects of cinema when distributors 'pulled' films that they believed were 'inappropriate'. Most of the time we watch buildings being blown up or hijackers taking hostages without a second thought – it is an accepted form of entertainment (see Chapter 3 case study on action films).

Classifying media institutions

Work on media institutions is similar to that on **genre** – the two concepts are
closely related. Like genre, institution is a fluid term. In our first example
above, everyone is part of several different institutions – as a family member, a
student, a patient etc. In the same way anyone working in the media or on any
media text needs to relate to more than one institution – more than one set of
relationships and processes. We'll explore what this means by working on an
extended example

An institutional analysis of photography

'Photography' is an example of a media *practice* – an organised set of media
activities which has developed over a long period and is easily accessible as a
means of creating a media text. Photography is also an institution, and that
means that photographers and photographs are in some way subject to
constraints.

It's an interesting example of a media activity because, although a
photograph can exist as a media text itself, most of the time we come across
photographs as collections in an album or an exhibition or as photographic
images which are used in other media texts such as magazines, newspapers,
posters, websites etc.

This dual role of the photographic image sets up a number of broadly
'institutional' questions, involving both the production and the reading of
photographs:

- Is the photograph on its own the same as the photographic image
  reproduced in a magazine or newspaper?
- Can the meaning of a photographic image change, depending on the type
  of media text in which it appears?
- Do photographs have a different value or status, depending on the context
  within which we see them?

See Chapter 1. An analysis of a specific image will enable us to explore these issues. Figure
7.1 shows a young woman kneeling by a flowerbed. She is in focus in the
foreground, looking not at the camera but to her left. Slightly out of focus, in
the background, other people are sat on benches – some of them might be
looking at the young woman. This is a description at the **denotative** level.
By analysing it carefully at the **connotative** level, we can interpret the image.
The young woman's clothes (especially the hat) and make-up suggest the
1950s. The formal flower bed, wide path and benches suggest a public park.
Foliage on the trees and the display of tulips suggests late spring or early
summer (further supported by the deep shadow thrown by the woman in the
strong sunlight). The framing draws attention to the woman and this is

emphasised by the use of depth of field which blurs into the distance. The woman's posture suggests a 'pose' in that it looks quite uncomfortable (although this might be because of her outfit) and arranged for the camera. She is kneeling on the cut grass, on the 'wrong side' of a wire in a very formal garden, suggesting that a rule has been broken and that her behaviour is in some way 'naughty'. So far, so good. But this is a photographic image, taken out of context.

- Where and when might the image have first appeared?
- What is the *purpose* of the image in that context?

These are interrelated institutional questions, and we can draw up a list of
   possible answers in relation to a third question:

- What type of photography is this?

Figure 7.1

See Chapter 3.

This is a familiar genre question, but we can turn it towards an analysis of institution by investigating what the genre classification implies about who took the photograph, who commissioned it etc.:

- *A snapshot.* Could this be a snapshot taken for a family album? It seems unlikely, partly because the woman doesn't look at the camera. Also we might expect a rather closer shot with less background. It could, however, be a 'staged' shot for the album – perhaps with some kind of story behind it?
- *A still from a film.* Could this be a photograph taken on a film location? Is it a film made in the 1950s, or a recent film set in the 1950s?
- *A paparazzi photograph.* Is the young woman famous and has the photographer caught her playing in the park?
- *A promotional photograph.* Perhaps she is famous and has posed for publicity photos?
- *A fashion photograph.* Although this is possible, the clothes are not given sufficient prominence for this to be very likely.
- *An advertising photograph.* Perhaps this is an intriguing image which is anchored by an advertising tag-line (supply your own!).
- *A feature photograph.* Newspapers and magazines often use photographs to improve the look of a page, and this may be simply meant to represent the picture editor's idea of a 'welcome to spring' image.
- *A documentary photograph.* Is this an attempt to 'document reality' – to record a moment in a park on a sunny day?
- *An art photograph.* Might this be part of a collection in a book or for a gallery exhibition, organised around a theme or a particular technique?

All of these are just about possible, although some seem much more likely than others. These types of photography might be seen as separate genres, but we should note that as genres they are distinguished only by sometimes quite subtle differences in understandings or 'framings'. We've shown that the same image could belong in several different genres and we won't be able to pin it down unless we know more about who the photographer was and the context of its publication. (We should also note that there are other types of photography which might have different subject matter or very different framings – portraiture, landscape, medical, industrial, news, wildlife etc.)

Bert Hardy (1913–95) was a self-educated photographer, who began work as a messenger boy and developed his expertise with the German Leica camera.

The original photograph was taken by **Bert Hardy**, and appeared in *Picture Post* magazine in May 1950. It features a young Audrey Hepburn, who a few years later would become an international star in films such as *Breakfast at Tiffany's* (US 1961) and *My Fair Lady* (US 1964). *Picture Post* was an extremely popular weekly illustrated magazine, published between 1938 and 1957. It specialised in news and current affairs and 'human interest' stories and carried many of the black and white images which have now become associated with the social history of the period. Bert Hardy was a 'staff photographer' on the magazine, who gained a high reputation with a recognisable style derived

from his innovative use of a small 35 mm camera. He pioneered
documentary-style shooting, making use of available light, especially in a
series of features depicting life in working-class communities. Many of his
best photographs capture the humanity and vitality of 'ordinary people'.
When *Picture Post* closed in 1957, Hardy became a sought-after advertising
photographer. He was one of the earliest photographers to have his work
collected and exhibited when, during the 1970s, photography began to gain
more recognition as an 'art form'.

What does this knowledge about photographer and publication context do
to limit the range of possible types of photography which might describe the
Audrey Hepburn photograph? It clearly rules out some categories and erects
barriers between others. The context suggests that this was a 'light feature'
item, a 'pretty girl greets the spring' story (Gardiner 1993). There is a hint of
the promotional tie-in, with the magazine giving a helping hand to
Hepburn's career and, despite the nature of the job, Hardy's style and interest
in documentary come through – this is also a study of Kew Gardens, a
popular place for Londoners to visit. In the 1990s the image appeared in a
collection of *Picture Post Women* (Gardiner 1993) and could conceivably appear
in an exhibition of Hardy's work. Thus as the context changes, so does the
category, and this image is now primarily an 'art' image or an historical
document. What do these changes tell us?

The categories of photography are based on *purpose*, and the purpose also
affects the practice or 'content' – how the photograph is taken – and its status,
both with other photographers and with audiences. There are clear
distinctions between an 'amateur' snapshot and a 'professional' feature
photograph – not least that the latter is a commercial operation.

There are also differences between 'commercial' photography and 'art' or
'documentary' photography. In the former, images may be cropped or
manipulated by a designer or picture editor – the photographer gives up
'ownership' in return for a fee or salary. In the latter, images are likely to be
published 'as is' or after processing by the photographer alone. Of course,
'amateur' photographs are sometimes published and commercial photographs
do appear in galleries, but the original status is maintained and the 'crossing
over' into a different category is noticeable. The definitions of categories
change over time and it is worth noting that a photograph is normally
accompanied by 'anchoring text' which makes the category explicit (even if it
is only 'Majorca 1996' scribbled on the back of a snapshot).

- Who makes the decisions about which category is appropriate for which
  kinds of photography?
- Who decides which category has higher or lower status?
- Can anyone become a photographer and contribute work in these
  particular categories?

Picture Post The archive of
photographs from the magazine is
now administered by Hulton
Archive, and several individual
images have become widely used
on postcards and posters. You
can view Hardy's work on
www.hultonarchive.com.

When *amateur* prints are used, a
publication may announce them
as such. A similar policy on
television news may add the title
'amateur video' to any footage
which has been accepted for
broadcast. This signals that the
poor quality is not the fault of the
broadcaster. The force of this
distinction is gradually receding as
more 'non-standard' video
material is shown.

These too are institutional questions. Photography is an *organised* activity. No matter that anyone can point a camera and press a button, we all recognise that a more formal media institution called 'photography' exists with its rules and regulations. At its simplest level, the distinction between amateur and professional is based on the organisation of professionals. You can't become a 'professional' simply by selling a photograph. The definition of professional is based on:

- status as an employed or self-employed person with a reputation for good work
- training and qualifications
- membership of a professional association
- competitions, awards and recognition
- access to 'industry standard' equipment and the skills to use it.

These criteria are important in excluding some people from becoming professional photographers and in 'standardising' expectations about what constitutes a 'professional photograph' or even a 'good photograph'. They are 'institutional constraints' within which photography practice develops.

- *Employment status* is important in that it will influence decisions about what will sell or what will meet a set brief. Most professionals are dependent on the work they produce having currency in the contemporary market. Some photographers might be 'grant-aided', enabling them to undertake 'avant garde' work, but they too will be constrained by the funding criteria.

See Chapter 8.

- *Training and qualifications* are important in photography, which, like journalism but unlike the film industry, has had a long history of 'scientific' and 'technical' training provision, as well as more art- and design-orientated education. There is a limited number of specialist courses at certain colleges which have become associated with certain types of photography, such as the documentary tradition at Newport (University of Wales College). Students are influenced by their tutors and the traditions of the department and carry these into their future practice. Assessment in the form of National Vocational Qualifications is a way of 'proving' professional competence.

'*Professional*' is an example of a term with two rather different meanings in everyday speech. It can refer to adherence to a code of conduct and a high level of skill – 'she is highly professional in her work' or to a rather automatic performance of the expected role – 'don't worry about him, he's a cynical old pro'.

- *Professional associations* support members and help to 'maintain standards'. They may operate a code of ethics which modifies behaviour and puts pressure on members to conform. They preserve the status of members by lobbying government in their interest and negotiating better deals and conditions with buyers of photographic services and equipment suppliers. They also publish journals and run conferences which act as a forum for discussion as well as the circulation of new ideas. What does the Code of Ethics below tell you about photography as an institution?

Like many other activities which began in Victorian Britain, photography has a 'Royal Society' which welcomes amateur and professional members. Compare this with the Royal Television Society, which is professional only. Film and radio don't appear to warrant royal patronage in the same way.

The Code of Ethics of the BIPP (British Institute of Professional Photographers)

- A member shall present himself, his work, his services and his premises in such a manner as will uphold and dignify his professional status and the reputation of the Institute.
- A member shall exercise all reasonable skill, care and diligence in the discharge of his duties, and, in so far as any of his duties are discretionary, shall act fairly and in good faith.
- Any confidential information acquired by a member in the course of his professional duties shall not be divulged by him to any third party.
- No member shall corruptly offer or accept any gift or inducement.
- A member may use in conjunction only with his own name the Institute designatory letters to which he is entitled; and he shall not use any other designatory letters or other description to which he is not entitled.
- A member shall at all times and in all respects conduct his professional and business operations within the law, both criminal and civil.
- A member knowingly condoning a breach of this Code shall be responsible as if he himself had committed the breach.
- A member shall cooperate fully with any investigations into an alleged breach of this Code.

The code can be found on the website at www.bipp.com.

- *Awards and prizes* are important in confirming which groups of photographers are recognised as being at the forefront of contemporary practice. They will receive publicity which will strengthen moves to change practice.
- *Industry standard equipment* is another barrier to new entrants to the profession, not just because of cost but also because of the training needed to use it – often, the necessary support to learn new techniques is available only through professional associations. It could be argued that digital technologies have eroded some of the 'mystique' of 'professional equipment' by making advanced features available at lower cost, but the issue of access to training remains important.

'Amateur photography' can also feel like an institution, especially if it excludes 'outsiders': there is little in amateur or popular photography magazines to help us map our course. There, the concept of photography is limited, being addressed mainly to white heterosexual males. Not much is offered to women and the existence of working-class, black, or lesbian

Awards are often given by the professional bodies and sponsored by major manufacturers – reinforcing the sense of an organised and institutionalised practice. The most famous awards ceremony is Oscars night, shown around the world. How much does this event 'represent' the institution of Hollywood cinema to the world audience?

Photography is very much associated with ideas of 'identity' and the politics of who controls the images which contribute to those ideas. You will find plenty of examples of photographers working against 'institutional' influences on identity.

'Disability imagery' is one example where the 'subjects' of institutional image-making have fought back: 'My personal journey of private crisis, of the slow gaining of understanding of disability as an external oppression, and on into the disability movement, vitally informs my photographs . . . Charity photography is a form which is at once stubborn and fragile. A photography which . . . is based on a medical view (or model) of disability cannot lead to the empowerment and liberation of disabled people' (Hevey 1992).

experience is barely acknowledged. It is orientated, primarily, to 'know-how' and assumes an interest in tourism, the landscape and glamour.

(Spence and Solomon 1995)

This quotation recognises the force of institutional factors in photography. It also emphasises how much they can be perceived as discriminatory. (It is useful here to refer back to the BIPP Code and its use of 'he' to describe photographers.) Various groups of photographers have recognised this and set up organisations or campaigns to promote their own interests, which would otherwise be seen as marginal.

ACTIVITY 7.1

Take any two contrasting types of photography (e.g. portraiture and sports photojournalism) – check out books and magazines dealing with photography and look at how the two types of work are presented. Try and list the differences between the two types in terms of:

- relationship with a client – who pays the photographer's fee?
- relationship with the subject of the photograph
- the environment in which the photographers work – how much control do they have?
- the equipment the photographers might use
- a description of a typical working day
- what the photographers might consider as a 'good photograph'
- the different markets in which publications carrying the photographs might be sold.

How important are these institutional differences in thinking about the photographs themselves?

Applying ideas about media institutions

From the analysis of photography, you should be able to move on to any other media institution using these points as a guide:

- *Establishment* Established institutions are *enduring* – they are recognised as having been established for some time. They have a history that informs (and perhaps constrains) the present and the future work undertaken by them. At best, because there are no overnight institutions, they have tried out ideas and established 'support systems' for members; at worst a sort of institutional inertia can operate within their norms. At the start of the twenty-first century photography is struggling to come to terms with digital imaging and the challenge to very long-held views about photographs as evidence. Most media institutions feel slightly threatened by ideas such as **convergence** because they appear to undermine long-established identities.

- *Regulation*   Institutions *regulate and structure* activities: they make rules and they suggest specific ways of working. In broad terms, institutions provide stability and preserve the status quo and of course, 'organise change'. The professional associations are important in regulating the behaviour of their members.

    See Chapter 18.

- *Collectivism*   Institutions are, in one sense, *collectivist*. They organise individuals and individuality in order to achieve a common goal. (This goal may be that chosen by a small group or even an individual at the top of the hierarchy – institutions are not necessarily democratic.) This is particularly important in media institutions in which individual creative ideas are prized, but may have to be sacrificed for the good of the group (often the financial security of the organisation).

- *Work*   Institutions develop *working practices* that have an underpinning set of assumptions about the aims of the institution and its ethos. They recognise training and qualifications in the specialist skills necessary for the job and will probably have developed specific job titles and descriptions (sometimes recognised by trade unions and staff associations and used as the basis for pay and conditions).

- *Values*   All the people associated with the institution – directors, managers, employees – are expected to share the *values* associated with the ethos and to behave accordingly in their relations with others, both inside and outside the institution. It must be staffed by recognised professionals, whose education and training will effectively exclude casual intruders as new staff.

    The reference to the BBC as 'Auntie' during the 1970s and 1980s is a good example of the audience view of a broadcasting institution. It suggested that the corporation was 'one of the family', but, worryingly for BBC executives, an older and perhaps more conservative relative than they might wish.

- *Status*   The wider public will be aware of the *status* of the institution and of their own expected relationship to it. Again this is particularly important for media institutions, because the audiences for media texts are 'organised' as part of the network of relationships.

ACTIVITY 7.2

Outlining media institutions

Using the bullet points above and thinking particularly about:

- regulatory bodies (Chapter 18)
- job descriptions
- training and qualifications
- professional associations and awards

sketch out your definition of the institution of 'radio' and 'journalism' as understood in the UK.

Can a single company be an institution?

When you come to study media institutions, you may find that you are asked to write about institutions using a single media text or a single company as a starting point. It's important that you recognise that the company and the text exist in an institutional framework and that means a framework within which all the companies producing similar products are also working. The *Sunday Times* is constrained in the way it approaches journalism by an understanding of the standards of journalism appropriate for a broadsheet newspaper. Similarly, its parent company, News Corporation, is a major global corporation which is also constrained by the ways in which such corporations are expected to behave. This particular company and newspaper title may be at the forefront of trying to shift institutional boundaries, but we still want to study them as part of a group.

One example of an organisation that might itself be an 'institution' is the BBC, because of its uniquely long-established position in the UK system in terms of funding and self-regulation. But the BBC has to deal also with other institutional constraints, e.g. it also uses journalists who are constrained in aspects of their behaviour by the same code of ethics that impinges upon journalists at the *Sunday Times*.

Media institutions and society

Human society has always had the means to express ideas and emotions through forms such as storytelling, dance, music and art. Modern media have extended those capacities, in terms of realism, reproduction and distribution to mass audiences. The institutional questions which arise are not necessarily 'new', but they arouse concern and interest because their potential impact is so great. Consider the following issues about the role of the media and the nature of media texts:

- the 'truth' of claims to represent 'reality'
- the hurt and damage to individuals caused by offensive media texts
- the potential damage to society inflicted by stories celebrating corruption and depravity
- the potential loss of national, regional and cultural identity through submission to dominant culture.

Some of these issues are raised in other chapters and case studies as well, and in some cases they are linked with questions of economics – what kinds of media activity can we afford, what are the implications for employment or balance of trade? Here, we will consider two broadly based issues relating to journalism:

- 'truth' and partiality
- ethics and work practices

The case of journalism

Journalism is the practice of reporting and commenting on events. We can think of it as a set of working practices and an institution like photography, though one which is even more bound up with that hotly contested concept of 'truth'.

The cub reporter at the gardening club show, the columnist on a national paper, the sub-editor who writes the captions on pin-ups, the film reviewer on a website and the foreign correspondent reporting for the BBC in a war zone are all journalists. They share certain values and are subject to similar institutional constraints, but there are also important differences.

Journalism is one sector of the UK media industries with a history of clearly defined training routes for entry and progression through the profession. The NCTJ (National Council for the Training of Journalists) and the large regional newspaper groups have organised training schemes which allow journalists to start 'at the bottom' and learn their trade 'on the job'.

To some extent these schemes are now in competition with degree and postgraduate level courses which produce highly qualified entrants with less experience (an innovation not warmly welcomed in some parts of the industry). Nevertheless, most journalists receive an introduction to acceptable working practices with a strong institutional sense of what it means to be a journalist. This introduction is not value-free, and discrimination based on gender or race has been identified and challenged by journalists who established new codes of conduct within the profession. Campaigns against racist reporting have been developed (see Figure 4.7 for National Union of Journalists guidelines) alongside pressure groups designed to promote opportunities for black media workers or workers with disabilities. More subtle forms of 'gendered' training expectations tend to prepare women to work on 'human interest' stories rather than, for example, on sports reporting.

In an illuminating study of *Women in Radio*, the gendered nature of radio work was confirmed, with women less likely to present current affairs, but contributors noted a number of changes in the image of the news reporter. The hard-bitten hack in the raincoat found in the pub has given way to the dedicated young professional more likely to be found in the gym when not working late – young women are possibly more likely to fit this ideal. Also, new technology in the news room means that more interviews are conducted over the **ISDN** line rather than 'foot in door' or 'face to face'. Again, women are thought to be better at this form of work than men (Mitchell (ed.) 2000: 252).

A beginning on a local newspaper is often the first stage on a progression through different media institutions, including local radio, regional television and then national newspapers, radio or television. This has happened for many

'In this business, you have to think like a man, act like a woman, and work like a dog' (Martha Jean Steinberg, quoted in Mitchell (ed.) 2000: 205).

'Women leapt in to fill these [radio] vacancies and they were largely university-educated women who were not there because they had financed their own trip abroad, or because their husbands, fathers or brothers had played any role in their career' (Sebba 1998).

See Chapter 2 on 'story construction'.

years but has been further encouraged by the 'convergence' of media forms. Journalists in any medium are expected to share skills, knowledge and understanding about what makes a 'good story' and how to produce accurate and interesting material to deadlines. However, the different media have different institutional constraints. Broadcast journalism has traditionally operated 'impartially', drawing on a sense of 'balanced reporting' as required by the charter of the BBC or by the Independent Television Commission (ITC) and Radio Authority in the case of other broadcasters. By contrast, print journalists work in a more politically charged environment where stories clearly have *angles* and columnists in particular are expected to represent the editorial *line*. This isn't expressed as partiality, of course, but as 'comment'.

A tabloid might list 'ten things you never knew about salmonella' – another angle.

An *angle* on a story refers to the direction from which the journalist approaches the material. A news item on the agency wires might refer to an outbreak of food poisoning. One journalist might decide to follow up the story by concentrating on the issue of public health: which shop, factory etc. might be responsible, how are the local authorities handling the outbreak of infection? Another journalist might approach the same material by linking it to other recent outbreaks and asking questions about central government food policy. These are two angles on the same story.

Editorial 'lines' are sometimes discussed on television current affairs programmes. A useful summary of editorial decisions can be found in the 'Editor' section of the Saturday *Guardian*.

A *line* is a policy set down by the editor (perhaps at the behest of a proprietor such as Rupert Murdoch) stating what the paper believes in and therefore how stories will be presented. The idea that such a line exists will be denied by many editors and journalists, but it becomes apparent whenever the paper decides to go against its usual line. The most obvious example of a line is the general support for one particular party at election time. In 1997 the *Sun* surprised most readers by switching allegiance from Conservative to Labour.

ACTIVITY 7.3

Editorial policy

Over a couple of weeks try to follow the same few big news stories in two newspapers with strong identities (e.g. the *Sun*, *Mirror*, *Daily Mail*, *Guardian* and *Daily Telegraph*).

- Can you identify an editorial line in any of the papers on a particular story?
- Can you find examples of reporting or comment which appear to contradict the editorial stance of the paper?

Although it is still possible to find writers with different political views working on the same broadsheet paper (especially the *Guardian* or the

Independent), it is increasingly the case that the press is seen to be 'partisan'. This emphasises the difference between print and broadcast journalism, but also puts pressure on the broadcasters. Newspapers can 'set an agenda' on a particular story which is picked up by radio and television. Viewers and listeners then expect impartiality from broadcasters, but, with the context of the story already set, it is difficult to 'reset' it. And, with the increased competition in news presentation, ignoring the story may not be possible. The result is that broadcasters can be sucked in to a style of coverage they may not be trained or professionally inclined to handle.

Broadcasters can also claim to be 'agenda-setting': *'Breakfast With Frost* is BBC Television's agenda-setting news and current affairs programme' – introduction to the programme's page on the BBC website.

Paedophiles and the *News of the World*

An 'editorial campaign' is often a means by which a new editor can 'make their mark' and at the same time promote the paper, perhaps 'repositioning' it in the marketplace. Rebekah Wade was appointed as editor of the *News of the World* in the summer of 2000 and she soon launched a controversial campaign against anonymity for registered paedophiles, publishing names and addresses. Roy Greenslade, the *Guardian*'s 'industry watcher', commenting on the affair, noted that a young and inexperienced editor had surprised the industry with a carefully thought-out strategy that survived a critical backlash and raised interesting questions about government policy (source: *Guardian Unlimited* website, story posted 31 July 2000).

A famous fictional editorial policy was set out as a front-page manifesto by Orson Welles as Charles Foster Kane in the film *Citizen Kane* (US 1941).

The broadcasters' aim of impartiality is put to the strongest test when news stories involve issues of 'national interest' or 'national security'. In these circumstances there is a temptation to slide into an 'us against them' style of reporting. During the Cold War (i.e. from the late 1940s through to the end of the 1980s) there was some (but not total) agreement as to who the 'bad guys' were (i.e. the Soviet Union and its allies), and this allowed a certain amount of positioning of the journalist without breaching the impartiality code. In recent struggles, such as the civil war in Bosnia, the position of journalists has become more difficult. There is no meaningful balance between superpowers, and no immediate bad guy. Surely this means that impartiality is a given – the journalist reports what he or she sees? In reality this is (1) difficult and (2) not necessarily 'good television'.

Journalists in Bosnia found themselves involved in the war – used as hostages, shot at and generally not able to 'stand back'. The war itself was seen as so confusing that to grab attention news editors were looking for angles on stories which increasingly attempted to determine who the bad guys were. In 1996, at an international conference on news reporting in

Berlin, the BBC journalist Martin Bell made a protest about what he termed
'bystander journalism' – the reduction of the 'objectivity' of the reporter to an
onlooker's role. Bell went on to leave the BBC and to get elected to
Parliament as an 'anti-sleaze' candidate, but his comments ignited a debate
about the 'journalism of attachment'. 'In the news business it isn't
involvement, but indifference that makes for bad practice. Good journalism is
the journalism of attachment' (Bell 1997).

> a UN unit was despatched by an officer from another nation to deal with a
> protesting crowd of hungry civilians . . . The UN unit, the 'Blue Berets'
> happily beat them to a pulp. Asked why, they said 'This is how we do it at
> home.' Are they the 'good guys'? . . . War zones are deceptive, and eye-
> witness reports sometimes need to be verified even when it is your eyes.
>
> (Adie 1998).

Figure 7.2 Welcome to Sarajevo
(UK 1997) deals with many of the
issues surrounding contemporary
broadcast journalism.

James Cameron (1911–85) was
a journalist with a high reputation
for integrity, commitment and
courage. An annual award for
foreign correspondents is named
after him.

This debate is important in terms of the state of contemporary journalism,
but it is not a clear-cut issue. Bell was supported and attacked with equal
force by distinguished journalists. He maintained that he was not arguing
against objectivity or hard factual reporting. It emerged that one of his targets
was the concept of rolling news (BBC News 24 was then being developed),
which critics argue is reliant on ill-prepared, 'instant' reports, rather than the
deep coverage provided by the traditional professional foreign correspondent.

Rolling news is a response to a competitive international news market
driven by different communications technology, but also by changes in
definitions of news and editorial policies. It is tempting to polarise the debate
surrounding Bell's remarks as traditional factual reporting versus attached,
committed journalism. But this would be misleading. Perhaps the most
celebrated foreign correspondent of the last fifty years was **James Cameron**,
who saw 'this famous "objectivity" as not only virtually impossible, but
maybe even undesirable' (Cameron 1980). On the other hand 'commentators'
who are given the space to step outside 'reporting on events' to write or
broadcast about issues more generally may have few worthwhile opinions
about important issues and therefore tend to support the status quo by
default.

One of the features of contemporary newspapers is the rise of the
'columnist', which to a certain extent has matched the decline of the 'reporter'
and the general move to more 'entertainment' (or 'infotainment') forms.
Newspapers have responded to what their proprietors have seen as the market
trends by shifting resources away from large numbers of relatively poorly paid
reporters 'on the ground' to a smaller number of highly paid commentators
based in London (most national daily papers are now entirely London
operations, whereas they once operated out of large bases in Manchester,

Birmingham and other cities). This change has had an impact on, and has in turn been influenced by, changes in journalism training and the consequent 'institutionalisation' of the new forms. To a certain extent the same process is evident in local newspapers where 'features' have grown at the expense of 'news'.

'11 September' and the 'war on terrorism'

The attack on the World Trade Center and the Pentagon on 11 September 2001 and the subsequent call by President Bush for a 'war on terrorism' provided a challenge to journalism practice. It is tempting to say that these events were a significant 'turning point', but it is probably too early to judge. There are three observations we can make in the light of the comments above:

- The 'war on terrorism' was, from an American perspective, clearly a case of being able to identify the 'bad guys' again after the end of the Cold War. It was noticeable that in the UK print and broadcast media there were some journalists who adopted this position and others who were much more cautious. Those who criticised American policies, even if it was done implicitly, were sometimes put under significant pressure by other journalists, readers and Americans in the UK.
- The events in New York and Washington prompted publication of 'thought pieces' by both columnists and novelists, many of whom were familiar with life in the American cities. Many of these pieces were both revealing and moving about the impact of the events. However, when attention shifted to Afghanistan, a country few journalists have visited, and Muslim culture, again a subject with which few had much contact, it was clear that the 'comment' columns in many newspapers were misleading at best.
- There was a rush to endorse what now look like wild estimates of the numbers killed in the attacks. This is understandable given the horror of the events, but the early estimates have not been emphatically corrected. Very few accounts compared them to other events in which large numbers died, e.g. the gas leak from a Union Carbide plant in Bhopal, India, in 1984 in which over three thousand died.

In the aftermath of '9:11' we can note that there have been significant changes in the way that journalism is presented to us, not least in the rise of Internet-based coverage of events and the possible intervention of non-journalists, particularly academics in ongoing debates. 'National' newspapers are now widely available around the world via the Internet, as are 'national' radio broadcasts. E-mail allows responses to be 'posted' to newspapers and

The *Guardian* now has many American readers via the Internet who are perhaps unaware of its history and political liberalism. Seamus Milne's post-11 September article 'They can't see why they are hated' elicited two thousand e-mails direct to the author.

television stations almost immediately – and if the originating publication won't take the response, there are numerous other electronic outlets that will.

There are three institutional categories of newspapers in the UK press:

*   *Broadsheet newspapers* are so called because of the large size of the pages – the largest size commonly available for print products. (Ironically, the sheets are 'tall' rather than 'broad'.) In the UK the national broadsheets (*The Times, Daily Telegraph, Guardian* etc.) are all treated as 'serious news' papers, with a reading age commensurate with higher education. This leads to the alternative term **quality press** (i.e. the high quality of journalistic writing).

*   *Tabloid newspapers* are smaller in page size, roughly half as big as broadsheets and more square in shape. The term 'tabloid' has generated a second meaning which refers to sensational stories and striking page layouts with large images and headlines, exploiting the shape of the page. This second meaning tends to push tabloids 'downmarket' and has also been carried over to television, where it again implies sensation and screaming headlines. The tabloids have also been termed the **popular press**. But beware. In Europe it is commonplace to find a 'tabloid-sized' paper which is 'serious', and the **mid-market** papers in the UK such as the *Daily Mail* and *Daily Express* decided that the gain from the 'manageability' and layout features of the tabloids outweighed the pejorative image when they moved from broadsheet to tabloid size in the 1980s. In order to distinguish this middle market from the *Sun, Mirror* and *Star*, the latter group are now being referred to as the *red-top* tabloids (following their use of a red background on the masthead). Notice too that the *Independent* and *The Times* have followed the *Guardian* in producing tabloid 'second sections' (although not with the *Guardian*'s success). 'Tabloid' and 'broadsheet' are also misleading when considering the regional press.

*   The *regional press* describes most UK newspapers apart from the twenty or so national titles based in London (or Scotland). These may be different sizes and morning or evening dailies or weeklies, but institutionally they all differ from what used to be called the 'Fleet Street nationals' because of their recognition of a specific 'local' audience and, most importantly, a local advertising market (see Chapter 12). Ownership of the regional press is concentrated in a few large companies with some involvement by the same groups who own the nationals and the recent arrival of the American group Gannett.

In April 2002 the *Daily Mirror* redesigned its masthead (now white on black with a red stripe) to distinguish itself from the *Sun* and *Daily Star*.

'Fleet Street' refers to the location of the national dailies in central London before the new technologies prompted them to move out (e.g. to Wapping).

Ethics and values

One of the main institutional constraints in any media practice is a shared sense of the values. This often translates into a set of ethics, perhaps inscribed in a Code of Conduct such as the Photographers' code outlined above. The difficulty with ethical behaviour is that it often runs counter to what might produce a 'good story' (another institutionalised feature of working in many media) and in turn ensure higher circulation, ratings etc. and both professional kudos and financial reward. This is the basis for the narratives of much of the literature and film based on journalistic adventures. Few media practitioners set out to behave unethically; most media organisations attempt to deal with such behaviour through some form of redress and also try to prevent it happening again.

In the film *Under Fire* (US 1982) a photojournalist fakes an image persuading revolutionaries that their inspirational leader is still alive – they go on to defeat the evil dictator.

Radio

In January 2002, Radio 4's *Feedback* programme which airs listener's comments, ran a piece on Radio 1 DJs. Listeners, including a parent of an eighteen-year-old, had complained about references to excessive drinking over the Christmas holiday. One DJ had run a competition for the most 'evil' cocktail made up from left-over Christmas drinks. Another had boasted about how much she had drunk the night before, inviting listeners to phone or e-mail with their own exploits. The implied question was, "is this celebrating dangerous drinking?" Or was it just a bit of fun, as the Radio 1 producer concerned suggested?

- What do you think?
- What would be the advice to DJs that you would give?

As a public service radio producer you wouldn't want to encourage dangerous drinking. Equally, you would want a slight edge of danger to a Radio 1 show in order to keep up the audience's interest.

Press

Another institutional shift: the *Guardian* established a Readers' Editor (an American idea) in 1997. Although an employee, the Readers' Editor is given complete independence to investigate a whole range of questions about material in the paper. He has a column every Saturday in which an issue is discussed in detail and a Corrections and Clarifications column on the centre page each day. So successful has the post been that the *Independent on Sunday* and the *Observer* have also started something similar.

Often, the issues under investigation run over a long time. In January 2002, the Saturday column referred to a court case involving Leeds footballers and an alleged racist assault. A parallel story covered the attempts to outlaw racism at Leeds United's ground where non-white supporters make up only a small proportion of the match crowd. To illustrate the story, the *Guardian* had used a photograph of a fourteen-year-old Asian boy in the Leeds crowd, taken with a long lens. The photograph was used in a positive way, and at first the boy in question was happy to see himself in the newspaper. However, later on he began to worry about being picked out in the crowd and he ended up not wanting to go to matches any more. His father complained to the newspaper, suggesting that it should have known better in such delicate circumstances. The Readers' Editor agreed with the father and the photograph was deleted from the newspaper archive. The Press Complaints Council Code was not totally helpful in this case, but it does suggest that permission should be sought before someone under sixteen is depicted.

We've argued that 'journalism' is recognisable as a set of work practices and ethics which runs across different media. The process of **convergence** of technologies and ownership has been matched by a similar convergence of attitudes towards previously distinct forms of journalism in press and broadcasting. A useful summary of where journalism is heading is provided by Michael Bromley (1997) who argues that debate over the state of journalism and its likely future in the early part of the twenty-first century involves four interrelated areas:

- technological change
- new business structures
- the functions of news
- the coherence of journalism as an occupation.

ACTIVITY 7.4

The state of journalism

Taking Bromley's four points above, check through the preceding section and the relevant sections of other chapters and case studies in this book to put together a coherent view of the 'state of journalism'. You should look in particular at the News case study, Chapter 8 and Chapter 16.

References

Adie, Kate (1998) 'Dispatches from the front: reporting war' in Mike Ungersma, *Reporters and the Reported*, Cardiff: Centre for Journalism Studies.

Bell, Martin (1997) *In Harm's Way*, London: Hamish Hamilton.

Bromley, Michael (1997) 'The end of journalism? Changes in workplace practices in the press and broadcasting in the 1990s', in Michael Bromley and Tom O'Malley (eds) *A Journalism Reader*, London: Routledge.

Cameron, James (1980) *Point of Departure*, London: Granada.

Carter, Cynthia, Branston, Gill and Allan, Stuart (eds) (1998) *News, Gender and Power*, London: Routledge.

Gardiner, Juliet (1993) *Picture Post Women*, London: Collins & Brown.

Hevey, David (1992) *The Creatures That Time Forgot: Photography and Disability Imagery*, London: Routledge.

Holland, Patricia (1998) 'The politics of the soft smile: soft news and the sexualization of the popular press', in Cynthia Carter, Gill Branston and Stuart Allan (eds) *News, Gender and Power*, London: Routledge.

Mitchell, Caroline (ed.) (2000) *Women in Radio*, London: Routledge.

O'Malley, Tom and Treharne, Jo (1993) *Selling the Beeb*, London: Campaign for Press and Broadcasting Freedom.

O'Sullivan, Tim, Hartley, John, Saunders, Danny, Montgomery, Martin and Fisk, John (1994, 2nd edition) *Key Concepts in Cultural and Communication Studies*, London: Routledge.

Sebba, Anne M. (1998) 'Women and the fourth estate', in Mike Ungersma *Reporters and the Reported*, Cardiff: Centre for Journalism Studies.

Spence, Jo and Solomon, Joan (eds) (1995) *What Can a Woman Do With a Camera?*, London: Routledge.

Ungersma, Mike (ed.) (1998) *Reporters and the Reported: The 1998 Vauxhall Lectures on Contemporary Issues in British Journalism*, Cardiff: Centre for Journalism Studies, Cardiff University (also available on the Internet at www.cardiff.ac.uk, as are the 1999 and 2000 collections of lectures).

Further reading

The Media Handbook series from Routledge provides useful material on institutional issues, especially:

Holland, Pat (2000, 2nd edition) *The Television Handbook*, London: Routledge.

Wells, Liz (2000, 2nd edition) *Photography: A Critical Introduction*, London: Routledge.

Free Press, the Newsletter of the Campaign for Press and Broadcasting Freedom, is a good source of information on stories concerning industrial relations, regulation and other institutional issues. Visit the CPBF website for updates on Campaign policies. As well as the Michael Bromley article cited above, there are several other useful articles in *A Journalism Reader*.

Websites

www.cjr.org

www.cpbf.org.uk

www.nnj.org.uk

www.presswise.org.uk

www.reportingtheworld.org

CASE STUDY: TELEVISION AS INDUSTRY AND INSTITUTION

- The current television environment
- Public service broadcasting (PSB)
- Digital broadcasting and global media

- References
- Further reading

Television is arguably the medium that is central to most people's lives in the developed world (see Chapter 18). Most of us watch television for a minimum of three hours per day and television provides us with information and ideas as well as entertainment. In the UK, television as a 'mass medium' is less than fifty years old, but in its life span it has changed several times, both as an industry and as an institution.

An outline history of UK television

The early years 1936–55

In the beginning, the new television service was constrained, in terms of both geographical and social 'reach'. Initially a limited service for the metropolitan middle class, it was a long time (including closedown from 1939–46, because of the disruption of the Second World War) before the single BBC channel was widely available. It was 1952 before the signal was available for 81 per cent of the population. The television service required a viewing licence on top of the existing radio licence, and by 1955 the number of television licence payers had risen to four and a half million (out of around fourteen million households).

A universal public service 1955–82

The highly controversial introduction of 'commercial' or 'independent' television (ITV) in 1955, in London and then around the country (set up partly with public service rather than simply commercial principles), did much to fire up the BBC, which was

allowed to introduce a second channel with colour and a higher resolution picture in 1964. Colour transmissions began in 1967 but the 'switchover' to the new 625 lines of UHF from the original 405 lines of VHF took over twenty years. It was 1985 before the old system was finally switched off – an interesting comparison with the current debate about switching to digital broadcasting in a very different television environment. In this period, ITV companies were obliged to operate on a purely regional basis, serving a distinctive community and abiding by tight regulatory controls laid down by the franchising authority, the IBA (Independent Broadcasting Authority). (See the Selling audiences case study following Chapter 6 and the discussion of 'Wales and West'.)

The beginnings of pluralism 1982–90

Channel 4 went on air in 1982 with a new remit, to widen the range of programming and to serve a diverse range of audiences not served by the BBC and ITV. Channel 4 was innovative in several different ways (see Holland 2000: 17). It was a public sector organisation that was funded via advertising revenue, initially sold by the ITV companies. It didn't make its own programmes, but commissioned independent companies as a 'broadcaster-publisher' and created a new form of television channel. In Wales, S4C was also set up as a public service broadcaster-publisher. This period also saw the UK introduction of satellite broadcasting (two companies, Sky and BSB began broadcasting, but Sky soon took over BSB to form

BSkyB) and the re-emergence of cable television (it had previously been used to relay terrestrial signals and some local services) offering a variety of channels on broadband cable.

The multi-channel environment, 1990 onwards

The Broadcasting Acts of 1990 and 1996 legislated for a new television environment in which regulation of 'independent television' was loosened, Channel 4 gained control over its own advertising revenue from ITV, and digital broadcasting promised to provide even more channels than analogue cable and satellite, as well as 'interactivity' and computer services. Channel 5 was launched as a final terrestrial channel (i.e. analogue bandwidth was now used up). Throughout the previous thirty-five years, the BBC and 'independent television' (i.e. ITV and later Channel 4) had shared the audience on a roughly equal basis. From now on, the audience share of 'other broadcasters' would grow steadily, undermining the settled terrestrial broadcasting environment.

A similar history is observable in most other developed countries, with technology and economic activity being the driving force for change and the US usually leading in terms of innovation.

Various commentators have found ways to analyse this history. John Ellis (2000), one of the foremost academic analysts of UK television, has represented the history like this:

- the era of scarcity
- the era of availability
- the era of plenty.

'Scarcity' refers in most countries to the restricted number of channels available up to the late 1970s (terrestrial broadcasts are limited by the availability of suitable 'bandwidths' of radio waves). New technologies such as broadband cable and DBS (direct broadcasting by satellite) allowed the move to the era

of 'availability'. But in the early years of the twenty-first century, Ellis suggests, television is moving towards a future that is being promoted by producers and distributors, but which audiences have yet to recognise completely.

In Ellis's terms the producers and audiences are actually 'working through' an 'age of uncertainty' as television begins to redefine itself. We can see this in the refusal by a large section of the UK audience to 'buy in' to the new world of plenty – after a decade of promotion, 'multi-channel television' has managed to attract only ten million households out of a total of twenty-four million UK television households (BARB figures, March 2002).

If we recognise that 'uncertainty' is a feature of the UK television environment, we can recognise two of the questions relating to how the television industry and the institution of television will develop over the next few years:

- What is the pattern of ownership in the UK television industry – does it have an effect on the range and quality of programming?
- What is the role of **public service broadcasting** in a multi-channel television world?

The current television environment

Whilst these are questions that have been asked consistently over the last few years, some of the features of the general media environment have changed quite recently and it is worth running through these changes before we tackle the debates.

Levels of economic activity

At the start of the twenty-first century, most of the advanced economies began to 'slow down' in terms of economic growth. The sudden collapse of some of the 'tiger economies' of the Pacific Rim, the American downturn and the events of 11 September 2001 have all had an impact on advertising revenue. As the economy slows, advertising dries up. This affects some media, such as television, radio and the press, quite quickly.

What is bad for commercial television is paradoxically good for cinema and for public sector broadcasting. In 2001, cinema audiences and ticket revenues rose to record levels – the UK cinema box office hit $1 billion for the first time. Although the BBC's revenue from the licence fee did not rise, it didn't fall either. ITV, by contrast, saw a massive fall in advertising revenue. When the economy is booming, ITV has traditionally 'bought' success. Bolstered by advertising revenue, it has lured both stars and producers away from the BBC. That isn't possible when revenue is falling.

Political will and ideologies

The accession of Labour to power in 1997 did change attitudes towards UK television ownership and control and regulation. To a certain extent, expectations were justified in a retreat from the previous Conservative government's attacks upon the BBC and the attempts to 'privatise' Channel 4. However, there were also signs of a willingness to relax cross-media ownership rules and in other industries private–public partnerships began to be promoted. UK government policy recognised the economic and cultural importance of 'media and cultural industries' and the Department of Culture, Media and Sport and the Department of Trade and Industry were charged with promoting the move to digital television: 'We want every home to be able to enjoy the present and future benefits of digital television' (from the government website at www.digitaltelevision.gov.uk).

Management styles and personality politics

As 'celebrity culture' gains a hold in the UK media (see Stardom and celebrity case study following Chapter 4), it is perhaps not surprising that media corporations are sometimes now judged by the personalities who lead them. Rupert Murdoch of News Corporation has become demonised as the 'media mogul' to be feared in the UK as CEO of News Corporation. It is also significant that Greg Dyke has replaced John Birt as Director General of the BBC.

Dyke is a well-known figure in the television industry, primarily in commercial television. He is best known, thanks to a characteristic *Sun* headline, as 'Roland Rat's Dad'. This refers to his successful introduction of a puppet character to the ailing TV-AM breakfast show in the mid-1980s. Dyke is 'high-profile' and his actions in moving the BBC back towards more popular programming are inevitably going to be seen in light of his own background. In a corporation previously known for the 'mandarin' tendencies of its senior staff, Dyke's lower-middle-class 'blokeishness' and his support of the Labour Party stand out.

Dyke arrived at the BBC in 2000, and just over a year later Michael Jackson left Channel 4 for the US, having personally led the station in pursuit of the youth audience and entertainment shows such as *Ali G, So Graham Norton* etc. Jackson, like Jeremy Isaacs and Michael Grade before him, was a high-profile Channel 4 boss, and it will be interesting to see what Mark Thompson does with the channel.

'Who is going to articulate Channel 4's modern public service role before government? "C4's image is all wrong. It has managed to look rich and commercial when in fact it's a public service broadcaster," says one of Jackson's contemporaries. You would never know it is spending £70m a year on education. Jackson tossed a grenade into the debate with his farewell speech in October when he said, "That ancient phrase, public service broadcasting is a battle standard we no longer need to rally around. It's become a pointless juju stick." Someone has to pick up the debate about public service broadcasting where Jackson left off. Someone also has to decide what to do with Channel 4's push into the new multi-media world, where it needs partners' (Maggie Brown, *Guardian*, 10 December 2001).

The personalities at the top of UK television companies do not just lead their own teams; they are also the focus for public expectations about their various channels. Greg Dyke, for instance has to present the BBC case for renewal of its charter in 2006 and the continuation of the licence fee.

New technologies

The move to digital broadcasting is the single biggest change in nearly fifty years of UK television. The UK is actually well ahead of other countries in the switchover, but millions of pounds are being wasted in persuading the audience to make the move. We may have reached a point where technological development has moved ahead of audience demand. Video on demand (VOD), interactivity, computer services, shopping and banking, hard drive recording:

which of these will attract a mass audience? So far only the chance to vote on *Big Brother* and *Pop Idol* seems to have made an impact.

Public awareness and involvement in debate

The BBC has made efforts to talk to licence payers and Channel 4 has made some attempts to involve audiences through interactive programmes and education, but commercial broadcasters appear to be interested only in existing methods of audience research (see case study Selling audiences following Chapter 6). Where pressure groups have in the past campaigned on television issues, it has often been to uphold 'quality' and preserve public service broadcasting (see below). Will this continue? Figure 7.3 shows how audience share for different channels varies across the country. This suggests that

Region	ITV % share	C4 % share	C5 % share	BBC1 % share	BBC2 % share	Other % share
London	22.3	10.0	6.3	28.8	12.2	20.4
Midlands	25.1	8.6	7.2	27.1	11.4	20.6
North West	25.8	8.9	5.3	26.0	11.3	22.7
Border	33.7	8.9	2.9	24.0	11.9	18.6
Scotland	23.7	9.7	6.5	25.5	10.6	23.9
North East	27.0	9.4	7.1	26.2	10.9	19.4
Yorkshire	26.3	9.5	5.4	27.8	11.5	19.6
East	24.6	8.6	3.9	28.5	11.6	22.8
South & South East	25.5	10.0	1.9	31.5	12.7	18.4
South West	26.6	10.9	2.8	33.5	13.7	12.5
Wales & West	23.7	7.3	4.0	30.4	11.2	23.5
Ulster	26.5	8.1	3.5	23.8	9.2	28.9

Figure 7.3 Television viewing across UK regions in December 2001. The table shows the share for each of the five terrestrial channels, of the total audience watching television in each ITV region. 'Other' refers to the share held by all satellite and cable channels (source BARB).

- households that choose a multi-channel service might watch non-terrestrial channels for up to 30 per cent of the time
- access and/or take-up is not evenly spread across the country.

How will government policy reflect these regional differences (i.e. in supporting PSB or not)?

Ownership and control

After a long period of relative stability, the UK television sector has livened up since the launch of digital services in 1998. Compared with other television markets, the UK has several distinctive features:

- the relative strength of the BBC as the organisation with the largest audience share, but with restrictions on revenue and investment
- a strong PSB tradition and an assumption (by producers and audiences) about the 'high quality' of UK television production
- a relatively tight control (compared to the US) on the amount of advertising on commercial channels and the disruption of programmes for advertising breaks
- a large number of small 'independent' producers, some of which are now being bought by the majors
- ownership restrictions which have slowed the process of 'consolidation' of ITV (i.e. reducing the number of companies through mergers) and which have kept the major global media player, News Corporation, out of terrestrial television
- digital growth dominated by Sky Sports and Sky Movies
- very recent entry into the market by other major media corporations (e.g. Bertelsmann).

The major players in UK television

The figures shown for approximate audience share relate to April 2002.

BBC (all BBC channels 37 per cent)
The BBC remains one of the major audio-visual corporations in Europe. BBC1 overtook ITV as the most watched channel in 2001 when BBC2 also moved ahead of Channel 4. Although the new BBC digital channels have yet to make much impact, the various 'UK Gold' channels in which the BBC has a stake, are amongst the most successful of cable/satellite channels. The BBC also broadcasts BBC World and operates a highly successful on-line service and a publishing and merchandising division.

ITV network (all ITV channels 25 per cent)
By 2000, ITV had reduced from a network of fifteen regional companies to one dominated by two companies, Granada and Carlton, with all but the smallest two of the English franchises under their

control. The Scottish Media Group, Ulster Television and GMTV are the other significant ITV companies.

Carlton and Granada are big media companies by UK standards, but not by the standards of global players. At the time of writing, plummeting advertising revenues and a vicious circle of falling audiences and further falls in revenue have been compounded by the disastrous failure of ITV Digital. Carlton and Granada poured money into a terrestrial digital television service that failed to compete with Sky Digital.

Channel 4 (10 per cent)
Channel 4 has been hit by the advertising downturn, but because it is a public sector organisation it has not had to placate shareholders and the stock market. It has introduced new pay channels, Film Four and E4, with limited success. A gamble on targeting the young adult audience (i.e. for E4) may backfire if other audiences are lost.

Bertelsmann/RTL (Channel 5) (6 per cent)

One of the most significant moves in the UK television was the almost unnoticed takeover of Channel 5 in early 2000 by Europe's largest audio-visual group. RTL is the biggest commercial television broadcaster in Germany and is now in a group which includes Pearson Television (home of *Neighbours*, *The Bill* etc.). The major shareholder in the group is German media conglomerate Bertelsmann, a global media company only lacking a Hollywood studio in order to join Sony, Vivendi, Disney etc. RTL operates in France and the Netherlands as well as Germany and the UK.

BSkyB (7 per cent)

Sky began satellite broadcasting in 1989 and in 1998 launched Sky Digital. Over ten million UK households can now access Sky channels, with Sky Movies and Sky Sports proving the most popular channels in multi-channel homes. BSkyB is effectively controlled by News Corporation, even though only 37.5 per cent of shares are directly owned by Rupert Murdoch's company. BSkyB is less affected by the advertising downturn because revenue comes mainly from subscription. BSkyB is finally moving towards profitability after many years of losses brought on by investment in digital delivery etc. News Corporation has had other European interests channelled through BSkyB, including an abortive link-up with Kirch TV in Germany.

Other players (all other satellite and cable channels: 15 per cent)

NTL and Telewest control most of the UK's cable franchises. Telewest also operates some channels directly through Flextech (Bravo, Living, UK Gold etc.). Global media conglomerate Vivendi Universal has no direct control over UK television, but it has significant stakes in BSkyB (22 per cent) and RTL as well as interests in cable and satellite channels. The US majors, Time-Warner, Disney and Viacom, all have a significant presence in UK multi-channel homes through music and entertainment channels such as MTV, Nickelodeon (both Viacom) and Cartoon Network (Time-Warner).

As well as the advertising downturn, the main problem for distributors (i.e. as distinct from content providers) is the enormous cost of the switch to digital. The percentage of new customers who fail to stay with the new service and are later disconnected reflects the so-called **churn** rate, sometimes as high as 23 per cent, which has caused problems for NTL and Telewest in particular. The two cable companies are already carrying huge piles of debt (billions of pounds) and, as well as worrying about churn, they have had to negotiate content.

Sport and Movies have been the biggest attractions on new television services and most options have already been taken up by BSkyB, which, having paid very high prices, is beginning to be rewarded by low churn and increasing revenue from subscribers. ITV frantically bought football outside the Premiership at a high price. Some of the audiences for ITV Sport when it began as a pay-per-view service were so small that critics noted that it would have been cheaper to take customers to the matches, paying for hotel rooms and other extras.

The cost of the move to digital may well be the factor which delivers Carlton and/or Granada into the hands of a US major. The BBC did not attempt to build its own digital platform, but instead ensured that its channels were available on all the existing platforms. When the new digital channels (CBBC, CBeebies, 3 and 4 etc.) were announced, the commercial companies cried foul – and the government did temporarily withdraw permission for BBC3. The assumption that BBC channels must be 'universally available' like other public utilities such as water, electricity etc. is a feature of PSB principles.

The effect of ownership patterns on output

There isn't space here to give even a broad-brush summary of what is available on UK television channels. We can, however, make some observations about the distinctive programming that attracts high ratings or significant specialist audiences, and relate these to ownership

- A significant proportion of 'quality' drama is produced by UK independents commissioned by ITV, Channel 4 and BBC, e.g. Red in Manchester responsible for *Clocking Off* and *Queer as Folk*. If the UK broadcasters are forced to reduce costs, these programmes and the independents who make them may have to seek new outlets.

- 'In-house' productions by ITV are not shared out equally. Granada companies (e.g. Yorkshire, LWT, Anglia) produce the vast majority of ITV Network programmes. As advertising revenue falls, more pressure falls on flagship Granada programmes such as *Coronation Street* to 'prop up' audience share. There are signs that, by trying too hard for ratings, the programme is losing popularity.

- A number of succesful UK programmes are based on 'formula' or format programmes created by international production companies such as Endemol (*Big Brother*) and RTL/Pearson/Grundy (*The Bill*, *Neighbours*). RTL is showing an interest in developing Channel 5's programme range and programmes such as these could lure audiences away from ITV.

- The potential for exploitation of programme material across broadcast television and 'new media' is likely to be an important factor in future.

- No British broadcaster can now afford to be sole producer of high-cost drama series and more partnerships with overseas producers are inevitable (with possible implications of less culturally specific (i.e. less 'British') content?).

- As a major UK broadcaster, BSkyB has a poor record as a producer, and the overall proportion of British-produced material across Sky channels is small.

Ideas about the quality and diversity of programme material on UK television depend on matters of personal taste. However, the observations here suggest that, whilst there is clearly competition in the television market and innovation in new programme types, there is some pressure on the British producers of expensive forms such as drama.

Public service broadcasting (PSB)

The current PSB sector in the UK comprises:

- BBC Television and Radio
- Channel 4 and S4C.

The BBC was established by Royal Charter, which has been renewed on a ten-yearly basis (2006 is the next renewal date), in order to provide radio and television services in the UK plus the World Service. Governors are appointed by the Crown (i.e. effectively the government) and they in turn appoint the executives. The Corporation is, in theory, 'independent' of, or 'at arm's length' from the government. In practice, pressure can be exerted on BBC management in two ways:

- Governors may be appointed because of their sympathies for government policies.
- Parliament must agree any increase in the licence fee, and there is no guarantee that the BBC will automatically be able to increase its income in line with inflation.

The BBC is self-regulating (see Chapter 18). Responsibility for all broadcasts lies with the senior management. There are relatively few external restraints on BBC operations, and BBC Worldwide, a separate organisation in financial terms, exploits BBC programme material, selling to subscription channels in the UK and abroad and direct to the public in magazines and videos. Profits from this venture are fed back into programme-making, supplementing the licence fee.

Channel 4 has a remit first established by Parliament in 1981 and then revised in the Broadcasting Acts of 1990 and 1996. Initially a subsidiary of the Independent Broadcasting Authority (the forerunner to the Independent Television Commission), Channel 4 became a public corporation in 1993 with a ten-year licence from the ITC. The non-executive directors who make up the majority of the Board of Directors are appointed by the ITC, which is also the regulator for Channel 4. Channel 4 is funded by sale of advertising time. Originally this was organised via the ITV companies, which took some of the income, but Channel 4 is now able to sell time on its own behalf and to keep all the income.

S4C is a statutory authority set up in Wales to provide a service using programme material from the BBC and Channel 4, as well as commissioned work, and it is obliged to broadcast some programmes in the Welsh language. It is like the BBC in being a self-regulating broadcaster (even though it must follow ITC rules on advertising).

Defining PSB

This checklist of features is based on work by an independent agency, the Broadcasting Research Unit, during the 1980s (see O'Malley and Treharne 1993). Although the overall media environment has changed dramatically since the 1980s, the list remains useful. PSB should:

- provide a full range of programming to meet audience needs for education, entertainment and information
- be universally available (i.e. throughout the UK)
- cater for all interests and tastes
- cater for minorities
- have a concern for 'national identity' and community
- be detached from vested interests and government
- be one broadcasting body financed directly by the body of users
- promote competition in good programming rather than in numbers of viewers
- be run on guidelines which liberate and do not restrict programme-makers.

This is a more useful set of criteria (which we shall now examine separately) than traditional definitions which simply quote the relevant sections of broadcasting legislation or the BBC's Charter. It refers to many of the debates about the institution of broadcasting which have developed since the mid-1980s, when a 'free market philosophy' was first brought to bear on all aspects of public provision by the Thatcher government. It also helps us think about changes in technology and global issues of media production and distribution as they affect the UK.

Range of programming

The BBC and Channel 4 are both required to carry educational programming and significant news and current affairs. This is written into the BBC charter and the Channel 4 licence. The removal of education programming from the ITV network after the 1990 Broadcasting Act was both a symbolic move away from an ITV PSB role and an opportunity to develop morning and afternoon programming.

Universal access

A universal service is one provided according to need rather than profit and is based on 'equality of access'. The same argument applies to most of the now privatised utilities, implying that every consumer is entitled to the same service, despite the difference in cost of supply – the low-cost services effectively subsidise the high-cost ones. A good example is postal services. We all expect to send and receive letters with the same charge for a stamp and the same guarantees on delivery whether we live in a London suburb or on a remote Scottish island. However, this 'public service' monopoly is not guaranteed for ever, and the current Blair government has already started to think about privatisation. The telephone network was once in the public sector. Supporters of privatisation point to the rapid expansion of mobile phone services which have become 'essential' for many users as a triumph for the 'free market'. Yet they work only where a mast has been erected, which excludes parts of the UK, and which needs public agreement for health and other reasons.

The 'capture' of exclusive screenings of popular sporting events by BSkyB is a good example of the 'equal access' to broadcasts received as part of a public service being replaced by willingness to pay for an **encrypted service** (i.e. one requiring the viewer to pay a fee to decode the signal). It has therefore become a matter for parliamentary debate as to which sporting events are of special national interest and should therefore be reserved for 'free access' terrestrial television. (See list on www.culture.gov.uk.)

This has proved to be a difficult debate. The enormous growth in the revenue possibilities for Premier League football clubs in England has had an impact on many other sports. Television and sport are inextricably linked. The cricket authorities have argued successfully that, without the freedom to sell television rights to the highest bidder, the game might not be able to maintain the standard of test cricket in the UK (i.e. not enough money comes in via the gate receipts and sponsorship).

The BBC has itself entered into various agreements and deals which see it participating in delivery of programming on cable and satellite which is restricted in some way. In partnership with Flextech, now a content provider owned by the cable company Telewest, BBC material now appears on UK Gold, UK Horizon etc.

Access also relates to physical location. The postal analogy is useful here. A broadcast signal (as distinct from satellite or cable) is notoriously difficult (and expensive) to deliver in parts of the country where hills prevent reception. Should broadcasters receive extra public funds to make transmission to these areas possible? Channel 5's launch suffered from difficulties in delivering a worthwhile signal to around 30 per cent of the population. Channel 5 is a private-sector organisation, but should government have done more to enable potential viewers to receive the signal (some areas cannot be covered because a broadcasting frequency is not available)?

Catering for all interests, tastes and minorities

Equality of access also extends to consumer tastes. Does the public service provider broadcast 'something for everyone', including some programmes which have limited appeal or which need to be given time for the taste for them to be acquired? There is a limit to the range of specialist interests which can be included (and some may be deemed offensive to other groups) but there is a clear duty for both BBC and Channel 4 to act in such a way to guarantee a range of programming, from *EastEnders* to *The Late Review*, *Countdown* to *World Cinema*.

The BBC aims to provide a broad spread of popular programming on BBC1 and to supplement this with more varied material on BBC2. Channel 4 has the licence requirement to cater for interests beyond those targeted by ITV, in terms of both programme content and 'experimental and innovative approaches to broadcasting'. But both the BBC and Channel 4 have shifted some of their 'niche programming' to digital channels that are not accessible to half the population. Where world cinema or an arts documentary might have appeared on BBC2 or Channel 4, it has now been replaced by a 'lifestyle programme' about gardening or interior decorating. World Cinema is now on BBC4 or Film Four (a subscription channel). Does this mean that the equal access requirement has not been met?

How does PSB work in a multi-channel television environment? There are contradictory messages coming through to broadcasters and regulators. On the one hand, there is plenty of evidence that the expectations of digital television pioneers are not being met – the number of UK satellite and cable subscribers is growing more slowly than the major players have forecast. Yet, when viewers are offered a choice, they are increasingly finding other channels to watch. In 2001 the total share of viewing held by BBC1 and BBC2 was under 40 per cent. Can the BBC still justify the licence fee if only a third of licence fee payers are actually watching? What does PSB mean if, even with Channel 4 included, less than half the audience is watching?

One of the ironies of the 'competitive market conditions' which have developed in recent years is that this requirement to cater for more specialised tastes has not, at first sight, been the weak point of PSB provision. The commonly held view, that 'dumbing-down' in the face of commercial competition from satellite and cable was inevitable, can be challenged. The figures show that it is ITV which is losing audiences while BBC2 and Channel 4 are keeping roughly their share (see Table 7.1). 'Others' includes all non-terrestrial satellite and cable viewing. The 2002 figures are for a single month and use the new BARB system introduced in February 2002.

Table 7.1 Audience share for UK broadcasters 1997–2002

	BBC1	BBC2	ITV	C4	C5	Others
2002 (April)	26.2	10.9	24.8	9.6	6.4	22.1
1999	28.4	10.8	31.2	10.3	5.4	14
1997	31.8	11.4	35.2	10.3	n.a.	11.2

ACTIVITY 7.5

Audience share

Look at Table 7.1 carefully.

- What has been the main impact of the arrival of Channel 5 on the audience shares of the other broadcasters?
- Has broadcasting funded primarily by advertising increased its share since 1997?
- Has the PSB share changed significantly?
- Try to check the current figures in *Broadcast* or on the BARB website – what has happened since 2002?

There is an argument that suggests that the relative success of Channel 4 and BBC2 is indeed due to their having gone for more popular programming. However, advertisers are pleased to see that in relative terms (i.e. as a proportion of any audience) Channel 4 attracts more ABC1s than other channels, considerably more sixteen- to twenty-four-year-olds and nearly 25 per cent more of the hard-to-capture 'light viewers' (Channel 4 Annual Report 1997). This is an issue about 'niche' or specialised markets. As long as these markets are supported by ABC1 consumers, there is going to be a demand for programming to target them (and by extension, a case for BBC2 to offer a service). The problem comes when the 'minority taste' is shared only by relatively poor consumers who are not of interest to advertisers.

The segmenting of audiences by ethnic or language grouping is interesting in that providing programming for all so-called 'minority communities' was a main aim of Channel 4 programming in the 1980s but has arguably been less noticeable since the early 1990s. In the meantime, several satellite and cable channels have developed to serve South Asian communities in the UK, all on subscription only. It is difficult to obtain viewing figures for these channels (they are not published regularly by BARB), but there is a large potential market, partially served by video rental and the resurgence of cinemas showing Bollywood films. Looked at a different way, there are over a million Muslims in the UK – a sizeable market with at least one common interest in religious festivals.

ACTIVITY 7.6

Minority audiences

What is a 'minority audience'? Which audiences deserve to be supported by licence payers? When BBC4 was launched in March 2002 its first few nights attracted a maximum of 180,000 people for three consecutive minutes or more (the definition of 'audience reach') (Report, *Guardian* 7 March 2002).

- Bearing in mind the comments about 'minority tastes' above, draw up a list of types of programming which might appeal to specific minority tastes.

- Draw up a second list of criteria to use in deciding which programmes should be broadcast on a public service channel. What would be your cut-off point for audience numbers?

Concern for 'national identity' and community

This issue has already been broached in relation to the 'reserve' list of television events, especially sporting events. Its long history and its active role in supporting morale during the Second World War helped to create a sense of the BBC as a 'national institution', which has great resonance for older viewers and listeners. Some of this has been passed on to younger audiences (not least because the BBC is able to use its archives to support or even help create commemorations such as those for Queen's Golden Jubilee in 2002 and thereby to re-establish its reputation). 'The BBC helps to sustain a uniquely British, immensely varied national identity, across every part of the United Kingdom. We try to stretch audiences and to stretch talent. We are the bridge between the two' (John Birt, Director-General of the BBC, 75th Anniversary Lecture, January 1998).

Whenever there is some form of 'national event', the BBC is still most likely to be the 'natural' access point for most viewers and listeners. (Which media source did you turn to when the events of 11 September 2001 unfolded?) But what is a 'national event'? Increasingly, broadcasters are looking for what has become called a 'watercooler' programme – an American idea referring to any programme that people in an office feel compelled to discuss when they meet around the water machine. The most significant such programmes in recent years have arguably been *Big Brother* and *Pop Idol* – on Channel 4 and ITV respectively.

But this sense of national leadership can also provoke resistance to a sense of stuffiness or superiority (particularly a sense of metropolitan condescension for audiences outside London). As if to counter this perception, the ITC licence was amended to require Channel 4 to originate more than 30 per cent of UK production from outside London by 2002.

Channel 4 has a PSB role to 'innovate', not an assumed leadership role – indeed, it could be argued that its role is to counter the BBC's appeal and offer a different sense of national identity, which it has done at Christmas with an alternative 'Queen's Speech'. Do you see this as a bit of fun, mildly offensive or as making a serious point? Certainly, there is an obvious question about what is the 'national identity' for audiences in the UK, especially since Scottish and Welsh devolution (see Chapter 15). The more difficult aspects of the question arise with the coverage of the death of members of the royal family. The reactions to the coverage of the funeral of Diana, Princess of Wales and the much more muted response to Princess Margaret's funeral suggest that 'reading the public mood' may be difficult.

The main point here is that the PSB dimension does give an advantage to the BBC, and perhaps, to a lesser extent, to Channel 4. Private sector companies like BSkyB would find it difficult to present a case for their own programming to be seen as representing national identity, especially when the major interest in the channel is held by Australian-American Rupert Murdoch (although it has to be said that the *Sun* newspaper has often been successful in waving the Union Jack). Similarly, the separate companies which make up ITV have rarely managed to compete effectively with the BBC over coverage of national events via the operations of ITN and ITV Sport.

ACTIVITY 7.7

Idents

Refer back to Chapter 1 and discussion of logos. Consider the 'idents' or channel logos for the main broadcasters (and cable stations if possible).

- What do the idents signify about the ethos of the programming on the channel?

- In particular compare idents for the PSB and private sector channels – is there an obvious difference?
- Do any of the idents pick up on ideas of national identity?

Detachment from vested interests and government

At the centre of the PSB argument is the idea of an independent and impartial broadcaster, serving the interests of the whole population of the UK, not just the government of the day or private shareholders.

The system works by vesting the legal authority for the operation of the PSBs in legislation or Royal Charter. This in turn sets up management structures independent of government and a reasonable period of guaranteed 'licence' in which to operate. It is worth remembering, however, that a government minister, in 2002 the Secretary of State for Culture, Media and Sport, effectively appoints the Chair of BBC Governors and of Channel 4. The government is also able to determine the BBC licence fee and to change the rules governing Channel 4's finances.

One broadcasting body financed directly by users

This criterion perhaps best reveals the 1980s arguments which underpin the list. In relation to the increasingly global media production and distribution environment and the similarly 'open' financial environment (i.e. the absence of protective legislation against multinational corporations moving into national markets), it is difficult to predict the future of PSB.

The principle at stake is clear. The use of the term 'one body' states a case for a dedicated PSB provider, unencumbered with distracting and possibly conflicting aims in other sectors or territories or with partners of any kind. Both the BBC and Channel 4 have found it necessary to seek partners in order to finance productions. Often this is with other PSB providers in

North America or Europe, but the BBC sees itself as a major 'player' and has made deals with a number of private-sector organisations, including Discovery Channel and Flextech.

The licence fee does see the BBC funded directly by its 'users', whereas Channel 4 relies on sale of advertising. The BBC also raises revenue from the sales of programmes and related material. Subscription income has come from encrypted programming, and the Flextech package takes advertising.

If the principle is clear and the danger identified – a broadcasting environment dominated by multinational media corporations unlikely to conform to PSB strictures – the direction of future policy is not so clear. The cultural importance of a securely financed 'British broadcaster' is such that any UK government is likely to feel that it is in the public interest to allow the BBC to make its deals and to retain a place in the international market. This might also explain why governments have been amenable to the 'consolidation' of the ITV network companies into two main groups – rather domination by Granada and Carlton than possible entry by larger American players. Stopping a European company such as Bertelsmann from getting control of both ITV and Channel 5 may be more of a problem.

Competition in programming rather than numbers of viewers

UK television moved during the Thatcher years from programme-led production to advertising-led production. This was the inevitable result of the promotion of the market as determining factor. It is difficult to assess exactly how the 'ethos' of an organisation changes, but in Chapter 8 there is an analysis of the changing 'culture' of production. If contemporary television is compared to the so-called 'Golden Age' of the 1970s, there is little doubt that current producers are much less likely to be supported by management if risky ventures don't show immediate returns in terms of audience numbers. The future of PSB is in doubt if 'ratings' become the only basis for judging the success of programmes.

Liberation not restriction for programme-makers

This criterion follows on from the last one. Again, it suggests harking back to a Golden Age when programme-makers were supported and nurtured. The impact of the 25 per cent production quota has been to:

* create a group of small independent production companies with loose ties to broadcasters
* assist in the breaking-up of the long-established production units in the BBC.

While it will still be possible to maintain short-term relationships with creative partnerships of writers, directors and producers, there is no going back, and, as the BBC continues to become more 'efficient' it risks alienating many of its previous supporters. This is a trend which Greg Dyke set out to reverse.

Digital broadcasting and global media

The ideas about PSB discussed above were all developed before the 1980s when broadcasting remained largely a concern of nationally defined organisations. (One feature of the earlier period was the limited number of broadcast frequencies allocated by international agreement and then internally by national governments – 'spectrum scarcity'.) The loosening of regulatory controls, government policies fostering competition and the development of new technologies for programme delivery (i.e. satellite, cable and digital broadcasting) means that all territories are opening up to penetration by global rather than solely national broadcasters.

In this context the BBC seems, at first glance, in a stronger position than Channel 4. The BBC is a 'global broadcaster' and has been so for longer than any other body. The radio World Service has been for many critics the epitome of a PSB ideal, offering news which

attempts a real degree of impartiality and comment on events in all parts of the world, delivered in many languages. But it has become increasingly short of resources, as well as being marginalised by the expansion of television services such as CNN. In order to fund BBC World Television, the corporation has had to divert resources from other areas or raise extra money (PSB critics ask why UK licence payers should fund a 'World Service').

A different challenge comes in the home market, where PSB faces a difficult future. In order to get some perspective on this debate it is helpful to compare the UK situation with that of other countries. Television Studies has often tended to compare the UK and the US, partly because of the familiarity of some of the programme material, partly because the difference in status for PSB in the two systems is so great.

In the US, broadcasting is dominated by four commercial networks: ABC (owned by Disney), CBS (owned by Viacom), NBC (owned by General Electric) and Fox Television (owned by News Corporation). Two new networks, WB TV (Time Warner) and UPN (Viacom), have been targeted mainly at younger viewers. All these networks have local 'affiliates' who take their programming and they also compete with independents, cable and satellite in terms of entertainment and news services. The Public Broadcasting System (PBS) is an affiliation of small television and radio stations in the major cities, with limited budgets (from donations and endowments) and small (but elite) audiences. They have limited capacity to make programmes and buy in material such as *Absolutely Fabulous* from the BBC and other larger producers. (They also co-produce with the BBC.)

The PSB situation in the US is so 'bad' (i.e. so limited by lack of resources) that in the UK it is assumed that 'it could never happen here', or the situation is used as a dire warning about what might happen if competition gets out of control. This was also the prediction of some commentators when commercial radio was launched in the UK. It has gradually moved towards American-style 'format radio' (i.e. playing a single type of music on a specific station), but the BBC has maintained a high profile and has even increased audiences for some network services such as Radio 5. American experiences do not necessarily travel to the UK.

The PSB funding dilemma

The major advantage of the licence fee to the BBC is a guaranteed income. The disadvantage is potential interference from the legislators in terms of setting fee levels. In return for the fee, PSB must be universal and accountable to the general audience.

The private-sector competition has for long been dependent on advertising income. We've noted that this can rise or fall with the strength of the economy and it is always vulnerable to competition from other media selling space. Some of the newer private services are funded by direct fee for each programme watched (Pay Per View, PPV) or subscription to a channel (BSkyB now gets an annual income from movie subscription channels which is greater than the annual UK cinema box office). These new methods mean that viewers are now more closely tied to 'products purchased' than to a PSB ideal.

The dilemma for PSB is clear. Stick with the licence fee and watch production values fall and audiences with them (the rise in the licence fee has failed to match inflation in production costs for several years now) or go for more popular programming ('dumbing down'?) and face criticism from important political supporters? BBC attempts to find new partners and increase commercial revenue are similarly fraught with dangers. Seeing the BBC logo associated with a commercial venture might make some audiences think about 'selling-out', while others will wonder why they pay a licence fee if the corporation can make money through charging for its services.

ACTIVITY 7.8
Paying for television
There are several ways to pay for television services:
- advertising, e.g. current ITV, Channel 4 etc.
- licence fee, e.g. BBC
- PPV, e.g. 'one-off' sports events, concerts
- subscription, e.g. Sky Movie Channels.

Think about your own viewing habits. Imagine that you could have only one form of television service, paid for by only one of these methods. Which would you choose? Now think about two other groups of viewers: a family with young teenagers, an older person living alone. What would be best for them?
- What does this exercise tell you about the dilemma for PSB?

In the global/regional media market the future of UK broadcasting is to a large extent tied up with Europe and the EU. Policies relating to PSB are discussed at EU level and are to a certain extent 'built in' to regulatory duties expected of appropriate agencies in all EU member countries (similar PSB and private sector issues are found in most parts of Europe). It is no surprise then, that Rupert Murdoch has made several attempts to counter the views of the BBC and to woo EU commissioners. Murdoch is watched with some trepidation by European television companies.

Jeannette Steemers (1998) is a useful source on the European dimension of this issue as well as the future of PSB in the digital world. This is a very complex debate, and we can pick out only a few main points here, but they will act as a summary of this case study and should be considered in relation to other parts of the book:
- The digital 'revolution' has already shown that it will take longer to 'work through' than many commentators first thought.
- The BBC and Channel 4 have participated in the revolution so far.

- The future of the licence fee is still doubtful; subscription is becoming an important revenue source for broadcasters.
- The principle of PSB still has mileage in the twenty-first century, but the PSB institutions of the last twenty years may not be the most appropriate organisations for the future.
- The convergence of media technologies means that other forms of public access to media may be appropriate as well as, or instead of, PSB (e.g. guaranteed Internet access for all households).

References

Ellis, John (2000) *Seeing Things: Television in the Age of Uncertainty*, London: I. B. Taurus.

Holland, Patricia (2000, 2nd edition) *The Television Handbook*, London: Routledge.

O'Malley, Tom and Treharne, J. (1993) *Selling the Beeb*, London: Campaign for Press and Broadcasting Freedom.

Steemers, Jeannette (1998) 'On the threshold of the "digital age": prospects for public broadcasting', in Jeannette Steemers (ed.) *Changing Channels*, Luton: University of Luton Press/John Libbey Media.

Further reading

Abercrombie, Nicholas (1996) *Television and Society*, Cambridge: Polity.

Crisell, Andrew (1997) *An Introductory History of British Broadcasting*, London: Routledge.

Geraghty, Christine and Lusted, David (eds) (1998) *The Television Studies Book*, London and New York: Arnold.

Hood, Stuart and Tabary-Peterssen, Thalia (1997, 4th edition) *On Television*, London: Pluto.

O'Sullivan, Tim, Dutton, Brian and Reyner, Philip (1998, 2nd edition) *Studying the Media: An Introduction*, London, New York, Melbourne and Auckland: Arnold.

Scannell, Paddy (1990) 'Public service broadcasting: the history of a concept', in Andrew Goodwin and Gary Whannel (eds) *Understanding Television*, London: Routledge.

Thompson, John B. (1997) *The Media and Modernity: A Social Theory of the Media*, Cambridge: Polity.

Websites

www.barb.co.uk

www.culture.gov.uk

www.digitaltelevision.gov.uk

8 Industries

Depending on your course, you may find discussion of media 'industries' is subsumed under the heading of 'Media Institutions'. We think these are best kept distinct. Institutions are discussed in Chapter 7.

The common view of 'the media' equates their activities with glamour and excitement, creativity and controversy. There are such moments, of course – more perhaps than in other types of work. But, crucially, media activity is a commercial, industrial process, whether by major corporations or small producers. In this chapter we explore their processes, using some of the tools of economic analysis.

Economic activity can be roughly divided between the production of *goods* and *services*. In most 'developed' economies (e.g. those of North America and western Europe), the emphasis has shifted away from manufacturing goods, which often now takes place in South East Asia or eastern Europe where labour and other costs are lower, towards the provision of *services*. Take the provision of telephone services or supermarket retailing. In both there is a heavy emphasis on 'serving the consumer' but the provision of that service is often dependent on the global economy (telephone help lines set up in India, supermarket green beans flown in from Africa).

Are modern media industries producing goods or services? The simple answer is both. They certainly represent a modern form of economic activity, spanning the globe, utilising the latest technology and constantly innovating in order to stimulate and then attempt to satisfy consumer needs and 'wants'. These industries produce '*goods*' – you only have to wander round an HMV or Virgin Megastore to realise just how many tapes, discs, magazines etc. are available – and *services*: a trip to the cinema means being offered an entertainment service. If we enjoy it, we may buy the product (i.e. the video or DVD) for our own use later. Media industries make money from 'communication' of entertainment and information to a mass market. Different sectors are organised like manufacturing plants or like service providers.

Media production as a factory process

Some media activity can be related to traditional forms of 'factory
production'. We can even compare production of a daily newspaper with that
of, for example, tinned baked beans. They share:

- initial investment in plant and machinery – fixed assets
- a daily demand for the product, requiring continuous production and a
  constant supply of raw materials (paper, ink and 'raw news'; beans and
  cans)
- distribution of the product to all parts of the economy
- stimulation of demand, including market research to ensure up-to-date
  information about performance of the product and the satisfaction of
  customers
- advertising the product to keep it in the public eye and to attract new
  buyers.

See Chapter 13.

These common features are important – media industries usually make
decisions based on standard business principles. Yet media industries are
different from most other forms of manufacture, and it is these differences
(sometimes called 'specificities') which we want to explore in more detail.
Let's stay with the production of print-based news:

- The 'raw material' is not homogeneous – skill and cultural, aesthetic and
  political judgements are necessary in selection of events which will be
  marketed as 'news'.
- The price of news varies – some is free, some (especially if celebrity-related)
  may be very expensive to purchase or access.
- The product is not always a necessity and demand can fall if consumers'
  tastes change.
- Production and distribution patterns are not fixed – the product can be
  transmitted electronically and reproduced locally.
- Staff costs will generally be greater than in other forms of manufacture
  because a greater variety of skills are required in the process.
- This particular product has a shelf life of only one day (really, only half a
  day).
- Revenue from sale of the product is only part of the business – a large
  proportion comes from the sale of advertising space. Advertisers therefore
  have influence on the fortunes of the product.

These points suggest that managing this kind of media production process is
a particularly complex (and risky) business. The two most important
considerations for the newspaper producer are:

- the collection and processing of suitable news material
- the distribution of the finished product.

The actual production (i.e. page make-up and printing) of the newspaper is perhaps not as crucial as you might think in determining the success of the product. Certainly, the quality of the feature material and the 'look' of the paper will contribute greatly to its long-term reputation, but they won't necessarily boost the circulation as dramatically as a sensational story. Nor will they immediately impress the advertisers. Media products such as newspapers depend on a complex mix of factors for their success – it's the same news and similar features most of the time, so why the different circulation figures and different advertising revenue for individual newspaper titles?

Part of what makes commercial media products different is the definition of the target audience. It doesn't just matter that the product is sold, but that it is sold to a specific readership. *The Times* distributes roughly twice as many copies of each edition as the *Guardian*, but the *Guardian* is able to offer advertisers a more clearly defined readership group with specific interests. The Selling audiences case study following Chapter 6 suggests some ways in which audiences can be specified. If poor distribution means that the product doesn't get to the customer in time, all the production effort will be wasted. All industries depend on good distribution, but there are special considerations for many kinds of media products.

The *Guardian* sells at a higher price and also takes more advertising, especially specialist advertising, in G2 sections such as Media, Education etc. *The Times* gives away 'bulk copies' to boost circulation.

Long-life media – a different process?

In film or music production there is a rather different production process, or at least a different emphasis, from that of the daily newspaper, or even the daily or weekly television programme. Purchase of a CD or a ticket for the cinema has to be a more calculated decision (measured against a higher price and a greater commitment of time and effort). The 'product' is not 'consumed' completely – we may return to experience the film again at a later date and we will listen to the CD repeatedly. With a shelf-life longer than the single day of the newspaper, there is the possibility of building an audience for a film or a musical performance over several weeks as well as developing a number of associated products.

It is even possible that as a collector's item the product will increase in value over time. Since the product is also reproducible from a 'master copy', it can be 'relaunched' again in the future at minimum cost and attract a new set of buyers. Walt Disney was the first to recognise this phenomenon, and in by using it saved his film studio. He saw that animated films did not date as quickly as live action features and that, since a large part of his audience was made up of young children, he could rerelease classic films such as *Snow White and the Seven Dwarfs* (US 1937) and *Pinocchio* (US 1939) every seven years to a new audience. This strategy has been altered by the advent of video, but it is still relevant and has been applied to other classic films such as *Gone With the*

Wind (US 1939) and *Star Wars* (US 1977). A recyclable product is also a recyclable **brand** name, and the modern Disney company has benefited further from **merchandising** spin-offs. Like Warner Bros, Disney has recognised the value of its brand names and has opened retail outlets to maximise profits. Music companies have also realised that 'classic recordings' can be digitally re-mastered and re-packaged for collectors and for new audiences.

> Newspapers have a short life as consumer products, but they have always had a long-term value as **archive** material. Possibilities for this were once limited by storage space but can now be commercially exploited on CD-ROM and on-line.

Types of activities

So far we have referred both to 'media industries' and to specific production activities. Up until the 1990s, each medium of production was seen to involve distinct industrial processes:

- film
- television
- radio
- newspapers
- magazines
- music recording.

(We might also include book publishing, although this has traditionally been kept outside 'the media' – why do you think this might be?)

Now, we commonly refer to the **convergence** of different industrial processes so that similar activities are common to more than one media industry. The main technological engine for this development is digital media production. Workers in all the six industries above sit concentrating on very similar computer screens, manipulating a mouse and 'dragging' files whether they contain sounds, images or text. At the other end of the process, the pattern of ownership and control across media industries means that most of the major companies involved have an interest in at least four out of the six traditional industries as well as in the 'new' industry of electronic media (i.e. Internet services, computer games etc.).

But it is still worth exploring the differences that remain between the two main groups of media activities.

Gone with the Wind is still the most successful film ever made (adjusting box office for inflation) and has been rereleased many times. In 1998 it was released by New Line, the 'independent' arm of Warner Bros. Time Warner acquired the rights when they merged with Ted Turner's company. Turner had bought *Gone with the Wind* as part of the MGM film library and it was the most valuable asset in his portfolio. The new release added twelve minutes of new footage in a digitally re-mastered version. Two hundred prints were released (*Screen International*, 12 June 1998).

Merchandising The marketing of a wide range of consumer goods bearing images from a specific media product has a very long history, but the sheer scale of current merchandising dates from the release of *Star Wars* in 1977.

Newspapers and live broadcasting: radio and television

- continuous production and distribution – steady cash flow

- high fixed costs (printing plants, studios)

- high proportion of revenue from advertising

- universal distribution in a restricted area (i.e. national, regional or local)

- output taken to be entertainment and 'information'.

Recorded music and film production

- sporadic production, regular but not daily distribution, possibility of interrupted revenue flows

- each production has a separate budget (fixed costs can be avoided)

- revenue from 'rentals', merchandising, product placement

- no limits on potential global distribution

- output taken to be entertainment and 'art'.

There are other differences but these five oppositions raise interesting questions. To some extent 'new'(ish) technologies such as DVD, videotape, CD-ROM etc. have bridged some of the gaps (e.g. television programmes on tape are sold like films).

Film companies are now exploiting their archives of past productions, repackaging them for retail on DVD and selling rights to broadcast to specialist satellite and cable television channels. As films now go on to make as much money from television and video as from theatrical release, if not more, the major film companies do in fact achieve a steady flow of income, allowing them to survive a string of failures. Without this 'subsidy' from past successes, companies such as 20th Century Fox might have collapsed.

At the same time, television companies have moved away from producing their own programmes and have begun to buy in more programmes made by smaller 'independent' production companies. Channel 4 was the first UK television channel to be set up as a 'publisher broadcaster' – making no programmes itself and avoiding the burden of paying for expensive studio facilities. Television companies have also tried to break out of the restrictions of a local market by selling certain prestige programmes abroad. However, only the BBC in the UK is large enough to sustain an international broadcasting presence (through BBC World and the World Service on radio).

Newspapers have attempted, with various levels of success, to exploit their brand names and extend their market reach through use of new technologies, making archives available on CD-ROM and setting up electronic titles on the web. The *Guardian* has been particularly successful in attracting a much wider readership for its 'Guardian Unlimited' website than for the paper itself (which also prints in Europe and in its *Guardian Weekly* format for distribution worldwide). These activities definitely help secure the *Guardian's* reputation with readers and therefore with advertisers.

ACTIVITY 8.1

How do you think the magazine industry fits into this analysis? Does its reliance on advertising make it more like newspapers and broadcasting? Or does the relatively high cost of a magazine and its potential status for collectors make the industry more like film and music?

Six stages of media production

No matter what the media product or the industry sector, there tends to be a similar production process in each case, and you need to be aware of the stages of production as set out in the box below. The terms used by professionals in each industry sector differ but the most-often-studied industry is film production, and we will use that industry here to explore the questions raised by its specific organisation of the process. There is further discussion of the production process in Chapter 10.

Six stages of media production

- negotiating a deal
- pre-production and preparation
- production
- post-production
- distribution and marketing
- exhibition.

Negotiating a deal in contemporary Hollywood

The international film industry is dominated by a handful of major companies, still referred to as 'studios', even though they do not all own studio facilities as such and the majority of films they handle are actually made by small production companies. A film begins as an idea, 'pitched' to a studio. It is conceived as an individual product and put together by a producer as a 'package' of a story, stars and a director and crew. There are a number of ways in which the package can be financed, but for big-budget films the 'deal' will nearly always involve one of the major studios.

The six Hollywood majors have survived seventy years or more. Few other industries have such established brand names and it is the exploitation of this brand via global distribution of films (and videos) which keeps the majors ahead of the pack of smaller companies.

Major studios

- Warner Bros
- Sony Pictures
- Universal
- Disney
- Paramount
- 20th Century Fox

These are the six **majors**, which are all part of media conglomerates. MGM/UA is still technically a major but operates with a precarious business base – at the time of writing, rumours about a possible takeover are circulating. DreamWorks, the studio owned by Steven Spielberg, Jeffrey Katzenberg and David Geffen, is a major film producer, but acts as a distributor only in North America.

The concept behind a new film could be developed from many sources, but to interest the studios in the relatively 'conservative' atmosphere of Hollywood it will probably need to be supported by evidence of previous success associated with the ingredients of the proposal:

- a sequel to a recent box-office hit (e.g. sequels such as *Men in Black 2* and the next episodes of 'franchises' such as Harry Potter and James Bond)
- a remake of a European box-office hit (e.g. *Open Your Eyes* (Spain 1997) remade as *Vanilla Sky* (US 2001))
- an adaptation of a best-selling book (e.g. *Chocolat* (US 2000) from the Joanne Harris novel or the *Harry Potter* series)
- an original story by a proven scriptwriter such as Alan Ball (*American Beauty* (US 1999))
- an original idea from a successful director/star team, e.g. Steven Soderbergh and George Clooney
- a new twist on a story from a currently popular genre cycle
- any combination of the above.

It isn't always easy to work out why a deal 'seemed like a good idea at the time'. It can take as long as two or three years for a 'deal' to produce a finished film. In that time the 'big star' attracted to the project might have faded from view or public taste might have changed. Film producers have to make educated guesses about what will work with audiences a year or more in the future, and they have to gamble with very large sums of money.

This gamble is taken by a normally conservative financial sector which can take enormous risks in terms of production budget, when the chances of success at the cinema box office are actually quite small – most films lose money on theatrical release. (The combined total of *expenditure* on new films by Hollywood studios is often not much less than the total box-office *receipts* in the same period.) There are, however, good reasons why Hollywood continues to make profit.

Each of the major Hollywood studios finances a **slate** of seven or eight big films every year at a budget of around $50 million or more each, aiming for a smash hit during the two critical seasons which run in North America from May to August and Thanksgiving (late November) to Christmas. Some critics refer to these as '**ultra-high-budget films**' (see Maltby 1998). The studio will also probably release another dozen or so 'medium-budget' films. The budget for each film will include half as much again to spend on *P&A* (prints and advertising), giving an average of $75 million per film across the slate. With an outlay of over $1 billion on the slate, at least one film must be a big hit (grossing $200 million or more) for the studio to cover its costs. If a studio is very lucky and has a record-breaking blockbuster (e.g. *Titanic* with $1.3 billion in 1998), then profits can be substantial (*Titanic* was so expensive to make and market that it took two studios to distribute it). However, many films flop completely at the cinema box office (losing $50 million or more on a single picture is not unknown – the most recent disaster was *Town and Country* (US 2001), a romantic comedy with Warren Beatty).

'Tentpole movie' is another term for the 'ultra-high-budget' film, presumably on the grounds that one big blockbuster provides the support for the whole slate, just as the pole holds up the big top in the circus. This is one of the slang terms in the famous entertainment paper *Variety*.

Film rentals

It is common practice for the film industry to publish box-office figures, and they appear in the weekly '*Top 10*' as published in newspapers and on the Internet (see www.boxofficeguru.com). However, these figures are misleading as evidence of profitability. The 'rental charge' (what the exhibitor pays to the distributor) starts high on the first week and gradually falls. Around 50 per cent of final box-office is retained by the cinema exhibitor, and $100 million at the box office means that only $50 million is returned to the distributor (usually the studio that produced the film). This explains why for most films it takes the international and ancillary markets revenue to push the final total into profit.

The most dramatic example of box-office failure was the epic western *Heaven's Gate* in 1980. So much was lost that the studio, **United Artists**, collapsed completely and is now little more than a name. That was at a time when the majors were financially vulnerable. The relative stability of the majors' more recent operations is explained by two developments in the 1990s:

- the increase in the importance of the *international* theatrical (cinema) market, which is now roughly equivalent in value to North America (the 'domestic' market)

United Artists The sorry tale of the decline of United Artists is told in one of the best books about the studios, *Final Cut* by Bach (1985).

For Hollywood, 'domestic' describes the US and Canada; everything else is 'international'.

Video rentals and the majors
Hollywood once believed that the VCR could kill the industry (see Gomery 1992). But by the late 1980s video retail and rental on films had passed cinema box office. It is now recognised that audiences love movies so much that those who rent or buy videos also tend to go to the cinema most often (*Screen International*, 8 March 2002).

- the development of ancillary markets in video, pay television, computer games and merchandising, which are now more important than the traditional test of success at the North American box office.

(The situation in the UK mirrors the American experience. UK audiences pay most to watch films on satellite and cable. Video retail comes next. Cinema box-office revenues have been rising and now compete with video and DVD rentals. See the annual *BFI Handbook* for figures.)

The result of these changes in markets is that a higher proportion of ultra-high-budget features are likely to go into profit eventually. Richard Maltby (1998) suggests that as many as half the blockbusters will turn a profit, compared to one in ten in the pre-video days. What we should note is that, in economic terms, the majors can expect very long 'streams' of income from a successful film, so that in any single financial year they are guaranteed some income even if all the current releases are relative flops. It is this guarantee that keeps them in business and allows them to price out competitors by pushing up budgets.

The 'pitch' process is brilliantly satirised in Robert Altman's film *The Player* (US 1992). One of the best explanations of 'the deal' is in Pirie (1981).

The guarantee is valid only for what have been termed '**high-concept**' movies. Justin Wyatt (1994: 8) suggested that these represent "a style of film-making modelled by economic and institutional forces". High concept emphasises:

- successful pitching, especially via market research, and pre-sold marketability
- easily summarised idea (in twenty-five words or less, according to Steven Spielberg)
- successful saturation advertising. (See Branston 2000: 48.)

The six bullet points at the beginning of this section refer to the basis of this process (i.e. by reference to a proven source) and, if you add big stars and spectacle to the mix, you should be able to 'pitch' your own ideas.

ACTIVITY 8.2

The pitch

What ideas have you got for a new film – one which would definitely interest a Hollywood studio?

- Look back through the section above and develop your idea along the suggested lines.
- Think carefully about whom you would cast and, most important, try to sum up the idea in a single line (e.g. *Alien* = *Jaws* in space).
- Test out your outline on a friend. How well does it stand up?

This strange business, in which producers feel more secure with a large budget, sees investors nervous about 'low-budget' pictures. The budget may be artificially forced up towards the average (a form of 'institutional constraint'?) and star names added at large fees, even when the story doesn't necessarily need stars. What might be a 'big-budget' production in Europe – $10–20 million – is automatically seen as a 'small film' in Hollywood and thereby marginalised for North American distributors.

There are some small independent producers and distributors who succeed outside the orbit of the majors. Sometimes they can spot new markets ahead of the majors, or they are prepared to take on controversial issues or even controversial audiences. It is still possible to make low-budget films on strict production schedules and to sell them to specialist markets without the massive P&A spends of the majors. But it is becoming much more difficult. By the late 1990s nearly all the successful independent distributors had been 'acquired' by the majors, who continue to run them as separate businesses to maintain their image of 'independence' and, arguably, as their 'Research and Development' arm (see Wyatt 1998 on Miramax and New Line).

Given this background, it is not surprising that the setting-up period can be lengthy, and scripts may pass through the hands of many studio executives before they are 'greenlighted'. The gestation period for some films may be ten years or more. During this time a good deal of development money may have been spent by a studio on an **option** on the rights to the idea (known as the **property**) without a foot of film ever having been shot. What the owner of the property fears most is it being put into **turn-around** – a limbo-land for script ideas which languish with one studio until another comes along which is prepared to pick up the option (i.e. to pay enough to cover the development money paid out by the first studio). It's a wonder films get made at all.

Pre-production

Once the go-ahead has been given, the production team has a great deal to do before shooting begins. Parts must be cast (the lead players were probably decided as part of the original deal), locations chosen, costumes researched, dialogue coaches and wranglers (animal handlers) hired, hotel rooms booked etc. All this may take several months, during which time the script will be reworked and the direction of the project may be altered. A starting date is announced and reported in the trade press (*Hollywood Reporter*, *Variety* etc.) and eventually the cameras will roll (although it is not unknown for the plug to be pulled on the whole enterprise at this stage).

This preparation period is crucial to Hollywood production, and many commentators have identified the extra work on polishing the script and preparing storyboards for action sequences as the key to the high technical

---

Six stages of media production

The Full Monty (UK/US 1997) is a film 'without stars' in an American sense. The budget was low, allowing a very big international spend on promotion by distributor Fox Searchlight (an 'independent' operated by a major).

French producer/director Luc Besson made *The Fifth Element* (France 1997) in English on an $80 million budget. A relatively modest hit in North America, the film did Hollywood blockbuster-style business around the world and Besson has gone on to produce more films in this way.

See the British Film Industry case study following Chapter 12 for an example of this process with *Iris* (UK/US 2001).

Since a trade announcement is part of the process of drumming up interest in a production project, many more films are 'announced' than are actually made.

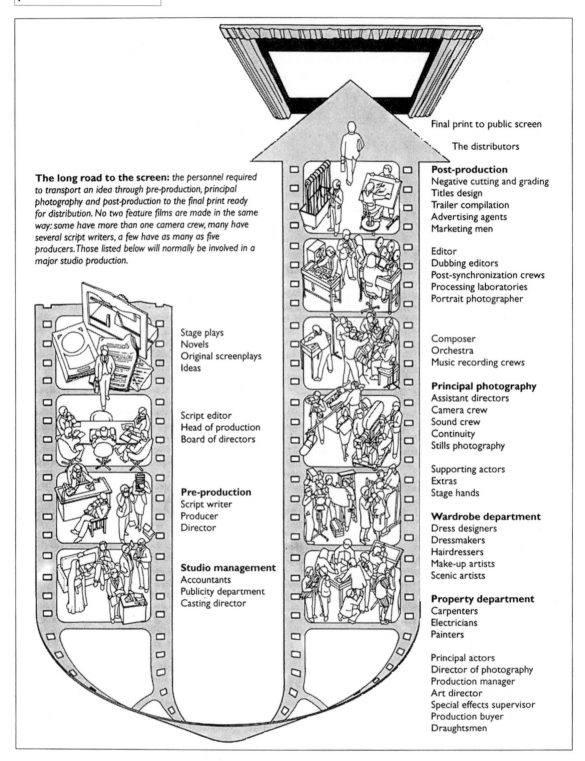

The long road to the screen: the personnel required to transport an idea through pre-production, principal photography and post-production to the final print ready for distribution. No two feature films are made in the same way: some have more than one camera crew, many have several script writers, a few have as many as five producers. Those listed below will normally be involved in a major studio production.

Stage plays
Novels
Original screenplays
Ideas

Script editor
Head of production
Board of directors

Pre-production
Script writer
Producer
Director

Studio management
Accountants
Publicity department
Casting director

Final print to public screen

The distributors

Post-production
Negative cutting and grading
Titles design
Trailer compilation
Advertising agents
Marketing men

Editor
Dubbing editors
Post-synchronization crews
Processing laboratories
Portrait photographer

Composer
Orchestra
Music recording crews

Principal photography
Assistant directors
Camera crew
Sound crew
Continuity
Stills photography

Supporting actors
Extras
Stage hands

Wardrobe department
Dress designers
Dressmakers
Hairdressers
Make-up artists
Scenic artists

Property department
Carpenters
Electricians
Painters

Principal actors
Director of photography
Production manager
Art director
Special effects supervisor
Production buyer
Draughtsmen

Figure 8.1 The long road to the screen from *Anatomy of the Movies* (Pirie 1981). This is still the same basic production process over twenty years later, although post-production has 'gone digital'.

quality of the finished product. But it isn't the only way to make a film – there are several highly regarded European and independent American films which have been made without a finished script.

At this point the producer should have a clear idea of the final budget. This will be used in the monitoring of progress on the shoot. If any costs look like over-running, changes to the script may have to be made. Figure 8.2 shows the outline for a feature film budget. The 'below the line' costs refer to the running costs of production. 'Above the line' costs refer to creative inputs.

Production

This stage is often called **principal photography**, and it is likely to be the shortest period of all. Modern films usually **wrap** in around fifty days of shooting – an average of two to three minutes a day – depending on the demands of the script. The low-budget producer will aim to halve that time by clever use of **set-ups** and tight scripting. Efficient directors are those who can come in 'on' or even 'under' budget. Keeping a whole crew on location a day longer than the planned schedule can add considerably to the overall cost, and directors and crews who can stick to schedules will be rehired.

Special effects which require shooting with actors can be a major problem and cause some productions to come back to studio lots or specialist facilities (including those in Britain); others go to locations offering cheaper labour or good deals on **permissions** (using famous buildings or locations), taxation etc. Hollywood has at various times made films in the south-eastern United States (Florida, Georgia, Alabama) or Canada, Europe and now Australasia.

'Shooting' is the most visible aspect of the production process and is frequently itself filmed in order to be used for publicity purposes. It therefore generates the most interest from the public. It also involves spending money 'on location', and there is a great deal of competition between locations to attract Hollywood productions.

	$ million
Above the line costs (ATL)	
1. Story rights	1.00
2. Writers' fees	1.00
3. Producers' fees	2.50
4. Directors' fees	2.50
5. Actors' fees	26.00
6. Stunts etc.	0.50
7. Subsistence	1.00
Total ATL	**34.50**
Below the line (BTL)	
8. Extras, stand-ins	0.75
9. Wardrobe, make-up etc.	1.70
10. Camera and film	1.50
11. Building sets	3.00
12. Set operation	1.00
13. Lighting	0.50
14. Sound	0.13
15. Special effects ('physical' – snow etc.)	0.25
16. Locations	0.60
17. Transport	1.75
18. Second Unit	0.90
19. BTL subsistence	1.40
Post production	
20. Digital effects	0.10
21. Editing	1.50
22. Titles	0.10
23. Music	1.20
24. Sound	0.60
25. Previews	0.10
26. Labs	0.25
Completion and miscellaneous	
27. Insurance, royalties etc.	0.40
28. Publicity	0.10
29. Miscellaneous expenses	0.10
Total BTL	**17.93**
Grand Total	**52.43**

Figure 8.2 Budget outline for a typical Hollywood feature film. This is based upon figures published in *Premiere* in July 2000.

New York is often impersonated in American films by Toronto. Liverpool and Manchester have represented European cities in several films.

Video recording of the shoot is now almost routine, providing some of the 'extra material' to be included on the DVD release.

Film equipment American companies dominate equipment supply, although French and German companies have also been important. UK-produced equipment has often copied American designs.

See Chapter 11 for more on Foley work.

Film production services

The film production process depends on access to a wide range of specialist services, and it is the provision of these which is another factor in preserving the dominance of Hollywood in the industry. Technology for filming (cameras, lenses, lighting, mounts etc.) and for post-production (editing and film-processing) is a specialised industry which requires high levels of investment and close co-operation between film-makers and technologists. The major studios have sought to maintain these relationships – even to the extent of buying into the companies involved.

Other services (e.g. financial, legal and promotional) are perhaps more mobile and more flexible, but their concentration in Los Angeles remains an important factor in maintaining the 'Hollywood community'.

Post-production

The longest stage in the process may well be post-production. Here the film is edited – some might say this is where the film narrative is actually created. The relationship between the director and the editor (or 'cutter') may be relatively distant or it may be very close, as in the case of Martin Scorsese and Thelma Schoonmaker, who work together for many months to complete a picture.

The increase in the importance of film sound during the last ten years has added to the work in post-production, with more time spent on tidying up dialogue through 'looping' or Automatic Dialogue Replacement (**ADR**) (actors record their lines again while watching themselves on a loop of film, played through until they can lip-sync perfectly) and adding sound effects using the **Foley Studio**. Special visual effects are also added at this stage. The completed film then goes to the laboratories for **colour grading** and other adjustments required to produce suitable screening prints.

Distribution and marketing

Every part of the process is important. The success of a film can depend at least as much on how it is handled by the distributor as on the film itself – indeed many experts call distribution the key to power in the media industries. Distributors promote and market films in particular **territories** and negotiate **release patterns** with exhibitors. The distribution of most big-budget Hollywood films is directly controlled by the majors themselves. In North America each major studio usually distributes its own pictures. In the UK, Paramount and Universal, with MGM-UA, are joint owners of the biggest distributor, UIP. In the other important cinema markets around the world the majors may have an agreement with a local distributor, but as the international market grows they are increasingly opening their own offices in every territory.

In 2001 the 'major studios', through their own distribution companies or in partnership, took over 80 per cent of the North American (US and Canada) market. A majority share for American films is evident in most territories in the world, with rare exceptions such as India and China (although Hollywood distribution is growing here). The growth of exhibition sites, especially in Europe, South East Asia and South America, has seen the international box office matching the domestic market. (For more on film distribution see Chapter 12.)

Exhibition

In the US the major studios were barred from ownership of significant cinema chains (following the **anti-trust legislation** at the end of the 1940s which signalled the decline of the studio system – see Maltby (1995) for a detailed account of the way in which Hollywood studios were organised between 1930 and 1950). Overseas there were no such restrictions, and in the last few years Warner Bros and UCI (owned by Paramount and Universal) have built multiplexes in many cinema markets, including the UK, where other US chains such as Showcase (owned by Viacom/Paramount's parent company, National Amusements) are also receptive to Hollywood films.

Ownership or control of every stage of production is known as **vertical integration**, and it has obvious advantages for the majors in ensuring that they will have a cinema available to take a film when it is ready for release. This isn't always the case for independent distributors who are trying to find outlets for their films. Coupled with the cost of advertising and prints, this lack of access to cinemas is one of the main ways in which new entrants to the film business are kept out. In 2001 six major exhibitors in the UK (Odeon, UGC, Showcase, Cine-UK, UCI and Warner) dominated the market and sold 70 per cent of the tickets.

The lack of cinema screens on which to release new films became a problem in the UK in the mid-1980s and was a factor in the building boom within British exhibition. The producers and distributors of art films tried to respond to the majors by copying them and becoming integrated distributors themselves (e.g. Artificial Eye and Curzon, with screens in London available for openings).

The distribution pattern of films and the exhibition practices in the UK have changed significantly since the American exhibitors moved in, and now much more resemble what happens elsewhere in Europe and North America.

UK cinema audience The class base of the audience has been a factor in the changing nature of film exhibition in the UK since the earliest days. The location of the multiplexes favours cinemagoers with transport and the extra spending power to pay higher admission prices. Research released by CAVIAR (Cinema and Video Industry Audience Research) in 2001 clearly shows that, even though more people were recognised as belonging to C2DE socio-economic groupings, the cinema audience was skewed in favour of ABC1s, who were much more likely to be 'frequent cinemagoers' (see also Chapter 13).

See Chapter 12 on Specialist Cinema Distribution.

Attendance habits have changed as a result. Although there are more screens, there are fewer cinemas (older cinemas have continued to close as multiplexes open) and virtually none in suburbs or small towns. Even in larger towns there may be only a single cinema. People will travel further to the cinema and most of us now have a multiplex with ten or more screens within half an hour's drive.

The major change for the exhibition sector will come with digital projection, which will require all cinemas to invest in new equipment. In the past with CinemaScope (a new screen in the 1950s) and Dolby Sound (new sound systems in the 1980s), this proved to take quite a long time and exhibitors took some convincing. **Digital projection** may be similarly a long time arriving, but new cinemas may have the equipment from the off.

Digital projection is being promoted by key industry figures such as George Lucas, who has had to pull back from making future *Star Wars* films 'digital only' because of slow progress in installing cinema equipment. In 2001 only three UK cinemas were available for commercial digital projection.

ACTIVITY 8.3
The production process model

To test out your understanding of the six-stage model, jot down some notes on what would happen in each stage of the production process for

- a new magazine for dance enthusiasts
- the first recordings by a new band.

You might have difficulty in deciding into which stage to put a particular activity – don't worry about this: using the model is not necessarily about getting 'right answers' but more about helping you to understand the process. This exercise should help in both your industry studies and your production work.

Organisation of production

Once we have been able to develop a model to describe the production process, what kinds of issues can we explore? Here are some from an industry approach.

Structure

How significant is the structure of the industry (the pattern of large and small companies in different sectors) in determining how media products are produced and what kinds of products appear? Two important questions centre on integration and regulation.

Integration refers to the growth of organisations by means of acquisition of other organisations in the same industry. **Vertical integration** refers to an organisation established in one part of the production chain gaining control of the other parts of the production process, e.g. a Hollywood studio being bought by a cinema chain (see Viacom Case Study below). A fully integrated media organisation would control every aspect of the production process. In the past, this has meant newspapers being produced by companies who even owned the trees from which the paper was made.

Horizontal integration   refers to media organisations acquiring control of their competitors within that segment of the production process (it is theoretically possible for an organisation to be both vertically and horizontally integrated, but that would mean that one organisation was effectively the whole industry). Ultimately, one organisation may control a majority share of the market – a **monopoly** position. More usually, there is at least one other competitor – creating a **duopoly**, as in UK cinema exhibition for many years, or UK television – or a small number of competitors of roughly equal status: an **oligopoly**. Most media industries – indeed most large-scale industries of any kind – are oligopolies.

Economists refer to the relationships between organisations in an oligopoly situation as **imperfect competition**. There are likely to be unwritten agreements between the oligopolists as to standards, pricing policies, labour relations etc. Because governments are likely to be concerned at the political implications of media monopolies, action is likely to be taken against 'too much' integration. This concern has increased as traditionally separate industries such as publishing, broadcasting and film have moved closer together.

Cross-media ownership has been a sensitive issue in the UK, which is unique in having a history of a strong national press with large circulations and a public service broadcasting environment. Fears grew of monopoly power in the mid-1990s. Tight controls have since been relaxed but the resistance to any move into terrestrial television by the dominant newspaper group, News International, is strong.

'Exactly half of this week's top 40 [bestselling books] are published by companies owned by just three global media groups: Pearson, Bertelsmann and News Corporation' (Joel Rickett, *Guardian* 17 August 2002).

ACTIVITY 8.4

Researching ownership

Use the newspaper archives in your library and/or the Internet to trace the changes in ownership and control of UK media activities in the last few years involving any one of these groups: Carlton, Pearson, EMAP. This should give you some idea of the complexity of UK media business.

Control of acquisitions in the media industries and subsequent oligopoly practices can be exercised in two ways:

- **Public sector** media organisations, financed and controlled by the public purse and public accountability, can be set up. Nearly all countries have some form of public broadcasting (radio and television) and many have set up government agencies which play an important role in financing and distributing films and other media products.
- The activities of media organisations can be **regulated** by government or

public sector 'watchdogs'. Regulations often cover not only monopoly ownership or control and financial dealings but also the range and 'quality' of products (including technical quality) and sometimes the sensitive content of products.

See Chapter 18 for more detail.

Location and local–global relations

The location of media industries is important for two main reasons:

- As a major employment sector (possibly the largest in some parts of Europe), the location of media production facilities is a contentious issue in many countries where the 'spend' of media industries is a major factor in the local economy.
- If the media producers are all located in one area, then their media products are likely to be influenced by the culture of that area, which may or may not align with that of media consumers elsewhere.

The Hollywood studios have always prided themselves on the international appeal of their products. Yet, within the US, studios have traditionally been careful to censor material in order not to offend audiences in more conservative areas. Once, of course, this meant pandering to a form of apartheid in the Southern states. Getting the balance right (between culturally conservative and liberal parts of the country) is difficult. Films and television programmes are usually financed in New York and made in Los Angeles, and this twin axis has traditionally controlled the US media. The location of Ted Turner's operation (CNN especially) – a new competitor based in Atlanta – was therefore of some significance. The South (from Florida across to New Mexico) is both the area of economic expansion and the home of even more conservative political views. The phenomenon of bigoted talk-radio 'shock jocks' (another Southern strength) is also a symptom of a shift in the geography of the American media.

Regional production In the UK, 'national' agencies such as the BBC are sensitive to the charge of **metropolitan bias**. Specialist departments have been developed in or moved to Manchester, Birmingham and Bristol in order to demonstrate commitment to the regions. Often, however, guests and presenters are sent from London to appear on programmes.

The *Guardian* 'North' has recently been introduced, with some regionally focused news and sport. The difference may be slight, but the new 'masthead' on the paper is symbolically important.

In the UK the concentration of media production in London and the south-east has led to many complaints about **metropolitan bias**. The growth and spread of a new speech pattern – so-called 'estuary English' – has been blamed on the London base of media commentators, and the restructuring of both ITV and the BBC has been scrutinised for the guarantee of **regional production**. Similar arguments could be made about national newspapers, which once had major regional editorial offices – Manchester, for instance was the base for several dailies (including the *Manchester Guardian*, which moved to London).

Perhaps the major concern over location is the fear that media production in one country may be completely controlled from another country. This fear extends to both the news media and to media seen to be important agents in building a cultural identity. It can be argued that the spread of 'international news services' such as CNN has had a beneficial effect in those parts of the world where repressive governments can muzzle their own media but cannot stop the inflow of satellite images (or indeed BBC World Service radio broadcasts). On the other hand, most western countries have expressed concern about the ownership of media companies operating within their national boundaries being held by non-nationals (Rupert Murdoch had to take out US citizenship in order to acquire his US television holdings). This fear relates to anxiety over the 'unregulated' international media market outlined in the previous section.

See also Chapter 15.

The economic benefits of attracting media business into an area can be considerable. With a weak sterling/dollar exchange rate, the choice of the UK and Ireland as the base for Hollywood feature film production in the early 1990s generated a great deal of local business in some of the more remote parts of Wales, Scotland and especially Ireland (where government policy has been to invite production companies in directly and to offer a range of incentives) (see Chapter 10). In the late 1990s the strength of the pound raised fears that American producers would move to cheaper locations.

ACTIVITY 8.5

Media industries in the local economy

Investigate your local authority (at a county or city level) and its attitude to media development.

- Does it operate a film office?
- Does it have a media policy? Or does it refer to 'cultural industries'?
- What kind of economic benefits are expected?

Work patterns and employment

Work in the media is often perceived as glamorous and highly paid. In reality, this description fits only a small percentage of the workforce. We can recognise different groups of workers:

- technical (production, transmission etc.)
- creative (writers, performers, designers etc.)
- production organisation and management
- professional services (finance, legal etc.)
- auxiliary support services (clerical, administrative, catering etc.).

Technical staff represent a problem for employers in terms of both initial training and reskilling and the associated costs. The move to new technologies has produced conflicts in all sectors. Introduction of computerised processes has in some instances led to 'de-skilling' of tasks.

See Chapter 16.

Like every other industry in the UK, the film, video and broadcasting industry has been required to develop 'standards' and recognised qualifications for various job functions. These National Vocational Qualifications (NVQs) (SVQs in Scotland) have taken several years to develop and are being slowly accepted by an industry unaccustomed to formal training.

Elsewhere it has opened up new production opportunities and led to skill shortages where existing technical staff need retraining (e.g. in broadcast television). Media corporations in some sectors (film especially) have a poor record on training, expecting staff to 'work up from the bottom' or simply recruiting staff trained by somebody else (the BBC used to train the majority of broadcast technicians before deregulation). This 'short-termism' (i.e. not worrying about the future) is now being addressed, but overall it remains a problem.

Differing labour costs for technical staff have led to shifting locations for media work: a common feature of globalisation. Much colour printing is now undertaken in the 'Pacific rim' countries, which have access to both high technology and lower wage costs (and digital material can easily be transmitted from editorial offices in Europe and North America). Hollywood productions are periodically attracted abroad because of lower staff costs. UK studios offer very highly skilled technicians, especially for big-budget productions with special effects (the *Star Wars* series is a good example – now lost to Fox Australia, part of News Corporation). Eastern Europe has become an attractive location with basic studio facilities at very low cost.

Creative personnel have usually been considered by media theorists in terms of how personal expression survives within an industrial system. Other issues, however, relate to the ownership of creative ideas and the rights which ensue. Media corporations attempt to control these as much as possible through contracts. Most of the high-profile cases of disputes over rights have come from the music industry (e.g. George Michael's famous battle with Sony in the early 1990s).

Production management staff are those who make sure that the project is completed and that it gets distributed. The most significant development in production management, as in the other sectors, has been the move towards freelancing or subcontracting to smaller independent production teams. The trend is perhaps most marked in film and broadcasting, with 50 per cent or more of staff in the UK freelancing, but is common also in newspapers and magazines. Media corporations tend to concentrate on ownership of properties and rights rather than direct control over employment. They do of course control what freelance staff and independent production groups do through contracts and financial support. Supporters of the system maintain that the arrangement means that production groups are 'lean and mean' and highly competitive, that they are not hampered by institutional inertia. One disadvantage is that training and retraining and other initiatives which require industry-wide action become much more difficult to organise.

The *professional services sector* in the media industries requires a high degree of specialisation, especially in legal and financial fields, and again tends to favour location in metropolitan centres (where specialist agencies will find

sufficient work to support a practice). More general *support services* are not so
location-conscious.

Technological development

Chapter 16 provides both background and analysis of technological change in
the media industries. Technological change affects every part of the
production process and not just the 'production' stage. As an example, the
development of **broadband cable** and the transmission of digital media
products at high speed around the world is primarily about distribution,
but there is equal interest in the exhibition of the product in the home
via a digital 'set-top box' or in the presentation theatre using digital
projection.

The 'deal', especially the international deal, will perhaps be aided by
video-conferencing and access to Internet sites making dissemination of
specialist information and research material possible. Post-production may
also benefit – digital video can be edited 'on location' and beamed back to the
studio.

The media business environment

Ownership and influence on products

The ownership and control of media companies is an issue in Media Studies
because of a belief that the nature of the product, and in particular the content
of news and factual material or the ideological limits of a whole range of
products, may be influenced by business considerations or the 'proprietorial'
whims of chief executives. Conversely, the lack of production opportunities
for smaller and non-commercial producers means that only a narrow range of
media products are easily available to audiences.

See Chapter 5.

Recognising the possibility of proprietorial control was relatively
straightforward when newspapers were run by 'press barons' and Hollywood
studios by autocratic moguls. Or at least that is the stereotypical view of these
entrepreneurs. In the Viacom case study below, we allude to one example of
individual proprietorial power.

Does ownership influence products? Certainly newspapers sometimes
develop a distinctive editorial line that can be traced back to a proprietor or
leading executive. There are some specific examples of this, such as Conrad
Black's newspapers in Canada (he also owns the *Daily Telegraph*), but
sometimes the editorial line has been developed over many years and may stay
much the same if ownership changes. Much more likely is that management
style and management aims will change the broad direction of a media

company's activities (e.g. the impact of Rupert Murdoch's takeover of British newspapers such as the *Sun* and *The Times*).

Ownership and control is primarily about costs and market share and the potential for profit. It is to achieve these two economic aims that companies grow through takeovers and mergers. Vertical integration makes sense if costs are reduced because each process is kept within the company. Horizontal integration should mean more market share and a reduction in average costs. If two music companies merge, they can use one headquarters building, one marketing team, merge some labels etc. and sell the same number of records as a joint company as when they were separate companies.

The product will be changed if doing so makes it less costly to produce or more likely to attract an audience/readership. Certain kinds of ownership, such as transferral to the public sector, may mean that 'non-commercial' products, meeting social objectives or regulatory requirements (e.g. education projects), become possible.

Modern media companies are most likely to be part of a **conglomerate** – a division within a much larger company, 'organised on the principle of multiple profit centres which reinforce each other – designed not only to generate revenue and profits, but to keep such monies within the corporation' (Robert Gustafson quoted in Izod 1988). The parent company is likely to be engaged in several different media sectors and probably related sectors such as the manufacture of technology or the provision of telecommunications (see The Majors case study below). The range of activities encompassed by the widest definitions of 'media' is vast and includes some of the fastest-growing industrial sectors. It is inevitable that our representation will need updating by the time you read this, but it should still give you a good grasp of the international market. Note these features:

- The Hollywood studios are often the most familiar names in the group of brands.
- The major media corporations span North America, Europe and Japan.
- It still isn't clear whether we should include computer and telecommunications companies as 'media corporations', but companies such as Microsoft are bigger than the purely media companies.

Financial control

Modern media corporations are owned by shareholders. The 'cross-holding' of shares of one media corporation by another is widespread (especially in Europe). The major shareholders are often 'institutional' – insurance companies or pension funds far removed from the production which generates the profit. Thousands of small shareholders are represented by 'fund managers' and have little chance to influence corporate affairs. The future of the corporation lies very much in the hands of accountants and financial advisers who look at the balance sheets rather than the product as an indicator of the health of the company. Ultimately, stock exchanges can determine the fate of corporations.

This observation, which is relevant for all modern corporations, shouldn't be seen as 'proof' that all industrial media production is devoid of creative work or that because it is industrial it will all be the same. It does, however, suggest the kinds of influences which are present when media corporations make decisions to buy or sell subsidiary companies or to cease production (i.e. close down a newspaper title or shelve a feature film). There are a few media industry figures with a personal fortune big enough to enable them to become significant 'players' in the media market, and there are a handful of executives whose reputation is such that their activity (or even their presence) can dramatically affect the financial status of a company, but even so the accountants set the 'bottom line' on most projects.

'Industry players' include Silvio Berlusconi, Michael Eisner, Steven Spielberg, Bill Gates, Summer Redstone etc.

Media production takes place in what can sometimes seem a quite contradictory business environment. Financial security matters more than individual creativity, yet in the mid-1990s a financially secure company (Sony) made a mess of operating two Hollywood studios, Columbia and Tri-Star, while good creative management turned round a company in difficulty (Disney). We might argue that some management strategies are more effective in allowing the development of an environment in which creative decisions can be made. We might also note that the attitude of financial markets towards media industries is important. In the US there is a positive attitude towards investment in the media industries, especially Hollywood, despite the disasters. For good or ill, US investors seem to be attracted by the glamour (see the increasingly high profile of the Oscars ceremonies each year) and will risk their money accordingly. Contrast this with the UK, where it has proved very difficult to persuade financial institutions to finance British films or new media generally.

The contemporary media business environment is in a constant state of turmoil as conglomerates buy and sell companies in an attempt to keep on board the bandwagon – a wagon which is surely rolling, but no one is sure in exactly which direction. The failure of the so-called 'dot.com' revolution (i.e. to launch Internet-based businesses) to sustain growth has injected some reality into the claims for future growth, but still industry executives speak enthusiastically about 'new products' and 'new opportunities'. We have picked out four trends which do seem to be important and which we think you should study: libraries, brands, distribution and synergy.

Several media conglomerates have lost large amounts of money investing in 'new media' ventures, e.g. Vivendi Universal in Vivazzi.

Libraries

New distribution systems and the multiplication of channels on digital television have been developing faster than the output of new product. Anyone who controls a library or 'back catalogue' of recognisable media products is now in a good position to exploit these resources. Hollywood film libraries, the rights to well-known popular songs, photographic archives – all these are being snapped up by the large media corporations. They are catalogued and presented on-line in different collections, generating revenue as immediate product and then again as they are reproduced by their media users.

Libraries are also a form of security for the major corporations in a precarious business such as film distribution. DreamWorks is in a relatively precarious position as a 'new' studio because, if its new releases fail at the box office, it does not have revenue from library material coming in at a steady trickle – the lifeblood which sustains the established majors.

Brands

As the international media market grows and companies attempt to operate in several different countries, the marketing of new products becomes more problematic. If a company wants to build its presence in Poland, Thailand and South Africa, will it need different logos, a different company image to appeal in different cultural contexts? Brands are expensive to develop (See Chapter 13). The power of the international brand, instantly recognisable everywhere, goes some way to explaining the longevity of the Hollywood studios. There cannot be many parts of the world where Warner's shield, Paramount's mountain and MGM's lion are not familiar to a mass audience. (Many of MGM's famous films are now owned by Time Warner, but the lion stays on them.) The move to merchandising, utilising the studio logo to the full, is evidence of the new importance of the logo.

Conglomerates think carefully about brands and company names. When Canadian drinks company Seagram bought MCA, it changed the film operation back to 'Universal Pictures' – the traditional studio name. But when Disney bought Miramax, it kept the name alive because it was a strong 'brand' in the 'independent film' market. Now that French company Vivendi has bought Universal, it will be interesting to see whether it keeps the name in Europe or uses its European brand Canal Plus or Studio Canal.

New distribution formats

Chapter 16 analyses the move to digital media products, all of which (sounds, pictures and text) move down broadband cable. The companies which control the cable systems are in a powerful position. Once again, the world market is very much dominated and influenced by the major North American companies which have prospered in the largest telecommunications market.

There are big corporate battles ahead in Europe with the privatised state monopolies competing with new companies such as Vodaphone, but it is the American telecommunications market which still holds the key, with the prospect of mergers between the cable companies and telephone companies on the one hand and mergers, or at least close co-operation, between the owners of digital networks and the 'software' providers such as Microsoft and the Hollywood studios on the other.

The other noticeable feature of the television industry is the takeover of small specialist film and video equipment suppliers by larger companies with more broadly based business telecommunications or information-handling concerns.

Synergy

Synergy is media industry jargon for the extra 'energy' produced by linking two complementary companies or products. The marriage of cable television and telephone supply is a good example. Selling telephone services helps reduce the cost of installing cable; installed cable allows attractive pricing of telephone services etc. In the Viacom case study below we discuss a conglomerate that tries to create synergy between its different operating divisions.

See Chapter 13.

The attractions of synergy are obvious, but achieving a profitable outcome is not straightforward. Sony has struggled to make ownership of 'hardware' and 'software' companies pay off. Making movies is not necessarily going to make selling DVD players any easier. Matsushita and Philips both tried and gave up, selling their interests in MCA/Universal and Polygram. Sometimes, concentrating on doing one thing well can pay off. Nevertheless the potential benefits of synergy are too good to turn down and there will inevitably be further attempts, not least because the convergence of media industries will throw up more opportunities.

Case study 1: The major players

The global media conglomerates which dominate the media industries are shown in Figure 8.3. By mid-2001, after a series of mergers and acquisitions, a new media environment emerged. The economic recession, especially in advertising, has since taken some of the value away from the biggest companies, but the trend towards bigger conglomerations is likely to continue. There are anomalies. EMI remains marooned as a music major without other interests. Viacom, Disney and News Corporation lack a record label. Surprisingly, the main attempts to grab EMI have come from the majors who already have music interests. MGM/UA looks like a weak film studio, Bertelsmann is the only conglomerate without a studio. But Bertelsmann has no other film or television interests in North America and may have its hands full with television in Europe. Vivendi-Universal is the conglomerate with the strongest link between European and American interests.

	Bertelsmann	Disney	News Corporation	Sony	AOL Time Warner	Viacom	Vivendi Universal
Film Studios Cinemas		Disney Miramax	20th Century Fox	Columbia TriStar	Warner Bros New Line Warner Cinemas	Paramount Showcase UCI (50%)	Universal USA Pictures UCI (50%)
Television	RTL Group (across Europe) Pearson TV	ABC Disney Channel ESPN	Fox TV BSkyB Star TV	Columbia Television Studios Sony TV (Asia)	CNN Cartoon Network (Turner Broadcasting) WBTV HBO Cable systems	CBS, MTV Nickelodeon UPN, BET Paramount	USA Studios Canal +
Radio	RTL Group	ABC Radio				Infinity Radio	
Music	BMG (RCA, Arista)			Sony Music	Warner Music Division		Universal Music Group
Print	Gruner + Jahr Magazines Springer Business Media Random House		Newspapers Harper Collins		Time Warner Book Group Time Magazine DC Comics IPC Magazines	Simon & Schuster	Vivendi Universal Publishing
New Media	Interactive Television Music			Video Games Digital Pictures Entertainment	AOL		Vivendi Universal Net Vizzavi MP3
Live Entertainment		Theme Parks Hotels Cruise Line				Theme Parks	Theme Parks
Other	Arvato printing	Merchandising Stores		Electronics Hardware and Consumables	Merchandising Stores	Infinity Advertising (Outdoor)	Telecomms Environmental Services

Figure 8.3 The 'major players' – media conglomerates with interests in three or more different media.

Does this 'consolidation' of corporate power in a handful of companies matter? The debate between media academics on www.opendemocracy.com suggests that it does. There are plenty of critics who want us to beware of the concentration of ownership because it reduces the number of 'voices' and viewpoints. They point out that criticism of Hollywood's activities on American television is less likely when five out of six networks share ownership with the studios. Opponents suggest that there is competition and that the strength of the corporations means that we get the chance to choose from an array of high-quality products.

There is also an argument about the actual power of so-called 'media moguls' and their Goliath-like presence in the face of much smaller 'David-like' companies who are struggling to share markets. The opendemocracy site is well worth investigating in order to follow these arguments.

European media corporations

Now that Vivendi and Bertelsmann have broken into the American–Japanese group of majors, attention is turning to European media markets and the battles to control pan-European services such as television and telecommunications. The major players in Europe differ from their American counterparts in the following ways:

- Public sector broadcasters have had a central role in European media. ARD (Germany), BBC and RAI (Italy) up to now have been more secure within their home markets than the private-sector American broadcasters. The Japanese public sector broadcaster, NHK, is another major player, but the future for public service broadcasters is doubtful (see Television industry case study following Chapter 7).

- Broadcasting and publishing are much more important for European media corporations (i.e. more than 'filmed entertainment'). This is partly a matter of 'own language/culture' markets, less easily penetrated by American producers, and some of these companies have a long history in industries such as printing and publishing. The French company Hachette claims to be the world's biggest magazine company with titles such as *Elle*. National barriers are starting to come down with digital media processes.

- European corporations (especially German groups) have tended to expand within Europe rather than to look more widely for opportunities. There is a complex web of cross-ownership of shares in different European media corporations. The high start-up costs of new technologies such as satellite and the long-established practices of film and television co-productions have led to various partnerships. UK media groups, sharing a common language with the Americans and with a history of overseas investment, have been more international in outlook. Once again, this situation is changing. The Americans are looking towards new European television markets in cable and satellite, and the German corporations (especially Bertelsmann) are looking to North America. BSkyB (News Corporation) and Liberty Media are two

In 2002, the chief executives of Bertelsmann and Vivendi who had driven the companies into North America were both forced out. This could signal another change in the media business environment.

See Miller *et al.* (2001) for more on Hollywood and Europe.

It's worth exploring the metaphors of these activities: 'major players', a 'level playing field' and a 'free market place'. Can you think of others that present very hard-headed business practice as if it was a game played with rules of fairness?

of the US conglomerates circling around European pay television services.

- The European Union has recognised the vital importance of 'media industries' and has developed policies and funding arrangements to assist future growth. European co-operation is seen as the only realistic response to the power of US corporations represented by trade associations such as MPAA. Generally, Europe is thought to be 'tightly regulated'. The US government, though concerned about monopoly power at home, is generally supportive of US media corporations trading abroad.

There is a seemingly inevitable move towards an increased domination of media activity by a group of 'major players'. Convergence and the attractions of synergy point to a future where conglomerates straddling print, music, film and broadcasting will predominate. The shift of focus from 'production' to distribution and the exploitation of archives of existing products suggests that 'delivery' companies in telecommunications and digital systems will become important partners for media conglomerates. Against this inevitability, we should also recognise that the media environment is volatile. New technologies do not automatically succeed and there is always the possibility of new companies which innovate successfully coming along.

ACTIVITY 8.6

Industry profile

One of the major corporations is covered in detail in the Viacom case study below. Take any of the other 'major players', American or European, and research the following:

- How did the company start and what are the significant moments in its history? (Does anything explain why it grew so big?)
- What are its main activities and how does it organise them (e.g. in separate divisions)?
- What kind of results did it achieve in the last financial year?
- What is the latest news story featuring the company?

You should be able to find all this information on the Internet.

'Independence' and 'alternatives' in the media industries

So far we have discussed media production and consumption in terms of the
mainstream: large-scale activity, with a clear commercial purpose, driven
primarily by a profit motive and representing mainly dominant views in
society. This is the province of the major players, but these aren't always the
same companies in each media industry. A film and television 'major' such as
Disney is known as an 'independent' in the music industry (see Music
industry case study following this chapter). Sometimes, the majors brand
some of their output as 'independent' by setting up or acquiring a separate
company (e.g. Disney acquired the 'independent' film company Miramax and
kept its identity separate).

Being 'outside the mainstream' often simply means a more localised form
of production, and may include educational and training material, parish
newsletters, fanzines etc. But sometimes 'outside the mainstream' is a more
conscious decision by a professional producer – an attempt to distinguish
media output or to offer something which is alternative in some way.

Using the term 'independent' and linking it to alternative media
production is problematic. Most media productions require collaboration
between creative and technical teams, and they need an organisation to
distribute the work. All media work is 'dependent' on technology, funding
etc. What we are concerned with here is how producers approach such
dependencies. There are a number of options:

- the 'maverick' (the word means a stray animal without a brand) doesn't
  want to be part of the mainstream because, for example, s/he finds
  oppressive the 'bottom line' structures of profit and the resulting
  constraints on risk, or perhaps on the ability to make local or topical
  references which this can involve. Such media-makers find ways to
  continue working with the minimum of compromise over the content and
  style of the work. This may mean targeting a niche audience, working for
  only a select group of funders or making use of the idea of 'art', which can
  invoke and support different kinds of practice.
- 'The artist' wants to maintain control, usually working with a small group
  of regular collaborators, but will be willing to see her/his work being
  discussed as art and therefore outside mainstream commercial markets.
  The art market, in film, video or audio is just as institutionalised as the
  mainstream but involves slightly different activities for the media
  producer (e.g. festivals, exhibitions, different spaces for review and
  publicity etc.) as well as different forms of financing (sponsorship, public
  and other arts funding etc.).
- The 'politically committed' media producer has the aim of making some
  kind of statement or working with particular groups of collaborators on

'Although independent publishers
have had a bleak few years, some
are growing fast, adapting quicker
than their larger rivals to new
niches and the shifting demands
of readers' (Joel Rickett, *Guardian*
17 August 2002).

245

social issues, and will look for opportunities to do this, perhaps via forms of distribution not controlled by the majors or by accessing different funds (public funding, arts foundations etc.).

At various times media producers working in this way have been 'ahead of the game', creating media products in new ways or with new forms. This has been called the **avant garde**. The mainstream takes a little time to catch up, but then often 'incorporates' aspects of such work into mainstream production (see the comments on extending the boundaries of the mainstream above). If there is any form of avant garde in contemporary media production, it might be expected to be found in the 'new media', utilising digital technology and perhaps drawing on 'high art' modes such as video art.

Alt. culture

See Chapter 16.

Digital media technology has the potential for exploitation in new kinds of media work. Music and video producers have clearly benefited from access to relatively inexpensive but good-quality equipment. If the majors won't distribute the music conventionally or it is too expensive to use them, distribution is possible via the Internet. This won't necessarily be a big market, but if costs are kept to a minimum it can be viable. It also offers a chance to producers in different parts of the world to reach new audiences.

The changes in political activity, moving away from traditional political parties to so-called 'single-issue' campaigns and new alliances, possibly across national boundaries, has produced a range of websites offering both different ideas and new ways of presenting them. Circulating images, songs, jokes and web-links is an integral part of Internet culture. In the early days of the Internet one of its most attractive features for many users was the array of

See examples listed at the end of the News case study on page 147.

news groups, the most popular of which the were the 'alt.' groups in which, possibly, 'alternative' views might be found.

The 'alt.' tag has been taken up in other media so that alt. country has emerged as a new music genre clearly defined as 'not Nashville'. However, as it begins to produce its own stars such as Ryan Adams, interest from the majors is likely. 'Independence' is often presented as an attractive, rebellious place completely outside the commercial compromises of the mainstream. This is, unfortunately perhaps, a rather romantic notion, but nevertheless one you need to consider.

ACTIVITY 8.7

Alt. culture

Survey your recent media activities and purchases.

- How many of them might be described as 'independent' or 'alternative'? Do
  they fit any of the three categories above (maverick, art or politics)? Do any of
  them consciously use the 'alt.' or 'indie' tag?
- Was this description part of their appeal to you?

Use a search engine such as Google (see Chapter 9) to look for 'Alternative Music'
and 'Alternative Politics'.

- What kind of website do you find? Do your findings suggest that there is a form
  of 'alternative culture' and potentially alternative production?

Case study 2: Viacom: profile of a media conglomerate

Viacom is a name that is not known to the general public in the UK, even
though the brands it owns appear regularly on film and television screens.
Yet this global media corporation vies with Disney as the number two to
AOL-Time Warner.

Originally, Viacom was a television company created in 1971 when CBS,
one of the three US national television networks, was forced to 'spin-off'
some of its cable and television interests to satisfy the US regulator, the
Federal Communications Commission. Viacom developed two significant
cable and satellite channels, MTV (which was launched in 1981) and
Nickelodeon. In what was a 'new media' venture in the 1980s, Viacom
had partners in the form of Warner Bros, but they pulled out in 1982.

Viacom had a future in television, but in the 1980s there was no sign
that it would become involved in other media. Enter Sumner Redstone and
changing times. Redstone is something of a celebrity in the US media
business world. After Harvard and war service as a codebreaker he had an
early career as a lawyer and took over the family business in 1967 at the
age of forty-four. The business was cinema exhibition, and Redstone has
developed National Amusements into a global chain operating in North
America, the UK, Argentina and Chile under the Showcase and Multiplex
brands. In 1987 Redstone used National Amusements to buy a 68 per cent
controlling interest in the publicly quoted company, Viacom.

Many commentators thought that the $3.2 billion that Redstone paid for
Viacom was far too much, but Redstone saw a great future in specialist
cable and viewed Viacom as a means to build up a media corporation. In
1994 he swooped and in two major deals gained control of Paramount
Communications (including the film studio, one of the original Hollywood
'Big Five') and the video store empire of Blockbuster. In 1999 he engineered

Figure 8.4 Sumner Redstone, architect of the transformation of Viacom into a media conglomerate.

a merger with CBS television, with Viacom now buying its parent, and in 2000 completed the takeover of Infinity, the largest company controlling advertising on US radio and 'outdoor' sites.

Viacom today is a typical media conglomerate in its global presence in a number of different media sectors, but unusual in the control held by National Amusements over voting stocks. (National Amusements is what in the US is called a 'closely held' company – a 'private company' – and as such does not have to release business accounts for public scrutiny.) Sumner Redstone has more power than most of the other media industry leaders. He doesn't act in the publicly aggressive way of Rupert Murdoch, but he does represent the traditional values of the American entrepreneur, claiming to be a 'Liberal Democrat' and to 'take risks and work hard'.

Viacom owns a wide range of brand names. The company is divided into several divisions:

- publishing and on-line: Simon & Schuster, music publishing, on-line services
- recreation and retail: Blockbuster, Famous Players Cinemas (Canada), UCI (UK, shared with Universal), theme parks, sports franchises
- motion pictures: Paramount Pictures, Paramount Home Video
- broadcast television: CBS, UPN, Paramount Television, Viacom television stations
- cable television: MTV, Nickelodeon, VH1, movie channels, BET (Black Entertainment Television)
- radio and outdoor: Infinity.

One of Sumner Redstone's often quoted remarks in the late 1990s was 'Content is King', i.e. creating and owning valuable programme material is what makes a conglomerate powerful. In some ways this is an odd remark for someone who began commercial media life as a cinema exhibitor and whose company gains its largest slice of revenue from selling advertising space. Viacom is the biggest provider of advertising space across North America – something which does not bode well for the company during a period of economic recession. However, Viacom is a 'conservatively managed' company and has so far managed to survive, despite carrying huge burdens of debt from purchases such as that of Blockbuster. What the 'content' quotation really means is that the key to success is exploiting content across as many distribution channels as possible.

Integration

Figure 8.5 shows Viacom as a modern 'integrated' media conglomerate. In terms of vertical integration, original content such as a feature film is generated by production units such as MTV (see below) or acquired or commissioned by Paramount. The film is then distributed by Paramount, exhibited in Showcase and UCI cinemas in the US or the UK and sold or rented through Blockbuster.

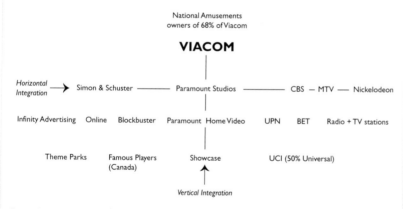

Figure 8.5 The structure of Viacom as an integrated media conglomerate.

Viacom is also 'horizontally integrated', especially in television. The same television material can be delivered via terrestrial networks CBS and UPN, often via television stations owned by Viacom and by BET on cable. Horizontal integration allows Viacom to maintain a significant share of television revenues and therefore to compete with Time Warner, Universal and Disney.

Global branding

There is some dispute amongst media commentators as to what constitutes
a 'global' media player amongst the large corporations. News Corporation
is often quoted as the defining example because of its strong presence in
Australia, the US and the UK via 20th Century Fox, BSkyB and its
newspaper groups. All the major Hollywood studios have a global presence
through the distribution of their film titles, but do they need more than
simply the distribution of their product to count as 'global corporations'? In
the case of Viacom, the two concrete global operations are Blockbuster and
MTV, which guarantee a place in video and television markets across the
world alongside the film business dominated by the major distributor UIP
and cinema chain UCI (both jointly owned with Universal) across Europe
and other territories. If Viacom has a weakness in global terms, it is the lack
of a music label to complement MTV.

What makes Viacom unique is the way that the concept of 'synergy' has
been taken on board and used to maximise the potential of the company's
content production. For example, by comparison with the other majors,
Paramount has fewer big budget releases – the aim appears to be to make
the money go further.

Synergy and Jimmy Neutron

In December 2001, Paramount released *Jimmy Neutron*, an animated feature
aimed at a 'tweenager' market of six-to-twelve-year-olds. Its Christmas
opening was somewhat overshadowed by *Lord of the Rings* and *Harry Potter*,
but it registered a healthy $60 million-plus at the box office. Unlike other
films that have proved themselves at the box office and then fostered 'spin-
offs', *Jimmy Neutron* was conceived as a synergistic project from the outset.
When the script arrived at Nickelodeon in late 1999, the potential was
recognised and a proposal was discussed by all of Viacom's producing
companies. The first public launch was a series of 'inter-programme'
broadcasts of between one and two minutes on Nickelodeon in January
2001 with the intention of pushing viewers towards on-line games related
to the shorts and then to print material in Nickelodeon's subscriber
magazines. All this was prompted by research that suggested the target
viewers wanted something on all media. Books for slightly younger readers
using the Jimmy Neutron character were released at the same time by
Viacom's publishing division, Simon & Schuster.

The first three 'release platforms' were all Viacom-owned, but in
November 2001 a soundtrack album for the film (using star names such as

Patrick Stewart and featuring tracks by artists such as Britney Spears) was released on Jive Records leading into the film release (see the Music industry case study following this chapter for more on Jive). Meanwhile the shorts were being aired internationally. The international roll-out for the film was scheduled for March 2002, to be followed in autumn 2002 by the television series, with pre-sales across international markets already tied up. Merchandising was already in place by June 2001. Whether or not *Jimmy Neutron* became an instant 'franchise' spawning further features and series, the whole industry was watching Viacom's strategy carefully.

This was not the first time that Viacom had used its different producing sectors in combination to produce profitable content. Paramount has seen several releases, such as *Varsity Blues* (1999), *Election* (1999) and *Save the Last Dance* (2001), all with 'teen content', originated by MTV. At a time when the average Hollywood mainstream movie costs around $50 million, these films represent extremely good business. *Varsity Blues* cost $16 million and grossed $53 million, *Election* $8.5 million cost, $14.8 million at the box office, *Save the Last Dance*, $13 million and $91 million. Add in *The Original Kings of Comedy*, Spike Lee's performance documentary in 2000, budget $3 million and box office $38 million and it isn't difficult to see why MTV Films is causing a stir. Another surprise hit, *Orange County* in January 2002, rounds out a slate of nine features, none of which has lost significant money at the box office and some which have been very profitable. *Save the Last Dance* shows a ratio of 7:1, production budget to box office.

All these shows are teen/twenty comedies and four of them feature African-American stars, attractive to Black Entertainment Television. They all have an 'afterlife' on Paramount Video and are distributed via Blockbuster. *Election* also helped the status of MTV by providing a critically acclaimed hit film.

The big money in film releases is linked to family films and children's films. *The Rugrats*, developed on Nickelodeon, have also graduated successfully to feature film status with a fourth feature in 2002. These films cost more but their appeal is wider (significant overseas sales). Nickelodeon has so far produced fourteen titles and enabled Viacom to compete with Disney and DreamWorks (*The Rugrats Movie* (1999) grossed over $100 million).

A further Viacom producing unit is Comedy Central, the cable channel that brought the world *South Park*. This channel is, however, shared 50 per cent with Time Warner and points towards the ways in which the global corporations both compete and co-operate. When *South Park: Bigger, Longer and Uncut* was released in 1999, Paramount took 'domestic' (i.e. North American) distribution and Warner Bros took international. Paramount got the better deal in this case.

Viacom and the global media market

Despite its global presence, Viacom is essentially a US company with the bulk of its revenues coming from US advertising, television, film and video operations. It certainly uses its global brands and distribution systems to exploit 'content' as effectively as possible, but much of its operating energy is in maintaining US market share and to that end it is constantly buying and selling television and radio stations and engaging in a watchful game with its main rivals. Where Rupert Murdoch's News Corporation is the target for critics of media concentration in the UK, Viacom is beginning to be discussed in the US in similar terms to those applied to Time Warner-AOL – as a dominant force in the American market.

References and further reading

Most of these references are also suitable for further reading:

Bach, Steven (1985) *Final Cut*, London: Jonathan Cape.

Balio, Tino (1998) '"A major presence in all of the world's important markets": the globalisation of Hollywood in the 1990s', in Steve Neale and Murray Smith (eds) *Contemporary Hollywood Cinema*.

Branston, Gill (2000) *Cinema and Cultural Modernity*, Buckingham: Open University Press, London: Routledge.

Gomery, Douglas (1986) *The Hollywood Studio System*, London: BFI/Macmillan.

Gomery, Douglas (1992) *Shared Pleasures*, London: BFI.

Gomery, Douglas (1996) 'Toward a new media economics', in David Bordwell and Noel Carroll (eds) *Post-theory: Reconstructing Film Studies*, Madison and London: University of Wisconsin Press.

Izod, John (1988) *Hollywood and the Box Office 1895–1986*, London: Macmillan.

Lacey, Nick and Stafford, Roy (2000) *Film as Product in Contemporary Hollywood*, London: British Film Institute.

Maltby, Richard (1995) *Hollywood Cinema*, Oxford: Blackwell.

Maltby, Richard (1998) '"Nobody knows everything": post-classical historiographies and consolidated entertainment', in Steve Neale and Murray Smith (eds) *Contemporary Hollywood Cinema*, London: Routledge.

Miller, Toby, Govil, Nitin, McMurria, John and Maxwell, Richard (2001)
Global Hollywood, London: British Film Institute.

Neale, Steve and Smith, Murray (eds) (1998) *Contemporary Hollywood Cinema*,
London: Routledge.

Pirie, David (ed.) (1981) *Anatomy of the Movies*, London: Windward.

Seguin, Denis (2001) 'Survivor: National Amusements at 65' *Screen
International*, 2 March.

Seguin, Denis (2001) 'All systems go', *Screen International*, 12 October.

Wasko, Janet (1994) *Hollywood in the Information Age: Beyond the Silver Screen*,
Cambridge: Polity.

Wyatt, Justin (1984) *High Concept: Movies and Marketing in Hollywood*, Austin:
University of Texas Press.

Wyatt, Justin (1998) 'The formation of the "major independent": Miramax,
New Line and New Hollywood', in Steve Neale and Murray Smith (eds)
Contemporary Hollywood Cinema, London: Routledge.

The business operations of the media corporations are best followed in the
trade publications for each industry. *Screen International*, *Variety* and *Billboard*
are particularly useful in that they cover a wide range of 'entertainment
media'. For a more defined UK perspective look at *Broadcast*, *Media Week*, *UK
Press Gazette* etc. Many of these publications operate a website – it will
probably require a subscription to get at detailed information, but there are
'free' headline news stories as well. All the corporations mentioned in the
chapter have websites giving useful information (sites that may be listed as
French or German often have links to English versions on the index page, or
you can use the rough translation services offered by some of the search
engines).

Use Google to find the websites of the companies (see Chapter 9).

CASE STUDY: MUSIC INDUSTRY, TECHNOLOGY AND SYNERGY

- An outline history
- The structure of the industry
- Synergy, convergence and the contemporary music industry

- References
- Further reading

The music industry is an integral part of the broader media industries sector, but it is also an industry with some unique features. In this case study we look at those unique features and focus on the way in which music products have been so important in the introduction of all kinds of media technology. The music industry has arguably always been concerned with synergy and convergence – helping the development of other media industries through the sales of related music products and through the incorporation of music performances in other products.

An outline history

Beginnings

The gramophone was invented at roughly the same time as film projection, and together the new technologies spread around the world at the start of the twentieth century. The first companies to exploit the possibilities of the gramophone produced both the machines themselves and the 'software' – cylinders at first, but then the familiar discs. Some well-known names were involved from the beginning: HMV (His Master's Voice), Columbia, Victor etc. Recorded music was one of the first forms of mass-produced 'home entertainment'. Previously, music-making in the home had required both the musical skill and the resources to purchase instruments and learn to play them.

As we might expect, some of the first companies involved in the new industry were already involved in

publishing sheet music or manufacturing musical instruments. One company made billiard tables for wealthy homes, but in another case gramophones were produced alongside typewriters – another key example of technology for the period. This link between business and media technologies was revived in the 1990s when music moved to computers first developed as business tools. The early growth was not confined to North America. Companies developed quickly in Europe and around the world – HMV India was founded in 1901.

1920s – radio

The gramophone industry was boosted in the 1920s by the arrival of commercial radio services. Not only did the new services (primarily in North America) offer the opportunity for recorded music to be played to a mass audience, but the manufacturers of gramophones found themselves well placed to become involved in the production of radio sets. This period saw the foundation of RCA-Victor (the Radio Corporation of America joined with the Victor Record Company in 1929).

The rapid development of radio had helped to create the 'boom' which eventually ended with the Wall Street Crash of 1929 and the start of the Great Depression. But this was also a period in which sound was developed in the cinema – first on disc and later on film. RCA became part of one of the first modern media corporations when in conjunction with theatre chain Keith-Albee-Orpheum it formed RKO Radio Pictures, partly to promote its own 'sound on film' system. RKO was one of the 'Big Five' major studios that established the Hollywood studio system in the 1930s. It was also one of the first media conglomerates encompassing radio, recorded music, vaudeville (live light entertainment) and cinema with its showcase at the six-thousand-seat Radio City Music Hall in New York. (An outline of RCA history is available on the website at www.rca.com.)

> The early record companies established themselves overseas in all the principal markets. The Victor Company of Japan was bought by the Matsushita Electronics Company in 1954 and as JVC introduced the VHS cassette in 1977.

1930s and 1940s – jukebox and Hollywood

Record sales plummeted at the start of the 1930s with the impact of the Depression. But still the influence of recorded music spread. The jukebox, a striking example of 'new technology' playing sixteen or twenty-four different records, became an alternative to radio as a means of both providing entertainment in bars and clubs and creating interest in particular performers (i.e. a second way of assessing popularity). Music was an important element of films in the 1930s and 1940s, with musicals and music performances featured in other genres. There were also 'musical shorts' featuring popular music stars.

One important development in this period was the 'institutionalising' of different genres of popular music, particularly black music (known at the time as 'race music') and 'hillbilly' or country music. Supported by a distinctive culture and a chain of dedicated radio stations and record labels, these were the first indications of both 'market segmentation' and 'roots culture' in the commercial media environment. Both black music and country music found their way into Hollywood, although the films that featured the music were usually B pictures or independent productions (black cinema existed to a certain extent outside the

mainstream at this time, with segregated audiences in the southern states). Mainstream popular music was dominated by 'big bands'.

1950–60s – Hollywood and rock 'n' roll

The music industry expanded in the 1950s with the explosion of rock 'n' roll (a fusion of the black music and country music which had been 'marginal' in the 1930s) and the growing affluence of young record buyers. It was also encouraged by

- the replacement of heavy, brittle shellac discs that stored only a few minutes of music by more durable (and more portable) vinyl 'singles' and 'long-play' albums (LPs) capable of storing up to twenty minutes per side.
- the increasing focus on the youth audience by Hollywood studios
- the development of television as home entertainment with its own need to attract younger viewers (a need further promoted by advertisers).

The links between music, radio, film and television grew strong in the 1950s and 1960s. A good example would be the career of pop singer Ricky Nelson. He first appeared as a child in a television sitcom, the *Ozzie and Harriet Show*, featuring his real-life family, headed by bandleader Ozzie Nelson. As a teenager he became a 'teen idol', combining good looks with country-tinged rock 'n' roll and in 1959 he appeared in a major Hollywood western with John Wayne (*Rio Bravo*). This period also saw the first chart-rigging and 'payola' scandals, in which radio DJs were accused of artificially creating hit records, and the establishment of television variety shows.

Television 'specials' hosted by leading mainstream singers such as Nat King Cole and Perry Como were ratings winners, but the most important shows were those like *The Ed Sullivan Show*, which introduced new 'stars'. Up until this point, popular music, apart from the biggest mainstream acts whose national profile was reflected through Hollywood, was primarily a regional affair. Records were promoted by local radio stations and often by local record labels. These would be picked up and distributed by bigger labels, but often an artist would remain a 'regional star' especially if the music genre was not nationally followed (i.e. blues, country, soul etc.) But when early rock 'n' roll performers such as Elvis Presley appeared on *The Ed Sullivan Show* (shown only from the waist up – conservative American television decreed that his act was 'lewd'), they were immediately seen across America on networked television.

1970s Hollywood and the soundtrack album

Hollywood embraced pop stars in the 1950s and 1960s, mainly because they attracted a youth audience. But they put the stars into conventional genre vehicles (see any of the Elvis Presley films, most of which stripped the star of any musical excitement) and made little attempt to use the the music itself as part of the product (what today would be called 'synergy' – see below). It was not until the post-Beatles period in the late 1960s that the studios began to recognise that the performers and their audiences were far more sophisticated than they had imagined and that successful films would be those that were sensitive to the new pop culture.

Significant films were *The Graduate* (1967), which featured new songs by Simon and Garfunkel and saw both single and album success working to help the film, and *Easy Rider* (1969), a low-budget success that put the 'counter-culture' of sex, drugs and anti-war protest on screen and produced one of the first hit 'soundtrack albums'. Soundtracks had sold before, but usually they were based on previous stage musicals etc. The early 1970s was a very bad time for Hollywood (i.e. before the arrival of *Jaws* and *Star Wars*). Rock music looked like the future.

There are various 1970s films which have been cited as 'turning points' in the relationship between Hollywood and the music industry. *American Graffiti* (1973), *Saturday Night Fever* (1977) and *Grease* (1978) in their different ways (*American Graffiti* was a nostalgia

film using 1950s music. The other two were more traditional in genre terms) all suggested that synergy could work. Sell the film, sell the album – the two could not be separated. Where previously the studio had commissioned a songwriter, there was now a prolonged negotiation over music rights to existing titles. Music companies were talking to studios. Sometimes they were part of the same company (e.g. Warner Bros) – but sometimes the cost of rights proved too much. Music companies were becoming more powerful, and in 1962 MCA (Music Corporation of America, home of Decca Records etc.) had bought Universal Studios.

At the end of the 1970s, music on film also benefited from the introduction of Dolby Stereo into theatres. After nearly fifty years without any major developments in cinema sound, the success of films such as *Star Wars* in 1977 convinced cinema owners to invest in the new system. It is significant that *Star Wars* produced a successful soundtrack album of 'theme music' and that composer John Williams became a new 'star' name.

1980s – MTV

During the 1980s, music companies benefited from three separate technological innovations:
- the CD
- the videocassette
- cable and satellite broadcasting.

The CD represented a major opportunity to persuade customers to re-equip with new audio technology and to buy new versions of old favourites in the new format. At the same time, the videocassette increased interest in the possibility of collecting video recordings of music stars and helped to launch the new format (Hollywood was initially reluctant to release films on cassette, so 'music videos' were needed to drive the new market). The new format also encouraged the concept of 'music television' with an increase in the demand for film and video recordings to be made. The music companies wanted such recordings to help market the performers and their new material. The fans wanted the recordings to keep. In retrospect, the potential for 'music television' was there for all to see, but when MTV was launched it took some time to become a success. The music television concept needed a dedicated channel, and this was provided by the developments in satellite broadcasting and cable television (see the Viacom case study in Chapter 8).

A further innovation in this period was the portability of recording and playback devices, especially the Sony Walkman. The Walkman allowed music fans to change the way they listened to music – in effect to consume more music, because they were not restricted by location. Initially a cassette technology, Walkmans moved to CD and then to Mini-Disc. This last was not ultimately successful, partly because the smaller size did not offer a major benefit to compensate for the loss of compatibility with other systems. That would come with computer files.

1990s – music goes digital

Compact disc technology offered a means of storing music in a digital format. Digital recording techniques were also developing in the 1980s. However, the innovation that would revolutionise 'digital music' was the development of suitable hardware and software for *distribution* of digital files over computer networks. This was achieved largely through compression techniques that eventually produced the MP3 standard. MP3s could be used by everybody, whereas other compression software worked only on particular computer platforms.

MP3 may destroy the music industry as such or it may simply open up new possibilities. So far, MP3 has seen the development of a means of:

- converting existing digital music tracks to computer files that can be played on any computer
- 'burning' a new CD of collected files (or 'copying' an existing CD)
- transferring files to a portable MP3 player (lighter and holding more tracks than a Walkman)

- 'swapping' MP3s with other users over the Internet. The latest developments have seen the music industry both benefiting from the expansion of Internet services as a means of promoting artists and also driving that expansion (searching for music and information about performers is one of the most popular activities on the Internet).

ACTIVITY 8.8

The outline history above refers to the biggest music market in North America. In the UK, the history is similar, but often with events lagging a few years behind. Use the Internet and reference books to find out about the following and try to outline some of the important events in the history of the music industry in the UK:

- Radio Luxembourg (1930s–60s)
- *NME* and *Melody Maker* – first charts (1950s)
- Radio Caroline and Radio 1 (1960s)
- *Ready, Steady, Go!* (1960s television)
- Rough Trade and Beggars' Banquet (1970s record labels).

The structure of the industry

Given this history of development, closely tied in with other media, how is the music industry organised today? Not surprisingly, the same handful of large media conglomerates discussed in Chapter 8 are the 'majors' in the music industry worldwide:

- Time Warner as Warner Bros
- Sony as Sony/Columbia
- Bertelsmann as RCA/BMG
- Vivendi Universal as MCA.

In addition, there is a fifth major company in the form of EMI. The existence of a British company which concentrates solely on music in the ranks of the majors is an indication of the importance of the UK music industry – the UK has the highest per capita sales of recorded music and overall counts as the third biggest market. UK government statistics suggest that 41,000 musicians, performers and composers work in the UK industry (see DCMS website at www.culture.gov.uk/creative/music).

Two 'major' Hollywood-based groups, Disney and Viacom/Paramount, are classed as 'independents' in the music industry. News Corporation is the only media conglomerate without a significant music industry interest apart from its Fox Television interests.

The music industry is not 'integrated' in quite the same way as cinema. The 'majors' are primarily distributors, but not so much 'exhibitors' – in the case of the music industry, the exhibitors are effectively the radio and television stations and the retail outlets. Note here that Disney (owner of American broadcaster ABC) and Viacom (owner of CBS, MTV, VH-1 and Blockbuster Video) have a major presence as exhibitors.

The importance of 'independents'

In one sense the music industry is still a 'cottage industry' since the vast majority of the 41,000 'creative talents' in the UK work alone or for small companies. Ninety per cent of the UK industry is classed as 'SME' (Small or Medium Enterprises). It is these SMEs who produce the music which is eventually distributed by the majors and who organise local gigs and manage new acts. One of the features of the industry over the past twenty years has been the trajectory of performers, often starting with a small independent record label and gradually moving to a contract with one of the majors. The majors have also created their own small specialist labels in the hope of finding new talent.

In Chapter 8 we discuss the concept of 'independence' in the media industries. Here we simply want to note that the most successful current music company, at least in terms of record sales, appears to be the Zomba Group with its Jive Records label. In 2000, according to IFPI (International Federation of the

Phonographic Industry), the artist who appeared in the top album lists of the most countries around the world (nineteen) was Britney Spears. Also in the IFPI's chart were the Backstreet Boys, another Jive Records act. Still based in north-west London, Zomba is now established worldwide with a roster of stars covering 'pop, progressive urban, street and rap' on Jive, plus other labels such as Silvertone (blues, rock and alternative). Zomba has companies in the US, Australasia and Singapore and it deals with the majors. Bertelsmann holds 20 per cent of Jive and Viacom has made deals with Zomba to promote Jive artists on film and to use Zomba for soundtrack tie-ins (see Viacom case study in Chapter 8).

A global industry

It is in the global market that the music majors differ from the usual approach of the multinational conglomerates. The Hollywood studios rarely attempt to make films directly (i.e. to finance a local operation) in overseas territories (apart from the UK). Infrequently, they pick up local films for possible international distribution, but mostly they deal in American films. By contrast, the music companies tend to buy local record labels and to acquire a roster of local artistes in addition to their marketing of global acts.

Historically, the music industry has been able to develop in all parts of the world, partly because, unlike film and television, audio recording is a relatively simple and inexpensive process with minimum requirements for technology. It also requires far less organisation of talent and can draw upon deep reservoirs of local performance skills and musical knowledge.

Hollywood became dominant in international cinema by the late 1920s in most territories, taking a significant share of each market, usually through dubbing. But although the large American and European music companies set up operations in most territories worldwide, 'domestic' artistes and repertoire have managed to remain important, especially in Asia, the Middle East and Latin America. In 2000, 68 per cent of repertoire was 'domestic' across the world (see Figure 8.6). This figure is slightly misleading because the biggest market is North America, where nearly 90 per cent is 'domestic' compared with Australasia where the figure is only just over 20 per cent. Even so, this is a very healthy situation for 'home' artistes by comparison with film and television.

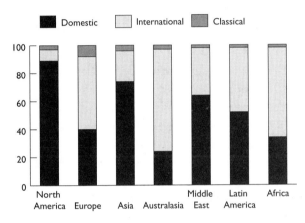

Figure 8.6   The share of domestic, international and classical music repertoire in different parts of the world in 2000 (source: IFPI).

Significant profits are made around the world, but overall the music market is static, if not falling in value. The global sales total was $37 billion in 2000, a fall of $2 billion since 1995. The industry is suffering badly from two forms of 'piracy'. In poorer countries where prices are low, piracy means the illegal mass duplication of tapes. But this is rapidly developing into production of CDs. In North America, by far the biggest market, and in Europe, the fear is that digital copying and swapping of audio files on the Internet is undermining the industry. Very large amounts of money are involved. In 2000 an IFPI Piracy report suggested that one-third of all recording 'units' (i.e. singles, albums etc.) sold worldwide were pirated. Pirate products have been valued at over $4 billion,

but the actual lost sales represent a much bigger loss to the industry. Mass duplication is the problem in Asia and eastern Europe. In North America and Western Europe, the loss comes from individual computer users making digital copies (see below). The extent of this is far more difficult to calculate, but in February 2001 2.8 billion songs were freely distributed on the Internet (www.ifpi.org).

The North American music market

The latest figures from the RIAA (Record Industry Association of America) suggest that the industry is indeed in crisis. The value of the market has declined, with falling CD sales the main concern (vinyl is making something of a comeback on a small scale, and DVD growth is very rapid). New products such as audio DVD offer some hope of reviving the market, but the threat from Internet swapping and CD burning is real.

To put the market in perspective, in 2001 it was running at around $10 billion, a significant decline on the late 1990s but still an industry worth more than the cinema box office. However, cinema box office is rising, and films go on to make as much money again on video or DVD and television. Music is not in the dominant position it was in the 1970s and 1980s. An indicator of the problem is that the industry has been unsuccessful in developing new artists with guaranteed sales in the millions of units. The most profitable way for the industry to work is to concentrate on relatively few artists and to promote them heavily, hoping for massive sales of a small number of titles. (The logic of this is that promotion of lesser-known acts can be just as expensive but is unlikely to produce the volume of sales.) In 2001 EMI decided to cut its losses by withdrawing from a major contract with Mariah Carey – it was prepared to pay her a reported $20 million rather than lose the money in the future, when they believed her records wouldn't sell. (Carey's 2001 album sold poorly and her film debut was not successful.)

Figure 8.7 Sales figures for different music formats showing the changes in consumer demand between June 2000 and June 2001 (sales of singles are excluded) (source: RIAA).

| Format | January – June 2000 | | January – June 2001 | | % Change |
	Units (millions)	$ millions	Units (millions)	$ millions	Change in Value
CD	420.0	5,681.2	397.9	5,528.0	-2.7
Cassette	38.6	303.2	22.0	176.0	-41.9
Vinyl LP/EP	1.0	12.4	1.0	12.9	3.3
Music Video	5.1	68.6	4.8	65.5	-4.0
DVD	1.4	35.2	3.0	70.1	99.2
Totals	466.1	6,100.6	428.7	5,852.9	-4.0

Synergy, convergence and the contemporary music industry

What we've tried to show in this case study is that the music industry has been uniquely placed to help each of the other media industries at crucial stages of their development. It has provided opportunities for synergy that have been exploited by radio, television and cinema and now by 'new media'. In 2002 the excitement in the UK over the voting for ITV's *Pop Idol* and the subsequent release of the winner's first single showed benefits for television, phone companies and the music industry.

Convergence means that what were once separate industries are 'coming together', converging on a common platform of 'digital media forms'. This sounds attractive if it will mean greater access for music users and new music products, but there is also the worry that convergence will lead to the disappearance of the distinct industry.

Music and the Internet are both natural and un-natural bedfellows. The creation and consumption of music is a personal, cultural experience, and the technology of the Internet changes the mode of consumption in a way that is both appealing and threatening – and certainly disruptive.

(Martin Mills of Beggars Banquet Records Group, in the Introduction to *Consumers Call the Tune*, Department of Culture Media and Sport, April 2000)

The digital threat

The Internet could be the means to open access to new music products for both producers/performers and consumers. Or it could undermine the current industry structure and threaten the livelihoods of producers/performers who in the long term may be unable to continue.

The problem is how to develop a market for digital music that guarantees a royalty payment to the creative talent (composer or performer or producer). There are two parts to the problem. First, MP3 files are often available free from other users. Napster software could search the Internet, find a supplier of a specific MP3 and arrange a transfer to anyone on-line who wanted it. Napster.com was effectively 'bought out' by a consortium including the major Bertelsmann, who recognised its appeal, but determined to set up its own system on which it could charge a fee. Universal bought the original site at MP3.com, and two other commercial sites were announced by consortia of the other majors. Successful legal actions against Napster and other companies looked like slowing down the pirates, but other similar programs exist. The pirates got there first on the Internet, and the industry is now trying to create a legitimate business. Users have remained reluctant to pay for MP3s and they continue to look for the free option. If the majors want to stay in business they must eventually find a scheme that works and on which they can charge a fee that customers will pay.

The second part of the problem is that it is now very easy to 'rip' a music track from a CD, store it as an MP3 and then burn it to a new CD. Blank CDs cost less than £1, and software such as Apple's iTunes is very easy to use. Alternatively, MP3s can be downloaded to portable players such as the iPod or its PC equivalent. As mobile phone technology advances, it is already producing small 'combi' devices that will act as phone, Internet connection (WAP), pocket computer and MP3 player.

It is clear from what is happening that some industry players are making good profits out of the current situation (the manufacturers of blank CDs and CD writers for instance). But the question remains, why spend £15 on a CD when for less than £1 and a few minutes' work you can borrow one from a friend and copy it?

The problem facing the industry has arisen before with the copying of CDs to tape. That produced a campaign, 'Home taping is killing music', sponsored by the industry and the musicians themselves. However, the industry weathered that storm – partly because it emerged that 'home tapers' were actually also heavy purchasers of CDs. The same problem of piracy in all its forms faces the Hollywood film studios. They have taken various measures, including a coding signal on videotapes that stops them being copied to most modern VCRs, which are factory programmed to read the code. The first attempt to try a similar scheme on CDs failed because the code also prevented customers who bought the CD from (quite legitimately) playing the CD on their computer. Using a computer CD drive as a music source is important to a significant part of the market: thousands of returned CDs embarassed the major label, who withdrew the release.

Do the companies really have to worry about the impact of copying? The latest Hollywood audience research suggests that people who buy or rent most videos and DVDs actually go to the cinema more often than those who buy fewer. Could it be that people who copy CDs also buy more and go to more concerts?

From a sample of 834 interviews with US Internet users in 2001, the international research firm Ipsos-Reid concluded that

- only 8 per cent of users who had ever downloaded music had paid for it
- 84 per cent were not prepared to pay for downloads, even if no free music was available;

but

- 81 per cent had either increased or maintained their purchase of CDs, despite downloading free material
- 84 per cent were avid users of the Internet in researching information about bands, tours and albums before purchase.

(www.ipsos-reid.com)

What this research appears to show is that the dilemma for music companies is very real. There may be something in Internet use that refers back to a time when the Internet was less commercial – we all like 'free downloads' and they are often what sends us back to a particular Internet site. But does offering something free to encourage visits to a site translate into sales? What do you think?

ACTIVITY 8.9

Do your own Internet research. Look for MP3s by well-known artists.

- Are they freely available on 'pirate sites'?
- Are they available on legitimate 'pay sites'?
- How does the payment scheme work? (e.g. Is it a subscription or a single payment?)
- Canvas your friends. How many of them would pay for an MP3 in this way?

References

This case study was researched solely on the Internet. The following websites proved useful:
www.culture.gov.uk/creative/music
www.ifpi.org
www.ipsos-reid.com

www.rca.com

www.riaa.com

Further reading

Du Gay, Paul *et al.* (1996) *Doing Cultural Studies: The Story of the Sony Walkman*, London; Sage.

Negus, Keith (1996) *Popular Music in Theory*, Cambridge: Polity.

Negus, Keith (1999) *Music Genres and Popular Cultures*, London: Routledge.

Shuker, Roy (2001) *Understanding Popular Music*, London: Routledge.

Part II
Media Practices

primary or secondary research

9 Research

In Part II we are concerned with 'media practices' – considering both how media organisations go about their business and also how you will be expected to approach your own media productions and academic studies. We have organised the chapters to follow the production process roughly, and we begin with the essential preparatory work of research.

Research is crucial to every form of media production, and the role of researcher is clearly identified in some media industries (e.g. television). In other industries research is perhaps less visible, but think of the work that goes into art direction and costume design on a feature film or the hours of listening that inform the decisions of a record producer. In this chapter we will refer to:

- content research
- production research
- audience research
- academic research

These definitions refer to the *purpose* of research, and you need to make sure that you can distinguish between them. There is also an important distinction between *primary* and *secondary* research and between different research *methodologies*.

Primary or secondary research

Since this distinction applies to any form of research, let's clarify it first. **Primary research** implies that the researcher is the first agent to collect and collate material. An interview is the clearest possible example of primary research – asking questions and obtaining responses which are 'original'. Interviews may be used to form the background material from which a script or an article is written. Alternatively, the interviews may appear in the finished text, as in the traditional Sunday magazine profile of a prominent figure. A genre of film documentary has also developed where eye-witnesses describe what happened at the time. Such interviews are usually rerecorded for the production itself.

The distinction between primary and secondary research is not always clear-cut. Is a photograph in a newspaper archive secondary or primary? Once it has been 'collected' with other similar photographs in a book, it definitely becomes secondary. The distinction is really about whose interpretation of the material comes first.

Other primary sources may be government records, such as the register of births and deaths or the correspondence and personal papers of individuals or organisations. These are sometimes formally organised into '**archives**' (see below). Other forms of primary research can include taking photographs or making sound recordings (of folk songs or birdsong perhaps).

'Deep' research, rather like the **ethnographic** studies carried out by academic ethnographers, may begin by the researcher living in a community for some time and recording aspects of daily life (see Chapter 6). This is the kind of research novelists might undertake to 'get the feel' of a location.

Secondary research implies that someone else other than the researcher has collected and organised material and made it available for research, usually in a library or archive. It often means using compiled records such as reference books. Sources need not be reference books as such – you could look at the novels and magazines written in a particular period, or at films, or television advertisements.

Secondary research material has connotations of being somehow less authentic because it has already been mediated in some way. So, if you look up the letters of a famous novelist, published in book form, they will have already been selected and edited and introduced by someone else – you won't be responding to them directly. In some ways this is a specious argument since every 'record' is a mediated account of something that has happened, but it is still a useful distinction since a reliance on secondary material alone is unlikely to provide as much sense of personal involvement in a story as research that includes some first-hand experience and contains the possibility of finding something which perhaps didn't 'fit' previous researchers' expectations.

Content or background research

Some research is likely to take place even before a programme is commissioned or a film 'greenlighted'. This is background research that helps to set up the proposal – to find out if there really is an interesting story to back up that good idea in the pub. Sometimes the background research has been carried out for another purpose and then used to inform a new proposal. A university thesis might become the basis for a book and then a television programme.

Once the proposal has been accepted, further research will be needed, not only to inform the script but also possibly to provide sounds and images that might appear in a film or radio or television programme. Media production relies heavily on specialist archives.

Picture libraries

Many newspapers and magazines as well as television companies have an in-house picture library where they keep carefully filed copies of images they own (or where they have acquired reproduction rights), covering topics such as famous personalities, important buildings, locations etc. Most of these libraries now have been digitised so that images can be traced through multiple searches, e.g. all images of women in uniform in the Second World War. These are then instantaneously available if a news story breaks. All photographs taken by staff reporters on a newspaper are automatically filed for possible future use. These libraries represent important assets for the media corporations and can be sold or leased for considerable sums. In some cases libraries have survived the deaths of the publications which created them and have become profit-earners in their own right.

The market for images is such that photographers have built up their own archives of standard shots (sunsets, cute babies etc.) which they offer as commercial library pictures. With the growth of CD technology and on-line services via the Internet, there are now many ways in which media producers can acquire high-quality images for advertising or promotion at a relatively low cost. The 'international image market' is such that a small group of companies are carefully buying up the rights to an enormous range of images, all available in digital form – credit card account permitting. In all these cases, users of images will pay for different services (see the section on copyright in Chapter 10).

Some of the major commericial picture libraries have developed out of newspaper collections, like the Hulton Archive which derived originally from the *Picture Post* and *Daily Herald* archives from the 1930s–50s. Check the library on www.hultongetty.com.

Corbis is the image company set up by Bill Gates. See www.corbis.com.

Sound libraries

'Library sounds' – collections of mood music and sound effects at relatively low cost – are available on CD to be used by corporate producers via various licence agreements. Other audio recordings are owned by the broadcasters or the large recording companies. The BBC has extensive archives of past recordings, and these sometimes form the basis of entire radio programmes. There is also the National Sound Archive in the UK which holds a collection of historic and representative recordings.

Film and video libraries

Until the 1940s film companies often threw their products away once their initial release was completed. Early television recordings often went the same way. Now the companies have recognised the value of their products and have begun to archive them carefully and in some cases have bought other collections as well.

Regional film archives Your region may have established a film archive, possibly associated with a university or a library. Films made in the region by professionals and amateurs may be held, along with stills and production materials. Some material is being issued by archives (e.g. Scottish and North West Film Archives).

The British Universities Film and Video Council (BFUVC) offers an on-line service for students using a connection from an 'ac.uk' address www.bufvc.ac.uk/databases/rgo.html.

Insight at the National Museum of Photography, Film and Television in Bradford is a new attraction which opens up the collections of the museum to public access. Individuals and groups can view materials by appointment. See the website at www.nmpft.org.uk/insight.

Film archives have the advantage over video in that the basic technology has not changed over a hundred years and, provided that the film has survived physically, it is usually possible to make a viewing copy of any footage. Video formats change frequently and it is already proving difficult to replay material on some of the older formats because the relevant video players are no longer in working order.

The National Film and Television Archive provides a service for film students and researchers, and other national and regional organisations have now begun to market their materials for educational and commercial use. Film research is a highly specialised business, and the British Universities Film and Video Council publishes a guide for researchers. Archiving has a recognisable career structure and the University of East Anglia for example now offers a postgraduate course.

ACTIVITY 9.1

Research project

Set yourself a research project aimed at collecting material for a magazine article. Choose something general such as 'National Lottery winners' or 'medical stories'.

- Compile a cuttings library over a couple of weeks, looking through newspapers and magazines for text and photographs (look at a good spread of papers). Alternatively, download stories from Internet sites and store them on disk.
- Tape television or radio programmes or use a notebook to jot down programme details. Make sure you always record your source reference, including the names of photographers or the rights holders for images.
- At the end of your allotted time, review your material. Do you have enough material to help you generate ideas for an article?
- Have you found good images or quotations?
- Have you got all the references?

This is a good practice exercise for all media students – at some stage in your course you will probably have to do this as an assignment.

ACTIVITY 9.2

Research sources

1 Next time there is a broadcast of a documentary series covering a historical period, check the credits for details of the research sources (if you have satellite or cable, try the Discovery Channel).

- How many different film archives have been used?
- Are there individuals who have contributed material?
- How many researchers are named?

2   Watch any major political interview on television (e.g. with a government minister).

- What kinds of questions does the interviewer ask?
- Which questions would have needed some form of research – is there a named researcher for the programme?

Other specialist sources

Some forms of research also require knowledge of specific procedures. Political commentators know to go to *Hansard* for a record of parliamentary business and to look up the decisions of parliamentary special committees as well as debates on the floor of the House of Commons. Similarly a great deal of useful information can be found in government statistical reports, court proceedings etc.

Background research now regularly takes place on-line using the Internet. If you know your way around a search engine and useful portals (websites that guide you through links to other sites in defined areas of interest) you can achieve a great deal without leaving your computer terminal.

Internet details

In the material that follows, to avoid confusion, everything that you need to type into a search engine dialogue box is shown between these signs: < >. Most of the time, you don't need to use upper case letters in your search, so <titanic> should find exactly the same material as <Titanic>. When we refer to a website or webpage we will only give the main part of the address, e.g. www.google.com – you still need the first part of the address as well, e.g. http://www.google.com. In most cases, we list only the homepage of the website and you may need to search through the site to find what you want.

Searching on the Internet

The Internet is a valuable source of material for research exercises – much of the information in this book has been discovered on, or checked against, a wide range of Internet sites.

If you are going to find useful material on the Web, you need to learn to search effectively. There are dozens of search engines and tools to choose from and they aren't all equally useful. So, don't expect that the network you use in college will necessarily be set up for the kind of research you want to do.

We have been reluctant to give too many web addresses simply because they do change over two or three years. A quick search is often more rewarding than typing in a 'known' address.

Search engines

There are three types of search engine:

- *simple word search* You type in a keyword and the software looks for that word across millions of pages on the Internet. It will return to you all the 'hits'. They may be in order of the most relevant sites where the word appears in a page title or name – or sites may have paid a fee to be 'placed with' the search engine. The likelihood is that you will receive far more hits than you need and you will need to try to refine the search. Google at www.google.co.uk is the most efficient general search tool – fast and comprehensive.

- *metasearch engine* In this case the software sends your keyword to several other search engines at the same time and sorts the results for you. This will also return many hits and because it uses several different engines, you may pick up webpages missed by the single engine. But it may also be more cumbersome to use. www.search.com is an example of a metasearch engine.

- *portals or 'subject' search engines* offer you a presorted catalogue of websites. The search engine's human staff have set up the categories. This allows you to narrow your search and to avoid a great deal of irrelevant material. However, it may be a less productive search and also less up to date. It may also suggest a simple search if it can't find something to match your query. Yahoo! (www.yahoo.com) is the best known portal.

In most cases, the quickest and most effective way to find anything is to type it in Google. You are almost guaranteed to find something useful in a matter of seconds. But if your research is going to be successful, you need to develop some strategies for refining your search. In Part II our case study is the British film industry. We'll organise a search for information on one of the films discussed in the case study.

Sexy Beast (UK 2001) is directed by Jonathan Glazer and stars Ben Kingsley and Ray Winstone. To get some basic details about the film we could start with the entry in the Internet Movie Database at uk.imdb.com. This is a portal and will allow us to use the database and give us links to other sites. It is a well-presented site with lots of information, but it won't tell us everything we want to know.

The IMDB started in the UK (at Cardiff University), but now it is skewed towards US production. It makes sense, therefore to try a more specialised site at www.britfilms.com which holds a catalogue of recent British films. This gives some useful information on the production company, but it doesn't tell us what the budget for the film was. A general Google search might find this out.

By putting double quotes around the film title you can reduce the number of irrelevant hits. <"sexy beast"> will look only for the specific title and not for the two words separately. Depending on the search engine, you can sometimes select 'the complete phrase' rather than 'any word' to get a similar effect.

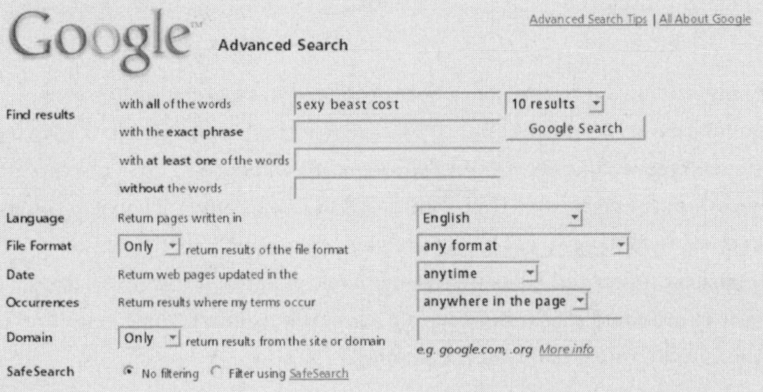

Figure 9.1a The settings for a Google search for <sexy beast cost>.

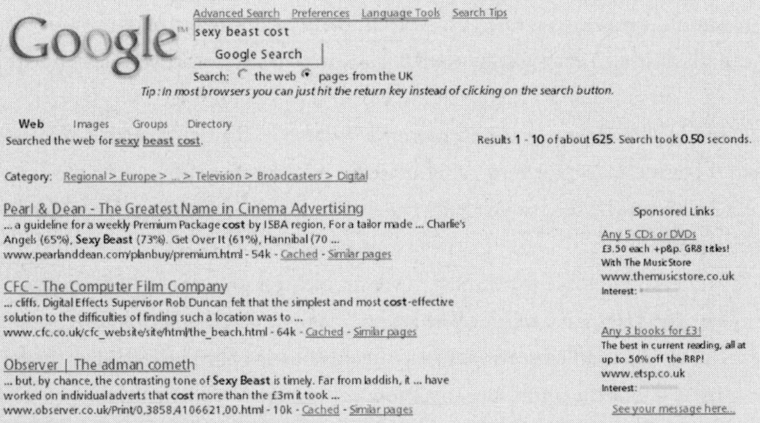

Figure 9.1b The top results of the search.

A simple name search like this will still throw up thousands of 'hits', most related to the film. How can you reduce the number quickly?

- On Google, select 'UK only', if you think that overseas sites will be less useful.
- Go to 'Preferences' or 'Advanced Search' and select 'only English' (or whatever other languages you want).
- Try using some 'Boolean operators', such as '+'. This requires the search engine to look for sites that include all the terms on the same page. The search engine should guide you in how to use symbols such as this.

<sexy beast + budget> throws up plenty of hits but no clear answer. But <sexy beast + cost> finds an interview with Jonathan Glazer which reveals the answer – £3 million. The site that carries this interview is the *Observer* section of the *Guardian/Observer* site. It might have been sensible to look here first, since this is one of the largest and best sources of recent news and features on the Web.

As you visit sites, you can take a note of them and store the addresses as 'bookmarks' or 'favourites', but, if you are working on a network, it may be easier to keep a paper record. As a shortcut, all you need to do is to keep the keyword in the address or *URL* ('unique resource locator'). Then you can use that word in Google to get to the site you want quickly. For example <"guardian unlimited"> should immediately produce www.guardian.co.uk. You may even find that simply typing <guardian> into Google brings up the *Guardian* site immediately as the first hit.

How useful is the information you find?

You should be able to refine your search using a combination of the methods above so that you find what you are looking for. If you have a hundred hits to plough through, even after you have refined your search, it is likely that the most useful material will be in the first few that the search engine lists. But how reliable is the information? Anyone can put a website up on the net, so you will need to verify the statement. Check the following:

- Who is responsible for the site? – it should tell you on the home page.
- Does the URL give a clue? The last part of the address should tell you. 'edu' or 'ac' is an educational institution (but it could be a student page), 'org' is a 'not for profit' organisation, 'gov' is government. 'com' or 'co' is a commercial site, 'net' is a network provider and 'mil' is military.
- Does the site have a specific viewpoint?
- How up to date is the page? 'Dead pages' can linger on otherwise live sites for a long time and may now be factually incorrect or misleading.

Finding material on the web is sometimes exciting – there is enormous satisfaction in finding something after a long search. But you need to step back. Would it have been easier to look it up in a reference book in the library? How time-consuming is it, if you feel that you have to verify what you find? What you need is experience of using the Web to conduct meaningful research and practice at refining searches. There is one area in which the Web excels, and that is up-to-date figures. Often these are on-line before they are published in hard copy. Look for sites involved in media business dealings. Often the trade association for that sector, or companies offering market research or industry analyses are most useful. We've put a list of suggested websites in the resources section of the book.

Using your Web findings

You may be using a network or your own computer, Explorer or Netscape as a browser on a PC or a Mac, so we can't advise you on how to store your material. But the main point to remember is to keep track of where you have been visiting. It's so easy to use links from one site to another that you can easily lose track of where you have been. You need the URL of each site you have visited for the references listing in your work. You could print out the relevant pages (checking that you have the URL printed on them). But if there is material that you want to quote, this means re-keying it later on. If you can 'cut and paste' from the web page into an open file in a wordprocessor (with the URL pasted in as well) you may save yourself time. You can also save the file direct from the web, but you need to check how the software you are using does this – saving a file as HTML will save all the codings amongst the text that you want.

What is worth downloading is any material offered as a '**pdf**'. This is a computer file which works on any computer with Acrobat Reader (freely downloadable from www.adobe.com). If your browser has Reader installed, the file will open on your computer and you can save it to disk as well (some pdfs are too big for a floppy disk). You can then read the publication later, exactly as it appeared on screen. Pdfs are increasingly being used for company statements, reports, statistics etc. and we have used many of them in preparing this book.

Referencing and bibliographies

Research is an essential academic skill, and you will no doubt be expected to provide full references for any sources you have consulted in preparing essays or reports. There are three reasons for doing this:

- References allow anyone reading your work to refer to your original sources, perhaps to find out more background.
- The references you provide are essential in order to avoid any charges of plagiarism – passing off someone else's work as your own.
- A good range of references demonstrates your wide background reading – often part of the assessment criteria for courses.

There are several different methods for referencing academic sources. It doesn't necessarily matter which one you use, although some academic institutions specify a preferred option. It is important to be consistent and thorough. We have used the 'Harvard' system. You'll see the name of an author next to a quotation, followed by a year and sometimes a page number. We like giving the full first name of authors, though often only initials are used. You can then go to the references at the end of a chapter and look up the full entry which will give you author, year of publication, title, place of publication and publisher. Magazine articles are also listed with the magazine issue number and date. You should give the full URL of any web page you quote, and it may also be useful to give the date on which you visited the site (it may disappear in the meantime).

Production research

This refers to a whole range of logistical issues, some of which, concerning information needed by the production crew, are discussed in Chapter 10 under the heading of 'Recce' and Location. But there are also research tasks concerned with the 'talent' on a programme – finding contestants for a quiz show, compiling possible interview questions or a dossier on a studio guest. Here, background research will be worked on to produce something usable in a live show.

Other forms of production research may refer to props, costumes etc. and how these are to be used in the final programme. You may have to find not only authentic swords and armour but also trainers to show actors how to use them. The various guides to career opportunities stress that production research in television especially requires a high level of interpersonal skills and that much of the working day is spent on the phone persuading people to do things for the programme. The researcher may also be responsible for checking out all the potential legal, ethical and regulatory issues that may arise if research material is used.

ACTIVITY 9.3

Production research

Tape five minutes from two different television programmes – a consumer affairs or 'lifestyle' programme and a 'costume drama' (anything not set in the present day).

Make a note of all the different production research activities that each programme may have involved, including:

- props, clothes, vehicles etc.
- personality backgrounds
- experts needed
- permissions, copyright
- legal, ethical, regulatory issues etc.

Does one type of programme require more research?

Audience research

Constructing an audience profile for a particular product or investigating a specific target audience is a specialised area of work. Some media producers employ market research companies to analyse markets and specific audiences for their products. You may be required to do this before undertaking a production – finding out what your target audience wants. You may also conduct some audience research after your production has been presented to an audience in an attempt to find out how it has been received.

Although they have different purposes, audience research may share a number of features with academic research (see below). Both distinguish **quantitative** and **qualitative** research.

See Chapter 6 for more on this.

Production companies want to know about a specific target audience, so they will want to be assured about the sample selected by the research company. It needs to include sufficient people to be representative of different age, class and gender divisions across the different regions where the media product may be experienced. Quantitative research is a number-crunching exercise and aims to produce audience figures for cinema and broadcasting, and readership figures for print products. Each industry follows different conventions: cinema is usually interested in 'frequency of visits to a cinema'; television looks at 'shares' of a potential audience achieved by a programme, and newspapers are interested in both circulation and readership.

See Chapter 12 for some examples of audience research.

In your own quantitative research you will necessarily lack the resources of a research company, but you can carry out worthwhile research if you remember these points:

- Think about your target audience and what you want to know. The more your sample reflects the composition of the audience, the more useful the results.
- The bigger the sample, the more likely the results will be credible;
- Ask 'closed' questions that will produce numerical data that can easily be input into a spreadsheet to produce analyses.

From these points it is clear that your research needs careful planning. If your target audience is shoppers or consumers it may be useful to ask simple questions in the shopping centre during the day. But this will not necessarily

'Closed' questions invite a simple 'yes' or 'no' or a definable number, e.g. "How many CDs did you buy last month?" None, one, two to five, more than five?

produce a useful sample if you need to include people in work. As you collect responses you need to note gender, age etc. if this is relevant.

Research organisations employ a range of methods to collect data. You may have been approached on the street by a researcher with a clip board or you may have been 'door-stepped' at home. Another possibility is a 'cold call' on the telephone. In all these circumstances, there must be some doubt as to the usefulness of the data since only those willing to spend time with the researcher will answer questions – many people will refuse to stop or decline to answer at the door or on the telephone. To get round these problems, 'consumer surveys' sometimes offer an inducement – shopping vouchers or free entry into a prize draw. One form of this is the 'reader survey' that you may have come across in specialist magazines. Here your tastes will be explored in terms not just of what else you read, but also of what other kinds of goods you buy. Research data can be sold to other companies or jointly sponsored by companies with interests in the same audience but in relation to different products.

One reason why you may be asked to take part in research is because research bureaux sometimes target communities by postcode. The **ACORN** system, used by marketing data firm CACI, groups consumers by the postcode. A postcode usually covers around fifteen households, who may be expected to share certain characteristics. A similar form of audience research is conducted via some film previews where audiences are offered a free screening in return for completion of 'scorecards' about a new film.

ACORN A Classification of Residential Neighbourhoods – you can look up your own street classification using www.upmystreet.com.

You can get a good idea of media industry research from the website of BMRB International, a UK company specialising in media research. www.bmrb.co.uk offers a wealth of information, including an indication of the costs of asking questions and purchasing reports as well as some free material. One of BMRB's strategies has been to develop a TGI (Target Group Index) for various groups including children and young people (partly because most media industry readership surveys ignore readers under the age of fifteen). By asking similar questions over a number of years the TGI can now show trends in reading behaviour.

Figure 9.2 shows how the 'Youth TGI' can be used to demonstrate how the age profile for readership of *Smash Hits* has changed over time. The chart shows that overall readership fell between 1994 and 1996, but has since recovered. However, the proportion of readers under eleven has risen dramatically, more than doubling from 24 per cent in 1994 to over 50 per cent in 2001. Knowing that the readership is getting younger is obviously important to the publishers, but also to everyone else wanting to sell media products to this age group. In her Youth TGI presentation, 'Young at Heart', Liz McMahon refers to a number of other interesting findings about 'young readers':

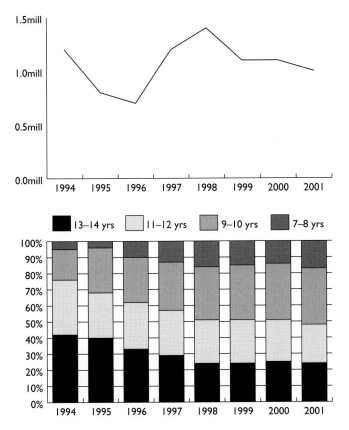

Figure 9.2 Trends in readership of *Smash Hits* between 1994 and 2001. The graph at the top shows the total readership for each year and the chart below shows how the 'age profile' has fallen with younger readers forming a greater proportion of the whole (source: the Youth TGI (Target Group Indicator) compiled by BRMB International).

- Girls and boys aged seven-to-fourteen read different magazine titles, except for a shared interest in *What's On TV*.
- Sixty per cent of seven-to-fourteen-year-olds had Internet access at home in 2001 and most used it to send e-mails and play games.
- If they had to 'give up' an activity, most seven-to-fourteen-year-olds would give up radio – they are least likely to give up using a phone.
- Only 51 per cent of eleven-to-fourteen-year-olds ever read a Sunday paper, but 90 per cent do 'ever read' a magazine.

(Presentation downloaded from www.bmrb.co.uk)

These findings give a good indication of the kinds of useful numerical data available to media producers, enabling them to focus investment and future planning on new titles etc. (Readership data is discussed also in Chapter 12.)

Ranking If you want to ask audiences to rank their feelings about a media product, it's a good idea to offer four options rather than three – otherwise many will opt for a non-committal 'answer in the middle'. With four options, they are forced to move towards 'liked' or 'disliked'.

'Open' questions usually begin with words such as 'how' or 'why' and invite a response that explores an issue.

Qualitative research suggests that it is not the number of responses that is important, but the opinions or ideas that respondents express. A questionnaire may still be useful if you offer multiple-choice-type questions (possibly a ranking of responses) and also allow some 'open' questions. Other possibilities are interviews or discussions ('**focus groups**' – see Chapter 13 – are observed discussions) or diaries written by audiences over a short period. Your aim here is to find out what the audience thinks about a media product. How you interpret your findings will depend on your objectives. If you want to use audience responses to help you with your next production, the most useful responses are those that tell you something that you don't already know.

If your only audience is other students on your course, you may face the problem that they are far too polite about your work. Anonymous response forms, direct questions ('What didn't you like about . . .') or observation may be needed. You can tell a lot by watching and listening to different audiences viewing your work – when do they laugh, groan, when do they fidget, when do they appear rapt? But you may well be better off with a different audience altogether.

Academic research

There is discussion of the most high-profile academic research concerning 'audience effects' in Chapter 6. Academic research uses both quantitative methods (in studying representation issues for instance – 'content analysis') and qualitative methods, and similar issues arise as to those discussed above in relation to audience research. What distinguishes academic research (most of the time, at least) is the purpose of the exercise. Most commercially funded audience research is designed to produce data to help media producers target audiences more effectively and for advertisers to identify products with advertising opportunities that can demonstrate their efficiency in 'delivering audiences'. Academic research is interested in how media communication works, how producers and audiences behave, how media products change over time and in different social, political and economic contexts etc.

Academic research begins with a *hypothesis* – 'a proposition or a question assumed for the sake of argument'. Material is then gathered in an attempt to demonstrate that the hypothesis can be proved. Research findings are collated and analysed and conclusions formed which are then published. Such work is essential to higher education and in recent years has become even more important as funding of universities depends to some extent on the research output of staff. You may well select a university on the basis of its specialisms in media research.

The likelihood is that you may be required to carry out a research project as part of the assessment of your course. An assignment may require you to carry out some form of primary and secondary research. Again, much of the discussion above is relevant in how you organise your work. You will probably be advised to discuss the title of your project with your tutor or supervisor and you should always try to argue a point, to have a definite initial question in such projects, not just collect as much information as you can. There are two good reasons for doing this at an early stage:

- Many students select very broad areas of research, possibly because they think it will be easy to find material (e.g. 'the representation of young men on British television') and won't need to do that tricky thing: formulate a good research question to which they're looking for the answer. The difficulty with broad areas of research is that it is difficult to produce worthwhile conclusions because it is too difficult to analyse all the available material and to make interesting comparisons. Cutting down the area to include one television genre in one time period might be a better bet.

- Some media texts are difficult to find. This is particularly true of films and television programmes, which are often inexplicably out of print. On the other hand, certain texts are not only widely available but have also been discussed in academic journals and on Internet mailing lists. Although you may want to find an obscure text, and can try advertising in Internet chatrooms, or other locations, good advice can point you to research topics that will enable you more easily to undertake effective primary and secondary research.

References and further reading

Chater, Kathy (2001) *Research for Media Production*, Oxford: Focal Press.

O'Sullivan, Tim, Dutton, Brian and Rayner, Philip (1998) 'Media research and investigation' in *Studying the Media*, 2nd ed., London: Arnold.

Websites

www.bfi.org.uk   Useful source of information about film and television, includes pages for the National Film and Television Archive, the BFI Library (the National Library for Film) and a Researcher's Guide. A good 'portal' for all searches on film and television.

www.radioresearch.co.uk   Scottish radio information.

www.skillset.org The Film and Broadcast Industry National Training Organisation with good links and offering access to career advice.

See Chapter 12 for industry audience research links.

10 Production organisation

- The production process in outline
- Setting out
- Negotiating a brief

- Pre-production
- Production
- Post-production
- References and further reading

In this chapter we deal with the organisation and management of media production tasks. Along with Chapter 11, the information and advice here will enable you to understand the production process and to approach your own productions with confidence.

The production process in outline

If you discuss the concept of the production process with professionals who work in different media (e.g. magazine publishing, television etc.), they will probably stress the differences – the specificities – of their particular work practices. In Chapter 8 we outline a six-stage production process which, while primarily concerned with film and television, will serve equally well for other types of media production, even if the professionals concerned would not necessarily recognise the terms used:

- development or negotiating a brief
- pre-production
- production
- post-production
- distribution
- exhibition.

These stages represent the production process for a single, coherent product. An established, daily, media product won't need to involve endless negotiation and pre-production (although the inclusion of some material will still need to be negotiated), but when the product was first devised the production team will have gone through these stages. A television or radio series is commissioned in blocks and can be treated as a single production.

'Development' is the term used in the film industry. A 'brief' is a design industry term, also used in video production. In many industries a freelance producer, writer or director hopes to be 'commissioned' by a 'publisher' of some kind.

Setting out

Whatever the production task, there are several important questions which need to be asked at the outset.

Purpose

Why are you producing a media text? Most likely it will be to 'educate, inform or entertain'. If it isn't one of these, then it is probably intended to persuade. All production must be entertaining to a certain extent or else readers won't persevere with the text. Your production will be assessed according to the extent to which it 'fits its purpose', and you should bear this in mind throughout each stage of the process.

Target audience

The meaning produced by a text depends to a large extent on the intended reader, and it's futile to try to construct a text if you don't know who that reader is. The audience profile will include the standard age, gender and class information as well as more culturally based distinctions which might include religion, sexual orientation, marital or family status etc., and environmental factors such as geographical location (see Chapter 6 for further discussion of the descriptions used by media industries).

Budget and funding

Media production requires money – large amounts in many cases. Where does it come from?

Direct sales Not many producers can be self-funding – generating enough income from sales to fund the next production. In most cases, the preparation costs and the delay in receiving income mean that the outlay is too big for a small company to cover.

There are then a limited number of options available. Borrowing the money from a bank will mean high interest payments, putting more pressure on the 'need to succeed'. Selling an interest in your production to a backer is perhaps a less risky venture, but of course it means that, if you do well, a share of the profits goes to your backers.

Pre-sales Continuing production can be guaranteed if you can 'pre-sell' your products at a fixed price. This way you may cover the whole of your budget with a guaranteed sale. The disadvantage is that, if your product is very successful and could command a higher price, you will have forgone potential profits.

'Now that farmers are being paid for not growing crops . . . might I suggest that this is a policy the Arts Council could adopt . . . they could pay writers not to produce books' (adapted from a letter by David M. Bennie to *The Literary Review*). The same view might be applied to a wide range of media products which don't have a clear purpose and a recognised audience.

Selling rights to a distributor   This saves you the trouble and the risk of selling your product in territories (or to other media) which you don't know much about. A distributor pays you a fixed sum. Once again, you lose profits if the product is successful.

Selling ideas   If you can sell your production idea, you can save yourself the bother of producing at all. You can also negotiate to make your product as a commission for a major producer, leaving someone else to worry about budgets while you just take a fee.

Sponsorship or advertising   You may get someone else to pay for the production (or part of it) as part of a sponsorship deal. Companies may be interested in being associated with a 'quality' product, especially if it addresses a specific target audience. A specialised form of sponsorship involves **product placement**. Print products and possibly radio broadcasts may be funded by the direct sale of advertising space. The danger of sponsorship is that the sponsors' views on the production may compromise your own aims.

Product placement This refers to the prominent position of consumer items in the decor of films and television programmes and crucially the use of such products by stars – Coca-Cola and Pepsi are reputed to have spent millions getting their products used by stars in Hollywood features (see Chapter 3).

Grant aid has enabled many currently successful film-makers to make a start. Lottery funding is a relatively new source of support, mainly for organisations, but also for smaller ventures – check with your local arts board.

Grant-aid   If you have no money and little experience, you may actually be better placed to get started on a project than if you have a track record. Many arts agencies offer grants to new producers. These may be quite small – a few hundred pounds up to a few thousand – but enough to get started. Look in the reference section for details of the British Film Institute, Arts Council and regional arts boards etc. Be warned, grant applications have strict schedules tied to annual budgets and quite detailed application forms. Make sure you have enough time to get advice and fill in the forms properly. You will also need to evaluate your work – you will probably find that your Media Studies work is useful in explaining what you want to do. Many grants are aimed at giving help to particular groups of new producers or new forms of production.

For many producers, 'independence' from control or 'interference' by funders is a big issue. On the other hand some funders can be helpful in budgeting for you (and also giving you 'backing' which will allow you entry into other negotiations with potential buyers etc.).

Style

What style or genre will you use? No matter how 'original' you attempt to be, you will be making references to media conventions – if you don't make these references your readers may have difficulty following the text. You will perhaps be warned not to imitate professional work slavishly, but, at least when you first start out, it is difficult not to draw on work you enjoy or admire. The best advice is to make open your intention to work 'in the style of' an existing producer and to begin by trying to understand all the conventions of a particular genre or style. If you want to go on and break with convention, it is useful to know which 'rules' need to be broken. If you are clear in the aesthetic or the formal approach which you wish to adopt, you will find it much easier to explain what you want to do, both to the commissioner of the work and to the rest of your production team.

Working in a familiar genre can mean greater 'freedom' because the conventions are so well known that audiences can be introduced to new ideas on the back of familiar ones.

Schedule

How long have you got to complete the production process? Planning and preparation are essential for a successful production, but even the best plans come to nothing if the overall task is impossible. Calculate the time each part of the process will take and ensure that you know everything about the schedule from the outset. For instance, you may be required to show the unfinished work to your commissioner in order to confirm the inclusion of contentious material, but will that person be available when you reach the crucial decision-making stage? Can your **schedule** be adapted to cope with these problems?

Your schedule will distinguish different parts of the process and you will be able to plan when and where each can take place. Be careful, because some aspects of production are more time-dependent than others, e.g. video post-production always takes longer than you imagine. Some parts of the production process are dependent on other parts having been completed first, so, for instance, if you want titles on your video production which 'overlay' the images in the opening sequence, you must prepare them before you start editing – you can't add them afterwards. 'Managing the schedule' is one of the most important aspects of production and perhaps the least appreciated by beginners. Check that you know, at the outset, all the stages your production needs to go through and include sufficient 'recovery time' for each stage in case things go wrong.

A schedule for magazine production

Imagine you are setting out to produce a fanzine or a small specialist magazine, say a sixteen-page, 'single colour' (the cheapest form of printing in which you choose just one ink colour) A4-size magazine. You have a number of friends who are going to contribute articles and you hope to distribute five hundred copies. All the desktop publishing (DTP) will be done by you and you will then take hard copy or a computer file to a printing company. How do you organise the schedule?

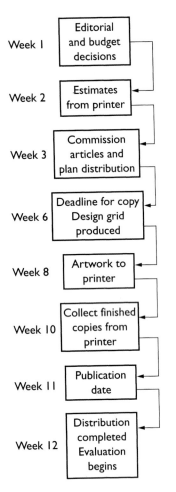

Week 1	Editorial and budget decisions
Week 2	Estimates from printer
Week 3	Commission articles and plan distribution
Week 6	Deadline for copy Design grid produced
Week 8	Artwork to printer
Week 10	Collect finished copies from printer
Week 11	Publication date
Week 12	Distribution completed Evaluation begins

Figure 10.1 Magazine production schedule.

The first decision will be the date of publication. This is the date when you want readers to have the magazine in their hands – you need to set a date well before the first date for any events or 'forthcoming attractions' you might list. You can then work backwards to set deadlines for each stage of the production process. You might come up with something like the schedule in Figure 10.1.

This might seem like a long production schedule for a small magazine and you might well be able to shorten some stages – but, even so, it will take you a couple of months to complete the process (in the professional magazine industry, each monthly magazine can take up to three months to produce, so that staff are working on two or three magazines at any one time, with issues being planned while one is being copy-edited and another is being printed). Notice the constraints. You can't be sure about commissioning pieces if you don't know the editorial policy or how much space you will have to fill given the budget. If you want to sell advertising, you must first give the advertiser a sense of what the publication will look like. Once the artwork (i.e. your designed pages) has gone to the printer, there isn't a lot you can do to affect the timing, so Week 8, 'going to print' day, is very important.

If you publish a magazine during your course it will need a schedule like this and you will probably need a whole term to do the job properly.

Constraints

Time and money are both constraints, but there are several others. Availability of appropriate technology is an obvious constraint and so is the availability of **talent** (actors or presenters in an audio-visual production) or creative people on the production team. There may be constraints on the availability of inanimate resources as well – locations, props or archive materials.

Less obvious, but equally important, are constraints on **permissions** – the rights to use a piece of music, a photograph, a poem etc. – and restraints created by law: slander, libel, obscenity, the Official Secrets Act etc.

Your ability to develop a production in relation to the imposed constraints is a major factor in demonstrating creativity in a vocational context. 'Problem-solving' or 'working within constraints' is what defines the effective media producer. Sometimes, working within constraints produces the most interesting work.

Constraints and creativity in film production

In the early days of the Soviet Union in 1919, when the new state was being blockaded by the West, a shortage of film stock prompted experiments by Kuleshov in which he spliced together 'offcuts' of exposed film and discovered novel effects of juxtaposing images. This was later developed into the celebrated Soviet 'montage' style. A more recent echo of this 'discovery' was the early 1980s 'scratch videos' produced by young and poorly funded video editors who 'stole' clips from broadcast television in order to produce satirical comments on contemporary society. Montage sequences are now routine in music videos.

More recently, the director and cinematographer of *Se7en* (US 1995), David Fincher and Darius Khondji, produced an original 'look' for their film, partly as a result of various constraints. 'The reason it rains all of the time is that we only had Brad Pitt for 55 days, with no contingency. So we did it to stay on schedule, because we knew that if it ever really rained we would have been fucked . . . We decided we wouldn't build any flyaway walls. If the kitchen is only 12 feet, then hem him in. We live in an age when anything is possible, so it's always important to limit yourself. It's important the blinders you put on, what you won't say. I wanted to take an adult approach – not, "Oh wow, a Luma crane".' (David Fincher interviewed in *Sight and Sound*, January 1996: 24.)

Figure 10.2 Morgan Freeman and Brad Pitt in a tight space in *Se7en*.

Important health and safety issues

You may not think of media production work as being particularly dangerous, but it can be in certain circumstances and, like every other 'public' activity, it is covered by a legal obligation on you to protect both yourself and others from injury.

The best way to learn about specific media production hazards is to address them 'on the job'. Your lecturer should always make clear the fire exits from any accommodation you use and should outline the particular safety requirements when dealing with equipment. These include electrical connections, trailing cables, very hot and fragile lights, noxious chemicals in photography etc. If you aren't told about these things – ask. Remember that the legal obligation can fall on you – you have a right to be told, but you also have a responsibility to act safely so that you don't injure anyone else. A good source of advice and information is often the appropriate union (e.g. BECTU for video), who may well have health and safety advisers. The technicians in your college should be well aware of potential hazards.

As a producer, you should be aware of some of the less obvious health and safety issues:

- *Stress* is a potential hazard for production personnel, who are often under pressure to make decisions or to operate equipment quickly and efficiently. You will notice this in 'live' television or radio productions. Stress can build up and affect performance (which in turn could lead to 'unsafe' decisions).
- *Public liability* requires you to be very careful when out on location, where you might cause an obstruction with cameras, cables, lights etc. As well as seeking permission, you need to warn passers-by of the hazards.
- *Special effects and stunts* can add a great deal to video productions, but there is a danger that in the excitement of creating an effect, you forget about the dangers, especially in driving or attempting falls etc.
- *Lifting and moving*   In the frenzy of getting equipment to where you want it and then how you want it arranged, it is all too easy to strain your muscles with heavy or awkward objects (and sometimes to damage expensive equipment). Learn how to handle equipment properly and find the crew and the time to move it safely.

Negotiating a brief

Once you have prepared your ideas by considering the issues above, you are ready to try them out and 'pitch' them to a potential funder or a commissioner for a publisher (e.g. a broadcast television or radio company or a print publisher), perhaps in response to a 'tender document' such as the one in Figure 10.3. To do this effectively you will need to encapsulate the main points of want you want to do into an **outline**, preferably no more than a couple of sides of A4 paper.

An alternative, when you have an idea but there is no specific tender document, is to send in a **proposal** suggesting something you could do. A proposal will include an outline and an argument as to why it would be successful with a specific target audience or readership. You should address the proposal to the relevant commissioner or editor, and it is sensible to study carefully which market a particular publisher targets. A proposal may also include a 'sample' of writing or script and will therefore be more substantial than a simple outline.

A term often used in television is '**treatment**'. The meaning of this term varies. Sometimes it refers to the style or approach which will be taken to a particular programme idea, and sometimes it is a full working through of ideas or a 'filling in' of the outline, describing what will happen. The production process may require an outline, which is developed into a treatment and finally into a production script.

Many proposals to write articles or stories are rejected by magazines because they are clearly unsuitable for the readership in terms of either content or style.

For more ideas about proposals for television see Holland (2000).

BBC Commissioning Brief Ref. 1/F52

CHANNEL
BBC ONE

CLASSIFICATION
Factual Entertainment

DAY
Weekday

SLOT
19.00

EDITORIAL GUIDE
Bathtime, cooking, eating, catching up with the family's day. It's tough enough to make your mark at seven o'clock – especially when so many soap fans are making a date with their favourites.

But there are plenty of people who don't or who can be tempted away if you can make yourself heard: rewarding information, a sense of event, a strong format with a twist of jeopardy or unpredictability, a compelling insight into other people's lives.

AUDIENCE
Available Audience Range: 19–24 million

Minimum Audience Target 30-33% share: 6–8 million

DURATION
30 minutes

EPISODES PER STRAND (SERIES)
8–13 with the potential to run 26

TOTAL SLOTS
100 open to Factual and Entertainment programmes.

PROGRAMME EXAMPLES
Holiday, Celebrity Ready Steady Cook.

PRICE/COST INFORMATION
- **Target price: £45,000–£70,000 net per episode. Most opportunities are at the lower end. A small higher end is reserved for exceptional profile in artist or format.**
- **To help with is, we are particularly interested in commissioning longer runs.**
- **Potential for third party investment (i.e. another broadcaster) is probably limited.**

Figure 10.3 A commissioning brief from BBC1 for 'factual entertainment'.

The process of 'negotiating a brief' will lead to a point where you will be offered a deal with a set of conditions on cost, schedule etc. Be careful not to accept unrealistic deadlines – it always takes longer than you think. Note also that the commissioner will probably specify points at which you will need to report progress and allow the commissioner to suggest changes. You have a deal and a brief, but remember that, unless you are publishing the work yourself, the commissioner can always decide to shelve your work rather than publish it, so you will need to argue your case carefully throughout production.

Pre-production

Research

Risk assessment You should draw up a detailed assessment of all the health and safety considerations at this stage. Don't proceed with production if the risks cannot be covered.

Sometimes a proposal will have come out of research – perhaps for another purpose. In this sense, research comes before the brief is agreed. Usually, research is a major component of 'pre-production'. Because research is such an important part of academic media work, as well as production, we have devoted Chapter 9 to all issues related to research. Please refer to that chapter now.

Recce

Good preparation is essential for effective media production, and before any audio or video or photography work takes place on location a production company will undertake a series of 'recces' (reconnaissance). These include checks on electrical power sources (often broadcasters' needs are so great that they bring their own generators), on access for people and equipment and on health and safety generally. Facilities such as changing rooms, refreshments and possibly press and public relations spaces are important too. These are the producer's main concerns. The director, camera and sound crews will also want to select locations for aesthetic reasons and to begin to build the constraints created by the location into the production schedule.

Film commissions Many UK cities and regions have recognised the economic benefits that film and television productions can bring to the local economy and have set up offices to help producers find locations, crews and facilities and to sort out permissions. Liverpool and Yorkshire have been particularly successful – look in the *BFI Handbook* for a full list.

ACTIVITY 10.1

Locations

Take a close look at any film or television series (tape it so you can study it in detail) and carry out an analysis of the locations used.

- How much of it is shot in a studio, how much on location?
- List all the separate locations. Could you find substitute locations in your locality?
- Now consider the task of the producer. Think of your substitute locations: how would you organise the shooting so that you cut down travelling between locations?
- What kind of permissions do you think you would need for the locations you have chosen?

Figure 10.4 A studio production like this requires crew of at least five – camera operator, floor manager, sound mixer, vision mixer and director – to keep them in order. Prior to recording, the lights have to be arranged and the 'talent' briefed (Solihull College, © Simon Derry).

Design

Every media product is 'designed'. Think of a couple of very different products – a magazine and a feature film. In both cases, an important member of the production team is the Art Editor or Art Director. They are responsible for the obvious art and design elements in the products – the dramatic layout of pages and the use of illustrations, especially on the cover of a newsstand magazine, the stupendous sets of a Hollywood musical and the credit sequence of the film. But they also contribute to a much broader concept of design – the overall fitness of purpose and coherence of the media product. The opening credit sequence of a film, the choice of typeface in a magazine, are not just attractive and appropriate in themselves. They are designed to announce and complement the other features of the product.

You might want to think about a media product in the same way as one of those exquisitely crafted Japanese lacquered boxes or a designer suit – whichever way you look at them as you turn them over, they present a

Saul and Elaine Bass are famous as designers of title sequences for Hollywood, in particular for Alfred Hitchcock (including *Psycho*) and Martin Scorsese. See Pat Kirkham, 'Looking for the simple idea', *Sight and Sound*, vol. 4, no. 2 (February 1994).

beautifully finished surface. And when you use them for their intended purpose, they do the job effortlessly. Good design doesn't have to cost a fortune, though. A zippo lighter or a box of matches can be designed well, and so can the supposedly insignificant media products, such as the continuity announcements and **idents** on television or the local football fanzine. And it isn't just in visual terms that we can detect design features. Radio programmes are designed as well and it will be quite apparent if the sound text is not coherent in its style and 'feel'. Good design means that products work well with users, and that must be the first priority for media production.

See Chapter 11 for more on design ideas. Note here that design issues need to be addressed at the preparation stage. Design needs to inform other aspects of production and to develop from the initial ideas about the product.

Similarly design-intensive are the animated **idents** used on television such as the long-running series of '2s' on BBC2.

Production

This is the stage when the main work is done on the material which will appear in the finished product – see Chapter 11 for details. It is useful at this point to discuss who does what and how the roles are defined and integrated as a part of a production team.

The production unit and production roles

The units which you form to undertake production tasks in education or training are not so different from their industrial counterparts. Even in very large media corporations, creative staff work in relatively small teams and in some sectors a production company may be just a couple of people, who hire freelances to work on specific jobs. In every case we can identify a close-knit production team, who work together over a period of time. They may be augmented at particular stages in production by larger groups of people who perform relatively routine tasks in an industrial process.

Let's take our previous example of a small specialist magazine and look at its production in more detail. Perhaps this is one of many titles produced by a large international publishing group such as IPC (owned by Time Warner) or perhaps it is a private venture. Either way, the 'production team' may comprise only a few full-time people such as the editor and an assistant, a couple of 'staff writers' and perhaps an art editor. Outside this circle will be others who, while committed to the magazine, may also be involved in other titles. The same commitment (i.e. to the individual title) will not be found in the printers and distributors, who deal with many different titles over the year. Each production unit is likely to include the following job roles:

Producer   Somebody must take charge of the production as the 'organiser of scarce resources' and the financial controller. This role will also usually require an overview of the purpose of the production and the creative intent. The term is used in both film and television and radio and sound recording, but there are differences. In film production, the producer is very much the provider of budget and the organiser of resources – in most cases the creative control of the project lies with the director, although there are some very 'hands-on' producers (including well-known directors who retain the producer role themselves, delegating some tasks to assistants). In radio and television, the producer is also usually the creative force behind a series. In sound recording too, the producer might be seen as a creative force. In publishing, the same role is likely to be shared by an editor and a production manager.

Director or editor   This role is about creative control – making decisions during the course of the production and maintaining a clear idea of the form and style of the product. In **time-based media** such as film, television or radio, the director is the co-ordinator of the creative process, literally directing the crew and the talent. In broadcasting, the creative controller tends to be termed an editor when the programme material is news or current affairs. The editor of a newspaper or magazine tends to oversee creative and production manager roles. The role of the director raises interesting questions about the managerial style of the decision-taker. The director or editor has to take decisions – 'the buck stops here'.

Researcher (see Chapter 9)   Every production needs some research, but not always a separate researcher. Most research is 'background' – the checking of information or the compilation of information and ideas on a specific topic. Some production research requires special skills and knowledge, first in the general academic skills of using and checking sources, second in relation to a specialist subject (such as military history).

Archives can be very specialised, and film, picture or sound researchers may be seen as specialised roles, perhaps undertaken by freelances or small research companies.

Finding contestants for *Blind Date* or guests for a talk show also seen as 'research', but here the skills are rather different. They may involve developing a 'feel' for what will be televisual, what will be popular, what will be a ratings winner. They may also include the ability to charm or cajole reluctant performers into appearing (for the smallest fee). This aspect of research may be performed by a production assistant – someone much closer to the producer role than the autonomous researcher.

Television is a producer-led medium according to Jeremy Tunstall in Holland (2000). This book has several accounts of what being a producer means written by well-known figures. A good example of the creative power of the producer in television is the rise of Phil Redmond, who gained a profile first as the writer who developed *Grange Hill* in the 1970s, but consolidated his position by forming Mersey Television and producing *Brookside* for Channel 4.

'Each picture has some sort of rhythm which only the director can give it. He has to be like the captain of a ship' (Fritz Lang from Halliwell's *Filmgoer's Book of Quotes* (1978)).

Time-based media a term used mainly by practitioners with art and design backgrounds to distinguish film, television and radio from photography. You may also hear *lens-based media* used to group film, television and photography.

Refer back to Activity 10.1 and compare a low-budget and prestige documentary in terms of the amount of research required to mount the programme successfully.

Investigative newspaper reporters may also be seen as researchers. They may also write up their own reports – something denied to most broadcast researchers.

291

Several writers have commented on the difference between television and film in terms of 'freedoms and opportunities'. Television drama can give writers time to develop characters and to hone dialogue, but the dramatic possibilities in visual terms are limited and the format length and structure of series or soaps is restricting. On a film there is more creative freedom to tell a story in visual terms but less time to develop characters. A bigger budget is also likely to mean that the script will be revised many times, perhaps against the writer's wishes.

Creative personnel This is a loose term and may include everybody involved in the production, but here we are referring to those members of the team who are charged with making specific contributions based on specialist skills such as writing, camerawork, design etc. The task for creative personnel is to carry out the wishes of the producer or director in a professional manner, contributing to the overall production as effectively as possible. Conflicts are possible if the individual contributors wish to 'do their own thing'. There are interesting questions about authorship here – once a scriptwriter has completed work on a film, does she or he have the right to be consulted if the producer or director then decides to cut from, add to or alter the finished script?

The director or producer will work hard to maintain a good working relationship with all the creative staff, consulting them (which means explaining *and* listening) on particular aspects of their work and perhaps incorporating their suggestions into the overall production. The director's role requires her or him to maintain the coherence of the whole media text, so if a particular contribution is threatening to upset the balance it needs to be corrected, even if, on its own, it represents a very effective and entertaining element. Here are the seeds of conflict, especially in the supercharged atmosphere of most production processes.

The success of a creative team will depend on good working relationships. This doesn't necessarily mean that everyone in the team likes each other, but they must respect each other's work and be prepared to submit to the 'general will' of the team and the ultimate decision of the acknowledged leader. The most successful producers tend to be those who have built up and maintained a creative team which has lasted several years.

Technical personnel Somebody must be responsible for the operation of equipment and for its efficient performance (i.e. they must maintain and set up equipment so that it performs to manufacturers' specifications). Variously described as 'technicians' or 'engineers', these people ensure that creative ideas can be realised within the constraints which the technology demands. Some technical operations such as maintenance and servicing may be required even when no productions are scheduled.

Camera crew on a film set normally comprise an operator and assistants to look after loading, focus pulling and camera movements (the job of the 'grip') etc. An electrical crew led by a 'gaffer' with a 'best boy' will set up lighting under the **DP**'s supervision. See the diagram of the film production process in Chapter 8.

It is a fine line which separates the 'creative' from the 'technical', and many media practitioners combine both roles. For example, a *director of photography* (**DP**) on a feature film is very much part of the creative team, responsible for the overall 'look' of the film and the supervision of camera and lighting operations. Operation of the equipment will be handled by the **camera crew**, but the DP, who will have begun a career as part of the technical crew, will select lenses and perhaps even override equipment specifications and solve technical problems, based on long experience. Some media practitioners are seen as possessing 'craft' rather than technical skills – implying a more personal, 'creative' skill with technology, beyond that of 'operation'.

In an ideal situation, creative staff have sufficient knowledge of technical operations to be able to communicate effectively with the technical team. In turn, technical staff are able to recognise the creative opportunities which their equipment makes possible and to advise accordingly. In the production unit, an integrated creative and technical team generally produces the best results. Often, however, the technical team is made up of freelances or in-house staff who are allocated to production units on a rota basis. The ability to communicate effectively and to develop working relationships quickly then becomes even more important.

The need for close communication between creative and technical teams raises two issues about media production training which are important for all media students:

- It helps if all production staff know something about each aspect of production – too much specialisation means that effective communication becomes more difficult.

- It isn't necessarily those with the most creative ideas or the best technical prowess who make the best production team members – good working relationships are also important, and training should be geared towards development of the appropriate personal and organisational skills.

Freelances   The **freelance** is a long-standing figure in many parts of the media industries. At one time the term referred to relatively well-known figures such as high-profile writers or journalists who were in such demand that they could afford to offer their services to whoever would pay, rather than relying on the security of permanent employment. This usage continues and now includes television personalities as well as film directors. However, the big growth is in the number of rather less well-known media workers who would probably prefer to be 'employed' as they were in the past by broadcast television companies or daily newspapers, but who now find themselves made redundant and perhaps offered work on a short-term contract basis – often for a series of articles or work on a television series. Whether this should be called 'freelance work' in the strict sense is debatable (they may in some cases be little better off than the notoriously badly treated 'homeworkers'), but in the film, video and broadcast industry freelances now constitute more than half the total workforce.

Freelances pose problems for the continuity of the production team, and they are less likely to be followers of a 'house style'. On the other hand, they may bring new ideas and ways of working to a team. In practice, freelances may end up working for a particular production unit on a fairly regular basis so this may not be a great change. What is likely, however, is a gradual

Freelance   The term goes back to the period when medieval knights returning from the Crusades would roam Europe offering their services to different rulers.

breakdown of the 'institutional' ethos of some of the large media corporations such as the BBC and a reliance on more generic output (i.e. an industry 'standard') from the host of smaller independent companies (see Chapter 7).

As a media student you should note that in your own productions it is often possible to 'buy in' some freelance help from students on another course who may have specific expertise (especially in areas such as design). Also, if you are looking for employment in the media industries, you should prepare yourself for possible freelance status. A good start is to begin preparing your portfolio of completed production work as soon as possible, keeping a CV up-to-date and looking for opportunities to gain experience and to acquire a wide range of skills. Freelances have to manage their own financial affairs and actively seek work – it is a very different life from that of a paid employee whose main concern is fulfilling a job description to the satisfaction of an employer. Many higher education courses now include units on business studies, personal finance, portfolio management and CV-writing which are designed to help the potential freelance to survive.

Administrative personnel   Media students are often told about the difficulty of obtaining employment in 'the industry' and the example of starting 'at the bottom'. Making the tea and being a 'runner' are quoted as the lowest entry points. At the other end of the scale, the accountant is sometimes seen as the villain, not only for curtailing creativity through budgetary control but for being 'boring' as well. Making tea and doing the books are of course essential elements in any enterprise, and media production is no exception.

A large-scale production such as a feature film involves hundreds of personnel with an enormous variety of skills and qualifications (see Figure 8.1). Even a small production needs an 'office'. For convenience we have termed these 'administrative' in that they are primarily concerned with making sure that production can go ahead with all the needs of the creative and technical teams catered for. Again, we can distinguish between administrative personnel who are integral to the production team – very often in roles as the extra arms and legs of producers – and those who are brought in as needed, either as freelances or from some central, in-house, agency.

Some roles may be termed 'organisational' rather than administrative in that they are directly concerned with the operation of the production process. The floor manager in a television studio or the continuity role in feature film production are good examples of such important roles where an understanding of the production process is central. It is also worth pointing out that, while the skills necessary for the other administrative roles are generalised rather than specific, the roles do allow new personnel to pick up a great deal of knowledge about the production process.

Presenters One aspect of production work that many of us fear is presenting – speaking on radio or television (especially direct to camera) or introducing events at screenings or exhibitions. No matter how embarrassed you feel, you should try it a couple of times for the experience and so that you have some idea about what presenters feel in the situations which you might create for them as writer or director. If you are going to become a presenter, then you will need to seek out specialist advice on how to train your voice, how to breathe, how to use a microphone and how to read a script. You will also want to study a range of professionals (not just one, or you might end up a mimic).

If you are a writer, the most important thing to remember is to provide the presenter with 'spoken language'. A speech may look great on paper, but it may sound laboured when read out. If you can't find a presenter amongst the other media students, look elsewhere, just as you would for actors. Because you study the media, it doesn't necessarily mean you want to appear as the 'talent'.

Figure 10.5 Be prepared for your stint before the microphone! (Solihull College, © Simon Derry).

Production roles in education and training So what should you take from these role descriptions in terms of your own education and training? First, wide experience of different production contexts will help to develop your theoretical understanding, and your preparation for 'post-entry' training in any specific production role. Try as many roles as possible. You may have thought that being a writer was your dream, only to discover that you have a real flair for sound recording and that the radio studio gives you a buzz.

Copyright and permissions

Media products are often referential or intertextual, making use of previously recorded material. In a highly commercial industry, almost anything that has any kind of commercial potential – i.e. it could be used in another publication – will be 'owned' in terms of the rights for reproduction.

If the reproduction rights on a work have lapsed (which in Europe means seventy years after the author's death) and have not been renewed, the work passes into the **public domain** and anyone can reproduce it without charge. There is a difference, however, between the work of art and the physical media product. For instance, most nineteenth-century novels are now in the public domain, and this means that any publisher can sell a new edition of Dickens etc. But the 'Penguin edition' will remain in copyright as a printed text – you cannot simply photocopy it. If you want to use an image in a magazine article, you will need to do three things: get a copy of the original photograph (you may need to pay a fee for a 10×8 inch print, the preferred size, or for a high resolution digital image); obtain permission from the rights holder; and probably pay a further reproduction fee based on the nature of your

Public domain and digital technology Digital versions of images and text (and software) are easy to distribute and copy. Public domain (PD) material is distributed free of charge as long as the distributor does not attempt to make a profit. 'Shareware' allows products to be used free, but business users are expected to pay a small fee.

publication, the size of the image on the page and the position of that page in the publication (you pay most for the front cover).

Audiovisual recordings can involve you in several different sets of 'permissions' and rights issues. Say you want to use a recording of a popular song in a video programme. There are three potential rights holders here. First, the person who wrote the song will want a 'reproduction fee'; next, the singer will need payment for reproduction of the performance; and finally the record label will want a fee for reproduction of their specific recording. In practice two of these may be dealt with by the same agency.

Music rights Performers' rights are handled by the Performing Rights Society (PRS). Recordings are handled by the Mechanical Copyright Protection Society (MCPS). PPL handles Phonographic Performance Licences for use by broadcasters etc.

> A conversation about permissions for material in an earlier edition of this book: 'I'm trying to get permission to use a few stills from the Creek ad for Levi's jeans . . . $5,000 each for the last educational publisher in the US? We need to ask everyone involved in the ad? Does that include the horse? He has an agent?' (This last bit is a joke – but only just.)

The industry has developed specific paperwork for media producers to use to request permissions – usually producers don't buy a whole song but only a few seconds. One solution for small producers is to use 'library music', specifically written and recorded for audiovisual productions and catalogued on CDs according to themes. A producer buys the CD and then pays a set fee for a track. This is usually cheaper and less administratively complex than using well-known pieces. Use this resource carefully, though, as overfamiliar library music can sound bland.

Post-production

Once the main material has been produced, or 'found' and collated, it must be shaped into the final product. This involves several different activities.

Rewriting and editing

Authors' rights are negotiated by the Society of Authors and the Publishers' Association, and copying fees are collected by the Author Licensing and Collecting Society.

It's very unlikely that you will get your production right first time. Sections in this book have gone through several versions – sometimes altering radically, sometimes just a tweak. During your academic career you have probably suffered from constant pressure from teachers to check your work and, even when you think you've finished, to go back and rewrite parts or even the whole of your work. If you took that advice and got into good habits, you are now going to reap your reward.

Figure 10.6 The edit suite is where a video production is shaped and structured. This is a nonlinear suite using Media 100 hardware and software.

Rewriting shouldn't be seen as simply a process of spotting mistakes and correcting them. It should also be a creative process – material is 'shaped' during production. Both the original writer and the editor will be involved in trying to work on the script or text. It is worth reminding yourself here that editing is a constructive process, not just a 'cutting out' of the bad bits. It is also time-consuming, and a sensible schedule will take rewrites into account. Do be careful about labelling each version of your text, especially when working on a computer allows you to create several versions of the same picture or text extract in a few minutes – there is nothing more frustrating than finding that, when you want to go back to a previous version, you can't easily distinguish which is which.

Editing is usually carried out by someone other than the writer or director. This means that it is important to establish good communication within the team. There has been a tendency to think of print editing and audio-visual editing as rather different activities. The move to digital production, using a computer interface, means that such differences are disappearing and all forms of editing now involve structuring the text and selecting the most appropriate material to be juxtaposed (Figure 10.6).

Copy-editing is a specialist editing role in print production. It ensures that the raw text is checked for spelling mistakes, inaccurate information and adherence to house style. A similar aspect of video editing might be a check

A good slogan for you: 'Writing is rewriting' – whether for academic essays or 'creative writing'.

to ensure that colour grading was matched on separate video sources.
Sub-editing is a specific newspaper production activity in which experienced
staff cut stories to fit the space available and write headlines and captions.

Special effects and graphics are prepared and added to programmes at the
editing stage. In print production, the typesetter attempts to combine text
and graphics according to the laid-down design grid.

Proofing

'Proofing' refers also to checking
the correct colours to be printed
in a magazine etc. Designers use a
carefully calibrated printer to
produce a proof for a client
before releasing the work for
publishing. (Colours look
different on a computer screen.)

When you get very wrapped up in a production project it is sometimes
difficult to be objective about your own work. Sometimes it is even difficult
to see what is there at all, and this is where a 'proof reader' comes in. Their job
is simply to spot unintentional errors. Ideally, someone who proofs not only
has a sharp eye (or ear) but knows something about the subject as well.
Authors of printed material are usually supplied with proof copies of their
work to check.

> *Now, Voyager* is a famous 1940s Hollywood melodrama, starring Bette Davis. In
> an American film magazine, an advertisement for film soundtracks listed two
> separate films, 'Now' and 'Voyager' under a 'classics' heading.

Test marketing or previewing

Sunset Boulevard (US 1950) is
narrated by a corpse floating in a
swimming pool. Director Billy
Wilder originally opened with
two corpses discussing the story
in a morgue, but the Illinois
preview audience thought that
was too much (according to Otto
Friedrich in *City of Nets* (London:
Harper Collins 1987).

If you are unsure about your product in some way (perhaps the design features
are not quite right or you simply panic about your great idea), it may be
possible to test a draft version of the product on a small selected group of
readers and see what kind of a response you get. This isn't foolproof, and you
could select the wrong test group. Some may argue as well that you shouldn't
be frightened of making mistakes and that the previewing policy leads to very
bland products.

Finishing

The most successful media products offer the audience a special pleasure
which derives from a quality 'finish'. This means that presentation is as good
as it can be within the constraints of the format and the medium. Good finish
means that your video begins from black with music and titles fading up
smoothly 'in sync'. Titles are accurate and carefully designed to complement
the visuals. If you have a great set of photographic prints, it does matter how

you present them. A good display with thought given to lighting and carefully printed captions or catalogue will enhance the experience for your audience. This should be the final production stage before the product is distributed for the eager public.

Distribution

If you don't present your product to your audience directly, you will need some form of distribution. Other chapters stress that in the media industries this can be the most important part of the production process. You don't want to produce a magazine only to discover that nobody gets to read it or to broadcast a radio programme which nobody hears.

Student productions can get a wide audience if distribution is organised in good time. Check back on the magazine schedule at the start of the chapter, which suggests organising the distribution at an early stage – perhaps finding shops, pubs, cinemas etc. who would be willing to display free copies of your magazine to be picked up by their patrons (you can afford to distribute free copies in this way if you sell advertising to cover your production costs). Several schools and colleges have taken the opportunity under the radio broadcasting legislation to apply for a Restricted Service Licence (RSL), allowing them to broadcast for a couple of days in a local area. Video productions can be timed to be ready for the various festivals of student work. If you have any ambitions to become a media producer, here is your starting point to get your work recognised. (See Chapter 12 for more on distribution.)

Exhibition

This stage is relevant only for film and video or photography, but it is very important to present your work to an audience in the best possible conditions – it is the equivalent of 'finishing' in print production. For a video screening you will want to make sure that your audience are comfortable and have good 'sight-lines' to see the screen. The sound and picture quality must be as good as possible with the monitor or video projector set properly and sound levels appropriate for the acoustics in the room. You will want the tape to start at exactly the right place, so set it up carefully beforehand. Would the audience benefit from some screening notes?

The development of digital video and video projection means that material edited on a computer screen is now being shown on large screens. Do leave yourself time to project on a big screen and see whether any adjustments need to be made. (And make sure the equipment and the software works!)

Think about your own experience of going to the cinema. What do you expect in terms of the best viewing environment?

Audience feedback

At the beginning of this chapter we made the point that media production is meaningful only if you know the audience to whom you hope to present your work. It follows that your production isn't finished until it has reached the intended audience and you have gained some feedback. Only then will you be able to evaluate the production decisions you have made. You will also be able to use the feedback material to inform your next production – audience feedback supplies the link which helps to make production a cyclical process.

There are numerous ways in which you can gauge audience reactions to your work. Sitting in with an audience can be useful. When do they go quiet and concentrate? When do they fidget and yawn? What kind of comments do they make to each other? You can formalise this by organising some form of discussion after a screening, or when everyone has read through your magazine. Get someone else to chair the session and be prepared to be open with your audience about what you were trying to do. If all of this sounds a little daunting, you can always devise a simple audience feedback questionnaire which can be given to everyone when they first come into contact with the product. Audiences will be happy to fill in questionnaires if the questions are appropriate and if the spaces for answers are inviting. If you are lucky, the questionnaire will produce a greater number of responses and perhaps a wider range of respondents than the face-to-face discussion. (See Chapter 9 on questionnaires.)

What will you expect from your audience feedback? We all like praise and to know that what we have produced has given people pleasure, but, more important, we want confirmation of what has worked and what has caused confusion or even misunderstanding. You should not be dismayed if audiences have read your work in very different ways (in Chapter 3 we have emphasised that this is a function of the reading process). Every response is useful and will make you more aware of the range of possibilities.

After studying the audience feedback, the final task is to undertake your own evaluation of your production experience. In order to help you do this, your tutor will probably want to organise a formal 'debriefing'.

Debriefing

Most media production courses operate a procedure whereby you are briefed before an activity on what you are required to do and what constraints you face. You are then debriefed at the end of the activity. This is an important part of the process – perhaps the most important part, because it is here that you work out what you have learnt and identify your strengths and weaknesses. Most debriefings are group discussions – either everyone has worked individually on the same activity or work has been organised in groups.

Debriefings work best when everyone is committed to the activity and is supportive of each other. This means accepting criticism from the other group members and in turn making positive, constructive comments about their performance. This isn't easy. If the production has not gone well you might be sorely tempted to 'get your blame in first' or to defend your own actions. If it has gone well you might be tempted simply to tell each other 'you were great'. Neither of these approaches is particularly helpful. If it worked well, why was that? If it didn't, can you work out why, without apportioning blame? The likelihood is that you will have to follow up the debriefing with an **evaluation**, so you need answers to these questions.

It's more than likely that your **evaluation** of your own production work will form part of your assessment for the course. Examiners often comment that evaluations are the weak point in otherwise good production work. They want you to demonstrate that you are able to 'reflect' on the process you have gone through and that you have recognised what you have achieved and what you can learn from.

Learning from production

We hope these notes will be helpful, but there is no substitute for production work itself. Get involved as much as you can. Make things with a view to finding out about the production process as well as reaching an audience. Listen and learn from other producers. Above all, reflect on what you have done and try to do better next time. And have fun.

References and further reading

An accessible book with plenty of good ideas on relatively low-budget video production is:
Harding, Thomas (2001) *The Video Activist Handbook*, London: Pluto Press.

Rather more mainstream and industry-based is:
Jarvis, Peter (1996) *The Essential Television Handbook*, Oxford: Focal Press.

Job roles in film and television are well covered in:
Langham, Josephine (1996, 2nd edition) *Lights Camera Action!: Careers in Film, Television and Radio*, London: BFI.

For background on production organisation in different media sectors see the Routledge Handbook Series:
Brierley, Sean (1995) *The Advertising Handbook*.
Fleming, Carole (2002, 2nd edition *The Radio Handbook*.
Holland, Patricia (2000, 2nd edition) *The Television Handbook*.
Keeble, Richard (2001, 3rd edition) *The Newspapers Handbook*.
McKay, Jenny (2000), *The Magazines Handbook*.
Wright, Terence (1999), *The Photography Handbook*.

Useful reference sources, published annually:
BFI Film and Television Handbook.
The Guardian Media Guide.
The Writers' and Artists' Year Book, London: A.C. Black.

The Writer's Handbook, Basingstoke: Macmillan.

Technical manuals, dealing with different aspects of production and different technologies are published by:

BBC Enterprises (The full range of material can be seen in the BBC shop opposite Broadcasting House on Portland Place, London W1. Publications include guides to scriptwriting and training manuals which are listed in a catalogue obtainable from BBC Television Training, BBC Elstree Centre, Clarendon Road, Borehamwood, Herts WD6 1TF.)

Focal Press (This imprint specialises in media technical handbooks and manuals, in particular the Media Manuals series. A catalogue can be obtained from: Focal Press, Linacre House, Jordan Hill, Oxford OX2 8DP. Most of these manuals are written for professional or semi-professional media users.)

Useful addresses (see also p. 521)

Mechanical Copyright Protection Service, Elgar House, 41 Streatham High Road, London SW16 1ER – information and advice available on request.
Performing Right Society, 29–33 Berners Street, London W1P 4AA – information available from the Public Affairs Department.

11 Production techniques

This chapter will help you to make informed choices when you select and use materials and equipment for media projects. It should also help you to read other media texts in terms of their technical codes.

This chapter is intended both as an extension of 'Production organisation' (Chapter 10) and as a complement to 'Meanings and media' (Chapter 1 and case study) and 'Narratives' (Chapter 2). There is also some discussion of production techniques in 'Realisms' (Chapter 17) and in the British Film Industry case study.

Technical codes

In Chapter 1 codes are defined as systems of signs – allowing meanings to be communicated. Technical codes are the choices that can be made in selecting or using materials and equipment on the basis of the technical qualities of the **format** or the technical qualities of the sound image or visual image created. For example you can select paper for printing a magazine on the basis of its colour, weight (thickness) and porosity (the extent to which the ink is absorbed). The quality of presentation of the text or photograph printed on the page will depend on the settings of the printer in terms of resolution, number of colours etc.

There are several meanings of '**format**'. Here it means a different size of paper or type of recording medium, e.g. VHS video or DVD. But see also Chapter 3.

You won't make your production choices in isolation, but in the context of a specific brief and mindful of the **cultural codes** of the content of your programme. Sometimes, the association of specific technical decisions with particular subjects has become conventionalised so that stylistic or aesthetic decisions have come to signify a certain mood or atmosphere (the low-key lighting of a *film noir*, the jaunty music of a television quiz show); a particular format or shape that has been adopted for a specific function (the small portrait photo for a passport). The strength of the technical or cultural connection is revealed when conventions are broken – in comedy texts for example. Technical codes are helpful in providing a convenient shortcut for

A good example of restrictive
technology is the development of
film and video cameras and
lighting techniques which suit
northern European skin tones
and which are therefore not ideal
for showing darker skin.

Look at some of the issues in
Chapters 7 and 16. Technology
may be 'value-free' but it is used
in value-laden institutional
contexts, e.g. there are relatively
few women cinematographers or
sound editors.

presenting conventional texts, but they can also provide an excuse for not
thinking about how to represent something, so that the technology is allowed
to dictate the creative decision and effectively restricts choice.

We've also decided to include a section on *narrative codes* in film and
television in this chapter, linked with the discussion in Chapter 2. Although
these are not strictly technical codes, such has been the power and global
spread of narrative cinema that they have developed into a series of
conventions related to shot sizes and camera movements that have become
formalised as part of 'film language', and it makes sense to deal with them
here. Such narrative codes are more difficult to distinguish in print and audio
texts, but where possible we have included these in the general discussion.

This chapter concentrates on the technical decisions which you as producer
are going to make, mindful that in your proposal you have identified a
purpose, a target audience and a genre or style.

Technical codes in print products

A print product requires ink and paper. There are many different kinds of
paper and several different ways of getting ink on to them. Try to begin a
print production with a sort through paper samples and possibly a discussion
with a print professional about what kinds of paper are available.

Paper

The paper used in this book is 90 gsm, 'coated'. This was changed from the
first edition, in an attempt to make the book lighter and easier to handle.

Weight   Paper is classified in 'grams per square metre' or 'gsm'. Standard
photocopying paper is 80 gsm. Glossy brochures may use 120 gsm. Above
about 150 gsm, paper becomes more like thin card. Weight is important for a
number of reasons. At a very practical level, heavier paper means a heavier
product and, if it is going to be mailed out, this could mean greater postal
costs (heavier paper is already more expensive to buy). However, heavier paper
can feel more luxurious. Thinner paper can suffer from 'see-through' or 'bleed'
– if it is printed on both sides, heavy black text or illustrations will be visible
through the paper and perhaps spoil the visual appeal of the page. This is also
affected by coatings (see below).

Coated or uncoated?   The cheapest paper (e.g. newsprint) is 'uncoated' and
porous. This means that it feels a little rough between the fingers (ask a
printer about paper and she or he will perhaps rub it between the thumb and
first finger). It also means that, when ink is applied, it will tend to spread,

because it is absorbed by the fibres. You will see this if you use cheap paper on
an inkjet printer – the problem is exacerbated because the ink is very wet.
Better-quality papers are coated with a layer of non-porous material (or are
treated to have the same qualities). Ink is far less likely to spread and coated
papers give much better reproductions of photographs, as well as feeling
smoother. You can choose between 'glossy' or 'shiny' and 'matt' or 'velvet',
according to taste (and what you think your readers will like).

Texture, colour and other qualities   Some expensive papers have a textured feel
like old parchment or cloth-based paper. These can be absorbent, but can also
look stylish. Paper doesn't have to be white. Different colour ranges are
possible, including pastel shades, strong colours and fluorescent colours. If
you are a real print fanatic, you may even consider the smell of the paper – it
could signify luxury or suggest that it is only a 'throwaway' product. Another
technical consideration is the form of binding. If pages are glued together
along one edge and the publication has a flat spine, it is known as 'perfect-
bound'. Other methods 'stitch' or staple groups of double-page spreads along
the central fold, and another option is to 'spiral bind' with a strip of flexible
plastic or coated wire.

Size and shape   UK paper sizes are now standardised into the 'A' and 'B'
series. You will be familiar with the A4 standard for photocopy paper and A5
for leaflets. The equivalents in the 'B' series are slightly larger. Books and
magazines may use older sizes such as 'quarto' or 'royal'. Newspapers are
usually **tabloid** (slightly smaller than A3) or **broadsheet** (slightly smaller
than A2). Depending on your computer software, you may be offered
templates for American paper sizes, which are noticeably different.

Often you will make a decision about size and shape on the basis of purely
functional criteria – A5 for a booklet, A4 for a magazine. If you are printing
on your school or college inkjet or laser printer, a sheet of A4, or possibly A3,
paper can be folded to give four pages of A5 or A4. If you go to a professional
printer, who uses rolls of paper, there are fewer restrictions, and you can use an
'odd' size or shape. This could mean that your product stands out. A4
magazines tend to signify an educational or 'amateur' product – a good
example of an institutional sign. (See also the comments about tabloid and
broadsheet newspapers in Chapter 7.) Most print products are 'portrait'
(height greater than width), but some are 'landscape' (width greater than
height). Some are square and others very tall and narrow. They don't have to
open as double pages – they can have two or more folds. All of these
considerations affect the way the product is 'read'.

Paper is usually purchased by the
ream – 500 sheets.

Half A4 is A5. Twice A4 is A3.
Using A4 sheets you can work up
or down to see what A1, A2, A6
and A7 might look like.

ACTIVITY 11.1

Decisions on paper types

Collect a wide variety of magazines and books and try to distinguish between them in terms of paper size, shape, colour, weight etc. What conclusions do you come to about the institutional conventions – the 'rules' which enable a product to address a particular audience? Are there examples of products you immediately like or dislike because of the paper choices? If you can find examples, try to compare the same advertisement on different paper stock (e.g. in the matt format of weekend magazines such as the *Independent* and in a shiny, glossy style magazine).

Text and images

It helps to think about the printed page as a single image. Forget about what the words say for a moment: think about text in terms of shapes on the page. This will lead you into consideration of *typography* and **typesetting**, as well as **grids** and **white space**.

Look at the information at the front of the book, opposite the Contents page, to see how the typesetting has been organised.

Typography   As a 'print designer' you have the choice of hundreds of different **fonts**. A computer font comprises up to 256 alphabetic, numerical and punctuation characters plus various symbols and accented characters. Fonts come in 'families' of different weights and styles, such as **bold**, light, roman ('upright'), *italic* etc. A **typeface** is another name for a font family.

There are four main categories of typefaces. The main two, used for *body text*, to be read in small sizes, are known as **serif** and **sans-serif**. The serif is the bar across the ends of the 'arms and legs' of the character. Typefaces used primarily for posters and signs are known as **display** and may be ornate and therefore unsuitable for sustained reading. Typefaces classified as **script** are based on styles of handwriting.

Some typefaces are very old, dating back centuries. Others were designed last week. Classic faces such as Gill, designed by Eric Gill in the 1920s, have moved in and out of fashion. If you are interested, there are several good catalogues or dictionaries of typography in reference libraries. You will find your own favourite faces, but you need to be aware of some typography conventions before you start to experiment, even if you want to break with them. Most typefaces are available in two standard formats – 'Postscript' for professional printing and 'TrueType' for more general use (they are also available for both Windows and Macintosh use).

Fonts were originally 'founts' – from the foundry, where they were cast in metal type. Germany and North America were the main producers of metal type – e.g. Agfa, Monotype, Linotype etc.

'Times' is a **serif** typeface

Helvetica is a **sans-serif** typeface

Broadway is a **display** typeface

Zapf Chancery is a **script** typeface

The credit sequence of the film *Gattaca* (US 1997) makes clever use of typography to distinguish the letters A, T, C and G, which are always shown in a different font. The name 'Gattaca' is derived from the four 'letters' of the DNA code; they stand for the chemicals Adenine, Thymine, Guanine and Cytosine.

The same idea is observable in *Brassed Off* (UK/US 1996), which features a brass band contest. In the credit sequence all the letters *f* and *p*, the musical symbols for 'loud' and 'soft', are shown in bold italic and a different colour.

- Serif faces are said to be best for long runs of body text, because the serif helps to distinguish the characters in a block of text and makes sustained reading easier.

- Sans-serif faces are commonly used for headings where immediacy and clarity are important. But they are now often used for body text as well – sans-serif has tended to mean a more 'modern' look in recent years.

- In any single document, you should not use more than two typefaces for body text and headings. (You can use display fonts in adverts and you can make use of different styles and weights within the two typeface families you select.)

Typesetting   With a desktop publishing programme such as PageMaker or Quark Xpress, you can manipulate text with great precision and create exactly the look you want. You can choose the size of the type in **points** and the space between each line of text (known as **leading**). A common choice for a book would be 10 point type with 2 points of leading, known as '10 on 12'. Type size does matter – if you make it too large, your product may suggest that its readership is young children. If it is very small, it may be difficult for older people to read (your eyes start to weaken in your forties!). Type can be squeezed up or strung out along a line, either by selecting a specially designed 'extended' or 'compressed' typeface or by manipulating the space between characters (sometimes known as *tracking*).

The look of a column of text is also affected by the use of alignment or **justification** (also referred to as 'ranging'). If you justify the text to both the left and right side (sometimes known as 'flush') the result will be a smooth edge, but on each line the space between words will be adjusted, and between some lines it will be noticeably different. The alternative is standard spacing between words, but a ragged right edge to the column of text. This choice is said to be personal (we like it ragged), but be careful of using justification with narrow columns.

Grids and white space   Before you start designing a page or a poster, it is worth thinking about a grid – a basic structure of columns and rows. This will determine the shape and feel of the page, with the body of text sharing space with drawings, photographs etc. and balanced with open spaces – so-called *white space*.

Again there are some basic conventions. If a column is too wide, the scanning-eye can lose the position of the start of the next line. A single column of small type across an A4 page is not advisable. On the other hand a very narrow column may not work if you get only two or three words per line. Horizontal grid divisions will produce a page with a series of boxes which can

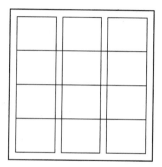

Figure 11.1   A simple layout grid.

be used for text and illustrations. Three columns and three horizontal grid divisions on an A4 page give a range of options with plenty of flexibility.

ACTIVITY 11.2

Grids

Devise a selection of grids on a desktop publishing program. Create or find some text and **clipart** and try laying out a page using different grids. Which do you find easiest to work with? Which gives the most attractive result? Compare your own efforts with the layouts in the publications you selected for Activity 11.1.

Refer to Figure 11.2 as an example of a page layout. In DTP terminology the space between columns is the **gutter**. Note the margins. This particular design uses a thin line to mark the margin on three sides. You can probably guess that the side without the margin is where the fold comes. This means that this is a **verso** or left-hand page. The right-hand or **recto** page will have the left margin 'open'. The design here is for an eight-page leaflet, but if it was more pages, the designer would need to think about making the inside margins slightly bigger to compensate for the part of the page we can't easily see as it disappears into the fold (see what happens yourself if you take several sheets of A4 paper and fold them to make an A5 booklet). Desktop publishing software allows the designer to set up 'master pages' for these left and right pages, so that each page can be automatically set up. A separate design can be used for the centre pages, because here it may be possible to run text or images across two pages – a *double-page spread*. This term applies to any two facing pages which have material designed across the fold; however, it works best in the middle pages of a folded or stapled publication because these will be printed as a single sheet – elsewhere in the publication facing pages will be the right or left hand sides of different sheets that require careful alignment of page elements and accurate assembly by the printer. Again, it is best to look at a range of print products to see how page designs work – take an old magazine apart to see how the pages fit together.

The text in Figure 11.2 is attempting to persuade readers to think about buying 'e-books', downloaded from the Internet. The design must therefore suggest the modernity of the subject. The designer has made a number of decisions. First, the thin line for the margins has also been used to divide up the page into a series of rectangles, including two photographs, one small and landscape and one larger and portrait. There are also three rectangles holding 'headline' text in larger sizes. The grid is not conventional, but it does present the body text in two columns. These are pushed to the right to allow space for the main figure in the photograph.

Blue text is set in OCR-A at 18 on 26 pts on a yellow background

...reading will never be the same again

Blue text in Neue Helvetica 65 medium at 14 on 18 pts on a lighter yellow tint

eBooks are, quite simply, one of the most exciting innovations in the history of publishing. They extend and enlarge the reading experience, and they improve the accessibility of information.

Body text is set in Neue Helvetica 55 roman at 8.5 on 12 pts (colour black)

Instead of having a paper volume, bound into a cover, you have an electronic copy that's filed on your computer like any other document. To read it you use a special 'reader' application that displays the text, page by page – without scrolling – on the screen of your PC, laptop or handheld device.

No one seriously suggests that eBooks will take the place of printed versions, but they do have a number of advantages for students, academics, researchers and others who need rapid access to a wide variety of published – copyright – information.

The eBook, for example, can be searched in a similar way to an encyclopaedia on CD-ROM, so you can quickly locate a reference such as a date, place name or event – and you can easily bookmark related information.

Blue cap

For frequent travellers, eBooks are a tremendous asset: they enable you to carry a basic reference library with you that weighs next to nothing. If you normally travel with a laptop or similar device, you can take as many books with you as will fit on your hard disc. What does this mean in practice? Well, on average, a megabyte of storage will hold two books – and most laptops now come with thousands of megabytes of disk space.

Total commitment

Neue Helvetica 75 bold at 9.5 on 12 pts

At Taylor & Francis we are totally committed to the eBooks concept. We have over 200 years of publishing experience and we're convinced that eBooks will be an extremely popular innovation. In fact we are currently producing electronic versions of several thousand books on our backlist.

Storage and display technology will clearly change in the future but you can rest assured that we will support all major eBook Reader formats.

eBooks are one of the most **exciting innovations** in the history of publishing.

Yellow text in Neue Helvetica 65 medium at 11 (line 1), 26 (line 2) and 15 (line 3) on 26pts

Yellow lamp   Gutter   A 'rule' used to create a margin

Figure 11.2 Sample page from a leaflet about e-books.

The type size for the body text is quite small at 8.5 but it is set on 12 points, giving plenty of space between the lines and a general sense of 'openness' (the page reproduction in this book is not full-size – you can use any DTP software to reproduce the type size and leading yourself for comparison). The 'auto leading' for 8.5 would be 11.2. The headlines are similarly set with plenty of leading. The body text and all but the top heading are set in 'Neue Helvetica', a more modern and lighter version of the most common sans-serif type family. There are three different weights of this face in use on the page. The top heading '. . . reading' also looks stretched out, but this is a property of the typeface, OCR-A BT. The 'BT' refers to the foundry, Bitstream and the name OCR indicates that this was a face designed for Optical Character Readers – i.e. for computers to read automatically. It works well in this mode because it is a 'proportional' font – each character takes up the same amount of space. This means there is as much space for an 'i' as for a 'w'. Because of this, such fonts are not good for body text as they take up more space overall, but they do suggest 'computer' very well. (The *tracking* here is minus 11.)

The page also uses colour, with yellow for the background to boxes, and both yellow and blue text. These colours also dominate the photographs. You will want to think about the choice of photographs in relation to the overall meaning of the page (see Chapter 1), but here you should also note the use of a shallow field of focus to distinguish the young woman from both background and foreground.

Images   There are two kinds of images which you can use in a dtp program. The first is called a **bitmap**. This is an image made up of an arrangement of pixels of different colours – a 'map' of '**bits**' of information. Bitmaps usually start life as photographs which are scanned in to the computer, but you can create them yourself using a 'paint' package. The quality of the bitmap as a printed image depends on two factors – the number of colours and the size of the individual pixels. A very high-quality image in a fashion magazine will have 'millions of colours' and a massive bitmap of very small pixels. The result is that you cannot see the individual pixels in the image on the page, and the vast range of colours means that the reproduction will be as close as possible to the original colours of the photograph. This is a *high-resolution* image. At the other end of the scale is an image with a limited number of colours and a relatively small bitmap. When a bitmap is enlarged or reduced (scaled up or down) the individual pixels are each enlarged or reduced, so that, if the printed image is larger than the original, it is possible to see the individual pixels in a very 'blocky' presentation. This is a *low-resolution* image, which you will sometimes see in newspapers when the content is so important that the picture editor is prepared to accept the low quality.

Figure 11.3 A low-resolution bitmap showing the pixels.

Scanning and printing photographs is a tricky business, and there is not enough space here to go into detail. As a producer, you will usually want to get the best-quality image into your publication. Unfortunately, high-resolution files are very large (several megabytes) and your equipment may not be able to handle them easily. Go for the best quality you can handle and scale down, never up.

The second type of image is known as a **vector** drawing or 'structured' or 'outline' drawing. Instead of the fixed bitmap, a vector drawing is made up of a set of points which are joined by curves. These are stored in the computer file as a formula. When the vector drawing is used in a dtp program, it can be scaled up or down and the computer recalculates the formula for the curve. This way, the image will always be high-quality. This is the basis for much of the **clipart** you will find on your computer. The image is high-quality but often has few colours and does not attempt to replicate a photograph. You can draw such images yourself, but you need great skill and knowledge of the drawing software. The industry standard drawing programs are Illustrator and Freehand.

There is another form of 'image' which you may wish to use, called an **EPS** or 'encapsulated postscript' file. This isn't an image file as such, but rather a text file describing an image in great detail for a print program – on a similar principle to the vector drawing. **Postscript** is a print description language used extensively in publishing (largely on Macintosh computers). The files are very good for printing, but are sometimes difficult to load into dtp programs.

Text as image   Fonts for dtp should always be 'outline' fonts which can be scaled like the vector drawings or Postscript files described above. Beware of bitmap fonts which work only at a set size – if you enlarge them they become blocky. You can use certain fonts in a drawing program and then manipulate characters or whole words as if they were images.

Manipulation of images   One of the great benefits of computerised page layout is the range of possibilities for manipulating text and images – changing colour, shape, texture etc. in a seemingly unlimited number of ways. This boon is also a curse if you let it run away with you. Just as in video production (which includes many of the same effects), it is important to have a purpose rather than just to create an effect for the sake of it. Why might you want to manipulate or distort images and/or text?

First, you may simply want to 'enhance' or improve the image. There are many tools available to do this, including colour controls and balance of light and dark in an image ('equalisation'). Often enhancements may not be obvious at all and so may not act as a code (except in coding 'perfection' or

Clipart is commercially produced artwork – drawings of a wide range of objects and people, available copyright-free on CD-ROM.

EPS clipart, like this Illustrator drawing, will retain its detail when scaled up or down.
   Clipart is useful in relatively informal documents but can look out of place in formal publications.

Figure 11.4a and 11.4b A wave distort digital effect has been applied to this photographic image.

'high standard of finish'). You may wish to use effects to emphasise text, such as shadow or outline, or a 'fill' pattern instead of solid black or colour.

You may also wish to distort the shape of images or construct new images by putting together a collage of some kind. Many of these effects are already programmed for the industry standard image manipulation package, Adobe Photoshop. New effects are known as 'plug-ins' for the program. These effects are noticeable, and you might need to be careful not to follow trends just because there is a new plug-in. You can see these trends developing in the magazines – such as the use of soft grey shadows for headline text a little while ago. Ideally, you want to appear contemporary – clearly up with trends – but also distinctive.

Electronic publishing

It is increasingly likely that you will be undertaking projects that end with a digital file rather than a print product. You may be asked to create a series of pages for a website, a slide presentation or an 'e-booklet', all designed to be 'read' on-line. Apart from being interesting examples of 'new media', these are also formats that can potentially be e-mailed to other parties or made available via websites.

There are various software packages available to create these products, but you need to be aware of the professional packages if you want to go further with your practical work.

Web pages   The industry standard software packages such as Macromedia's Dreamweaver and Adobe's GoLive will allow you to compile text in HTML format and combine it with graphics, animation etc. They should also help to manage your pages (keeping links up to date etc.) and upload to a website.

All of the conventions that apply to DTP apply to web pages as well, although you can use colour without worrying about who is paying the print costs. Think about the following points:

- The software will probably offer you 'default' type sizes and faces. Don't get too adventurous, because what you select may not appear on someone else's computer.
- The computer screen shape is 'landscape' rather than portrait – don't make your reader scroll down a long page.
- Don't make your page too 'busy' and beware of large animations etc. – many readers will just go somewhere else if your page takes a long time to load.
- The only image formats you can use are **GIFs** (for colour line art) or **JPEGs** (for photographs).
- All images on the Web are 'low-resolution' (72 dpi), so you may need to 'optimise' your images in Photoshop.

The drawback to working in HTML on a web page is that you cannot control
how your page will be seen on another computer. Depending on the browser
(Explorer or Navigator), the platform (Windows or MacOS) and the screen
resolution of the monitor (800 × 600 is a kind of standard, but many people
don't use it), your page can look very different. Try viewing it on a range of
browser/platform combinations. The best advice is to keep it simple. If you
really want a particular typeface for a logo, save it as an image rather than text.

A common print format   There is a solution if you want what you produce to
be seen by everyone in the same way. Adobe's 'portable document format'
(**pdf**) is a development from the Postscript printing language. If you have
software that can produce a Postscript file (such as PageMaker or Quark), it
can be 'distilled' by Acrobat into a pdf and then read on any computer by
Acrobat Reader (which is free from Adobe). You will notice that quite a few
web pages now include pdfs to download. Once downloaded, the file can be
read on screen or printed out (as long as it has been prepared for 'print'). A pdf
can include text, photographs, tables etc.

Presentation   Acrobat is also an excellent package for presenting slides, but
the choice by most people in business is Microsoft Powerpoint. Again the
usual DTP conventions hold good, but if you are going to project slides on to
a big screen as part of your presentation, here are a few tips:
- Think about type size and face – on a big screen you don't want too much
  text and a sans-serif face at a large size (16 points or more depending on
  how far away the viewer is sitting) is best.
- White or yellow on a black background works well on a big screen.
- Avoid red (it 'bleeds' badly on a video projector).
- Go easy with the animated transitions between slides – they can get
  boring.

On all electronic publishing work, remember that it is the quality of the text
and images that matters, so design your page to show them off. The best way
to learn is to visit different kinds of website and make a note of what you like
about a particular page design.

Technical codes in video production

A video image is actually made up of a matrix – a set of rows and columns of
pixels – which can be individually charged to show a particular colour. Your
computer screen offers a video image of a specific resolution – in effect a
bitmap (which is why you can 'grab' your computer screen as an image and
use it in a print product, as we have done in this book). 'Full motion video'

PAL Video standard, as used for UK television, has a bitmap of 720 × 576 pixels. Most computer screens offer higher resolutions.

At a basic level, digital video is similar to analogue in terms of resolution (see Chapter 16), but some high-resolution video cameras are now approaching film resolutions (e.g. the equipment used by George Lucas on *Star Wars Episode 2*).

The term **lamp** describes the physical device which provides the 'light' and is used to avoid confusion.

changes the image twenty-five times per second to give the impression of continuous movement. Each full frame of video corresponds to a single frame on a strip of film, which passes through a projector at the slightly slower speed of twenty-four frames per second.

The two main differences between analogue video and film are that the video image is relatively low-resolution (i.e. a small bitmap – see print image section above) and exists only when a timing signal can stabilise the image (i.e. it is difficult to distinguish the single frames easily). Film is high-resolution and stable. Digital video is beginning to close the gap in many ways, so for our purposes we can for most of the time treat film and video together. (Much of this section is also relevant for still photography.)

The single most important element in the film or video image is light, or more specifically, light captured by a lens. Technical codes can therefore be classified as follows:

- light
  - sources (positions)
  - type of **lamp** (colour of light, area covered)
  - brightness, intensity
- lens or aperture
  - focal length
  - size
- sensitivity of film or light sensor
- shutter speed
- special effects.

These are all codes relating to the contrast between light and shade and the effect of light in 'modelling' or shaping figures in an environment. There are some basic rules for a lighting set-up as shown in Figure 11.5. Traditionally, film and television uses a **set-up** with three kinds of **lamps**, placed in specific positions. The **key light** is a bright, powerful light which illuminates a person or object and throws a deep shadow. It usually comes from a lamp above and at an angle to the subject. **Fill light** comes from smaller lamps placed at complementary angles to 'fill' the shadows created by the key light with a softer light. Finally **back light**, from a lamp above and behind the figure, helps to bring it forward from the background and create some depth in the image.

In mainstream film and television, most comedies, musicals, talk shows and light entertainment are presented in *high-key* lighting. This means that the ratio of fill to key is high – most of the shadows are filled in. Light has a texture which is either 'hard' – producing deep and sharp shadows – or 'soft', creating only slight shadows. The texture depends both on the intensity of the lighting element (brightness) and the extent to which the light is 'direct' or diffused in some way with a 'scrim' (a fine mesh) or gauze.

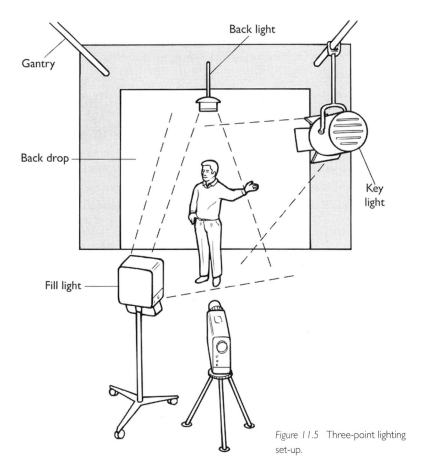

Gantry

Back light

Back drop

Key light

Fill light

Figure 11.5 Three-point lighting set-up.

Figure 11.6 This crowded shoot on location shows a white reflector and a 2,500-watt key light with 'barn doors'. The umbrella is for the rain, but white umbrellas can be used as reflectors.

Light is brighter when it is concentrated on a 'spot'. This can be achieved with lenses in the lamp or with 'barn doors' (metal hinged flaps). Softer light can be achieved by 'bouncing' or reflecting light off the ceiling or a white sheet.

Light is angled on to its subject, and the texture can be controlled. A third factor is 'colour' – depending on the power of the lamp, light has a **colour temperature**. The most powerful light is bright daylight, which is 'hot' and produces a blue sky. Artificial lights are by comparison 'cold' and tend towards reddish yellow. (You'll notice that this is the opposite of what you would expect, since we tend to equate blue with cold and red with heat.) If you shoot in colour, you must ensure that either the film stock or the video camera is adjusted for indoor or outdoor lighting. The video camera adjustment is known as **white balance**. If these adjustments are not made, the image will have a blue or yellow cast.

Fine gradations of light are difficult to distinguish on a video screen, but are revealed in all their glory in the classic black and white cinematography of 1940s cinema. It is worth trying to see re-issued 1940s films on a large

The origins of *film noir* lighting are argued to be in German cinema of the 1920s and 1930s – the practice spread to Hollywood and other European cinemas with the emigration of talent following Hitler's seizure of power in 1933, and became prevalent in drama and horror.

cinema screen to get the full effect. *Film noir* lighting was '*low key*' – so called because of a low 'fill' to 'key' ratio – often dispensing with fill and back lights altogether to produce stark images with single, hard key lights. Thus 'low' fill to key ratio.

Many different kinds of lamps were used in classical cinema, and you may find references to some exotic names, such as 'pups' or 'babies', 'inkies', 'scoops', 'juniors' and 'seniors'. These refer to lights of different power and purpose. During your course, if you do get access to lighting equipment it is likely to be a kit of 'redheads', so named because of the reddish colour achieved at relatively low power. You will see these in use by some news crews in an interview set-up on location. The more powerful portable light is a 'blonde' (again because of the colour of the brighter light).

Natural light also varies in power and texture and film-makers often choose to shoot at only certain times of day to capture a particular lighting effect. Natural light can be used indoors (i.e. through windows, doorways) and can be manipulated via reflectors (and suitable adjustment for colour temperature).

Figure 11.7 Out of the Past (US 1947) is a classic film noir. In this shot, a table lamp is offscreen to the right, throwing a bright light up on to Robert Mitchum.

ACTIVITY 11.3

Experiment with lighting

The best way to learn about lighting and lenses is to experiment. Unfortunately, many inexpensive video cameras are designed to prevent you doing just that. Equipment for 'home' use has automatic controls which try to standardise the image. Look for a video camera with 'manual' iris or aperture control, or at least some means of altering the aperture setting.

- Try to create a *film noir* image, applying some of the lighting techniques described above. Start with a set as dark as possible – a studio or a room with blackout – gradually adding 'lamps' to achieve effects of light and shadow typical of the *noir* image.

Any video camera will be worth using for the next task:

- Try to manipulate natural light by shooting in a room where you can control sunlight through a window to act as a key light. Use a reflector to act as a fill source.
- What happens to the lighting on your subject if you are pointing the camera towards the window or at a white wall? You should be able to work out what is happening (and learn to avoid it – unless you want to create an effect).

Figure 11.8 A colour film which used film noir techniques was Blade Runner (US 1982). Here lighting is used to create metaphorical prison bars across the lovers.

PRODUCTION TECHNIQUES

Lens and aperture

Light is captured by the camera via the lens and passes through the aperture to reach the film or video light sensor. The lens and aperture function just like your eye in focusing on the subject and controlling the amount of light. When you are faced with a bright light your iris contracts. In the same way the camera aperture can be made smaller. The smaller the aperture, the longer the focal length achieved by the lens. A longer focal length means a greater depth of focus in the image. Conversely, a shorter focal length means only a limited field of focus.

It's easy to be confused by the terms photographers use. 'Depth of field' is also a function of the type of lens. A 'standard' lens for a film or still camera is given as 50 mm focal length – the distance between the lens and the film on which a sharp image is focused. This lens produces an image with roughly the same perspective as your own view of a scene. A shorter or **wide-angle** lens of 25 mm produces a scene which seems further away, but which 'crams more in'. A long lens, often called a **telephoto** lens, of 80 mm or more will compress the distance between you and the scene. The confusion comes when you realise that the long lens means a shallow field of focus while a short lens means very deep focus. You don't need to know all the details about lenses (unless you want to be a director of photography), but you should be able to distinguish between the use of a wide-angle and telephoto lens as shown in the examples here.

You can check out some of these ideas about lenses with a video camera. Modern video cameras use a **zoom** lens to simulate shorter and longer lenses, so a typical small video camcorder will have a zoom lens offering 'lengths' from, say, 10 mm to 120 mm (these are the equivalent of 20 mm to 240 mm on a 35 mm camera), with controls often marked 'W' and 'T' for wide-angle and telephoto. If you want to create great depth of field in a scene, use a relatively short lens with characters relatively close to the camera and plenty of action in the background.

One of the disadvantages of a wide-angle lens is that objects very close to the camera can become distorted, even when still in focus. This can work well in a horror film or *film noir* where the face looming into the camera with bulging eyes etc. can be quite shocking. Other distorting lenses can be used to create more obvious effects, such as the circular or 'goldfish bowl' effect.

Our striking still from *The Good, the Bad and the Ugly* (Figure 11.10) shows the dramatic effects of a wide-angle lens and a small aperture. The foreground and the deep background are both in sharp focus. This is an extraordinary shot and was achievable only with the bright desert sunlight and a particular widescreen film format called Techniscope (see Salt 1992) which used a half-size film frame, effectively doubling the focal length.

Technical codes in video production

You will recognise the long lens used by the sports photographer to take close-ups of the action. Some are so long that they need a separate support without which the camera would be impossible to hold.

Figure 11.9 Wide-angle distortion in *La haine* (France 1995).

In the *film noir Crossfire* (US 1947), the 'villain' is photographed with different lenses as the film progresses. Each time, the lens is slightly shorter, so at the climax of the film his appearance is very disturbing.

Figure 11.10 *The Good, the Bad and the Ugly* (Italy 1966).

The widescreen formats introduced in the 1950s all required more light through the lens to capture and project a bigger image. At first it was thought that 'epic' pictures would all be set outdoors or on sets with very shallow fields of focus. The lens manufacturers improved their products dramatically, and improvements in the other parts of the system meant that, eventually, everything that studio cinematographers of the 1940s had achieved could be replicated in widescreen and Technicolor.

You should note from this that the history of technical codes in cinema and television has been largely concerned, in terms of the image, with the problem of light. There are three aspects of the problem:

- getting enough light, of the correct intensity, tone and texture on to the scene, where it is required
- developing a lens to capture the light
- developing the 'light-sensing' device in the camera.

'Film' is a photochemical technology. An emulsion of chemicals on a celluloid base reacts to exposure to light and changes colour. Throughout the history of the cinema, the basic technology has remained the same, but improvements have been made to the emulsion to make it more sensitive and to respond to a wider range of lighting possibilities. Video cameras have light-sensitive chips which transmit information to be stored on tape or disk. Again their development involves increasing the data flow – the lighting information to be recorded. Film or video sensing devices can be ranged from 'fast' to 'slow' in terms of how quickly they can capture light. A fast film can operate in relatively poor lighting conditions, but the resulting image is quite 'grainy' – a feature you might notice in newsreel footage from the 1940s or 1950s. Slow film needs plenty of light to produce very smooth and glossy images.

Colour film depends on chemical processes which can produce different palettes. If you read what successful cinematographers and directors say about their films, you will sometimes find references to a choice of Eastmancolor or Fujicolor because they favour one group of colours rather than another. It is also possible to alter the way the colour is to be recorded, by use of filters on the camera or lamps, or the way it is 'printed' on the final film, by adjusting the developing time or temperature.

Figure 11.11 The Battle of Algiers (Algeria 1965) was a famous example of a feature film with a 'feel' of actuality, achieved partly through documentary camera techniques and a grainy fast-film appearance.

Cinematography

You can find out a great deal about the work of the cinematographer from websites such as those of the American Society of Cinematographers (www.cinematographer.com) or the International Cinematographers Guild (www.cameraguild.com). Roger Deakins, the British cinematographer who

shot *The Shawshank Redemption* and many of the Coen brothers' films, has
been interviewed on both sites. He explains how he achieved the sepia toned
look of *O Brother, Where Art Thou?*, which was printed from film to a digital
format. All the greens were manipulated using the computer and the result
then transferred to the final film print.

Speed of shooting and projecting

A film camera has a shutter which closes the aperture and allows the film to be
fed through the gate at a rate of twenty-four frames per second. This speed is
matched by the cinema projector. But speeds can be manipulated in a number
of ways to speed up and slow down the action. Some cameras allow the film to
be 'overcranked' so that thirty or even forty frames are recorded each second.
When this footage is played at 24 fps, it produces 'slow motion', used to great
effect by action director Sam Peckinpah for scenes of violence, such as the
climax of *The Wild Bunch* (US 1969) (Figure 11.12). The opposite effect is
achieved by undercranking the camera or speeding up the projector. Such
techniques can now also be imitated in digital editing.

Figure 11.12   *The Wild Bunch* (US
1969).

Special effects

Some of the digital effects used in photographic images for print are also
relevant for video and film, and, as edit suites move from analogue to digital
nonlinear, more and more effects become available. Entire films can now be
made using computer-generated animated sequences such as those in *Monsters
Inc.* (US 2001), and others include spectacular digital sequences such as the
morphing liquid metal in *Terminator 2* (US 1991). It is worth remembering,
however, that special effects using double exposures, glass **matte** screens and
front or back projection have been common in cinema since 1896 – modern
effects are often based on the same ideas.

Matte   an opaque shape that
masks off part of the image
captured by the camera lens.
Used from early cinema onwards
in creating effects by combining
images (i.e. partial images
combined to make one complete
image). Glass mattes, on which
elaborate sets can be painted,
were still in use on *Star Wars* (US
1977), having been introduced
early in the century.

ACTIVITY 11.4

Lenses, shutters and film stock

It is difficult to experiment with these codes (although some of you may be lucky
and have access to video cameras with a range of controls). It is also quite difficult
to recognise some of the subtleties of film stock and colour palettes when
watching films on video. But you can learn something by watching a variety of films
from different periods.

> Watch the openings of three or four films from the history of cinema, ideally
> one from silent cinema, one from the 1940s, one from the 1970s and one from
> recent cinema. Note the differences in
> - depth of field
> - use of wide-angle or telephoto lenses
> - quality of the image – colour, grain etc.
> - use of special effects.
>
> What conclusions do you draw about changing techniques?

'Narrative' codes in film and video production

Some decisions about the images which appear in print or in a film or
television programme depend not on technical issues but on selection of
framings, angles, shot 'size' etc. for the sake of the narrative flow. We're
including them here because they have become so closely bound up with the
routines of 'technical' film knowledge. Because all of them are in some way
concerned with manipulating narrative 'space', we've included them under
the heading of narrative codes.

When moving images were first presented as 'films' in the nineteenth
century, the camera was stationary and action took place before it. The action
recorded was continuous and lasted for as long as the roll of film in the
camera. Even when the idea of filming a series of actions developed, the
camera was at first simply placed where the audience might be – in the front
row of the theatre stalls. Very quickly, however film crews learnt how to make
the story much more interesting to watch by:
- changing the framing and composition (moving the camera and the
  actors)
- changing the angle of view
- shooting while the camera is moving.

Framings and composition

These early innovations in camerawork became 'codified' into a 'film
language' with precise terms for different *framings*. The basis for the system is
the framing of the human body as shown in Figure 11.13. Terms also
developed for groupings of people and angles on the action. Notice that
although these are 'narrative codes', they are also related to technical codes.
A framing of a face in 'big close-up' can be achieved either by moving the
camera close to the subject with a standard lens or by using a telephoto lens
from some distance away. The effect won't be exactly the same. Using a
wide-angle lens close to the face may produce distortion.

PRODUCTION TECHNIQUES

'Narrative' codes in film and video production

Extreme Close-Up (ECU)

Medium Long Shot (MLS)

Interviewee looks into space in the frame (and towards the interviewer)

Big Close-Up (BCU)

Long Shot (LS)

Moving subject walks into space

Close-Up (CU)

Very Long Shot (VLS)

High Angle Shot (looking down)

Medium Close-Up (MCU)

Two Shot (could be CU/MCU/MS)

Low Angle Shot (looking up)

Medium or Mid-Shot (MS)

'Over the shoulder shot'

Tilted frame

Figure 11.13 Shot sizes and framings.

Composition refers more to the shape of the subject within the frame or
where objects are placed in relation to each other. Ideas for composition (like
some ideas about the use of lighting and colour) have developed from
concepts of beauty developed in fine art (see Rose 2001).

> *Mise en scène*, or the 'setting up of a scene', is a term borrowed from theatre
> which is sometimes used to refer to the way in which the visual image has
> been organised in a film. Its original use was confined to production design,
> decor, costume, colour, lighting etc. (i.e. theatrical elements). Some
> commentators have included all the elements of camerawork mentioned
> above. In practice it is difficult to distinguish 'camera effects' from the
> organisation of the scene in front of the camera. When we discuss the
> 'disturbed *mise en scène* of *film noir*', we mean both the dark shadows and
> bright pools of light and the tilted frame, high angles, distortions etc. found in a
> film such as *Crossfire*.

Figure 11.14 shows how different camera postions and movements are
achieved. Again, some of these seem to refer to more or less the same effect,
but the differences can be important. *La haine* (France 1995) is distinctive
because of its long travelling (or 'tracking') shots. These could have been
attempted with a **Steadicam**, but the director wanted the control that
genuine tracking would give him.

Editing transitions

Changing camera set-ups means that editing is required. This is also an issue
about manipulating 'narrative time'. There are two aspects to consider:
- the nature of the 'transition' between shots
- the relationship between different scenes.

The most common transition is the simple cut – one image replaces another
immediately. Careful framing (which means shifting the angle or changing
the shot size) can disguise a cut's abruptness and aid the audience's absorption
into the narrative, especially when the sound track of music and dialogue is
continuous. The **cut** has no special meaning except to 'move the narrative
forward'. In modern cinema and television, 'fast-cutting' at the rate of every
five or six seconds also has the effect of generating a fast pace to the narrative
(which in turn can make a '**long-take**' style of shooting feel leisurely).

Every other form of transition is more noticeable and tends to have a more
specialised meaning. Sometimes one image slowly fades away at the same
time as another fades up, allowing a short period when the images overlap.

CAMERA MOVEMENTS and POSITIONS

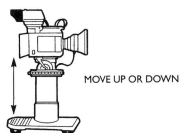

MOVE UP OR DOWN

The height of the camera position dictates the *viewpoint* – perhaps of a character looking at something or someone. It also provides the viewpoint of the audience on the action.

The convention is that the height of the camera will correspond to the 'eye-line' of characters on screen (whose eyes will usually be in the top third of the screen). Cutting from one character to another will usually require an '*eye-line match*'. Forgetting to raise or lower the camera during shooting is a common mistake of student operators.

The camera can move up or down as characters rise or sink to their knees, maintaining the same eye-line.

A *tilt* of the camera can give the impression of looking down (into a well?) or upwards (to the top of a tower?) – the *angled framing* of which may suggest the inferiority or superiority of the viewer to the subject.

Not to be confused with a *tilted frame*, in which the camera 'lists' to left or right.

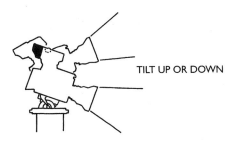

TILT UP OR DOWN

A common movement is the **pan**, when the camera swivels on its axis to describe an arc which displays a 'panorama'. The arc is usually not more than 270° – a full 360° pan is quite disorientating. Pans are usually slow and smooth, but a very fast 'whip pan' can be effective in action sequences.

CAMERA 'PANS' LEFT OR RIGHT

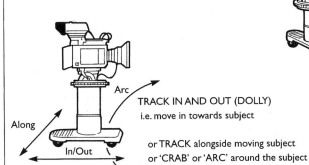

Arc
TRACK IN AND OUT (DOLLY)
i.e. move in towards subject

or TRACK alongside moving subject
or 'CRAB' or 'ARC' around the subject

Along

In/Out

One of the most exhilarating experiences for audiences is when the camera physically moves across terrain, drawing the viewer into the action. Traditionally, this was done with a camera on a wheeled device running on tracks – thus a *tracking shot*. In a studio, cameras might be on a trolley able to move in different directions – known as a 'dolly' – or on a 'crane' able to rise way above a scene and 'swoop' down.

In recent years, cameras have been freed from restraints and can be carried by the operator, almost anywhere, with a smooth action thanks to the **Steadicam**.

With a 'STEADICAM', a camera operator can move with the camera in any direction

Figure 11.14 Camera movements.

Bloody Sunday (UK/Ireland 2002) is a film about events in Derry in 1972. Fades to black are used between scenes to suggest that only the crucial scenes are being shown – an attempt to create 'authenticity' (see Chapter 16).

This is a '**mix**' in television and a '**dissolve**' in the cinema. Traditionally, a dissolve has been a softer kind of transition, often within a sequence signifying time passing. It may also be the signal for a flashback or a dream sequence, usually with some other visual clue. A more marked signal of time passing, and possibly location change, comes with the fade to black and then the slow fade up to a new scene. The **wipe** was popular in cinema during the studio era (some of the most effective wipes are in the films of Akira Kurosawa, such as *Seven Samurai* (Japan 1954)). It involves pulling or pushing an image out of the way to reveal another beneath, rather as the windscreen wiper on a car reveals the road ahead. Digital editing software offers numerous different kinds of wipes, and used with care they can be very effective.

New forms of transition and new ideas about editing are emerging in contemporary cinema and television. Most of these, like the freeze frames in Steven Soderbergh films (e.g. *Out of Sight*, US 1998) or the speeded-up sequences in Wong Kar-Wai's *Chungking Express* (Hong Kong 1994), are variations on older ideas. Others are developing in music television. One way of avoiding camera movement or doing away with the need for a transition is the use of the zoom lens. In several science fiction films this has now produced the effect of a zoom across space (see the ending of *Men in Black* (US 1999)).

Parallel editing

Very early in the cinema, the idea of showing two strands of a story happening at the same time was developed. This allows the parallel development of stories and builds up the excitement of suspense stories or chase sequences. Sometimes this is called 'cross-cutting' as attention crosses from one location to another where linked events are being played out. Another possibility, briefly popular in the late 1960s, is the split screen, with different stories occupying different parts of the screen. This technique was successfully revived in *Lola rennt* (*Run Lola Run*) (Germany 1998).

Continuity 'rules'

Some film theorists (especially Bordwell, Staiger and Thompson 1985) have argued that 'Studio Hollywood' used various rules for framing and combining shots. These combined to form a 'continuity system' or an 'Institutional Mode of Representation'. Some of these rules are still largely in place because they help audiences make sense of what is going on – thus the '180 degree' or 'crossing the line' rule. This is illustrated in Figure 11.15 and demonstrates how camera set-ups must be organised to avoid confusion over narrative space.

Camera A   Camera B

When Cameras A and B are kept on the same side of an imaginary 180° line, the two actors walk towards each other.

Camera A   Camera B

When the 'line' is crossed, both actors appear to be moving in the same direction and the audience is in danger of misreading the scene.

Figure 11.15 The 180 degree rule is designed to prevent confusing transitions by not allowing the camera to 'cross the line'.

Other conventions such as avoiding the 'jump cut' (caused by cutting together shots that are only slightly different in content and shot size so that the image appears to jump) are gradually falling away as they become accepted in a range of films. The best advice is to try to develop a consistent style – if you decide to make unusual transitions or to use different compositions, do it for a reason and think about what you are doing. If the images themselves and the story you are telling are interesting, 'breaking the rules' may enhance the audience's enjoyment.

ACTIVITY 11.5

Take any scene from a recent film or television fiction; or look at a television ad. Take notes on:

- how it has been edited
- how the *mise-en-scène* contributes to the narrative.

Now examine the sound track:

- What are the components of this track: music? voices? noises? sound effects including distortion? How have they been chosen and arranged? Are some louder than others? Why do you think each has been included? Do any seem accidental?

- How have they been shaped around the action or talk in that scene? How close do the voices seem? How have they been chosen, or constructed? How does all this help construct the narrative?

Technical codes in audio production

It is possible to think about sound in much the same way as light. The cinematographer 'models with light'. The sound designer models with sound. It isn't very likely that you will have access to full **Dolby** Stereo sound recording for your productions, but it is important that you should know something about the principles of sound design in film and television and the work of the recording engineer in the music or radio studio.

It may be helpful to begin by thinking of a radio broadcast or a film sound track as representing a 'soundscape' (like a visual landscape) or a 'sound stage' (like a theatrical stage). On this stage will be a number of performers, a distance apart, with background sounds such as traffic, birdsong etc. How can this be represented to an audience? The secrets are in the capture of particular sounds via microphones and then the mixing and editing process.

Ray Dolby (born 1933) An American working in the UK in the 1960s, Dolby pioneered work on noise reduction and revolutionised the quality of sound from cassette recorders and, later, cinema projection.

Recording sounds

The nature of recorded sound is a function of the microphone, the acoustic qualities of the location and the sensitivity of the recording medium. There are several different kinds of **microphones**, categorised by different mechanisms for capturing sound and by different pick-up or *response* patterns (see Figure 11.16). A directional microphone with a very tightly defined response captures dialogue without background sound. This 'cardioid response pattern' indicates sound picked up from immediately in front of the microphone with limited responses to each side. The same effect can be achieved with a microphone positioned close to the speaker's lips like a 'tie-clip' microphone. By contrast, an omni-directional microphone picks up dialogue plus all the background noise. Some microphones can be 'switched' between different responses.

The sound that is 'picked up' has various qualities determined by the frequency range of the microphone – its capacity to pick up high- and low-frequency sounds such as a whistle and a bass drum. Other qualities are more difficult to describe, but sound engineers refer to the texture of sound – 'hard' or 'soft', 'fat' or 'thin' – or the 'colour' of sound – 'warm', 'bright', 'round' etc. Some of these qualities are emphasised by particular types of microphone. For example, the large microphones which you might see in newsreels from the 1940s are renowned for giving a rich fruity sound. If you are interested in developing audio production ideas, you should investigate the different kinds of microphone available for your practical work, but note that professional microphones are expensive and you may find only a limited choice.

More controllable, and equally important in terms of the quality of sound, are the acoustic qualities of the recording location. Sound is carried in waves created by pressing air. When the sound waves meet a soft absorbent surface they are effectively 'soaked up'. You've probably been at a party where, as more and more people arrive, the music has to be turned up louder – almost as if the bodies soak up the music. Conversely, when sound waves meet hard, shiny surfaces, they bounce back and in some cases produce echoes. If you set out to record a conversation in a student canteen, with vinyl floors, formica tables and large glass windows, you will probably get a terrible clattering noise, even with a reasonable-quality microphone. But the same conversation in a room with carpeting and curtains may be perfectably acceptable. Just as a television director or film-maker may elect to shoot in a studio, where the lighting can be set up very precisely, sound recordists may use a studio space which is designed to be acoustically 'dead' – i.e. there is no background '**noise**' or atmosphere. Suitable sounds can then be added to create the finished product.

The recording format is important because it too has a frequency response and may alter the quality of the sound. You may have several options on your

See Chapter 1 and Chapter 16 for further discussion of the sound image.

microphone types 'omni-directional': for vox pops – interviews in the street. Directional 'shotgun'-style microphone: on a 'boom' (pole) or with a pistol-grip, pointed at the action in a drama or interview. Tie-clip: used in a studio. Radio microphone: used by a performer on stage.

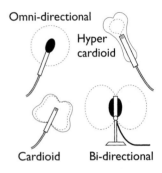

Figure 11.16 Microphone response patterns (cardioid = 'heart-shaped').

Noise in sound recording is a term used to describe any unwanted sound.

course including traditional formats such as cassette or open-reel tape, digital
audiotape (**DAT**), **MiniDisc** or hard-disk recording on the computer. Formats
tend to be chosen for specific purposes and the current situation is very
flexible. You will find professionals who favour one format over another.

Editing and mixing

Until quite recently it was standard practice for all radio interviews and
features to be physically edited by 'cutting and splicing'. Disk-based editing
has now largely taken over, but you may come across both. As well as
assembling the audio material you want, the editing stage also allows you to
'process' the sound and to add sound effects.

We've noted that one practice used to achieve the effect of a 'location' is to
record the dialogue in a studio and add the atmosphere as a sound effect. This
involves using an **audio mixer**, which allows different sound sources on
separate 'tracks' to be mixed together. The 'level' and frequency ranges of
sounds can also be manipulated to produce a fluid 'soundscape', analogous to
an edited visual sequence.

Audio mixers range from
simple 4 track machines to much
larger 8, 16 or 32 track machines.

ACTIVITY 11.6

Compiling a radio sequence

Again, your opportunities to experiment will depend on the equipment available. In
order to develop audio skills, tape two or three short interviews (a couple of
questions only) with a range of people. If possible, conduct one interview in a
location with 'atmosphere' and one in a 'dead' acoustic space.

- Try to add some atmosphere to the 'studio' interview.
- Edit the interviews together and add an introduction and a link.
- Listen to your edit. Are the 'levels' (the loudness) consistent throughout?
- Are the joins noticeable – how could you make them less obvious? (This will
  depend on your equipment.)

Stereo means 'solid' – i.e. sound
with width and depth.

Stereo and the sound stage

All of the comments above apply to 'mono' recordings, where the sound has
been recorded at a single point via the microphone. It is also possible to use a
stereo microphone to record sound 'in depth' – not only to record the sounds
but to place them in position on the sound stage. It is also possible to take a
mono recording and to place it within a stereo sound stage set-up using an
audio mixer. The creation of the stereo sound stage is at the creative heart of
modern stereo radio, television and cinema sound. The sound designer

attempts to create a 'sound image', which means that every person who speaks and every significant sound (a footstep, a phone ringing etc.) is heard clearly, but also in the context of a believable background – a city street, a busy office etc. This is all possible with modern technology, which has allowed a greater frequency range and less noise through the use of noise-reduction systems such as Dolby.

Modern film sound is highly sophisticated and usually is carefully rerecorded after shooting using 'looping studios', where actors repeat under studio conditions their lines spoken on location. **Foley** technology is then used to add the sound effects (Figure 11.17). Typical effects produced by Foley artists are footsteps and the rustle of clothing etc., which is difficult to 'close mike'.

In terms of 'technical audio codes', it is useful to have a set of terms to describe sounds used in a mix, based on a combination of the technology used to create or capture them and their narrative function (see Chapters 3 and 16). In a mix for narratives (in drama or advertising?) in radio, film or television, we can distinguish

- dialogue spoken by the important characters in a scene
- sound effects – the specific sounds which carry narrative information, such as a knock on the door
- background or ambient sound which gives the scene atmosphere – the general hubbub in a bar
- 'non-**diegetic**' sound – sound which doesn't come from the fictional world of the narrative. The clearest example is theme music. Music playing on a jukebox in the scene is diegetic.

Sound is one of the areas of film studies which has received less attention than it deserves. Since the success of *Star Wars* and Dolby Stereo in 1977, film producers and cinema managers have recognised its importance (see Murch 1995). The recent introduction of digital sound systems has enhanced its importance, and, with DVDs and digital broadcasting, television sound is also improving. Next time you go to the cinema, especially to see a Hollywood blockbuster, try to listen carefully to the sound track, along the lines suggested in Activity 11.7. You will notice how the opening music tries both to wake you up – pay attention, back there! – and to pin you to your seat with sheer volume. But in the main narrative it is the range of sound frequencies which is important. Watch out for moments when the movement of the narrative hangs on a sound. Walter Murch describes his work on the opening of *Apocalypse Now* (US 1979):

You are looking at Saigon, you are in a hotel room, but you begin to hear the sounds of the jungle. One by one the elements of the street turn into jungle sounds: a policeman's whistle turns into a bird, the two-stroke

Jack Foley was a Universal Studios sound engineer who developed techniques for recording sound effects.

Figure 11.17 Preparing to lay down sound effects in a Foley studio at Lucasfilms.

The classic 'sound recording' film is *The Conversation* (US 1974) with Gene Hackman as the surveillance agent who becomes obsessed with a recording.

Living in Oblivion (US 1996) is a more recent 'independent' film, about a low-budget film producer, with interesting and amusing sequences about sound recording.

Traditional dialogue recording in film or television allows each character to talk in turn. More 'realistic' is the technique which 'overlaps' lines by different characters. This can be achieved by miking each character in a scene and allowing each a track on a mixing desk. An appropriate balance can be achieved later. This multitrack technique was pioneered by director Robert Altman.

Wonderland (UK 1999) is an innovative film in terms of sound. Much of the action is set in London bars and cafés. Instead of taking over a bar and using 'extras', the director shot scenes in which the actors mingled with the usual bar patrons and the sound crew captured the dialogue (and some of the ambient sound) via radio microphones.

motorcycles turn into insects, and item by item each thread of one reality is pulled out of the tapestry and replaced by another one. You are looking at something very improbable which is a man sitting in an hotel room . . . Although his body is in Saigon, his mind is somewhere else.

(Murch 1996: 161)

ACTIVITY 11.7

Sound and vision

Take a short sequence (two or three minutes) of video, either something you have shot yourself or a sequence copied from a film or television programme.

Play the sequence without sound and concentrate on the meaning suggested by the images alone.

- Take two or three very different music tracks (or sound effects) and play them in conjunction with the visuals.
- How much difference does the sound make?

Skills development

The only way to develop your skills in using sound (and print and video) is to practise and to explore new techniques and approaches. Don't be afraid to fail – if it doesn't work, try something else. Even if you don't intend to become a media practitioner, the more you know about production techniques, the easier you will find it to understand how media texts produce their meanings.

References and further reading

Bordwell, David, Staiger, Janet and Thompson, Kristin (1988) *The Classical Hollywood Cinema*, London: Routledge.

Chion, Michel (1994) *Audio-vision: Sound on Screen*, Chichester: Columbia University Press.

Hedgecoe, John (1979) *Introductory Photography Course*, London: Mitchell Beazley.

Malkiewicz, Kris (1989) *Cinematography*, London: Columbus Books.

Rose, Gillian (2001) *Visual Methodologies*, London: Sage.

Salt, Barry (1992) *Film Style & Technology: History & Analysis*, London: Starword.

Books by practitioners or interviews with them are sometimes useful in revealing how they work. The *Projections* Series edited by John Boorman and Walter Donohue for Faber & Faber carries excellent materials on film production techniques, e.g.:

Projections 4 (1995): Walter Murch, 'Sound design: the dancing shadow'.

Projections 6 (1996) has a section of interviews with cinematographers such as Vittorio Storaro and Freddie Young as well as Walter Murch on sound in *Apocalypse Now*. The film *Visions of Light: The Art of Cinematography* (US/Japan 1992) is available on video and demonstrates techniques from the history of Hollywood cinema.

Websites

www.filmsound.org
www.howstuffworks.com

See also references for Chapter 10.

12 Distribution, promotion and selling advertising space

- Distribution structures in media industries
- Case Study 1: Film distribution in the UK
- Distributing 'advertising-led' products
- Case Study 2: A local media market
- Promotion
- References and further reading

The last stage of the media production process involves getting the product to the target audience. Often, this is the least analysed part of the process and also the one which media practice courses are least likely to feature in detail. To try to redress the balance, we've decided to make it the focus for a separate practice-based chapter (Chapter 13 and the Selling audiences case study following Chapter 6 address related 'theory' issues).

There are two main problems that we need to face. First, the distribution practices of some media industries are very specialised, so we will look in detail at just one example, the distribution of 'specialist films' in the UK. Second, most media production in television, radio and the press is concerned with selling advertising space as well as selling the product. (Even when advertising is not carried, as on BBC programming, distribution is influenced by the rest of the market which is advertising-led). We'll look at the example of the regional press and the relationship between the sale of advertising space and circulation and readership.

Distribution structures in media industries

In most media industries, the majors are concerned to control distribution of their product – either directly or through some form of partnership. They know that success depends on getting the right product to the target audience at the right time. Mainstream media products in all media industries are delivered to audiences along well-organised distribution channels.

National newspapers

Distribution in the print publishing industry involves a three-stage process, from publisher to wholesaler to retailer. As outlined in Chapter 8 newspapers have a shelf life of less than a day, so efficient distribution is important. The UK system falls within definitions of a **monopoly** situation because one company, W. H. Smith, has 33 per cent of the wholesale market, by value. Two others, John Menzies (29 per cent) and Surridge Dawson (18 per cent) have a significant share and the remainder is taken up by a group of twenty-six small independents.

A **monopoly** will be investigated by the Competion Commission at the request of an industry regulator if any company holds a 25 per cent share by value of a specific market.

The system is deemed to serve the public interest, since the wholesalers work on a regional basis. All retailers (mostly newsagents) in a particular area get their newspapers from a single wholesaler at agreed rates. The publishers organise getting each edition to the wholesalers as quickly as possible. This means finding a printer in each major region so that transport time is reduced to a minimum. Sometimes a newspaper title is printed by a rival group if that means more efficient distribution.

W. H. Smith moved towards disrupting the system in 2000 with a suggestion that it would deliver nationally to supermarket chains such as Tesco, but this was resisted. In 2001 W. H. Smith was accused of inefficiency by the main newspaper groups. The dominant position of W. H. Smith is inevitably going to cause some concern. The Office of Fair Trading's conclusion that the current system works to the customer's advantage does not cover questions of 'diversity'. A similar distribution system operates for magazines, and, with a 33 per cent share, it is clear that if W. H. Smith (or John Menzies) refused to distribute a particular title, it would make it very difficult for the title to succeed in the marketplace. (Local agreements prevent retailers from going to other wholesalers or to publishers direct.) (All figures from Office of Fair Trading 2002)

In 2002 W. H. Smith refused to distribute books that didn't carry a barcode and therefore could not be processed automatically at a cash till (*Guardian* 31 August 2002).

The war of the freesheets

If you live around London or another major city, you may pick up a free newspaper such as *Metro* on a local train or bus ride. These papers use material processed by their parent newspaper group and sell advertising. The whole operation depends on getting the newspapers into the hands of commuters, who may then read the ads.

At the end of 2001 Rupert Murdoch announced plans for a London
freesheet produced by News International (publisher of *The Times* and the
Sun). Immediately, he was warned off by Associated Newspapers, the
Daily Mail group that also owns the *Evening Standard* and the successful
Metro freesheet. Most copies are picked up as commuters enter Tube stations,
and Associated had an exclusive deal with London Underground to
distribute copies. In this case distribution is the main consideration for the
publisher.

Newspaper distribution has not, as yet, been significantly affected by digital
transmission. This has been important in the production process (news arrives
as digital data) and newspapers have electronic versions on the Internet, but
these are not as convenient to read as the printed version. Would you be
willing to download a daily paper from the Internet, rather than buying one
from the newsagent?

Radio and television

Television transmitters in the UK
are now all operated by either
Castle Communications
(purchasers of the BBC's
transmitters) or NTL (purchasers
of ITV transmitters).

BSkyB broadcasts from the Astra
satellite, owned by SES-Astra, a
Luxembourg company with
satellites over western Europe
and North America.

Distribution of broadcasting services is completely governed by technology
and regulation. The 'deregulation' and 'liberalisation' (or possibly
'reregulation') of broadcasting in the 1990s (see Chapter 18) completely
changed the broadcasting environment in the UK. We can think about
distribution in the following terms.

- *Analogue versus digital*   Broadcasting is shifting from analogue to digital
  with an 'analogue switch-off' anticipated around 2010.
- *Delivery 'platforms'*   In many parts of the country, viewers and listeners
  have the option to choose from 'terrestrial' (i.e. received via an aerial),
  satellite or cable. All require some form of 'tuner' or 'decoder' and all are
  currently available as analogue or digital.
- *Content and carriers*   Few television broadcasters have direct control over
  the carrier of their signal. BBC and ITV had to give up ownership of the
  network of transmitters across the UK as part of the 1990s shake-up of the
  industry. BSkyB effectively rents space on the Astra satellite that gives a
  'footprint' over the UK. The cable companies are involved in only a small
  selection of the many channels they carry. Regulation means that most
  carriers must offer viewers all the main BBC channels plus Channels 4, 5
  and ITV1. Otherwise 'content' owners or channels must negotiate
  distribution deals with carriers.

The situation in the radio industry is more straightforward, with 'free-to-
air' radio transmissions under the control of the broadcasting station and
further distribution negotiated with satellite and cable. Regulation of

broadcasting means that although there are disputes between content provider and carrier, most can be resolved by the regulator.

Recorded music

The Music Industry case study (following Chapter 8) explores the issue of free distribution of MP3s over the Internet. This is the industry in which distribution has been most affected by Internet usage. CDs are one of the main commodities purchased on-line. This is partly because an on-line retailer can carry a much greater range of product than a traditional retailer.

Record stores have perhaps been most affected by general conditions in retailing. This means fewer, but bigger, stores with pressure on small independents. In addition, a small range of 'chart music' is increasingly available in supermarkets, petrol stations etc. All of this means that, if your tastes go beyond chart music and you have lost the services of a knowledgeable local dealer, the chances are that you will be better off buying on-line, or through conventional mail order. In the sense of finding specialist material, these comments about music recording also apply to video (VHS/DVD) and specialist magazines.

Digital media

Digital transmission has had an impact on all the traditional media industries, but it also offers the possibility of new media products. Making a distinction between what is a 'new product' and what is simply an electronic version of an existing product is not straightforward. For instance, in the case of electronic versions of existing print publications, if this means that the publication is distributed over the Internet, but the reader then prints out the publication and reads it as hard copy, all that has happened is that the mode of distribution has changed (presenting a print publication, the equivalent of exhibiting a film, has stayed the same). If, however, the reader 'uses' the publication 'on screen', then a new exhibition practice is developing. So-called 'e-zines' or 'e-books' hold the promise of further developments (see Chapter 16).

Digital transmission and digital distribution systems have undoubtedly changed the media environment significantly in music and broadcasting, and the next area for possible change is in film distribution. See Chapter 8 for comments on digital projection. Digital distribution may mean that films can be 'downloaded' to cinemas direct from the distributor (with in-built codes which render the film unviewable after the rental expires, or if the film is copied). If you visit your local cinema and speak to the projectionists, you'll discover that cinema operation hasn't changed significantly over a hundred years. Films still arrive in several reels in large metal cans. The reels have to be spliced together before projection and the whole operation reversed before the reels are packaged up and sent to the next cinema. Digital distribution could mean:

- cost savings on transporting cans of film
- no physical damage to delicate prints (they wear out after a limited number of screenings)
- greater security from piracy, since physical prints could not be stolen.

This is a big and expensive change to implement, even if the long-term benefits are great. Cinema history and the recent history of technological innovation suggest that this move (and the take-up of new media products) may take longer than predicted.

Cinema prints Each time a film is run through a projector it is subject to some damage. Most film prints are destroyed after the initial release in cinemas. A few that have the least damage are stored for occasional 'repertory' screenings. A later 're-release' will mean striking new prints.

Case study 1: Film distribution in the UK

Film distribution (i.e. delivering prints to cinemas) has its own unique system. As the first stage of a three-part process the success or failure of a cinema release determines how the video and television releases are organised within their respective sectors (see above).

In the international film business, the rights to screen a film are sold in respect of distinct 'territories' such as the UK (which includes Ireland in this context). Most major Hollywood films are distributed directly by the studio which financed the film. In the UK this means that the cinema box office is dominated by a handful of major distributors as shown in Figure 12.1.

Any mainstream film not taken up by these five (e.g. some of the other studio brands such as New Line etc.) will probably go to Entertainment, a UK independent specialising in Hollywood films. In 2001 only one film in the UK top twenty was not distributed by these companies. *What Women Want*, starring Mel Gibson, was distributed by Gibson's own company, Icon. In any year, the six major distributors will account for around 90 per cent of the box-office rentals.

The distributors have to place films with cinema chains – the exhibitors. The exhibition sector was shaken up in the late 1990s by both new multiplex building and changing ownership. The distribution of cinema screens at the end of 2001 is shown in Figure 12.2. These six chains control all the largest and most modern multiplex cinemas. Showcase, UCI and Warner Village are all controlled by corporations that also own Hollywood studios. The other three chains all have established relationships with the studios. UGC is a French company and also offers a different possible set of relationships.

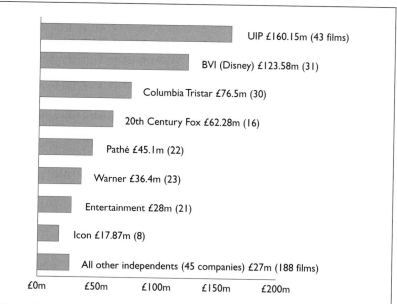

Figure 12.1 Distributor share and number of films released in the UK in 2000, showing the dominance of five Hollywood majors and three 'independents' (source: *British Film Institute Handbook* 2002).

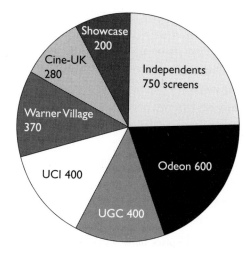

Warner Village is a joint venture between Warner Bros. International Theatres and Australian company Village Roadshow.

Figure 12.2 UK cinema circuits by number of screens at December 2001: approximate screen numbers (taking account of openings and closures) based on figures published in *Screen International*, 1 March 2002.

Cine-UK was founded by a former Warner Bros. executive.

A Hollywood blockbuster is released 'wide' with one or more prints being sent to each multiplex. *Harry Potter and the Philosopher's Stone* (2001) was released on over a thousand prints in the UK. A more usual figure would be four to five hundred. Each print costs over £1,000 so this is a significant investment. The wide release depends on blanket promotional and advertising coverage for the first weekend, and produces a 'buzz' or 'word of mouth', which means you may find yourself seeing a film you'd not initially have chosen to see in order to discuss it with friends. Free trailer packages are sent to television stations. Stars give interviews and newspaper and television advertising guarantees exposure. This package of measures will cost the distributor over £1 million, but if it ensures an opening of £2 million or more the spend will be justified and the impetus will have been given to a final box-office total of £5 million to £10 million.

Specialist cinema

The distributors of non-Hollywood product cannot afford to adopt this policy. They must work under very different conditions. The term 'specialist cinema' was coined by the Film Council in 2001 to describe what is sometimes called 'arthouse cinema' and includes European and world cinema alongside low-budget British films and so-called 'American Independents'.

Most of the time, specialist film titles are handled by independent distributors. Some of these, such as Pathé and Film Four International, may handle as many films as the 'majors' – twenty or more per year earning perhaps £1 million per picture on average. But these are exceptions. Forty or more small distributors share a few percentage points of the box office – sometimes earning only a few thousands per film.

All the independents face two problems:

- They can't afford to send out more than a handful of prints at any one time.
- They are often dealing with many smaller independent cinemas rather than a handful of big chains.

The strategy adopted is therefore to open a small number of prints in London and selected cities and let them run for a few weeks before sending the prints out on a long tour around the other specialist cinemas in different parts of the country.

This strategy is very difficult to support with promotional activities. Specialist films rely heavily not only on festivals and awards but also on reviews, yet these appear in the first week of release and probably only in the London broadsheets. Their impact will have lessened when the film reaches cinemas in some parts of the country several weeks later. Similarly, advertisements in specialist magazines are timed for the London release. Local media give little space to specialist films (which often require a specialist reviewer to cover them adequately) and they are the main source of film reviews for cinemagoers in the UK (source Newspaper Society Market Research).

In January 2002, the Film Council, the UK body charged by government with promoting film culture in the UK, announced a package of support for specialist film distribution, suggesting three possible strategies:

- setting up a 'virtual circuit' of specialist cinemas to make booking of film titles both more efficient and less risky – this could include existing cinemas plus some new ones in places such as Leeds and Birmingham
- designating a 'circuit' of specialist screens in commercial multiplexes (something already tried by the British Film Institute with inconclusive results)
- inviting bids for Lottery funds from new operators of specialist cinemas.

In addition, the Film Council announced an intention to support the distribution of twenty specialist films per year – a total of £1 million.

The Film Council measures are an attempt to address the question so many people ask: 'I heard about this really interesting film on Jonathan Ross, but it never seems to come to my local cinema. Why not?' Around four hundred films are released in the UK each year, but only about half of them reach most parts of the country. A large percentage of British films never get released at all. Film distribution is certainly a good example of the free market not delivering diversity of product, or at least not to all potential audiences.

ACTIVITY 12.1

Specialist film titles

Log the new film releases in any single month. The broadsheet newspapers should review each release (or look at the releases in a magazine such as *Uncut*).

- How many of the titles appear at your local cinemas?
- Are they shown at the multiplex or a specialist cinema? How many screenings do they get in total?
- Which films aren't shown in your locality – would you like to see any of them?

Distributing 'advertising-led' products

Film exhibition, like other public events, does offer advertisers a 'captive audience'. Unlike television ads that can be ignored, ads shown on the big screen before the feature can have considerable impact. The companies that sell this screen space are aware that particular cinemas attract certain kinds of audiences, but they have no input into film production in order to persuade producers to make particular types of films – Hollywood producers are not concerned to tailor their product to the needs of British advertisers. However, 'product placement' in films of internationally known brands such as Apple and Coca-Cola etc. is an important consideration for filmmakers.

The total UK spend on advertising in cinemas was £128 million in 2000, including production costs for the ads. This represents just 1 per cent of total annual advertising expenditure in the UK (source: *Newspaper Society Fact Sheet*, 2001). We can conclude that, as a medium, cinema is a market for advertisers to exploit, but not to 'lead' in terms of influencing production.

This is not so in other media, especially commercial television and radio, where the content of the programming is closely related to the needs of advertisers to reach specific audiences. A good example of this is the scheduling of programmes on Channel 4 to deliver a youth audience or an ABC1 young adult audience. Where film may be termed a 'producer-led' medium, television has tended to become 'advertiser-led'. A third possibility is 'audience-led' media – where audience demand leads producers to make particular kinds of products. 'Give the people what they want' is a phrase some producers use, but do you think this is actually what happens in practice?

In an advertising-led medium, the person in charge of production or publication has a difficult series of decisions to make:

- What is the source of revenue? Is it purely advertising revenue from selling space or sponsorship, or is there the chance of selling the media product as well? Will pursuing one source of revenue damage the chances of increasing the other?
- How will advertising revenues be maximised – by increasing sales as much as possible or by targeting particular audiences (i.e. those most prized by advertisers)?
- How important is the overall 'quality' of the media product in retaining viewers, readers etc.? Is there a regulator to be satisfied?
- How important are distribution and promotion issues in maximising revenues?

These points all come together in the regional newspaper industry. This sector is very important for advertisers, accounting for 19 per cent of all advertising expenditure and ranking second only to television as an advertising medium (i.e. ahead of national newspapers) with £2.76 billion (source: *Newspaper Society Fact Sheet*, 2001). The sector is dominated by large newspaper groups owning many titles across the country.

Local newspapers generally target a closely defined target readership – everyone who lives in the town and surrounding rural areas. The largest circulations are recorded by the truly regional papers – the morning or evening dailies in large cities and towns. But here, although circulation is large, 'penetration' – the percentage of the population who buy and read the paper – may be quite low. Regional evening newspapers such as the *Liverpool Echo* or the *Express & Star* in the West Midlands may sell 150,000 copies or more, but both are circulating in wide catchment areas with populations of up to a million. Weekly papers in small towns may sell only 15,000 copies, but two factors are likely to make the weekly more effective for advertisers:

- Most weekly papers have a high *readership* compared to circulation, so the 15,000 copies may be read by 45,000 people, a large percentage of adults in the town.
- Weekly papers have a 'shelf life' of six or seven days. They are less of an 'impulse buy' and they may be picked up and consulted several times in a week – and therefore any ads will be seen more often.

Weekly papers are an important advertising medium. How do editors approach the four questions outlined above in attempting to maximise revenue?

Advertising and editorial are interdependent. Advertising space sells because of the promise to reach the readers. If the editorial quality falls and circulation falls with it, advertising revenue will also fall. If advertising revenue falls, the cover price must rise, but this in turn will drive more readers away and so on. This is the vicious whirlpool of decline every publisher dreads. Get it right and it works the other way. New readers mean more advertising revenue and in turn more resources for editorial. Advertising revenue is far more important than the revenue from the cover price (the ratio is about 5:1 in favour of advertising). As a consequence, most local papers have a high proportion of advertising to editorial – 60 per cent advertising material is common.

In April 2002 Johnston Press became the fourth biggest regional press group, behind Trinity Mirror, Newsquest and Northcliffe. These four groups account for half the 71 million papers sold weekly in the UK.

ABC (Audit Bureau of Circulation), VFD (Verified Free Distribution) and NRS (National Readership Survey) are the official bodies providing statistics on newspapers. The Newspaper Society is the trade association for the regional press, and commissions its own research.

Display advertising

Most of what we think of as advertising across all media is **display** advertising, but in value terms **classified** advertising is often most important in newspapers. The easiest way to distinguish between the two is to remember that 'classifieds' (sometimes called 'small ads') are usually just a few lines of text in a tiny standard print size, grouped together in a separate section of the paper, whereas display ads can be any size and may use any typeface or graphics they choose in order to stand out or 'display' on the page. The advertising department will price display space according to the likely attention from readers.

The most obvious users of display space (i.e. the biggest ads) in local papers tend to be local supermarkets, furniture warehouses, garden centres etc. Display ads cost a great deal and in order to justify their cost they must reach a high proportion of potential buyers of the products being advertised. This explains why nationally available products are rarely advertised in local papers. There is little point in advertising a particular brand of car in a local paper since the ad would be seen by only a small fraction of the potential national market. Advertising in every local paper would not be as good value as advertising in one or two national papers. However, advertising a car as part of an ad for a local garage makes sense in a local paper, if 'two out of three' potential buyers at that garage get to see the ad.

Classified advertising

Hundreds of tiny two-line ads don't sound very glamorous, and 'selling classifieds' might be thought of as a very routine job. In fact, a successful classified section is often the basis for overall success on a newspaper. This is true of local and national papers. One of the strengths of the *Guardian* is its different specialist classified section for each day of the week (many of the job ads in these sections use illustrations and different typefaces, but they are still classifieds because of the way they are grouped and how the space is sold). Classifieds offer a very important service, and they may be the sole reason some people buy the paper.

We can split the classified section in a local paper into different functions. First, there are 'official announcements' – public announcements which must be made by law such as planning notices, licence applications etc. Then there are the more personal announcements, the 'hatched, matched and dispatched' as they are often called (births, marriages and deaths). We are all interested in what happens to friends and neighbours, and these are often the most eagerly scrutinised part of the paper.

The third function of the classified section is to advertise local products and services, and here again there are strong links to the local community. The local council is likely to be a big advertiser in relation to job vacancies, and this may create difficulties if the paper is also running investigative stories on the council. There have been several instances, especially in London and other large cities, where paper and council have fallen out so badly that the council has refused to advertise in the local paper. Both sides suffered badly in such disputes. The paper lost advertising revenue and the council found recruitment much more difficult. This is a good example of how commercial necessity may constrain (or help maintain) local press relations.

A successful classified section generates good business for the paper if it convinces readers that the goods and services on offer are worth pursuing, i.e. that everyone offering something uses the classifieds to sell it. The Classifieds Manager dreams of the situation where eager punters are waiting for the paper to appear so they can be the first to apply for the job, bid for the second-hand car etc. In big cities, where the evening paper may have several editions starting at around 11 or 12 noon, the first edition is likely to be bought either by people chasing jobs or flats or by gamblers checking the afternoon racing.

Advertising features

Part way between advertising and editorial copy is the advertising feature or 'advertorial'. This material is designed to attract advertising directly. The newspaper produces a general article, usually with an aim of giving information about a particular topic, and invites businesses with some link to the topic to advertise on a special deal basis. There are a number of standard ploys. For instance, when a new restaurant opens or is refurbished, a piece may be written about the opening and advertisements sought from the drinks suppliers, builders, furnishings suppliers etc. associated with the opening. Most of the parties concerned benefit from the arrangement. The paper sells space. The advertisers get a good deal and a little extra attention because of the focus on the page. The restaurant gets free publicity and even the reader gets useful information in terms of knowledge about a new facility. In order to preserve its ethical position the paper will print 'Advertising Feature' at the head of the piece to signify that what follows is not a news report or a food and drink 'review'. The reader must then accept that the information in the piece, though not factually inaccurate, will not be as objective as in other parts of the paper.

A comprehensive advertising sales and promotion policy

You will have noted that many aspects of selling advertisements are, like the news itself, relatively fixed. Many of the classifieds and even some of the regular display ads are placed week in, week out. However, in order to maintain a high level of ad revenue and to deter competitors (see below), it is important for the paper to be 'selling' space and not just 'renting' it out. In other words the paper must employ people to contact firms and persuade them of the value of advertising. Regular advertising supplements, such as 'education specials' that show group photographs from local schools, ensure that all those featured will buy the paper as a souvenir. They also give an

opportunity for schools outfitters, local newsagents etc. to advertise to parents
and friends.

ACTIVITY 12.2

Developing an ad feature

The advertising feature can be planned well in advance since retailers themselves
recognise certain times of the year when particular shopping needs are paramount.
Christmas, holidays, 'back to school' are obvious subjects for features.

- Draw up a schedule of twelve possible advertising features, one a month
  throughout the year. There are several ideas listed here, but you'll need
  to consider others suitable for less obvious months, such as October or
  March.
- Go to your local library (or direct to the paper itself) and check back to see
  what your local paper actually carried at different times.

The most competitive area of advertising is in the classifieds, and here the
paper must be sure that it is efficient (and accurate) in taking copy, i.e. it
provides a good service to users; but also it must sell new ideas and new deals
to business users of classifieds such as the estate agents and motor dealers.
A new deal such as discounts for long 'runs' over several weeks or for bigger
displays within the classified section can make a dramatic impact. There is
also a 'production constraint' factor.

Selling advertising space

Imagine you are the editor of a local paper and you plan a forty-page issue
with eighteen pages of classifieds. The deadline for copy to go to the printers
arrives and you have all the editorial material sorted out, but you have only
seventeen pages of classified ads. What do you do?

There are a number of options, but you certainly can't leave the page
blank. You can't drop the page because pages are printed in fours, at least.
You could spread the material more widely and lose the space, but this will
mean that you have lost potential revenue. The best move is to phone round
your regular advertisers and offer them lower and lower rates until you
persuade them to buy the remaining space.

Q Can you see any drawbacks in this?

A If you do it too often, the advertisers may start to think you are in some
   kind of trouble – or they may decide to withhold their ads until your
   prices fall.

Selling advertising space (and from the other side buying space – known in the industry as **media buying**) requires specialist knowledge and skills. A whole separate industry has grown up which supports the process, and you can get a good flavour of the business if you read the trade publication *Media Week*, which carries advertisements by newspapers themselves targeting media buyers and presenting information about their circulation figures (usually as audited by ABC) and their reader profile (i.e. the percentage of AB, C1 etc.). You may also come across reports from organisations who log the effectiveness of advertising campaigns in different media. Local newspapers want to show that they offer better value to advertisers, and they may commission research to prove it. This wouldn't normally be done by a single title, but may be undertaken by a newspaper group as a whole. Local reader panels often supplement larger group studies.

See Selling audiences case study.

ACTIVITY 12.3

Market research

Find out how people use your local newspaper. Create a questionnaire designed to address the following issues:

- How long do they spend reading the paper?
- How many people in the household read the paper?
- How long do they keep the paper in the house?
- How reliable and accurate do readers feel local news is compared to national or regional news?
- Why do they read the paper? Why do some people not read it?
- What kind of research findings would be most useful in persuading advertisers that local newspapers offer a good deal? Try to mock up an ad for the group which owns your local newspaper, to appear in *Media Week*.

The nature of media research is such that what may appear insignificant details can be crucial in persuading advertisers. For instance the reader profile may reveal that a particular paper attracts a high proportion of older middle-class people who take expensive holidays.

The saturated media market and advertising spend

The total 'advertising spend' in any locality is probably relatively fixed, i.e. there is a limit to how much businesses or individuals are prepared to spend on advertising at any one time. If a new medium or a new competitor in the same medium comes along, the same spend will be spread further and divided up between a greater number of media products. In 2000–1 regional newspaper advertising revenue rose, but with advertising generally falling (i.e. across all media) there is strong pressure on editors and advertising managers to promote the paper and fend off competitors.

So what competition might a local newspaper be afraid of? The obvious threat is a free newspaper, which in some parts of the country has taken away sufficient advertising business to cause the collapse of a 'paid-for' rival. However, since the same large newspaper groups publish both paid-for and free papers, it is unlikely that this will happen on a wide scale, since groups tend to have a monopoly in many areas and they can manipulate distribution. More problematic is commercial radio, which tends to be owned by non-newspaper media groups. We'll look at the situation in one small town.

Case study 2: A local media market

Keighley is a small town in West Yorkshire with a population in the town and surrounding villages of around 60,000. It is part of the Metropolitan District of Bradford, population upwards of 450,000. The key local newspaper is the weekly *Keighley News* with a circulation of around 16,000 and a 'penetration' in the town of 50 per cent of households. The regular claim of the paper is that 'two out of three local people are readers'.

There is also a local freesheet (20,000 copies midweek) and an evening paper, the *Bradford Telegraph & Argus*, which sells around 50,000 throughout the metropolitan area. Local newspapers are also published, by the same group, in two neighbouring small towns, Ilkley and Skipton which serve distinctive communities with rather different readerships (one more middle-class, the other more likely to live in a rural area).

All of the newspapers in and around Keighley are owned by the same group, Newsquest, now controlled by a major American newspaper and broadcasting group, Gannett. Newsquest is one of the largest UK regional newspaper groups, with interests across the country. This local monopoly means that resources can be shared and activities co-ordinated across the titles in the Bradford group. For example, the *Keighley Target* freesheet is delivered to households on a Wednesday. Editorial material is generally taken from the previous Friday's *Keighley News*, supplemented with a small proportion of updated material.

'Electronic publishing' has developed relatively slowly in the town. At first the paper had its own website, but now it is adminstered via the Newsquest Group and its successful 'This is . . . ' sites. The *Keighley News* contributes to the 'This is . . . Bradford' site.

Telewest operates the cable television franchise in the Bradford area, but at present there is no significant local advertising on a community channel. Yorkshire TV does not target advertising at a local level. The local commercial radio station in Bradford is The Pulse, owned by the Wireless Group headed by *ex-Sun*-editor Kelvin McKenzie. It broadcasts across the whole metropolitan district and tends to compete with the *Telegraph & Argus* in terms of local advertising, with a focus on Bradford.

District	Households	Circulation Jul–Dec 2001	Household Penetration %
Keighley town	16939	8729	51.53
Silsden	11338	3951	34.85
Haworth	5306	1892	35.66
Outside Keighley		1781	
Total		16353	

	Keighley	Silsden
Total pop. 15+	32,310	22,890
Total Readership	22,102	11,179
Men	10,119	4,774
Women	11,983	6,405
Readers per copy (RPC)	2.5	2.8
15–34	7,683	2,910
35–54	7,481	4,073
55+	6,938	4,296
ABC1	8,892	6,093
C2DE	12,210	5,086

Figure 12.3 Circulation and readership details, published by JICREG (Joint Industry Committee for Regional Press Research) and the Newspaper Society for the *Keighley News*, July to December 2001. The table on the left shows circulation in Keighley and its two adjoining districts. The table on the right gives the readership profile for Keighley town and the neighbouring district of Silsden.

Readership details in Figure 12.3 show important features about the population in Keighley and district. It is more working-class than the UK average (in which ABC1 and C2DE groups are roughly equal) and is divided into distinct communities – the town centre and outlying villages. These figures are used by Newsquest to plan development of the title and by potential advertisers to test for suitability in advertising their products.

The range of media products in the town has not changed for several years and, unless advertising revenues increase, a new competitor is unlikely. A local paper is often the main focus for interest in local affairs and as such offers a form of public service – this is another feature of its distribution policy. In maintaining its service to the community, the *Keighley News* will have an interesting problem in catering for both a growing younger population and a growing older population – how will both be targeted?

ACTIVITY 12.4
Find out about the demographics of your local area and the readership
profile of your local paper (go to www.adweb.co.uk). How does it compare
to the *Keighley News*? Does the profile suggest that any particular target
groups will be important for your paper?

Promotion

Advertising is a form of promotion, but there are other ways of increasing
both the circulation of local newspapers and audiences at local cinemas, as
well as persuading businesses to buy advertising space in both media outlets.
There are two ways to do this:

- *nationally*, through the support of trade organisations – if you go to the
  Newspaper Society's website at www.newspapersoc.org.uk you can
  download a Powerpoint presentation arguing why local papers are the best
  place to advertise.
- *locally*, through making sure that all local residents are constantly
  reminded of the importance of their local paper and cinema.
  One of the best ways to promote one medium is to use another:
- Host a local website.
- Use poster displays in the local area.
- Advertise in local tourist literature.
- Make sure the newspaper office or radio station has an attractive public
  display window or reception area – newspapers attract attention through
  local photographs in the window.
- Make links with schools, colleges (a 'young journalists' column or
  supplement in the paper).
- Utilise the 'point of sale' – provide newsagents with advertising boards or
  shop signs showing the newspaper title.

Newspapers and cinemas can form close relationships through 'entertainment
supplements' and specific promotions such as competitions, preview
screenings etc. (newspaper vouchers swapped for free cinema tickets). Radio
stations and cinemas will also consider cross-promotion, but radio and
newspapers are more likely to be competitive. Radio stations organise
'roadshows' and a presence at local events (summer shows etc.).

ACTIVITY 12.5

Survey the promotional activities of your local media outlets: newspaper, radio and cinema. Which of the strategies listed above do they use? Do they use any other ideas? How much do they compete with each other and how much do they co-operate?

References and further reading

Office of Fair Trading (2002) *Review of Undertakings Given by Newspaper Wholesalers*, consultation paper (see www.oft.gov.uk).

The most useful source is the spread of local newspapers in your area, and, if possible, some contact with the people who produce them.

Most text books and manuals are geared more towards the national press:

Keeble, Richard (2001, 3rd edition) *The Newspapers Handbook*, London: Routledge.

Franklin, Bob and Murphy, David (1998) *Making the Local News: Local Journalism in Context*, London: Routledge, in particular the opening essay by Franklin and Murphy: 'Changing times: local newspapers, technology and markets'.

Websites

www.adweb.co.uk

www.carltonscreen.com

www.newspapersoc.org.uk

These two sites are linked and through their menus: you can find out everything you need to know about the regional press in the UK.

www.pearlanddean.com

Invaluable source of information and ideas about cinema advertising and distribution.

www.rab.co.uk

Radio industry advertising site.

CASE STUDY: THE BRITISH FILM INDUSTRY

- Institution: what is a British film?
- British film culture
- British film-makers and film-making traditions

This case study allows us to apply some of the ideas developed in a wide range of chapters to a definable media operation – making 'British films'. It appears here alongside Distribution, Production Organisation and Production Techniques, but it might also be a case study of Institutions and Industries or Globalisation.

The British film industry is widely discussed in the UK press, often in terms of 'boom' or 'bust', characterised by the success of a single film on Oscar night or the revelation that so many 'publicly funded' British films have never even been released to cinemas. More intriguing are these two comments:

- The French New Wave director François Truffaut famously said that the terms 'British' and 'cinema' just didn't go together. Behind this statement is the generally accurate observation that there is an impoverished film culture in the UK – film is not treated seriously as an art form.
- A complaint by many British film-makers is that there is no UK 'industry' as such (i.e. compared to Hollywood). Film-making is a 'practice' with very little structure and no sense of continuity – it is more like a series of cottage industries.

And yet, the British film industry retains an importance in the global media economy. In terms of both the number of films produced and the size of the cinema audience, Britain may lag behind India and France, but London is in many ways the capital of the 'international film industry' ('international' = outside North America), and successful British films sell very well around the world. These contradictions stem in the most part from the relationship between British film production and the Hollywood studio majors. Sharing a language with the most successful international film industry is both a blessing and a curse.

Since the 1920s, when the Hollywood studios became established as the dominant force in cinema across the world, they have been active in the UK, making films in their own or rented studio facilities, distributing American (and some British) films and sometimes building cinemas to ensure that the films are shown. At the same time, the studios have lured British talent – actors, writers, directors, cinematographers etc. – across the Atlantic to Hollywood itself. Audiences have colluded in this process. By the 1930s it was obvious that working-class audiences in particular preferred American to British films. There have been periods when 'home-grown' British films have done particularly well at the box office, but the long-term bias is firmly in favour of Hollywood. In recent years the domination has been almost total. In 1999, 60 per cent of all UK admissions were to purely American films and a further 27 per cent were for joint US/UK productions.

In practice, it is difficult to distinguish between 'British' and 'American' film-making. Consider some of the biggest 'British' films of recent years: *The Full Monty* (1997), *Notting Hill* (1999), *Billy Elliot* (2000). All of these films benefited from Hollywood money – crucially they were all distributed by the Hollywood studios, as if they were American films. For the record, *The Full Monty* was technically an American film, financed directly by Fox Searchlight, one of the film divisions of Rupert Murdoch's News Corporation. *Notting Hill* was originally a production supported by the European 'major' distributor, Polygram, but that company was then sold to the American major, Universal. *Billy Elliot* counts as a genuinely 'British film', but it was distributed by the largest Hollywood distributor in Europe, UIP.

ACTIVITY 12.6

Think of any British films you have seen recently. How has sharing a language with Hollywood helped or hindered the success of your selected films?

Institution: what is a British film?

It seems reasonable then to ask the question, 'What is a British film?' This isn't just an academic question. In the UK as in the rest of Europe and elsewhere, governments are aware of the need to support 'indigenous production' for economic, social and cultural reasons and they may subsidise 'British'

production. The total 'spend' on films by consumers in the UK is around £3 billion. (Most is spent on satellite and cable film channels, followed by video retail, cinema tickets and finally video rental.) Every time you go to a Warner Bros cinema to see a George Clooney film, most of the £10–12 spent on ticket and popcorn etc. finds its way back to Burbank, California. Fortunately, Warner Bros may then spend some of that money making the next George Clooney film in the UK. Overall, the British film industry does not have such a disastrous effect upon the balance of payments as those in some other European countries and, with the television industry, which has tended to be a 'net earner' for Britain, film and television production roughly breaks even in the UK (i.e. imports of TV balance exports).

In an attempt to untangle the different ways in which a film may be 'British', the British Film Institute in its annual *Handbook* has suggested five categories.

Categories of 'British film'

Category A

Cultural and financial impetus and the majority of personnel from the UK. The largest group of British films (forty-seven in 1999), but most with very small budgets by Hollywood standards (an average of £2.24 million in 1999). These films are 'purely British'.

Category B

Majority UK co-production. UK cultural content, significant UK personnel and finance but foreign partners. Such co-productions have been common in Europe since the 1950s, but British companies were much slower in finding foreign partners. Sixteen films in 1999 with an average budget of £4.2 million (boosted by the £15 million spent on Sally Potter's *The Man Who Cried*).

Category C

Minority UK co-production. Foreign (non-US) films with a small UK involvement in finance or personnel. The obverse of Category B, twelve films in 1999 with an average budget of £3.94 million, boosted by $13.94 million spent on the Dutch/German children's film *The Little Vampire*.

Category D

American-financed or part-financed films made in the UK. Most titles have UK cultural content. This category comprises the films that belong to the tradition of 'Hollywood in Europe'. Some are relatively 'small' films, perhaps with promising directors or arthouse credentials, in which the studios invest. Others are blockbusters intended for US and international multiplex distribution. In 1999 there were twenty-three of these films with an average budget of £13.95 million. Again, this figure is distorted by two very high budget films, *Gladiator* at £92 million and *The World Is Not Enough* at £50 million. All but one of the American-backed films had a budget above that of the average of Category A.

Category E
American films made outside the UK, but in which

there is a minority UK financial involvement. In 1999 there were only two such films with an average budget of £4.24 million. Some British companies have been successful in what is essentially the American market. The Coen brothers' films, such as *The Big Lebowski* (1997), culturally a completely American film, have benefited from this kind of investment.

Funding issues

It is clear from the BFI breakdown that 'wholly British' films have the lowest budgets. In itself, this is not necessarily a 'bad thing'. Some of the films made in this category have been highly praised and have had relatively successful international distribution. But this is likely to happen only if they are picked up by a Hollywood distributor. Most of the films made in this category fail to find a release at all. In 1999, of all the British films (i.e. all five categories, one hundred films), only 22 per cent received a 'wide release' (on thirty prints or more); 22 per cent more received a 'limited release' (i.e. a handful of prints went out to art cinemas), but the remainder were unreleased in 1999. Even a year later, over a third of the films made in 1999 had failed to get a release – most of these were 'wholly British' films from Category A.

The financial dilemma

British film-makers face a number of problems in deciding what kinds of films to make. Most of these are problems associated with the size of the UK market compared to the American market. In simple terms, should film-makers aim to produce films for the UK market alone, or should they go for America and the international market? This question, which has faced the British industry since the 1920s, is in fact extremely difficult to answer. Throughout the history of the British cinema, the success of occasional British films abroad has tempted producers to go for the big

market. Invariably, they have been unable to sustain this policy for long, and many production companies have overreached themselves and collapsed. This is as true now as for previous decades. Why is the decision so difficult?

Budgets

We've seen from the *BFI Handbook* categories that budgets vary.

Average budget for Category A, 'wholly British film'	£2.24 million
Promotional spend on the film (estimate)	£0.01 million
	Total £2.25 million

Average budget of a mainstream Hollywood film	£36 million
Promotional spend (in the UK, following massive US spend)	£1 million
	Total £37 million

There is clearly a huge gulf between these figures. Any UK producer aiming for a large budget from UK sources alone is unlikely to be able to raise much more than £5 million. To compete with Hollywood probably means gaining access to American money and partnership with a Hollywood studio. Sample budgets for UK films made in 1999:

Kevin and Perry Go Large (Category A)	£4 million
The Beach (Category D)	£23.50 million

What does the 'Hollywood' budget pay for?

- *stars* – a major Hollywood star adds several million pounds to the budget, but also attracts the audience. Leonardo DiCaprio certainly boosted the costs of *The Beach*.
- *script development funding* – Hollywood spends as much on getting the script right as British films spend on the whole production
- *shooting time* and the possibility for reshoots
- *elaborate camerawork* (cranes, helicopter shots etc.) and stunt work
- *digital effects*
- *music rights* to popular songs.

All these factors 'show' on the screen: they help create the exciting gloss of a Hollywood production. British films can't compete on this level, unless there is a 'major' British studio capable of spending (and risking losing) around £200 million per year (i.e. making ten films at £20 million each). Consistent studio production hasn't been possible since the 1960s. (Film-making in the UK is relatively expensive compared to new studios in Australia etc. – another factor working against UK producers.)

So, the choices for British producers are:

- Make low-budget films targeted at mainstream British audiences, hoping that the 'peculiarly British' subject matter will attract overseas audiences who will see the films as 'unusual'.
- Make low-budget films for a niche 'arthouse audience' in the UK and abroad.
- Look for partners in Europe and/or America and aim more clearly for an 'international audience' with a 'medium-budget' film.

If the last option is selected, a further dilemma arises. Should the film remain 'British' and be 'true to itself', or should it take out difficult British features such as local accents and dialects, politics and cultural pursuits (audiences in America are unlikely to respond to stories about football or cricket, for example)?

The German connection: Road Movies

In the UK, it has been unusual for film directors to set up their own production companies, but in Europe this is not the case. Road Movies is a German company set up in 1976 by the director Wim Wenders (one of the major directors of the 'New German Cinema' of the 1970s) and two partners. Over twenty-five years, the company has continued to produce Wenders's films, but has also formed alliances with UK producers such as Parallax, best known as Ken Loach's producers, and Spanish company Tumasol. Road Movies has provided continuity for Parallax, co-producing Loach's films such as *Land and Freedom* (1995), *Carla's Song* (1997), *My Name Is Joe* (1998) and *Bread and Roses* (2000). This continuity has enabled Loach to keep on making films at slightly above the UK average budget without having to look for new partners each time. (Road Movies presence makes it easier for other partners to come on board.)

ACTIVITY 12.7

Using the Internet Movie Database, check the production details of recent films directed by Ken Loach. Look specifically at *Bread and Roses*. How many partners are needed for Parallax and Road Movies and how many different 'national industries' are involved in this 'British' film, set in Los Angeles?

The recent history of British films is littered with failed attempts to work within these options or to break out. There have also been some conspicuous successes.

Iris

Iris is an example of a particular kind of British film that provides an interesting case study in setting up a production:

- The subject matter (the early career and later physical decline of the famous novelist and philosopher Iris Murdoch) does not obviously appeal to the mainstream audience
  but
- There is certainly a niche audience for a story featuring a literary 'giant'.
- The 'property' (a memoir written by Iris Murdoch's husband) had already been widely discussed in the UK broadsheets.
- The project was 'fronted' by the noted UK theatre director and film-maker Richard Eyre.

Writing in the *Guardian* of 12 January 2002, as the film was about to be released in the UK, Eyre traced the development of the production.

March 1999: Eyre meets Judi Dench, already pencilled in for the starring role, and learns about the project which is being set up by the Hollywood studio Sony, with a proposed budget of $20 million (about £15 million) as a 'mainstream movie'. He lobbies his contacts to 'get him on board'.

November 1999: Eyre is offered the director's role and is asked to write the film as well. He accepts, but later contracts another writer to work with him. He also finds a producer.

May 2000: A script is completed and delivered to Sony, who find it too complicated.

June 2000: A revised script is delivered. Sony like it.

July 2000: Sony have decided to move the project from their mainstream studio to Sony Classics (their 'independent arm') and the budget is cut in half. Eventually it becomes clear that Sony will actually only put up $5 million. Another partner is needed. Channel 4 think the story is too 'old-fashioned', but the BBC are keen.

August 2000: Sony put the project into 'turnaround' – they will sell it to Eyre for $238,000 (i.e. the rights to the property). He must look for other partners and he teams up with a noted independent Hollywood producer, Scott Rudin. At first Paramount seem interested, but they drop out. Through his agent, Eyre contacts Mirage films, the production company set up by UK writer and director Anthony Minghella and Hollywood producer and director Sydney Pollack. A package is put together which includes the BBC (to take UK rights), Miramax (North America) and Intermedia, the Germany/US/UK film financers (the rest of the world). The budget is now nearer $7 million. This means:

- The film is being financed on the 'advance payments' for the three distribution territories.
- There are now six 'executive' producers representing the backers as well as the original two producers – decision-making may become more difficult.
- Some scenes that were to be shot abroad will have to return to the UK, where production will be dependent on the weather as well as the availablity of actors (e.g. Judi Dench, who is working on several big-budget films at the same time) – scheduling the production will be difficult.

December 2000: The script is up to draft ten, the budget has fallen further to $6 million – this means only thirty-nine days shooting, very tight for a film of this type. Shooting has been put off – the project has not yet got the final 'green light' – but Jim Broadbent has been signed and Kate Winslet is also being lined up.

February 2001: Pre-production begins at Pinewood studios. Next door is the *Tomb Raider* production that has been shooting for three months and has a budget ten times bigger than Eyre's.

April 2001: 'Principal photography' finally begins. Eyre comments that the film has had a 'charmed life' – only a year has elapsed since the first script was written.

May 2001: Shooting completed on time, the film goes into post-production.

December 2001: With the budget all gone, the editing has to stop even though there are more suggestions for changes. The film premieres in New York to ensure that it can be considered for Oscar and other award nominations (Miramax is famous for its Oscar campaigns).

January 2002: *Iris* opens in the UK. It is finally released by Buena Vista International, the distribution arm of Miramax's parent, Disney. (Miramax bought the rights from the BBC when it saw that the film would do well.) There are generally good reviews and box-office returns from a 'platform release' of eighty-four screens, mostly in London and the South (only one screen across the whole of the North of England). In America the film has only had a very limited release but Dench, Broadbent and Winslet are all nominated for a Golden Globe and Broadbent wins as Best Supporting Actor. All three are also nominated for Oscars and again Broadbent wins.

Iris is not a 'mainstream film' but in British terms it has an above-average budget and a 'star line-up'. From Richard Eyre's account, a number of points are worth commenting on:

- The time from Eyre's appointment as writer and director to the premiere of the finished film is two years. Of this, only thirty-nine days are actually spent shooting – this is not untypical of film production.
- Eyre's 'network' of contacts in the UK and US was essential to the project.
- The 'talent' in front of the camera and Eyre himself are well-known and could demand bigger fees, but they all take 'deferred payments', meaning that they will receive very little 'up front' and must wait to see whether the film makes a profit (this may be several years away).
- There is no sense of a production unit as such in Eyre's account. Meetings take place in his house or in hotels. Pinewood is rented when needed; the crew are freelances.

Is *Iris* a 'British' film? Most sources list it as a UK/US production, which means that under the BFI categories it will probably be listed as Category D, because of the Miramax involvement. This is slightly odd because it places *Iris* in the same category as *Sleepy Hollow* (also produced by Scott Rudin, for Paramount), a film most audiences would think of as 'American'.

By the time of the Oscar ceremonies in 2002, *Iris* had earned $5 million in the UK and $3 million in the US, where figures were holding up very well. A possible worldwide total of $14 million and a healthy afterlife on video means that it will be a modest success.

Government intervention in funding and support

There is a long history of government intervention in film production in the UK. Traditionally this has been in the form of small-scale investment funds for commercial film-making and funding for art or 'cultural' cinema in which the grant is a much larger proportion of the budget. By the late 1990s, there was a general recognition that public funding needed a rethink, and the new Labour government in 1997 promised to be more 'film-friendly'. As well as moneys distributed by the BFI and the Arts Councils of England, Scotland, Wales and Northern Ireland, Lottery money was awarded to three private production companies – the Film Consortium, DNA Films and Pathé Pictures – in the form of a 'franchise'. They were able to put up to £2 million towards the budget of several different films.

The Film Council was set up in 2000 to re-organise government support for the British film industry and British film culture and to oversee the use of National Lottery funds in film production. It has set up three separate funds. The Premiere Fund invests money in commercial British films with the intention of helping to create a viable production sector. The New Cinema Fund has a 'cultural' aim in supporting 'edgier' small-scale film-making. The Development Fund addresses the fundamental UK problem of poor script development by providing some money in the early stages of script preparation. (Finance in the film industry means that investment money doesn't usually start to be paid out until production actually starts.)

The Film Council is working against a background of mistrust. Support for film production is an investment and, if a film is commercially successful, the funders expect eventually to collect returns on that investment. In the most optimistic scenario, the commercial success of Lottery-funded films would help to pay for the more experimental work. Film financing is very complicated and it can take several years for the accountants to agree on profit or loss. The Lottery investors are first in line to get their money back, but even so only a handful (six out of 250 films according to the *BFI Film and Television Handbook 2002*) of Lottery-funded films since 1995 have been able to pay back Lottery funds with box-office receipts.

Given the high level of criticism in the press, the Film Council has announced that future funding would be on a more 'business-like' basis. One of the first films to receive Film Council funding, *Gosford Park* (2001), has indeed been a commercial success. But this prompts the question – how should public money be spent? A cultural project might be acceptable if public money ensured that certain kinds of 'cultural', 'art' films were produced, especially if they helped new talents to emerge and gain experience. But what would be the point in putting public money into a venture which, if it was an obviously 'commercial' project, would find American or European private funding anyway? The answer is that it might help to build the

infrastructure of the industry by encouraging production – unfortunately, the level of production is not the main issue. Remember, the majority of films made in Britain are not seen by the mass audience.

Distribution

The real problem for British films is not finding the money to make them, especially the low-budget films. The problem is to get them shown. Hollywood films are always going to take precedence in the multiplex. Many multiplexes are owned by Hollywood studios, but even in European-owned chains such as Odeon, UGC and Cineworld, the promotional support given to its films by the American distributor means that American films are always going to attract big audiences. The money spent on promoting Hollywood releases in the UK (£1 million plus for big films) is way beyond the financial resources of British distributors. (See Chapter 12.)

There is a link between funding and distribution in the sense that a British 'studio' with enough clout to fund a string of 'medium-budget' films would also be likely to have some clout as a distributor. This was certainly the case with Polygram (a Dutch-owned company with a film division largely based in the UK). At the time of its takeover by Universal in 1999 (which was more to do with the music interests of its parent company than with film as such) Polygram was in the process of setting up in North America as a 'mini-major' and had competed successfully with the Hollywood majors in the UK (one of Polygram's big successes was the distribution of *Trainspotting* in 1996). Before Polygram, two smaller companies, Goldcrest in the 1970s and Palace Pictures in the 1980s, had failed to 'stay the course'. The last time British studios had effectively competed was in the 1950s when ABPC and Rank (the owners respectively of the ABC and Odeon cinema chains) and the independent British Lion had successfully run Elstree, Pinewood and Shepperton studios and acted as major distributors.

Ancillary markets

Revenues generated by feature films are not confined to the UK and North American box office. Significant revenues can be earned also in other cinema markets, especially in Europe. Unfortunately, European film industries do not publish box-office information in quite the same way as the industries in the UK and North America. Therefore it is difficult to research the success of British films in Europe. For the more high-profile films, however, it is evident that UK films can earn as much revenue in France, Germany, Spain and Italy as in their 'home' market or even more. This explains why several British companies regularly enter co-productions with European partners.

As an EU member nation, the UK stands to benefit from substantial European funding for 'audio-visual' productions. However, it is fair to say that the British film industry overall still tends to look towards Hollywood rather than Europe as potential partners. This may change now that one Hollywood major, Universal, is owned by a French company (Vivendi).

The majority of the money earned by many UK films comes from television broadcasts (satellite, cable and terrestrial) and from the video market (although, again, poor distribution on video limits this potential). Television has always been a strong sector for UK audiences, and without television support, especially from Channel 4 and its commitment to making films, the British industry might well have died in the 1980s. BBC Films has also become important as a producer since the mid-1990s.

Summary of industry characteristics

The important characteristics of the British film industry at the start of the twenty-first century are:

- a home market that is not large enough to allow 'large'- or even 'medium'-budget films to make a profit in the UK alone
- the lack of any significant UK producing or distributing 'studio' on the American model

- statutory support for British film via the Film Council
- an uneasy relationship with European producers and European funding for production and distribution
- a disproportionate share of UK production, distribution and exhibition controlled by the Hollywood majors
- the importance of UK television channels in supporting film production, notably Channel 4 and the BBC, but also Granada and BSkyB.

British film culture

The audience for British films has an important influence on the kinds of films that are made. Historically, British audiences have behaved in ways quite different from audiences in Europe, and to a certain extent in North America. At the high point of cinema attendance in the UK in the late 1940s, Britain had larger audiences than anywhere else in Europe. This was also a period when British films performed reasonably well against Hollywood competition. By the late 1950s the mass audience was moving over to

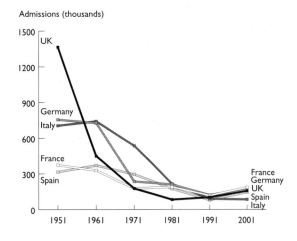

Figure 12.4 Cinema audiences in the five main European markets from 1951 to 2001, showing the massive declines for the UK and Germany and the relative stability of France (source: *Encyclopedia of European Cinema* (1995), ed. Ginette Vincendeau, London: Cassell; and *Screen International*, 1 March 2002).

television at a great pace at a time when audiences in France, Germany and Italy were still growing or were at least stable. Television became more important in people's lives in the UK and cinema took something of a back seat from the 1970s onwards.

Compared to a country such as France, film culture is not highly developed in the UK and, in particular, the idea of film as an 'art form' is not widely endorsed. This may seem a surprising statement in a country where Film and Media Studies are rapidly growing academic disciplines, but there are several important indicators:

- It is more difficult to persuade funders of the importance of 'cultural film' rather than straight 'commercial film' in the UK. (The Film Council is responsible for both 'industry' and 'film culture'.)
- The range of different kinds of films released in the UK is narrow by international standards.
- There are proportionately fewer 'independent cinemas' showing non-Hollywood films in the UK compared to other European countries.
- Foreign-language films perform less well at the UK box office than elsewhere in Europe, where both dubbing and subtitling are more readily accepted.
- Certain internationally respected British film-makers (e.g. Ken Loach, Mike Leigh) often earn more from overseas box offices than from the UK.
- There is currently no 'serious' programme on UK television dealing regularly and exclusively with film as an art form.

In this climate, it is perhaps not surprising that many UK film-makers either attempt to make Hollywood-style films in the UK or move to Hollywood themselves. Unless the British film audience becomes more aware of a wider film culture, it will remain difficult for British filmmakers to get innovative films into cinemas. 'Film education' is crucial to the future of the British film industry.

The current UK audience figures are rising, but this is mostly benefiting multiplexes showing Hollywood products. Overall, people in the UK still go to the cinema less frequently than in many other countries. In Ireland, for instance, the frequency rate has reached four times a year for every individual. In the UK the figure is rising but has not yet reached three visits to the cinema each year (2001 estimates based on admissions of 156 million and population aged four-plus of 55 million). Cultural factors can be summarised as follows:

- relatively low status of film within British culture, especially compared with most of the rest of Europe
- an 'undeveloped' UK audience in terms of interest in a diversity of film
- a weak distribution sector
- an exhibition sector which is still relatively 'underscreened' and therefore returns a very high 'per screen revenue' compared to most other territories (but also suffers from high land rents)
- an audience which attends cinema screenings less frequently than in most other English-speaking countries.

British film-makers and film-making traditions

The creative talent employed by the British film industry faces a number of constraints and 'institutional factors' that influence how films are made. Some of these derive from the cultural factors outlined above and the low status of film in British culture generally.

For example, theatre and television are relatively highly regarded in the UK compared to film. British actors are far more likely to be trained for the theatre than for film, and British writers are likely to gain more prestige from writing a successful television drama series than from scripting a successful film. As a consequence, it might be argued that it is more difficult to produce the kinds of film stars who grace Hollywood films or to develop a professional film scriptwriting industry along Hollywood lines. Familiar arguments about British cinema that might arise from the theatre background are:

- British films are more 'talky' and less at ease with dynamic movement.
- The acting is less fluid and spontaneous than in Hollywood.

These are quite old arguments and may be out of date in the twenty-first century – what do you think?

Having theatre and television as cultural resources for film production is not necessarily a bad thing, and UK theatre directors were at the helm of two high-profile films *American Beauty* (US 1999, director Sam Mendes) and *Billy Elliot* (UK 2000, director Stephen Daldry). In both cases, veteran cinematographers, Conrad Hall and Brian Tufano respectively, must have had a great deal to do with the look of each film. The theatrical background obviously helped with the excellent performances given by the actors, but it would be possible to mount an argument about how other aspects of the film narrative were handled. (*Billy Elliot* also had a first-time scriptwriter, the award-winning radio writer Lee Hall).

British films are perhaps more likely to be produced with this kind of 'imported' talent because of the relatively small number of graduates from the National Film School and the difficulties they face in getting a first job. Again, by comparison, American and French film schools produce more graduates who appear to get more opportunities. 'Training' for the film industry was almost non-existent (crafts were learnt 'on the job' – a job obtained often through nepotism or working up from being a 'runner') before the establishment of the Industry Training Body, Skillset, in the early 1990s. It is now being formalised, but the British industry still has some way to go to match other film industries.

The career route for aspiring film-makers is likely to take them through television or advertising before an opening in film becomes available. It is also likely that many British films will be made with funding from television companies with a view to a television screening soon after the theatrical release. This strong television and advertising link has led to two charges about the effects on British film:

- The scale and 'look' of British films is often 'televisual' rather than cinematic.
- Directors trained in advertising are more likely to produce 'glossy' and stylish films, possibly devoid of substance.

You will notice that these charges are to some extent contradictory – are British films visually dull or too frenetically busy? The charges are certainly worth investigating – might it be true that Ridley Scott's art school and advertising background is evident in his films? Tony Scott, Hugh Hudson, Adrian Lyne and Alan Parker all emerged from UK advertising in the 1970s and gravitated towards Hollywood. Below we look at Jonathan Glazer, another recruit with an advertising background but also with music video experience (a more recent source of directorial talent, given the strength of the UK music industry). Note also that two of the most 'cinematic' of British directors, Danny Boyle (*Trainspotting*, *The Beach*) and Michael Winterbottom (*Welcome to Sarajevo*, *Wonderland*), both came out of television.

Realism

One of the major factors in both the production of British films and their reception by audiences and critics is the legacy of 'realism'. (See Chapter 17.) The 'British documentary movement' of the 1930s and 1940s was the first significant British film movement to be recognised by critics outside Britain. Documentary gave the British film industry prestige, and this was further boosted during and just after the Second World War when British feature films learnt from the documentarists how to shoot on location and how to use 'authentic' props and costumes etc. Later, in the late 1950s, the industry went further and used more realist dialogue (and a wider range of actors). Since then 'British realism' has become associated with two types of films:

- *'costume' or 'period' films* displaying a very high level of 'authentic detail' – e.g. films based on nineteenth-century 'classic novels' or more modern novels about the 1930s and 1940s. This is an issue of 'surface realism', recreating period detail, and is recognised by some audiences as a mark of 'quality'.

- *'social realist' films* dealing with recognisable social problems, filmed in 'real' locations, often using some form of 'documentary style' camera and an avoidance of any notions of 'glamour' or false 'prettiness'.

To many older and more middle-class audiences, and certainly for many audiences overseas, these two types of films are what British cinema is all about. The approaches are epitomised for these audiences by the period adaptations of Merchant–Ivory productions and films such as *Brassed Off* (1996) or *Billy Elliot* which use social realism as part of a mix of elements.

Such recognition perhaps works in the opposite way for UK working-class audiences (who usually prefer Hollywood films). They may well steer clear of both period films and social realism. Nevertheless, 'popular British films' such as gangster and comedy films may still be influenced by a general British feeling for realist detail, and it is certainly true that determinedly 'fantastic' or expressionist film-makers in the UK, such as Terry Gilliam or Sally Potter, have had to work harder to gain critical acclaim. In one sense, the critical support for realism alone could be seen as a reflection of a narrow film culture.

British film scholarship has attempted to counter the critics' reliance on realism. Work on *Carry On* films and Hammer horror from the 1950s and 1960s is evidence of a recognition of the commercial success of these series and the ways in which they utilised traditional British genre forms on low budgets. Scholarship has perhaps been less successful in increasing the profile of contemporary British directors who take risks in developing new aesthetics for British films. Let's try to draw together some of these points in a brief look at three instances of British film-making.

Mainstream UK film-making

We've noted that the most commercially successful British films are the Category D films which see a major (Hollywood) studio offering financial support way above the usual UK budget. Four of the biggest domestic and international successes share a very similar production background. In 1993 *Four Weddings and a Funeral* was produced by Polygram (the film division of then Dutch media conglomerate Philips) with Channel 4 and Working Title, the UK production company headed by Tim Bevan and Eric Fellner. Working with only the average UK budget of the time of £2 million, the creative team produced a film that made over £200 million worldwide. In 1996 Working Title and Polygram, this time with UK independent, Tiger Aspect, spent considerably more money (£16.2 million) on sending Rowan Atkinson to America in *Bean*. Again worldwide box office topped £200 million. The trick was repeated with *Notting Hill* in 1999 and *Bridget Jones' Diary* in 2001, but by this time Polygram had been bought by Universal.

Bevan and Fellner are two of the most powerful men in the British film industry, but they are also Hollywood 'players' since Working Title is closely tied in to Universal. The films listed above are just the highest-profile titles in their portfolio (the 'low-budget' brand WT[2] produced *Billy Elliot*). They have worked consistently with a group of creative talents – the four films above were all scripted by Richard Curtis – but it is noticeable that they aim for the international rather than UK (or, indeed, American) market. In terms of British film culture, it is their smaller titles, including those from director Stephen Frears, that are perhaps more significant. Their most adventurous partnerships tend to be with the Coen brothers on resolutely American projects.

Working Title have succeeded in maintaining output where other UK production companies have failed. Arguably, this is because they have sheltered within the embrace of a major studio and applied Hollywood production methods: 'It's extraordinary to

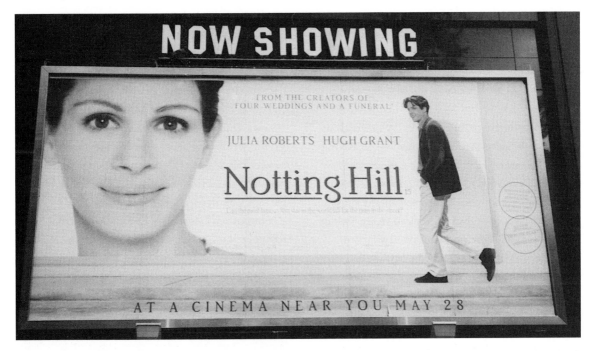

Figure 12.5a The poster for *Notting Hill* (UK 1999) on the wall of the Odeon Leicester Square during its opening run.

Figure 12.5b Tourists in Leicester Square outside the Odeon – the 'shop window' of British cinema.

all their films have been hits, but so far they have been able to 'cross-subsidise' hits and misses. In 2001 their biggest budget film so far, *Captain Correlli's Mandolin*, was less than successful, so caution and modest budgets remain important.

ACTIVITY 12.8

Research Working Title and the careers of Tim Bevan and Eric Fellner. What else can you learn from the long list of titles they have produced? To what extent does the list suggest that they have been crucial to a sense of the British film industry since the late 1980s – or are they more like an international film company that just happens to be based in London?

walk into a British film company on Oxford Street . . . and it's run with complete L.A. efficiency, instead of it being a bunch of ex-BBC, very nice amateurs' (Hugh Grant quoted in *Premiere* magazine, March 2001). Not

A British auteur

Few British film directors seek to emulate the auteurs of European art cinema and to try to make films in a distinctive style. Ironically, Michael Winterbottom our second example, learnt his trade in British television, directing on Granada TV's crime series *Cracker* and Roddy Doyle's Dublin drama *The Family* (1994), but he also made television documentaries, including one on the Swedish art cinema director Ingmar Bergman.

When he began to make features, Winterbottom made two decisions that were unusual for an aspiring British film-maker. First, he formed a production company, Revolution Films, with Andrew Eaton and, second, he set out to make uncompromising films, often with distinctive visual (and aural) styles. Two of Winterbottom's highest-profile films saw him re-invent the idea of a British costume film in *Jude* (1996) and explore the emotions of television reporters in Bosnia in *Welcome to Sarajevo* (1997).

In 1999 *Wonderland* offered a conventional drama about a working-class family in South London, but presented in an unusual way. Shot on film, but often hand-held with only 'available light', the visual style of the film nodded towards both the DOGME approach (see Chapter 17) and the highly stylised work of Hong Kong director Wong Kar-Wai and Australian cinematographer Christopher Doyle. Equally unusual was the decision to shoot in a Soho bar and café during 'normal' hours – i.e. not taking over the location. The actors used radio microphones and the camera picked them out in crowded locations. The resulting 'look' and 'sound' of *Wonderland* produced one of the most distinctive and compelling representations of London life that British cinema has ever produced. But this was not recognised by many critics: 'it felt like small-scale television; indeed the washed out, grainy quality of the camerawork sometimes looked like a television picture stretched to breaking-point' (Peter Bradshaw, *Guardian* 15 May 1999). What is so surprising about this comment (and there were others like it) is that the wide CinemaScope compositions, combined with the other elements, produce something completely unlike television. What are British film critics looking at? Outside the UK, Winterbottom is highly regarded –

one of the few British film-makers regularly screened at international festivals. In 2000, *The Claim*, a version of Hardy's *The Mayor of Casterbridge* set in California in the 1860s, became Winterbottom's biggest-budget film, but like the others it received poor distribution and made very little money, despite some very good reviews. *The Claim* is another film in which Winterbottom and his collaborators strove hard to rework our images of the western and the costume film. A failure at the box office like *The Claim* would perhaps slow down another film-maker, but Winterbottom is seemingly constantly at work – a tribute to the work of his production company colleagues.

Figure 12.6 Steve Coogan and Shirley Henderson in *24 Hour Party People* (UK 2002).

Due out as this book goes into production, *24 Hour Party People* looks as if it may finally bring Winterbottom a hit with its story about the Manchester music scene in the 1970s. Shot by the Dutch cinematographer Robby Müller, well known across European art cinema, and with more innovative sound work, this film may finally allow Winterbottom to receive recognition in the UK. If he was a film-maker in France, Germany or Sweden he would not have to had wait this long. Poorly served by distributors generally, Winterbottom's work is often not available on video or television in its usual CinemaScope format, but *Jude*, *Welcome to Sarajevo* and *The Claim* are now available on DVD. Revolution

Films has also created two of the best websites dedicated to a film's production yet seen:

- www.theclaimmovie.com
- partypeoplethemovie.com

These sites both gave details about the sound recording and camerawork as well as masses of production work detail. The site for *The Claim* was updated daily during the shoot. (The sites may have been removed by the time you read this, but check via the Internet Movie Database at uk.imdb.com.)

Figure 12.7 Jonathan Glazer on the set of *Sexy Beast* (UK 2001).

Distribution is crucial

Revolution films suffer from uncertain distribution, and in our final example, we'll look at a film where the importance of distribution was clearly demonstrated. Jonathan Glazer, who directed *Sexy Beast* in 2000, was already well known as the award-winning director of advertisements, such as the surreal 'The Surfer' and 'The Swimmer' for Guinness, and music videos for Radiohead. His first feature film was a British gangster film starring Ray Winstone as a British crook who has retired to Spain, only to be summoned back for one last job by a Ben Kingsley character who is very hard to refuse.

Following the success of *Lock, Stock and Two Smoking Barrels* (UK 1996) and the subsequent box-office failure of a host of other British gangster films,

the distributors of *Sexy Beast*, Film Four, were cautious about its release. It went out on a platform release in the UK in January 2001 on twenty-seven screens, scoring a high screen average that placed the film in the top fifteen chart. But four weeks later it slid out of the chart after widening to just seventy-two screens. The total UK gross was around £600,000. However, in North America, where the film opened in June, the release was handled very carefully and the film stayed in a small number of cinemas for the next six months, bringing in nearly $7 million and earning an Oscar nomination for Ben Kingsley as Best Supporting Actor and a slew of other awards.

What went wrong in the UK? Perhaps Film Four did not get enough bookings for the film in the first few weeks? Certainly there was excellent 'word of mouth' during the opening, but the film was not on for long enough to benefit. Perhaps too little promotion was put behind the release? Or did Film Four just get cold feet because of the recent poor history of gangster films at the box office? If so, this seems short-sighted. *Sexy Beast* mixes comedy, romance and some surreal sequences with its obvious generic markers. Besides its strong cast, the film also features a strong visual sense and an impressive use of music, with production values well presented by the well-known international producer Jeremy Thomas.

One of the strongest British film debuts in recent years, *Sexy Beast* has been acclaimed around the world, but will probably be known by most British audiences through its high-profile video and DVD release. And that's a shame for a film very much made for the big screen. The story of its release says much about the British film industry.

Further reading

Robert Murphy (ed.) (2000) *British Cinema of the '90s*, London: BFI.

Robert Murphy (ed.) (2001) *The British Cinema Book*, London: BFI.

The *Journal of Popular British Cinema* is an annual 'themed' publication from Flicks Books featuring many of the leading scholars of British Cinema and providing access to current debates. Volume 1 (1998) deals with 'Genre' and Volume 2 (1999) with 'Audience and Reception'. Volume 5 (2002) covers New British Cinema and provides an excellent resource for extending this case study.

The annual *BFI Film and Television Handbook* is invaluable as a reference source. Details about British films can also be found on the British Council films website: www.britfilms.com

Useful website

www.filmcouncil.org.uk

13 Advertising and branding

- Histories of advertising
- Marketing and branding histories
- The influence of advertising
- Case study: The ASA and debates on regulation
- References
- Further reading

To advertise originally meant 'to draw attention to something' or to notify or inform someone of something (Dyer 1982). It is now the media form most often encountered, most of the time – on billboards; on Internet screens; coming unsolicited through the letterbox; commercially funding most of the world's television, newspapers and magazines; and working within and around movies as product placement and tie-in product. Currently it is estimated that in the US alone close to $160 billion a year is spent on advertising (i.e. more than the Gross Domestic Product of any but the richest twenty-three countries). This is funded, of course, by us, the consumers, through the cost of the goods we buy. It is arguably the most powerful and pervasive form of propaganda in the history of the planet – try to avoid all advertising for a single day and you will probably have stayed in bed with all screens and radios turned off. Don Slater has defined its function, along with marketing, as 'the redefinition of market structures and relations (above all, competitive relations) through the . . . cultural redefinition of goods' (1997: 45).

The South African company De Beers sought in 1947 to redefine diamonds, saying they would 'make diamonds a cultural imperative in a woman's life'. Their advertising continues to try to redefine these small rocks in this way.

Yet it is also true that advertisers are now aware of audiences' awareness of their tricks and strategies, and they make endless, self-reflexive play with them, with amusing, enjoyable and often stunning-looking results. Some media theorists emphasise the 'freedom' of readers of ads to interpret them as they choose, or to simply ignore them. Others stress the broader power of brand advertising, as well as the corporate power that makes brands globally prevalent, to shape our deepest imaginings, anxieties and desires – a fascinating area for study, then.

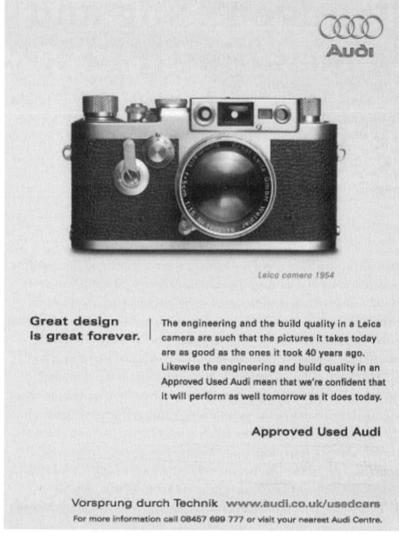

Leica camera 1954

Great design is great forever. The engineering and the build quality in a Leica camera are such that the pictures it takes today are as good as the ones it took 40 years ago. Likewise the engineering and build quality in an Approved Used Audi mean that we're confident that it will perform as well tomorrow as it does today.

Approved Used Audi

Vorsprung durch Technik www.audi.co.uk/usedcars
For more information call 08457 699 777 or visit your nearest Audi Centre.

Figure 13.1 A second-hand car ad. But one where a powerfully branded car, Audi, seeks to associate itself with a product which is so beyond 'second-hand' as to be – a 'classic'.

ACTIVITY 13.1

- How many forms of advertising have you encountered this week?
- Jot down where you encountered them.
- Have you ever advertised? Where: 'free', student or other local paper? Local cable television? The Internet? Postcards in a shop window?

There's a lot of emphasis on big, branded advertisements now. By contrast:

- What is the smallest ad you've ever seen? How would you explain what it seems to be trying to communicate, and to whom?

Advertising has drawn the attention of generations of analysts, especially in work on the effects of mass commercial culture. Often students are fascinated by tales of '**subliminal** ads' as evidence of the sheer power of this media form. But the major objections to advertising have included the following:

- It brainwashes its audience, not with subliminal ads but with base, deceptive promises and appeals, designed to promote consumerist materialism, waste, hedonism (pleasure seeking) and envy.

- It defends itself by arguing that it helps us to be 'rational consumers'. Yet even if this meant assessing all the claims of all the shampoos available (over four hundred at the last count) it would take more time than most people ever have.

- Related to such over-production of certain goods, advertising is part of the built-in drive to '**planned obsolescence**' and high consumption on which modern capitalism depends and which, in the fairly near future, may be fatal to the planet.

- It acts as an unnecessary business expense, which adds significantly to the costs of goods for customers. Large monopolies such as Proctor & Gamble spend millions advertising their own products (such as soap powders) against those of their own subsidiaries.

- For all its 'free market' claims, it produces barriers to competition because young companies cannot afford the expenditure needed to break into markets via the costly work of creating 'brands'. This of course relates directly to the processes known as *distribution* by which some products are made available to us and others are not.

- Its use of glamorous body images leads to ideological conformity, especially around already powerful identities such as the 'approved versions' of gender, class, ethnicity, disability and age differences.

Subliminal advertising associated with hypnosis and said to work by flashing barely perceptible messages to audiences in between frames of a film or advert. Some, very specialised evidence came from the US in the 1950s (flashing images of ice cream during a film were said to have encouraged sales in the interval!) but the myth persisted much longer. See Packard (1979), pp. 41–2.

'Planned obsolescence' phrase made famous by US consumer rights and Green campaigner Ralph Nader (see www.nader.org). In addition to supporting through advertising, the drive to keep up with fashions, manufacturers of certain products (especially cars) are argued deliberately to 'build in' an *avoidance* of lasting for as long as possible, thus encouraging (unnecessary) repeated acts of purchase – as the bodywork rusts etc.

Histories of advertising

Advertising can arguably be found as far back as Greek and Roman public criers, shouting the wares of local traders. But its recognisable modern form appears with the nineteenth-century industrial revolution; the over-production of goods for existing western markets through new manufacturing techniques; and then the drive to expand markets via imperialist conquest across the globe. In the 1850s in Britain, for example, the Prime Minister, Gladstone, removed regulations and taxes on advertising, and manufacturers were able to appeal to consumers over the heads of retailers, through the burgeoning media. In the US, with its huge capitalist economy, potential customers began to be educated (informally, by advertising) into the possibilities and attractions of consumption. You will find that many of the best recent histories of advertising are intimately bound up with analysing processes of distribution and consumer culture.

For many years ads were described as though they operated in trivial and irrational ways, and as though that was why they had a 'brainwashing' effect on women. 'Femininity' is often constructed as being irrational, and bound up with consumption (shopping and the work of the home) not production or 'serious', i.e. paid, work outside the home. But the influence of advertising cannot be understood outside other powerful contexts. In the nineteenth century, real gains and freedoms for women were represented by many new products, both in saving hard, repetitive labour in the home, and in the pleasures of the new shops where they were sold. These were, crucially, safe and pleasant public spaces for women who were often otherwise largely confined to the home. Goods were displayed, usually at fixed prices, in large, attractively laid-out department stores in safe shopping districts ('factories for selling' in Rachel Bowlby's (2000) words, and see also Pumphrey 1984). The attractions were like those of early picture palaces: attention paid to opulent visual display and comfort, with rest rooms, restaurants and polite service – a rare treat for many working-class people.

> Campaigning politics have also been conducted within 'consumption'. The suffrage movement (for votes for women) as well as the anti-slavery movement sometimes organised consumer boycotts and made their own plates, mugs etc. with appropriate colours (green, purple and white for suffrage) or slogans. Selfridges decorated its shop window in these colours for a time.

In step with these developments, by the end of the 1920s US advertisers, consciously or unconsciously, began to try to transform the buying habits of shoppers or consumers (largely women). The success of the US government's **propaganda** during the First World War convinced them that they too could use **social psychology** or **behaviourism**, the name given to research into human motivation and ways of associating (see Packard 1979). *Lifestyle advertising* developed, going beyond a simple outline of a product's uses towards encouraging potential buyers to associate it with a whole desirable style of life, and to feel that not owning the product would lead to personal failure, unpopularity etc. Along with this, the idea of fashion and keeping up with fashion through consuming goods was newly emphasised. This was done partly through the glamour of Hollywood movies and their product placement (see below) but also through the manufacturers' adoption of planned obsolescence for certain products, such as cars (see Packard 1984;

Nader website) which could otherwise easily be made to last a consumer's lifetime.

In the 1920s the positive connotations which fashion gave to change, novelty and youthfulness undermined traditional attitudes which endorsed 'thrift, self-sufficiency, home cooking, family entertainment, hand-made and hand-me-down clothes' (Pumphrey 1984). These traditional attitudes often had oppressive consequences for women, generally the ones expected to do the 'making' and the 'handing down'. The liberating roles of both advertising and the mass consumption of labour-saving goods have been hailed by theorists of consumption. But it is important to hang on to a more critical view of the role of advertising even as we realise the rational grounds for the appeal of many products to us.

For example, advertising in the 1920s (and since) has used *two* major figures for women to adopt as models. The first is the figure of the independent, unmarried *'flapper'*, found in films, magazines and books, offering a challenge to nineteenth-century constructions of femininity on the level of style, image and consumption (rather than in other areas such as political struggles for the vote or equal pay). The second model is the more traditional, though equally constructed, figure of 'the housewife', invited to feel she had sole responsibility for keeping the home and its inhabitants clean and the meals on the table at the right times. Interestingly, this figure too was (and continues to be) set up as 'modern'. Ads, even those encouraging the most paranoid levels of anxiety about 'germs' and 'dirt' in the home, in many ways seemed not to treat their addressees patronisingly. 'The Housewife' was constructed as having a *serious* responsibility (keeping the home clean and safe) and as *democratically* joining 'hundreds of thousands of American women' said to have benefited from this or that product. She was encouraged to think of herself as both a private *and* a public figure, one who was being offered the opportunity to take advantage of modern devices – in other words to be connected with technological and social advances.

As with the flapper though, there are gaps in this image. Why should such labour-saving devices actually mean more work for women, via the much higher standards of cleanliness expected of them? If women's work in the home was so important, why was it not counted or paid as work? Why could not men, or some children, share involvement with this work in the family?

For both these mythical figures, advertisers constructed a kind of *self-surveillance* in which women were repeatedly invited to take part, asking questions about how clean, how safe was their bathroom, kitchen, cutlery or toilet, and how appealing was their hair, skin, figure or personal aroma?

Figure 13.2 The Flapper's 'unencumbered simplified clothing, short hair and boyish figure, rebellious lifestyle and pursuit of pleasure . . . [along with] her hectic social life' (Pumphrey 1984) made her a key cultural figure, though one raising questions: Where does she work? Where does her money come from? What else is she interested in? How does she relate to the 1920s political women's movements?

'Dirt is matter out of place' (Mary Douglas (1996), *Purity and Danger: An Analysis of the Concepts of Pollution and Taboo*, London: Ark.

'The irony is that, as technology has improved, so that it is easier to wash, we insist on washing everything far too often. The increasing number of cases of asthma, allergic reactions . . . may be one side effect of removing all "dirt" from our lives' (Suzanne Moore (2001), *New Statesman*, 13 August: 28).

Of course such images of femininity have implications for dominant versions of masculinity. See Peugeot 607 ad, July 2001, picturing the car with the slogan: 'Now *that's* the man your wife married.'

'A woman . . . is almost continually accompanied by her own image of herself . . . She has to survey everything she is and everything she does because how she appears to others, and ultimately how she appears to men, is of crucial importance for what is . . . thought of as the success of her life' (John Berger (1972), *Ways of Seeing*, Harmondsworth: Penguin).

Figure 13.3 From *Good Housekeeping*: however dated and sombre she looks to us, the 1920s housewife here is being addressed as someone who is: (1) able to understand some scientific terms, and (2) eager to leave the kitchen for the more modern public activities of shopping and 'play'.

Marketing and branding
histories

ACTIVITY 13.2

Look through television ads during programmes which seem scheduled or
'channelled' to attract female audiences (e.g. morning or afternoon television).

- Do you think self-surveillance is still invited? How can you tell?
- How does the camera position viewers in relation to the women in the ads?
- Are there any ads addressing men in ways that encourage self-surveillance?
- How are they similar to or different from those addressing women?
- What kinds of questions are women shown putting to themselves in ads for:
  cosmetics, clothes, household cleaners?
- Are the two kinds of ads significantly different in their use of: fantasy situations,
  irony, wit, playfulness?

Marketing and branding histories

Marketing can be defined as the sum of the ways in which a product is
positioned in its particular market. This includes areas related to distribution
(many marketing courses start with the 'Four Ps: Product, Placement,
Promotion and Price: see Myers 1999) and often, now, to the 'brand' image of
the product or its owners. Advertising or marketing agencies co-ordinate
different kinds of activities, in competition with each other. **Public
Relations or PR** is one set of activities, involving the selling of persons or
companies, using many of same techniques as advertising – competitions, free
offers – but also arranging incidents, 'spontaneous' happenings, dates, even
staged relationships to be reported by the media as news (see the career of
publicist Max Clifford). Video PR companies, for example, may scan their
sales databases for the names of customers for science fiction videos (which in
1997 accounted for only 9 per cent of the total market, but has many 'hard
core' fans). The PR agency may then set up fan clubs for particular films (by
mailing purchasers) which can act as a further publicity mechanism. All of
these activities can overlap with those of the **advertising agencies** who make
ads and manage campaigns, 'placing' or buying space for ads in particular
media.

ACTIVITY 13.3

Companies such as Coca-Cola and Pepsi have their own in-house divisions
dedicated to product placement, including the influencing of scripts (see Wasko
1994). US television shows such as *Sex and the City* seem increasingly blatant
about the way they showcase and name expensive shoes, clothes and other
fashion items.

- Watch for product placement in the next movie or television programme you see.
- What do you think the product owners hoped to get from the placement?

See case study following Chapter 6.

Branding associates certain meanings with products. This will already be familiar to you from work on semiotics, but the economics of branding bring whole new dimensions to that study. At its simplest level branding involves trying to persuade customers of a product's quality prior to purchase or experience by means of the reputation or image of the producing company. Naomi Klein (2000) suggests that the current importance of brands goes back to the mid-1980s when management theorists began to argue that successful corporations must primarily produce brands, as opposed to emphasising their actual products. The partial recession in the US in that decade went hand in hand with the startling success of new kinds of corporation: Microsoft and Nike, and later Tommy Hilfiger and Intel.

> These . . . made the bold claim that producing goods was only an incidental part of their operations, and that thanks to recent victories in trade liberalisation and labor-law reform, they were able to have their products made for them by contractors, many of them overseas. What these companies produced primarily were not things, they said, but *images* of their products. Their real work lay not in manufacturing but in marketing.
>
> (Klein 2000: 4)

> 'Hear'Say is a branding miracle. Within the span of 15 weeks a group of young people has gone from obscurity to performing at the Brit awards, a number one single, an album, launching a line of clothing . . . As their licensing manager admitted, they were marketing the group before they even knew who was going to be in it. The brand came before the product' (Madeleine Bunting (2001), 'Hearts for sale', *Guardian*, 9 April).

Others have summarised this as 'not value for money but values for money'. Klein points out that

> creating a brand calls for a completely different set of tools and materials [from creating products]. It requires an endless parade of brand extensions, continually renewed imagery for marketing, and most of all, fresh new spaces to disseminate the brand's idea of itself.
>
> (Klein 2000: 5)

ADVERTISING AND BRANDING

Marketing and branding histories

What are Gary Lineker and Steve Redgrave doing advertising crisps, when you think about it?
How much fatty fast food like crisps did they eat in the training which produced their, now-branded, reputations?

A key moment came in 1988 when Philip Morris, the tobacco company, purchased Kraft for $12.6 billion – six times the valuation of the company but what Philip Morris were willing to pay for the word 'Kraft'. Great news for the ad world, which could now claim that advertising expenditure was an investment in real equity rather than an unnecessary 'frill' (see Klein 2000: 7–8).

Branding relates closely to the concept of synergy, which refers to

- the combined marketing
- of 'products' (such as 'Britney Spears' or *The Lord of the Rings*)
- across different media and other products (in music, toys, Internet and television programmes, T-shirts, theme park rides and so on)
- which are often owned by the same corporation (such as Time Warner or Disney)
- such that the total effect is greater than the sum of the different parts (see Wasko 2001).

Synergy has been around for some time. Indeed the 'escapism' of entertainment forms is often into worlds which turn out to have very recognisable products in them. Even fantasy forms, such as the James Bond films, have always blended conspicuous consumption, brand-name snobbery and product placement for certain luxury cars, champagnes and watches.

Hollywood and marketing

Early Hollywood movies very soon (there was alarm in England and Germany as early as 1912) were an important arm of American exports and their marketing. Fashions, up-to-the-minute kitchen technology and furnishings were showcased in 'women's films', establishing **tie-ins** with manufacturers. In the mid-1930s sketches of styles to be worn by specific actresses in films were sent to merchandising bureaux, which produced them in time for the film's release, then sold them in Macy's Cinema Fashions Shops, among others (see Branston 2000; Eckert 1990; LaPlace 1987). The cigarette industry regularly lobbied performers to smoke on screen. These tie-in products were controversial as early as the 1920s. By the late 1930s Hollywood occupied a privileged position in the advertising industry. As Tom Dewe Matthews (1998) points out, drawing on the work of Peter Kramer: 'Warners had million dollar contracts with General Electric and General Motors, MGM had a tie-in to Bell telephones as well as to Coca-Cola, Paramount was with Westinghouse and all the studios had links to radio networks like CBS and NBC . . . directors in the

Figure 13.4 An example of synergy: a New Zealand tourist board image advertising not only a hugely successful film and its locations, but also, through the 'Pure New Zealand' wording, the farm produce exported from that country.

twenties and thirties were encouraged to junk historical costume dramas and instead . . . [make films] which could show off the latest Bell telephone, General Electric oven or Westinghouse refrigerator' (cited in Branston 2000: 28).

But the strategy now is crucially linked to branding. Wasko quotes an article in *The Economist*:

> Such a strategy is not so much vertical or horizontal integration, but a wheel, with the brand at the hub and each of the spokes a means of exploiting it. Exploitation produces both a stream of revenue and further strengthens the brand. Thus when Viacom licenses Rugrats toothpaste and Rugrats macaroni cheese, it both makes money and promotes the direct-to-video movie launched last year and the animation feature due out later this year.
>
> (Wasko 2001: 71)

Klein suggests we 'think of the brand as the core meaning of the modern corporation, and of the advertisement as one vehicle used to convey that meaning to the world' (Klein 2000: 5). It is now often argued that the versatility of modern capitalism means that individual products (e.g. a bar of chocolate, or trainers) are not unique for very long: product specifications can be easily copied by rivals in a few days, and the difference between products anyway is often minimal – think of soap powders or shampoos. Brands, however, (e.g. Cadbury's, Nike), making a range of products, can be made to seem stable guarantees of 'quality' and sometimes indeed do provide that, though at some expense. The matter of reputation is crucial (some PR firms employ 'reputation management' experts) and has been shrewdly targeted by 'anti-globalisation' protesters including the lively interventions of Adbusters. Virgin is a good example of 'brand extension': from stores to air travel to finance and railways – as well as of the dangers that one part of the brand's operations (railways, say) can affect the rest of its reputation. Branding talk is now a regular part of the ways in which organisations previously thought of as non-commercial describe themselves. The amount of money which the BBC spends on the studio and logos for its main news programmes can be seen as a kind of 'branding as quality'. Some have suggested that, just as news or serious current affairs programmes such as *Panorama* used to act as 'flagship' programmes, now a prestigious soap such as *EastEnders* or *Coronation Street* can be understood partly as competitive 'branding' initiatives by the two main British television channels. Closer to home you may have experience of the efforts that schools, colleges and universities make to 'brand themselves' in particular ways, or your town or city may brand itself – as does the UK in certain trade and tourism contexts.

Figure 13.5 Parodying brand advertising: from the Adbusters website www.adbusters.org.

'Market research suggests that children often recognise a brand logo before they can recognise their own name. Much child-directed advertising aims to turn kids into fifth columnists within their families, nagging their parents to the checkout . . . In the US a typical child will watch more than 30,000 TV ads . . . every year, many made by the fast food industry which has an annual American TV advertising budget of about $3 billion. About a quarter of children in the US aged between two and five have televisions in their bedrooms' (Meek 2001: 4).

The influence of advertising

Many accounts of advertising analyse particular ads *outside* such full marketing, distribution and cultural contexts. Huge powers are then attributed to the ads themselves. Even in the 1980s, when study of the media included broader histories of advertising, there was still a tendency to assume the *effects of individual ads.*

To some extent such work was swayed by the well-established hype of advertising itself, crucial to maintain such a industry, selling promises of increased sales. In the 1950s, for example, advertising often succeeded in taking credit for stimulating British consumer demand after the Second World War, whereas it's arguable that the welfare state was at least as crucial in this change, giving millions of ordinary people proper health care, pensions and secondary education for the first time (see Brierley in Briggs and Cobley 1997). Such changes accompanied the rise of supermarkets and then hypermarkets (tending to privilege consumers with cars by inviting even larger amounts of shopping). These distribution outlets pile the goods high. Their initial novelty in the 1950s was to suggest by their very layout, as well as by accompanying advertising, that shoppers could choose for themselves the nature and number of items they would buy, rather than being advised by the corner shopkeeper or even the polite assistant in the department store and then constrained by having to carry the goods home by hand.

It is important to hold on to the fact that big brands have the power to distribute their goods in this way, now controlling for example much of agricultural production via their deals with supermarkets; insisting on the prized best positions on supermarket shelves, or succeeding with the nimblest of pricing policies across the globe (see Lang and Heasman 2001). The influence of advertising, powerful as it is, must always be seen in the context of such other kinds of consumer-capitalist power in acounting for why some products seem so 'popular'. It is never simply a matter of 'the power of the text', the advertisement itself, let alone the consumer's rather limited power to make fun with or ignore such messages.

ACTIVITY 13.4

Have you ever seen a major ad (with prime-time placement on television, for example) for a product which it has been difficult to obtain? Choose a prime-time television ad and research in your local supermarket:

- How easy is it to find the product?
- How does its pricing relate to its marketing, its position in the store etc.? Is it on special offer while being intensively advertised?
- How many other similar products (e.g. shampoos) could you count on display?

ACTIVITY 13.5

Find some writings on advertising which put a heavy emphasis on its power alone to influence people into buying certain goods.

- How would you want to qualify them?

Note when you next visit your local supermarket what we might call its careful *mise en scène*. (Slightly pink lighting over the meats? Smell of bread enticing you through the store towards the bakery? 'Dump bins' full of goodies, like a kids' party? Sweets to prompt tired children to exert their 'pester power' over parents at the check out? Muzak pacing your visit, its rhythm depending on time of day – slow to encourage you to shop, fast to encourage customers out?)

- How do its attractions, and the way it invites you to buy certain goods at certain points in your trip, relate to the power of ads and the products you in fact purchased?

> Research has shown that two thirds of children who asked their parents for advertised products ('pester power') were granted their request. See Sue Dibb on www.mcspotlight.org.

A purely text-based study of advertising, lacking interest in its fuller, distribution context, can lead, in some Media Studies, to the satisfying illusion that the media class can coolly examine the ways that advertising works *on the rest of* its audience, while we personally 'stay above all that'. This is made easier by the amount of knowledge which now circulates about ads, all the way from television programmes or press articles about them to the ironic self-reflexivity now built into many ads themselves (intertextual reference to other products; the use of deliberately puzzling 'messages' to draw the viewer in to identify the product, and themselves, as 'smart' etc.). This makes us all feel pretty sussed about advertising (though perhaps addicted to the next 'fix' of knowingness about them?). The brand 'textual' system itself does not operate completely freely, of course, however jokey or democratic its overall tone.

ABSENT SCHWEPPES BRAND AD

We wanted to print one of the series of very stylish Schweppes ads circulated around Christmas festivities in 2001 and in the summer of 2002. These

- were positioned in newspapers and magazines and also ran as television ads
- used an unexpected full-page slightly blurred and grainy black-and-white-news-style photo (unusual for advertising, and seeming to suggest they were 'caught' or *vérité* photos)
- involved a celebrity in an unexpected pose which had a witty or subversive relationship to their real life image (for example it seemed Camilla Parker-Bowles was caught putting on a wedding dress; Sven Goran Eriksson seemed caught entering a bathroom wearing Union Jack underpants; Cherie Blair seemed to be pinching Tony Blair's bottom, shot from behind as they face the press corps at 10 Downing St, etc.)
- printed the caption 'Sch . . . you know who?' on the familiar Schweppes logo in medium lettering. But in tiny letters at the top of the frames were the words 'Sch . . . you know it's not really her/him' to protect from claims against the celebrities impersonated and perhaps to confirm for readers fascinated enough to wonder or smart enough to suspect that, yes, they were faked.

But when we asked permission to use them we were told that Coca-Cola Great Britain and Ireland, the owner of the trademark, did 'appreciate your request but with regret cannot give permission for this proposed use. It does not currently fit into our plans for the use of the "Schweppes" trade mark.'

You don't have to share the extreme global pessimism of the **Frankfurt School** and its successors to argue for some key *influence* to the advertising-branding-consumer system as a whole (as opposed to the *effects* of individual ads):

- the power of the identities which advertising-branding (and other media images) keep on inviting us into
- the consequences of increasingly ad-funded cultures, from television to schools and colleges
- the persistence of older-style advertising in some parts of the world. Despite the ironic self-awareness and regulation of western advertising, many older-style ads and marketing ploys are still used in the 'Third World' and eastern Europe, as well as in poorer areas of the 'First World'. Cigarette companies for example, are rushing to ensure that their brands are known in Russia and China before more regulated health restrictions are imposed. New mothers in 'developing' countries are often encouraged in hospital to begin the habit of buying expensive packeted baby food milk instead of learning, like western women, the advantages of breast feeding as a cheaper and healthier practice.

'[In India] . . . television has brought the lifestyle of the urban middle class – with its electric kitchen gadgets, motor scooters and fancy furnishings – to villages where women still collect cow dung to fuel their cooking fires . . . Though [washing machines and fridges] have little practical use in a farm hamlet with no running water and only a few hours of electricity each night, they have become status symbols in one of the world's fastest growing consumer markets' (*Guardian*, 4 January 1995).

Figure 13.6 Old style, macho, no-health warning cigarette ad, Mauritius, 1997. Cigarette manufacturers in the UK are currently obliged to give 20 per cent of ad space to health warnings. These 'rotate' to contain messages about the several dire health effects of smoking.

Case study: The ASA and debates on regulation

Figure 13.7

The regulatory body the ASA (Advertising Standards Authority, founded in 1962) aims to ensure that the annual £30 million worth (2001) of press ads, plus other non-broadcast ads, are 'legal, decent, honest and truthful; that they are prepared with a sense of responsiblitiy to the consumer and to society; and that they are in line with the principles of fair competition generally accepted in the business'. (Television and radio ads are covered through the Broadcasting Act(s).)

See chapter 18.

The ASA's annual budget (£4 million in 2001) is funded by a small levy on display ads and direct mailing. It does not have the same powers as the ITC (Independent Television Commission), a statutory body which can ban the showing of certain advertisements. In addition ASA has far more material to monitor. Moreover, the ASA cannot enforce its decisions. Persistent offenders may be reported to the Office of Fair Trading, which can apply for an injunction, but such a sanction is difficult to impose, for example on issues of taste.

Much of the argument about regulatory systems such as this hinges on perceptions of public opinion. If complaints seem to be going up, then there is often a debate about whether 'public displeasure' is growing, or whether there is simply greater awareness of the channels for complaint.

ACTIVITY 13.6

Take an ad which you think contravenes the ASA's main principles (above) and make a complaint to the ASA.

> Assess the arguments which it makes in reply to your complaint. Compare it to other cases detailed on their useful website (www.asa.org.uk).
>
> You might also explore www.mcspotlight.org and www.aeforum.org.

Advertising has always been keen to locate, augment and profit from the cutting edge of cultural fashions and change. In the last twenty years this has been researched via processes such as **focus** groups and more recently 'viral' or 'peer to peer' advertising. Viral advertising is said to work like a virus in the community or computers – 'infect' one consumer who spreads it to others. This also uses the idea (see Gladwell 2001) that there is a 'tipping point' in any process, but especially the spread of good 'word of mouth' which successful ad campaigns try to build. It is all a long way from simple psychological or 'effects' models.

Focus groups are small groups of consumers of a product, usually chosen to be representative in terms of age, class etc. They are assembled to take part in guided discussion of the product, usually taped for later close analysis, so as to help producers assess the likely success of changes to that product. See Stoessl in Briggs and Cobley (1997).

Advertisers have also learnt from developing knowledge and discussions about the media. Media Studies, after all, started some fifty years ago, and many of its assumptions are embedded in journalistic and other popular discourses, and have usually been encountered by graduates working in PR. The processes of advertising's necessary attempts to keep up to the minute means that it has to take risks, such as pursuits of the so-called 'pink pound' of gay consumers via attractive images of gay people. Many would applaud this as giving visibility to identities whose very existence has previously been censored.

Ads, however, inevitably address us as shoppers, as consumers, promising to solve all the cutting-edge dilemmas they evoke simply by separate acts of shopping. In the process some rich contradictions are thrown up within their fantasy scenarios:

- Television car ads often work by showing speeding cars in pristine natural landscape – pristine because devoid of other cars and their polluting results.
- Women's magazines often produce challenging articles and even campaigns around topics such as date rape; women's guilt at their supposed inadequacy as mothers, wives, home-makers; child abuse; the dangers of sexualising very young children in advertising imagery, and so on. It's precisely on such topicality that they sell their space to advertisers.

But the bulk of those very ads appeal to readers on the basis of feelings such as anxiety about weight or housework, images of sexualised toddlers, of 'perfect' bodies, hair, kitchens, relationships – even if many of these are dealt with ironically and with a sense of humour.

A few examples of the possible influence of advertising:

- Research into anorexia suggests that young women's understandable absorption into representations of fashion can very easily lead to dissatisfaction with, and an inability to imagine as desirable, any but the most conventional (usually thin or at least adolescent) body (see Bordo 1993). '48% of women between 25 and 35 are on some kind of a diet and 20% of young women say they diet all or most of the time' (Orbach 2002).

- Research into housewives' attitudes to their work quickly reveals enormous amounts of guilt about the cleanliness or tidiness of their homes, even if they laugh at, or with, individual ad representations.

- Many men feel that the most compelling advertising representations of masculinity are ones that produce real levels of anxiety and inadequacy, even if male culture, with its emphasis on 'strong' silences or loud camaraderie, makes it difficult to talk about or explore such feelings.

- There is evidence (perhaps in your own family?) that even young children feel they have to wear the 'right' trainers, jeans, computers . . . or have the 'right' body shape.

- The tobacco industry, with proven connections to cancer and other diseases has a huge global advertising and sponsorship budget. With their health warnings against using the deadly product, even tobacco packets themselves continue to embody the contradictions of this addictive commodity, and of advertising itself.

Joke circulating in 2002 when Philip Morris (the $15 billion tobacco giant) changed the name of Marlborough cigarettes to Altria: 'We've shortened the name so it doesn't make you cough when you ask for a packet.'

References

Bordo, Susan (1993) *Unbearable Weight: Feminism, Western Culture, and the Body*, Berkeley: University of California Press.

Bowlby, Rachel (2000) *Carried Away: The Invention of Modern Shopping*, London: Faber.

Branston, Gill (2000) *Cinema and Cultural Modernity*, Buckingham: Open University Press, especially Chapters 1–3.

Brierley, Sean (1995) *The Advertising Handbook*, London and New York: Routledge.

Briggs, Adam and Cobley, Paul (eds) (1998) *The Media: An Introduction*, Harlow: Longman.

Dibb, Sue (1993) *Children: Advertisers' Dream. Nutrition Nightmare? The Case for More Responsibility in Food Advertising*, London: National Food Alliance.

Dyer, Gillian (1982) *Advertising as Communication*, London: Methuen.

Eckert, Charles (1990) 'The Carole Lombard in Macy's window', in J. Gaines and C. Herzog (eds) *Fabrications: Costume and the Female Body*, London: Routledge.

Gladwell, Michael (2001) *The Tipping Point: How Little Things Can Make a Big Difference*, London: Bantam.

Klein, N. (2000) *No Logo*, London: Flamingo.

Lang, Tim and Heasman, Michael (eds) (2001) *Public Health and the Battle for Mouths, Minds and Markets*, Sterling, VA: Stylus Publishers.

La Place, Maria (1987) 'Producing and consuming the woman's film', in Christine Gledhill (ed.) *Home Is Where the Heart Is*, London: BFI.

Matthews, Tom Dewe (1998) 'See the movie. Ogle the star', *Guardian*, 27 November.

Medhurst, Andy (1999) 'Day for night', *Sight and Sound*, June.

Meek, James (2001) 'We do Ron Ron Ron, we do Ron Ron', review of Eric Schlosser (2001) *'Fast-Food Nation'* (London: Allen Lane), *London Review of Books*, 24 May.

Myers, Greg (1999) *AdWorlds: Brands, Media, Audiences*, London: Edward Arnold.

Nader, Ralph, website www:nader.org

Packard, Vance (1979) *The Hidden Persuaders*, London: Penguin.

Pumphrey, Martin (1984) 'The flapper, the housewife and the making of modernity', *Cultural Studies*.

Slater, Don (1997) *Consumer Culture and Modernity*, Cambridge: Polity.

Wasko, Janet (1994) *Hollywood in the Information Age*, Cambridge: Polity Press.

Wasko, Janet (2001) *Understanding Disney: The Manufacture of Fantasy*, Cambridge: Polity.

Further reading

Coward, Ros (1984) *Female Desire: Women's Sexuality Today*, London: Paladin.

Goffman, Erving (1976) *Gender Advertisements*, London: Macmillan.

Marcuse, Herbert (1964) *One Dimensional Man*, London: Routledge & Kegan Paul.

Williamson, Judith (1978) *Decoding Advertisements: Ideology and Meaning in Advertising*, London: Marion Boyars.

Williamson, Judith (1985) *Consuming Passions*, London: Marion Boyars.

See also the excellent BBC series 'A Century of the Self' (2002).

Part III
Media Debates

14 Postmodernisms

- A period of social life – postmodernity?
- A form of cultural sensibility characteristic of this period?
- An aesthetic style?

- Debates
- Case study: *Pulp Fiction*
- References
- Further reading

'**Postmodernism**' is a word you will come across in many discussions of contemporary media, and you should be warned that, though frequently used, it signals a complex field of debate. It can be a confusing term, not only at first sight (Q: since 'modern' usually means 'now', how can we be living in the post-now?) but because it's often quite casually or loosely used, and is also used in different ways, which often overlap (see McGuigan 1996; Morley 1993; Sarup 1999). This chapter tries to explain its contexts and debates.

'Postmodernism' has been used to mean at least *four* different things, which David Morley usefully outlines as:

- a period of social life
- a form of cultural sensibility
- an aesthetic style (e.g. in media forms)
- a mode of thought useful for analysing the period (this is where 'postmodernism' overlaps with post-structrualist theories).

Let's focus only on the first *three* of these, though they involve the *fourth*.

A period of social life – postmodernity?

The prefix 'post-' clearly implies a break, a relation to a period which has gone before. In the case of 'postmodernism' the previous period is clearly 'the modern' or '**modernity**', whose definition again has involved heated debates. It is usually dated (see Giddens) loosely as starting with the industrial revolution, and the accompanying eighteenth-century European Enlightenment emphases on rationality, science-centred 'progress' and the importance of 'individualism' in place of older, feudal social structures with their deferences and reliance on tradition (see below).

Influential 'pomo' writers: Jean-François Lyotard (1925–98) (*The Postmodern Condition: A Report on Knowledge*, 1984); Jean Baudrillard (b. 1929) (see *Selected Writings*, ed. Poster, Mark, Cambridge: Polity, 1988). See www.scim.vuw.ac.nz/comms for reprints from these and other writers plus stimulating comments.

'The *Books in Print* index shows no book titles . . . on postmodernism between 1978–1981, but 14 . . . in 1988, 22 in 1989 and 29 in 1990 . . . 241 (articles) appear[ed] between 1987 and 1991' (Strinati 1995: 222; the term itself was first coined in the late nineteenth century).

Other terms which try to characterise the specific period we are living through include: the information society; late capitalism; post-industrial society; post-Fordist society; the society of the spectacle; late modernity; and even globalisation.

'There are precious few signs that [we] have recently entered a new age . . . What we need today is not a theory of a new age, but . . . a new theory of an age whose broad contours were laid down some time ago, and whose consequences we have yet fully to ascertain' (Thompson 1997: 9).

Fordism is a method of mass industrial production, established by Henry Ford in the US in the 1920s, using concentrated production in one enormous factory complex, the assembly line, via a specific division of labour by the workforce (called 'Taylorism'). 'You can have any colour as long as it's black': a saying attributed to Henry Ford about his newly mass-produced model T Ford car.

A further period (which is often what seems to be meant by 'postmodernity') within this 'modern' is that of computer technology and cybernetics. These have often replaced the early twentieth-century factory production line of standardised goods, made by (usually male) workers, each devoted to a specialised part of the whole labour of production. **Fordism** is one name for this, after Henry Ford and his factory production line methods of car making. We are now said to be living in *post-Fordist* times. The most adequate descriptive term for our world is still 'capitalist' but it is one where mass standardised production lines are obsolete, whether for cars or for films (as in studio Hollywood's output up to the 1950s). Production is now centred on smaller, more versatile units, closely integrated to the information technologies needed to respond flexibly to a highly developed set of consumer demands, like the 'package unit' system for making contemporary movies (or modules in many areas of education) or 'just in time' production of other goods. In a further step, *consumption* is often emphasised as an active process, indeed as both the equivalent of citizenship and as the major way we construct our identities. In this sense it has taken over the key role of production and our identities as workers or owners in Marxist acounts, and it relates to a celebration of audiences' activities in Media Studies.

Those who prefer 'late modernity' to 'postmodernity' as a name for our contemporary period, argue that:

- The term *postmodernism* over-dramatises the breaks from earlier periods. 'Heavy' capitalist industries and mass production lines have not disappeared into what's often called 'the weightless economy'. They have often simply been relocated into low-wage areas such as those of the 'Asian tiger economies' and Eastern bloc countries – or sometimes into the low-wage economy of homeworkers (usually female) in the West.

- It's also true that, for all the talk of differences, or of nation states being irrelevant in this 'postmodern' world, one supremely powerful nation, the US, is bidding for ever more global hegemony. It is the symbols of the US, and the brand identities of US corporations, which often appear as 'universal' symbols of this 'now' (see Billig 1995 Chapter 6).

- The emphasis on small-scale flexible capitalism ('**post-Fordism**') blurs perceptions of long-established huge power structures which are still alive and well. Contemporary Hollywood for example is not run by small groups

Post-Fordism method of commodity production which subcontracts parts of the production process to a number of firms, and uses new technology to make production more responsive to consumer demand. 'You can have any colour – and would you like a personalised number plate, a CD player, sunroof . . .?' – 'Post-Fordist' car dealer's pitch.

of equal individuals getting film 'packages' together (see *Pulp Fiction* case study below).

- And though the attention to the activities of consumers and audiences for popular media is a welcome move, we need to remember that the ability to consume certain goods is highly dependent on income, education and location – and this is true for media goods too. Not everyone is able to 'shut up and shop'; issues of who controls production and how it might be transformed are still key for many kinds of politics – and media.

A form of cultural sensibility characteristic of this period?

Writers on postmodernism (such as Lyotard, Baudrillard and Jameson) oddly enough often use a traditional Marxist base/superstructure model to argue that these social-economic changes produce particular 'structures of feeling' or a 'cultural logic'. Typical assertions include claims that, mostly thanks to television, we now live in a 'three-minute culture' (the length of most people's attention spans, it is said, shaped by advertising and now **zapping**); or that we are part of an over-visual society, a 'society of the spectacle' – again, due to the preponderance of television. This has implications for realist forms of all kinds, since our sense of reality is now said to be utterly dominated by popular media images; cultural forms can no longer 'hold up the mirror to reality', since reality itself is saturated by advertising, film, video games, and television images. Moreover the capacity of digital imaging makes 'truth claims' or the reliability of images tricky. Advertising no longer tries seriously to convince us of its products' real quality but, for example, just shows us a cool joke about the product.

In theories of postmodernism the important perception that our sense of reality is *always* partly formed by language and the media is taken to an absolute extreme. The self is imaged as nothing more than a hall of mirrors. This echoes positions from the **Frankfurt School** onwards, deeply distrustful of popular cultural forms and the people who enjoy them. It is a much more pessimistic position than, for example, the argument that it is because of bombardment by a multitude of media signs that the work of making meaning is often rejected – as a kind of defence against 'overload'.

Such theorists have also written of the 'death of the grand narratives' or the death of 'the Enlightenment project' (now often called 'modernity'). Very broadly, as we have seen, this refers to those movements in political thought and other ideas from about the eighteenth century onwards which proclaimed the importance of reason, and the knowability of the world through it. The next step was to argue that, if the world could be known, it could be changed – still a key component of realist media forms and, indeed, of any politics. Postmodernist critiques, however, describe Marxism, feminism, belief in

The power to *distribute* is still the key to power in the film industry, and still rests with the handful of majors, where you will still find names such as Paramount, Fox and Warners in association with huge conglomerates: Viacom, News Corporation, Time Warner.

Zapping rapidly cutting between television channels using a remote control device. Argued to undermine the authority and narrative hold of earlier ways of viewing, which was always of fewer channels, in a context of fewer media etc.

Digital imaging technology allows anything to be representable, from the feather in the 'impossible' title sequence of *Forrest Gump* (US 1994) to the convincing dinosaurs of *Jurassic Park* (US 1993).

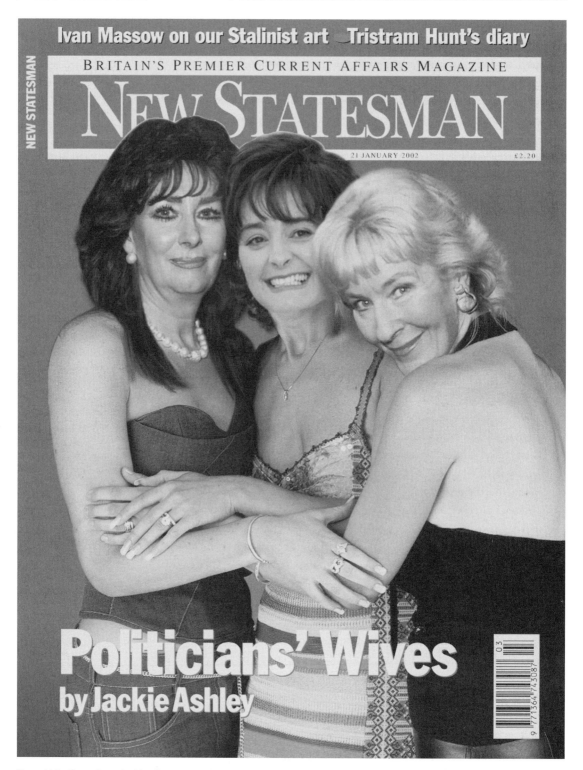

Figure 14.1 Cover from the *New Statesman*: an image, apparently of the wives of real politicians (Tony Blair, Neil Hamilton and John Prescott), posed and digitalised so as to make them look like part of the publicity material for the 2002 series *Footballers' Wives*.

scientific progress and so on as nothing more than '*grand*' or '*master-narratives*': stories about history, naively structured with happy endings. Instead postmodernism offers *micro-narratives* which do not necessarily add up, but which may be woven together (see Andermahr *et al.* 1997).

There is some truth in the perception that large claims to political truth are often narratively shaped, such as Marxism's claim that working people acting together will eventually bring about socialism. But however conscious we are now of narrative shapings in scientific and political rhetoric, it seems we cannot easily do without them and the meaning they give to experience. And what else is postmodern theory but another such story or image? Is it a very cynical one of course, pretending to be not a story, and in some versions seeing the whole of global culture as 'partying at the end of history', with politics pointless in the aftermath of the triumph of global capitalism? Which 'story' will you choose to try to live by, and how closely does it correspond to your experiences?

An aesthetic style?

Loosely, 'postmodernism' refers to several, now familiar, aspects of contemporary media:

- *hybridity* (the mixing and sampling of different kinds and levels – of hip hop music, of material in television ads, films, etc.). Also called cross-over, such forms are said to level hierarchies of taste. It is said that all distinctions between 'high art' and popular culture, have gone, or become blurred. Postmodern texts 'raid the image bank' which is so richly available through video and computer technologies, recycle some (but not all) old movies and shows on television, the Internet etc. Music videos often provide good examples of such processes, also called **intertextuality** and **bricolage**.

- *the blurring of real and 'simulated'*, especially in screen fictions, not only in CGI (Computer Generated Effects) in *Lord of the Rings* (US 2001), or the *Toy Story* films but also, for example, in the narrative questions of science fiction such as *The Matrix* (US 1999) or *Blade Runner* (US 1982): 'Is it human or not? If not, does it matter?'

- *'the erosion of history'* in non-fiction forms such as television news; in the blurring of time in films such as *Blue Velvet* (US 1986) or the extravagant play with historical fact in, say, *Elizabeth* (UK 1998) or *Saving Private Ryan* (US 1998) or *Pearl Harbor* (US 2001)

- *intertextual reference*, in films like the *Scream* series, or in the gangsters watching *The Godfather* films in *The Sopranos* television series (2001–2)

- *disjointed narrative structures*. These are said to mimic the uncertainties and extreme relativism of postmodernity (see *Pulp Fiction* case study at the end

Intertextuality 'describes the variety of ways in which texts interact with other texts, and in particular the interdependence between texts rather than their . . . uniqueness' (Andermahr *et al.*: 113).

of this chapter). Or else it is said that contemporary narratives often can't guarantee identifications with characters, or the 'happy ending' in areas such as love, the future, the Defeat of the Enemy, which have traditionally been achieved at closure. They often manage only a play with multiple, or heavily ironic, perhaps 'unfinished' or parodic endings – see *Fight Club* (US 1999), or the *Austin Powers* series, or *Blade Runner* (US 1982).

> **Bricolage**   a French word ('jumble') used by structuralists to refer to the process of adaptation or improvisation where aspects of one style are given quite different meanings when juxtaposed with stylistic features from another. The original meaning or signification is changed by the new, and the term implies a kind of creativity on the part of the '*bricoleur*'.
>
> For Dick Hebdige (1979) youth subcultural groups such as punks, with their bondage gear, use of swastikas etc., were bricoleurs when they took clothes associated with different class positions or work functions and converted them into fashion statements 'empty' of their original meanings. This emphasised *consumption* as part of processes of subversion and adaptation, rather than *production* (as in Marxist models of social change). A more recent, feminised example would be the combination of Doc Martens and summer dresses often worn by young women and girls (as by the central figure of *Amelie* (France 2001) or *Ghost World* (US 2001).

Confusingly, **modernity** is *sometimes* used to refer to the ideas and intellectual inheritance of eighteenth-century Enlightenment thinkers (think of the French Revolution's slogan 'Liberty, Equality, Fraternity'), and *sometimes* of a period of time which is clearly still going on. McGuigan (1999), Morley (1996) and Strinati (1995) are helpful on these distinctions.

But as specialist students you also need to know what is meant by the distinction indicated between postmodernism and **modernism** in the arts. The modernist movement is usually dated from around the First World War, as part of a huge set of social and economic changes (though some postmodern writers use it to refer to much earlier art work). These prompted new ways of expressing new ideas and sensibilities. In literature writers such as Virginia Woolf and T.S. Eliot ruptured existing traditions of 'good' taste, 'proper' rhyme schemes, and the settled ways of writing novels.

Such breaks often took the form of a kind of **avant-gardist** or experimental play with different media (often high-status media such as painting or classical music or literature). These might take the form of verbal playing with extreme puns and allusions (signifiers coming close to separating from their meanings or 'signifieds'), or the montage breaks of Eisenstein's editing in early Soviet cinema.

Tarantino for example is linked to the modernist period by his often-quoted reverence for Jean-Luc Godard, the 1950s 'New Wave' film director, though what attracts Tarantino is not the political, post-1968 Godard but the early Godard who 'played' with Hollywood conventions. Other directors, such as Scorsese, De Palma, Coppola, make references to 'modernist' New Wave films, though generally within a traditional Hollywood aesthetic and narrative shaping. Indeed, it might be argued that Hollywood has effectively swallowed some of the stylistic features of modernism without having gone through the pain of experimentation.

Part of *political artistic modernism* was often a **self-reflexivity**: a text makes open reference to its constructedness as a text and does not try to conceal it. Sometimes, as in the work of Brecht or later Godard, this was politically motivated, trying to demystify the production of art, showing it as a kind of work and trying to connect it to the rest of the real, political world. Contemporary media forms and techologies are now able to routinely play with this, from the open discussion of endings within the film, or of film projection in *Fight Club*, to the self-reflexive play of ads or television programmes such as *It'll Be Alright on the Night*. But they are rarely used for directly political purposes.

Debates

Realisms

Many postmodern emphases seem uninterested in the extent to which spectacle, special effects, remakes, generic mixing, have *always* been a part of Hollywood and popular genres, and have always been understood as such by audiences. It is assumed instead that audiences and the popular forms they enjoy are always to be distrusted and bemoaned. The extent to which special effects and spectacle are part of contemporary media may indeed be unprecedented. But do these changes render any kind of realist media work impossible or unattractive to audiences?

Blurring of boundaries

It's easy to see how many boundaries between 'high' and 'low' cultural reference have been eroded, and such emphases are alluring because of their democratic implications: there's no such thing as bad taste; you can enjoy (shop for?) what you like; class hierarchies have disappeared here, as everywhere else.

But paradoxically, for there to be any thrill in transgressing boundaries, like those between 'high' and 'low' forms in Baz Luhrman's *William Shakespeare's Romeo and Juliet* (1997), those boundaries need still to have some meaning – and indeed they do, if you think of the industry still associated

VANISHING CREAM.

BODDINGTONS. THE CREAM OF MANCHESTER.

BODDINGTONS. THE CREAM OF MANCHESTER.

THE CREAM OF MANCHESTER.

Figure 14.2 The play of the signifier and the 'empty referent' in contemporary advertising. Instead of making direct claims for the product, the ad plays to the knowingness of an audience assumed to be saturated with advertising images.

with the status and name of Shakespeare, the cultural importance of being able to influence what appears on school and college syllabuses, and so on.

Camp

Other writers have pointed to the similarity between postmodern approaches and **camp**, understood not as cross-dressing but as a particular sensibility.

They share:

- a delight in surface, style
- a delight in trivial rather than dominant forms: conversations about burgers in *Pulp Fiction* or hairstyles in John Waters's camp film *Hairspray* (US 1988).
- an off-centring, giddying tone involving a scepticism about serious value, a refusal of depth.

Andy Medhurst (1997) has argued, however, that there are important differences, which are to do with where the two approaches emerge from. Where 'pomo' will collapse and relativise value, camp laughs at certain values, especially those of straight society. As he points out, no camp man can claim the pompous authority of many white males, so he may as well laugh at things that are taken seriously.

> 'Camp, eludes a single, crisp definition . . . It is a configuration of taste codes and a declaration of effeminate interest . . . It revels in exaggeration, theatricality, parody and bitching . . . [in 1990] I [argued that] "postmodernism is only heterosexuals catching up with camp" . . . But . . . I was wrong: postmodern aesthetics can easily be confused with camp, but while camp grows from a specific cultural identity, postmodern discourses peddle the arrogant fiction that specific cultural identities have ceased to exist' (Medhurst 1997: 290).

Case study: *Pulp Fiction* (1994)

Many critics have called this a typically **postmodern** product, so it seems worth testing it against some of the questions above:

- In what sense can it be called postmodern?
- What does this term describe here?
- Through what other theoretical approaches can the film be usefully discussed?

Applying postmodern textual criteria

Intertextuality is evidently in play. The film makes references to gangster, blaxploitation, boxing, war, musical, romance and even arthouse genres (in its homage to the French (modernist) director Jean-Luc Godard). The references include possible ones across to other Tarantino films. (Is Vince the cousin or brother to Vic, 'Mr Blonde' Vega in *Reservoir Dogs*? Or related to Suzanne Vega, the singer, as he says at one point?) They include the stars' other performances: Harvey Keitel as 'cleaner-up of murders' in *The Assassin* (US 1993); Travolta possibly acting here the future of Tony Manero from *Saturday Night Fever* . . . the potential references are almost infinite, and certainly partly intended by Tarantino.

Figure 14.3 The scene in the trendy diner Jack Rabbit Slims, full of references to 1950s stars and movies. Said to celebrate 'style', surface, 'empty' communication.

The name of the production company for the film, 'A Band Apart', is the title of a film by Godard; Vincent and Mia's dance in Jack Rabbit Slim's is a pun on the title of a film by Godard, and Mia/Thurman's hairstyle and 'look' deliberately echo that of Anna Karina, an actress closely associated with Godard's life and work.

'Yeah. Keep it in the shot. Movie geeks like me'll be analysing this scene for years to come' (Tarantino on the accidental inclusion of an orange balloon in a shot from *Reservoir Dogs*, quoted in Clarkson (1995): 161).

Modernist techniques   Though *Pulp Fiction* makes fairly traditional use of editing for continuity and cinematography for 'legibility' of meaning, conventional lighting etc. of stars, the film also represents some variation on these. There is some use of disruptions to the 'Hollywood style' (though compare the much-lower-status *Naked Gun* spoofs or *Wayne's World* films); the film occasionally works with some odd angles (such as the shots of the backs of Jules's and Vincent's heads), some unusually long takes, and moments such as the one where Mia/Thurman mimes drawing a 'square' which unexpectedly appears on screen, or where the exact time it takes Mr Wolf to get to the house is flashed up.

Absence of history   The film has no specific location or setting in time or history. The present or early 1990s seem to be referenced in the McDonald's chat, Jules's cellular phone, the talk of body-piercing, but a lot of the retro-cultural references (music of the 1960s and 1970s; Vince's 1974 Chevy car and the style of some of the dialogue) meld into an ambiguous area of 'no-time'.

Hybridity   As well as intertextual references, the tone of the film is disorienting in the way it clashes different kinds and levels of feeling. Thus Vincent is killed, absurdly, while on the toilet, reading a piece of pulp fiction just as Butch's toaster alarm goes off, in fact, *because* it goes off. Several scenes feature offhand shootings (deliberate and accidental) where the killer does not even look at the victim in a shocking juxtaposition.

> *Butch doesn't move, except to point the M61 in Vincent's direction.*
> *Neither man opens his mouth.*
> *Then . . . the toaster loudly kicks up the PopTarts.*
> *That's all the situation needed.'*
>
> (from the screenplay of *Pulp Fiction*)

'Narrative structure   It's argued that the narrative of the film is fragmented and disorienting in terms of time and space (giving a fragmented sense of location and history?) – and therefore postmodern.

The relationship of plot and story

One of the favourite aspects of the film for fans is the way that much of it is devoted to 'trivial' conversations – about foot massage, burgers, pot bellies or tummies etc. This, however, does not have the same narrative function as the time given in *Psycho* to the apparently trivial action of Norman cleaning up the bathroom, for example. The latter serves the narrative by giving audiences relief after shock and swerving suspicions away from Norman. But in *Pulp Fiction* real screen or **syuzhet** time is given to mundane discussions – interestingly often about verbal definition, and the difficulty of defining (what *is* the status of a foot massage? the difference between a tummy and a pot belly?). These conversations about trivial meanings seem to relate both to a kind of realism (most of us spend quite a bit of time in trivial conversations) and to postmodernism's sense of the slipperiness of the signified, of words – like Jules's puzzling over the meanings of the Bible, or the opening title's double dictionary definition of 'pulp'.

Plot order

- 'Prologue' (Honey Bunny and Pumpkin in diner, up to the start of the robbery)
- 'Vincent Vega and Marcellus Wallace's Wife'
- 'The Gold Watch' (including death of Vincent)
- 'The Bonnie Situation'
- 'Epilogue' (in the diner, during the robbery and its aftermath, taking us to a few minutes after the end of the 'Prologue').

The final film story order

- Early section of 'The Gold Watch' with Butch's father's friend giving him the watch when Butch was a child
- 'Vincent and Marcellus's wife'
- 'The Bonnie Situation'
- 'Prologue'
- 'Epilogue'
- The ending of 'The Gold Watch' and the escape of Butch and Fabien

Q Which is the last event of the story?

A Fabienne and Butch making their getaway on the chopper, at the end of 'The Gold Watch'.

Q Which is the last event in the plot?

A Vincent and Jules walking out of the diner (well before Vincent is killed during 'The Gold Watch').

Q Is the complex narrative structure unprecedentedly random?

A No, several other Hollywood (and independent) films have been comparably complex, including *The Killing* (US 1956), which Tarantino acknowledged as one of many influences.

Far from being a random ending (with Jules having turned his back, perhaps temporarily, on violence, and Vince jauntily walking out of the diner (to be shot on the toilet a little later), the Brookers (1996) argue that it is arranged so as to emphasise transformation and 'new lives', for example:

- Butch's decision to act honourably, save Marcellus and begin a new life free of boxing with Fabienne (at the end of the *fabula*)
- Mia's resurrection (brought back from the dead) from the overdose, in a scene whose tone shifts the film's generic base almost to that of a vampire or horror movie
- Vincent and Jules's gaining of new purpose as they stride out of the diner at the end of the *syuzhet* (instead of the film ending close to the time when Vince is slumped dead in the toilet).

Q What do you think of this way of understanding the narrative's shape? Does it suggest a 'random postmodernity' 'about nothing but style'?

The production and promotion history

One of the problems of postmodernism as a theory is that it tends to be uninterested in histories of production, preferring to imply that a successful film somehow mysteriously expresses the 'spirit of the age'. The production history of this film suggests another way of understanding it: as a post-studio independent movie – remembering the complexity of that term 'independent'.

See Chapter 8.

Pulp Fiction was assembled as a package deal: after the success of *Reservoir Dogs* (1992) Jersey Films (with Danny de Vito a key player), owned by Tri-Star, paid Tarantino $900,000 in advance. This enabled him to go to Amsterdam to work on a screenplay. However, when Tri-Star saw the script, it was anxious about the film's length, and the scene where Vincent injects himself with heroin. Tri-Star sold it to Miramax who had bought *Reservoir Dogs* and knew the foreign earnings potential of its successor. Pre-sold foreign sales in fact covered the $8 million production costs of *Pulp Fiction*.

However the success of the film was also partly determined by the fact that just before its US release (May 1993) Miramax was bought by Disney. This meant that Disney's huge conglomerate clout (through its distribution company Buena Vista) allowed the expensive gamble of releasing what was basically an arthouse movie into 1,300 US cinemas. The gamble paid off; the film opened with $9.3 million receipts, top of the US charts, which allowed further publicity and marketing possibilities. Disney exploited these with a promotional budget eventually as big as the production costs, and Tarantino proved a talented salesman for the film, especially on the festival circuit after it won the Palme D'Or at Cannes Film Festival. (A further historical determinant: some sceptics pointed out that the jury at Cannes was headed by Clint Eastwood and ignored the claims of more obvious contenders.

Others suggested that the Cannes award was a French effort to sweeten the Americans after rumours that they would in future boycott the festival in retaliation for the GATT controversy.)

Thus the film was able to appeal to several different potential audiences. In addition, Disney launched it with a US television ad campaign promoting its humorous aspect, with posters featuring Travolta dancing. Disney coped with the fear of controversy about its violent content with the slogan 'YOU WON'T KNOW THE FACTS UNTIL YOU SEE THE FICTION'.

The success of the British release partly ensued from Tarantino's previous notoriety: the release of *Reservoir Dogs* in 1992 had overlapped with the James Bulger trial (when two young boys were convicted of brutally murdering a two-year-old child) and an accompanying moral panic over the effects of violent film material. This ensured high media coverage and cult status (as 'forbidden texts') for both films. In addition, *Reservoir Dogs* had still been refused a certificate when *Pulp Fiction* was released on video (though with one well-publicised alteration: a change of the angle of shot when Vincent plunges the heroin needle into his arm).

Tarantino, authorship, postmodernism

Oddly enough, for a figure so often called 'postmodern', Tarantino has been marketed as, and talks of himself as being, very much an 'auteur-star-director', like others in post-studio Hollywood (Scorsese, Coppola, Spielberg). Certainly his use of music; of tie-in albums which include key dialogue sections of the films; and of casting decisions can be argued as innovative (though you might like to debate how far they are 'postmodern'). Like Hitchcock and others he often makes appearances in his films (here as a polite, domesticated coffee geek).

It is possible to read the adulation of him in a number of ways:

- as generational: a delight by the young in anti-authority figures, and also in someone who's 'made it' in ways many (young men?) could hope to emulate. The idea of a smart kid from a single-parent family, a one-time videoshop salesman, 'the slacker as auteur' (Brooker) is one which understandably appeals, and is a refreshing change from ideas of 'genius' and pompous celebrations of authorship.

This career is also striking in not beginning in elite film schools, or with privileged access to the industry, let alone the family links which so many film industry figures now seem to possess (see the powerful Coppola, Scorsese, Redgrave etc. clans). It works with a sense of the world as risky, as full of nooks and crannies and possibilities, not simply old-established certainties. (Though see the role of 'that old certainty' Disney's distribution clout in his career above.)

The adulation also seems to work

- as a search for stable meanings by some fans (*'what is in the suitcase? Tarantino can tell us'*) among the sliding signifiers and relativism of the film
- to express a sense of the individual as the producer of meanings, intention, which, contradictorily, postmodern theorists have suggested has vanished from the world.

> Tarantino himself takes a postmodern stance on meaning and authorship: of Oliver Stone's more political films (*Platoon, JFK, Wall Street, Nixon*) he has said: 'He wants every single one of you to walk out thinking like he does. I don't. I made *Pulp Fiction* to be entertaining. I always hope that if one million people see my movie, they saw a million different movies' (quoted in Brooker 1996: 142).

Questions of representation

Postmodern approaches, while claiming to delight in the breakdown of old hierarchies, are not much interested in questions of representation, since they do not believe either in 'the real' or in the ability of language, or media to represent it.

In contrast to this ('it's all ironic' 'it's all postmodern play') are questions of *representation*:

- Though young women often enjoy the film, some have seen it as yet another male-centred story revelling in violent action and talk, in a cinema dominated by such films. It seems to construct its female characters as either the femme fatale (Mia) or the child-woman (Fabienne), and even the vivid 'Honey Bunny' of the first scene is reduced to hysterical screeching in the last one, as though the film doesn't know quite what to do with her. They also point to the phenomenon of 'laddishness', and suggest there are problems in the kinds of jokes which particular films (and DJs, writers, singers etc.) circulate, however the films situate them. This raises one of the central riddles of postmodern textuality: is the 'ironic' reading of a 'reactionary' character, text or joke necessarily a progressive thing? (See debates on Eminem's lyrics.)
- Opponents of this position have suggested that both men and women enjoy the film, and the key status of the bulk of its fans is as *students*

rather than male or female. They'd also say you have to take each film on its merits, and *Pulp Fiction* is not sexist or racist in its totality.

Tarantino's repeated scripting of *racist language* in the mouths of his black characters caused most controversy in relation to *Jackie Brown* (1998). He has argued:

- The black actors involved do not object, therefore why should anyone else?
- Such language is natural for his characters, and does not mean the same in the mouth of a black American as it does for others.
- Critics such as Spike Lee are jealous of his standing in the Afro-American community (interview with Barry Norman, BBC, March 1998).

'Sam Jackson uses "nigger" all the time in his speech, that's just who he is and where he comes from . . . I'm a white guy who's not afraid of that word. I just don't feel the whole white guilt and pussy-footing around race issues. I'm completely above all that' (Tarantino, *Sight and Sound*, March 1998).

His critics argue as follows.

- The characters are constructed, not described by Tarantino: to argue 'that's just how they are' is thus a cop-out.
- Spike Lee has said that if he had put antisemitic words (such as 'kike') into the mouths of his black characters in *Mo' Better Blues* to the extent that Tarantino does in his films, he would have been in deep trouble.
- Tarantino seems to be fascinated by, deeply desirous of having, 'black cool' – but this is defined in very stereotyped, some would say negative, ways: as meaning coping with violence, being street-smart, 'dealing' with women (see Willis 2000).
- Gay viewers have felt his films to be unsympathetic if not threatening, in their unproblematic sympathy for violently macho characters. The location of 'the heart of darkness' in the grotesque rape scene could also be said to recirculate the oldest prejudices about the 'redneck' South of the US.

References

Andermahr, Sonya, Lovell, Terry and Wolkowitz, Carol (1997) *A Concise Glossary of Feminist Theory*, London and New York: Arnold.

Baudrillard, Jean (1988) *Baudrillard: Selected Writings*, ed. Poster, Mark, Cambridge: Polity.

Billig, Michael (1995) 'Postmodernity and identity' in *Banal Nationalism*, London: Routledge.

Branston, Gill (2000) *Cinema and Cultural Modernity*, Buckingham: Open University Press.

Brooker, Peter and Will (1996) 'Pulpmodernism: Tarantino's affirmative action', in Deborah Cartmell, I. Q. Hunter, Heidi Kaye and Imelda Whelehan (eds) *Pulping Fictions: Consuming Culture Across the Literary/Media Divide*, London: Pluto.

Clarkson, Wensley (1995) *Quentin Tarantino: Shooting from the Hip*, London: Judy Piatkus.

Hebdige, Dick (1979) *Subculture: The Meaning of Style*, London: Methuen.

Lyotard, Jean-François (1984, originally published 1979) *The Postmodern Condition: A Report on Knowledge*, Minneapolis: University of Minnesota Press.

McGuigan, Jim (1999) *Modernity and Postmodern Culture*, London: Open University Press.

Medhurst, Andy (1997) 'Camp', in A. Medhurst and S. Lunt (eds) *Lesbian and Gay Studies: A Critical Introduction*, London: Cassell.

Morley, David (1996) 'Postmodernism: the rough guide', in James Curran, David Morley and Valerie Walkerdine (eds) *Cultural Studies and Communications*, London and New York: Arnold.

Strinati, Dominic (1995) *An Introduction to Theories of Popular Culture*, London: Routledge.

Tarantino, Quentin (1994) *Pulp Fiction* (screenplay), London: Faber and Faber.

Willis, Sharon (2000) '"Style", posture and idiom: Tarantino's figures of masculinity', in Christine Gledhill and Linda Williams (eds) *Reinventing Film Studies*, London and New York: Arnold.

Further reading

Brooker, Peter and Brooker, Will (eds) (1997) *Postmodern After-images*, London and New York: Arnold.

Cartmell, Deborah *et al.* (eds) (1997) *Trash Aesthetics: Popular Culture and its Audiences*, London: Pluto.

Connor, Steven (1989, revised edition 1997) *Postmodernist Culture*, Oxford: Basil Blackwell.

Hebdige, Dick (1988) *Hiding in the Light*, London: Comedia/ Routledge.

Jameson, Fredric (1991) *Postmodernism, or, The Cultural Logic of Late Capitalism*, Durham: Duke University Press.

Sarup, Madan (1993, 2nd edition) *An Introductory Guide to Post-structuralism and Postmodernism*, Hemel Hempstead: Harvester.

15 Globalisation

> The UN Human Development report, July 1999: 'the combined wealth of the world's richest 3 families is greater than the annual income of 600m people in the least developed countries' *Guardian* (12 July 1999).
>
> 'it is as if globalisation is in fast forward, and the world's ability to understand and react to it is in slow motion' (Ted Turner, commenting on the UN report, July 1999).

This chapter explores debates around

- what is meant by **globalisation** and the emphasis on global–local relations in Media Studies
- theories which try to understand the history, structures and consequences of 'globalisation'.

What is meant by 'globalisation'?

Power structures and activities on a larger than national scale have existed for many centuries (e.g. the Chinese, Persian and Roman Empires and the Roman Catholic Church across medieval Europe and beyond). Globalisation is something rather different, and distinctively modern. It grew from the expansion of trade in the late Middle Ages which itself was accompanied and followed by the growth of western imperialist and then post-imperialist power over the rest of the world.

Globalisation has been said to occur when activities:

- take place in a global (not national or regional) arena
- are deliberately organised on a global scale
- involve some interdependency, so that local activities in different parts of the world are shaped by each other

- often involve technologies which make possible instantaneous, as opposed to simply speedy, communications.

The speed of global processes now

The electronic demands of supermarket shoppers are scanned *instantaneously* at checkouts and relayed to the shop's storerooms. This has abolished dependence on local growth and harvesting cycles – for some people. For others 'agribusiness' means near-constant labour, oppressive contracts with supermarket chains, and water dependency. Salads picked and washed in Kenya, on estates using huge amounts of precious water, are air-freighted in forty-eight hours to 'save the time' of British consumers.

'Big' news items are now broadcast instantaneously, twenty-four hours each day, globally. They often have direct, international effects on jobs and sometimes governments, e.g. news of the 11 September 2001 terrorist attacks on the US led to stock market collapses, huge job losses, especially in the air travel and tourism industries, and so on.

'Television . . . now escorts children across the globe even before they have permission to cross the street' (Meyrowitz 1985: 238).

Communications technologies have been crucial to the development of this 'international' economy, beginning with the invention of paper and printing in China, traded with Europe, allowing books and pamphlets to circulate well beyond the places where they were produced. Crucial for later expansion were the development of underwater cable systems by the European imperial powers and companies such as Cable and Wireless (still a global player in telecommunications) and the establishment of international news agencies (see Thompson 1997: 152–9). It may come as a surprise to learn that underwater cables were so important, yet, until the 1850s, telegraph systems were land-based and thus quite restricted. By the 1870s submarine cables had been laid throughout South East Asia, along the coast of Africa. Europe was soon linked to China, Australia and South America. It was the first global system of communication which separated the sending of messages from the need to transport them physically.

News agencies likewise gathered and disseminated news over huge areas, and eventually, in 1869, agreed to divide up the world into mutually exclusive spheres of operation. These more or less corresponded, like the reach of the underwater cable systems, to the spheres of influence of the major European imperial powers.

'In 1924, at the British Empire Exhibition, King George V sent himself a telegram which circled the globe on all British lines in 80 seconds' (Thompson 1997: 154).

McWorld (and associated terms such as McJob, for low-wage, non-unionised repetitive work): coined from the worldwide spread of McDonald's food chain. Because of the standardisation of a narrow range of product in the twenty thousand worldwide McDonald's outlets, and its identification with US capitalism, the term often signifies a completely standardised, Americanised world, despite slight 'local' variations.

Some accounts of globalisation characterise it as a homogenising process, leading to '**McWorld**' (see Herman and McChesney). Others suggest that 'local' characteristics persist, sometimes in the form of fierce religious or ethnic loyalties; sometimes in the form of local foods, costumes, customs and versions of history.

Figure 15.1 'McWorld': the global/local economy.

Figure 15.2 2000 Sydney Olympics: the spectacles of sport within globalised media.

ACTIVITY 15.1

Use a videotape or photos of the opening ceremony of the latest Olympic Games (or any other world sports event). Research the following

- What are the ratings figures for the ceremony?
- How are 'Third World' nations represented or orchestrated in the ceremony?
- How is the 'local' place of the ceremony represented?
- How, if at all, are differences, disputes between nations represented?
- What are the 'production values' of the event?
- Which countries do these represent?
- How is the spectacle 'gendered'?

If you can, record coverage of the Para-Olympics (for athletes with disabilities) and note the main differences in the ways this event is constructed.

Globalised 'messages' from globalised sporting spectacles

'The wave of Amercian security and intense jingoism that has marked the first
week of the Winter Olympics here [Salt Lake City, 2002] has led to senior
officials of the [International Olympic Committee] wondering . . . whether the
US can ever stage another Olympic event . . . "This is a show designed to send
a message to Osama Bin Laden" said one IOC member . . . there are more
American security personnel here than in Afghanistan . . . President Bush broke
with protocol by opening the games from a position among a group of US
athletes . . . NBC [referred] to the Iranian team as part of the "axis of evil" . . .'
Duncan Mackay, 'Chariots of ire: is US jingoism tarnishing the Olympic ideal?',
(*Guardian*, 15 February 2002).

Mostly there is an interplay of 'global' and 'local', especially given the
abiding importance of nation states and their legislation which is needed to
help manage global capitalism. It is true that very often US money and
imagery are dominant, and increasingly taken for granted as part of the 'local'.
The film industry is a good example of the interplays within 'globalised'
media. To get a big co-production financed, there will usually need to be
complex pre-production negotiations with television, video, cable etc. funders
sometimes based in the overseas market where the film will have to sell to
recoup its profits. This means that the resulting film may have unexpected
elements in it which are far from being 'local', even 'local to the US'. However
this limited degree of diversity will tend to go along with the need for at least
one 'US' star, though, again, this may be someone like Catherine Zeta Jones,
or Sean Connery, originally coming from outside the US. Then, in production,
the global–local logic of selling big-budget blockbusters tends to mean that
films, however 'local' the subject matter, are shot and made globally, across
the world. But this is far from a globally uniform process: the 'global'
locations of such movies are often used at the cost of some damage to local
environments, damage which is unlikely at a 'First World' location like Times
Square, New York for example (see Branston 2000, Chapter 3, and Miller
et al. 2001: 197).

The golfer Tiger Woods, subject of huge sponsorship deals by Nike, describes himself as 'Cablinasian' (a mix of Caucasian, Black, Indian, Asian) or one quarter Thai, one quarter Chinese, one eighth Native American, one eighth white European (see Coakley 1998: 251). Clearly this multiple ethnic identity is a crucial part of his global marketability for Nike.

The cultural imperialism debate

From the outset the global spread of media corporations has been intimately
linked with imperialist histories. In addition there is ample evidence of a
highly profitable, mostly one-way flow of news, information and
entertainment from the major western countries, led by the US, to the rest of
the world. Importantly, more 'regional' flows now also exist, often dependent

'The sun never sets on the British Empire.' 'Because God doesn't trust the British in the dark' (joke circulating in Hong Kong, 1997).

on the global spread of imperial languages such as Spanish, English, French and Arabic – see the importance of Mexico and Brazil as producers and exporters of 'telenovelas' or soap operas to the rest of Latin America and parts of Europe.

To theorise the media in fully political ways, political economy approaches of Armand and Michele Mattelart, Janet Wasko, Toby Miller and especially Herbert Schiller have argued that much of the globalisation of communication has been driven, since the Second World War, by the commercial interests of the large US-based corporations, especially those based in oil and arms manufacture. These often act in collaboration with the US state as political and military interests which have replaced the British, French, Dutch and other older empires. It is not a giant leap, then, to argue that US media power is a form of **cultural** or **media imperialism**. Traditional, local cultures are argued to be destroyed in this process, and new forms of cultural dependency are shaped which mirror older imperialist relations of power.

Herbert Schiller was one of the best known of those making the 'cultural imperialism' argument. He argued that the dominance of US advertising-driven commercial media not only forces a costly US model of broadcasting, print, radio etc. and its technologies on the rest of the world, including indigenous, non-commercial cultures, but also drives to inculcate the desire for American-style consumerism in societies which can ill afford it. Several criticisms have been made of his approaches.

First, he developed his case in the 1950s and 1960s when US economic dominance in the global system seemed secure and unchallengeable, the very 'heart of the beast' that was also fighting a brutal war in Vietnam. Later theorists have argued that it does not adequately describe the shifts of the post-1945 period, nor the significance and persistence of other systems of belief, such as religious and nationalist thought.

Second, it is even more difficult, as Schiller recognised, to apply the theory to the 1990s and after. Global restructuring has now to *some* extent eroded the economic pre-eminence of the US (though see below). Some major US media have been bought by foreign companies: Japanese Sony bought Columbia and TriStar pictures in 1989, to add to CBS records; Bertelsmann bought RCA and Random House publishers; the then-Australian Rupert Murdoch bought 20th Century Fox in 1986; and the French company Vivendi bought the (Canadian Seagram-owned) Universal Studios in 2000. We will discover whether such accounts of a less dominant US are premature in the aftermath of 11 September 2001 and the George W. Bush presidency.

Third, Schiller later argued that the idea of American cultural imperialism should be replaced by the (unwieldy) term 'transnational corporate cultural

These have been called the 'military-industrial complex' first by President Eisenhower and later by more critical analysts.

The USA . . . still excels in producing missiles, and selling entertainment commodities' (Wasko 1994). Media products are often said to be America's second largest export area, though see Gomery (1996).

In many countries creams are on sale to lighten black skins, straighten black hair. Plastic surgery is available to widen 'oriental' eyes. How might all this relate to global media imagery and advertising?

domination' (which can be shortened to 'TNC cultural domination', given the accepted abbreviation for Trans-National Corporation). Critics argue that even this is an inadequate term for the complex flows, networks and uses of media products in the contemporary world.

Fourth, Miller *et al*. (2001) argue that it is not so much the external reach of an 'imperialist' distribution system which is at stake but what they call the 'new international division of cultural labour' involving employment practices within production itself. These operate above all with an eye to costs, meaning that jobs perceived as less crucial will go wherever the corporations can get to pay the lowest wages. The better-paid decision-making and post-production industries are still localised mostly in California and Canada, though even there workers are feeling the pinch of these policies (see the voices cited at the end of Miller *et al*.'s book).

Fifth, the cultural imperialism thesis implies in almost romantic fashion that, before the arrival of US media, Third World countries were enjoying a cosy golden age of indigenous, authentic traditions and cultural heritage, untainted by values imposed from outside. Critics argue this risks patronising what are seen as weaker nations. It often describes as 'indigenous' those cultures whose sophisticated traditions and 'heritages' have been shaped by very long and brutal processes of cultural conflict and exchange from before the years of US intervention, often including hundreds of years of European colonial 'enterprise'.

Finally, such a US-focused model underplays the pleasures of the rich hybridities, parts of 'global–local' cultures which have been formed, even within the US, as a result of the painful **diasporas** of modernity.

A reminder from Chapter 5: 'In 1993 [Michael Eisner, the head of Disney] received more than $203 million in salary and stock options' (Wasko 2001: 42).

Bodily adornment and cover are called 'fashion' (and linked to modernity) in the West, but 'tradition' (and linked to the past, and to tourism) in the 'developing world'.

Diaspora dispersal across the globe of peoples who originated in a single geographical location, e.g. the dispersed community formed from the black diaspora of the African-American slave trade. Contemporary diasporic movements are plural, pushing whole peoples 'to and fro' through unemployment, political repression, famine etc.

Some terms in the debate

- Who gets to define what counts as 'development' or 'progress'?
- Why do we assume that one form of 'development' (i.e. a highly industrialised consumer-capitalist economy) is best for all countries – including the most 'developed'?
- What terms are to be used within these power relations– the 'Third World'? the 'Global South'? the 'developing world'? the 'poorer countries'? the 'majority world'?

Some critics of 'globalisation' call 'the Third World' *underdeveloped*, i.e. deliberately starved of investment, and exploited for raw materials (food, oil, minerals which are now key to information technologies) needed by western powers in the interests of the *overdeveloped* world.

Visual images can give a
misleading sense of these
relations. A photo of a woman
using a mobile phone in
Bangladesh might suggest
'western' scale privilege in the
midst of poverty. Yet she might
be using it to save enormous
amounts of time and energy by
avoiding a wasted journey in
areas without transportation.

Progress towards what? Must 'development' always means a 'progress'
towards western capitalist standards of inequality, stress, competitiveness,
damage to the planet, job insecurity?

Media Studies on its own cannot alter these inequalities – but it can point
out the images and words which help sustain them.

Figure 15.3   One of the Baka people, in the Sudan, who in his handling
of technology seems to refute the idea of 'primitive tribes'.

A perhaps unexpected example of hybridity: 'traditional British' customs such
as Christmas celebrations result from histories of conquest, incorporation and
adaptation. They are a hybrid, or mixture, emerging partly from

● ancient Latin celebrations, from the Roman conquest, called Saturnalia, which fell towards the end of December, when agricultural labours were over and there was a need to brighten the darkest point of the year (the winter solstice)

- Christian religious imagery, imposed on these pagan festivities during the Roman conquest of Britain
- the nineteenth-century Germanic custom of the decorated indoor Christmas tree, introduced by Prince Albert
- the adoption of a bird discovered in America, the turkey, as centre of the 'traditional' British Christmas meal
- huge commercial pressures since the 1950s to celebrate via spectacular and expensive gifts, street lights in the shopping districts, overeating, lots of television-watching, a well-publicised and expensive battle between television companies for the 'big Christmas films'

In some parts of Britain the 'Christmas' lights are now preceded by those for Diwali (a Hindu festival) in a further hybrid refreshing of traditions.

Rigging the 'free market'?

However, we don't need to adopt the full-blown media imperialism model to argue that conglomerates such as News Corporation or AOL-Time Warner do not foster a global and truly 'free market' (or 'level playing field', as it's sometimes called, another cosy image for often brutal commercial force: see MacArthur 2000).

Key phrases here are loaded with connotations: '**the free market**' evokes images of a friendly rural marketplace on a sunny day. 'The **level playing field**' is many miles away from the clamour of stock exchanges, the brutal employment practices of some global corporations and the secret meetings of powerful cartels.

'even if we note . . . the lack of precise coincidence between ownership and content, the equation does not always work out in favour of diversity and openness. Sony do not, by and large, produce Japanese culture for the world . . . The music of Soweto as expressed in the *mbube* of Ladysmith Black Mambazo entered global space with Paul Simon's . . . appropriation of it on his *Graceland* album' (Silverstone 1999: 108).

Media conglomerates operate as **oligopolies** – a few large organisations together dominating the market. They often work together (like **cartels**) to co-operate on perpetuating 'free trade' treaties which will further their interests (see Klein 2001). (Though far from being 'free' or 'deregulated', these depend on thousands of pages of regulations, and the co-operation of nation states to implement them.)

See Chapter 5.

The media corporations that control the market are mostly owned by American, European and Japanese capital, though they are usually based in the US and, importantly, tend to use US stars, high-paid personnel and consumerist imagery. (Even the Australian Rupert Murdoch has had to take on US citizenship in order to acquire more large US interests.) It's also worth pointing out again that the term 'globalisation' makes the process seem like a 'force of nature', spread right over the planet. In fact the multinational corporations divide the world into a series of regional markets or 'territories': in descending order of 'market importance' these are:

1   North America (US and Canada)
2   western Europe, Japan and Australia
3   developing economies and regional producers (including India, China and Brazil, and eastern Europe)
4   the rest of the world.

AOL (America On Line)-Time Warner is the largest media corporation in the world. Time Warner alone held this title previously. Formed from the merger between Time Inc. and Warner Communications Inc. in 1989, it acquired Turner Broadcasting (CNN etc.) in 1996. Its 1997 sales were $25 billion, that is, a tenth of the GNP (Gross National Product) of India.

(These categories are based mainly on film and television distribution, but are useful indicators for all media markets. They can also be usefully explored in terms of 'the labor market' or what people can expect to be paid for working in the industries. See Miller *et al*. 2001.)

'Reading' global box office

A report (May 2002) by *Screen Digest* on exhibition and distribution, 1997–2002, of eighteen cinema markets across Asia, the Pacific rim, the Middle East and Africa revealed some surprising contradictions. Although total cinema admissions for the eighteen countries generated $3.8 billion in 2000, this was down in dollar terms on the previous year. However, for many countries, box office revenue was up, at least in their local currencies, suggesting that fluctuations in dollar exchange rates distorts the true picture of global market growth.

Japan, for example, accounts for some 4 per cent of admissions in the region as a whole, yet takes nearly 42 per cent of all box-office revenues.

China accounts for 72 per cent of screens across the entire region, but only 12.7 per cent of the total admissions. Similarly, India accounts for 77.4 per cent of all admissions across the eighteen markets, but only 12.3 per cent of the box office. *Screen Digest* also records the screen growth in several Asian markets, driven by economic regeneration and multiplex development. The follow-on effect of increasing admissions, and ultimately increased investment in local production, is also analysed, with South Korea being a recent example. (Summarised from *Screen International*, 8 May 2002.)

There are many media producers located in groups 2 and 3 who are able to operate in different regional markets such as Latin America – very effectively in many cases. However, they have little chance of penetrating the major market in North America. US-based corporations, in contrast, can market effectively in all the markets, including the poorest. Why is this? Powerful US media figures often talk as though US products themselves simply and effortlessly win global assent and popularity, that they have 'universal appeal'. It is important to realise the huge experience which the US entertainment giants have accumulated in making successful products. In cinema, for example, the early 'American' makers and exhibitors in the 1890s were often first- or second-generation immigrants to the US, and thus in very close contact with European popular taste to which they were exporting.

But what is key to understanding their global penetration now is the role of commercial strategies of employment and distribution such as **differential pricing** and wages. This deserves as least as much emphasis as the better known strategies of adaptations to titles, casting, plots chosen to appeal to as broad a market as possible etc. Pricing strategies mean that once a US television series, for example, has been distributed in the North American continent (which usually allows it to recoup its production costs), it will be offered to every broadcaster in the world, but at different(ial) rates. The money made thus is often clear profit. In the 'developed' countries these charges are based on audience size (e.g. on the relatively affluent and concentrated audiences who can be contacted by media in big cities). But in Africa the rates may be lowered dramatically so programmes can be virtually given away for relatively little cost.

Such low charges are not inspired by charitable motives. The process both ensures *overall* profitability and also consolidates habits of enjoying US-style entertainment forms. It also seems to help develop an appetite for the products placed in them, by audiences whose lifestyles are usually remote from those targeted in US advertising-funded programmes. Rates are so low that they impact on local production, since African or West Indian broadcasters, for example, cannot hope to produce programming of a similar

'It is not "domination" by American cinema. It's just the magic of story-telling, and it unites the world.' Steven Spielberg quoted in Branston (2000: 61).

For global television documentaries as much as for 'global' feature films the motto is often: 'let's make it "language neutral" i.e. with as little sync [sound] as possible and no talking heads. They can add those later for different national markets' (discussion at Sheffield International Documentary Film Festival 2001).

READER'S DIGEST IS READ BY MORE AFFLUENT ASIANS THAN ANY OTHER PUBLICATION (21%). MORE LUXURY WATCH OWNERS, CAR BUYERS, FREQUENT FLYERS AND SCOTCH WHISKY DRINKERS THAN TIME, FEER, NEWSWEEK, ASIAWEEK AND YZ! IF YOU REALLY WANT TO COMMUNICATE WITH YOUR MARKET TALK TO THEM IN THEIR OWN LANGUAGE! ONLY 20% OF ASIA'S ELITE USE ENGLISH AT HOME. READER'S DIGEST PUBLISHES 17 ASIAN EDITIONS IN 4 LANGUAGES - CHINESE, THAI, KOREAN AND ENGLISH. FOR DIRECT ACCESS TO THE LATEST ATMS CALL PENNY MORTIMER OR KAREN FAIRBROTHER (44) 171 715 8170

 **Reader's Digest**

ASIA'S BIGGEST SELLING MAGAZINE

Figure 15.4 The global/local faces of a 'big one': *Reader's Digest* has 97 million readers in 46 countries around the world.

technical quality at a lower price, and their station managers cannot afford *not* to buy in.

In addition, in many African countries, for instance, film distribution is almost entirely in the hands of overseas companies which are unwilling to distribute African films, even though local producers are not lacking in creative ideas or production skills. Several theorists argue that this distribution imbalance could be tackled, especially with government support for organized resistance to international trade agreements which always favour US interests and, for example, alliances to build satellite and digital transmission and distribution systems. Others urge western educationalists, in Media Studies for example, to teach about cinemas other than Hollywood entertainment forms so as to help develop an understanding and appetite for films which are trying not to copy that model but to do something different.

'TV [Zimbabwe television] can only afford to produce about twelve hours of indigenous drama a year, albeit incredibly cheaply, with the actors also doing day jobs and providing their own costumes. [Such] drama series are very popular with the majority black audience but ...' (Dowmunt 1993: 6).

Q How do you think this sentence might end, given the ways US media corporations price their 'product' for such markets?

'The problem with the American dominance of global cinema ... is not that it prevents Britain (and other countries) from developing cultural identities for themselves but ... it also threatens to deprive America itself of views of

America from the outside. American dominance simply reinforces America's own powerful, yet provincial cinematic myths about itself, . . . structured around terrifying misrecognitions and appallingly narcissistic fantasies . . . harmful not simply to everyone else . . . but also, above all, to America itself'
(Peter Wollen in Nowell Smith and Ricci: 134).

Figure 15.5 International box-office charts from *Screen International*: a vivid example of the dominance of US distributed and advertised films globally. How many non-US products can you make out?

NORTH AMERICA Weekend Jan 25-27 — TOP 30

Rank		Film (Country of origin) Distributor	Week	Theatres	Three-day total $ Jan 25-27	% change from prior weekend	Theatre $ avaerage	Total $ gross Jan 27
1	(1)	**BLACK HAWK DOWN** (US) *Sony Pictures*	5	3,101	$17,012,268	−49	$5,486	$58,893,074
2	(2)	**SNOW DOGS** (US) *Buena Vista*	2	2,440	$13,079,373	−45	$5,360	$38,811,967
3	(−)	**A WALK TO REMEMBER** (US) *Warner Bros*	NEW	2,411	$12,177,488	—	$5,051	$12,177,488
4	(4)	**A BEAUTIFUL MIND** (US) *Universal*	6	2,237	$11,531,735	−22	$5,155	$92,887,746
5	(−)	**THE COUNT OF MONTE CRISTO** (US) *Buena Vista*	NEW	2,007	$11,376,150	—	$5,668	$11,376,150
6	(−)	**THE MOTHMAN PROPHECIES** (US) *Sony Pictures*	NEW	2,331	$11,208,851	—	$4,809	$11,208,851
7	(−)	**I AM SAM** (US) *New Line*	5	1,268	$8,315,581	+32,454	$6,558	$8,506,955
8	(3)	**THE LORD OF THE RINGS: THE FELLOWSHIP..** (NZ-US) *New Line*	6	2,703	$7,803,075	−49	$2,887	$258,449,272
9	(−)	**KUNG POW: ENTER THE FIST** (US) *20th Century Fox*	NEW	2,478	$7,017,474	—	$2,832	$7,017,474
10	(5)	**ORANGE COUNTY** (US) *Paramount*	3	2,317	$4,418,401	−58	$1,907	$34,046,523
11	(6)	**OCEAN'S ELEVEN** (US) *Warner Bros*	8	2,010	$3,176,373	−53	$1,580	$175,974,750
12	(7)	**THE ROYAL TENENBAUMS** (US) *Buena Vista*	7	999	$3,084,804	−42	$3,088	$41,495,735
13	(9)	**GOSFORD PARK** (UK-US) *USA Films*	5	756	$2,782,555	−33	$3,681	$15,980,889
14	(13)	**IN THE BEDROOM** (US) *Miramax*	10	465	$1,941,677	−32	$4,176	$14,449,092
25	(8)	**JIMMY NEUTRON – BOY GENIUS** (US) *Paramount*	6	1,802	$1,777,704	−59	$987	$76,221,724
16	(11)	**VANILLA SKY** (US) *Paramount*	7	1,640	$1,654,127	−54	$1,009	$96,076,019
17	(18)	**BROTHERHOOD OF THE WOLF** (Fr) *Universal*	3	292	$1,608,920	+5	$5,510	$4,258,413
18	(14)	**BEAUTY AND THE BEAST** (SPECIAL EDITION) (US) *Buena Vista*	4	68	$1,470,492	−40	$21,625	$12,543,294
19	(10)	**KATE & LEOPOLD** (US) *Miramax*	5	1,540	$1,448,767	−65	$941	$45,023,594
20	(12)	**HARRY POTTER...** (UK-US) *Warner Bros*	11	1,202	$1,402,381	−59	$1,167	$311,573,984
21	(20)	**AMELIE** (Fr) *Miramax*	13	275	$900,775	−32	$3,276	$22,389,459
22	(19)	**THE SHIPPING NEWS** (US) *Miramax*	5	421	$879,705	−42	$2,090	$9,259,705
23	(15)	**MONSTERS, INC.** (US) *Buena Vista*	13	627	$555,368	−72	$886	$250,676,747
24	(17)	**HOW HIGH** (US) *Universal*	6	510	$502,310	−68	$985	$30,240,430
25	(−)	**LANTANA** (Aus) *Lions Gate Films*	7	84	$383,948	+106	$4,571	$1,104,696
26	(16)	**ALI** (US) *Sony Pictures*	5	473	$324,270	−81	$686	$57,880,790
27	(21)	**BEHIND ENEMY LINES** (US) *20th Century Fox*	9	503	$320,488	−67	$637	$57,460,084
28	(23)	**STATE PROPERTY** (US) *Lions Gate Films*	2	63	$216,074	−61	$3,430	$864,606
29	(27)	**SHALLOW HAL** (US) *20th Century Fox*	12	323	$194,469	−40	$602	$69,935,950
30	(30)	**MONSTER'S BALL** (US) *Lions Gate Film*	5	17	$193,982	−2	$11,411	$1,079,270
TOTAL				37,363	$128,759,585		$3,446	$1,827,864,731

Note: Domestic total includes US and Canada. (©) Copyright 2001 AC Nielsen EDI, Inc (1) 323 860 4600. Last weekend four-day percentage change does not apply.

NORTH AMERICA Jan 25-27 — TOP 10 INDEPENDENT RELEASES

Rank		Film (Country of origin) Distributor	Week	Theatres	Three-day total $ Jan 25-27	% change from prior weekend	Theatre $ avaerage	Total $ gross Jan 27
1	(−)	**I AM SAM** (US) *New Line*	5	1,268	$8,315,581	+32,454	$6,558	$8,506,955
2	(1)	**THE LORD OF THE RINGS: THE FELLOWSHIP..** (NZ-US) *New Line*	6	2,703	$7,803,075	−49	$2,887	$258,449,272
3	(2)	**GOSFORD PARK** (UK-US) *USA Films*	5	756	$2,782,555	−33	$3,681	$15,980,889
4	(4)	**IN THE BEDROOM** (US) *Miramax*	10	465	$1,941,677	−32	$4,176	$14,449,092
5	(3)	**KATE & LEOPOLD** (US) *Mirimax*	5	1,540	$1,448,767	−65	$941	$45,023,594
6	(6)	**AMELIE** (Fr) *Miramax*	13	275	$900,775	−32	$3,276	$22,389,459
7	(5)	**THE SHIPPING NEWS** (US) *Miramax*	5	421	$879,705	−42	$2,090	$9,259,705
8	(−)	**LANTANA** (Aus) *Lions Gate Films*	7	84	$383,948	+106	$4,571	$1,104,696
9	(7)	**STATE PROPERTY** (US) *Lions Gate Films*	2	63	$216,074	−61	$3,430	$864,606
10	(9)	**MONSTER'S BALL** (US) *Lions Gate Film*	5	17	$193,982	−2	$11,411	$1,079,270
TOTAL				7,592	$24,866,139		$3,275	$377,107,538

Note: Domestic total includes US and Canada. (©) Copyright 2001 AC Nielsen EDI, Inc (1) 323 860 4600. Last weekend four-day percentage change does not apply.

BRAZIL Week ending Jan 17 — TOP 10

Rank		Film / Origin / Distributor	Week	Seven-day gross REAL	Seven-day gross $	Screens	Screen $ average	% chg	Total $ gross to Jan 17
1	(1)	**The Lord Of The Rings** (NZ-US) Warner Bros	2	REAL 4,730,499	$2,004,449	372	$5,388	–50	$6,018,790
2	(–)	**Ta Todo Mundo Louco** (Br) Art/Eur/Man	NEW	REAL 2,255,488	$955,715	141	$6,778	—	$955,715
3	(2)	**Xuxa E Os Duendes** (Br) Warner Bros	5	REAL1,651,314	$699,709	293	$2,388	–14	$3,541,281
4	(3)	**Monsters, Inc.** (US) Col TriStar/BVI	5	REAL1,165,921	$494,034	270	$1,830	–31	$4,253,281
5	(4)	**American Pie 2** (US) UIP	4	REAL930,982	$394,484	180	$2,192	–42	$3,089,736
6	(–)	**From Hell** (US) 20th Fox	NEW	REAL757,874	$321,133	90	$3,568	—	$321,133
7	(5)	**Harry Potter...** (UK–US) Warner Bros	8	REAL717,770	$304,140	192	$1,584	–44	$9,748,503
8	(–)	**Jason X** (US) Playarte	NEW	REAL658,051	$278,835	102	$2,734	—	$278,835
9	(–)	**Zoolander** (US) UIP	NEW	REAL429,069	$181,809	104	$1,748	—	$181,809
10	(–)	**Trapaceiros** (Br) Art/Eur/Man	NEW	REAL396,785	$168,129	23	$7,310	—	$168,129

$1 = REAL 2.36   Source: Jornal Do Video

HONG KONG Week ending Jan 24 — TOP 10

Rank		Film / Origin / Distributor	Week	Seven-day gross HK$	Seven-day gross $	Scrs	Screen average $	% chg	Total gross $ to Jan 24
1	(6)	**Black Hawk Down** (US) 20th Fox ††	2	HK$4,148,524	$531,862	36	$14,774	+446	$629,353
2	(2)	**Harry Potter...** (UK-US) Warner Bros	5	HK$1,299,098	$166,155	30	$5,552	–43	$5,475,296
3	(1)	**Second Time Around** (HK) OHY	2	HK$1,244,630	$159,568	21	$7,598	–55	$513,490
4	(5)	**Spirited Away** (Jap) Intercontinental Films	6	HK$734,448	$94,160	23	$4,094	–40	$3.208,879
5	(4)	**Vidocq** (Fr) Intercontinental Films	3	HK$501,657	$64,315	12	$5,360	–62	$255,160
6	(–)	**Time 4 Hope** (HK) Emperor Multimedia Group	NEW	HK$472,961	$60,636	9	$6,737	—	$67,081
7	(–)	**Chingu** (Korea) MAD	NEW	HK$376,366	$48,252	11	$4,387	—	$54,999
8	(7)	**Y Tu Mama Tambien** (Mex) Edko Films	2	HK$280,792	$35,999	8	$4,500	–45	$111,536
9	(–)	**Donnie Darko** (US) Panasia Films	NEW	HK$262,330	$33,632	11	$3,057	—	$37,614
10	(–)	**Beauty And The Breast** (HK) MSP †	NEW	HK$261,651	$33,545	31	$1,082	—	$33,545

$1= HK$7.8   † One-day on release only   †† Eight days on release only.   Source: MPIA

SPAIN Three-day weekend Jan 25–27 — TOP 10

Rank		Film / Origin / Distributor	Week	Three-day gross €	Three-day gross $	Screens	Screen avg $	% chg	Total gross $ to Jan 17
1	(1)	**Ocean's Eleven** (US) Warner Sogefilms	2	€2,288,656	$1,978,095	330	$5,994	–26	$5,378,028
2	(2)	**The Lord Of The Rings...** (NZ-US) Aurum	6	€1,082,990	$936,033	385	$2,431	–25	$23,088,799
3	(–)	**13 Ghosts** (US) Col TriStar	NEW	€1,009,535	$872,545	202	$4,320	—	$872,545
4	(3)	**Shallow Hal** (US) 20th Fox	3	€987,653	$853,633	250	$3,415	–30	$4,250,132
5	(–)	**Vidocq** (Fr) Vertigo	NEW	€624,813	$540,029	180	$3,000	—	$540,029
6	(–)	**Behind Enemy Lines** (US) 20th Fox	NEW	€600,121	$518,687	260	$1,995	—	$518,687
7	(–)	**Serendipity** (US) Lauren Films	NEW	€348,954	$301,602	151	$1,997	—	$301,602
8	(4)	**Harry Potter...** (UK-US) Warner Bros	9	€270,922	$234,159	202	$1,159	–44	$23,119,590
9	(8)	**K-Pax** (US) Lauren Films	2	€265,061	$229,093	146	$1,569	–27	$653,800
10	(6)	**The Hole** (UK) Warner Sogefilms	4	€237,321	$205,118	144	$1,424	–48	$2,080,963

$1 = €1.157   Source: ACNielsen/EDI Inc

Local producers have two other main problems: training and equipment. Training needs to be 'on the job' for at least part of the time on (expensive) broadcast-quality equipment. Most readers of this book will take for granted access to videotapes, batteries, cables etc. But broadcasters in some parts of the world may be hundreds of miles from mains electricity and water, let alone such equipment. And cameras etc. designed for broadcast use in North America, western Europe and Japan will not necessarily perform efficiently in tropical conditions. The upshot is that trainees are sent to North America or Europe or the training is offered by the equipment manufacturers on their terms.

Current debates

Let us come back to the debates we outlined earlier. First, other questions have been posed of the media imperialism model. Its ownership emphasis can imply that all US television, for example, unavoidably expresses only consumerist values, both in the programmes themselves and via the advertising which finances them. This ignores the diversity of images, themes and information which can, and indeed has to, appear on commercially funded television (the media's insatiable need for *repetition and difference* again), including occasional material which is critical, up to a point, of corporate interests.

Second, it's sometimes the case that the very power of global-but-centralised processes such as branding can work against the interests of their owners. Global branding of sporting spectacles such as the Olympic Games means not just wonderful publicity for Nike and others but, simultaneously, the possibility of a 'high news profile' to stories of exploitation of child labour in Indonesia, Pakistan etc. by the same corporations. Those possibilities can then be made tangible by the ingenuity and commitment of design workers such as Adbusters, by trade unionists and other anti-corporate protesters (see Klein 2001). They may also be able to build on the claims of some corporations to be operating policies of 'corporate responsibility', and the desires of many of those working within them to work for a properly respected brand.

Third, the media imperialism model can imply that audiences inevitably become, or want to become, consumers *simply as a result of watching such programmes*. Audience research suggests a more complex situation. Roger Silverstone suggests that a metaphor of translation would be a better way to understand what goes on in these global flows: 'globalisation is a process of translation. We believe that . . . Hollywood or Disney is the same in Paris or Penang as it is in Poughkeepsie. We believe that the news of the world is the same wherever it is received. But we know that it is not' (Silverstone 1999: 109).

ACTIVITY 15.2

'When people watch international news . . . they pay as much attention to street scenes, housing and clothing as to the commentary which accompanies the pictures from foreign lands' (Thompson 1997: 176).

• Does this apply to your viewing? Make notes when you next watch international news coverage.

• If you know anyone who has come to Britain from another country, ask them whether they ever made this use of news before they came here.

However, it seems more than one step too far to leap from this to the argument that 'we' are now living in a 'global village' (the influential phrase of the 1960s Canadian theorist Marshall McLuhan), all of us cosily sharing the same imagery and products, warming our hands by the fireside of our democratic screens. Talk of the 'freedoms' of the Internet and broadband are now part of this kind of rhetoric, but often works at the expense of understanding key inequalities in media power relations.

First, who is the 'we' that has access to literacy, telephones, let alone the computers and modems needed to 'surf the global Net' (again, a very US image)? Of course this inequality applies to parts of the 'First World' as well as the 'majority world'. As one critic has said: 'the distribution of television is very uneven world-wide; in countries like Britain, it is close to saturation, while in the non-Arab countries of Africa, there are only 13 sets per thousand people' (Abercrombie 1996: 95).

Second, in whose interests is the Net being shaped? Who controls the agenda of which entries pop up first when you type a particular category into a search engine, for example?

The Lone Ranger and his trusty sidekick Tonto face an overwhelmingly large posse of hostile Apache. 'We're in real trouble Tonto' says the Ranger. Asks Tonto: 'Who's this "we", Paleface?'

Examples though which to think about 'globalisation'

You can trace in ad imagery some of the 'naturalising' of the feeling that 'There Is No Alternative' (or 'TINA', as this slogan of Margaret Thatcher's was once dubbed) to globalisation. From the 1970s hugely increased advertising and PR budgets went along with newly globalising images and appetites. Coca-Cola was one of the first to launch a television commercial aiming at a single global image and product. It used an image of the globe itself in its 1971 'I'd like to teach the world to sing in perfect harmony' ad (see Myers 1999: 55). Several others have followed suit and the combination of an image of a globe in space, a montage of people of different races in diverse clothing, arrows such as the ones in airline maps, is now a familiar part of 'commercial speech' or advertising. McDonald's, Fuji film, British Airways and, more surprisingly, the Halifax bank and the Norwich Union insurance company have recently followed suit.

Some news coverage of so-called 'anti-globalisation' demonstrations emphasises, for example, that the protesters wear trainers manufactured in the sweatshops they so object to, or that they travel many miles by polluting air transport. These are shrewd points about the extent to which even dissidents in the 'West' have to make use of advanced capitalist production. But it also embodies the way the media insist on using 'globalisation' rather than 'corporate power' as the key term for description of such protest. Look at coverage of the next such demonstration for these accounts.

The same inequalities occasionally apply to permission to access the computers themselves: 'In Myanma (formerly Burma) only 11 people have Internet access – the military rulers' (Radio 4 *From Our Own Correspondent*, 23 June 2001, Jonathan Head reporting).

Third, there are risks in *uncritical* celebrations of active audiences across the world, argued to be able to construct resistant meanings no matter what is on their screens. It is one thing to point out what audiences seem able to do with the most unexpected news images, or how creatively fans can work with their favourite fictions. It is quite another to argue that 'the global market' will do it all for us, that there is no need for also having high-quality national investigative journalisms, or easily available, well-researched and regulated media. This is especially true given the amount of regulation and state
co-operation which the multinational corporations depend on.

Fourth, some critics of global metaphors, while agreeing about the importance of instantaneous global technologies, such as the Internet, ask whether evidence of such changes has been exaggerated. 'Local' or national boundaries, religions, laws, media institutions, taxation structures etc. still exist, and have huge economic and ideological power. Indeed, national identities seem transformed, but not obliterated, by globalisation. Perhaps the world economy is best thought of not as global but as centred on regions or networks (see Tomlinson 1999) which can be defined:

- as areas of advanced consumer-capitalist power (North America, Europe, and East Asia before the collapse of the so-called 'tiger economies')
- by language use (regions often inherited the languages of the imperialist powers, such as the Hispanic or Spanish-speaking areas of 'Latin' America)
- by religions and cultures (the Islamic 'Middle' East)
- by technological factors such as the 'footprint' of a satellite (MTV Europe or Star TV in Asia – or television signals in parts of the UK).

See Chapter 3 and especially the discussion of *Big Brother* (see Chapter 6).

'A supposedly exemplary open market specimen, the North American Free Trade Agreement . . . needs a . . . thousand pages of protocols, weighing 850 kilogrammes! So far as investment is concerned, this is an international not a global age – and governments continue to matter' (Miller *et al.* 2001: 41).

ACTIVITY 15.3

List the number of ways in which your experiences of the media over the last week have been affected by:

- living in a *global* media economy
- living in a *national* media economy
- living with media which *mix global and national* characteristics
- living with media which cross huge spaces instantaneously.

References

Abercrombie, Nicholas (1996) *Television and Society*, Cambridge: Polity.

Appadurai, Arjun (1996) *Modernity at Large: Cultural Dimensions of Globalization*, Minneapolis: University of Minnesota Press.

Branston, Gill (2000) *Cinema and Cultural Modernity*, Buckingham: Open University Press.

Coakley, J. (1998, 6th edition) *Sport in Society: Issues and Controversies*, New York: McGraw Hill.

Dowmunt, T. (ed.) (1993) Channels of Resistance, London: BFI/Channel 4.

Gomery, Douglas (1996) 'Towards a new media economics' in *Post-theory: Reconstructing Film Studies*, Madison and London: University of Wisconsin Press.

Hall, Stuart (1991) 'The local and the global: globalisation and ethnicity', in A. King (ed.) *Culture, Globalisation and the World System*, London: Macmillan.

Herman, Ed and McChesney, Robert (1997) *The Global Media: The New Visionaries of Corporate Capitalism*, London: Cassell.

Klein, Naomi (2001, 2nd edition) *No Logo*, London: Flamingo.

MacArthur, John (2000) *The Selling of 'Free Trade': NAFTA, Washington, and the Subversion of American Democracy*, London and Berkeley: University of California Press.

McLuhan, Marshall (1964) *Understanding Media: The Extensions of Man*, London: Routledge and Kegan Paul.

Meyrowitz, Joshua (1985) *No Sense of Place: The Impact of Electronic Media on Social Behaviour*, New York: Oxford University Press.

Miller, Toby, Govil, Nitin, McMurria, John and Maxwell, Richard (2002) *Global Hollywood*, London: BFI.

Myers, Greg (1999) *Ad Worlds: Brands, Media Audiences*, London and New York: Arnold.

Schiller, Herbert I. (1996) *Information Inequality*, London and New York: Routledge.

Schiller, Herbert I. (1991) 'Not yet the post-imperialist era', in Tim
   O'Sullivan and Yvonne Jewkes (eds) *The Media Studies Reader*, London:
   Routledge, 1997.
Silverstone, Roger (1999) *Why Study the Media?*, London: Sage.
Thompson, John B. (1997) *The Media and Modernity: A Social Theory of the
   Media*, Cambridge: Polity.
Tomlinson, John (1999) *Globalisation and Culture*, Cambridge: Polity.
Wasko, Janet (1994) *Hollywood in the Information Age*, Cambridge: Polity.
Wasko, Janet (2001) *Understanding Disney: The Manufacture of Fantasy*,
   Cambridge: Polity.

Further reading

Beck, Ulrich (2000) *What Is Globalisation?*, Cambridge: Polity.
DFID (2001) *The Media in Governance: A Guide to Assistance*, London: DFID.
O'Sullivan, Tim and Jewkes, Yvonne (eds) (1997) *The Media Studies Reader*,
   London and New York: Arnold (esp. Section 5).

Useful websites

www.caslon.com.au/mediaprofiles/overview.htm
www.charter99.org – the Charter for Global Democracy
www.dfid.gov.uk
www.opendemocracy.com – see its strand covering debates on globalisation

16 | Technologies

- Outlining debates about 'media technology'
- Technology: focus of conflict
- Technological change
- Technology and the media workplace

- Case study: Cybercultures – living in an Internet world
- Digital imaging
- References
- Further reading

Issues related to 'technology' cause all kinds of problems for Media Studies. Not least is the 'wow' factor and the difficulty in making sensible judgements and predictions about the impact of technological change. In the second edition of this book, we covered the widespread adoption of Internet services in some detail. A few years later it is clear that Internet access has increased and more users are familiar with the range of services. Yet, at the same time, the bubble of hype that surrounded the Internet has burst – 'dot.com millionaires' have faded away and many of the assumptions about how we would all use the Internet have proved to be false. Something similar could be argued about other 'digital media revolutions', especially in film and television. In this chapter we will try to be careful not to make too many assumptions, but to trace some of the recent history of technological change in the media industries and relate it to the range of issues explored in other chapters. Technological change is also addressed in the case studies following Chapters 7 and 8.

The *Guardian Online*'s deputy editor reported in March 2002 that he had abandoned his palmtop computer and reverted to a 'pen and paper' organiser as it was quicker and more reliable.

Science fiction dystopias offer a discourse on 'technology out of control' – a good example is *The Matrix* (US 1999).

Luddites Textile workers in the early nineteenth century who, fearing their jobs would be taken by machines in the new factories, organised themselves and destroyed the new machines if they were used in this way. Ned Ludd was a fictitious name used to protect the leaders of the struggle. 'Luddite' is generally a term of abuse, but the workers were correct in their analysis – the machines were used to replace their skilled labour.

Outlining debates about 'media technology'

Ideas about media technology have been developed in a wider discussion about contemporary society. Some of the expressed concerns are that

- technology is developing too quickly, it is affecting all of us (and particularly children) to an unknown extent – it is 'out of control'
- technology is gendered and not universally available and accessible, whether in terms of class or region
- the 'user-friendliness' of computer technology is deskilling workers
- 'new technologies' are a threat to established employment patterns, on the reasonable assumption that technology usually replaces human labour eventually. Thus the historical basis for the jibe about 'new **Luddites**' to describe critics of computer technologies.

But, equally:

- Technology might be liberating in allowing us to participate more in production and learn more about the world.

- 'New' technologies will lead to 'new' products and these will power the
  new industries of the developed world (with older industries moving to
  'lower-wage' economies).

Other ideas are concerned more specifically with media work:

- Artists and producers must change their methods and patterns of work and
  perhaps their whole approach to 'creativity'.
- Technology threatens the link between 'reality' and media representations.
- New technologies and new products may produce new forms of
  communication – will they be 'institutionalised' quickly or allow new
  forms of 'accessible democracy'?

Defining 'media technology'

Technology isn't just about machines or equipment – the **hardware** aspect
which puts off many people. Technology is also about *methods*, *means* and *skill*
– essentially about how we can exploit our knowledge in order to produce
something which in economic terms has a direct use or an exchange value.
These form the **software** in modern systems such as a computer game or a
machine operating system. Some people also refer to the 'liveware' or
'wetware' – the human beings who are part of the system. The relationship
between human activity and machine activity is known as **cybernetics**,
which has often been represented in terms of virtual reality – human
interaction with fictional worlds created by computers.

The concept at the centre of
The Matrix (US 1999) is an
example of a virtual reality.

Take a junior reporter attending the local Magistrates Court. He or she
uses simple but effective technology – a pencil and a notepad – to record what
is said. Of course, these may seem simple, even primitive, technologies, but
the modern pencil and paper are the result of hundreds of years of
technological development in the application of chemical knowledge about
graphite and wood pulp and techniques for manufacture and good design, to
allow them to be 'operated' effectively.

Technology: the practice of any or all of the applied sciences that
have practical value; technical methods in a particular field of
industry or art; technical nomenclature; technical means and skill
characteristic of a particular civilisation, group or period (from the
Greek, techne = art)

(*Chambers 20th Century Dictionary*)

'Art' has an original meaning
which includes the application of
practical skills: at one time 'artist'
and 'technician' may have had a
similar meaning. See entries in
Raymond Williams, *Keywords*
(revised edition, London:
Fontana, 1988).

The technological input does not stop there. A special system of writing,
shorthand, with its own set of characters, was developed to enable the
reporter to record material more quickly. In this example we have a marriage
between hardware (the equipment – pencil and paper) and software (the
systemised applications knowledge – shorthand), which we can recognise in

There is even a book devoted to the pencil and its history: Henry Petroski's *The Pencil: A History of Design and Circumstance* (London and New York: Faber & Faber and Knopf, 1990).

See Chapter 7 on journalism as institution.

Images of scientists and technicians In *The Man in the White Suit* (UK 1951) Alec Guinness plays an inventor of a cloth that never gets dirty and won't wear out. He is bewildered when laundry workers and textile workers attack him because of the risk to their jobs, but saved, in this social comedy, when the cloth disintegrates after only a few days – though not before his invention has created social and economic upheavals.

Most stereotypes of scientists and technicians present them as a far more malign threat to society – one of the points where SF and horror often overlap. How do they relate to the scientist heroes featured at the end of news bulletins etc. who find cures for diseases?

Anorak What does this term of abuse say about general attitudes towards detailed knowledge of specific technologies? Is it a recognition that an obsession about technology is anti-social and unhealthy or does it suggest that those who use it as abuse are fearful of technology?

all forms of media production. Finally, we can note that the reporter works within the **institution** of journalism, with its developed techniques for constructing news stories – a further extension of the idea of news technology.

ACTIVITY 16.1
- Can you list the different technologies used in a local radio studio?
- Can you divide them into software and hardware?

Technology: focus of conflict

The 'methods, means and skill' definition of technology is not always appreciated. This is the result of a mix of factors which tend to obscure the real issues and to promote cruder, more simplistic ideas.

- *Class* undoubtedly plays a role in this. In Britain, class positions depend largely on education and occupation. Technologists have traditionally had lower status than professionals such as doctors or lawyers. This is perhaps a uniquely British problem in that, despite their importance in creating the industrial revolution or developing the infrastructure of modern society, 'engineers' have never gained the status they have achieved elsewhere in Europe. You will also be aware that 'vocational' courses, which imply a closer attention to technology, have less status in education than 'academic' courses.

- These class differences perhaps lead on to distinctions between '*doers*' and '*thinkers*' in media production and media education. Sometimes it is the commercial producer, who sees 'new' technology as either cost-cutting or possessing a 'wow' factor, versus the creative artist, who wants to retain 'ideas' and traditional skills. (Be careful here, though: **avant-garde** artists often embrace new technologies first – see the Independents section of Chapter 8). Sometimes it is the pragmatic broadcaster versus the academic theorist. Much of the time it boils down to a difference between those who actually use the technology on a daily basis and those who don't.

- Media technology is *gendered*: in many cases girls are put off media production work because of its association with 'boys' toys' and a macho culture of bigger, faster, louder etc.: some boys have suffered from taunts about their excessive interest in equipment rather than people, 'the trainspotter syndrome' or the '**anorak**'. These gender differences are not all clear-cut. In the film industry, it is not unusual to find women film editors, and there are now a handful of successful women directors, but women cinematographers (i.e. the persons in charge of lighting and camerawork) are very rare. There is evidence to suggest that this wasn't always so and that in the early years of cinema women were very active. Indeed the first director of a narrative film may well have been a woman, Alice Guy Blach, who directed a short feature in 1896. In 1911 she wrote: 'There is nothing connected with the staging of a motion picture that a woman cannot do as easily as a man, and there is no reason why she cannot completely master every technicality of the art' (quoted in Acker 1991).

But these early roles for women were not maintained. Women (the stereotyped view says) have traditionally 'worked well with people' (director) or 'at a bench on a production process' (editor), but not in a role which requires application of both technical knowledge and artistic vision. The prejudice against women artists and composers has perhaps passed across to cinema. A more obvious reason is that camera operators have traditionally needed knowledge of optics and women have suffered from lack of access to the necessary school physics.

Women in Hollywood 'Guy power dominated the business, as it still does: to this day it is rare to have women running studios or directing films, and unknown – for here lies the voyeur's magic – to let them photograph a movie' (critic David Thomson on contemporary Hollywood, *Independent on Sunday*, 8 January 1995).

ACTIVITY 16.2

Technical roles for women

Is this criticism of the film industry also applicable to television? Have a look at the credit lists of a range of television programmes and films.

- How many women are listed as camera operators or directors of photography?
- How many women write the music for films and television (as distinct from performing it)?
- Which jobs are most likely to be filled by women?

The first woman member of the BSC (British Society of Cinematographers) was Sue Gibson, who worked for director Marleen Gorris on the Virginia Woolf adaptation *Mrs Dalloway* (UK/US 1997).

Technology is a potential stumbling block in the path of good working relationships. If you know about technology, you will think it is important and want to consider its implications. If you don't feel happy with it you will perhaps try to ignore those implications. This will be a real issue for you when you begin to produce your own media texts.

Many media producers and critics would agree that technology *in itself* is not very interesting; what is important is *what is produced as a media text*. A pamphlet which has changed history, a photograph which will always be remembered, a sound recording which moves a listener to tears, may all have been produced on primitive equipment with basic techniques – the lack of sophisticated technology did not stop them communicating. On the other hand, would you choose to ignore the most modern technology if it was available to you (even if it meant tackling something you didn't totally understand)? We won't solve this dilemma, but we should be sensitive to the issue. The best we might hope for is for everyone to agree to select the most appropriate technology for the job, rather than allowing the technology to do the selecting for us.

Technological change

Technology interests us most when it changes. From the first cave painting to the latest hi-tech feature film, media producers have striven to develop both hardware and software in order to achieve a better product. In media studies we want to ask: 'What does "better" mean? – less expensive to produce, more realistic, more beautiful, more easy to understand, more exciting, more uplifting, more easily available (and who decides the standards against which these are to be judged)?'

Early in the twenty-first century, the 'technological imperative' – the general feeling that we are being driven forward by the increasing pace of technological change – is perhaps more evident in relation to media and communications than to any other area. In past decades attention has centred on the 'space race', weapons technology, new cars or medical breakthroughs. Now the biggest industry in the world produces 'information' and 'entertainment', and more people are employed in it than in any of the traditional industries. In Chapter 8 we discuss the activities of the 'media industries', but we should also note that companies concerned directly with computing, telecommunications and information handling, such as Microsoft, are much bigger and more profitable than those concerned with media products such as entertainment or news.

Your studies are likely to include reference to 'new media technologies'. This is a slightly misleading term in that it refers to a process of change that began nearly twenty years ago.

Analogue to digital

Computer design Early computer graphics showed their origins clearly (suggesting a 'technology-driven' product). The software could not produce 'realistic' colours and textures, but looking 'futuristic' was then fashionable, so the product was acceptable. Now, design philosophies and computer power allow more 'naturalistic' images (i.e. as if painted with an analogue paintbrush).

The revolution in media technology largely took place between the mid-1980s and late 1990s. Anyone born since 1985 is likely to have experienced **digital** media as almost commonplace and to have been aware of computers from starting school. There are one or two aspects of media technology where the changes are still working through, and it is important to be aware of what the 'revolution' from analogue to digital has achieved so far.

> **analogue**   that which is analogous to something else (bearing some correspondence or resemblance), from the Greek *analogia* = 'according to' and *logos* = 'ratio'.
> **digital**   represented by numbers (digits = fingers).

An analogue device works by recording and storing or displaying information in a suitable 'physical' form, after first converting measurements from their original 'real world' state. In this way, what is mediated by the device is an 'analogy' of the real thing in another physical form.

The oldest such devices are measuring instruments such as the sundial or the hourglass. The 'chronometer' in all its guises is a good guide to developing technology. The ability to measure time accurately changed the way we live dramatically (timed hours of work were a major feature of the factories built in the industrial revolution). Devices developed from reliance on the sun to mechanical springs of great precision and finally to the digital accuracy of microchips.

At one time, all media technologies were based on analogue processes. 'Chemical photography' relies on light-sensitive chemicals reacting differentially to the reflected light from a subject captured by the lens. Microphones capture sound by measuring vibrations caused by sound waves and then converting them, first to electrical impulses and then to magnetic charges which can be stored on tape. In each case, the information stored is a physical representation of the original 'image'. Analogue media are each distinct with different modes of representing a signal. They are also 'continuous' in tone – a photograph moves smoothly from one colour shade to another.

Digital technology is concerned only with numbers – everything which is captured must be converted to numerical data. The microphone and the camera lens are still used, but a sensing device 'reads' the information about sound waves or patterns of light and converts it to numerical form. From then on all processing is done by means of computation – the device contains a computer. Digital media are no longer distinct – they are all represented by numbers and they are no longer 'continuous' but broken down into patterns of data. (So a digital photograph is a '**bitmap**', a matrix of dots – see Chapter 11.)

In every aspect of media production there has been a shift from 'analogue to digital', and understanding what this shift means will help us to recognise the interrelationship of many of the debates about technology.

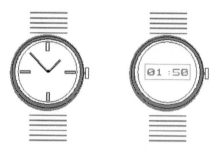

Figure 16.1 Analogue and digital watches.

The story of the CD and DVD

Digital television offers many
extra channels provided by a
multiplex system: 'In the analogue
era, we called them repeats, in
the digital age, it's multiplexing'
(Adam Singer, then of Flextech,
quoted in the *Economist*, March
1998, and proving that 'new'
technology does not necessarily
mean 'new' products).

The first digital media technology to catch the attention of the general public
was probably the compact disc. Since its appearance in the early 1980s, the
CD has had various 'ups and downs' in the market place, but the rapid
acceptability of the first audio CDs was straightforward to explain:

- They offered higher definition sound on relatively cheap equipment (i.e.
  compared to top-range analogue equipment).
- They were less likely to be damaged accidentally or to wear out.
- Up to 75 minutes of music could be stored (vinyl rarely went beyond 40
  minutes per disc).
- They could be 'programmed' to play tracks in any order.
- They were much smaller and easier to store than the traditional black vinyl
  discs.

The appeal can be summarised as 'reliability, convenience, modern design and
new features'. The main barrier to swift acceptance by the mass consumer
market was the cost of the CD player and the relatively high cost of the discs
themselves. Here is the dilemma for every media producer wanting to
introduce new technologies into the consumer market. The new product
needs to be cheap enough to attract the average consumer, but that means
possibly losing large sums of money subsidising the price of hardware and
software in the early stages. At least part of the success of CDs was the 'repackaging' of existing recorded music on discount labels or 'giveaways'. The
actual CDs cost very little to produce so this was affordable. Note that the
market was older consumers – the youth market in the 1980s was still on
cassette.

With CDs established, various
companies tried to introduce
other digital audio products such
as DAT (digital audio tape), digital
compact cassettes and Mini-
Discs. None of these succeeded
in the mass market, although
DAT and Mini-Disc did carve out
a niche in professional audio
work.

In the meantime, the CD developed in another guise – as a computer
storage device, the CD-Rom. This time, the advantage was more storage than
a 'floppy disk' (or even a hard drive in the early days) and more portability
than a fixed hard drive. The big market that was predicted was for
'interactive' CD-Roms – games, stories, education etc. To some extent this
did happen but not as much as the developers hoped, and money was lost in
CD 'publishing'. What was necessary was a CD drive as standard in every

computer. This came when computer software grew in size so that it could be supplied only on CD-ROM. When everyone had a drive, the future for CDs became brighter and, once the drives could become 'writers' as well as 'readers', the market was secured.

Disc or **disk** The American spelling here is used to refer to computer disks. Those used in audio equipment are discs.

Familiarity helped the DVD

Digital video first appeared on Laser Discs. These caught on in America, where a sufficiently large group of film fans were willing to buy a player and expensive discs in order to get superior-quality image and sound played through a television. But in the UK, this new technology failed to sell. When DVDs appeared, they offered the same advantages, along with 'familiarity' – they looked like CDs and the new DVD player could take CDs as well.

At the time of writing, the 'combo' drive – a computer drive that will 'read' and 'write' both CDs and DVDs – is already appearing on home computers and will probably become standard in the future. Apple, the most innovative computer company in design terms, announced the concept of the 'digital hub' with the introduction of the **iMac** in 1999. This computer was designed to accommodate every aspect of digital media 'built-in', and the appropriate software began to be distributed with the machine – iMovie, iTunes, iPhoto etc. Here is one sense of **convergence** – a single platform for every kind of media production activity.

The integrated digital media suite on the iMacs released in 2002 allows a user to connect a still or video camera and download images. These can be edited and 'printed' to a CD or DVD. Music and other sounds can be recorded to hard disk or imported via CD or the Internet and again edited and printed to CD or DVD. All of this is possible at home or in a Media Studies classroom or workshop. Costs are relatively low, and the potential quality of the final product is high. The hardware and software designers have done their jobs well. Apple has probably one of the most comforting images of the future embedded in its products and advertising. Consumers and small media producers are impressed by technology that is affordable, easy to use and produces good results. But what of the wider implications?

Does 'digital' give better quality?

The manufacturers claim that digital audio gives a clearer, more 'authentic' sound because nothing is lost or added to the original performance. This claim is worth investigating. If a sound has been produced in a studio, it will have been captured by a microphone and then recorded – in this sense there is no difference between analogue and digital recording. Some musical

Figure 16.2a Convergence on the Mac: an iBook showing free iTunes software and an iPod, a compact storage device and player of MP3s.

Figure 16.2b The digital editing software iMovie is also 'bundled' free with iMacs and iBooks.

instruments are digital themselves – a digital keyboard can be programmed to sound like other instruments, because the 'sound' it produces is initially in the form of digital information rather than soundwaves. It comes from the on-board computer's memory rather than, say, from a vibrating piano wire, and the digital information can be recorded directly. In this latter case, the recorded data is certainly a replica of what the musician 'played'. (Another way to think of this is that you can 'make music' without musical instruments at all – simply by 'playing' the sounds already stored as digital 'samples' in the computer memory.) A microphone can, however, produce only a representation of a sound image (just as a camera can produce only a representation of a visual image).

There are some philosophical arguments here – can any natural sound be recorded 'authentically'? Leaving this aside, the major difference comes during the next two stages of the process.

An analogue recording requires a physical transfer of data during the editing and mixing stage and then again during the duplication stage. Every time this physical exchange takes place some data is lost and some extra noise is added. The tape, the recording heads, the cables, the electrical wiring and earthing – all of these can be the source of 'noise' (noise is any unwanted sound). The digital process may use similar media – tape, cables etc. – but since it is numerical data which is being transferred, the computer can monitor the data exchange, constantly checking that the data 'adds up' (computer data has 'check numbers' inserted in the data stream which allow number checking and correction). In this way the digital recording process can guarantee that degradation of data and the presence of 'noise' are kept to an absolute minimum.

This isn't quite the end of the story, however. Digital processes share one feature of analogue processes – the more detail you want in the recorded 'image', the more storage space you need. In analogue terms this means that the area of tape needed to record music is so great that the tape must be passed at high speeds across the recording heads. In digital terms it means that, in order to fit all the necessary data on to a suitable disc (or disk), it may be necessary to leave out some of the very high or very low frequencies of a sound recording or to 'compress' the data so that it takes up less space.

Both these actions alter the original recording and this means that it is still possible that the analogue equipment with the highest specification (and the highest price) can produce a more 'authentic' sound than many digital systems.

Samples are analogue sounds, captured and stored on a computer disk as digital data. They can be manipulated, edited together and turned into new music productions. Use of samples not only provides the means for the 'bedroom recording star' to make music – it also raises interesting questions about the copyright on sounds.

See Chapter 17 and Analysing images case study.

'Domestic' or professional?

Quality is also a matter of the expertise needed by the user and the technical specifications of equipment. Media technology has for many years been categorised by manufacturers as suitable for 'domestic', 'semi-professional' or 'professional' use. For many years BBC and ITV technical officers decreed what was suitable for broadcast use, but the multi-channel television and radio environment has introduced a greater range in acceptable technical 'standards'.

The distinctions are based on a number of factors, the most important being the quality of the audio or video signal that can be recorded and input to an edit suite. In simple terms, the professional technology provides more information from larger-**format** media.

Formats In this context, 'format' refers to different sizes and types of data storage devices e.g. film as 16 mm or 35 mm.

The domestic equipment designed for the home user often has fixed or automatic controls which limit the possibilities of creating certain types of images (audio or visual). Conversely, professional equipment, which allows great control over the recording process, also requires considerable skill on behalf of the operator. Perhaps the major distinguishing feature, however, is cost – £600 for a domestic camcorder, £10,000 or more for a broadcast machine.

An indication of how these distinctions are breaking down is the use of relatively inexpensive (i.e. £2,000) digital video cameras on feature films such as the DOGME film *Festen* (Denmark 1998) – see Chapter 17.

Digital technology threatens many of these distinctions. Format is less of an issue, even if the price differential still means that domestic users are limited by what they are able, and prepared, to pay for. But as we've noted in our iMac example above, professional quality work is attainable: here is one source of the argument that says that new technology can provide greater **access** to media production.

But can the professionals 'allow' this gap to be closed? Almost certainly not. The broadcasting industries compete by seeking to maintain leadership in 'quality' sounds and images by developing new delivery systems such as stereo broadcasts and 'high-definition' images on widescreen television sets. 'Professionalism' is an important part of the institution of television or radio or any other media industry (see Chapter 7). A regulated industry with its conventional modes of operation must distinguish itself from what it sees as 'amateur' production. The Internet is an interesting test case of this with its thousands of websites. Websites are 'new media' products which come from an industry sector that is yet to be fully 'institutionalised'. Instead, it is rather like the cinema at the end of the nineteenth century. There are many small producers using a wide range of software tools with varying degrees of proficiency. The result is enormous variety. This gives any Internet surfer the chance to find some exciting and innovative ways of accessing information, but also some frustrating and time-consuming experiences of downloading badly scanned images that are too large or trying to read purple text on a pink background.

Nonlinear editing Traditional analogue video editing requires each shot to be copied in sequence (i.e. in a 'linear' mode) to a master tape. Digital video editing allows shots to be digitised and then compiled using a 'timeline'. Shots can be 'cut and pasted' as in a wordprocessor before the final version is 'rendered' or 'printed'. Not only does digital processing mean less degradation of the image, but it gives much more flexibility. Film editing has always been 'nonlinear' but transferring to a digital process still confers advantages of flexibility and efficiency.

Figure 16.3 Media 100 is one of the leading 'nonlinear editing' systems that have brought digital editing to audio, video and multimedia applications.

Intelligent machines?

If the stored data is digital it can be accessed and used in many other ways. Digital devices can provide information about what they are doing and can perform automatic operations – in effect they can be programmed to perform, just like any other computer. At the simplest level, a CD player can play the tracks on a disc in any order. At the most complex level, a digital video edit suite can read an edit decision list and put together an entire programme while you go off for a cup of tea ('auto-conforming'). All of this makes digital technologies potentially more creative in the sense that they can make possible new ways of doing things and even suggest new things to do with spin-offs from the extra information they provide.

Miniaturisation

Digital storage, via compression, can lead to smaller devices and, as we have noted, consumers moved to CDs from vinyl discs because they were more convenient to handle. Digital processing is controlled by microchips which get smaller and more powerful, seemingly day by day. The process of miniaturisation goes on non-stop. This means that new consumer products and especially new portable products will continue to appear. The most recent example of this is the 'third generation' of mobile phones that are effectively 'micro computers'.

Convergence

Because digital media technologies treat text, graphics, photographs and
sounds in the same way, the differences between texts in different media have
disappeared. The 'essence' of each separate medium has disappeared and with
it many of the institutional aspects of media production in that area. The
consequences of this are not yet clear. Take the example of the 'e-book' – a
portable device that can be loaded with text and image (and possibly audio)
files and 'read' via the screen.

Traditional book purchasers have scoffed at the possibility of reading a
novel 'on screen' – an unappealing proposition? Yet the e-book has many
advantages for kinds of text access. If you own this book for instance, you
might be frustrated when a new edition comes out. What if you could simply
'download' the new bits from the Internet and update your copy? Did you
curse your teachers when you had to lug a huge bag of books round school?
What if all of them could fit on an e-book reader?

Sound editing technology now looks the same as video editing or
photographic retouching technology: all data appears on a computer screen
and is manipulated via mouse and keyboard (as in Figure 16.3). Multimedia
programs are 'authored' by someone who writes a script comprising a set of
instructions which in effect command the software to play a video sequence or
a sound sequence or to display text or still images, all of which are just
datafiles to be 'called up'.

> just as cut-and-splice methods in sound recording suggested an intriguing
> link with film in the sixties, the exact equivalence of digital 'composing'
> programmes like Cubase and video editing programmes like AVID placed
> the two disciplines within morphologically similar techno-grids. In both
> cases the praxis is the same – bunch of folks in an airless city room staring
> at a screen.
>
> (Sinker 1995)

Technology and the media workplace

We have already noted that attitudes towards technology vary enormously.
Some of us are 'anti' (technophobes), others are 'pro' (technophiles). Partly it
is a matter of how comfortable we feel with new equipment. But some of the
ways in which technology changes our lives are not immediately apparent.
Pam Linn, an educationist writing in the mid-1980s, referred to this as
technological immanence – the invasion of our world by an intelligence we don't
immediately recognise. Computer technology has changed the way we work,
bringing 'liberation' and new creative opportunities, but also anxiety and
insecurity. A good example of this is our approach to writing. In a world of

Photography is considered to be
no longer a useful term by many
critics and has been replaced by
'electronic imaging or digital
imaging'. Traditional photography
is a medium of photochemistry. In
the new 'digital darkroom' images
from different sources (video,
computer, chemical photography)
are combined.

Technology and the media workplace

word processing and e-mail it is difficult to imagine how books were ever written using a typewriter or even pen and ink. But if a pen nib broke or a typewriter key jammed, the author still had the 'hard copy' of what had already been written. If a computer file is corrupted, everything may be lost, and after years of using a keyboard handwriting skills deteriorate. Our reliance on computer systems has changed our way of working.

Transferable skills are highly valued by governments and employers who want workers to be able to move easily between different jobs. Computer skills are potentially 'transferable', but most training emphasises understanding of specific software such as Microsoft Word, rather than how the technology works. So, is the understanding transferable to other packages and other computer platforms? Are keyboard operators more or less 'skilled' than the typists of previous generations?

Linn also raised the issues of *user-friendliness* and effective *deskilling*.

- Modern machines have several automatic functions and 'default settings', which allow anyone to use them without having to learn how to operate them fully or to understand how they work.

- Computer displays are designed to be user-friendly by presenting the user with a screen which effectively mimics the environment which it has replaced. A desktop publishing program mimics the designer's desk and the software is designed to be 'intuitive' so that the user can move objects about the screen without having to understand what the computer is doing. This feature has been a major factor in the success of the new technologies, but Linn argued that it is based on a 'deficiency model' of the user's competence: 'In practice "user friendliness" makes a program easier to use at the cost of understanding how the program actually achieves its effects. Ease of use is related to powerlessness, rather than to control' (Linn 1985).

The issue here is 'skill transfer'. If you learn to use one software package, can you transfer your skill to another package on another machine? And do you know what to do if the computer does not perform as you expect? You cannot transfer your skills if you do not 'own' them, and skill ownership is another important issue. Linn might argue that the skills are 'owned' by the software.

It is worth noting that 'professional' media technology has fewer 'automatic' settings and allows greater control over actions. This is good for the designer or editor, but 'dangerous' for the keyboard operator in the office, who is expected to follow routines – software as 'control'?

ACTIVITY 16.3
Skill ownership

Think about the media technology you use on your course.

When computers were first introduced into offices in the 1970s, there was much talk of 'the paperless office' of the future. In fact two aspects of computer work – unreliability and ease of amendement and reprinting – increased the amount of paper in offices quite dramatically.

- How much do you know about how it works?
- Can you distinguish between decisions you make about how to use the equipment (altering sound levels, changing camera lens settings) and settings given to you automatically?
- How much do you need to know before you can feel 'in control' of the technology you use?
- Try to think of one production you worked on. Could you describe how you could have achieved a similar result using different technology?

You may well have already come to this conclusion if you learnt how to use one computer in lower school and then found that the computers in the sixth form or college did not use the same software. The computer manufacturers and software writers could make your life easier, but often it suits them to frustrate you into buying their product and then sticking with it. Your ability to transfer skills is a potential loss to them because you could easily transfer your allegiance. These questions of skill ownership and operator's 'control' over the technology are important in all areas of media production. A similar set of questions underpinned the US government's legal action against Microsoft when it succeeded in installing its internet software on all new computers so that new users would accept Outlook Express and Internet Explorer as 'defaults'. Microsoft knew that most users would not want to move to another software package which required them to 'transfer skills'.

One of the drawbacks in the 'default setting' of most computers to use Outlook Express is that it has made it much easier to spread viruses, many of which operate like Microsoft 'macros' – software routines that are automatically launched when an infected e-mail is opened.

Deskilling and 'multiskilling'

These questions of skill ownership and 'empowerment' lead us to a general discussion about 'deskilling'. The invention of this term implies that jobs are becoming less reliant on specialist craft skill and more on a range of lower-level general skills. It's interesting to note that various groups have 'turned' this concept to argue for 'multiskilling', which has special resonance in the media industries where one or two 'generalists' can now manage the work previously carried out by several specialists. For example, the traditional crafts of typesetting and picture retouching required highly skilled staff with years of training. These have now been replaced by computer software. With the two 'industry standard' software packages, Adobe **Photoshop** and **Quark Xpress**, any reasonably computer-literate person can learn the basics of how to lay out a page and how to manipulate an image after only a few days' tuition – the software has effectively given us a concentrated version of all the skills and knowledge which the craft operatives have learnt over many years.

But does this make us 'typesetters'? Are we really capable of 'desktop publishing'? Well, sort of. What we don't know is what makes a good page

Lightbulb joke: 'How many Microsoft engineers does it take to change a lightbulb? None – Bill Gates will just redefine darkness as the industry standard.'

Quark Xpress This is the software used by nearly all magazine publishers for sophisticated page layout. The only serious rival is Adobe's InDesign. Image manipulation is dominated by **Photoshop**. Although the Macintosh is the usual computer for publishing, all three programs are available on 'Wintel' PCs as well.

layout, why some typefaces are not appropriate for particular uses – in short we are not trained designers (see Chapter 11). The software will actually try to do this for us as well, suggesting standard layouts. Unfortunately, most software has bland standard settings which mean that there are now many examples of badly designed leaflets and posters, immediately recognisable as 'dtp' publications. The same is true of images, thousands of which are available on CD-ROMs. This use of **clipart** means that many people without developed drawing skills are able to produce illustrated work (as we have done with two drawings in this chapter). We could see this as increased access to opportunities for a wider range of people to engage in production, but some employers may see an opportunity to pay less for skills and reduce staffing levels. Introduction of new technology inevitably leads to redundancy and redeployment – investment in capital equipment displaces labour.

The end of hot metal

The introduction of new technology has led to the disappearance of many traditional job roles. The clearest example of this was the war waged by proprietors such as Rupert Murdoch on the Fleet Street print unions in the newspaper industry in the 1980s. When the national newspapers were based in Fleet Street in central London, typesetting machines such as the Linotype produced metal type 'set' in lines in a tray from which the pages could be printed. The alloy type was melted for reuse and the Linotype actually spat out **'hot metal'**. This process required skilled print workers. Murdoch broke them by moving out to Wapping and computerising the whole process, which also meant that journalists found themselves increasingly responsible for the initial preparation of their copy.

'Hot metal' is now used to refer to newspaper practices before Murdoch's battle with the unions.

In some local newspapers, the picture editor has gone and the news editor now selects the images. In broadcasting, the television four-person film news crew (two on camera plus a sound operator and a reporter) has been reduced to a video team of two – and some stations have experimented with 'videojournalists'. What were once specialist 'graded posts', fought for by craft unions, are being replaced by 'multiskilling'.

In North America some radio stations are completely automatic, broadcasting from computer files with pre-recorded continuity announcements and not a DJ in sight. In the better radio stations the computer has not replaced staff, but has instead enabled them to work more quickly and therefore to spend more time 'getting it right'. Technology in itself is not a threat to labour – it is always a case of how management

Videojournalists were employed briefly by a local cable company, Channel 1, in London, working on their own as combined reporter, camera operator and sound recordist. See Griffiths (1998).

TV-AM, which held the franchise for breakfast television on ITV during the 1980s, used to operate a series of remote studios in various provincial cities. These studios had make-up rooms, reception areas for guests and a single set with a lighting rig and a camera 'remotely controlled' from London. One full-time employee operated the studio.

attempts to use it. 'Things don't take less time. Instead you get people doing things in more detail, more accurately and better than they did before. These days most stations are pretty slim, and on air you're using the same number of people' (Paul Fairburn, Programme Controller of Heartland FM interviewed in *Broadcast*, 21 April 1995).

Case study: Cybercultures – living in an Internet world

> Mankind's extended electric nervous system, rustling data and credit in the crowded matrix, monochrome nonspace where the only stars are dense concentrations of information, and high above it all burn corporate galaxies and the cold spiral arms of military systems.
>
> (Gibson 1986)

William Gibson created the idea of 'cyberspace' in his science fiction stories of the early 1980s. Here was a whole new world in which human experience was 'digitised' and interaction took place in the 'virtual reality' of datastreams. We haven't quite reached that point yet, but millions of us 'jack in' to the Internet each day and explore what the digital world has to offer. And many of those who work at the frontiers of the digital world are conscious of the ideas explored by Gibson and other 'cyberpunk' writers.

The Internet has become 'established', and slowly it is beginning to become 'institutionalised'. Is it really offering something completely new in terms of media and communications or should we treat it just like any other form of media distribution system? How have media and cultural theorists discussed what the Internet might mean?

Universal access

The world of 'new' media on the Internet is at least in theory available to everyone, but in practice it depends on a range of factors. In the UK, the Blair government made access to the Internet an important feature of its overall approach to the new digital environment:

> We want to ensure the widest possible access to a choice of diverse communications services of the highest quality. All of us can benefit from new services – as citizens, as parents, as workers, as students, and as consumers. We want to include every section of our society in the benefits of these services, and use to the full the opportunities now available for enhancing their diversity and quality.
>
> (Introduction to the Communications White Paper, 2000)

The evidence of this desire is evident in the National Grid for Learning with
investment in ICT networks and Internet connections for schools and
libraries. But even if the physical infrastructure for Internet access is
available (and there are questions about this – see below) there are
important social, cultural and political questions to ask. Are we all aware of,
and equipped to use, the opportunities available? Alessandro Aurigi and
Stephen Graham identified a new 'class system' operating in cyberspace:

- *the information users* – an elite of transnational service workers with the
  skills and knowledge to achieve a dominant position (the *digital elite*)
- *the information used* – less affluent and less mobile workers whose main
  connection with the Internet is as *digital consumers*
- *the 'off-line'* – marginalised groups of the underemployed or unemployed
  or the technologically intimidated who are unable to participate in
  cyberculture – the *digital underclass*.

(adapted from Bell 2001: 131)

This is a useful observation about the new media environment generally, but
it also links to a central argument about the Internet – does it provide
opportunities for a new form of democracy or its opposite, a new form of
oppression? There are links here to a number of arguments throughout this
book. Are music 'pirates' opening up the music industry and lifting the
tyranny of the record companies with free downloads of music? (See Music
Industry case study following Chapter 8.) Does the new technology allow
'independent producers' to make new kinds of products outside the
mainstream? (See Chapter 8.) Does it offer political campaigners
('hacktivists') a whole new world of online protest and activity, whether
around anti-capitalist global protest or local issues? (See Branigan 2001.)
Then again, is the Internet just another means of 'selling audiences' to
advertisers? (See Chapter 6 and case study.)

Another way to think about the new Internet technologies is in terms of
'push' and 'pull' technologies. Several media technologies began as
interactive, 'two-way' modes of communication. Radio is a good example,
and the Internet was certainly conceived in this way. What is the Internet
after all, except a 'network of networks' – a means to link your computer
with thousands of others across the world? Initially, Internet connections
were sought by users who wanted to 'explore' and to find things that they
could bring home, or to find like-minded people with whom they could
share experiences. In effect, they were using the Internet as a *'pull'*
technology. The new language of the Internet referred to 'surfing' websites
or 'browsing' them. It isn't quite clear how these terms arose but one
implies the surfer riding the wave looking for the 'big one' and the other the

book collector searching through second-hand stores. Both these are 'active users' looking for something.

Figure 16.4
A cybercafé. Is this just another consumer entertainment outlet or a new form of participation in a community?

As the Internet expanded and businesses became interested in the new 'dot.com' economy as a means of making money, the culture began to change. The technologies offered opportunities to promote goods and services, to '*push*' material to users. Junk mail appeared on the web as 'spamming' – unwanted e-mails, often offering pornography (pornography has always been an 'early adopter' of new technologies). Less obvious was the growth of 'portals' (gateways to on-line services) and Internet Service Providers (**ISPs**) who offered not just a connection but also an array of tailor-made web pages. AOL, the largest of these ISPs, became part of the biggest media conglomerate when it merged with Time Warner.

The new users of the Internet were less 'adventurous' and more consumer-orientated. They gained access through Microsoft or AOL and they approached what was offer as if it was another type of consumer technology. The expansion of Internet access was based largely on 'push' technologies and these are also a feature of access via the television 'set-top box'. 'Consumers' are offered goods and services, and it is surprising what information is collected about everyone of us as we make 'transactions' in the digital world. Consider the following:

- Your credit card records details of what you buy.
- Your name on a mailing list can be sold to someone else.
- A supermarket smart card records every item you buy.
- A '**cookie**' placed on your computer by a website helps 'personalise' your next visit (see Selling audiences case study following Chapter 6).

Cookies are tiny programs that are placed on your hard drive to send information back to an Internet site. Your web browser should enable you to decide whether you wish to accept them.

Note, that in many cases, the 'default' set by your computer or your contract with a supplier assumes that you give your permission for these details to be used. You have to act if you want to stop it.

Some successful consumer websites, such as Amazon, are now able to offer you new items to buy on the basis of what you have bought before.

But many such sites have closed down because we have been more
reluctant to part with our money than was previously assumed. (Most
'e-commerce' is 'b2b' (business to business) rather than 'b2c' (business to
consumer). So perhaps we are not so easily led – not so 'passive' as
consumers?)

There are aspects of the new technologies that are more positive. The
explosion of text messaging was an unexpected phenomenon – a new
communication form taken up and developed by users rather than
'providers'. We might also point to the positive aspects of the
interactivity with popular television shows such as *Big Brother* and *Pop Idol*.
Discussions about these shows took place in 'real life' and in 'virtual life' on
bulletin boards and in chatrooms. Will or could such interactivity and
democratic decision-making be applied to political issues, in all their
complexity?

Language and culture

The Internet is predominately a medium of written English. American
websites dominate the Internet, but elsewhere any language that cannot be
displayed in a standard western alphabet is at a disadvantage. English is one
of the four most used languages in the world, as is Spanish. But the other
two most used languages, Chinese and Arabic, are much more difficult to
display on websites because their written forms require a different system
of characters and a different mode of reading. Is the Internet 'globalising
culture' through its promotion of English? Another group of users who may
be excluded are the visually impaired. But if technology is developed to
support visually impaired users, it may open up whole new fields of
discovery for such users. This is another example of how a new technology
can be both threatening and potentially liberating.

In parts of the world where even electricity is a luxury, the Internet may
not seem very relevant, but it is worth referring to earlier debates about
television services and pointing out that just one computer linking an
isolated community to the Internet could introduce a whole range of
information resources.

We began with a government statement of intent to make access to
digital services possible for everyone, but that statement has been criticised
as too 'consumerist' (see Chapter 18 for discussion of the White Paper)
and too negative, too much about protecting citizens and not enough about
empowering them to be active in the new environment. The Internet is not
just another communications technology, but a new cultural form.

ACTIVITY 16.4

Conduct your own qualitative research (see Chapter 9) on Internet usage. Select a sample of Internet users to represent a broad spread of society (not just fellow students). Devise a list of open questions to enable you to discover how they use the Internet. How do they connect? What are they looking for? etc. Summarise your findings and decide whether your group is mostly 'push' or 'pull' in their use of the technology.

Digital imaging

> The drive behind much of the technical development in cinema since 1950 has been towards both a greater or heightened sense of 'realism' and a bigger, more breathtaking realisation of spectacle . . . towards reducing the spectators' sense of their 'real' world, and replacing it with a fully believable artificial one.
>
> (Allen 1998: 127)

> The reduction of the photographic image to numbers implies the possibility of its reversal, in other words the creation of fictional, but photographically 'real', imagery (and spaces).
>
> (Henning 1995: 218)

These two quotations neatly represent major concerns within what might now be termed 'image technologies'. They both play with the idea of the **photorealistic** – the achievement of an iconic image which attempts to represent the 'real' world. We explore the issue of 'realisms' and their importance within media studies in Chapter 17, but what interests us here is the impact of technological change and the difference between the attitudes developed within photography and cinema.

The drive for greater realism has propelled technological development in cinema throughout its history. It is not just a question of a bigger, brighter, more sharply focused image with more 'natural' colours, but also a depth and clarity of sound. Somehow, Hollywood has managed to contain the contradiction of a more 'realistic' image associated with an extraordinary spectacle – culminating in the massive investment in special effects technology to create the spectacle of *Titanic* (US 1997).

Allen goes on to point out that, although we recognise that the spectacle is created by new technologies, we still insist that the effects are seamlessly melded into the fictional world of the film – we know that '**morphing**' isn't possible, but if it was it would look as 'real' as it does in *Terminator 2* (US 1991). By contrast, when the material of a film is actuality, one of the dominant conventions is to foreground the construction of the image by emphasising the hand-held camera and the use of the interviewer's microphone.

Morphing is a technique ideally suited to computer operation. It refers to the process of changing the shape of an object in a smooth, continuous process. The computer is given the original image and the 'changed' image and then calculates the frames in between, each of which shows a slight alteration.

Photography starts from a different position. The 'dominant' mode of photography for most of the history of the medium has been the documentary strand which upholds the photographic image as 'evidence' of something which has happened. Perhaps because the photographic print is a 'fixed' permanent record (unlike the 'time-based' status of film, which exists only as a flickering and temporary image on a screen), it is seen as 'capturing' reality in a 'decisive moment' (the phrase made famous by **Henri Cartier-Bresson**).

There are other modes of photography, and several photographic artists have embraced new technologies and used them to develop a wide range of techniques in order to produce innovative work for exhibitions and commercial (advertising, fashion etc.) work. But though these works attract interest and debate, they do not represent the challenge which the latest digital imaging has brought to the status of the photograph as evidence.

The quotation from Henning refers to an anxiety about a 'post-photographic world' in which there is no certainty. What appears 'real' may be a fiction. Of course, it has long been possible to 'doctor' a photograph, but before digital **manipulation** the procedure was quite difficult and the results often less than satisfactory. In Figure 16.4 a simple manipulation has been carried out – the lamp-posts have been 'rubbed out'. This casual editing is now a commonplace. If you check the newspapers when a big story breaks, you will sometimes see the same agency photograph used in different newspapers with different 'digital enhancements'. These are often designed to clarify the meaning of an image with some background details removed. How do you feel about this? Have we finally reached the dreadful world of Orwell's *Nineteen Eighty-Four* – or perhaps we have been freed from the tyranny of 'real images'? Some critics recognise this as another feature of a 'postmodern' condition (see Chapter 14) – a world of surfaces with no fixed meanings.

Pleasantville (US 1999) uses digital image manipulation to create the fictional world of a 1950s black and white television sitcom that is gradually 'coloured in', but the colours used are quite different from the 'realist' colours of scenes set in contemporary America. This film was one of the first to transfer film to high-resolution digital video for manipulation. *O Brother, Where Art Thou?* (US/UK 2000) was similarly transferred to video to allow the 'greens' of the landscape in the film to be presented as 'dusty yellows'.

Henri Cartier-Bresson (born 1908) French documentarist with an enormous impact on photography practice. His first collection of photographs was published in America in 1952 under the title *The Decisive Moment*.

Manipulation In July 1995 Russian President Boris Yeltsin returned to public duty after treatment for heart disease. A photograph was released as proof of his recovery. Much discussion followed, in which some observers claimed that they remembered the photograph from an earlier period – only the shirt he was wearing had been changed.

Figure 16.5a and b It is a simple task to 'rub out' the lamp-posts in the image – and to remove individuals from the march if necessary.

Conclusion

We've tried to deal in this chapter with a wide range of issues to do with technological change. In doing so we've tried to avoid some of the glib determinist statements in which the impact of technology has easily recognised effects (usually bad). We've presented a series of sometimes contradictory analyses that are relevant to many media debates. The pace of change is so great that you will need to be on the lookout for news stories in order to keep up-to-date. Try to use this chapter to develop a starting point for your own analysis.

References

Acker, Ally (1991) *Reel Women*, London: Batsford.

Allen, Michael (1998) 'From *Bwana Devil* to *Batman Forever*: technology in contemporary Hollywood cinema', in Steve Neale and Murray Smith (eds) *Contemporary Hollywood Cinema*, London: Routledge.

Bell, David (2001) *An Introduction to Cybercultures*, London: Routledge.

Branigan, Tania (2001) 'Net tightens around the hacktivists' *Guardian*, 2 January.

Gauntlett, David (ed.) (2000) *Web.Studies: Rewiring Media Studies for the Digital Age*, London: Arnold.

Gibson, William (1986) *Burning Chrome*, London: Panther.

Griffiths, Richard (1998) *Videojournalism*, London: Focal Press.

Henning, Michelle (1995) 'Digital encounters: mythical pasts and electronic presence', in Martin Lister (ed.) *The Photographic Image in Digital Culture*, London: Routledge.

Linn, Pam (1985) 'Microcomputers in education: dead and living labour', in Tony Solomonides and Les Levidow (eds) *Compulsive Technology: Computers as Culture*, London: Free Association Books.

Lister, Martin (ed.) (1995) *The Photographic Image in Digital Culture*, London: Routledge.

Lister, Martin (2000) 'Photography in the age of electronic imaging', in Liz Wells (ed.) *Photography: A Critical Introduction*, London: Routledge.

Sinker, Mark (1995) 'Music as film', in Jonathan Romney and Adrian Wootton (eds) *Celluloid Jukebox*, London: BFI.

Further reading

There are very few books which address new media technologies in an accessible form for students – and many that do soon become out of date. Articles in newspapers (i.e. the broadsheet dailies and Sundays) and magazines (both 'hobbyist' and professional) are sometimes more useful, but beware exaggerated claims about the possibilities of change.

Websites

www.gn.apc.org/pmhp/ehippies is cited by Branigan as the electrohippie collective website

hacktivism.tao.ca is the hacktivism discussion list

17 Realisms

Why realisms?

In the first two editions of this book, we felt the need to explain why 'realisms' needed a separate chapter. The significance of realist approaches seemed to have diminished. In the last two or three years; however, questions of realism have returned with a vengeance. Audience participation in, and interaction with, so-called 'reality' television shows is common across the schedules. In drama the first few weeks of 2002 saw two different documentary/drama mixes about 'Bloody Sunday', based on classic models from the 1960s, and the 'real' charge of such accidental footage as that capturing the attacks on the World Trade Center on 11 September 2001 suggests that authentic footage, however rough, retains a huge fascination (see Bruzzi in Creeber 2001: 133).

- **Realism** is a concept which writers and producers fight over – a politically charged term with an apparently obvious meaning, but also a long and varied history, which needs to be understood if it is going to be used effectively in media studies.

What is in dispute? Look at any historical drama on television. A programme which depicted life at the court of Elizabeth I would be ridiculed if someone was wearing a wristwatch, but we would accept that all the characters speak a recognisable English, even though we know that the people of the time spoke something we would find hard to follow. The wristwatch breaks the rules of historical detail, but the dialogue translation is an acceptable realist convention, which has been rendered 'invisible':

- Realism is something we have learnt to decode.

A similar point arises with the selection of colour or black and white filmstock in an image. For readers over fifty, black and white photography often denotes realism. They are familiar with events from wartime in which they have a personal emotional investment, being documented in monochrome in family snapshots or newsreels, whereas colour images of the same events seem like a fiction. Younger readers are likely to reverse this meaning and to take colour as 'real' and monochrome as a style feature.

- Realism as a term draws attention to a desire to connect with the rest of the real world especially around broad social questions such as unemployment, war, homelessness etc.

However, you can't simply point a camera at such events and expect to produce realism:

- Realism is an **aesthetic** construct, produced by means of recognisable codes and conventions which change over time.
- There is no single 'realism'; different cultures and different contexts produce different 'realisms'.

The controversy around realism is explained by its connection to social issues – which themselves are often the basis for conflict – and by the contradiction inherent in its use as an approach to media production, i.e. that a **realism effect** requires careful preparation and perhaps considerable artistry on behalf of the producer: it is never just a case of 'simply capturing reality'.

- In the 1994 film *Forrest Gump*, Tom Hanks shakes the hand of President John Kennedy, thirty years after Kennedy's death. We can now produce **photorealistic** images of events that never happened – not even as an acted-out scene, never mind as documented **actuality**. The technique is applied here in an entertainment film and audiences were amused rather than threatened, but it does raise the question: If we break the link between concrete reality and its representation, where does this leave our trust in **documentary** evidence? (See Chapter 16 for more on this issue.)
- Most viewers react to depictions of violence on the cinema or television screen, but some argue that 'realistic' violence is acceptable because it enables us to understand what the effects of violence really are, whereas 'cartoon violence' is simply gratuitous and likely to corrupt because it asks us to enjoy someone else's pain through a fantasy. Others argue the opposite – that, because we know that some violent acts we see are a fantasy, they do no real damage; but realistic violence appeals to our prurient, voyeuristic nature.

Whether or not children can distinguish between the 'real' and the 'fantastic' in this context is an important consideration, but this point tends to be lost if the two sides of the argument don't share a common understanding of the various modes of realism. (See Chapters 3 and 6, comments on this issue and verisimilitude.)

Newsreels during the 1930s and 1940s were all presented in monochrome and remained as 'evidence' of the period until the 1970s and 1980s, when researchers discovered 'amateur' or 'military' film footage of the war years, shot in colour.

Aesthetics refers originally to the 'principles of taste and art' or the 'philosophy of the fine arts'. It has come to be used to refer to an interest in visual style or 'the look' of something. A realist aesthetic is an approach to media production which consciously attempts to use a visual style which will help to produce a realist effect.

Actualities was the name given to the first short films of 'real events'. The term documentary appeared during the 1920s and has tended to be reserved for films over a certain length (perhaps twenty minutes).

Documentary 'The use of the film medium to interpret creatively and in social terms the life of the people as it exists in reality' (from the title page of *Documentary Film* by Paul Rotha (London: Faber & Faber, 1939)). 'The creative treatment of actuality' to refer to documentary was first suggested by John Grierson in 1926 in a review of Robert Flaherty's film *Moana* (see Hardy (ed.) 1966).

Historical background

Realism as an artistic movement is associated with the rise of capitalism and the industrial revolution of the 1840s in western Europe. As a movement in painting it is seen as predominantly French, covering the period 1840–80 (Nochlin 1971). Some of the techniques used in realist painting (e.g. perspective and accurate scale) had been known since the Renaissance, but their application now coincided with the birth of photography – the first technology to offer a direct representation of 'reality'. Novels such as those by **Charles Dickens** and **Elizabeth Gaskell** were notable for attention to detail in the descriptions of the characters' lives and an interest in the social conditions of contemporary society at a time when two new classes, the industrial poor and the urban bourgeoisie, were becoming established. Earlier novelists had tended to use characters to explore either emotions or moral values, whereas the realists were interested in their material lives (which isn't to say that realist novels were lacking discussion of values).

We can trace many of the contemporary debates around realism back to these two forms – the photograph and the 'bourgeois novel'. The two central issues might be:

- the use of technology to get us closer to 'reality'
- the debate about an aesthetic which constructs narrative time and space so that it seems to represent the 'real world' *transparently* to us as readers, inviting us to identify with an individual hero (rather than the exemplary 'everyman' of earlier stories).

We can see these two issues in play in current debates about reality television, in the 'realism effect' of hidden cameras ('undercover') and surveillance video footage and in the 'narrativisation' of ordinary lives and mundane events on 'confessional shows' like Jerry Springer or reality game shows such as *Big Brother*.

Realisms and technology

Photography is a process involving drawing ('graph') with light ('photo'), and the first photographic technology was used to help artists to draw more realistic pictures. The concept of a '**camera obscura**' (literally a dark room) into which light can be introduced through a tiny aperture to create an inverted image on a white background was first suggested by the Arab scientist Alhazen in the ninth century and 're-discovered' during the Renaissance. In the late eighteenth century, portable 'light-boxes' with a focusing lens (known as 'camera lucida') were introduced, and eventually the image was captured on light-sensitive materials – photography was born.

Charles Dickens (1812–70) wrote about the experience of 'ordinary' people in London. **Elizabeth Gaskell** (1810–65) wrote about the cotton workers of Manchester.

Transparency the idea that the reader or viewer treats the constructing devices in a text as invisible and sees only the 'reality' which is represented. It is opposed by the idea of foregrounding the construction (as when we see a microphone boom in shot).

A camera obscura is included in some museums or specially constructed towers and these are worth visiting for the insight they provide into the pre-electronic 'worldview'. Try Edinburgh or Dumfries among others.

A photograph is a two-dimensional image of a three-dimensional reality, and this requires an understanding of certain 'ways of looking' in order to understand how to 'read' the image as if it were 3D. We could argue that this is what visual realist conventions allow us to do. The optical devices of the eighteenth century introduced artists to new ways of producing images cast on paper, which could then be sketched or traced to make a permanent record. They were particularly useful in making possible accurate reproduction of *monocular perspective*. Perspective describes the angle of view which changes as lines are drawn towards a point on the horizon. Monocular perspective implies a single point from which these lines are drawn – i.e. the representation is constructed such that a single viewpoint is allowed. The viewer is 'in control' of the world he or she surveys.

In earlier painting styles, perspective was treated quite differently. If you go to an art gallery and look at pre-Renaissance paintings or those from non-European cultures (see Figure 17.1), you will find the size and placement of figures in a landscape presented in various ways. We are so used to the constructed sense of 'depth' in a photographic image that we find it difficult to 'read' these earlier images. Yet they serve to remind us that what we see in any representation is an artificial construction. The realist image is a 'learnt' image – it is not something 'natural' (see Neale 1985 for more on perspective).

Social issues

The nineteenth century not only saw technological developments which allowed the detail of 'reality' to be represented to an extent never before contemplated, it also saw new industrial and social conditions which changed so quickly and so profoundly that they in turn prompted a demand for new ways of classifying and communicating the extent of that change. Journalistic writing and photography were developing alongside social investigations (into public health, poverty etc.) and industrial warfare. Two good examples are the coverage of the American Civil War (1861–5) – documented in great detail by contemporary photographers and journalists – and the work of Dr Barnado's in creating a photographic archive of the street urchins 'rescued' in Victorian London (55,000 photographs between 1874 and 1905). This realist approach to social science and journalism supported the more openly emotional appeal of realist art and literature. If the realist movement in painting and literature was over by the end of the century, the use of photography and film to represent social issues has persisted and produced fierce debates over 'realist aesthetics' during the twentieth century (see Chapter 14 for more on this history).

A Matter of Life and Death (UK 1946) is a famous fantasy film by Michael Powell and Emeric Pressburger. It includes a striking scene in which a country doctor uses a camera obscura to spy on his neighbours. Powell was an 'anti-realist' in style, but was fascinated by the camera as 'controlling eye'.

Figure 17.1 A fourteenth-century representation of samurai warriors from *Kitabakate monogatari* which uses different perspective and scale.

Some of the photographs commissioned by Barnado's were used in campaign leaflets showing the 'before' and 'after' images of boys rescued from the street. Already in the nineteenth century there were accusations that the images had been 'doctored' to make the transformation more dramatic.

Major technological advances in sound recording have concentrated on clarity and the establishment of a realistic stereo 'soundscape' – see Chapter 11.

See Chapter 1, and its case study.

Sound recording and realism

Much of the argument about realist aesthetics is taken up with visual codes, but we will begin with 'aural realism'. The later nineteenth century saw the development of sound recording technology, and with it arguments about 'realist sound'. We can talk of the 'sound image' in much the same way as the visual image. Our problem is that the terminology for discussion of sound images is not so well developed as for that of visual images, and as a consequence we are far less confident about discussing the realism of sound reproduction. A simple test will demonstrate the strangeness of discussing realist sound.

The sound of your own voice

Look at a recent photograph of yourself. Is it a good likeness? Most of us recognise ourselves in photographs. We might not like what we see, but we can accept it as a resemblance. Now listen to yourself recorded on tape. This is much harder to accept. Is that strange voice really you? Why are we so surprised to hear ourselves? Possibly, because our ears are less trained to listen to voices than our eyes are to look at pictures. There is also a physiological reason. When we speak we push out or pull in air which in turn creates sound waves. As a consequence we feel the vibrations from the act of speaking. When we hear our voice coming from speakers we don't feel anything (unless the speaker is so large and powerful that it makes the floor quake).

Perhaps this is what makes our own voice sound so alien – because it isn't accompanied by the familiar sensations of speaking. What would be even more strange would be to play a recording of ourselves backwards. This would be unintelligible. Yet, the visual equivalent would be simply to look in a mirror – a perfectly ordinary thing to do, but in fact an inverted representation of how we look, which we have learnt to 'read'.

Tuning in to sound effects

Andrew Crisell (1994) makes the point that a particular sound on the radio works quite differently on television. The radio sound is more appropriately called a **sound effect**. Galloping horses being simulated by the production assistant banging together two halves of a coconut shell is a good example. On radio we accept this sound as a realistic representation. If we were offered an authentic recording of 'real' horses galloping along 'real' highways, we might not even recognise the sound, without its accompanying visual signifier. So, as well as the 'quality' of sound reproduction, we must consider the realist codes necessary to convey meaning.

For the visual image, realism would normally imply that most of the component signs were **iconic**, i.e. they physically resemble real-world objects they represent. A realist visual account of horse-riding would show real horses and would use the iconography of 'horse culture' – bridles, saddles, stables etc. In the sound image, icons are much more problematic. All the associated sounds of horse riding, such as the heavy breathing of the horse, the squeak of the leather saddle, the clomping of hooves etc., are 'mixed' within the sound image and we may be unable to distinguish one from another. Their resemblance to real sounds becomes a problem. We are more likely to respond to an identifiable sound (perhaps a single whinny followed by a snort of breath) which signifies the presence of a horse, than a *mix* of sounds. In this case the sound image is more **indexical** than iconic, an index being a sign that works by establishing a relationship between itself and reality rather than simply offering a resemblance. The horse sound tells us about the presence of a horse. This whole exercise serves to remind us that we also use abstract signs – a character could use the word 'horse', the sound of which has neither resemblance nor indexical relationship to the real animal.

The history of media technology during the twentieth century was dominated by the drive for 'greater realism'. At the start of the twenty-first century it is difficult to imagine how much 'better' sound and image can get in the cinema auditorium, the main showcase for such technological advances. This doesn't mean that there will not still be an incentive to 'wow' audiences with even more startling realism effects. Putting the technology issue aside, we should recognise that realism will remain an issue of aesthetics – which approach to take – and a social and cultural issue about representing events and ideas.

Follow the debate in Chapter 16.

Realisms in film and video

Cinema has developed over a hundred years with a constant tension between its twin roots of 'photorealistic' image technology, capable of documenting reality, and a fairground mentality of fantasy and magic. For every **Lumière** 'actuality' there is a **Méliès** fantasy with special effects and trick photography. This might suggest that the history of cinema is of documentary or fantasy, and of course it isn't. Instead, film-makers moved between the two and combined elements of both to present a remarkable range of different kinds of film texts (including documentaries with the appearance of fantasy and vice versa), in which the distinction between 'fiction' and 'fact' is blurred. This diversity is something to celebrate. We are discussing 'realisms' as part of a range of different approaches to the medium.

We've noted that ideas about realism in the nineteenth century were based on a recognition of photography's ability to represent reality directly and also

Lumière brothers Auguste and Louis, French brothers often credited with the first cinema screenings in 1895. *Workers Leaving the Factory* and *A Train Arriving in the Station* were two of the 'actualities' of a few minutes' length which comprised the opening programme.

George Méliès was the great 'showman' of early cinema. His short films included *A Trip to the Moon* (France 1902).

on the desire by writers, photographers, social campaigners etc. to document social conditions. We might add that this was usually from a liberal perspective and accompanied a desire to 'change the world'. When 'realism' was recognised as an aesthetic in cinema it was in relation to a wide range of realisms and purposes, not all of which have been 'liberal' or 'progressive'. Often, however, the term *realist* has been reserved for films that not only represented social conditions but in some way saw them as the subject of the film or at least a major factor affecting the lives of the characters. It is useful, therefore to comment on two classifications of film aesthetics, Hollywood realism and social realism.

Hollywood realism

Most Hollywood films are 'realist' in terms of the transparency concept outlined above. Hollywood entertainment films create fictional worlds which are internally consistent. There is linear continuity in the narrative, reasonably authentic surface detail in locations and sets, and audiences are willing to 'suspend disbelief' in order to follow the plot. Even in genres such as science fiction, this kind of consistency is expected. A good way to 'foreground' how Hollywood creates this transparent realism is to compare a Hollywood film with a similar form of entertainment cinema such as Hindi Cinema ('Bollywood'). *Asoka* (India 2001) deals with one of the legendary figures of Indian history and his exploits two thousand years ago. Apart from anachronisms such as stitched cloth, this film includes a dance to modern music in which the dancer changes her outfit several times, and various swordfights that use the choreography of Hong Kong martial arts movies. It is difficult to imagine a similar Hollywood film such as *Gladiator* (US 2000) including such features, because they would detract from the consistency of the fictional world, however unlikely the actual story being told.

Hollywood deals in entertainment. Studios are rarely interested in mundane or everyday stories. Representations of social issues such as drug abuse or working conditions are usually included to provide an appropriate milieu for individual stories about heroism or triumph over adversity, rather than as the focus for the narrative. An interesting comparison might be between *Erin Brockovich* (US 2000) and *Bread and Roses* (UK/US/Germany/2000). Both films have female lead characters who become involved in 'struggles' against large companies in California, and both use a similar visual style that has sometimes been called 'social realism'. However *Erin Brockovich* ends up being mostly about the triumph of its eponymous heroine in winning a legal battle and asserting herself as an untrained but hardworking and intelligent legal executive, whereas *Bread and Roses* is primarily about the struggle of immigrant workers from Latin America and their successful union organisation in a series of strikes in Los Angeles.

Steven Soderbergh became a very successful Hollywood director with *Erin Brockovich, Traffic* and *Ocean's 11*. He began as an 'independent' director with an interest in European New Waves, including the work of Ken Loach. In *The Limey* (1999), Soderbergh used footage from Loach's *Poor Cow* (UK 1967) to show a young Terence Stamp.

Hollywood has also been concerned to use 'realism effects' to heighten the emotional intensity of the spectators' experiences in the cinema. *Saving Private Ryan* (US 1998) was widely admired for the sequences which represented American troops going ashore on D-Day. Veterans of the 'real' landing said that it took them straight back to the beach in 1944 and also enabled them to talk about the experience with younger audiences shocked by the vivid scenes. However, the sequence is used within the film to tell a familiar story of American combat troops in action. The use of mobile cameras (including underwater cameras) and sound effects represents how the men felt, rather than presenting an exploration of social conditions in the Army or explaining the military and political background to the event.

Social realism

The British tradition of cinematic and televisual realism has developed over many years via different 'movements' such as the 1930s Documentary Movement, 1950s 'Free Cinema', 1960s 'New Wave' and the 1960s and 1970s television play (*Play for Today* etc.). Many commentators have singled out Ken Loach as the leading active proponent of what has come to be known as '**social realism**', with the following distinctive features:

- films set in recognisable authentic locations, usually industrial cities
- authentic regional dialects and cultural references
- non-professional actors (although often other kinds of performers such as comedians) or actors who are associated primarily with this kind of work
- narratives based on the hardships of social disadvantage
- lead characters who are 'ordinary' and working-class
- 'observational', 'documentary' style of camerawork
- 'spontaneous' naturalistic acting style (Loach shoots scenes in chronological order and actors are unaware of the outcome of their character's actions)
- characters walk in and out of frame, dialogue overlaps.

The term social realism has been applied quite loosely to a wide range of realist styles in contemporary cinema but primarily to European cinema. Sometimes only one or two of the elements listed above may be present, but there is sufficient to distinguish a film from 'Hollywood realism'.

During the shooting of *Carla's Song* (UK 1996) Ken Loach told Robert Carlyle that 'something' would happen in the next scene when he was sleeping in a hammock. The explosion which followed threw Carlyle out of the hammock and he gave a believable response.

Social realism is sometimes confused with '**Socialist Realism**', which was the officially approved style of film-making (and other artistic practices) in the Soviet Union in the 1930s, under Stalin. This tended towards a romanticised view of heroic workers and was a 'conservative' and restrictive approach. (See Blandford *et al.* 2001.)

Different 'realisms'

As well as these rather loose usages of 'realism' as a descriptor, we can define specific realisms, all of which display one of these two features:

- The film-makers are concerned to capture something about the experience of real events, to represent them as faithfully as possible for the audience and to **mediate** them as little as possible.

- The film-makers have something specific to say about the real world and have developed a specific style, using realist conventions.

The first of these is a pragmatic approach which tries to get as close as possible to an event in a physical sense and tends towards a documentary approach. The second is a more obviously 'political' position and is likely to encompass 'realist fiction' as well as documentary. Again, we might see the former as developing from photography and journalism and the latter from literature – but it isn't quite as simple as that. We will investigate two celebrated historical examples, selecting from a wide range of possibles. We think you need this detail in order to explore ideas about realism. Both examples have resonances in contemporary media production which we hope you will pick up, but please be careful not to take either of them as representing 'fixed' positions about realistic aesthetics – this is one of the dangers of superficial studies which look for easy categorisations. You will find contradictions between approaches, but also similarities.

Case study 1: Documentary mode – direct cinema

The high point of the 'direct approach to recording reality' came in the early 1960s and was known in North America as Direct Cinema. The modern term is 'fly on the wall' to describe standard television documentary techniques which enable viewers to eavesdrop on what appear to be 'real events' (i.e. not specially staged for the camera). You might like to compare this with the multiple surveillance camera technique of television shows such as *Big Brother*.

Similar work (but with a different underpinning philosophy involving more interaction with the subject of the film) was also carried out in France and an alternative title is **cinéma vérité** (cinema truth).

The simple premise of this approach is that a camera and microphone are as close to events as possible and that the film or tape is running continuously. Everything that happens is recorded. The pioneers of this work had three main problems:

- finding camera and microphone technology which was lightweight and sensitive
- avoiding becoming part of the events and causing subjects to 'play to the cameras'
- deciding how to reduce the hours of footage to a reasonable length for audiences while avoiding a particular editorial position.

The early 1960s was the period when lightweight 16 mm film cameras could for the first time be combined with good-quality lightweight audio recorders for synchronised sound. With film stocks sensitive enough to provide reasonable monochrome picture quality under most lighting conditions, including small hand-held lights, the documentary crew were ready to go almost anywhere – and they did.

The new approach began with *Primary* (US 1960), in which a crew followed Democratic hopefuls John F. Kennedy and Hubert Humphrey during the Wisconsin 'primary' election for the presidential candidate. The film was made by an independent television producer Robert Drew, working with three documentary film-makers who would become the core of Direct Cinema – D. A. Pennebaker, Richard Leacock and Albert Maysles. As Monaco (1980) points out, the aim of Direct Cinema was a sense of '**objectivity**' – the events and people who were the subjects of films were able to speak for themselves, avoiding voice-over narration (the conventional accompaniment to many documentaries up to that point).

Conventions can soon develop and become 'naturalised' as part of the medium. We have now become used to the presence of the camera in all kinds of unlikely places and we have also grown sceptical about the 'objectivity' of documentary approaches. In 1960 not only was the technology new but the eavesdropping on ordinary lives was also novel.

The problem of subjects who 'played to the camera' and therefore behaved 'unnaturally' was partly avoided by selecting subjects for whom 'playing to an audience' was simply part of their usual behaviour. Politicians were followed by performers of various kinds, including Bob Dylan in probably the best-known and commercially most successful Direct Cinema feature, D. A. Pennebaker's *Don't Look Back* (US 1966) and the Rolling Stones in the Maysles brothers' *Gimme Shelter* (US 1971). *Nobody Someday* (2002) is a recent documentary on Robbie Williams which could usefully be viewed in comparison with the earlier work. Performers are now much more conscious of what the camera can do.

Problems were faced by Frederick Wiseman, who began a series of 'institutional' documentaries in the late 1960s. Wiseman tackled a police force, a high school and various other welfare agencies. His aim was to spend long enough with his subjects, filming all the while, for them to begin to feel that he and his crew were 'part of the furniture'. When he eventually came to the editing stage he had miles of film to sift through and the question of mediation became crucial. The initial approach of Pennebaker and Leacock was to try to subordinate editing decisions to the flow of events – i.e. not to develop a particular viewpoint through selection of shots but simply to show whatever the camera 'captured'. The emphasis is on 'capturing' rather than 'creating' images. Wiseman couldn't do this with his hours of film – he was forced to make decisions and effectively to enter

Shooting ratios for *vérité* documentaries are very high – 20:1, twenty or thirty hours of film for a one-hour programme. The programme is really 'scripted' in the edit suite.

into the relationship between the camera and the subject, in other words to mediate, to edit in both senses of the word.

Wiseman's films were controversial, and it is worth considering the links between his approach and other media forms. The 'closeness to the subject' and the revelations which might ensue were associated with photojournalism – as were many of the technological developments in cameras, lenses and film stocks. A parallel 'movement' to Direct Cinema was 'New Journalism', a development in newspaper and magazine journalism in which feature writers began to adopt some of the strategies of realist novelists in order to present stories. This meant detailed descriptive writing and also the possibility that the journalist could become part of the story, recording how he or she felt. In a sense this was in conflict with the 'objectivity' of Direct Cinema. Yet, in another way it shared what we might see as an immersion in the issue, especially following the Wiseman approach. Some of the better-known New Journalism pieces by **Hunter S. Thompson** and **Joe Eszterhas** belong to a 'counter-culture' view of America in the late 1960s and early 1970s (i.e. writing opposed to the values of the establishment). They display the first signs of a coming together of television, cinema, rock music and magazine writing which is now commonplace in 'style' magazines and a range of 'lifestyle' television programming (such as the Louis Theroux programmes). A marker of this synthesis is *In Cold Blood* (US 1967), a Hollywood feature based on a New Journalism 'documentary novel' about a pair of murderers, by Truman Capote.

> 'Many of them seem to be in love with realism for its own sake . . . They seem to be saying: "Hey! Come here! This is the way people are living now – just the way I'm going to show you! It may astound you, disgust you, delight you or arouse your contempt or make you laugh . . . Nevertheless, this is what it's like! It's all right here! You won't be bored! Take a look!"' (Tom Wolfe on the 'New Journalists' (Wolfe and Johnson 1975)).
>
> The 'excitement of the real' has been recognised by Hollywood film-makers who can use Direct Cinema techniques in features to add to the controversy of stories based on real events. Oliver Stone's films such as *JFK* (1991) and *Natural Born Killers* (1994) provide good examples.

The other important feature of Direct Cinema was that it was conceived in terms of television screening. The Drew Associates films were destined

Joe Eszterhas is now well known as the Hollywood scriptwriter of *Basic Instinct* etc. A film of **Hunter S. Thompson**'s best-known work, *Fear and Loathing in Las Vegas*, was released in 1998.

for television, and Wiseman was commissioned by National Educational Television. Crucial features of television in the 1960s were:

- poor picture quality – fuzzy black and white
- the importance of the soundtrack: many theorists believed that it carried more weight with audiences than the image track.

These two factors meshed with the approach to camera framings and editing – a direct style was suitable, as any complex compositions and framings would be lost on the small television screen while the jerky hand-held camera was acceptable – and the innovation of live 'direct' sound. The films were also assured a relatively large audience and one used to the 'live' feel of television.

This distinction between television and cinema in terms of audience involvement is important for the direct approach. A cinema audience, sitting in the dark in a secluded environment, can become immersed in the film, a feeling of 'being there'. But where is 'there'? The cinema also suggests that the whole experience is 'magical' and 'special' and that the events we experience are somehow happening out of time. By contrast, the television broadcast suggests that we are able to eavesdrop on an event which is happening *now* in a place which we could visit.

By the early 1970s the Direct Cinema pioneers were already looking to video and the first portable 'rover' packs (a hand-held video camera and a portable reel-to-reel recorder in a leather case that could be slung over a shoulder). Leacock in particular has continued to argue for more access to production for more people. The contemporary heirs of Direct Cinema are not too difficult to find. The early techniques quickly passed over into the current affairs documentary (e.g. *World in Action* in the UK) and then into both the 'safe' and the controversial **institutional documentary** series. *Video Diaries* and other similar 'camcorder documents' on contemporary television are in a direct line of descent from Direct Cinema.

The legacy of the Direct Cinema approach is a wide range of different television documentary forms, many of which have jettisoned the philosophy of attempting to limit the mediation of 'real events', but still offering a coherent 'story'. Instead, the hand-held camera has gone in search of 'police action' or eavesdropping on celebrities, primarily for the entertainment of the audience (i.e rather than 'information' or 'education'). For a period in the late 1990s a new hybrid form emerged – the documentary series, related to the *vérité* institutional documentary, but with the narrative pleasures of the soap opera, and christened **docu-soap**.

In the early 1970s, the leading 'fly on the wall' documentarist working in the UK, Roger Graef, found the BBC to be institutionally opposed to the Direct Cinema approach: 'The BBC published the Green Book on how to make documentaries: do a few days research and then restage what was "typical". Such a process involved the invasion by a crew of technicians, moving the furniture and turning each location into a film studio' (Graef 1995).

Institutional documentaries following the Wiseman lead have been popular on UK television. Mostly the exposure of institutions at work is informative or amusing, but those looking into the police and education have created great controversy – which probably says more about those institutions than about the documentary technique.

ACTIVITY 17.1

The fly on the wall

Where would you like to be a fly on the wall? Select a subject which you think would interest an audience and which you could visit with a camcorder. Ask yourself the questions posed by the Direct Cinema approach.

- Where would you place yourself to capture sound and image effectively? Could you capture all the material you would need to represent your subject to your satisfaction?
- What strategies would you use to ensure that your subjects did not 'perform' for the camera?
- Do you think your subject would automatically produce a story, or would you have to restructure the events during the editing process?

In this first example of cinematic (and televisual) realism, we have emphasised a number of factors:

- the role of technology
- the importance of a practice – how to do it in practical terms
- the importance of institutional links to other media forms (which in turn suggests something about how audiences will engage with the material).

Documentary practice and forms

The concept of 'documentary', both as a practice and as a type of film, has developed over the seventy-five years since John Grierson first coined the term in 1926. In the 1920s, feature-length documentaries were being made in all of the major film-making countries. In the Soviet Union the purpose of such films was educative, informative and propagandistic – taking the revolution to far-flung corners of the Russian Empire. In America the aim was more entertainment-orientated, with the allure of the exotic in **Robert Flaherty**'s trips to the Arctic and the South Seas or **Schoedsack** and **Cooper**'s films about rural life in Persia (Iran) and Siam (Thailand). European and Russian documentary features were also experimental as in the work of **Walther Ruttman, Jean Vigo** and **Dziga Vertov**. In this early period, with relatively primitive cameras, documentarists effectively laid out the whole range of documentary ideas – representing the 'real world' on the big screen.

In the 1930s the scope of documentary became more constrained by institutional factors. Grierson's productions for various public sector organisations in Britain were much shorter and operated on a smaller scale to educate the citizenry about aspects of modern life. Their intended outlet was the 'alternative circuit' of 'schools, film societies, YMCAs, women's

Robert Flaherty was a Canadian who specialised in documentaries about remote communities (e.g. in *Nanook of the North*, 1922). **Merian C. Cooper** and **Ernest Schoedsack** went on to make the fantasy film *King Kong* (US 1933). **Walther Ruttman** made an influential 'symphony of the city' with *Berlin* (1927). **Dziga Vertov** made the avant-garde *Man With the Movie Camera* (USSR 1929) and **Jean Vigo** made the similarly experimental *A propos de Nice* (France 1930) – another 'city symphony' photographed by Vertov's brother).

organisations, trade unions' (Lovell and Hillier 1972). They were propagandistic in their promotion of government policies, state enterprises and industrial sponsors, and later the same practitioners would produce propaganda in the Second World War. British documentaries included a wide range of documentary types including experimental animation (the work of Len Lye and Norman McLaren) and early 'witness interviews' (*Housing Problems*, 1935) as well as 'dramatised documentaries' using non-professionals (*The Saving of Bill Blewitt*, 1936). Subsequently, most attention was reserved for the 'poetic documentaries' of Humphrey Jennings which worked mostly at the level of emotion and ideology, using fluid montages of image, music and sound effects as in *Listen to Britain* (1942).

Some of the same concerns were evident in North American documentaries of the 1930s, especially in Pare Lorentz's independent films that supported the ideas of President Roosevelt's 'New Deal' (the Hollywood studios were opposed to any kind of state sponsorship of cinema). In all the major cinema territories the commercial newsreels presented a form of film reportage mostly presenting trivial items for entertainment (celebrities, royalty etc.) but also dealing with international affairs. The influential American series *The March of Time* broke new ground: it 'used actuality sequences but combined these with freewheeling dramatizations. Events were re-enacted not only by participants – this had often been done – but by professional actors in scenes scripted, directed, edited and scored by professonals, in a manner established in a radio series also titled *The March of Time*' (Barnouw 1993). Produced by *Time Magazine*, this controversial series pointed forwards towards television 'investigations' that would appear in the 1960s.

Grierson's productions in Britain were short, but elsewhere feature documentaries, shown in cinemas survived if the market was there or if government propaganda campaigns merited feature length (as they did in Germany and Italy in the 1930s and in all the belligerent nations during the Second World War). By the late 1940s many of the documentary techniques of location filming, mobile cameras and use of non-professionals had migrated to fiction film-making. In the 1950s documentary practice itself began to move to television, where a new set of technical and institutional restraints became important – the reduced size and resolution of the image and the politics of scheduling. Our discussion of Direct Cinema is concerned with a film-making practice developed specifically for television. The scheduling of documentary became an issue of 'entertainment', but also of a 'public broadcasting service' with objectives such as information and education. In other words, the same arguments about purpose were once again marshalled. The big difference between television and cinema was that the documentary on television was less of a single 'event' and more an element either of other programme types (such as the current affairs magazine programme) or of the 'flow' of nightly programming. Coupled with the degraded image, this made it difficult for the more 'poetic' documentaries to gain a screening. Television inevitably turned documentary more towards journalism and entertainment and away from any pretensions towards 'art'.

Theorising documentary practice

In his influential writings on documentary during the 1980s and 1990s, Bill Nichols developed a classification of what he called 'documentary modes' (Nichols 1991):

- *expository* – characterised by the 'voice of authority' on the soundtrack and a general attempt to present a fixed meaning about the 'reality' that is represented
- *observational* – the 'fly on the wall' approach
- *interactive* – the presence of the documentarist is represented in the film, 'selection' of material is foregrounded
- *reflexive* – the process of film-making is not only represented but 'interrogated' so that the reflexive documentary is as much about 'making a documentary' as about the ostensible subject material.

This classification has since been strongly criticised by Stella Bruzzi (2000: 2), who sees it as responsible for discussion of documentary practice as a form of linear progression from the 'primitive' expository documentaries of the 1930s to the modern 'reflexive' mode. Bruzzi identifies early 'reflexive' practice in the films of Dziga Vertov in the 1920s and argues that 'voice over' and other forms of controlled narration were everywhere in 2000. She also identifies a major problem with the polarisation of much of the discussion about documentary, between those who believe that technology will one day allow the 'perfect' representation of reality and those who believe that reality can never be represented in an objective way (and that, therefore, all documentaries 'fail'):

> The pact between documentary, reality and spectator is far more straight-forward than these theories make out . . . the spectator is not in need of signposts and inverted commas to understand that a documentary is a negotiation between reality on the one hand and image, interpretation and bias on the other.
>
> (Bruzzi 2000: 4)

A good example of Bruzzi's approach is the way that she explores a fifth 'mode' that Nichols introduced in 1994 – the '*performative*'. She sees Nichols as concentrating on the importance of 'performance' within an expository or observational documentary (e.g. in the Direct Cinema films outlined above, perhaps) – a 'negative' trait that reduces the objectivity. In contrast, Bruzzi looks at performance in a positive way in the films of documentarists who themselves become performers in their own films (e.g. Nick Broomfield and Molly Dineen). In so doing, the documentarist does not disguise the process of selecting from reality, but instead 'performs it' for the camera. It is as if the film-maker says to the audience: 'Look, I'm trying to make an objective statement, but this is what happens when I do.' The audience is offered a much freer relation to the film than Nichols's categories suggest.

Stella Bruzzi's work provides two important conclusions that you can apply in your own analysis of documentary texts:

- Over the whole history of documentary practice, film-makers have mixed documentary modes.
- There is a real world with social issues that can be represented as long as audiences recognise that such representations are negotiated by film-makers.

The impact of scheduling practice

Television programmers have used different documentary modes in a wide range of non-fiction programmes:

- sports
- natural history
- current affairs

- travel
- history
- artist biographies etc.

Each of these has developed its own set of codes and conventions, and you can recognise when footage from one type is used in another. This sometimes happens within a documentary about a particular person or historical event, where 'archive material' is being used to tell a story.

ACTIVITY 17.2

Analyse a documentary sequence from any programme using archive material. Note the use of different documentary modes and sources of 'actuality' footage. Look out for:

- 'witness interviews'
- 'expert statements'
- voice overs
- 'news' footage
- amateur film
- any of the programme material listed above.

How do these different types of material signal 'realism'? Do they all have the same status as 'documents'? Interesting films to study are *When We Were Kings* (US 1996), about Muhammad Ali's boxing match in Zaire in 1974, and *One Day in September* (Switzerland/UK/Germany 1999), about the hostage crisis at the 1972 Munich Olympics. Both films open with a mixture of several different modes and sources.

Mixing fiction and non-fiction

'Drama-doc' and 'docudrama' are terms used to describe the mix of fact and fiction in television productions. Unfortunately, there are no agreed definitions of these terms, which are used very loosely, but we can suggest that a 'dramatised' documentary (a drama-doc) is a documentary reconstruction using the techniques of a fiction film-maker (such as identifiable lead characters, continuity editing etc.) to represent historical, documented events, as in *One Day in September* or *Bloody Sunday* (UK 2002).

> the biggest single issue in public discussion of drama-documentary is that of possible confusion among the audience. In fact, a confusion about the fundamental nature of what is being watched is far less likely than a confusion about how what is dramatically depicted relates to what did actually happen – or might well have happened.
>
> (Corner quoted in Creeber 2002: 32)

A documentary drama is then a fiction which is presented using documentary techniques (location filming, non-professional actors etc.). A recent example is the BBC film about a smallpox epidemic created by bio-terrorism. *Smallpox 2002 – Silent Weapon* was introduced by a continuity announcement on BBC2 explaining that it was a 'functional film, made to look like a documentary'. The same technique was used in *The War Game* (BBC 1965), which purported to show what would happen during a nuclear attack. This film was thought so shocking that it was banned from being broadcast until the 1990s. John Corner (quoted in Creeber 2002: 34) suggests it was the film's implications for government defence policy that were unacceptable rather than that audiences would be frightened (the official explanation). Audiences are now assumed to be more sophisticated, and twenty-four-hour news coverage of such issues perhaps more familiar, so the smallpox film was far less controversial.

André Bazin (1919–58) An influential critic whose essays are collected in two volumes published in English in the late 1960s under the title *What is Cinema?* They are still in print (Bazin 1967, 1971).

Case study 2: Neo-realism and the realist fiction film

Less pragmatic film-makers than the Direct Cinema group have at various times attempted to develop approaches which would combine an exploration of social issues using the full range of the possibilities of cinema. This is a less 'pure' and more sophisticated position than that of Direct Cinema in recognising that 'Realism in art can only be achieved in one way – through artifice' (**André Bazin**). This emphasises that realism is about a set of conventions – or rather, sets of conventions since different realisms can use different conventions.

The central issue is about how to involve an audience, not in terms of identifying with the individual hero of a conventional narrative but in social issues, albeit played out in the lives of ordinary people. A realist film-maker is making a contract with the audience which implies a joint project to explore the real world through the medium of film. We've chosen to look at an influential historical figure and to relate his work to contemporary work in the mode he championed.

Roberto Rossellini

Rossellini is best known as one of the founders of **Italian neo-realism** – an approach to film-making which flourished in the immediate aftermath of the Second World War and which was characterised by very low budgets, location shooting, non-professional actors and 'real' stories.

> The subject of the neo-realism film is the world; not story or narrative. It contains no preconceived thesis, because ideas are born in the film from the subject. It has no affinity with the superfluous and the merely spectacular, which it refuses, but is attracted to the concrete . . . It refuses recipes and formulas . . . neo-realism poses problems for us and for itself in an attempt to make people think.
>
> (Roberto Rossellini in *Retrospective*, April 1953,
>
> reprinted in Overby 1978)

This argues for cinematic realism as a **progressive aesthetic** opposed to 'entertainment cinema' and in favour of 'education'. (Rossellini was taken up by Marxist critics in the 1970s, but he remained a Catholic humanist intellectual throughout his life.)

Neo-realism represents a mix between the pragmatic (in 1945 the Italian film industry was, like the rest of the country, in ruins with abandoned studios and a lack of basic film-making materials) and the idealistic. The aesthetic had been developed first in France during the 1930s and later under the fascist regime in Italy, for which Rossellini began his career with documentary-style stories about the armed forces. The stylistic feature we want to highlight is the use of the long shot and the long take.

The **long shot** is the ideal framing device to show crowds and the movements of soldiers in battle. Its use in Hollywood tends to be restricted to **establishing shots** and genres such as the western where 'figures in a landscape' are important. Usually, however, stories are told in mid-shot and medium close-up with attention paid to individual characters. Long shots are also difficult to organise on studio sets, where framing is often required

Roberto Rossellini (1906–77) a film-maker for forty years, constantly changing his approach to realism. Also an important teacher and lecturer on film and a major influence on younger film-makers such as Jean-Luc Godard.

Rossellini's first postwar film, *Rome Open City* (Italy 1945), shot under difficult circumstances on the streets of the newly liberated city, caused a sensation in France and the US.

Deep-focus is covered in Chapter 11.

Shot length   Various film scholars, including Bordwell, Staiger and Thompson (1985), have undertaken surveys of shot lengths from a range of films and production periods. The Hollywood average in the studio period was around twelve seconds, but is currently much less, perhaps six seconds.

to disguise the fact that a set is just a collection of 'flat' walls without a ceiling. Allied to the long shot is the use of **deep-focus**, which allows the film-maker to compose a shot in depth with objects in the foreground and the background, both in sharp focus. Different actions can take place within the frame, and the audience can select to look at the foreground or background. Deep-focus works well on location and, like the long shot, was common in silent cinema before bulky sound equipment began to restrict camerawork.

A **long take** is any shot lasting longer than about twenty seconds. For the film-maker, the long take poses problems because all the actions must be carefully worked out in advance. Long shots and staging in depth help because they give greater possibilities of movement in the frame. Alternatively, moving the camera by panning or tracking allows greater freedom. The panning and tracking camera, shooting in long takes, is a feature of Rossellini's films at various times.

Paisà was made in Italy in 1946 (the title refers to a colloquial Italian word for 'countryman' or simply 'friend') and represents the best example of Rossellini's approach to realism in this period. It is concerned with the story of the Allied advance through Italy at the end of the war. Different characters appear in each of six separate episodes – there is no possibility of us identifying with an American hero who 'makes it through'. The story derives, in Rossellini's terms, from the concrete reality of the situation, and the approach he takes to the production supports this aim. The six episodes are intercut with actual newsreel footage, titles and voice over in such a way that it is difficult to distinguish 'real' from staged footage. The Americans in the film are professional actors (but not 'stars'), but many of the Italians are played by local people in the 'real' locations which Rossellini uses whenever possible. In the final episode, the incidents are very much based on events recounted by the 'real' partisans.

At the end of the final episode, which features Italian partisans and American and British agents fighting the Germans in the Po delta, the partisans are captured and shot and the protesting American leader is executed. The film ends with a partisan's body floating out to sea and a title explaining that the war ended a few weeks later. This bleak ending would not be possible in a Hollywood film, but for Rossellini it is not the end of the 'story'. As Bondanella (1993) points out, for Rossellini the 'reality' is the triumph of the human spirit over adversity as understood in Christian philosophy.

The argument in favour of the long take and the long shot is clearly demonstrated in Figure 17.2. We are presented with a series of long takes in which the action unfolds, often in relatively long shot. The scenes are carefully orchestrated to flow almost seamlessly. Although there is clearly a 'leader' (the American officer), we are not invited to adopt his viewpoint. When mid-shots or medium close-ups are used, they pick out particular narrative incidents rather than develop individual characters. Most of all, the camera is used to create for us the viewpoint of the partisans who live in this unique environment. As Bazin writes:

> the horizon is always at the same height. Maintaining the same proportions between water and sky in every shot brings out one of the basic characteristics of this landscape. It is the exact equivalent, under conditions exposed by the screen, of the inner feeling men experience who are living between the sky and the water and whose lives are at the mercy of an infinitesimal shift of angle in relation to the horizon.
>
> (Bazin 1971: 37)

Figure 17.2 A typical shot from the last sequence of *Paisà* (Italy 1946). Note the camera angle which effectively mimics the partisans' view of their world and the long shot which encompasses the mixed band of partisans and British and American special forces – privileging no single character.

There are two important features about Rossellini's visual style in *Paisà*:

- The style attempts to 'reveal' the reality in the story; it doesn't draw attention to itself. It does, of course, 'construct' a representation of reality, but in doing so it fits Bazin's maxim that the representation of reality requires artifice.

- The relationship between film-maker and audience is such that the audience is invited to select where to look in the long-shot composition and is allowed to follow the action in the long take. The director, by avoiding close-ups and fast cutting, is not shouting 'look here!', 'look at that!'.

Fiction from fact

The basis of the neo-realism approach was neatly encapsulated by one of the main scriptwriters of the period, Cesare Zavattini. He referred to a typical starting point for a neo-realist film:

> A woman goes into a shop to buy a pair of shoes. The shoes cost 7,000 lire. The woman tries to bargain. The scene lasts perhaps two minutes, but I must make a two-hour film. What do I do? I analyse the fact in all its constituent elements, in its 'before', in its 'after', in its contemporaneity. The fact creates its own fiction.
>
> (Quoted in Williams 1980)

Zavattini did this to great effect in the celebrated *Bicycle Thieves* (Italy 1948), in which an unemployed man can't look for work unless he finds his stolen bicycle. Jim Allen used a similar starting point for the Ken Loach film *Raining Stones* (UK 1993), which was based on an unemployed man who wants to buy a communion dress for his daughter. *Bicycle Thieves* was also a model for the first African feature film Ousmane Sembene's *Borom Sarret* (Senegal 1963).

If you are interested in scriptwriting, trying out Zavattini's method is excellent practice. Take a simple action like the above and work backwards and forwards from it to create a story.

Rossellini went on in the 1950s and 1960s to explore ideas about realism in many different ways. His 1953 film *Viaggio in Italia* was a particular influence on Jean-Luc Godard and the French New Wave. For this film, Rossellini applied the idea of the story developing out of reality in a new way. He cast Ingrid Bergman and George Sanders as an English couple on holiday in Italy. Their marriage is breaking up, and to aid spontaneity Rossellini made up the script as shooting progressed, at one point making use of an archaeological find at the location spot. Sanders was bewildered by the experience and this comes across in his performance.

In the last part of his career, Rossellini turned to educational films about important historical figures. He took the technological aspect of creating the realism effect very seriously and invented his own zoom lens control mechanism that allowed him to alter lens settings seamlessly while moving the camera in a relatively confined space. This proved effective for both the large-scale battles in *Viva Italia* (1960) and the deathbed of Louis XIV in *The Rise to Power of Louis XIV* (France 1966).

Neo-realist practice in contemporary cinema

From the 1950s on, film-makers all over the world have found neo-realism to be an effective means of representing social issues. It has been particularly important in relatively poor countries with serious social disadvantage and poverty (e.g. in Africa, Latin America and India). The model has allowed powerful political films to be made on relatively low budgets. As we noted in relation to 'social realism', Ken Loach has developed a shooting style that derives many of its ideas from neo-realism, and elements of the approach are found in the work of various contemporary European film-makers.

In contemporary cinema, some critics have referred to neo-realism in attempting to explain the international success of Iranian films that deal with everyday events in an uncomplicated but often engrossing way (e.g. *The White Balloon* 1995). Similarly the Chinese director Zhang Yimou, previously mainly known for sumptuous melodramas, made an exemplary neo-realist film in *Not One Less* (1999). This tells the story of a teenage girl who is put in charge of a primary school in a remote village when the teacher is away. She will only be paid if all the children continue to attend. When one boy goes missing, she sets off for the city to look for him.

In the mid-1990s the signatories of the 'Dogme '95' declaration vowed to make films that were free of pretension and all the indulgences of Hollywood film-making.

Robert Guédiguian and Sandrine Veysset are two contemporary French directors whose work has been discussed under the heading of 'social realism', e.g. for *Where the Heart Is* (1998) and *Will It Snow For Christmas?* (1996).

The Dogme '95 'Vow of Chastity'

I swear to submit to the following set of rules drawn up and confirmed by DOGME 95:

1 Shooting must be done on location. Props and sets must not be brought in (if a particular prop is necessary for the story, a location must be chosen where this prop is to be found).

2   The sound must never be produced apart from the images or vice versa. (Music must not be used unless it occurs where the scene is being shot.)

3   The camera must be hand-held. Any movement or immobility attainable in the hand is permitted. (The film must not take place where the camera is standing; shooting must take place where the film takes place.)

4   The film must be in colour. Special lighting is not acceptable. (If there is too little light for exposure the scene must be cut or a single lamp be attached to the camera.)

5   Optical work and filters are forbidden.

6   The film must not contain superficial action. (Murders, weapons, etc. must not occur.)

7   Temporal and geographical alienation are forbidden. (That is to say that the film takes place here and now.)

8   Genre movies are not acceptable.

9   The film format must be Academy 35 mm.

10 The director must not be credited. Furthermore I swear as a director to refrain from personal taste! I am no longer an artist. I swear to refrain from creating a 'work', as I regard the instant as more important than the whole. My supreme goal is to force the truth out of my characters and settings. I swear to do so by all the means available and at the cost of any good taste and any aesthetic considerations. Thus I make my VOW OF CHASTITY.

Copenhagen, Monday 13 March 1995

On behalf of DOGME 95

(Signed) Lars von Trier, Thomas Vinterberg

(Dogme website)

In the event, the Dogme vow turned out to be largely a (very successful) means of promoting a group of film-makers and their films through generating a controversy. But if you look at the 'rules' above, you'll see that most of them fit the neo-realist approach very well. They also tune in to some of Rossellini's arguments about entertainment cinema. What is missing is any sense of addressing 'social issues' as a key concern – the Dogme group was not radical in a conventional 'political' sense.

The official Dogme films, including the one which most closely conformed to the rules, *Festen* (*Celebration*) (Denmark 1998), tended to focus on individual characters in fairly traditional cinematic narratives. Others, such as those directed by Lars von Trier, used sensational stories and broke the rules. Nevertheless, Dogme had an impact, especially on young film-makers with little money and a willingness to try new digital cameras as an entry into feature film-making. The 'rawness' and 'authenticity' of any shoot following the Dogme rules still has an impact and proves that different 'realisms' remain possible in contemporary cinema.

Realism and politics

Most realist film-makers, writers and documentarists are 'progressive' to some extent – their desire to represent 'the real' very often derives from a wish to expose something and thereby to help to get the situation changed.

It may be confusing then that some of the critics who support 'the realist aesthetic' are 'conservative' rather than 'progressive', especially in the UK. They tend to be keen on authentic detail, especially if a film celebrates their view of British history. There have been some very odd controversies over the 'political' films made by Ken Loach and others, where, in order to to undermine the potential exposure of 'real issues', critics have dismissed the authenticity of the films on the grounds that soldiers are 'wearing the wrong buttons'.

Realist approaches have also been criticised by more radical critics who object to the transparency of the representation of the real world that realism offers. This was particularly the case in the 1970s when social realism was not distinguished from Hollywood realism and the preferred way of making a 'political film' was to foreground the 'constructedness' of the film image. Films made in this way proved very difficult to watch unless the audience was already committed to the ideologies explored in the film. Realist films, by contrast, are usually easily understood and engaging. In contemporary film and television, the political debate has shifted somewhat. 'Social realism' is generally accepted by critics if it is an element in a comedy or feelgood film such as *The Full Monty* (UK 1997) or *Billy Elliot* (UK 2000), or a crime series such as *Cops* (UK 1998), but if the main thrust of the film is a study of a social issue, the charge is likely to be that the film is 'grim' or 'miserablist'.

The 'grim' charge has been particularly aimed at Ken Loach, who remains a committed political film-maker who rather unfashionably believes that it is possible for ordinary people to take control of their lives to achieve things. He works with a group of colleagues who have been able to find sufficient backing outside the Hollywood system to keep on making films which have something politically worthwhile to say, utilising a clearly defined approach. In this sense he is a realist film-maker.

ACTIVITY 17.3

Try to look at two or three of Ken Loach's later films (*Raining Stones* (1993), *Ladybird, Ladybird* (1994), *Land and Freedom* (1995), *Carla's Song* (1996), *My Name is Joe* (1998), *The Navigators* (2001) are all widely available on tape or DVD).

- All the films include at least some scenes set in contemporary Britain. Do they represent a Britain you recognise?
- If they do, which particular aspects of the films carry the connotations of 'realism'? Is it:
  - the casting?
  - the dialogue?
  - the locations?
  - the camera style?
  - references to particular 'real-world' political issues?
- Are the references to neo-realism helpful in understanding the films? Or are there other distinctive features which distinguish them from 'mainstream' contemporary films?
- Is the charge of 'grim and miserable' justified for the films?
- To what extent do you think the films are 'political'?

Figure 17.3 The volunteers to fight fascism in *Land and Freedom* (UK/Spain/Germany 1995).

Realist media texts are predicated on the assumption that they say something about the real world. In some cases this is simply a matter of stressing the

Figure 17.4 The Trench, transmitted by BBC2 in 2002, is an example of the new category of 'reality television'. Compare this image with that from the realist feature film, *Land and Freedom* on page 470.

credibility of the story; in others there is an appeal to audiences in terms of the social importance of the issue and the object is information more than entertainment. But we also need to recognise that arguments have been made that it is impossible to represent the 'real world' at all. These are taken up in Chapter 14 with its case study on *Pulp Fiction*.

References

Barnouw, Erik (1993) *Documentary: A History of the Non-fiction Film*, New York: Oxford University Press.

Bazin, André (1967 and 1971) *What is Cinema?*, vols I and II, London: University of California Press.

Blandford, Steve, Grant, Barry Keith and Hillier, Jim (2001) *The Film Studies Dictionary*, London: Arnold.

Bondanella, Peter (1993) *The Films of Roberto Rossellini*, Cambridge: Cambridge University Press.

Bordwell, David, Staiger, Janet and Thompson, Kirstin (1985) *The Classic Hollywood Cinema: Film Style and Mode of Production to 1960*, London: Routledge.

Bruzzi, Stella (2000) *New Documentary: A Critical Introduction*, London: Routledge

Corner, John (2001) 'Form and content in documentary study' and 'Documentary realism (documentary fakes)', in Glen Creeber (ed.) *The Television Genre Book*, London: BFI.

Crisell, Andrew (1994, 2nd edition) *Understanding Radio*, London: Routledge.

Graef, Roger (1995) 'Flying off the wall', *Guardian*, 6 October 1995.

Hardy, Forsyth (ed.) (1966) *Grierson on Documentary*, London: Faber and Faber.

Lovell, Alan and Hillier, Jim (1972) *Studies in Documentary*, London: Secker & Warburg/BFI.

Monaco, James (1980) 'American documentary since 1960', in Richard Roud (ed.) *Cinema: A Critical Dictionary*, vol. 1, London: Martin Secker & Warburg.

Neale, Steve (1985) *Cinema and Technology: Image, Sound, Colour*, London: BFI/Macmillan.

Nichols, Bill (1991) *Representing Reality: Issues and Concepts of Documentary*, Bloomington and Indianapolis: Indiana University Press.

Nichols, Bill (1994) *Blurred Boundaries: Questions of Meanings in Contemprary Culture*, Bloomington and Indianapolis: Indiana University Press.

Nochlin, Linda (1971) *Realism*, London: Penguin.

Overby, David (1978) *Springtime in Italy: A Reader on Neo-realism*, London: Talisman.

Williams, Christopher (ed.) (1980) *Realism and the Cinema*, London: Routledge & Kegan Paul/BFI.

Wolfe, Tom and Johnson, E. W. (eds) (1975) *The New Journalism*, London: Picador.

Further reading

Barsam, Richard M. (1992) *Non-fiction Film*, Bloomington: Indiana University Press.

Creeber, Glen (ed.) (2001) *The Television Genre Book*, London: BFI.

MacDonald, Kevin and Cousins, Mark (1998) *Imagining Reality: The Faber Book of Documentary*, London: Faber.

McKnight, George (ed.) (1997) *Agent of Challenge and Defiance: The Films of Ken Loach*, Trowbridge: Flicks Books.

Rosenthal, A. (ed.) (1999) *Why Docudrama?*, Carbondale and Edwardsville: Southern Illinois University Press.

Winston, Brian (1995) *Claiming the Real*, London: BFI.

18 Regulation

Many of the contemporary debates about media practices focus on the potential power of media industries with their large resources and new technologies. In Chapter 7 we suggested that 'constraining' the power of organisations was one of the main functions of the process of institutionalising them. But how should this take place and who should implement the constraints? Such questions are usually expressed in arguments about **regulation**.

Why regulate?

The arguments in favour of some form of regulation refer to two broad areas of activity:

- *public safety and the 'quality' of media products*; what is being offered to audiences, is it 'fit for purpose', is it offensive, is there diversity?
- *economic competition and the provision of goods and services*; does one organisation dominate the industry, does competition stimulate a range of organisations to better meet the needs of the consumer and society?

The first of these is concerned with institutional questions (see Chapter 7), the second with industrial questions (see Chapter 8). In both cases regulation is argued to be beneficial for the individual and for society. Is it as simple as that? How would you respond to these statements:

- Free speech means that racists must be allowed to use the media to express their views.
- Pirate radio must be closed down if it interferes with emergency services or military frequencies.

Both statements have been fiercely debated at various times. They involve legal questions (i.e. legislation can be invoked in both cases) and institutional media questions. What is less clear, perhaps, is that there are broader issues of how far we are prepared to allow other people to have a say in how we conduct our media activities. How do we resolve the conflict between the public and private aspects of our media use?

Is the best form of regulation organised by:

- governments?
- the media institution itself?
- the operations of the market?

Before we try to explore these questions, we need to sketch in the historical background to the regulation of media industries, since without it you will find it difficult to understand contemporary debates fully.

Historical background

Knowledge is power and has been recognised as such throughout history. Rulers and powerful classes have always tried to keep the mass of the population away from 'dangerous knowledge' – in Europe in the Middle Ages this meant a Christian Church which attempted to maintain a 'priestly language', Latin, as the basis for theological and academic texts. Making available scriptures in local languages, understood by all, was a revolutionary act and church authorities attempted to maintain control over education as long as possible, i.e. controlling how people learnt to read. The invention of the printing press promised to introduce the first 'mass medium', circulating ideas to everyone who could read. It is no surprise that governments of every kind immediately saw the importance of exerting some form of control over what was printed. Sometimes they banned titles; sometimes they altered them and sometimes they taxed them – raising revenue as well as limiting their availability by artificially raising prices.

The history of media activities in the twentieth century is in some ways about the struggle between European and American models of control that mirror political economy models of economic activity. In Europe, this saw a tendency towards social democratic models with a significant public sector and a role for government in overseeing broadcasting in particular. By contrast, American models stress 'unfettered' capitalist enterprise and only a limited role for state intervention.

Political events in Europe were important in establishing models, e.g. the British Broadcasting Corporation began as a private company but was taken into the public sector after the General Strike of 1926, in which the government and the trade unions both used the media to try to get their point across to the general public. An 'independent' but publicly funded broadcaster offers at least the potential for objective reporting. In West Germany, after the Second World War, the occupation forces re-organised broadcasting along BBC lines in an effort to prevent another takeover of the airwaves by an extremist political party. European countries have generally

Stamp duty is still levied on certain legal documents in the UK, but in the early nineteenth century it was used as a means of suppressing radical newspapers. The Newspaper Stamp Duties Act of 1819 was an effective means of 'regulating' newspapers by making them too expensive for working people to purchase. After newspaper and advertising duties were removed in 1855, the popular press began to grow.

had a strong tradition of **public service broadcasting**. (This is also true of other developed countries such as Canada, Australia and Japan.) Broadcasting in the public sector is generally regulated by a set of requirements laid down in a founding charter or licence and then monitored for performance.

See the Television Industry case study following Chapter 8.

In the US, political events did give rise to some public-sector media activities, such as the theatre programme devised as a means of entertaining and educating the poor as part of Roosevelt's New Deal during the 1930s Depression. This movement promoted the careers of many writers and directors, including Orson Welles, but was viciously attacked by some Hollywood executives. Many of those who took part in the programme were later attacked as dangerous radicals during the McCarthyite anti-Communist witch hunts of the late 1940s. In the US, publicly funded media activities have remained marginal – media activity is essentially a business enterprise. From the development of radio stations in the 1920s onwards, American broadcasting has been dominated by networks selling advertising. Public service broadcasting on European lines has been limited. This means that regulation of broadcasting in the US has been conducted by a federal agency more concerned with maintaining competition than in laying down requirements about programming.

Outside of broadcasting, the other media such as cinema, press and advertising developed systems of **self-regulation** as part of their instutionalisation in the twentieth century. Self-regulation means that institutions appoint committees or panels of individuals drawn from within the industry (and sometimes 'independents' from outside) who are charged with enforcing a code of behaviour.

The tradition of certificating films for cinema release dates back to 1912 in the UK, and Hollywood introduced a restrictive Production Code in 1930, designed to head off criticism and potential boycotts from religious groups. The press and advertising industries have also developed 'codes' of behaviour as a defence against critics, and like cinema they have been subject to forms of censorship. However, they have not been subjected to the same regulatory environment that has faced broadcasters. (See the list of self-regulating institutions and their codes below.)

The centrality of broadcasting

Broadcasting has usually required some form of **statutory regulation**. Jostein Gripsrud (2002: 260) suggests several reasons why broadcasting is often seen to be the most important medium and therefore as giving the most

Statutory regulation means that the powers of the regulator are provided by Act of Parliament and are therefore enforceable by law. In the case of the BBC, it has traditionally been allowed to self-regulate, with that status being conferred by Royal Charter.

concern to governments (this would have applied to radio in the 1930s–50s, but is now more a feature of television):

- Enormous 'reach' – accessible to almost everybody.
- People spend more time with radio and television than with any other medium.
- Television is located centrally in every country (despite local services, it is the medium which represents a national focus on events).
- Television dominates the agenda of the public sphere.
- Television is the most important medium for culture, both in the sense of a 'way of life' and in the sense of art – we get our sense of who we are and how we live primarily from television.

For all these reasons, television (and, to a lesser extent, radio) is considered too important to 'leave to the market', and governments have decided they should be regulated. We should also note the public safety issue of the control over radio frequencies (i.e. interference with vital services).

public sphere a concept associated with the work of Jürgen Habermas, who used the term to refer to a social space in which everyone should be able to communicate their ideas about the state and the economy. In practice, the opportunities to do so are limited.

Changes in the 'orthodoxy' of economic policy

From the end of the Second World War up until the early 1980s, the prevailing economic ideology in the developed world was 'Keynesianism' (named after the British economist John Maynard Keynes), a set of ideas that saw government intervention in the economy as an essential tool in controlling inflation and unemployment across all the major economies. Keynesian policies saw governments 'regulating' their own spending so that, if a depression in the economy threatened, spending would be increased on public sector goods and services. The aim of government policy was to maintain economic prosperity and the general economic welfare of all aspects of society.

For thirty years up until the mid-1970s, Keynesian policies provided relative economic stability. In Europe this allowed governments to fund public service broadcasters adequately so that programming could be 'producer-led'. Producers had budgets that allowed them to make a full range of programmes. The UK stood out in Europe as having a 'mixed economy' in television with a strong commercial sector in ITV, but one which was regulated alongside the BBC and had certain public service broadcasting obligations.

In the US, television broadcasting was a relatively stable market up to the 1970s, with two, and later three, big commercial networks competing across the country and an array of local channels in each major city. The different approach to regulation in the US did not affect Europe. In the era before full globalisation of media activity, the main issue for Europeans was the import

of Hollywood films – at various times imports were restricted in an attempt
to protect local markets. The activities of American broadcasters were not yet
important in Europe.

The Canadian economist J. K. Galbraith was a staunch supporter of Keynesian
policies and of the welfare programme, 'The Civil Society' introduced by the
Democrats in the US in the 1960s. This was a hugely controversial government
intervention in American life along European lines, tackling poverty, housing
etc. Galbraith's 1958 book *The Affluent Society* predicted what he saw as the
future problems of any society which ignored the 'public good' in favour of
'private pleasure'. He coined the term 'private affluence/public squalor'.

Nearly fifty years later this comment seems remarkably prescient in relation
to the US and the UK. A revealing insight into debates about government
intervention in the US economy can be found in readers' comments on the
republication of Galbraith's book in 1998 (look up the book on
www.amazon.com). From a European perspective, the fierce attacks on any
kind of government intervention as delivered by many commentators in
America seem extreme.

In the late 1970s, the economic orthodoxy shifted towards monetarism and
the promotion of so-called 'free market capitalism'. This meant that
governments intervened only in the flow of money in the economy – money
was all that mattered, and investment decisions were made only by referring
to the prevailing money market conditions and the potential profit from
investment (i.e. rather than if they would produce a social benefit). This is not
the place to discuss the rights and wrongs of these policies, but we need to
note that the changing orthodoxy in economic thinking had an effect on
government attitudes towards the media industries as businesses, and that
this was a change across all media markets.

Deregulation and liberalisation

What happened in the 1980s stemmed from a combination of different
factors:

- The new economic orthodoxy saw a move away from government funding
  of public-sector organisations towards support for more 'open',
  competitive markets.
- New technologies – cable, satellite and cheaper broadcasting technologies
  – offered a sudden increase in the possibilities for new channels, more
  choice, but fragmentation of the market.

(See Chapter 16 and the Television Industry case study following Chapter 7.)

- New global media players emerged, capable of moving across national boundaries. In some cases they were welcomed by national governments and sometimes accepted reluctantly.

The result of these changes was the destabilising of the existing broadcasting environment, with public service broadcasters having to react to the presence of American companies or new European private sector companies working to the American model.

In economic terms the introduction of new channels and new services meant that television was no longer something that governments saw as a 'public good', to be treated as a special form of media activity in which everyone shares. Instead, it became a 'private good' just like any other media product such as a newspaper or magazine. (See Küng-Shankleman 2000: 29.)

The UK Thatcher government (1979–90) supported this general trend and, with other parts of Europe following, the media market across the world moved into a phase of what some commentators called **deregulation** and **liberalisation**. Linked government policies saw:

In 1984 in the new 'free market',
the UK government ironically
decided that so-called 'video
nasties' should be censored by
law.

- the privatisation of what had been public sector monopolies in broadcasting and telecommunications. In the UK, the two best examples of this were the sale of the telecommunications business developed by the Post Office to form British Telecom and the sale of the national network of television transmitters that eventually produced NTL. These new private sector companies were free to attract investment into new media products and services
- the 'loosening' of regulatory controls, especially in broadcasting, which allowed previously tightly regulated ITV to lose some of its public service obligations
- the 'opening up' of UK media markets with new licences for broadcasting services, particularly in radio, satellite and cable. Restrictions on 'cross-media ownership' were also gradually lifted. This was the liberalisation of the market.

Oftel The Office of
Telecommunications started a
trend for regulators to be call
'Of . . .', e.g. the proposal for
OFCOM or Office of
Communications.

Ironically, this period actually saw an increase in the number of regulators, with the creation of Oftel to look after the new telecomms industry and the creation of new regulatory responsibilities for the certification of video releases. Nevertheless, the effect was 'less restriction' on media activity, and this was the purpose of deregulation.

The contemporary regulatory environment

Since the 1990s there have been changes in government and some changes in the approach to the surviving public sector in the UK. However, the media environment created by the arrival of new technologies and new broadcasters is here to stay for the foreseeable future. If the UK government decides to regulate, it must take account of European Union policy and the implications of the global media market. We can identify six different types of regulation, distinguished by how the power to regulate is located:

1 Direct control by government

Some countries are controlled by authoritarian regimes which intervene directly in the activities of the media industries (Myanmar, Iraq etc.). But such intervention isn't unknown in democracies. It isn't so long ago that the UK government prevented the voices of IRA spokespersons being heard on radio or television or issued 'D' notices warning that news stories were covered by the Official Secrets Act and should not be published. In this respect the UK has a relatively 'closed' form of government, which is often revealed as such in comparison with the 'open' US system. The Radiocommunications Agency in the UK is currently part of a government department.

2 Delegation by government to an independent statutory regulator

This is the current system used in the UK for commercial radio and television and it is proposed for the new agency OFCOM (see below).

3 Self-regulation by media producers

This has two meanings. In a formal sense the media institution appoints a panel to oversee regulation. But it also works through individual producers constraining themselves to avoid any chance of later demands for changes or cuts.

4 The general legal framework as a restraint

This is still the case in the UK in relation to obscenity and blasphemy. If legal charges are made against media producers, the results are often not satisfactory for either side. This issue is being addressed under the OFCOM proposals.

5 'Market forces' regulate

Audiences using their own judgement over purchases affect future industry activities through the **price mechanism**. This assumes a 'free market' with perfect competition which is very difficult to create. In practice, most markets are 'skewed' by price fixing or lack of knowledge by consumers about competing prices.

price mechanism Some economists refer to consumer actions in relation to prices as the means by which the laws of 'supply and demand' work in the marketplace. If a media product is poor-quality and does not offer what the market wants, people will not buy it unless the price falls. But then it will not be profitable to supply and so it will disappear from the market. Conversely if people find the product acceptable at the price, it will continue to be produced.

6 Audience pressure regulates

There is a long history of religious and 'culturally conservative' groups in the US, which have identified various media products as 'morally dangerous' – cinema, rock music, television, video games. In the UK, there have been similar but less powerful groups, as well as others more concerned with ideas of quality.

UK regulators

In the UK, as in most other countries, regulation at the start of the twenty-first century represented a 'rag-bag' of different strategies. All of the six types of regulation operate in some way.

UK Regulators

Self-regulation

See the Advertising case study re the ASA.

ASA   The **Advertising Standards Authority** is an example of self-regulation by the advertising industry. An independent panel drawn mainly from outside the industry uses an agreed Code to monitor advertisements placed in the press, on posters, Internet sites and other electronic media and cinema screens. It also covers sales promotions. Website: www.asa.org.uk.

BBFC   The **British Board of Film Classification** was set up as a self-regulating agency by the UK film industry in 1912. Under the Video Recordings Act of 1984, the BBFC became the agency for the compulsory certification for all video (and now DVD) titles in distribution. In this sense, the BBFC has a statutory role. Website: www.bbfc.co.uk

See the Stardom and celebrity case study re the PCC.

PCC   The **Press Complaints Commission** represents self-regulation for the newspaper and magazine industries. It undertakes to investigate complaints about editorial material in all UK national and regional newspapers and magazines, through application of a Code drawn up by editors. Website: www.pcc.org.uk.

Statutory regulators

ITC   The **Independendent Television Commission** is a statutory regulator with powers laid down by the Broadcasting Acts of 1990 and 1996. Its work includes:

- licensing television broadcasters based in the UK who deliver terrestrial, satellite and cable services (excepting BBC1, BBC2 and S4C)
- monitoring commercial television output, including advertising
- ensuring fair competition amongst commercial television broadcasters
- ensuring universal access to a wide range of commercial television broadcasting services
- investigating complaints and publishing findings about the content of commercial television programmes.

Website: www.itc.org.uk.

BSC The **Broadcasting Standards Commission** is a statutory body set up under the 1996 Broadcasting Act and charged with monitoring 'standards and fairness' in all UK broadcasting (i.e. all forms of radio and television, including the BBC). This entails:

- producing codes of conduct
- investigating complaints
- undertaking research and producing reports.

Website: www.bsc.org.uk.

The **Radio Authority** is the statutory body set up under the Broadcasting Acts of 1990 and 1996 to regulate all independent (i.e. non-BBC) radio broadcasting in the UK. Its remit includes:

- planning the use of broadcast radio frequencies
- licensing independent radio broadcasters
- monitoring radio programmes and advertising
- supervising the radio ownership system.

Website: www.radioauthority.org.uk

Oftel is the statutory body set up by the 1984 Telecommunications Act to regulate the telecommunications industry. It is a government agency charged with:

- protecting the interests of consumers
- maintaining fair competition
- ensuring access in the UK to the full range of telecommunications services.

Website: www.oftel.gov.uk.

The **Radiocommunications Agency** is part of the Department of Trade and Industry (DTI). It is charged with 'keeping the radio spectrum clean', allocating radio frequencies for different uses and representing the UK in global discussions about radio use. The **RA** deals with all non-military radio. Website: www.radio.gov.uk.

The coming of OFCOM

In late 2000, the UK government announced a Communications White
Paper laying out its intention to bring together all the statutory bodies
concerned with broadcasting and telecommunications under one umbrella
organisation to be known as 'OFCOM'. This was scheduled to be a reality by
the end of 2003, when the new regulator was expected to replace the ITC,
BSC, Radio Authority, RA and Oftel. The main objectives of OFCOM as set
out in the White Paper are:

- *furthering the interests of consumers*, especially through choice, price, quality
  of service and value for money
- *encouraging dynamic and competitive markets*, in both communications services
  and broadcast media
- *securing the continuing availability of high-quality broadcasting* content,
  satisfying a wide range of tastes and interests and a plurality of public
  expression
- *protecting the interests of citizens*, by maintaining generally accepted standards
  to protect the public from offensive and harmful broadcast content and
  ensuring protection of fairness and privacy – whilst balancing against this
  the need for an appropriate level of freedom of speech
- *encouraging efficiency and innovation in the management of radio spectrum*, and of
  other limited resources used for communications services and
  broadcasting.

(as presented in the Towers and Perrin Consultant's Report to the
Regulators' Steering Group, October 2001)

How do we make sense of these objectives? Is every aspect of regulation
covered? These objectives don't give the full flavour of the report, which does
also refer to ideas of 'universal access' to a range of important services and
guarantees a future for public service broadcasting. We can, however, try to
read between the lines and also look for how debates about the White Paper
developed.

The language of the objectives is interesting. Note the use of 'consumer'
and 'citizen' rather than 'audience' and the stress on 'dynamic and competitive
markets'. Commercial broadcasters took up the invitation to 'dynamic'
markets and immediately began to discuss the lifting of regulatory controls –
in particular, the possibility of a single owner of ITV. Other commentators
noted the references to **diversity** and *plurality*.

By diversity, we mean the range of different programmes and services
available to viewers and listeners. Plurality, on the other hand, is about the
choices viewers and listeners are able to make between different providers
of such services. Society benefits from both a diversity of services between

and within genres (such as news, entertainment, documentaries etc.) and a
plurality of suppliers of such services (since this increases exposure to a
variety of editorial styles and a range of views and opinions).

(Chapter 4 of the White Paper)

Figure 18.1a

Figure 18.1b

The Campaign for Press and Broadcasting Freedom, a UK pressure group
with an aim to promote 'accountability, diversity and plurality in mass
communications', targeted this statement and linked it to the support for the
market as a 'democratic weakness':

> We take the view that the number of channels, web-sites, radio stations
> and publications should be sufficient to generate a wide variety of different
> perspectives on society and culture. We do not think this means
> encouraging unlimited outlets. We think that the government should be
> concerned with preventing a concentration of ownership and using its
> legislative and economic power to promote a plurality of outlets.
>
> The media should not only have a sensible plurality of outlets, it should
> also be an arena in which a diversity of perspectives and viewpoints can be
> encountered. This means that governments have to take action to
> encourage participation in the media by the range of different
> communities in our society and also enforce, across the media, obligations
> on providers of services to promote key values of accuracy, impartiality and
> public service principles. We do not think that diversity is served by
> encouraging the spread of market driven services and leaving public
> service and community media on the margins of the system.

(CPBF Response to the White Paper, February 2001)

The response by the CPBF is long and detailed, offering a valuable critique of government thinking. At the heart of the objections is the shift to support markets, which assumes that plurality and diversity will be served by 'a competitive free market'. There are two problems with this:

- The loosening of ownership controls is likely to reduce the number of providers (one owner of ITV, one cable provider etc.).
- Whichever global media corporations remain in the newly consolidated UK market, they will be likely to share the same editorial 'lines' (see Chapter 7) on major issues and the same basic attitudes towards broadcasting services. If free market competition is encouraged, the public service providers will be marginalised and plurality will be reduced.

The CPBF response also includes a number of further issues:

- The White Paper suggests a negative view of regulation, especially in relation to 'protecting consumers' and ensuring competition. This might be expected if we read regulation as a means of constraining, but public service broadcasting has in the past been seen as a means of promoting public interest in mass media – constraint leads to creativity in programming.
- The White Paper is confusing in including newspapers under 'ownership rules' but not under 'content regulation'.
- There is an assumption about the future take-up of digital television and interactive services. This includes a definition of convergence (see Chapter 8 and Chapter 15) that refers only to computers, television and telecommunications. Will OFCOM be an appropriate body for the existing discrete media such as radio?

What does a free market mean for the UK?

Censorship and sex and violence

In a 'free market' we might expect to see a thriving trade in pornographic material, as in many European countries, if that is what people wish to buy. However, the very advocates of the free market are often amongst those who wish to control access to the marketplace for certain kinds of products. The result is that in terms of 'sex and violence' we expect to see the development of some form of *self-censorship* in all media, whereby the distribution companies in that medium agree to set standards for acceptable products. This has happened with film, magazines and more recently video and computer games.

The oddity of the debate about sex and violence in broadcasting (or in print or on film) is that the issue is rarely put to the market test. We don't know what would happen if 'hard' material were freely available – if it is unacceptable to a large number of media consumers, perhaps 'the market' would drop it from general release when it didn't sell? There are many pressure groups arguing for censorship but few actively campaigning against. One argument might be that the current attitude to self-censorship is patronising towards the audience. If someone is capable of making a decision about whether a media product represents 'value for money', why can't they also decide whether or not it is offensive and 'liable to corrupt'? And if they can't decide, what makes a programme-maker better qualified to decide? This is the argument as presented by the libertarian right and is a complete refutation of public service broadcasting, without the qualifications of the social market position.

In some respects this libertarian position looks very attractive (assuming that children are protected from 'offensive' material). However, 'freedom to choose' is also the freedom to be assailed by fierce marketing and the possibility that the acceptability of more explicit sex or violence will lead to more of such programming and less overall variety of material.

The power of different discourses to either permit or condemn sexual images is given in the jokey line: 'If I like it, it's erotic, if I don't, it's pornographic.'

ACTIVITY 18.1

Censorship of offensive material

How do you think censorship of offensive material should be handled in the media? How would you define 'offensive material'?

- What would be the consequences of a media environment without any censorship of offensive material? What do you think would happen in a free market?
- What are the arguments for and against such material being available only through licensed outlets at premium prices (could it be taxed like cigarettes and alcohol)?
- What are the arguments for banning such material altogether?
- Why is self-censorship preferred to an 'official censor' in non-broadcast media industries?

This topic is a good one to choose if you want to try producing a video or audio 'debate'-style programme. You should quite easily find people prepared to adopt specific positions. But first you will have to decide whether it is going to be a 'balanced' programme, or whether as producer you want to slant it in any particular way – in other words, you need to think about the institutional factors.

In March 2002, a court found against the BBC after an election campaign broadcast for an anti-abortion group was not broadcast because it contained 'offensive material'.

'Dumbing down' and programming aims

Much of the UK debate about television (and radio) is about the 'level' or 'seriousness' of programming and scheduling. Public service broadcasting in the period up to the 1980s was heavily geared to ensuring that certain kinds of programme were scheduled on all channels in peak time. Current affairs and news and arts programming were all prescribed and education during the day and at other times. The loosening of such requirements allowed ITV and then Channel 5 and the satellite and cable companies to target BBC programmes in the schedule with more 'ratings-friendly' programmes. The BBC struggled within its remit to compete, and towards the end of the 1990s various 'test cases' were widely discussed in the press and by regulators:

- the disappearance of current affairs programmes from peak time
- the disappearance of arts programmes from peak time
- reduction of news programmes and the move to 10 p.m. by the BBC.

In the free market, are these changes inevitable? The market is reflected in ratings and these in turn are used in negotiations with advertisers. Scheduling is a strategy game in which the scheduler makes an 'educated guess' about how well a programme will fare in a particular time-slot. Because an instant response is important in ratings terms, the scheduler is likely to

- risk only those programmes which are formulaic (have worked before)
- take off very quickly any programmes which don't achieve the target rating.

In the regulated market with strong support for the public broadcaster, the scheduler would often allow the programme to 'build' an audience – especially if it was a new kind of programme. This was 'production-led' scheduling rather than 'ratings-led' television.

How do you see the current schedule on BBC1 and BBC2 compared to ITV and Channel 4? Is it full of programmes looking for 'easy acceptance'? The proponents of the free market in broadcasting are likely to offer these observations:

- People want popular programmes, why shouldn't they have what they want? (This argument is often couched in class terms, with the public service supporters represented as being middle-class and out of touch with the tastes of the majority.)
- The market is very conscious of 'niche audiences' who want very different kinds of programmes. These audiences are often ABC1 and attractive to advertisers. As such they are targeted by schedulers, probably on specific channels.
- The market makes producers more focused and more efficient (an argument often made to explain the success of American imported programming).
- Were the majority of programmes any better under the old system? Yes, there were some great television plays and some classic sit-coms, but what about the rest?

The battle between 'public servants' and 'free market capitalists' has been fought for a very long time. Recently, a cable television executive resurrected the distinction between 'herbivores' (those who support public service ideals) and 'carnivores' (the beasts of the capitalist jungle) first used in the 1950s.

BBC1	BBC2	ITV
5.50 Wonder Woman (US series) 6.40 Jim'll Fix It (Jimmy Saville gameshow) 7.15 All Creatures Great and Small (UK comedy drama series) 8.05 Dick Emery Show (UK comedian) 8.40 Dallas (US series) 9.10 News 9.40 Match of the Day 10.50 Parkinson (Chat Show) 11.50 Weather and Closedown	5.50 Mr Smith's Indoor Garden 6.15 Open Door (Community access programme) 6.45 Test Cricket (Australia v. West Indies) 7.15 News and Sport 7.30 International Table Tennis 8.05 Film: *The Petrified Forest* (US 1936) 9.25 Animated Conversation 9.30 Playhouse: *Lifelike* by John Challen (single drama) 10.25 Something of a Miracle: 1979 Eisteddfod at Llangollen 11.15 News on 2 11.20 Film: *Rosemary's Baby* (US 1968) 1.35 Closedown	6.00 Happy Days (US sitcom) 6.30 Film: *The Valley of Gwangi* (US 1969) 8.15 The Faith Brown Chat Show 8.45 Enemy at the Door (UK WWII drama series) 9.45 News and Sport 10.00 *Heartland: Family* (UK single drama) 11.00 Film: *Licensed to Kill* (UK 1965) 12.35 Closedown

Figure 18.2 The evening television schedules for Saturday 26 January 1980. There were then only three channels.

ACTIVITY 18.2

Comparing schedules

Compare the schedules shown in Figure 18.2 with those for a Saturday evening on the same three channels today. How do the arguments above work out? Was there a greater diversity in the 1970s with evidence of the public service requirement? Or are the free marketeers right?

References

Campaign For Press and Broadcasting Freedom (2001) 'Response to the White Paper: *A New Future for Communications*, CM5010 (DTI/DCMS, London, HMSO, December 2000)', London: Campaign for Press and Broadcasting Freedom, February.

Gripsrud, Jostein (2002) *Understanding Media Culture*, London: Arnold.

Küng-Shankleman, Lucy (2000) *Inside the BBC and CNN*, London: Routledge.

Tom O'Malley (2001) *Communications Revolution: Who Benefits?*, London: CPBF.

Further reading

Lees, Tim, Ralph, Sue and Langham Brown, Jo (eds) (2000) *Is Regulation Still an Option in a Digital Universe?*, Luton: University of Luton Press.

Useful website

www.communicationsbill.gov.uk

Part IV
Reference

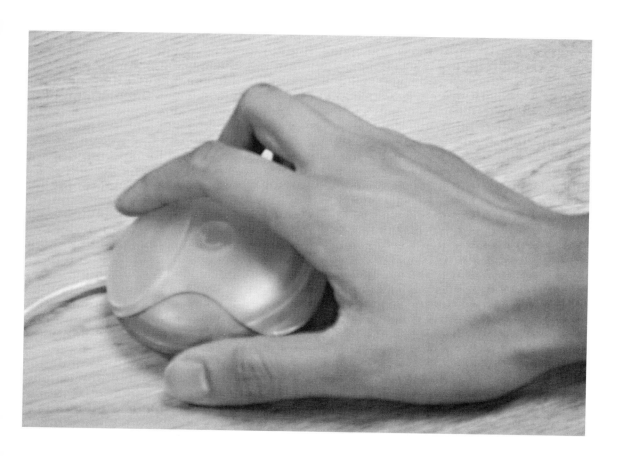

Glossary of key terms

Listed below are some of the key terms we have used, and which you will need to know, with short 'thumb-nail' definitions. Some common words are referenced only when they have special meanings in Media Studies. Use this glossary in conjunction with the index, contents page and chapter 'menus' to find the material you want.

180 degree rule   narrative continuity 'rule' on the placement of the camera in film-making (also known as 'not crossing the line')

25 per cent production quota   requirement for British broadcasters to commission 25 per cent of programmes from 'independents'

A&R   'Artists and Repertoire' represent the main assets of companies in the music industry. Performers are signed on contract and rights are held on recordings

ABC   Audit Bureau of Circulation – independent body which provides circulation figures of newspapers and magazines for advertisers

access   media slots or opportunities enabling audiences either to become producers or to have some form of right to reply to dominant media producers

acoustics   the science of sound – here, a consideration of the environment for sound recording

Acrobat   Adobe software that allows **pdf** files to be produced and read on any computer

actuality   term used in early cinema to describe recording of 'real events' – tended to be replaced by 'documentary' in the 1920s

ADR   Automatic Dialogue Replacement – a process during feature film production, also known as 'looping', which allows actors to rerecord dialogue for greater clarity while watching themselves on screen

advertising agencies   organisations which create and manage advertising campaigns, from conception to placement

aesthetics   activities which try to understand or evaluate the sense of beauty, or of form in a text or art work

age profile   the audience for a particular media text, classified according to age group

agenda   prioritised list of items dealt with by a media text, especially in news – hence the term 'agenda setting'

analogue   any device which represents a quality or value by a physical change in a measuring agent, e.g. the silver nitrate on photographic film which changes colour in response to light

anamorphic lens   distorting lens which 'squeezes' an image – used in widescreen film projection

anchoring   written or spoken text (e.g. caption, voice over) used to control or select a specific reading of a visual image

anthropology   study of the human species – applied in audience studies

anti-realism   an aesthetic based on denying any attempt to represent surface reality

anti-trust legislation   US government action taken to break up the monopoly power of large producers, e.g. the Paramount decision in 1948 forcing Hollywood studios to sell their cinema chains

arbitrary signifiers   term used in semiotics; signifiers with no resemblance to the referent or the signified; see **iconic**, **indexical** and **symbolic**

archive   any collection of similar material which can be used in future media productions, e.g. a film archive

artwork   term used in printing to describe any material which will be used to make a printing plate – could be text or illustrations

ASA   Advertising Standards Authority: regulator of advertising in newspapers and magazines

aspect ratio   the ratio of height to breadth of a cinema screen, or breadth to height of a television screen

audience ethnographies   research using ethnographic approaches; joining a specific audience group and working 'from the inside'

auteur   French term for author, used in 'la politique des auteurs', a debate from 1950s–60s film theory (see **authorship**)

authorship   approach originating in film studies which places emphasis on an individual author (usually the director) rather than the collective and collaborative nature of production; see **auteur**

avant garde   an artistic movement which is 'ahead of the mainstream' and usually experimental

AVID   name of the market leader in provision of

non-linear editing equipment. Often used as a generic term for computer editing of video or film

'B' picture   in the studio era, the shorter and less important feature in a cinematic double bill

back light   the third light source in a conventional three-point lighting set-up for film and video. The back light helps the subject to stand out from the background

BARB   Broadcasters' Audience Research Board, the body in Britain which produces television viewing figures

base–superstructure   critical term from early Marxism referring to the economic base on which is built the 'superstructure' of cultural and ideological institutions and assumptions

BBFC   British Board of Film Classification

behaviourism/behaviourist   movement in psychology which sees human behaviour as something which can be moulded by punishment and reward

bias/biased   ideological 'slant' in debates around factual reporting. Questioned in the light of pluralist rather than binary ('two sides to every question') models of news

bi-media journalism   a BBC policy to train journalists for television and radio under the same scheme

binary oppositions   sets of opposite values said to reveal the structure of cultures and, by extension, media texts; see structuralism

biopics   'biographical pictures' – a traditional Hollywood film genre

bit   corruption of 'binary digit', the '0' or '1' in a stream of binary data. Often used as an indicator of 'quality' or 'resolution', e.g. '24 bit colour image' implies a palette of millions of colours described by different combinations of primary colours, whereas a '1 bit' image can be only black and white

bitmap an image stored on a computer in the form of a matrix of '**bits**'. Bitmaps cannot be enlarged without losing quality

branding attaching powerful meanings or associations to products; persuading consumers of a product's quality prior to purchase or experience, usually by the reputation or image of the producing company

bricolage French term for 'putting together different articles', as in punk fashion

broadband cable modern telecommunications and television cable which allows more separate signals (channels) to be transmitted

broadsheet type of 'serious' newspaper with larger, less square pages than tabloids

browser computer software used to look at pages on the World Wide Web

BSC Broadcasting Standards Commission

burden of representation the problem posed for media worker when a previously under- or misrepresented group begins to be imaged in the media, and a few characters and producers have to bear the burden of being seen to represent the whole group – as 'positive role model' etc.

byte computer term (not the same as **bit**), referring to the basic unit of data storage for characters. File sizes and the capacity of computer memory are measured in kilobytes (a thousand bytes – KB), megabytes (MB) or gigabytes (GB)

camera obscura literally a 'dark room', the precursor of the modern camera

camp a sensibility, emerging from male gay culture, which revels in surface, style, theatricality, and exaggeration or parody of 'straight' forms of life

capitalism a competitive social system, emerging in the seventeenth century in Europe, based on commodification and the drive of the owners of the means of production to maximise the profits of their companies

cartel a group of organisations in an industry which secretly agree on maintaining high prices and effectively killing competition; see also **oligopoly**

CCCS Centre for Contemporary Cultural Studies at Birmingham University, 1964–2002

CD compact disc (or disk), a digital data storage medium. CD-ROM is a 'read-only' disk. CD-R is 'writable', CD-RW is 're-writable'

celebrity a figure understood as having the same access to fame as stars, but not always as closely associated with specific areas of achievement especially in cinema

censorship decisive acts of forbidding or preventing publication or distribution of media products, or parts of those products, by those with the power, either economic or legislative, to do so

CGI (1) Computer Generated Imagery, a term sometimes used for digital special effects; (2) Common Gateway Interface, an agreed standard that defines how a web page can allow users interactivity with an external program, e.g, using a search engine or shopping over the Internet

churn measure of the rate at which media service providers lose customers compared to the number of new customers signed up

cinéma vérité literally 'cinema truth' – an approach to documentary film-making aiming to get as close to events as possible, often producing very high shooting ratios of footage shot to that used in the final edit. Sometimes describes fiction narratives which attempt to resemble documentaries through use of hand-held cameras etc.

CinemaScope trade name for the **anamorphic** widescreen process introduced by 20th Century Fox in 1953

cinematography the art of lighting the set and photographing a film

class (1) one of the groups into which people are divided as a result of socio-economic inequality; (2) a specific group of consumers as recognised by advertisers, six classes now usually grouped into ABC1 ('upmarket') and C2DE ('downmarket'); (3) one of the groups assigned to occupational categories for statistical purposes as defined by the UK Registrar-General, changed in 1998 from six to eight categories

classical reference to the art and style of Greek and Roman civilisation; used to describe the Hollywood cinema of the studio system, which had developed into a form generally accepted as 'mature' and 'stable'. Contemporary forms which have changed this form radically are thus 'post-classical'

classification placing into categories. Sometimes used as synonymous with censorship, though the ratings are only one of the ways in which understandings of texts are prepared by different ways of classifying them

classified advertising advertising expressed in a few lines of text with ads grouped according to subject matter, also known as 'small ads'

clipart commercially produced artwork, available at low cost to enhance business and semi-professional print and electronic publications

closed term used of a narrative which is 'resolved' or comes to a conclusion, as opposed to an '*open*' or more ambiguous narrative ending

codes systems of meaning production

cognitive psychology movement in psychology (opposed to **behaviourism**) which argues that human behaviour is changed by appeals to thought processes

colour grading final process in preparing a feature film print for screening

colour temperature a measure of the lighting source on a film or video shoot, which affects the colour cast of white parts of the image and needs correction via filters (see **white balance**)

commodification a **commodity** is anything which can be bought and sold, usually within capitalist relations; **commodification** and the idea of **commodity fetishism** are terms used, often in Marxist theory, to argue against the undue spread and valuation of services, items, values

common sense in discussions of ideology, a set of assumptions that the world's meanings are obvious and can be understood without recourse to analysis or theory

commutation test a critical test used in semiotics, involving the substitution of one element in a complex sign

composition concept used in analysis of visual images referring to the position of objects in the image, their shape and the use of various devices to divide up the available space

conglomerate large industrial corporation, usually involved in several different industries

connote/connotation in semiotics, the meanings interpreted from a sign which link it to other concepts, values, memories

construct/construction semiotic term used to emphasise that media texts are 'made' and not simply 'taken from the real world'

consumers term for media audiences which emphasises the commercial aspects of distribution and exhibition, thus production and **consumption** of media texts

content analysis   see **quantitative analysis**

content provider   media companies who produce programme material for specific delivery or distribution systems, especially cable, satellite and Internet

continuity editing   editing techniques which are said to disguise the ways that narratives are constructed filmically. Sometimes called the 'continuity system' or 'continuity rules'

conventions   'unwritten rules' in the production of mainstream texts. Conventions are the dominant codings in any media

convergence   describes the 'coming together' of previously separate industries (computing, printing, film, audio etc.) which increasingly use the same or related technology and skilled workers. A feature of contemporary media environment, convergence is a product of mergers between companies in different sectors as well as a logical outcome of technological development

copy   (1) text written to support an advertisement; (2) the 'raw material' for journalism

copy-editing   checking the accuracy and legality of text intended for publication and its adherence to house style

CPT   advertisers' term standing for 'Cost Per Thousand' or the cost of reaching each thousand people in the target audience

critical pluralism   a theoretical approach which acknowledges the co-existence of different sets of ideas (as in pluralism) but recognises that some are more powerful than others, and that they are in a struggle for ascendancy

cropping   cutting parts from an image

cross-cutting   technique of sequencing images from different narrative spaces so that stories run in parallel, e.g. 'meanwhile, back at the ranch . . .'

cross-generic   blending different genre elements

crossing the line   'rule' for ensuring narrative continuity – 'not crossing the line (of action)' (also known as the **180 degree rule**)

cross-over   a media text which gains acceptance in a different genre market

cult   term used of media texts around which 'cults' or communities of enthusiastic users have developed. Often now used to signal the virtual communities possible via the Internet.

cultural codes   meanings derived from cultural differences; see **codes**

cultural competence   from Bourdieu, the idea that ease of access to media texts depends on cultural difference and experience

cultural imperialism   position that the globalisation of communication has been driven, particularly since the Second World War, by the 'military industrial complex' of the large US-based corporations and state. Sometimes used interchangeably with **media imperialism**

cut   a transition between two different visual or audio images in an edited sequence in which one image is immediately replaced by another (see **fade**, **dissolve**, **wipe**)

cutaway   an extra shot inserted between two visual images in a sequence which prevents a jarring transition (see **jump cut**)

DAT   Digital Audio Tape. Compact cassette housing tape suitable for digital recording. Used for some forms of professional audio recording and also for computer data storage

decoding   semiotic term for 'reading' the codes in a media text

deep-focus   technique in photography or cinematography, producing 'depth of field' – everything in shot in focus

demographics measurement of a population (from Greek *demos* = people) in terms of occupational class, age, sex and region (usually to ascertain their values and assumptions about spending)

denote/denotation in semiotics, the work of that part of the sign (the signifier) which is immediately recognisable to the reader and which has a direct relationship to a real-world entity (the referent)

deregulation removal of government restrictions on media industries

design grid the page layout design in a magazine

desktop reference to the way in which traditional media activities have been simulated on the computer screen, as in desktop publishing (DTP) or desktop video (DTV)

development media media production associated with aid programmes (in ex-British colonies especially)

dialectical montage juxtaposition of sequences in Soviet cinema representing the 'struggle' of opposing ideas

dialectics Marxist term to describe the process of change: the struggle of opposing ideas (thesis and antithesis) produce synthesis

diaspora dispersal, often forced, across the globe of peoples who originated in a single geographical location, e.g. the dispersed African communities formed as a result of the nineteenth century European slave trade

diegesis the time and space of the world of the audio-visual narrative. Most useful in distinguishing between diegetic and non-diegetic sound

difference key part of structuralist and semiotic emphases, arguing that meaning is produced largely in the difference between units such as words, rather than what they have in common. Has important (often destructive) consequences for thinking about

identification with 'sameness', important for social and political struggles

differential pricing means of accumulating maximum profit on a product by differentiating its price depending on what different markets (i.e. the wealth of potential consumers) will allow

digital based on numerical information, distinguished from **analogue**

digital editing editing using audio and/or video images which have been **digitised** (converted into computer data). Digital audio editing is sometimes called 'hard disk recording'. Digital video editing is usually termed **nonlinear** editing

digital imaging used to describe 'photography' which involves capture, manipulation or exhibition of images using a computer or other digital device. Some critics argue that this term should replace 'photography' altogether

Direct Cinema documentary movement in 1960s US

disc English spelling used here to refer to analogue recording devices

discourse any regulated system of statements or language use (e.g. in the law, or medicine) which has rules, and therefore exclusions and assumptions. For media it is extended to include visual as well as verbal languages, and also Foucualt's work on discourses' different connections to power

disk American spelling used here to refer to digital (computer) devices

display advertising advertising using a substantial area of a newspaper page (including graphics)

dissolve film term for the transition between two images in which one fades out as the other fades up (usually called a **mix** in television)

diversity the range of different types of programmes available on broadcast networks

division of labour work organised in specialist roles – traditional in the Hollywood studio system

docu-drama fiction narrative using documentary techniques

docu-soap a broadcast hybrid blending elements of soap (serial nature with character driven narratives ; a focus on emotional or 'gossipy' aspects of everyday life) with the codes and conventions of one kind of documentary (*vérité* camera work; real people not actors; real places not locations)

documentary media text dealing with 'real-world' events; see also **actuality**

dominant referring to the most powerful ideas in society at any time – expressed in **discourse** and **ideologies**

download transfer a file from a remote website to a desktop computer

DP Director of Photography – the person responsible for camerawork and lighting on a film shoot. British term used instead of *cinematographer*

drama-documentary documentary which uses techniques from fiction drama (also *drama-doc*)

duopoly an industry in which two companies control the market

DVD Digital Video Disc. A storage device for digital data which through **MPEG** compression allows video copies of feature films to be carried on a single 'compact' disc. Also used as a removable storage device for computer data. Attempts have been made to market DVD as 'Digital Versatile Disc' to emphasise the different uses

dystopia term used in science fiction; a dreadful future society, the opposite of **utopia**

economic determinist theory in political economy which looks for economic conditions as the basis for explanations of the social, cultural etc.

economies of scale cost savings which can be made by large organisations on the basis of the size of the operation, e.g. 'bulk buying'

editing sequencing of text, images and sounds; see **continuity editing**

editorial either a statement in a publication by the editor or any feature material (i.e. not advertising)

effects model model concerned with how the media 'does things to' audiences

empirical relying on observed experience as evidence for positions. A controversial term, often caricatured by opponents to imply an approach opposed to any kind of theory and relying on sense experience or simplistic facts alone

encrypted service a television broadcast that requires both a decoder (set-top box) and a specific subscriber number to unlock the signal

EPS Encapsulated Postscript – a computer image format used for placement of images in print documents

equilibrium the initial status quo which is 'disrupted' in a narrative

escapist seeking escape, especially from reality, a term used disparagingly of mass cultural forms. Often used as synonymous with 'entertainment'

establishing shot the opening shot of a conventional visual narrative sequence showing the geography of the narrative space

ethnography a method of deep research, involving spending considerable periods of time with a particular community or group of people. Audience ethnography was important in establishing Cultural Studies, and then in developing work on audiences within Media Studies

evaluation the process of reflecting on how well a media production has met its original aims. Often required by public sector funders as a condition of grant aid and by examiners as part of student assessment

expressionism aesthetics in which ideas and feelings are shown through exaggerated elements in the image (lighting, decor, sound etc.)

fabula term in narrative theory – Russian for 'story'

fade a production direction in audio and video editing in which an image gradually disappears

fan from 'fanatic': term for one who is passionately attached to a media text or performer. Originally often used derogatively, it now signals an interest in the varied activities of fans, especially over the Internet.

feminist belonging to movements and ideas which advocate the rights of women to have equal rights and opportunities to those possessed by men

fibre optic technology using glass fibres to carry data

fill light one of three lighting sources on a film **set-up**, used to 'fill' shadows created by the **key light**

flow term coined by Raymond Williams, after his first experience of US television in the 1950s, to suggest that broadcast media are experienced not as separate items but as a flow of similar segments

focal length the distance between the lens and the sensing device in a camera

focus groups method of audience research which assembles small, representative groups whose fairly informal discussions are facilitated, taped and analysed by, e.g., the producers of a television series seeking guidance on how to increase viewing

figures, or by advertisers researching associations etc. for the launch of a new product

Foley refers to technology used in feature film production to create sound effects. **Foley artists** work with a variety of materials to produce sounds mixed by a **Foley editor**

Fordism ideas about industrial production (including film etc.) derived from the concentrated large-scale assembly line established by Henry Ford in Detroit and then internationally from the 1920s

formal referring to the characteristics of a media text concerned with shape, colour, length etc., rather than content

formalist theoretical approach which privileges form over content

format (1) different size or shape of common media products (video is formatted as Betacam, VHS; newspapers as tabloid or broadsheet; film as 35 mm or 16 mm etc.); (2) a TV category allowing for the international trading of TV show concepts and set-ups: e.g. both *The Weakest Link* and *Who Wants to Be A Millionaire?* belong to the genre 'quiz show' though their formats differ; (3) 'format radio': station using only one kind of music or speech

framing referring to an image selected to show a person or object. Various framings from 'long shot' to 'extreme close-up' are defined by the size of the human body in the frame. Framing forms part of the process of composition of the image

franchise generally a licence to use a brand name in retailing or the service sector. Now used in Hollywood to describe a successful film title that can be developed into new films and associated products, e.g. *The Matrix*

Frankfurt School German critical theorists of mass culture working from the 1920s and 1930s, and later in the US in exile from German fascism

ftp   Internet **protocol** controlling file transfers between computers

GIF   Graphics Interchange Format: originally developed by Compuserve, GIFs are the standard format for non-photographic images on web pages, offering high compresssion and small file size

gatekeeping   process of choosing certain items for inclusion in news programmes and rejecting others

genre   theoretical term for classification of media texts into type groupings

globalisation   a process in which activities are organised on a global scale, in ways which involve some interdependence, and which are often instantaneous around the world

grid   basic design of a 'page' in a print or electronic publication, showing columns, margins etc.

gutter   in DTP, distance between two columns of print on a page

hardware   the physical equipment used to produce, distribute and exhibit media products

HDTV   High Definition Television. Standard for video images with a resolution in 'lines' which is double current norms (i.e. 1250 lines in the UK, 1050 lines in Japan and US)

hegemony, hegemonic   concept from Gramsci suggesting that power is achieved by dominant groups through successful struggles to persuade the subordinate that arrangements are in their interest

high-concept movie   the modern high-budget Hollywood film, based on a single strong idea which is easily 'pitched' and can be effectively marketed

homophobia   fear of homosexuality, expressed in a spectrum of activities from hostile or demeaning vocabulary and images to discriminatory legislation

horizontal integration   when an organisation takes over its competitors in the same industry

hybrid, hybridity   combination of differences, often styles, or technologies or cultural forms; e.g. Bhangra 'cross-over hits' in pop music; *Buffy*'s complex mixes etc.

hypertext   computer language allowing readers options to read documents in any order, hypertext mark-up language (*html*) is used to write pages on the **World Wide Web**

hypodermic model   model of media effects on audiences, imaged as being druglike

iconic   (from semiotics) resembling real-world objects (of signs) – see also **arbitrary**, **indexical** and **symbolic**

iconography   art history term, used to describe the study of familiar iconic signs in a genre

ident   a logo or sound image used on television or radio to identify the station

identity   the characteristics of an individual human being which are most central to that person's self-image and self-understanding

identity politics   the values and movements which have developed since the 1960s around issues of identity, in particular gender, race, sexuality and disability. Class is not usually included as one of these key identities

ideology, ideological   complex term relating to ideas and understanding about the social world and how these ideas are related to the distribution of power in society; also about how ideas and values are posed as 'natural'

image   a 'representation' of something expressed in visual or aural terms

imperfect competition   in economics, any 'market' in which a group of buyers or sellers is able to influence market forces; the basic condition for **oligopoly**. The term implies (like 'level playing field') that there could be such a thing as 'perfect competition'

independent any company in a media industry which is not seen as a major

indexical (in semiotics) referring to concepts via causal relationships (e.g. heat signified by the reading on a thermometer)

institution complex term, used in Media Studies to refer to the social, cultural and political structures within which media production and consumption are constrained

institutional documentary common genre type, a documentary about school, hospital life etc.

Internet the global 'network of networks' offering a range of services governed by different protocols, such as the World Wide Web, e-mail, **IRC** etc.

intertextuality the variety of ways in which media and other texts interact with each other, rather than being unique or distinct. Greatly used now because of the proliferation of media forms and audience familiary with them.

IRC Internet Relay Chat: software which allows Internet users to join 'conversations' organised in an ad hoc way around particular topics

ISDN Integrated Services Digital Network – a high-speed digital version of the familiar telephone system

ISP Internet Service Provider: a company that provides access to Internet services through a telephone 'dial-up' link

Italian neo-realism national film movement of 1940s and 1950s

ITC Independent Television Commission

jargon derogatory word for specialised terms within a subject area

JICREG Joint Industry Committee of Regional Newspapers – industry body researching readership of the regional press in the UK

JPEG Joint Photographic Experts Group: a standard for compression of data in a computer image file. JPEGs use 'lossy' compression – some quality is lost. Used for photographic images on the Internet

jump cut a very noticeable edit between two images with the same subject and roughly the same framing. Can be avoided by use of **cutaways**

justification in typesetting, alignment of text to right or left or both ('flush'). Text which is not justified right is known as 'ragged'

key light the main light source in a film **set-up**, a bright hard light producing deep shadows

leader (1) another name for the main editorial statement in a newspaper; (2) coloured tape at the beginning of an audio tape reel

leading the space a typesetter creates between lines of text, derived from strips of lead placed on the frame when text was set in trays of metal type

liberalisation the loosening of controls over media markets by governments – a contentious term since this also involves new forms of **regulation**

light touch regulation a loosening of regulatory controls associated with 'free market' policies in the 1980s and 1990s

long shot shot size or framing which shows the full human figure

long take shots lasting twenty seconds or more

mainstream the most highly commercialised areas of media production, ones in which dominant cultural and industrial norms operate

majors the most powerful producers in any media industry, e.g. the Hollywood studios

market the total of all the potential sellers and buyers for a particular product (and the number of products likely to be exchanged)

market penetration   the extent to which a product captures the potential sales in a market – expressed as market share

marketing   the process of presenting a product to its target audience; the ways in which it is positioned in its particular market

media buying   the function of an advertising agency in buying 'space' in a media product in which to place an advertisement

media imperialism (also called **cultural imperialism**)   the argument that rich and powerful countries (or 'military industrial complexes'), especially the US, dominate poorer ones through control of globalised media industries

mediate, mediation   changing the meaning of any 'real' event through the application of media technology

melodrama   often used in very approximate ways to mean 'exaggerated', 'hysterical' or 'extreme', originally a kind of drama which, coming out of censored theatre in the seventeenth century, developed an elaborate language of gesture and used highly polarised scenarios often pitting 'vice' against 'virtue'

merchandising   the exploitation of a film, television etc. character or title through the marketing of a range of 'branded' non-media products, especially children's products. Has a long history, but increased dramatically after the success of *Star Wars* in 1977

metropolitan bias   the argument that too much of the UK media is based in London and takes little interest in affairs outside the capital

mid-market   in classifications of media texts (especially newspapers), the middle position between **tabloid** and **quality**

MiniDisc   format designed by Sony to provide both a smaller CD for consumer playback and a

recording medium for the audio industry. Only the latter use has been taken up widely

mise en scène   literally 'putting together the scene'; literally 'putting into the scene' or staging the events of the script for the camera. Usually refers to visual processes at pre-edit stage, though some critics include sound in this term

mix   in video, a transition between scenes in which one image fades up as another fades down; see **dissolve**

mode of address   the way a text 'speaks' to its audience

model   in social sciences, a way of imagining how a system might work

modernism   innovative, often self-reflexive artistic movements which ran roughly from the 1920s to the 1970s

modernity   (1) an alternative to 'postmodernity' as a way of describing the 'contemporary', emphasizing attempts to rethink Enlightenment values such as belief in progress, rationality etc.; (2) in postmodern theory such 'pre-contemporary' processes as **Fordism**

monopoly   any market situation where one seller controls prices and the supply of product. In the UK a 25 per cent share will attract the interest of regulators

moral panics   a sudden increase in concern about the possible 'effects' of media products, e.g. 'video nasties' in the 1980s; mobile phones more recently

morphing   the process of presenting a change in shape from one object to another as a single, continuous movement. Achieved by computer software, e.g. the shape-changing Terminator in *Terminator 2* (US 1991)

MPAA   Motion Picture Association of America is the trade association formed by the major

Hollywood studios to protect their interests. The Motion Pictures Association (MPA) is the international arm of the organisation which has successfully defended the studios' rights to free trade and exploitation of international markets

MPEG Motion Picture Experts Group: MPEG-2 is a standard for compressing video data for editing and playback

MP3 (MPEG-1 Audio Level 3) the standard format for compressing music files

multimedia referring to several traditionally separate media being used together, e.g. sound, image and text on computers

multiplex (1) multi-screen cinemas which have resuscitated cinema exhibition; (2) in digital broadcasting, the capacity for several different television or radio channels to be broadcast on the same waveband width as a single analogue channel

myths traditional stories through which societies reinforce and explore their beliefs about themselves; in Media Studies, associated with the work of the anthropologist Lévi-Strauss, and then Roland Barthes, who uses it to mean almost the same as **ideology**

narration the process of telling a story, the selection and organisation of the events for a particular audience

narrative complex term referring to a sequence of events organised into a story with a particular structure

narrowcasting term which contrasts itself with 'broadcasting' to draw attention to the assumed fragmentation of audiences addressed by much television now

national identity in terms of representation, the set of ideas constructed around the concept of 'nation' and the ways in which individuals and groups relate to them

negotiated in audience theory, the idea that a meaning is arrived at as a result of a process of give and take between the reader's assumptions and the 'preferred meaning' offered by the text

news agencies organisations which gather news stories and sell them to broadcasters and newspaper publishers

news professionals the media workers who are trained to process news stories according to institutional norms

news values the criteria used by editors, not always consciously, to select and prioritise news stories for publication

niche marketing the idea that there are very small, but highly profitable markets which could support specialist advertising-led media products

nonlinear editing (**NLE**) film and video editing performed wholly on a computer. Video and audio images are digitised and can be sequenced in a script. Several different scripts can be compiled for playback from the computer, before a final version is 'printed' to film or tape. Analogue video and audio editing are 'linear'. Film editing has always been 'nonlinear'

NRS National Readership Survey is the organisation supplying information on UK readership of national newspapers and magazines

objectivity an idealist aim for journalists – to report events without becoming involved in them (i.e. not being 'subjective'); see **bias**

OFCOM Regulator for the UK broadcasting and telecommunications industries proposed in 2000

oligopoly an industry controlled by a small number of producers

oppositional actively opposed to the dominant; in

audience theory describes a reading which rejects the 'preferred meaning' offered by the text

opinion polls quantitative polls, whose results are highly structured by editorial decisions about which results to emphasise, which give a 'snapshot' of how a supposedly representative sample of people feels about an issue (e.g. '60 per cent of UK voters would support a 1 per cent tax on incomes over £100,000 to support public services')

option in Hollywood, a purchased right to develop a property such as a novel for a new film

outline (1) term for an idea forming the basis for negotiating a production commission; (2) a drawing or a font used in desktop publishing based on a mathematical formula describing the shape, also sometimes known as 'vector graphics' (cf. **bitmap**). Outline drawings and fonts maintain the same quality if enlarged

package unit system the basis for Hollywood film production which replaced the studio system in the 1950s. Each film is treated as a 'one-off' and a package of director, stars and crew brought together for a specific production

PageMaker computer software used for desktop publishing. Now more a 'business and education' application. See Quark Xpress for the industry standard

pan and scan technique for showing widescreen films on a standard-shape television set

paradigm/paradigmatic a class of objects or concepts. Defined along with **syntagm**: an element which follows another in a particular sequence. For example in choosing from a menu, the paradigms (starters, main courses, desserts) are elements from which you choose, and the syntagm is the sequence into which they are arranged (soup/fish/ice cream). Sometimes these structures are treated as 'horizontal' (across time) and 'vertical' (along values) aspects of narratives

pdf portable document format, a computer file format that allows a document to be viewed correctly and printed out on any computer using an **Acrobat** Reader

permissions agreements to film on specific locations or by rights holders that images, sounds and text may be used in a media production

perspective a drawing convention which suggests depth in a flat image. Often associated with the Renaissance and the growth of individualism since it suggests a single viewpoint on a scene

photographic truth the belief that photography can produce documentary 'evidence' – now challenged by **digital imaging**

photorealistic referring to the realist effect achieved by photography

Photoshop computer software used for image manipulation

planned obsolescence phrase made famous by US consumer rights and Green campaigner Ralph Nader. In addition to the drive to keep up with fashions, manufacturers of certain products (especially cars) deliberately 'build in' an avoidance of lasting for as long as they could, thus encouraging (unnecessary) repeated acts of purchase

plot defined in relation to '**story**' as the events in a narrative which are presented to an audience directly (see also **fabula** and **syuzhet**)

pluralist used to describe a political position which allows for several competing ideologies to be accepted as valid

point size measure of the size of text characters in typesetting: 72 points is roughly one inch

political economy study of the social relations, particularly power relations, that together constitute the production, distribution and consumption of resources

polysemic   literally 'many-signed', a text in which there are several possible meanings depending on the ways its constituent signs are read. Often now abandoned in favour of the position that audience activity as part of meaning production means that no sign can have, securely, only one meaning

popular   widely used term, literally meaning 'of the people'. Negatively, in contrast to 'high culture', 'art', etc. and as synonymous with 'mass'

post-feminism   position which argues that the condition of women 'after' the successes of the 1960s and 1970s wave of feminist struggles means that they can take for granted respect and equality and enjoy ironic pleasures and playfulness around traditional 'femininity'

post-Fordism   method of commodity production which subcontracts part of the production process to a number of firms and uses new technology to make production more responsive to consumer demand

postmodernism   complex term used with several meanings, usually involving self-reflexive contemporary culture and media or, more widely, a set of attitudes to the contemporary world

Postscript   'page description language' used in print publishing which is 'platform-free' – not dependent on the type of computer used

PCC   Press Complaints Commission

PPV   Pay Per View: method of charging television viewers for a single viewing of a programme, rather than subscribing to a channel for a set period. Used first for sports events and concerts, now also for some film screenings

preferred reading   (from Hall's encoding/ decoding theory of audience readings): the most likely reading of a text by audiences, given the operation of power structures and dominant values both in the institution producing the text and in

audiences. Hall argues it always struggles with other possible meanings

pre-sale   the possibility of selling the distributions rights to a product before production is completed, giving some security to the production

Press Complaints Commission   newspaper industry body set up to monitor the publication of unethical material

price mechanism   the movement of prices in any market that some economists argue operates the 'laws of supply and demand'

primary research   research into the original source of a media story – an interview, personal letters or government records

prime time   that part of a radio or television schedule expected to attract the biggest audience, i.e. 19.30 to 22.30 p.m.

principal photography   the production phase on a film shoot

privatisation   process by which services or utilities in the **public sector** are transferred to private ownership

producer choice   BBC policy encouraging producers to consider less expensive non-BBC facilities

product placement   an unofficial form of advertising in which branded products feature prominently in films, etc.

production cycle   in the Hollywood studio system, the constant film production process involving strict division of labour

proofing   process of checking the text in the final version of a media product before publication for errors in placement, spelling etc.; test printing a colour image on paper (because colours on a computer screen are not reliable guides)

propaganda any media text which seeks openly to persuade an audience of the validity of particular beliefs or actions

property any original story the rights to which have been acquired by a production company

proposal idea for a new media product submitted speculatively by a freelance to a major producer, including an outline and an argument that a market exists

protocol software controlling the interface between computers in a network. Protocols cover every aspect of using the Internet

public domain describes any media product for which copyright has expired, or has never been claimed, implying that no payment to a rights holder is required. This applies only to the work itself and not to a particular publication of it – i.e. the text of a Dickens novel, but not the Penguin printed version

public relations professional services promoting products by arranging opportunities for exposure in the media

public sector the part of the economy comprising organisations funded by central or local government. A public limited company (*plc*), however, is in the private sector, being owned by shareholders (it is listed on the stock exchange with shares available for sale to the public)

public service broadcasting (PSB) regulated broadcasting which has providing a public service as a primary aim

qualitative research audience research based on discussion groups or one-to-one interviews with interaction between researcher and subject

quality document an audit document showing how an organisation maintains the integrity of its administration systems

quality (film and television) subjective term used by critics and commentators to describe certain types of films and television programmes. Although there are no strict guidelines, the concept has been used in the licensing of UK television channnels in the form of the 'quality threshold' – a commitment to broadcast a specified amount of 'quality programmes'. Could refer to high production values, popular appeal or unusual programmes

quality press the 'serious' newspapers – in the UK synonymous with **broadsheet** (but not in the rest of Europe)

quantitative analysis also called *content analysis*, based on counting the frequency of certain elements in a clearly defined sample, and then analysing those frequencies. The selected quantities must be 'coded', i.e. a set of descriptive categories or labels are attached to them (e.g. 'headlines involving the word 'asylum seeker'). These should be unambiguous such that different researchers at different times using the same categories would code the images in exactly the same way. What matters is the quality of the questions asked.

quantitative research audience research based on anonymous data with **samples** constructed to represent larger populations of viewers, listeners and readers in order to estimate the size of the audience

Quark Xpress industry standard computer software used in page layout

quota a designated amount of production, minimum or maximum, which is specified for purposes of regulation or to protect specific producers from competition e.g. attempts to limit Hollywood's share of film markets by insisting that cinemas show 'home' nation product

racism the stigmatising of difference along the lines of 'racial' characteristics in order to justify advantage or abuse of power, whether economic, political, cultural or psychological

RAJAR Radio Joint Audience Research, the industry body which collects and publishes data on radio audiences in the UK

ratings viewing and listening figures presented as a league table of successful programmes, depending on audience size

reader panels groups of readers who can be questioned about their responses to a media product

reader research research into who 'reads' a media product

real time time taken for an event in an audio-visual text which exactly matches the time taken for the same event in the real world

realism a fiercely contested term which emphasises taking seriously the relationship between media texts and the rest of the 'real world'

realism effect the real-seemingness image, achieved through artifice

realist aesthetic an approach to presenting an image which seeks to achieve realism

'reality' TV form of factual television on British television from about 1989. The term was first applied to magazine format programmes based on crime, accident and health stories or 'trauma television' (*Crimewatch UK*; *Lifesavers* etc.). Now used of television which blends apparently 'raw' authentic material with news magazine format and, even more loosely, of any unscripted programme

ream standard measure of paper – 500 sheets

recce 'reconnaissance' – part of pre-production, checking out venues for performances or locations for recording

recto the right-hand page in a print publication

referent in semiotics, the 'real world' object to which the sign or signifier refers

regional press newspapers (morning or evening dailies and/or Sundays) published outside London with a distinct regional circulation. 'Local' papers (daily or weekly) are included in the industry definition of the regional press.

regional production obligation by the BBC to spread production around the regions and nations of the UK

regulation the process of monitoring the activities of industries. Some media industries regulate themselves and others are regulated by bodies set up by legislation

release patterns the geographical patterns of the release of media texts, especially feature films

repertoire (music) see A&R

repertoire of elements the fluid system of conventions and expectations associated with genre texts

repetition and difference the mix of familiar and new characteristics which offer pleasures and attract audiences to generic media texts

replicability unambiguity of research findings such that different researchers at different times would interpret the evidence in exactly the same way (see **quantitative analysis**)

right of reply the idea that persons who feel that they have been misrepresented should have the right to challenge media producers on air or in a newspaper

romance fiction genre in which intimate personal relationships related to love and marriage are the central focus

samples (1) in digital audio production, sounds or sequence of sounds 'captured' by a computer for use in future productions; (2) carefully selected groups of people chosen in audience research to represent larger populations

sans-serif any typeface or font 'without a **serif**'

schedule as in 'production schedule', the careful planning of the production process

scheduling strategies adopted to place programmes in radio and television schedules to most effect

script (1) dialogue and production directions for a radio, film or television production; (2) arrangement of sounds, images and effects placed in sequence on a computer for presentation; (3) a typeface designed to resemble handwriting

search engine computer software used to find a specific word or phrase in a database or across a network such as the Internet

secondary research research using reference books or previously annotated or published sources (cf. **primary research**)

segment (verb) to divide up a target audience into even more specialised groups which can be addressed by advertisers

self-reflexive applied to texts which display an awareness or a comment on their own artificial status as texts

self-regulation cinema and the press are regulated by bodies set up by the industries themselves

semiotics/semiology the study of sign systems

serif the bar across the ends of the main strokes of a text character in a typeface

service provider see **ISP**

set-top box computer which sits on top of a television set and controls the variety of possible incoming signals

set-ups term for the separate camera, lighting and sound positions necessary for shooting a feature film

shot the smallest element in any film sequence, a single 'take' during shooting which may be further shortened during editing

shot/reverse shot term for the conventional way of shooting an exchange between two characters in a film or television programme

sign/signified/signifier the sign, in semiotics, is divided into the signifier or physical form taken by the sign, and the signified, which is the concept it stands in for

slate film industry term for the list of major features to be produced during a production period

soap, soap opera the radio and television multi-strand continuous serial narrative form originally designed as a vehicle for sponsorship by soap powder manufacturers

social psychology the study of human behaviour

Socialist Realism the prescribed realist form forced on Soviet film-makers by the Stalin regime in the 1930s – featuring romanticised heroic workers

software the programs written for computers, or the films, music etc. which could be played on them

sound effect frequently used to refer to artificially created 'sounds' produced for audiovisual texts; also can be extended to refer to all aural material in a production apart from dialogue and music

sound image term used to emphasise the possibility of analysing or reading sounds in the same way as 'pictures'

sound stages term describing the individual buildings available for shooting in a film studio – the name implies that they can be used for recording sound

spaghetti westerns a cycle of films made in Italy and Spain in the 1960s and 1970s, drawing on the Hollywood western for inspiration

spin activities of press or PR officers (also called 'spin doctors') employed to put a positive 'spin' or angle on stories about their employer or client. The term suggests an unjustifiable degree of intervention in the construction of news

standardisation has a double meaning: it can signify 'sameness'; but can also denote the maintenance of standards, in the sense of quality

star actor whose image, via accumulated publicity, debate etc., is strong enough to be valued as an added component of any performance, and which acts as a specific attraction for audiences

star image the constructed image of the star, usually in relation to film and associated 'secondary circulation'

statutory regulation regulatory powers established by law (e.g. the Broadcasting Acts of 1990 and 1996)

Steadicam trade name for a stabilising device allowing a camera operator to move freely without jerking the image

stereotypes, stereotyping originally a term from printing, literally a 'solid' block of metal type; then, a representation of a type of person, without fine detail

story all of the events in a narrative, those presented directly to an audience and those which might be inferred – compare with **plot**

structuralism an approach to critical analysis which emphasises universal structures underlying the surface differences and apparent randomness of cultures, stories, media texts etc.

structuring oppositions see **binary oppositions**

studio system Hollywood production system from about 1930 to 1950, in which 'vertically integrated' film companies produced, distributed and exhibited a constant stream of new films.

sub-editing process late in the production of a newspaper in which stories are shortened or rewritten to fit the space available and headlines and picture captions are written

subliminal advertising kind of advertising associated with hypnosis and said to work by flashing barely perceptible messages to audiences in between frames of a film or television advertisements

superstructure ideological structures built on an 'economic base' according to Marxist theory

symbolic used in semiotics of a sign (usually visual) which has come to stand for a particular set of qualities or values, e.g. the 'Stars and Stripes' for the USA; see **arbitrary**, **iconic** and **indexical**

synergy the combined marketing of 'products' across different media and other products (in music, toys, Internet and television programmes, T-shirts, theme park rides and so on) which are often owned by the same corporation, such that the total effect is greater than the sum of the different parts

syntagmatic see **paradigm**, with which it is often used in combination

syuzhet term in specialist narrative theory – Russian for 'plot'

tabloid The size of a newsprint page, half that of the 'broadsheet'; by extension: sensationalist media form (television and radio as well as the press)

talent anyone appearing in front of the camera or microphone, the performers

target audiences the specific audiences to be addressed by a particular media text

Technicolor colour film process developed for cinema in the 1930s

technophobia fear of machines or technology, especially in science fiction narratives

telephoto long camera lens which enables distant objects to be shown in close-up – has the effect of 'flattening' the image

tentpole movie a major film which a studio hopes will provide the support for its annual slate and almost guarantee box-office returns

territories geographical areas for which the rights to a media product are negotiated

text any system of signs which can be 'read' – a poster, photograph, haircut etc.

tie-ins corporate products which accompany and help publicise a major film or television release, e.g. cereal pack toys of animation characters

transparency the way in which media texts present themselves as 'natural'; their construction is invisible to casual readers

treatment document in the pre-production process for television and video which describes how the ideas in the outline will be developed into a programme, referring to genre, style etc.

turn-around film industry term for a script dropped by one studio and waiting for another to pick it up

typeface a complete set of text and numeric characters plus symbols and punctuation marks with common design features. A typeface may be available in different weights (bold, light etc.) or styles (italic, condensed etc.)

typesetting now completely computerised, the process of arranging text in precise positions on the page

unit production system, unit-based production way of organising production under the Hollywood studio system

universal service (in relation to public service broadcasting) a service available to everyone at the same price

upload to transfer data to a website on a remote computer (or to a satellite for broadcasting)

uses and gratifications model 'active' model of audience behaviour, emphasising the uses to which audiences put even the most unlikely texts

utopian associated with an ideal, if not impossible, social world

vector graphics see **outline** (2)

verisimilitude quality of seeming like what is taken to be the real world of a particular text; see entries around **realism**

verso left-hand page in a print publication

vertical integration business activity involving one company acquiring others elsewhere in the production process

violence debate recurring debates over assumed audience behaviour, focusing on the possible 'effects' of representations of violence

virtual something which is a representation rather than the 'real' thing, thus 'virtual reality'

voice over voice used in soundtrack as encouragement to viewers to interpret the visual images in particular ways; a kind of '**anchoring**' in semiotic terms

voyeurism the pleasure of looking while unseen; used in thinking about male pleasure in the ways cinema, especially, constructs women as 'objects of the [male] gaze'

white balance the process of correcting the sensitivity of a video camera to match a specific lighting source (see **colour temperature**)

white space the blank spaces on a printed page – considered to be an important component in the overall design and 'look' of the page

wide angle camera lens which is used with the subject close to the camera, but with the whole scene shown – can lead to distortion of objects very close to the camera

wipe   transition in video editing in which one image replaces another according to a specific pattern such as the appearance of a page being turned

word of mouth   informal way in which media products become known about by audiences

World Wide Web   the network of 'pages' of images, texts and sounds on the Internet which can be viewed using browser software

wrap   industry jargon for the completion of a film shoot

zapping   rapidly cutting between television channels using a remote control device

zoom   an arrangement of camera lenses, allowing the operator to change the focal length and move between **telephoto** and **wide angle** settings

Bibliography

For detailed lists of sources and ideas for further reading on specific topics, see individual chapters. The titles below provide general introductions to the major debates in the book. You can use them as starting points for background reading and consult their bibliographies for further ideas.

Abercrombie, Nicholas (1996) *Television and Society*, Cambridge: Polity.

Alasuutari, Pertti (1999) *Rethinking the Media Audience: The New Agenda*, London: Sage.

Allan, Stuart (2000) *News Culture*, Buckingham: Open University Press.

Allen, Robert C. (ed.) (1995) *Channels of Discourse, Reassembled*, London and New York: Routledge.

Andermahr, Sonya, Lovell, Terry and Wolkowitz, Carol (1997) *A Concise Glossary of Feminist Theory*, London and New York: Arnold.

Ang, Ien (1996) *Living Room Wars: Rethinking Media Audiences for a Postmodern World*, London and New York: Routledge.

Appadurai, Arjun (1996) *Modernity at Large: Cultural Dimensions of Globalization*, Minneapolis: University of Minnesota Press.

Baehr, Helen and Dyer, Gillian (eds) (1987) *Boxed In: Women and Television*, London: Pandora.

Balnaves, Mark, Donald, James and Hemelryk Donald, Stephanie (2001) *The Global Media Atlas*, London: British Film Institute.

Barker, Chris (1997) *Global Television: An Introduction*, Oxford: Blackwell.

Barker, Martin and Beezer, Anne (eds) (1992) *Reading Into Cultural Studies*, London and New York: Routledge.

Barker, Martin and Brooks, Kate (1998) *Knowing Audiences 'Judge Dredd': Its Friends, Fans and Foes*, Luton: University of Luton Press.

Barker, Martin and Petley, Julian (eds) (2001, 2nd edition) *Ill Effects: The Media/Violence Debate*, London and New York: Routledge.

Barker, Martin with Austin, Thomas (2000) *From Antz to Titanic: Reinventing Film Analysis* London: Pluto Press.

Barthes, Roland (1972; first published 1957) *Mythologies*, London: Paladin.

Baudrillard, Jean (1988) *Baudrillard: Selected Writings*, ed. Poster, Mark, Cambridge: Polity.

Berman, Edward S. and McChesney, Robert W. (1997) *The Global Media: The New Missionaries of Corporate Capitalism*, London and Washington, DC: Cassell.

Bignell, Jonathan (1997) *Media Semiotics: An Introduction*, Manchester: Manchester University Press.

Billig, Michael (1995) *Banal Nationalism*, London: Sage.

Blandford, Steve, Grant, Barry Keith and Hillier, Jim (2001) *The Film Studies Dictionary*, London: Arnold.

Bogle, Donald (1994, 2nd edition) *Toms, Coons, Mulattoes, Mammies and Bucks: An Interpretative History of Blacks in American Films*, New York: Continuum.

Bordo, Susan (1993) *Unbearable Weight: Feminism, Western Culture, and the Body*, Berkeley: University of California Press.

Bordwell, David and Carroll, Noel (eds) (1996) *Post-theory: Reconstructing Film Studies*, Madison and London: University of Wisconsin Press.

Bordwell, David and Thompson Kirstin (2001, 6th edition), *Film Art : An Introduction*, Maidenhead and New York: McGraw Hill, plus excellent related Online Learning Center http://www.mhhe.com/socscience/art-film/bordwell_6_filmart/

Bourdieu, Pierre (1980) 'The aristocracy of culture', reprinted in R. Collins, J. Curran, N. Garnham, P. Scannell, P. Schlesinger and C. Sparks (eds) *Media, Culture & Society: A Critical Reader*, London and Beverly Hills: Sage.

Bourdieu, Pierre (1984) *Distinction: A Social Critique of the Judgement of Taste*, London: Routledge and Kegan Paul.

Branston, Gill (2001) *Cinema and Cultural Modernity*, Buckingham: Open University Press.

Brierley, Sean (1995) *The Advertising Handbook*, London and New York: Routledge.

Briggs, Adam and Cobley, Paul (eds) (1998) *The Media: An Introduction*, Harlow: Longman.

Bromley, Michael and O'Malley, Tom (eds) (1997) *A Journalism Reader*, London: Routledge.

Brooker, Peter and Brooker, Will (eds) (1997) *Postmodern After-images*, London and New York: Arnold.

Brunsdon, Charlotte (1997) *Screen Tastes: Soap Opera to Satellite Dishes*, London and New York: Routledge.

Brunsdon, Charlotte, D'Acci, Julie and Spigel, Lynne (eds) *Feminist Television Criticism: A Reader*, Oxford: Oxford University Press.

Bruzzi, Stella (2000) *New Documentary: A Critical Introduction*, London: Routledge.

Buscombe, Ed (ed.) (1988) *The BFI Companion to the Western*, London: André Deutsch/BFI.

Carter, Cynthia, Branston, Gill and Allan, Stuart (eds) (1998) *News, Gender and Power*, London: Routledge.

Casey, Bernadette, Casey, Neil, Calvert, Ben, French, Liam and Lewis, Justin (2002) *Television Studies: The Key Concepts*, London: Routledge.

Chomsky, Noam (2001) *9–11*, New York: Seven Stories.

Coakley, J. (1998, 6th edition) *Sport in Society: Issues and Controversies*, New York: McGraw Hill.

Cohen, Stan (1972) *Folk Devils and Moral Panics*, Oxford: Martin Robertson.

Connell, Robert W. (2000) *The Men and the Boys*, Cambridge: Polity.

Connor, Steven (1989 rev. 1997) *Postmodernist Culture*, Oxford: Basil Blackwell.

Cook, Pam and Bernink, Mieke (1999, 2nd edition) *The Cinema Book*, London: BFI.

Corner, John (1996) *The Art of Record: A Critical Introduction to Documentary*, Manchester: Manchester University Press.

Corner, John (1998) *Studying Media: Problems of Theory and Method*, Edinburgh: Edinburgh University Press.

Creeber, Glen (ed.) (2001) *The Television Genre Book*, London: BFI.

Crisell, Andrew (1994, 2nd edition) *Understanding Radio*, London: Routledge.

Crisell, Andrew (1997) *An Introductory History of British Broadcasting*, London: Routledge.

Croteau, David and Hoynes, William (2001) *The Business of Media: Corporate Media and the Public Interest*, London: Sage.

Curran, James and Gurevitch, Michael (eds) (1991) *Mass Media and Society*, London: Arnold.

Curran, James, Morley, David and Walkerdine, Valerie (eds) (1995) *Cultural Studies and Communications*, London: Arnold.

Curran, James and Park, Myung-Jin (eds) (2000) *De-westernizing Media Studies*, London: Routledge.

Curran, James and Seaton, Jean (1997) *Power Without Responsibility: The Press and Broadcasting in Britain*, London: Routledge.

Dunant, Sarah (ed.) (1994) *The War of the Words: The Political Correctness Debate*, London: Virago.

Durkin, Kevin (1985) *Television, Sex Roles and Children*, Milton Keynes: Open University Press.

Dyer, Gillian (1983) *Advertising as Communication*, London: Methuen.

Dyer, Richard (1973) *Only Entertainment* (1992 revised edition), London: Routledge.

Dyer, Richard (1987) *Heavenly Bodies*, London: Macmillan/BFI.

Dyer, Richard (1997) *White: Essays on Race and Culture*, London: Routledge.

Dyer, Richard (1998, 2nd edition) *Stars*, London: BFI.

Eagleton, Terry (1983) *Literary Theory: An Introduction*, Oxford: Blackwell.

Eldridge, John (ed.) (1995) *The Glasgow University Media Reader*, vol. 1, London: Routledge.

Ellis, John (1992, 2nd edition) *Visible Fictions*, London: Routledge.

Ellis, John (2000) *Seeing Things: Television in the Age of Uncertainty*, London: I. B. Taurus.

Evans, Harold (1978) *Pictures on a Page: Photojournalism, Graphics and Picture Editing*, London: Heinemann.

Ferguson, Marjorie and Golding, Peter (eds) (1997) *Cultural Studies in Question*, London: Sage.

Foucault, Michel (1988) *Politics, Philosophy, Culture: Interviews and other Writings 1977–1984*, London: Routledge.

Franklin, Bob and Murphy, David (1998) *Making the Local News: Local Journalism in Context*, London: Routledge.

Frith, Simon and Goodwin, Andrew (eds) (1990) *On Record*, London: Routledge.

Gamman, Lorraine and Marshment, Margaret (eds) (1998) *The Female Gaze: Women as Viewers of Popular Culture*, London: Women's Press.

Gauntlett, D. (2000) *Web Studies: Rewriting Media Studies for the Digital Age*, London: Arnold and Oxford University Press.

Geraghty, Christine (1991) *Women and Soap Opera: A Study of Prime Time Soaps*, London: Polity.

Geraghty, Christine and Lusted, David (1998) *The Television Studies Book*, London and New York: Arnold.

Glasgow University Media Group (1976) *Bad News*, London: Routledge & Kegan Paul.

Glasgow University Media Group (1993) *Getting the Message: News, Truth and Power*, London: Routledge.

Gledhill, Christine (ed.) (1987) *Home Is Where the Heart Is*, London: BFI.

Gledhill, Christine (1991) *Stardom: Industry of Desire*, London: Routledge.

Gledhill, Christine (1997) 'Genre and gender: the case of soap opera', in Stuart Hall (ed.) *Representation: Cultural Representations and Signifying Practices*, London, Thousand Oaks, New Delhi: Sage.

Gledhill, Christine and Williams, Linda (eds) (2000) *Reinventing Film Studies*, London and New York: Arnold.

Glynn, C., Herbst, S., O'Keefe, and Shapiro, R. (1999) *Public Opinion*, Boulder: Westview Press.

Goffman, Erving (1976) *Gender Advertisements*, London: Macmillan.

Golding, Peter and Elliott, Philip (1979) *Making the News*, London: Longman.

Gomery, Douglas (1992) *Shared Pleasures*, London: BFI.

Goodwin, Andrew and Whannel, Gary (eds) (1990) *Understanding Television*, London: Routledge.

Gramsci, Antonio (1994) *Selected Writings from the Prison Notebooks*, London: Lawrence and Wishart

Gray, Ann (forthcoming) *Lived Cultures: Ethnographic Methods in Cultural Studies*, London: Sage.

Gripsrud, Jostein (ed.) (2002) *Understanding Media Culture*, London: Arnold.

Hall, Stuart (1974) 'The television discourse – encoding and decoding', *Education and Culture*, No. 25 (UNESCO), reprinted in Ann Gray and Jim McGyigan (eds) (1997) *Studying Culture*, London: Arnold.

Hall, Stuart (1991) 'The local and the global: globalisation and ethnicity', in A. King (ed.) *Culture, Globalisation and the World System*, London: Macmillan.

Hall, Stuart (1996) *Race, the Floating Signifier*, videotape available from the Media Education Foundation.

Hall, Stuart (ed.) (1997) *Representation: Cultural Representations and Signifying Practices*, London: Thousand Oaks and New Delhi: Sage.

Hawthorn, Jeremy (1998) *A Glossary of Contemporary Literary Theory*, London and New York: Arnold.

Hebdige, Dick (1988) *Hiding in the Light*, London: Comedia/Routledge.

Herman, Ed and McChesney, Robert (1997) *The Global Media: The New Visionaries of Corporate Capitalism*, London: Cassell.

Hesmondhalgh, David (2002) *The Cultural Industries*, London: Sage.

Hill, John and Church Gibson, Pamela (eds) (1998) *The Oxford Guide to Film Studies*, Oxford and New York: Oxford University Press.

Hillier, Jim (ed.) (2001) *American Independent Cinema: A Sight and Sound Reader*, London: British Film Institute.

Hills, Matt (2002) *Fan Cultures*, London and New York: Routledge.

Holland, Patricia (2000, 2nd edition) *The Television Handbook*, London and New York: Routledge.

Hood, Stuart and Tabary-Peterssen, Thalia (1997, 4th edition) *On Television*, London: Pluto.

Jameson, Fredric (1991) *Postmodernism, or, The Cultural Logic of Late Capitalism*, Durham: Duke University Press.

Jancovich, M. (1996) *Rational Fears: American Horror in the 1950s*, Manchester and New York: Manchester University Press.

Keeble, Richard (1998, 2nd edition) *The Newspapers Handbook*, London: Routledge.

Klein, Naomi (2001 edn) *No Logo*, London: Flamingo.

Kramer, Peter (2002) *The Big Picture: Hollywood Cinema from Star Wars to Titanic*, London: British Film Institute.

Lacey, Nick (1998) *Image and Representation*, Basingstoke: Palgrave.

Lacey, Nick (2000) *Narrative and Genre*, Basingstoke: Palgrave.

Lacey, Nick and Stafford, Roy (2000) *Film as Product in Contemporary Hollywood*, London: British Film Institute and Keighley: ITP Publications.

Langham, Josephine (1996, 2nd edition) *Lights, Camera, Action!: Careers in Film, Television and Radio*, London: BFI.

Lewis, Justin (2001) *Constructing Public Opinion: How Political Elites Do What They Like and Why We Seem to Go Along with It*, New York: Columbia University Press.

Lister, Martin (ed.) (1995) *The Photographic Image in Digital Culture*, London: Routledge.

Lovell, Alan and Kramer, Peter (1999) *Screen Acting*, London: Routledge.

Lull, James (1995) *Media, Communication, Culture: A Global Approach*, Cambridge: Polity.

Macdonald, Myra (1995) *Representing Women: Myths of Femininity in the Popular Media*, London and New York: Arnold.

McGuigan, Jim (1992) *Cultural Populism*, London: Routledge.

McGuigan, Jim (1999) *Modernity and Postmodern Culture*, London: Open University Press.

McKay, Jenny (2000) *The Magazines Handbook*, London: Routledge.

Malik, Sarita (2001) *Representing Black Britain: Black and Asian Images on Television*, London: Sage.

Maltby, Richard and Craven, Ian (1995) *Hollywood Cinema*, Oxford: Blackwell.

Marcuse, Herbert (1964) *One Dimensional Man*, London: Routledge & Kegan Paul.

Marx, Karl and Engels, Frederick (1965: first published 1888) *The German Ideology*, London: Lawrence and Wishart.

Masterman, Len (1984) *Television Mythologies: Stars, Shows and Signs*, London: Comedia.

Medhurst, Andy and Lunt, Sally R. (eds) (1997) *Lesbian and Gay Studies: A Critical Introduction*, London: Cassell.

Miller, Daniel (1998) (ed.) *Material Cultures: Why Some Things Matter*, London: UCL Press.

Miller, Daniel, and Slater, Don (2001) *The Internet: An Ethnographic Approach*, Oxford: Berg.

Miller, Toby, Govil, Nitin, McMurria, John and Maxwell, Richard (2001) *Global Hollywood*, London: British Film Institute.

Miller, Toby (ed.) (2002) *Television Studies*, London: British Film Institute.

Moores, Sean (1993) *Interpreting Audiences: The Ethnography of Media Consumption*, London: Sage.

Morley, David (1980) *The Nationwide Audience*, London: BFI.

Morley, David (1986) *Family Television: Cultural Power and Domestic Leisure*, London: Comedia.

Morley, David (1996) 'Postmodernism: the rough guide', in James Curran, David Morley and Valerie Walkerdine, *Cultural Studies and Communications*, London and New York: Arnold.

Morley, David and Brunsdon, Charlotte (1998) *The Nationwide Television Studies*, London: Routledge.

Morley, David and Chen, Kuan-Hsing (eds) (1996) *Stuart Hall: Critical Dialogues in Cultural Studies*, London: Routledge.

Myers, Greg (1999) *Ad Worlds Brands, Media, Audiences*, London and New York: Edward Arnold.

Neale, Steve (1990) 'Questions of genre', *Screen*, vol. 31, no. 1.

Neale, Steve and Smith, Murray (eds) (1998) *Contemporary Hollywood Cinema*, London: Routledge.

Nelmes, Jill (ed.) (1999, 2nd edition) *An Introduction to Film Studies*, London: Routledge.

Noelle-Neumann, Elizabeth (1993) *The Spiral of Silence*, Chicago: University of Chicago Press.

Nowell-Smith, Geoffrey and Ricci, Steven (eds) (1998) *Hollywood and Europe: Economics, Culture, National Identity 1945–1995*, London: BFI.

O'Sullivan, Tim, Dutton, Brian and Rayner, Philip (1998, 2nd edition) *Studying the Media: An Introduction*, London, New York, Melbourne and Auckland: Arnold.

O'Sullivan, Tim, Hartley, John, Saunders, Danny, Montgomery, Martin and Fiske, John (1994, 2nd edition) *Key Concepts in Cultural and Communication Studies*, London: Routledge.

O'Sullivan, Tim and Jewkes, Yvonne (eds) (1997) *The Media Studies Reader*, London and New York: Arnold.

Packard, Vance (1979) *The Hidden Persuaders*, London: Penguin.

Perkins, Victor (1993) *Film as Film*, London: Da Capo.

Philo, Greg (1990) *Seeing and Believing: The Influence of Television*, London and New York: Routledge.

Philo, Greg (ed.) (1995) *The Glasgow Media Group Reader*, vol. 2, London and New York: Routledge.

Pines, Jim (ed.) (1992) *Black and White in Colour: Black People in British Television since 1936*, London: BFI.

Pirie, David (ed.) (1981) *Anatomy of the Movies*, London: Windward.

Rose, Gillian (2001) *Visual Methodologies*, London: Sage.

Rosenbaum, Jonathan (2000) *Movie Wars: How Hollywood and the Media Conspire to Limit What Films We Can See*, Chicago: A Cappella Press.

Sartelle, Joseph (1996) 'Dreams and nightmares in the Hollywood Blockbuster', in Geoffrey Nowell-Smith (ed.) *The Oxford History of World Cinema*, Oxford: Oxford University Press.

Sarup, Madan (1993, 2nd edition) *An Introductory Guide to Post-structuralism and Postmodernism*, Hemel Hempstead: Harvester.

Scannell, Paddy (1996) *Radio, Television and Modern Life*, Oxford: Blackwell.

Schatz, Thomas (1989 and 1998) *The Genius of the System: Hollywood Filmmaking in the Studio Era*, London: Faber & Faber.

Schiller, Herbert I. (1991) *Not Yet the Post-Imperialist Era*, in Tim O'Sullivan and Yvonne Jewkes (eds) 1997 *The Media Studies Reader*, London and New York: Arnold.

Schiller, Herbert I. (1996) *Information Inequality*, London and New York: Routledge.

Schlesinger, Philip (1987) *Putting 'Reality' Together*, London: Methuen.

Schlesinger, Philip *et al.* (1992) *Women Viewing Violence*, London: BFI.

Shohat, Ella and Stam, Robert (1994) *Unthinking Eurocentrism: Multiculturalism and the Media*, London and New York: Routledge.

Silverstone, Roger (1999) *Why Study the Media?*, London: Sage.

Slater, Don (1997) *Consumer Culture and Modernity*, Cambridge: Polity.

Spence, Jo (1986) *Putting Myself in the Picture*, London: Camden Press.

Sreberny-Mohammadi, Annabel, Winseck, Dwayne, McKenna, Jill and Boyd-Barrett, Oliver (eds) (1997) *Media in Global Context*, London and New York: Arnold.

Stacey, Jackie (1993) *Star Gazing: Hollywood Cinema and Female Spectatorship*, London: Routledge.

Stafford, Roy (2001) *Representation: An Introduction*, London: British Film Instute and Keighley: ITP Publications.

Staiger, Janet (1992) *Interpreting Films: Studies in the Historical Reception of American Cinema*, Princeton: Princeton University Press.

Stam, Robert and Miller, Toby (eds) (2000) *Film and Theory: An Anthology*, Oxford: Blackwell.

Stokes, Melvyn and Maltby, Richard (eds) *Identifying Hollywood's Audiences: Cultural Identity and the Movies*, London: BFI.

Strinati, Dominic (1995) *An Introduction to Theories of Popular Culture*, London: Routledge.

Thompson, John B. (1997) *The Media and Modernity: A Social Theory of the Media*, Cambridge: Polity.

Thompson, John B. (2000) *Political Scandal: Power and Visibility in the Media Age*, Cambridge: Polity.

Thompson, Kenneth (1998) *Moral Panics*, London and New York: Routledge.

Thornham, Sue (2000) *Feminist Theory and Cultural Studies*, London: Arnold.

Tolson, Andrew (1996) *Mediations: Text and Discourse in Media Studies*, London and New York: Arnold.

Todorov, Tzvetan (1977) *The Poetics of Prose*, Oxford, Blackwell.

Turner, Graeme (1999 edition) *Film as Social Practice*, London: Routledge.

Van Zoonen, Lisbet (1994) *Feminist Media Studies*, London: Sage.

Wasko, Janet (1994) *Hollywood in the Information Age: Beyond the Silver Screen*, Cambridge: Polity.

Wasko, Janet (2001) *Understanding Disney: The Manufacture of Fantasy*, Cambridge: Polity.

Wasko, Janet, Phillips, Mark and Meehan, Eileen R. (eds) (2001) *Dazzled by Disney? The Global Disney Audiences Project*, London: Leicester University Press.

Wells, Liz (ed.) (2000, 2nd edition) *Photography: A Critical Introduction*, London and New York: Routledge.

Wilby, Peter and Conroy, Andy (1994) *The Radio Handbook*, London: Routledge.

Williams, Kevin (1998) *Get Me a Murder a Day!*, London: Arnold.

Williams, Raymond (1958) 'Culture is ordinary' in *Resources of Hope: Culture, Democracy, Socialism*, London and New York: Verso, 1988.

Williams, Raymond (1976) *Keywords: A Vocabulary of Culture and Society*, London: Fontana/Croom Helm.

Williams, Raymond (1979) *Politics and Letters: Interviews with New Left Review*, London: Verso.

Williams, Raymond (1974, 2nd edition 1990) *Television: Technology and Cultural Form*, London: Fontana.

Williamson, Judith (1978) *Decoding Advertisements: Ideology and Meaning in Advertising*, London: Marion Boyars.

Winston, Brian (2000) *Lies, Damn Lies, and Documentary*, London: British Film Institute.

Wyatt, Justin (1994) *High Concept: Movies and Marketing in Hollywood*, Austin: University of Texas Press.

Wyatt, Justin (2002) *Marketing, The Film Reader*, London: Routledge.

Zelizer, Barbie and Allan, Stuart (eds) *Journalism after September 11*, London and New York: Routledge.

For specific technical manuals, please see the catalogues published by Focal Press, Linacre House, Jordan Hill, Oxford OX2 8DP; and by BBC Training, BBC Elstree Centre, Clarendon Road, Borehamwood, Herts WD6 1JF.

Useful information

Magazines

The following magazines are very useful sources of specialist material on the industries concerned. The North American magazines are all available in the UK, although outside major city centres they would need to be ordered. Trade magazines are expensive, but access to only one or two copies can give you a valuable insight into industry concerns, unavailable elsewhere.

Billboard, American music and related entertainment industry trade paper.

Broadcast, the trade magazine for the UK broadcasting industry.

Campaign, the trade magazine for the UK advertising industry.

Free Press, magazine of the Campaign for Press and Broadcasting Freedom (CPBF), available from 8 Cynthia Street, London N1 9JF.

Hollywood Reporter, American film industry paper.

The Journalist, magazine of the National Union of Journalists.

Marketing Week, the trade magazine for the UK marketing industry.

Media Week, the trade magazine for UK media buyers.

Music Week, trade paper of the UK music industry.

Screen, academic journal for film and television studies in higher education.

Screen Digest, monthly international television industry news magazine.

Screen Finance, fortnightly news and financial analysis of UK and European film and television.

Screen International, the trade magazine for film production, distribution and exhibition (includes video and television films).

Sight and Sound, monthly magazine from the British Film Institute, giving details of film and video releases plus critical writing and features.

Stage, Screen and Radio, journal of the media union BECTU.

UK Press Gazette, trade paper of the UK Press.

Variety, the American trade paper for the entertainment industry generally.

Yearbooks

BFI Film and Television Handbook.
Guardian Media Guide.
The Writers' and Artists' Year Book, London: A. C. Black.
Writers Handbook, London: Macmillan.

Doing your own research

To assist in your own research for essays, projects and seminars, we have listed organisations which offer useful advice and information for media students. We have included e-mail and website addresses where these are available but do check these since they may change after publication.

Useful addresses

The following organisations all offer advice and information which may be useful for media students.

Advertising Standards Authority (ASA)
2 Torrington Place
London WC1E 7HW ☎ 0207 580 5555
e-mail: inquiries@asa.org.uk

Arts Council of England
14 Great Peter Street
London SW1P 3NQ ☎ 0207 333 0100
e-mail: enquiries@artscouncil.org.uk
(Contact the Arts Council for details of your own Regional Arts Board.)
website: www.artscouncil.org.uk

Arts Council of Northern Ireland
MacNeice House
77 Malone Road
Belfast BT9 6AQ ☎ 02890 385200
website: www.artscouncil-ni.org

Arts Council of Wales
9 Museum Place
Cardiff CF1 3NX ☎ 02920 376500
website: www.ccc-acw.org.uk

BBC
Television Centre
Wood Lane
London W12 7RJ ☎ 020 743 8000
website: www.bbc.co.uk

Broadcasting House
Portland Place, Oxford Circus
London W1A 1AA ☎ 020 7580 4468

British Board of Film Classification (BBFC)
3 Soho Square
London W1V 6HD ☎ 020 7439 7961
website: www.bbfc.co.uk

British Film Institute (BFI)
21 Stephen Street
London W1P 2LN ☎ 020 7255 1444
website: www.bfi.org.uk

Broadcasting, Entertainment, Cinematograph and Theatre Union (BECTU)
111 Wardour Street
London W1F 0AY ☎ 020 7437 8506
website: www.cpbf.org.uk

Broadcasting Standards Commission
7 The Sanctuary
London SW1P 3JS ☎ 020 7808 1000
website: www.bsc.org.uk

Campaign for Press and Broadcasting Freedom (CPBF)
Second floor, Vi and Garner Smith House
23 Orford Road, Walthamstow
London E17 9NL ☎ 020 8521 5932
website: www.cpbf.org.uk

Channel 4 Television
124 Horseferry Road
London SW1P 2TX ☎ 020 7306 8333
website: www.channel4.com

Community Media Association
Head Office, The Work Station
15 Paternoster Row
Sheffield S1 2BX ☎ 0114 279 5219
e-mail: cma@commedia.org.uk
London office:
Resource Centre
356 Holloway Road
London N7 6PZ ☎ 020 7700 0100 ext 234
e-mail: cmalondon@commedia.org.uk

Film Education
20–21 Poland Street
London W1V 3DD ☎ 020 7851 9450
website: www.filmeducation.org

Independent Television Commission (ITC)
33 Foley Street
London W1W 7TL ☎ 020 7255 3000
website: www.itc.org.uk

Institute of Practitioners in Advertising (IPA)
44 Belgrave Square
London SW1 8QS ☎ 020 7235 7020
website: www.ipa.co.uk

Mechanical-Copyright Protection Society (MCPS)
Elgar House
41 Streatham High Road
London SW16 1ER ☎ 020 8664 4400
website: www.mcps.co.uk

Media Education Wales
UWIC
Cyncoed Road
Cardiff CF2 6XD ☎ 02920 689101/2
website: www.mediaedwales.org.uk

National Union of Journalists
Headline House
308–312 Gray's Inn Road
London WC1X 8DP ☎ 020 7278 7916
website: www.media.gn.apc.org/nuj.html

Northern Ireland Film Commission
21 Ormeau Avenue
Belfast BT2 8HD ☎ 02890 232444
e-mail: info@nifc.co.uk
website: www.nifc.co.uk

The Performing Right Society (PRS)
29–33 Berners Street
London W1T 3AB ☎ 020 7580 5544
website: www.prs.co.uk

Press Complaints Commission
1 Salisbury Square
London EC4Y 8JB ☎ 020 7353 1248
website: www.pcc.org.uk

Radio Authority
Holbrooke House
Great Queen Street
London WC2B 5DG ☎ 020 7430 2724
website: www.radioauthority.gov.uk

Royal Photographic Society
Milsom Street
Bath
Avon DA1 1DN ☎ 01225 462841
e-mail: info@rpsbath.demon.co.uk

Scottish Arts Council
12 Manor Place
Edinburgh EH3 7DN ☎ 0131 226 6051
website: www.sac.org.uk

Scottish Screen
Second floor, 249 West George Street
Glasgow G2 4QE ☎ 0141 302 1703
e-mail: Kathleen.Smith@scottishscreen.com (Information Officer)
website: www.scottishscreen.com

Sgrin (Media Agency for Wales)
The Bank
10 Mount Stuart Square
Cardiff Bay
Cardiff CF10 5EE ☎ 02920 333 300
e-mail: sgrin@sgrin.co.uk

Skillset National Training Organisation (NTO)
Second Floor
103 Dean Street
London W1V 5RA ☎ 020 7534 5300
www.skillset.org

Useful websites

www.aber.ac.uk/media/Functions/mcs.html – Daniel Chandler's Media and
Communication Studies site, highly recommended for media students

www.mediavillage.co.uk – UK media industry portal with database of links
to other media sites

www.newmediastudies.com – David Gauntlett's interesting and entertaining
website, looking at how the web has changed ways of thinking about Media
Studies

www.produxion.com – UK television production portal

www.theory.org.uk – entertaining site on popular culture and social theory

www.whatis.com – US site offering to explain new technology terms

Index

This index lists page references to four different kinds of information: key terms, media organisations, people and titles of films, radio and television programmes etc. It isn't exhaustive but, used in conjunction with the Glossary, should help you find out what you want. Definitions (either in the chapter or in the Glossary) will sometimes be signalled by **bold numbers**, illustrations by *italic numbers* and margin entries by '(m)'.